SAGE was founded in 1965 by Sara Miller McCune to support the dissemination of usable knowledge by publishing innovative and high-quality research and teaching content. Today, we publish over 900 journals, including those of more than 400 learned societies, more than 800 new books per year, and a growing range of library products including archives, data, case studies, reports, and video. SAGE remains majority-owned by our founder, and after Sara's lifetime will become owned by a charitable trust that secures our continued independence.

Los Angeles | London | New Delhi | Singapore | Washington DC | Melbourne

It's Not Just Academic!

It's Not Just Academic!

Essays on Sufism and Islamic Studies

Carl W. Ernst

SAGE | YODAPRESS

Los Angeles | London | New Delhi
Singapore | Washington DC | Melbourne

First published in 2018 by

SAGE | YODAPRESS

SAGE Publications India Pvt Ltd
B1/I-1 Mohan Cooperative Industrial Area
Mathura Road, New Delhi 110 044, India
www.sagepub.in

SAGE Publications Inc
2455 Teller Road
Thousand Oaks, California 91320, USA

SAGE Publications Ltd
1 Oliver's Yard, 55 City Road
London EC1Y 1SP, United Kingdom

SAGE Publications Asia-Pacific Pte Ltd
3 Church Street
#10-04 Samsung Hub
Singapore 049483

YODA PRESS
79 Gulmohar Enclave
New Delhi 110049
www.yodapress.co.in

Published by Vivek Mehra for SAGE Publications India Pvt Ltd, typeset in 11/13 pt Gentium Plus by Zaza Eunice, Hosur, Tamil Nadu, India and printed at Chaman Enterprises.

Library of Congress Cataloging-in-Publication Data

Name: Ernst, Carl W., author.
Title: It's not just academic! : essays on Sufism and Islamic studies / Carl W. Ernst.
Description: Thousand Oaks, California: SAGE Publications Inc, [2018] |
Includes bibliographical references and index.
Identifiers: LCCN 2017032994 (print) | LCCN 2017033853 (ebook) |
ISBN 9789352800100 (Web PDF) | ISBN 9789352800094 (ePub) | ISBN 9789352800087 (hardback : alk. paper)
Subjects: LCSH: Sufism—Miscellanea.
Classification: LCC BP189.23 (ebook) | LCC BP189.23 .E76 2017 (print) |
DDC 297.4—dc23
LC record available at https://lccn.loc.gov/2017032994

ISBN: 978-93-528-0008-7 (HB)

SAGE Yoda Team: Arpita Das, Ishita Gupta, Apoorva Saini and Sandhya Gola

Contents

Part 3
Sufism, Art, and Literature

Part 4
Contemporary Sufism

Part 5
Persianate Themes

Preface

This volume, *It's not Just Academic: Essays on Islamic Studies and Sufism,* is a collection of essays produced over the past three decades, and it is a companion to *Refractions of Islam in India,* also published by Yoda Press with SAGE Publications. Unlike the other volume, this book is not dominated by the problem of understanding Islam in the prism of a particular regional culture. Instead, it addresses basic and critical issues relating to the study of Islam, and it contains a wide range of particular examinations of Sufism, the tradition of spiritual and ethical practice that is so prominent in Muslim societies. As with *Refractions,* collecting these essays furnishes the occasion to reflect on the trajectory of inquiry which they illustrate.

Above all else, as the title indicates, these studies are animated by the conviction that scholarship in the humanities matters, and that it is important to communicate its conclusions clearly to the reading public. There are plenty of reasons to acknowledge these points when it comes to the study of Islam. During the years when I was completing my graduate studies at Harvard University (1975–81), two significant events highlighted the political relevance of Islamic studies in unprecedented ways. One was the outbreak of the Iranian revolution in 1978–79, which inspired intense and ongoing debates about Islam, politics, and violence. Suddenly scholars who specialized in the study of medieval manuscripts were being called upon to explain to journalists the raging ideological battles of contemporary Iran. The other event was the 1978 publication of Edward Said's *Orientalism*, with its critique of the colonialist engagements of Islamic studies. Academics accustomed to considering themselves as neutral observers now had to defend themselves from the suspicion of being supporters of imperialism. Scholars of Islamic studies now faced a much wider set of demands than their Orientalist predecessors had imagined.

The field of Islamic studies scholarship remained small despite the controversies of the late 1970s, and even the first Gulf War, in 1990–91, created only a temporary jump in publications relating to Islam, and very little increase in the number of trained specialists in Islamic studies in American colleges and universities. During the 1990s, however, the field began to grow perceptibly, and then the shock of the 2001 terrorist attacks on American targets led to more extensive development of academic Islamic studies, now increasingly integrated into the humanities and social sciences instead of being isolated as a foreign subject, although narrower specialized philology persists in some institutional frameworks.[1]

But the quest for more extensive academic expertise in Islamic studies was not the only response to crises relating to Islam. At the University of North Carolina at Chapel Hill, where I have been a faculty member since 1992, the 2002 Summer Reading Program for newly admitted students unexpectedly became a major controversy, when on my recommendation the book adopted was a poetic translation of selections from the Qur'an.[2] A firestorm of criticism was directed at UNC for requiring first-year students to read and discuss the book, less than a year after the 9/11 attacks, providing clear evidence of the deep suspicion of Islam that was emerging among the American public. Indeed, it was obvious that the mere existence of the Qur'an, as a post-biblical revelation, was a source of considerable anxiety. And for many who

---

[1] Carl W. Ernst and Richard C. Martin, "Introduction: Toward a Post-Orientalist Approach to Islamic Religious Studies," in *Rethinking Islamic Studies: From Orientalism to Cosmopolitanism*, ed. Carl W. Ernst and Richard C. Martin, Studies in Comparative Religion (Columbia, S.C.: University of South Carolina Press, 2010), pp. 1–22; Charles Kurzman and Carl W. Ernst, "Islamic Studies in U.S. Universities," in *Middle East Studies for the New Millennium: Infrastructures of Knowledge*, ed. Seteney Shami and Cynthia Miller-Idris (New York: Social Science Research Council, 2016), pp. 320–50.

[2] The book was Michael Sells, *Approaching the Qur'an: The Early Revelations* (Ashland, OR: White Cloud Press, 1999); see references in "Yacovelli v. Moeser," *Wikipedia*, October 9, 2016, https://en.wikipedia.org/w/index.php?title=Yacovelli_v._Moeser&oldid=743367244.

lacked any knowledge of the recent history of Muslim-majority societies, it was tempting and convenient to blame problems like contemporary terrorism on a text from fourteen centuries ago. From a scholarly perspective, it was astonishing to see how swiftly these ideological attacks on Islam swept away any consideration of recent history and politics; many were seemingly unaware of the sweeping conquest and colonization of Muslim countries by Western powers in the era leading up to the First World War. I ended up responding to this anti-Islamic prejudice in several publications addressing questions surrounding Islamic civilization, the Qur'an, and the opportunistic character of this overall hostility toward Islam. One of these responses was a fresh interpretation of Islam in the contemporary world.[3] Another was a book proposing a literary and historical approach to reading the Qur'an.[4] The most recent item was a collection of essays on Islamophobia in the US, for which as editor I wrote the introduction.[5] At the same time, I continued with a series of focused essays on particular texts and topics that to my mind provided compelling examples that challenged stereotypes of Islamic culture, and demanded serious rethinking of assumptions.

The title of this volume, *It's not Just Academic*, is an acknowledgement of the political context that surrounds any discussion of Islam, an atmosphere of negativity for which it is difficult to find any equivalent in other fields of religious studies. This does not mean that scholarship on Islam means defending Islam from all criticisms. But it does mean that the normal standards of humanistic scholarship, including fair-minded representation of culture and empathetic understanding, need to be affirmed. The title itself is taken from chapter 5, "It's Not Just Academic: Writing Public Scholarship in Middle Eastern and Islamic Studies." That essay is also in part a critique of the kind of scholarly writing that is opaque and inscrutable to a general

---

[3] Carl W. Ernst, *Following Muhammad: Rethinking Islam in the Contemporary World*, Islamic Civilization & Muslim Networks (Chapel Hill: University of North Carolina Press, 2004).

[4] Carl W. Ernst, *How to Read the Qur'an: A New Guide, with Select Translations* (Chapel Hill: University of North Carolina Press, 2010).

[5] Carl W. Ernst, "Introduction: The Problem of Islamophobia," in *Islamophobia in America: The Anatomy of Intolerance*, ed. Carl W. Ernst (New York, NY: Palgrave Macmillan, 2013), pp. 1–19.

audience, and it is also a call for clear and compelling writing that avoids unnecessary jargon.

The title essay is one of six that comprise Part 1, on "General and Critical Issues in Islamic Studies." It is accompanied by two essays on how to teach Islamic studies. "Between Orientalism and Fundamentalism: Problematizing the Teaching of Sufism" (chapter 1) questions the presentation of Sufism as a private form of mysticism, insisting on the importance of social and political context. "Reading Strategies for Introducing the Qur'an" (chapter 2) clarifies the non-theological approaches I tried out in my class on the Qur'an for several years, before I wrote the book *How to Read the Qur'an*. "'The West and Islam'?" (chapter 3) argues that the terms "East" and "West" perpetuate colonial conflicts through the myth of the clash of civilizations. Chapter 4 on "Muḥammad as the Pole of Existence" explores the underappreciated role of the Prophet as the guide of spiritual experience. The essay on "The Global Significance of the Arabic Language" (chapter 6) shows how Arabic has had a major cultural role not only for Arabs and Muslims, but also for Christians, Jews, and many non-Arab peoples.

The majority of the essays are concerned with Sufism, in three parts. Part 1 focuses on themes and figures from premodern Sufi traditions. These include an analytical reflection on "Esoteric and Mystical Aspects of Religious Knowledge in Sufism" (chapter 7) and a study of the definitions of mystical terminology in the "Early Lexicons of Sufism" (chapter 9). Two chapters (11 and 13) address Sufi theories of love, with special attention to the Persian master Rūzbihān Baqlī. Other themes include Rūzbihān's visionary ascensions (chapter 12), the relationship between Sufism and philosophy (chapter 14), and the counterintuitive claim by Ibn `Arabi that the unrepentant Pharaoh in fact achieved salvation (chapter 8). Two other essays deal with the controversial early Sufi Bayazid (or Abu Yazid) Bistami, as interpreted by the important later figures Ibn `Arabi (chapter 10) and Shams-i Tabriz (chapter 15).

Part 3 then shifts to Sufi engagements with art and literature. Two essays examine important Persian texts on the mystical understanding of Arabic calligraphy, one from Safavid Persia (chapter 16) and another from the Indian Deccan by an author from Shiraz (chapter 20). These are accompanied by thematic explorations of "The Symbolism of Birds and Flight" according to Rūzbihān (chapter 17) as well as the role of beauty and the feminine in Sufi thought (chapter 19). Persian Sufi poetry is scrutinized in the way that `Attar interprets the early Sufi martyr Hallaj (chapter 18), and with a close reading of a commentary on poems by Hafiz (chapter 21). Two companion pieces (chapters 22 and 23) lay out the role of the prefaces to the separate books of Rumi's *Masnavi*, including his skillful command of Arabic expression in one of the great classics of Persian literature.

Part 4 brings Sufism up to date, through investigations of the impact on Sufism by modern ideologies and technologies (chapter 24) and globalization itself (chapter 25). Part 5 concludes with reflections on Persianate themes in Islamic studies (chapter 26), concepts of religion in the esoteric teachings of the *Dabistan* (chapter 27), and the proto-Orientalist views of Sufism expressed by early travelers to Persia and their scholarly successors (chapter 28).

Throughout these essays, the basic method followed is to begin either with a question or with a striking example—a text or topic—that calls out for further examination. The questions themselves come from philology, literary theory, comparative religion, and the social sciences, although theory is handled lightly and not as an end in itself. I have found it especially rewarding to come to terms with cases that do not fit our common expectations, which therefore force us to revise conventional assumptions. For that reason, the interpretations of contested issues and controversial individuals are particularly fertile subjects to consider. It is my contention that this rich and complex tradition, still barely known to educated Europeans and Americans, is not "just academic" in the dismissive sense in which the term is sometimes used. Islamic culture and its Sufi dimension clearly form a major heritage for humanity, which is intrinsically interesting and worthy of consideration by anyone concerned with questions of culture and spirituality.

In general, the essays have been only lightly edited for consistency and style. Within each Part, essays are arranged roughly in chronological order. Although diacritical marks in the transliteration of Arabic and Persian terms are probably superfluous in a book intended for a wider audience, in a number of essays they were required by the original publishers, and they are retained here partly as a convenience and partly to acknowledge the academic venues in which they first appeared. While the use of a specialist tool like diacritics may appear to be inconsistent with the volume's title, it would be foolish to deny that these studies originated in a scholarly environment. But it is my hope that non-specialists will find them to be intriguing gateways to previously unknown cultural riches, which demonstrate the relevance of deep academic research for expanding our access to previous civilizational achievements.

Here I would also like to acknowledge my debts to many scholars I have worked with over the years, without whose encouragement these essays would not have come to light. My thanks go particularly to John Hick, Zafar Ishaq Ansari, Azizan Baharuddin, Jonathan Brockopp, Ahmet Karamustafa, Fatemeh Keshavarz, SherAli Tareen, Brannon Wheeler, Jane I. Smith, Muhammad Qasim Zaman, Arthur Buehler, Omid Safi, William Chittick, James W. Morris, Seyyed Hossein Nasr, Ghasem Kakaie, Nasrollah Pourjavady, Sheikha Hussah al-Sabah, Franklin Lewis, Yanis Eshots, Cemil Aydin, Juliane Hammer, Richard Martin, Bruce Lawrence, Miriam Cooke, Ahmed Moustafa, and Stefan Sperl. Leonard Lewisohn deserves special thanks for inviting and editing half a dozen of my contributions to the conferences he organized on the subject of Persian Sufism. Thanks also to Cemalnur Sargut, TÜRKKAD, and the Kerim Vakf for their support. I would also like to acknowledge the support of the Fulbright program and University of North Carolina at Chapel Hill for making possible the research on which the studies are based.

As before with *Refractions of Islam in India*, I want to thank Arpita Das, publisher of Yoda Press, who proposed both publications in the first place; and I would also like to thank several UNC doctoral students who assisted in the preparation of the text, including Brian Coussens for valuable editing, Micah Hughes for handling permissions, and SAGE Publications for indexing. I am particularly grateful to Jay Bonner for providing the cover artwork. Finally, I would like to take this opportunity to dedicate these essays to my undergraduate and graduate students at UNC, who in many cases have been the first audiences for the ideas presented here.

Carl W. Ernst
Chapel Hill, North Carolina
January 2017

Acknowledgments

Permission is gratefully acknowledged for the reprint of these articles and book chapters, as indicated below.

"Between Orientalism and Fundamentalism: Problematizing the Teaching of Sufism." In *Teaching Islam*, ed. Brannon Wheeler (Oxford: Oxford University Press, 2002), pp. 108–23. Reprinted with permission of Oxford University Press.

"Reading Strategies for Introducing the Qur'an as Literature in an American Public University." *Islamic Studies* (Islamabad) 45:3 (2006), pp. 333–44. Reprinted with permission of the Islamic Research Institute, International Islamic University, Islamabad.

"'The West and Islam?' Rethinking Orientalism and Occidentalism." *Ishraq: Islamic Philosophy Yearbook* (Moscow/Tehran), vol. 1 (2010), pp. 23–34. Reprinted with permission of LRC Publishing.

"Muhammad as the Pole of Existence." In *The Cambridge Companion to Muhammad*, ed. Jonathan Brockopp (Cambridge: Cambridge University Press, 2010), pp. 123–38. Reprinted with permission of Cambridge University Press.

"It's Not Just Academic – Writing Public Scholarship in Middle Eastern and Islamic Studies." *Review of Middle East Studies* 45/2 (Winter 2011 [published 2012]), pp. 164–71. Reprinted with permission of Cambridge University Press.

"The Global Significance of Arabic Language and Literature." *Religion Compass* 7/6 (2013), pp. 191–200. Reprinted with permission of John Wiley & Sons.

"Mystical and Esoteric Aspects of Religious Knowledge in Sufism." *The Journal of Religious Studies* XIII (1984), pp. 93–100. Reprinted with permission of *The Journal of Religious Studies*.

"Controversy over Ibn Al-'Arabi's *Fusus*: The Faith of Pharaoh." *Islamic Culture* LIX (1985), pp. 259–66. Copyright © Carl W. Ernst.

"Mystical Language and the Teaching Context in the Early Sufi Lexicons." In *Mysticism and Language*, ed. Steven T. Katz (Oxford: Oxford University Press, 1992), pp. 181–201. Reprinted with permission of Oxford University Press.

"The Man without Attributes: Ibn `Arabi's Interpretation of Abu Yazid al-Bistami." *Journal of the Muhyiddin Ibn `Arabi Society* XIII (1993), pp. 1–18. Reprinted with permission of the Muhyiddin Ibn `Arabi Society.

"Ruzbihan Baqli on Love as 'Essential Desire.'" In *Gott is schön und Er liebt die Schönheit/God is Beautiful and He Loves Beauty: Festschrift für Annemarie Schimmel*, ed. Alma Giese and J. Christoph Bürgel (Bern: Peter Lang, 1994), pp. 181–89. Reprinted with permission of Peter Lang.

"Vertical Pilgrimage and Interior Landscape in the Visionary Diary of Ruzbihan Baqli." *Muslim World* 88/2 (1998), pp. 129–40. Reprinted with permission of John Wiley & Sons.

"The Stages of Love in Persian Sufism, from Rabi`a to Ruzbihan." In *The Heritage of Sufism*, Volume 1, *Classical Persian Sufism from its Origins to Rumi (700–1300)*, ed. Leonard Lewisohn (Oxford: One World, 1999), pp. 435–55. Reprinted with permission of One World.

"Sufism and Philosophy in Mulla Sadra." In *Islam-West Philosophical Dialogue: The Papers presented at the World Congress on Mulla Sadra (May, 1999, Tehran)* (Tehran: Sadra Islamic Philosophy Research Institute, 2001), 1: 173–92. Copyright © Carl W. Ernst.

"Shams-i Tabrizi and the Audacity of Bayazid Bistami." In *Şems: Güneşle Aydinlananlar/Enlightened By The Sun* (Istanbul: Nefes Yayınevi, 2010), pp. 286–95. Reprinted with permission of Nefes Yayınevi.

"The Spirit of Islamic Calligraphy: Baba Shah Isfahani's *Adab al-Mashq*." *Journal of the American Oriental Society* 112 (1992), pp. 279–86. Reprinted with permission of the American Oriental Society.

"The Symbolism of Birds and Flight in the Writings of Ruzbihan Baqli." In *The Heritage of Sufism*, vol. 2, *The Legacy of Mediaeval Persian Sufism (1150–1500)*, ed. Leonard Lewisohn

(Oxford: One World, 1999), pp. 353–66. Reprinted with permission of One World.

"On Losing One's Head: Hallajian themes in works attributed to `Attar." In *Attar and the Persian Sufi Tradition: The Art of Spiritual Flight*, ed. Leonard Lewisohn and Christopher Shackle (London: I. B. Tauris, 2006), pp. 330–43. Reprinted with permission of I. B. Tauris.

"Beauty and the Feminine Element of Spirituality." In *Women and Tasawwuf* (Istanbul: Nefes, 2008), pp. 147–54. Reprinted with permission of Nefes Yayınevi.

"Sufism and the Aesthetics of Penmanship according to Siraj al-Shirazi's *Tuhfat al-Muhibbin* (1454)." *Journal of the American Oriental Society* 129.3 (2009), pp. 431–42. Reprinted with permission of the American Oriental Society.

"Jalal al-Din Davani's Interpretation of Hafiz." In *Hafiz and the School of Love in Persian Poetry*, ed. Leonard Lewisohn (London: I. B. Tauris, 2010), pp. 197–210. Reprinted with permission of I. B. Tauris.

"'A Little Indicates Much': Structure and Meaning in the Prefaces of Rumi's *Masnavi* (Books I-III)." *Mawlana Rumi Review* V (2014), pp. 14–25. Reprinted with permission of *Mawlana Rumi Review*, Exeter.

"Wakened by the Dove's Trill: Structure and Meaning in the Arabic Preface of Rumi's *Masnavi*, Book IV." In *The Philosophy of Ecstasy: Rumi and the Sufi Tradition*, ed. Leonard Lewisohn (London: World Wisdom, 2015), pp. 259–68. Reprinted with permission of World Wisdom.

"Ideological and Technological Transformations of Contemporary Sufism." In *Muslim Networks: Medium, Metaphor, and Method*, ed. Miriam Cooke and Bruce B. Lawrence. Islamic Civilization and Muslim Networks Series, 2. Chapel Hill: University of North Carolina Press, 2005), pp. 198–207. Reprinted with permission of University of North Carolina Press.

"Sufism, Islam, and Globalization in the Contemporary World: Methodological Reflections on a Changing Field of Study." In Memoriam: The 4th Victor Danner Memorial Lecture (Bloomington, IN: Department of Near Eastern Languages, 2009). Reprinted with permission of Department of Near Eastern Languages, Indiana University.

PART 1

GENERAL AND CRITICAL ISSUES IN ISLAMIC STUDIES

1

Between Orientalism and Fundamentalism: Problematizing the Teaching of Sufism

In late twentieth-century America, teaching or writing about Islamic religion is inescapably caught up in political controversy. Everyone who has taught a class on Islam has had to deal with the powerful stereotypes of terrorist violence and gender inequality that pervade media representations of Islamic societies. In the academy, it has long appeared that a conveniently non-political alternative subject could be framed in terms of the study of Sufism, or Islamic mysticism. Many Islamicists have offered courses on Sufism at North American colleges and universities, or have discussed Sufism in their classes on Islam, and a number of academics who offer courses on mysticism have attempted to incorporate some Sufi material into their surveys on this topic. Despite lively debates over the nature of mysticism in recent years, there has been hardly any reflection on the category of Sufism, considered as Islamic mysticism. This means that courses dealing with Sufism have been unable to provide any problematization of this concept—and that sort of reflection is necessary for any course in religious studies that aspires to be critical.[1] In this essay, based on a forthcoming study of Sufism, I would like to argue that the non-political image of Sufism is illusory.[2]

The history of the study of Sufism shows how powerfully the Orientalist discourse on religion reformulated aspects of Islamic culture into a separate category called Sufism. At the same time, growing "fundamentalist" movements in Muslim countries have isolated and rejected many aspects of what we call Sufism, as part of a struggle over the ownership of Islamic religious symbolism. The fact that these debates have taken place in the colonial and post-colonial periods indicates that modernity is crucial to the understanding of Sufism. Yet the classicist bias of Orientalism, and the strikingly similar "golden age" historiography of fundamentalism, have conspired to keep Sufism separate from modernity. Here I would like to show how it is possible to deal with Sufism critically in terms of religious studies, by introducing to the classroom some of the highly charged ideological interpretations of Sufism that have been offered by Orientalists and fundamentalists. When juxtaposed with the ways in which Sufis themselves have actively engaged with the ideologies and technologies of modernity, these "political" readings of Sufism make the subject far richer than the default hagiographic approach that limits itself to "classical" texts.

I would like to frame this discussion in terms of several outcomes that seem to me important in teaching courses relating to Islam:

- to acquaint students with religious practice, not just theological doctrine;
- to illustrate the contemporary relevance of the religious tradition, not just its "classical" past;

[1] Critical reflection and problematizing of categories, in my opinion, should be part of even the most elementary introductory courses in religious studies. They are all the more necessary in specialized and advanced courses.

[2] Carl W. Ernst, *Sufism: An Introduction to the Mystical Tradition of Islam* (Boston, Mass.: Shambhala, 2007). Further specific discussions of the problem of Sufism and modernity are to be found in Carl W. Ernst and Bruce B. Lawrence, *Sufi Martyrs of Love: Chishti Sufism in South Asia and Beyond* (New York: Palgrave Macmillan, 2002).

- to create an immediacy for students by employing multimedia resources (film, music, and internet) in addition to written texts;
- to complicate the picture of monolithic Islam by illustrating difference through categories such as ethnicity, gender, class, and nationality;
- to avoid privileging one Islamic perspective over another as being "orthodox", while clarifying the issues under debate; and
- to problematize the study of Islam as an example of the modern conceptualization of religion.

It is still necessary to provide a synthetic textbook presentation and some primary texts in translation, and my syllabi and readings still contain the standard narratives on the importance of the Qur'an, the Prophet Muhammad, etc. But a course on Sufism or Islam can end up being an Orientalist catechism, rather than a critical course in religious studies, unless objectives like these are part of the picture. The following remarks sketch out ways in which the modern ideologies surrounding Sufism may be integrated into the subject.

Sufism as an Orientalist Category

The standard presentation of Sufism as Islamic mysticism can be easily recognized in the venerable textbooks and anthologies that have been in use for decades in North American universities. A. J. Arberry's *Aspects of Islamic Civilization as presented in the Original Texts* (1956) is one of the best examples. It presents Sufism as a classical literary phenomenon best illustrated by the great Sufi poets (Rumi, Ibn al-Farid, etc.) or by prose works on discipline and metaphysics. This portrait was an intellectual achievement made possible by the deep erudition of sympathetic Orientalists who specialized in the study of Sufism (R. A. Nicholson, Arberry, Louis Massignon). Yet this concept of "Islamic mysticism" had a genealogy worth considering.

The term and category "Sufism" was first coined for European languages by British Orientalists based in India, particularly

Sir William Jones.[3] Before the nineteenth century, many European travelers had remarked upon "fakirs" and "dervishes", but only as exotic curiosities. Orientalists applied the term "Sufi" primarily to the literary phase of Sufism, particularly as expressed in Persian poetry. These European scholars were uniformly persuaded that the elegant poems of Hafiz and Jalal al-Din Rumi could have nothing to do with the Islamic ("Mahometan") religion. The so-called "Sooffees" were poets, after all, and they composed odes to the joys of wine-drinking, something no pious "Mahometan" would do. Furthermore, as anyone could see from their poems, they were fond of music and dance, they were great lovers, and their bold declarations were an open affront to the Qur'an. The Orientalists saw them as free-thinkers who had little to do with the stern faith of the Arabian Prophet. They had much more in common, so went the argument, with true Christianity, with Greek philosophy, and with the mystical speculations of the Indian Vedanta. Until rather recently, it was unanimously believed that Sufism was derived from Indian sources.[4] Thus the term "Sufi-ism" was invented at the end of the eighteenth century, as an appropriation of those portions of "Oriental" culture that Europeans found attractive. British colonial officials, who were the main source of European studies of Sufism in the nineteenth century, thus maintained a double attitude toward Sufism: its literary classics (part of the Persian curriculum required by the British East India Company until the 1830s) were admired, but its contemporary social manifestations were considered corrupt and degenerate in relation to what was perceived as orthodox Islam.[5] Thus the essential feature of the definitions of Sufism that appeared at

---

[3] Sir William Jones, "The Sixth Discourse, On the Persians," and "On the Mystical Poetry of the Persians and Hindus," in *Works* (London, 1807).

[4] Lt. J. W. Graham, "A Treatise on Sufiism, or Mahomedan Mysticism", in *Transactions of the Literary Society of Bombay* 1 (1819), 89–119. This attempt to find an extra-Islamic origin for Sufism has had defenders as recently as R. C. Zaehner, *Mysticism, Sacred and Profane: An Inquiry into some Varieties of Praeternatural Experience* (London: Oxford University Press, 1961). A detailed discussion of this issue is presented in my *Refractions of Islam in India: Situating Sufism and Yoga* (New Delhi: Yoda Press / SAGE Publications Inc, 2016).

[5] Sir R. F. Burton, *Sindh* (London, 1851), 198–231.

this time was the insistence that Sufism had no intrinsic relation with the faith of Islam.

The literary aspect of Sufism was thus considered by Orientalists to be separate from its contemporary institutional base, which was consigned to colonial administrators to worry about. In many Muslim regions, the Sufi orders, often referred to as "brotherhoods" or "confrèries" by Europeans, were the only local organizations to remain intact after the onset of colonial rule. In North Africa, French officials paid close attention to "marabouts" (from Arabic *murabit*, a resident in a Sufi lodge known as a *ribat*), fearing charismatic leaders who might organize local tribes. In places like the Indian Punjab, the descendants of Sufi saints were caretakers of what had become popular pilgrimage sites, and the British concocted a strategy of co-opting them into the system as influential landlords. In other cases, Sufi leaders who had extensive followings led campaigns of resistance to European conquest. In Algeria, the Emir `Abd al-Qadir fought the French for years until his defeat in 1847; in his exile in Syria, he wrote extensively on Sufism and supervised the publication of important Arabic Sufi texts. In the Caucasus, Shaykh Shamil of the Naqshbandi Sufi order set up an independent state that frustrated Russian attacks until 1859. The messianic movement of the Sudanese Mahdi, destroyed by British forces in 1881, originated from a Sufi order; British accounts of the defeat of the "dervishes" at the battle of Omdurman formed one of the high points of colonial triumphalism.

By the end of the nineteenth century, the study of the "brotherhoods" had become a necessary subject for European colonial administrators. In these circles the study of Sufism became a cross between the assembly of police dossiers and the analysis of dangerous cults. Sufi leaders like the Pir Pagaro in Sind were described as hypnotic demagogues whose fanatic followers would kill themselves at a hint from the master. In Somalia, the British dismissed the conservative Sufi leader Shaykh Muhammad `Abd Allah Hasan as "the mad mulla", though he was neither mad nor a mulla (traditional religious scholar); he is remembered today by his countrymen as the father of the Somali nation. In any case, there is considerable proto-anthropological material on Sufi saints and shrines compiled by British and French colonial officials, often drawing upon local oral tradition.

Neither the Orientalist nor the colonial-administrative approach to Sufism was very close to the sense of the word "Sufi" in Arabic and allied languages. The literature of Sufism that began to be produced in the tenth century CE employed the term Sufi in a deliberate and self-conscious fashion to orchestrate the ethical and mystical goals of the growing movement in a prescriptive fashion. A series of writings, primarily in Arabic, expounded the ideals of the Sufis and explained their relationship to other religious groups in Muslim society. The term Sufi in this way took on a didactic rather than an informational purpose. Answers to the question "What is Sufism?" multiplied and began to take on a new importance, as they nearly always were placed prominently at the beginning of every new treatise on Sufism. All these "definitions" are elusive from the perspective of descriptive history and social science. They do not have any clear reference to a defined group of people. Instead, they accomplish a powerful rhetorical transaction; the person who listens to or reads these definitions is forced to imagine the spiritual or ethical quality that is invoked by the definition, even when it is paradoxical. Definitions of Sufism are, in effect, teaching tools. References to individuals as being Sufis are comparatively rare. The actual terminology for different Islamic mystical vocations covers a wide range of semantic fields.

In the academy today, there is accordingly a fair degree of ambiguity attached to the concept of Sufism. As with other terms coined during the Enlightenment to describe religions, Sufism has now become a standard term, whether we like it or not. I would suggest that "Sufism" can best be used as a descriptive term of the "family resemblance" variety, to cover all the external social and historical manifestations associated with Sufi orders, saints, and the interior practice of Islam. Since this lacks the normative and prescriptive force of the ethical term "Sufi," it is important to point out to students the gap between outsider and insider perspectives, and to point out the objectives that govern any presentation of the subject.

Sufism, Fundamentalism, and Islam

While Islamic fundamentalism is certainly the aspect of Islam most frequently discussed in the Western media, it is unfortunately not much better known than other aspects of Islamic culture. The vagueness with which these terms are thrown around makes the average reader suspect that they are synonymous; one would assume that all Muslims must be fundamentalists. While it is usually recognized that there are Christian fundamentalists as well (indeed, the term originated in Los Angeles early in the twentieth century), the press have nearly given Muslim fundamentalists a monopoly over the term. Since the term has a fairly negative air, probably dating from the time when it was associated with anti-evolutionist forces at the time of the Scopes trial[6], Muslims who are tarred with this brush rightly resent it. Nonetheless, if it is carefully defined, "fundamentalism" can be used as a descriptive term with a specific meaning in a variety of religious contexts. Bruce Lawrence defines it as an anti-modernist ideology based on selective interpretation of scripture, used largely by secondary male elites in an oppositional role against the state.[7] It is important to note that anti-modernist does not mean anti-modern; fundamentalists are very much at home with modern technology and modern techniques of political struggle. Fundamentalists are instead opposed to the secularist ideology that has banished religion from public life; in this respect they are inescapably modern.

The relevance of fundamentalism for Sufism comes at the root of their belief systems. The selective interpretation of scripture that underlies the central authority of fundamentalism cannot afford to tolerate alternate interpretations. Since fundamentalists typically portray their interpretations as literal

---

[6] The 1925 trial of John Scopes in Tennessee was a challenge against the teaching of Darwinian biology in public schools, which has been a signature issue for the Christian conservative activists known as fundamentalists.

[7] Bruce B. Lawrence, *Defenders of God: The Fundamentalist Revolt Against the Modern Age* (San Francisco: Harper & Row, 1989), pp. 100–1.

and hence unchallengeably true, any kind of psychological or mystical interpretation of the sacred text is a basic threat to the monopoly that they wish to claim over tradition. Western journalists are too often content to accept the self-interpretation of Muslim fundamentalists as the sole authentic custodians of tradition. One would never guess from most media reports that fundamentalists usually constitute no more than 20 percent of any Muslim population, and that in this respect they are likely to have the same proportion as fundamentalists in Christian, Hindu, or Buddhist societies.

Like the spin doctors who attempt to mold public opinion through commentary, fundamentalist spokespersons attempt through their rhetoric of total confrontation to claim representation of Islam. For this effort to succeed, they must discredit and disenfranchise all other claimants to the sources of authority in the Islamic tradition. There is no stronger rival claim on these sources than in Sufism. Modern studies of Muslim fundamentalism rarely point this out, preferring instead to dwell on confrontation with European colonialism and the secular state as the proximate causes of this ideology. But the principal early fundamentalist movement, Wahhabism that swept Arabia in the nineteenth century, had nothing to do with responses to Europe. While resistance to the Ottoman empire may have been a factor, there was a basic religious struggle going on between Wahhabis and Sufis for the control of central religious symbols. Fundamentalists articulated their goal as the domination of the symbol of Islam.

The remarkable thing is that many of the leaders of Muslim fundamentalism were raised in social contexts where Sufism was strong. Both Hasan al-Banna, founder of the Muslim Brotherhood in Egypt, and Abu al-`Ala' Maududi, founder of the Indo-Pakistani Jama`at-i Islami, were very familiar with the authority structures of Sufi orders from their youth. From their writings it is quite clear that they admired the organizational strength of Sufi orders, and they acted in relation to their followers with all the charisma of a Sufi master in the company of disciples. They did not, however, adopt any of the spiritual practices of Sufism, and in particular they rejected the notion of any saintly mediation between God and ordinary humanity. In an attempt to destroy the accretions of history and return to the purity of Islam at the time of the Prophet, fundamentalists rejected the ritual and local cultural adaptations of Sufism as non-Islamic. From a political point of view, one must acknowledge that fundamentalists had sized up their opposition well. No other group held such a powerful hold on Muslim society and spirituality as the Sufi orders and saintly shrines.

Ironically, as a result of strategic successes by fundamentalist movements in certain key regions like Arabia, and the massive oil wealth that fell into the lap of the Saudi regime, many contemporary Muslims have been taught a story of the Islamic religious tradition from which Sufism has been rigorously excluded. It is ironic because as recently as the late eighteenth century, and for much of the previous millennium, most of the outstanding religious scholars of Mecca, Medina, and the great cities of the Muslim world, were intimately engaged with what we today call Sufism. It is doubly ironic because the fundamentalist story is belied by the religious practices of more than half of today's Muslim population. Veneration of the Prophet Muhammad and the Sufi saints is found as a major theme in every Muslim country from China to Morocco. On a more specialized level, millions have sought initiation in the multiple Sufi orders, which trace back a sacred teaching, generation after generation, all the way to the Prophet Muhammad. Techniques of meditation and chants of the names of God, sometimes in combination with music and dance, continue to be practiced as disciplines under the supervision of Sufi masters. Poetry, songs, and stories in dozens of local languages convey the lives and teachings of Sufi saints to a huge public. Despite the attempts of many postcolonial governments to regulate Sufi shrines and orders, because of their large followings and potential political clout, much of the activity connected with Sufism goes on regardless of attempts at interference.

The polemical attacks on Sufism by fundamentalists have had the primary goal of making Sufism into a subject that is separable from Islam, indeed hostile to it. This strategy permits fundamentalists to define Islam as they wish by selective use of certain scriptural texts. The novelty of this project has so far escaped the notice of most journalists and diplomats, since the study of Islamic cultures has not played a significant part in most Euro-American education. The Arabic term "islam" itself was of relatively minor importance in classical theologies based on the Qur'an; it literally means "submission" to God, and it denotes the minimal external forms of compliance with religious duty. If one looks at the works of theologians such as the famous al-Ghazali (d. 1111), the key term of religious identity is not "islam" but "iman" or faith, and the one who possesses it is the "mu'min" or believer. Faith is one of the major topics of the Qur'an, mentioned hundreds of times in the sacred text. In comparison, "islam" is a relatively uncommon term of secondary importance; it only occurs eight times in the Qur'an. Since, however, the term "islam" had a derivative meaning relating to the community of those who have submitted to God, it became practically useful particularly in modern times as a political boundary term, both to outsiders and to insiders who wished to draw lines around themselves.

Historically, the term Islam was introduced into European languages in the early nineteenth century by Orientalists like Edward Lane, as an explicit analogy with the modern Christian concept of religion; in this respect, "Islam" was just as much a neologism as the terms "Hinduism" and "Buddhism" were. Before that time Europeans used the term "Muhammadan" or "Mahometan" to refer to the followers of the Prophet Muhammad. The use of the term Islam by non-Muslim scholars coincides with its increasing frequency in the religious discourse of those who now call themselves Muslims. That is, the term "Islam" became popular in reformist and proto-fundamentalist circles at approximately the same time, or shortly after, it was popularized by European Orientalists. Both the outside "scientific" observers and the internal ideologues had found an ideal tool in the term Islam. Treated simultaneously as a set of changeless religious doctrines and as a sociological unit (now usually assimilated to the Arab minority), Islam became the eternal other opposing European civilization. The fact that much of Islamic history and culture was left out of the picture was not too great a price to pay for either of these constituencies.

Despite these historicist cautions about the use of religious terms, it must be acknowledged that the Orientalist and fundamentalist concepts of Sufism have coincided with the possibility of new alignments of Sufism with respect to Islam; once the two concepts emerge as separable, anything is possible. Contemporary Sufi groups are now called upon to make an explicit statement regarding the relation of the Sufi group with "mainstream" Islam, which may take the form of a non-relation. In premodern Sufism it was rare that any option but Islam could even be articulated. On the level of theoretical and literary mysticism, one can find some rare instances of Jewish Sufism, such as Maimonides' grandson Obadiah ben Abraham (d. 1265), or the Christian Sufism of Ramón Llull (d. 1316). In both these cases the authors in question were powerfully affected by reading Arabic Sufi literature, which inspired them to write new works in the same vein addressed to their co-religionists. As far as Sufi orders are concerned, in India there were a few instances of premodern Hindus who were initiated by Chishti masters without having to convert to Islam, but these were extremely few in number and by no means typical. On less formal levels, many non-Muslims have had contact with Sufi saints and have been impressed by them on a personal level. Such was the case, for instance, with the Christians and Jews who attended the funeral of Rumi; during the later Ottoman centuries, many Christians and Jews interacted with Sufism in this manner. Occasionally Zoroastrians did the same in Iran. The same kind of relationship still holds today for many Hindus and Sikhs who visit Sufi shrines in India. All this was made possible by the inwardness of Sufism, which tends to make external boundaries less significant. But prior to the nineteenth and twentieth centuries, it was scarcely necessary for a Sufi, steeped in the Qur'an and the example of the Prophet Muhammad, to have to define him- or herself in terms of Islam. Once Islam had been narrowly redefined as a legal and ideological system, however, the dual critique of Sufism by Orientalists and fundamentalists forced Sufis to justify themselves in terms of scriptural sources. Certainly there had been criticism of particular Sufi practices or doctrines prior to this, but never had the entire inner dimension of religion been called into question.

Today, particularly in Western countries, Sufi groups have to position themselves in relation to Islamic identity. Some are rigorous in following Islamic law and ritual, and this insistence is often combined with an adoption of the clothing and manners of the group's country of origin. Other groups are flexible for newcomers, on the theory that they can be gradually introduced to the outer dimension of religion later on after the inner aspect has been first absorbed. Yet other groups frankly relinquish Islamic law and symbolism, defining Sufism as the universal aspect of all religions. The most striking example of this universalist tendency is Hazrat Inayat Khan, who came to the West in the early years of this century. Trained both as a musician and as a Sufi in the Chishti order, he traveled in Europe and America giving performances of classical Indian music. Faced with the need to articulate a religious position, he presented Sufism in terms of universal religion, detached from Islamic ritual and legal practice. The groundwork for this position had been partly established much earlier by European scholars who viewed Sufism as a mysticism comparable to any other. More importantly, there was a universalist dimension implicit in Sufism as there was in the Islamic tradition, which recognized that every people had been sent a prophet. In all Muslim societies, there were significant continuities with pre-Islamic cultures, which guaranteed that Islamic culture was never merely Islamic.

In any case, there are excellent pedagogical opportunities to be found in raising the issues surrounding Sufism, Islam, and the fundamentalist critique of Sufism. What is important in this series of contested issues is to awaken students to the historical contingency of religious terminology. The semi-biological model of religious essences, which does not recognize significance in historical change, is simply inadequate to explain this sort of debate.

Sufism and the Modern World

Two major categories of modernity have already been touched upon in connection with the understanding of Sufism: Orientalism as the academic response to Europe's colonial expansion, and fundamentalism as a rejection of secular modernism. To this a number of other categories can be added, particularly the nation-state, science, and mass communication. While these have not eliminated the traditions of Sufi teaching and practice, they have added new concepts, relationships, and activities that should be acknowledged in any account of Sufism.

Most Muslim-majority countries gained independence in the years following World War II, and the new regimes in many ways continued the policies of the colonial regimes that preceded them. Colonial governments had typically eliminated or neutralized other sources of authority, and they centralized all functions of government under their own control. Formerly colonized countries have inherited authoritarian government structures that did not welcome competing political forces. In many Muslim countries one can see special government bureaucracies devoted to controlling Sufi institutions. In Egypt, this takes the form of a bureau called the Majlis al-Sufiyya or Association of Sufis, which lists and supervises some 80 "official" Sufi orders. As Valerie Hoffman has shown, however, some of the most popular Sufi orders, such as the Sudan-based Burhaniyya with a membership of several million, are not recognized by the state.[8]

The attempt to control Sufi orders and institutions by the state should be seen in the context of nationalism. In Pakistan, political leaders such as Ayyub Khan and Z. A. Bhutto attempted to redefine Sufi shrines in terms of a national ideology. Festivals at the tombs of important Sufi saints are regularly graced by provincial governors and even the prime minister, who give speeches describing how these saints were forerunners of the Islamic state of Pakistan. On the bureaucratic level, this relationship is paralled by assertion of the authority of the Department of Charitable Trusts over the operations and finances of major Sufi shrines. This same bureau is also responsible for a series of publications of official biographies of popular saints as well as

[8] Valerie J. Hoffman, *Sufism, Mystics, and Saints in Modern Egypt* (Columbia, SC: University of South Carolina Press, 1995).

devotional manuals, in this way indicating what constitutes officially approved forms of Sufism.[9]

Probably the most remarkable example of governmental conflict with Sufism occurred in modern Turkey, which banned all dervish orders in 1925; in a case of the internalization of European political anxieties, secular nationalism apparently attempted to eliminate a potential rival with strong claims on the loyalties of Turkish citizens. But after 1954, the Mevlevi or "Whirling Dervishes" were permitted to revive their ritual dance, on condition that it be a secular artistic performance and not a religious ritual. Rumi (Mevlana) is now celebrated as a hero of Turkish culture and religious tolerance. A similar case in the twentieth century was the attempt of the Soviet regime to control Sufism. With an official policy of promoting atheism, the Soviet government declared Sufi gatherings and rituals to be illegal. In the post-Soviet period, however, the Sufi shrines of Uzbekistan, particularly the tomb of Baha' al-Din Naqshband in Bukhara, have taken on considerable symbolic importance in the articulation of a new cultural and national identity.

Science looms large for Sufism in terms of the modernist critique of religion as superstition. This has been devastatingly effective in secularized circles in Muslim countries, where the issue of saintly miracles has come under attack. Modernist Muslim philosophers such as Sir Muhammad Iqbal and Mohamed Lahbabi blamed the mystically befuddled Sufi for the retrograde situation of Asian countries. It is instructive to offer to students a document that shows the response to such arguments. The author of an English biography of Shaykh `Abd al-Qadir Jilani published in Lahore in 1953 addressed skeptical readers by simply inviting them to apply scientific standards to these mind-boggling events.[10] The defenders of Sufism replied to the threats of Orientalism and science on modern terms. Some Sufi leaders have taken the step of undergoing university training in the sciences, particularly in the professional discipline of psychology.

---

[9] Katherine Ewing, "The Politics of Sufism: Redefining the Saints of Pakistan," *Journal of Asian Studies* 52 (1983), pp. 251–68.

[10] S. A. Salik, *The Saint of Jilan* (Lahore, 1953; reprint ed., Chicago: Kazi Publications, 1985).

The Pakistani Chishti leader Capt. Wahid Bakhsh Sial (d. 1995) is an example of a Sufi treating both Orientalists and Western scientists with their own medicine. In his English and Urdu writings he has systematically evaluated the theories and biases of European scholars of Sufism. On the one hand he has taken them to task for their tendency to separate Sufism from Islam. Over one-third of his book *Islamic Sufism* is devoted to disproving "That Myth of Foreign Origin of Sufism."[11] On the other hand, he has appropriated the rhetoric of science and uses it to undermine secularists who criticize religion. The first paragraph of his book's introduction announces this strategy:

> Sufism and science are striving for the same destination. Science wants to know: How did the universe come into being and what is its nature? Is there any Creator? What is He like? Where is He? How is He related to the universe? How is He related to man? Is it possible for man to approach Him? Sufism has found the answers and invites the scientists to come and have that knowledge.

This is the rhetoric of authority, well established by the prestige of medicine, science, and engineering. In Europe since the time of Comte, this rhetoric has been used to make religion irrelevant. Like other Muslim apologists who appropriate the language of science, Capt. Wahid Bakhsh seeks to turn the tables. While it has been possible for many Sufi leaders to accommodate their teachings in this way to the contemporary age, as will be shown below, modernism (whether religious or secular) is not comfortable with the spiritual authority, institutions, or practice of Sufism.

Perhaps the most remarkable aspect of the emergence of Sufism as a topic in the nineteenth and twentieth centuries has been the publicizing of a previously esoteric system of teaching through modern communications media. Today, Sufi orders and shrines in Muslim countries produce a continual stream of publications aimed at a variety of followers from the ordinary devotee to the scholar. Just as the recording industry

---

[11] Capt. Wahid Bakhsh Sial Rabbani, *Islamic Sufism: The Science of Flight in God, with God, by God, and Union and Communion with God, Also showing the Tremendous Sufi Influence on Christian and Hindu Mystics and Mysticism* (Lahore: Sufi Foundation, 1984), chapter 5, pp. 112–249.

democratized the private rituals of Sufi music for a mass audience, the introduction of print and lithography technology made possible the distribution of Sufi teachings on a scale far beyond what manuscript production could attain. As has been noted in the case of Ibn `Arabi's Arabic works, when they first emerged into print in the late nineteenth century, suddenly a work that had existed in at most a hundred manuscripts around the world (and those difficult to access) was now made easily available at a corner bookstore through print runs of a thousand copies.[12] Evidence is still far from complete, but indications are that in the principal locations for print technology in Muslim countries in the nineteenth century (Cairo, Istanbul, Tehran, and Delhi/Lucknow), the main patrons of publication, aside from governments, were Sufi orders.[13]

Although little work has been done on this subject, biographical sources can furnish valuable information about the role of print media in the development of a modern form of Sufism. Here we can see, for instance, how the Chishti leader Dhawqi Shah (d. 1951) was a university graduate and a reporter for an English-language newspaper prior to becoming a Sufi. He continued to publish newspaper articles throughout his life, both in Urdu and in English. His writings deal with such modern topics as racial theory, fundamentalism, comparative religion, and the Pakistan nationalist movement. Most remarkably, his chief successor, Shaykh Shahidullah Faridi, was a British-born convert to Islam originally named Lennard, who came to Pakistan after reading English translations of works on Sufism. His Urdu discourses, dictated in Karachi in the 1970s, are still available in print. The international distribution of printed books and periodicals was a necessary element in the lives of both men. The dramatic effects of print technology on subjects such as the Protestant Reformation and the development of nationalism have been

[12] Martin Notcutt, "Ibn `Arabi in Print" in *Muhyiddin Ibn `Arabi, A Commemorative Volume*, ed. Stephen Hirtenstein (Rockport, MA: Element, 1993), pp. 328–39.

[13] Muhsin Mahdi, "From the Manuscript Age to the Age of Printed Books," in *The Book in the Islamic World: The Written Word and Communication in the Middle East*, ed. George N. Atiyeh (Albany: State University of New York Press/Library of Congress, 1995), pp. 6–7. Mahdi suggests that the large followings of mystical orders made such publishing economically feasible.

frequently discussed, but the role of printing in the development of contemporary Sufism, including such modern forms as the periodical and the novel, still needs to be investigated.

In the late twentieth century, the other forms of publicizing Sufism has been through visual and electronic media. Most professionally made films relating to Sufism have fallen into the category of ethnographic or cultural documentary, although some governments (Turkey, India, Uzbekistan) have produced films that appropriate Sufi saints and Sufi-related culture as part of the national image.[14] The availability of movie and video cameras has made it possible to record the talks of Sufi teachers for several decades. But the recent explosion of Sufi-related home pages on the internet and in online discussion groups indicates that Sufism is going to be a very public part of the electronic age. The World Wide Web permits anyone to set up a home page without having to seek authorization from any particular religious hierarchy. It is accordingly receptive to a cheerful anarchy and a generally anti-authoritarian attitude. The principal divide that separates Sufi groups on the internet is whether or not they identify primarily with Islamic symbolism and religious practice; while this was not even an option in the premodern period, it is a major issue in debates about the nature of Sufism conducted in internet discussion groups. The internet is also a vehicle for advertising books and recordings relating to Sufism, so it continues to function as a marketing device.

The publicizing of Sufism through print and electronic media has brought about a remarkable shift in the tradition. Now advocates of Sufism can defend their heritage by publishing refutations of fundamentalist or modernist attacks on Sufism. In this sense the media permit Sufism to be contested and defended in the public sphere as one ideology alongside others. At the same time more personal forms such as the novel allow for an intimate expression of individual spiritual aspirations,

---

[14] Several documentary films on Sufism are available for loan to educational institutions, from the Non-Print Section, Undergraduate Library, University of North Carolina, Chapel Hill NC 27599. Some of these include: "For Those Who Sail to Heaven" (about an Egyptian saint's festival at Luxor), "Saints and Spirits" (about Sufi shrines and spirit possession in Morocco), and two films about the Mevlevis, "Turning" and "Whirling Dervishes".

which can be communicated to a large audience through the empathy created by the novelistic narrative. Biographies and discourses can also create an intimate relationship between readers and Sufi masters; although this was also the function of those genres in manuscript form, the wide distribution of print greatly enlarges the potential audience. Through these modern public media, Sufism is no longer just an esoteric community constructed largely through direct contact, ritual interaction, and oral instruction. Now it is publicized through mass printing, modern literary genres, and electronic technology, with all the changes in personal relationships that these media entail.

The transplantation of Sufism to Europe and America raises a number of issues, including the degree to which acculturation to a Middle Eastern or South Asian homeland is encouraged. One of the most distinctive developments of Sufism in the West is probably in the area of gender relations. Most Muslim societies where Sufism has been a living force have practiced some form of gender segregation. Female Sufi masters and saints, while known, have not been common in the past. But the social habits of the modern West are different, and it is not unusual to see men and women participating together in rituals, musical performances, and other gatherings held by Sufi orders. In some Sufi groups, women have quite naturally taken on positions of leadership. Just as American women are playing a notable and innovative role in the development of Buddhism in this country, so it may be expected that Sufism in the West will have to pay special attention to women's perspectives in order to succeed.

Above all, it must be pointed out that there are numerous points of contact between the Sufi tradition and the popular culture in which our students are immersed. Today in any music store one can buy fine audio recordings of music that originated in Sufi circles, now transformed into "world music" performances. The Pakistani qawwali singer Nusrat Fateh Ali Khan and the Moroccan musicians from Jahjouka have obtained the sponsorship of major recording labels and the enthusiastic support of successful European and American musicians, and their music has appeared on recent motion picture soundtracks (e.g., "Dead Man Walking"). The Persian poet Rumi in multiple

English versions is now the bestselling poet in America. The Whirling Dervishes from Turkey regularly perform tours in major concert halls in the West. There are dozens of internet websites linked to Sufi groups based in America. High-quality literary periodicals with glossy photographs and well-written articles are being produced by groups such as the Iranian Nimatullahi Sufi order, now based in London. I strongly urge that this kind of material (much of it easily available) be integrated into courses on Sufism and Islam, not only to provide access but also to stimulate debate on the nature of religion and culture in contemporary society.[15] Ignoring the contemporary dossier makes this subject a hermetically sealed vessel that is irrelevant to our students' concerns.

Problems with "Mysticism" as a Category

I would like to conclude with a brief reflection on how the study of Sufism can help alter the generic concept of mysticism with which it is often associated. Mysticism, although critically explored in a number of recent studies, is still often reduced to a bare universalism (with minor concessions to religious traditions) and, what is more, to the private experience of an individual. Not enough has been done to historicize and problematize the category of mysticism as it emerged around the turn of the century in Western thinking about religion. We still take for granted that terms such as "religious experience" are self-evident, though they in fact have historical genealogies.

It is important, for instance, to keep in view the political and social aspects of Sufism. Those who consider mysticism a private affair, and who view Sufism primarily through poetry or theoretical treatises, may feel that military and economic activities do not fit the picture of inner mystical experience. From this point of view, any accommodation with political power constitutes a fall from purity. It is difficult, however, to reconcile such a purely "other-worldly" perspective with either

[15] My *Sufism* includes a select discography.

the history or the teachings of Sufism. As one famous saying has it, "Sufism is all practical ethics (*adab*)." The prescriptive ethics that are bound up in Sufi rhetoric cannot be put into effect by isolated hermits. Sufis are constantly reminded of this by the model of the Prophet Muhammad, who plays for them the role of social and political leader as well as mystical exemplar. While there is certainly a tension between Sufism and "the world", illustrated most dramatically by the repentance that is the beginning of the spiritual stations, Sufism is also very much a community affair that is hard to separate from the rest of life. Students of Christian mysticism are well aware of the political and social activities of mystics like St. John of the Cross and St. Catherine of Siena. How would the textbook definition of mysticism change if these activities were connected more fully with their mystical writings? Joining the critical dimension of the study of religion with the comparative aspect may prove to be the most useful future agenda for the teaching of Sufism.

2

Reading Strategies for Introducing the Qur'an as Literature in an American Public University[1]

No Muslim encounters the Qur'an for the first time. It is part and parcel of life in Muslim societies from birth to death. In contrast, most Americans and Europeans have no acquaintance whatever with the Islamic sacred text, and it remains an enormous enigma, despite international controversies ranging from Salman Rushdie to Guantánamo. The educational task of introducing non-Muslims to the text of the Qur'an is evidently important, yet most English-language scholarship on the Qur'an either adheres to the forbiddingly technical norms of Orientalist scholarship or else serves an apologetic or polemical theological agenda. What is the best way of introducing readers to the Qur'an, who are not likely ever to become either specialists on the Qur'an or indeed Muslims?

By framing this as a pedagogical question about the goals of teaching a particular audience, I would like to suggest some

[1] An earlier version of this paper was presented at the conference on "The Qur'an: Text, Interpretation and Translation", held at the Centre of Islamic Studies, School of Oriental and African Studies, University of London, 12–14 November 2005.

effective strategies of literary interpretation that can actually be used in the classroom. The problem of understanding the Qur'an in a non-Muslim context is particularly relevant in the context where I work, the American public university. Religious Studies has become a typical and omnipresent discipline in the American academy. There are over 1,400 academic departments of Religious Studies in North American colleges and universities, yet barely 20 percent of these faculties claim to have a specialist in the study of Islam. At the same time, in face of high recent demand for Islamic Studies, it has become necessary for specialists from other fields to develop courses on Islam, the Qur'an, and related topics, as a secondary field. This pedagogical issue has recently been addressed by a volume entitled *Teaching Islam*, edited by Brannon Wheeler, which was published under the auspices of the American Academy of Religion's "Teaching Religious Studies" series.[2]

It may be that the peculiar political experience of North America, including both the "separation of church and state" doctrine in the United States and the results of immigration from Asian and African countries over the past four decades, has created the need for Religious Studies as a way of addressing pluralism and diversity. It remains the case that Religious Studies in this academic sense is hardly a dominant category for European universities, despite the existence of theological faculties and specialized departments devoted to international area studies. Religious Studies is even less visible as a discipline in the universities of Africa and Asia. The pedagogical problem I am addressing arises, not surprisingly, from the characteristics of a particular audience rather than from the inherent nature of the topic.

In any case, I have to deal with this as a practical issue, as for instance in my doctoral seminar at the University of North Carolina entitled "Pedagogy and Methodology in Islamic Studies," in which each of the 13 Religious Studies graduate students (only four of whom are specialists in Islamic Studies) had,

[2] Brannon Wheeler, ed. *Teaching Islam*, American Academy of Religion, Teaching Religious Studies Series (Oxford: Oxford University Press, 2002).

as a principal task, to construct a syllabus for an introductory course on Islam.[3] While methodology today is frequently used to describe scholarly research, I have reminded my students that the word methodology was introduced by Leibniz (in 1669) as the key element in teaching concerned with the form of pedagogical presentation, and that the great debates over method in the 17th century were all about the best method for teaching students.[4] I believe it is important to connect our most advanced research to the teaching process, and to discover methods for communicating the techniques of scholarship in a way that is accessible to non-specialists. Note that I do not advocate merely reciting the results or conclusions of scholarship in an authoritarian fashion, expecting students to regurgitate them as responses to exam questions; as Jonathan Z. Smith has cogently pointed out, we can only succeed in introducing students to the intellectual life of the university by allowing them to "problematize narratives", learning to think critically by analyzing selected examples and thereby understanding the consequences of particular arguments.[5] I take seriously the notion of intellectual responsibility as not merely announcing solutions, but as clarifying the differences between arguments and what is at stake. At the same time, it is important to disclose the toolkit of scholarship by a limited number of cases that can be investigated in depth (thus avoiding the doomed attempt to "cover the material" with its inevitable superficiality). I would argue that this method can work not only in the classroom but also with larger public audiences.

But the climate of opinion in America for the study of the Qur'an is complicated by a number of factors. Most forbidding

---

[3] The syllabus for this course, together with student projects, is available online at <http://www.unc.edu/courses/2005fall/reli/299/055/>.

[4] G. W. F. Leibniz, "Nova Methodus Discendae Docendaeque Jurisprudentiae" in *Sämtliche Schriften und Briefe*, Reihe 6, *Philosophische Schriften* (Berlin: Preussischen Akademie der Wissenschaften, 1930), I: 277; there he states of the three parts of teaching that "memory provides the material, methodology the form, and logic the application of material to form." See also Joannes Franciscus Buddeus, *Isagoge historico-theologica ad theologiam universam singulasque eius partes* (Leipzig: Thomas Fritsch, 1727), I: 251, where methodology is defined as a method of teaching (*methodum didacticam*) and an equivalent of the Greek *paideia*.

[5] Jonathan Z. Smith, "Narratives into Problems: The College Introductory Course and the Study of Religion," *Journal of the Academy of Religion*, 56 (1988), pp. 727–39.

is the pervasive negative stereotyping of Islam and Muslims in terms of terrorism and political violence. From this perspective, there is anxiety about the Qur'an primarily as a manual for the assassination of non-Muslims. More generally, a confused combination of enlightened secularism and unselfconscious Protestantism makes for a constant unease and anxiety about the very existence of the Qur'an, especially since scarcely anyone in the American political or cultural establishment seems to have any actual knowledge of the book at all. I was confronted forcefully with this issue in the summer of 2002, after I had innocently recommended to the Summer Reading Program Committee at University of North Carolina the assignment of *Approaching the Qur'an* by Michael Sells as the required book to be read over the summer by 3,500 incoming first-year students. My university was attacked as unpatriotic on right-wing television programs, sued in court by a Christian fundamentalist organization for trying to convert students to Islam, and accused in the North Carolina legislature of having assisted terrorism. Although the reading and discussion of the book in fact went off quite smoothly, the existence of this controversy indicates the magnitude of the problem of understanding.

In the popular sphere, the only way that non-Muslims generally encounter the Qur'an is in terms of readings of an extreme fundamentalist character, whether emanating from Islamist circles or from Christian evangelical opponents of Islam. The assumption is that certain selected verses from the Qur'an have an eternal and timeless authority which is blindly to be obeyed by Muslims in all circumstances; it is ironic that this extremist hermeneutic of the Qur'an is shared both by Usamah bin Ladin and by the Reverend Franklin Graham, a prominent evangelical leader and hostile commentator on Islam.[6] If these are the only perspectives on the Qur'an that our students have encountered, this makes our task all the more challenging. Then one must also consider the fact that, aside from our most advanced students, few in our classroom will have much acquaintance with the

---

[6] For a study of the extremist Qur'an interpretations of Usamah bin Ladin, see Rosalind Gwynne, "Osama bin Laden, the Qur'an and jihad," *Religion* 36 (2006), pp. 61–90.

vocabulary and conceptual apparatus of the study of religion in general.

On the most practical level of teaching a class, the question arises as to which books one will assign. Considerations of price and availability are nearly as important as the quality and persuasiveness of the argument. For reasons which are readily acknowledged, much of the scholarship on the Qur'an is difficult to locate and not written in a style that would be accessible to most readers. This is another example of the familiar distance between specialization and public knowledge. Yet there is a great advance in the current publication of the *Encyclopaedia of the Qur'an* (EQ), which is probably the most user-friendly encyclopedic work of reference ever published by E. J. Brill.[7]

Nevertheless, the most fruitful approaches to education begin not with the subject material considered in isolation but with reflection on the pedagogical goals and intended audience. I generally announce my goals for a course explicitly and list them on the course web page. In this case, goals would include gaining information and understanding about the Qur'an as a text, its literary structure, historical development, and later interpretation. More broadly, I aim for an understanding of problems related to Religious Studies as a discipline that is pursued in a modern university context. Since a course on the Qur'an will typically be an advanced class, one hopes that students will have taken an introduction to Islam previously. But in many liberal arts colleges, it is not possible to have prerequisites for humanities classes, and so instructors must face the possibility that students taking a course on the Qur'an may approach the subject with very little background on Islam. Nevertheless, relating the Qur'an to problems in Religious Studies suggests that students should become acquainted with the main scholarly debates over the Qur'an and their implications; more on that later. Finally, in my view all humanities courses should be devoted to developing analytical skills in reading, writing, and presentation of argument.

But matching these goals to the intended audience is a challenge. As already indicated, it may be that students take a

[7] Jane Dammen McAuliffe, ed. *Encyclopaedia of the Qur'an* (Leiden: Brill, 2001–5).

course on the Qur'an with little background in either the study of Islam or in the study of religion in general. It is worth pausing to observe how a class on the Qur'an differs both from courses on the Bible in American universities, and from courses on the Qur'an in Muslim societies. As Jane McAuliffe has pointed out, the study of the Bible is such a vast and specialized enterprise that it is broken down into many subspecialties, only a few of which could be mastered by the most ambitious scholar. Similarly, in universities in a country like Jordan, the study of the Qur'an is what she calls a "multifaceted academic discipline."[8] As a result, "any course on Qur'anic Studies must inevitably be shaped by the academic context in which it is offered."[9] In America, only in a handful of graduate departments of Near Eastern studies will one commonly find classes on the Qur'an in Arabic and the use of commentary literature.

The changing demographics of North American universities include a significant proportion of Muslim students taking courses on the academic study of Islam. While I will mention later on the comparative study of the Qur'an and Biblical texts, the presence of both non-Muslim and Muslim students in courses on Islam raises an issue that parallels the study of the Bible. North Carolina clearly belongs to the region of the US known as the "Bible Belt", and 83 percent of our students come from within the state. Among the 360 students who take my colleague Bart Ehrman's course in the New Testament every year, there are quite a few Christian fundamentalists, who reportedly form support groups to sustain their faith while taking this rigorously historical class.[10] He and many other scholars of Biblical studies for years have faced the gap between academic Biblical studies and the Sunday school interpretations of the Bible that many students bring with them to college. The political and legal solution that governs American education distinguishes the academic "teaching about religion" from the authoritative

---

[8] Jane McAuliffe, "Teaching Qur'anic studies in North America" in Wheeler, *Teaching Islam*, p. 97.

[9] Ibid., p. 98.

[10] Ehrman's enormously successful textbook is seen as the first to adopt a strictly historical perspective; see Bart D. Ehrman, *The New Testament: A Historical Introduction to the Early Christian Writings*, 3rd edn. (New York: Oxford University Press, 2003).

"teaching of religion" that takes place in faith communities. Thus, while the teachings that students have received are interesting and worthy of study in their own right, the academic study of religion does not permit authoritarian claims to privilege one perspective over another. While perhaps difficult to implement in practice, the principle that governs this approach to religious studies in no way differs, whether one is speaking of the Bible or the Qur'an. My assumption is that, while instructors certainly need to be aware of the sensitivities of all students, including Muslims, the organization of a class on the Qur'an has to be based entirely on academic rather than faith-based standards.

For this reason, in considering strategies and techniques for teaching the Qur'an in the American classroom, I propose concentrating on chronological reading of the text, non-theological analysis, and emphasis on literary and rhetorical interpretation, in the following manner.

The question of the chronological order of the appearance of the verses of the Qur'an is a thorny and contested issue. On the one hand, the 1924 Egyptian printed edition of the Qur'an canonizes a particular chronology of the Makkan and Medinan *sūrahs* that is widely accepted among Muslims. On the other hand, European scholars have built on the analyses of Theodor Nöldeke and his successors for a rather different chronology of the order of the *sūrahs* and indeed of individual verses. This problem needs to be faced directly, though it does not admit any easy solution.[11] That is, the standard order of the 114 *sūrahs* of the Qur'an may be described, as far as reading practice is concerned, as the ritual order of the recitation of the text. The division of the Qur'an into 30 equal parts for daily recitation during the course of a month illustrates this ritual practice quite clearly. As the Egyptian scholar al-Suyuti (d. 1505) observed, the late Medinan *sūrahs* so prominent at the beginning of the Qur'an were revealed to a Muslim society, unlike the Meccan *sūrahs* revealed in a non-Muslim context; therefore he argues that the canonical

[11] For a survey of the problem, see Gerhard Böwering, "Chronology and the Qur'an" in *EQ*, 1: 315–35.

sequence of *sūrahs* is indeed aimed at a Muslim readership.[12] There is thus no apparent justification for reading the text of the Qur'an in this order in an academic context, unless one has in mind its ritual performance. Thus in principle it is attractive to propose a reading of the Qur'an that follows its presumed historical sequence. If the academic study of the Qur'an does not aim to imitate the theological approach of the *madrasah*, I see no reason not to use the Nöldeke sequence as a baseline. The principle I appeal to here is that the academic study of religion does not simply replicate the views of any particular group of believers, though it certainly takes those views into account as an important factor; nevertheless, what distinguishes the academic study of religion is the impartial use of theoretical approaches without privileging one theological position over another.

Recent developments in this area of Qur'anic chronology have demonstrated effective results that can be obtained from using a literary analysis to develop a cumulative sense of the evolution of the Qur'anic text and its audience. An excellent example is Angelika Neuwirth's study of the "canonical process" illustrated by *Sūrat al-Hijr* (Qur. 15; no. 57 in the second Makkan period according to Nöldeke) as an epitome of the liturgical formation of the early Muslim community exemplified by the early Makkan *sūrahs*.[13] This formidable illustration of scholarship could be used as a model for directed student exercises of comparison and building up vocabulary as they follow a chronological reading of Qur'anic *sūrahs*.

To be sure, one should not ignore the fact of traditional exegesis of the Qur'an using the *sūrah* biographical tradition of the Prophet, and likewise one should draw attention to the "occasions of revelation" (*asbāb al-nuzūl*) literature as well as the doctrine of abrogation. At the same time, it is necessary to point out the measure of hermeneutical circularity that is inherent

---

[12] Jalal al-Din al-Suyuti, *Asrar tartib al-qur'an*, ed. `Abd al-Qadir Ahmad `Ata (Cairo: Dar al-I`tisam, 1396/1976).

[13] Angelika Neuwirth, "Referentiality and Textuality in *Sūrat al-Hijr*: Some Observations on the Qur'anic 'Canonical Process' and the Emergence of a Community" in Issa J. Boullata, ed. *Literary Structures of Religious Meaning in the Qur'an* (Richmond, Surrey: Curzon Press, 2000), pp. 143–72.

in any biographical or historical reading of the Qur'an. While it is essential to discuss the problems in European scholarship on Qur'anic chronology, from Nöldeke to Bell, one should note the comment of Neal Robinson: "I am bound to conclude that for all its faults, the Nöldeke-Schwally surah classification, occasionally modified in the light of Bell's insights, is a better working hypothesis than the standard Egyptian chronology."[14] I take this not as an authoritative conclusion, but as a good indication that there is evidence and argument in the Nöldeke-Schwally hypothesis. This historical principle should be employed in reading selections from the Qur'an just as if one were attempting to read the entire text sequentially. While such a selective reading cannot be exhaustive (and let us admit that it is not possible to read the entire Qur'an closely in one semester), it can nevertheless use illustrations to make significant points that accomplish the desired model of analysis. Ideally, one can put students onto research projects charting particular circumscribed topics according to both the Nöldeke and the Egyptian chronologies, to demonstrate the consequences of both hypotheses. Robinson has suggested this as an agenda for scholarly research, but there is no reason that this method cannot also be modeled in a pedagogical context.

In combination with this historical approach to the sequence of reading the Qur'an, an explicitly non-theological rhetorical analysis has much to offer. The renunciation of theological positions for pedagogical purposes can make it possible to move beyond what Arkoun refers to as the "dogmatic enclosure", in order to trace the genealogy of articles of faith from a historical and anthropological perspective, rather than assuming that there is such a thing as an uncontested notion of Muslim faith.[15] This does not require that Muslim students should give up their faith, or that anyone should dismiss the religious significance of the text. But for the time being, students will need to consider texts of the Qur'an while leaving aside debates about its status as the word of God. This is a well-established technique,

---

[14] Neal Robinson, *Discovering the Qur'an: A Contemporary Approach to a Veiled Text* (Washington, DC: Georgetown University Press, 2003), p. 95.

[15] Mohammed Arkoun, "Contemporary Critical Practices and the Qur'an" in *EQ*, 1: 427a.

though it can admittedly be fraught with consequences. To consider an example from the history of Christianity, the Spanish monk Fray Luis de Leon was imprisoned in 1562 by the Inquisition for composing an original translation of the Song of Songs directly from Hebrew, and for treating the text *as if* it were a non-allegorical pastoral poem.[16] Scholars such as Nasr Abu Zayd have undoubtedly experienced harsh criticism for their recent literary approaches to the Qur'an, even though Abu Zayd has not by any means renounced the sacredness of the text. Abu Zayd's insistence on pursuing a literary analysis in spite of controversy and persecution is a testament to his recognition of the importance of this task.[17]

Teaching the Qur'an in a non-theological fashion means that one does not need to force anyone to take a theological or religious position in discussing the text. In this respect, I cannot go along with Farid Esack's delineation of the five types of lovers of the Qur'an as a model for pedagogy. There are certainly some witty observations in his descriptions of the uncritical lover of the Qur'an, the scholarly lover, the critical lover, the friend of the lover, and the voyeur as types of readers of the Qur'an.[18] Yet it should not be necessary to put everyone into such a theological box before they can study the Qur'an. If the study of religion is to be a public space where differences can be discussed, there should not be a price of admission or precommitment. Literary analysis can proceed heuristically without dividing the world into a binary opposition between "Islamic" and "Western" scholarship, as if there were two totally opposed hermeneutics that were hermetically sealed from one another; the intellectual errors of Orientalism are only compounded by an Occidentalism that claims to understand an essentialized "West". At the same

---

[16] Fray Luis de Leon, *Obras Completas Castellanas* (Madrid: Biblioteca de Autores Cristianos, 1957), vol. 1, p. 70.

[17] Nasr Abu Zayd, "The Dilemma of the Literary Approach to the Qur'an," *Alif: Journal of Comparative Poetics*, Special Issue on Literature and the Sacred, 23 (2003), pp. 8–47.

[18] Farid Esack, *The Qur'an: A User's Guide* (Oxford: One World, 2005), pp. 1–10. Yet the psychoanalytic choice of a term for revisionists ("voyeur") clearly indicates a jaundiced view of that kind of scholarship.

time, one can advert to the possible theological implications of a non-theological analysis.[19]

On the rhetorical level, it can be a liberating experience to pursue a listener-response analysis of the process of transmission of the Qur'an; instead of employing direct theological language, one can assist students to analyse the text in terms of sender, addressee/transmitter, and community. Understanding the Qur'an as a living event of recitation is quite different from treating it as what Arkoun calls the Closed Official Corpus of later tradition. As Neuwirth points out, "Thus, with its final canonization the Qur'an as such had become *de-historicized*."[20] Therefore, a historicizing analysis implies de-canonization of the text, making it contingent rather than final and authoritative.

For a consistent avoidance of theology, I would also suggest that it is necessary to make an effort to detheologize the categories and genres of literary analysis. Literary genre is still to me the preferred mode of analysis, since thematic and topical approaches to the Qur'an lend themselves too easily to theological and legal conclusions. But even in literary analysis, the choice of terminology is a question of practicality and familiarity as much as it is of methodology. Terms such as eschatology, polemic, and apologetic are derived from the history of Christianity, as indeed is most of the vocabulary of religious studies. That in itself is not necessarily grounds for ruling out the use of these terms in Islamic Studies; the comparative approach to Religious Studies in fact demands that we use existing terms and refine them by stipulative definition. But in some cases, the technicality of language is in practice oppressive and not conducive to clarity for students, to whom the terms often remain arcane and forbidding. I base this on my own observation of looks of blank incomprehension when I use these terms with students. Moreover, I would argue that the theological aura of technical terms needs to be reduced whenever possible in this particular situation. This equally holds true for the vocabulary that Wansborough drew from the history of Judaism for his

---

[19] Nasr Abu Zayd, *Rethinking the Qur'an: Towards a Humanistic Hermeneutics* (Utrecht: Humanistics University Press, 2004).

[20] Neuwirth, "Referentiality and Textuality *in Sūrat al-Hijr*," p. 145; her emphasis.

discussion of early Islamic history (*midrash, halakhic, haggadah*). While an argument can be made for using such categories, they may come at a cost of foreclosing the possibility of a sui generis approach to the Qur'an. There are highly charged arguments about influence and authenticity that lend an air of religious disputation to many discussions of the relationship between the Qur'an and earlier scriptures. If serviceable technical terms can be used that do not invoke such theological arguments of precedence and priority, that would be a useful achievement. The same observation applies to the traditional doctrine of the miraculous inimitability of the Qur'an. Although phrased in terms of aesthetic appreciation, this is best viewed as a dogmatic assumption rather than an empirical conclusion.[21]

In terms of literary interpretation of the Qur'an, Robinson and Mustansir Mir have made persuasive arguments for the use of the *sūrah* as a literary unit. While it is true that this emphasis on the unity of the *sūrah* is relatively recent, it has practical advantages for literary analysis in the classroom. Particularly in the shorter *sūrah*s, one can address structural phenomena such as chiasmus to consider a reader response to the *sūrah* as a whole. This may not be identical with the most prominent ways in which these Qur'anic texts historically have been or are now being read, but this is how literary study differs from official commentaries. Other practical considerations for literary study would include taking seriously the issue of orality, and the way in which the word *qur'an* is used to signify the ongoing recitation as opposed to the Closed Official Corpus. There is also good reason for demonstrating the ritual use of the Qur'an, including playing recorded recitations to assist students to grasp the elements of sound and rhythm that permeate the text.

In any class that has an introductory element to it, no matter how small, the question arises to what extent one needs to include hypercritical and revisionist theories. An overly enthusiastic application of critical theory can leave students befuddled and confused rather than enlightened. Those who are not at all sure of the basic elements of a standard narrative are not

---

[21] Navid Kermani, "The Aesthetic Perception of the Qur'an as Reflected in Early Muslim History" in Boullata, ed. *Literary structures of Religious Meaning in the Qur'an*, 255–76.

the ideal audience for an argument that seeks to overturn that narrative. So to what extent is it useful or important to discuss hypercritical theories? The goal announced above, acquainting students with the chief academic debates on the subject, demands that we do not ignore the theories of the history of early Islam propounded by Wansborough and others. Keith Lewinstein has argued persuasively for the judicious introduction of "revisionist" scholarship on the Qur'an and early Islamic history in undergraduate courses, and Herbert Berg has suggested that Islamic Studies scholars have been reluctant to address these issues.[22] The important thing in this discussion is to model the relationship between evidence and argument, and to clarify the consequences that are at stake. While there certainly are invidious problems with the legacy of Orientalist scholarship, of which students should be aware, its polemical appropriation by ideologues should not in itself be the reason for ruling such arguments out of court. Rather, the merits and rhetorical claims of revisionist scholarship should be laid out in a clear fashion, as for instance Jonathan Berkey has demonstrated in his cogent discussion of early Islamic history.[23]

One more item which our American student audience requires, partly because of the dominant fundamentalist mode of interpretation that Christians often apply to Islam, is simply to introduce the notion of interpretation of the sacred text. That is, the notion that there is a fixed and standard meaning of the text that somehow floats above any historical context must be exposed to criticism. There are two principal ways in which this task may be accomplished. One is to have a minimum of two different translations in the classrooms at all times, and to call for frequent comparison of the translations to illustrate, from the difference between English versions, how the invisible and hidden original may be triangulated. The other way is of course to bring in

[22] Keith Lewinstein, "Recent Critical Scholarship in the Teaching of Islam" in Wheeler, ed. *Teaching Islam*, pp. 46–60; Herbert Berg, "The Implications of, and Opposition to, the Methods and Theories of John Wansbrough," *Method & Theory in the Study of Religion*, 9 (1997), pp. 3–22.

[23] Jonathan Berkey, *The Formation of Islam: Religion and Society in the Near East, 600–1800* (Cambridge: Cambridge University Press, 2003).

selected commentaries from different sources on the same verse, to see a few examples of how different readers have interpreted particular texts.[24] These are well-known and tested techniques.

Finally, it seems to me that the modern study of religion requires an effort of comparison. Once again, it is necessary to make strenuous efforts to free this term from the theological burden which it has often carried (i.e., to compare and discover which religious view is superior, generally one's own). All too often, when the Qur'an is to be compared to something else, the standards used are the conventional and official theological positions that in their current triumph are asserted to be the inevitable results of the history of religion. In other words, current forms of rabbinic Judaism, Catholicism, and Protestantism, are assumed to be somehow pre-ordained essences rather than contingent outcomes. Recent research on monotheism in the Mediterranean region offers intriguing examples that range beyond the charmed circle of the Bible and its Islamic successor.[25] While the debates embedded within the Qur'an have often lent themselves to stereotyped inter-confessional disputational arguments, it should be possible to envision the rhetoric of the Qur'an not simply in terms of the old argument of influence from biblical sources, but as an ongoing example of what Donald Akenson terms "Judahistic" (not Jewish) reflection on and creative retransmission of the scriptural mode of thinking in a contemporary vein.[26] It is in a similar sense, evidently, that Mohammad Arkoun envisions a comparative approach to monotheism in a global context, to dogmatic orthodox frameworks, and to the role of modern sciences, as the conditions for a comprehensive contemporary approach to the Qur'an.[27] The scope is obviously vast, and the challenge is considerable, in

---

[24] This has been done by Mahmoud M. Ayoub, *The Qur'an and Its Interpreters,* 2 vols. (Albany: State University of New York Press, 1984, 1992).

[25] Garth Fowden, *Empire to Commonwealth: Consequences of Monotheism in Late Antiquity* (Princeton, NJ: Princeton University Press, 1993).

[26] I owe this reference and the accompanying insight to Prof. Peter Wright of Colorado College. See Donald Harman Akenson, *Surpassing Wonder: The Invention of the Bible and the Talmuds* (New York: Harcourt Brace, 1998).

[27] Mohammed Arkoun, "Contemporary Critical Practices and the Qur'an" in *EQ*, 1: 412–31.

attempting to implement such a project in the framework of a classroom, but I believe it is worth the attempt.

I expect that this brief exposition of a pedagogical approach to the Qur'an for American university students may elicit some objections, particularly from those who are called upon to deal with a different sort of audience. I would be particularly interested to hear what sorts of strategies for introducing the Qur'an might be most appropriate, for instance, for British or French university students, with their different social legacies of the role of religion in education. But I will still argue that the most effective presentation of a challenging religious text like the Qur'an must be strategized not from the nature of the text itself but from an understanding of the capacities, history, and inclinations of the audience.[28]

---

[28] My own effort at an introductory course on the Qur'an may be seen at <http://www.unc.edu/courses/2006spring/reli/161/042/>.

3

"The West and Islam?" Rethinking Orientalism and Occidentalism[1]

"The West and Islam," as a pair of conjoined terms, confront each other as a dichotomy of opposition, creating through their juxtaposition a question that is full of tension. This may be illustrated by the following announcement by a spokesman for the Catholic Church:

> Msgr. Georg Gänswein, Pope Benedict XVI's secretary and close adviser, warned of the Islamization of Europe and stressed the need for the Continent's Christian roots not to be ignored. In comments released in advance of an interview to be published today in the German weekly *Süddeutsche Magazin*, he said: "Attempts to Islamize the West cannot be denied. The danger for the identity of Europe that is connected with it should not be ignored out of a wrongly understood respectfulness." He also defended a speech Benedict gave last year linking Islam and violence, saying it was an attempt by the pope to "act against a certain naïveté."[2]

The sharp note of conflict in this statement is striking. Not only has the papal representative described Islam as a danger to Europe, but also he has claimed Europe, in effect, as the rightful

[1] An earlier version of this essay was delivered as the 7th Tun Razak Lecture on 9 August 2007, at the University of Malaya in Kuala Lumpur.

[2] *New York Times*, 27 July 2007.

property of the Christian Church because of its historical roots in the region. It is my contention that this type of civilizational and religious conflict is built into the concept of "the West", particularly though not exclusively when it is put in opposition to Islam. This particular speech was protested by Muslim leaders both in Europe and elsewhere as a provocation that encourages Islamophobia. Those who do not wish to support an endless series of colonial-style conflicts between Muslims, Christians, and others, need to find ways to reconceptualize the world without relying upon the notion of the timeless East and West. In other words, it is time to move beyond both Occidentalism and Orientalism.

As I have argued in more detail elsewhere,[3] the concept of "the West" is to a certain extent fictive, in so far as it implies a unitary and homogeneous cultural identity that is vaguely ascribed to a number of countries in America and Europe and their would-be associates. Likewise, the notion of "the Islamic world" (interchangeable with Europe's Orient or "the East") can also be seriously misleading; it practically suggests that there is a separate planet that is somehow unconnected with Europe and America by political, economic, and military circumstances, and it glosses over as unimportant the many differences in history, ethnicity, language, and culture that characterize Muslim majority countries as well as the Muslim minorities elsewhere. From a historical point of view, the abstract notions of both "the West" and Islam leave out a great deal that is arguably significant. Both for Muslims and for European Christians, the historical roots of Abrahamic prophecy and Greek philosophy are a shared heritage, which neither can claim in an exclusive fashion. Muslims have been part of the fabric of European history for centuries, not only in al-Andalus but also in the Ottoman territories. And Muslims have also played a part in America over at least the past two centuries, as we must recognize if we note the existence of African Muslims, including scholars (like Omar ibn Sayyid) who were enslaved and sold in America. The dramatically increased Muslim populations of America and Europe are only the most

[3] Carl W. Ernst, *Following Muhammad: Rethinking Islam in the Contemporary World* (Chapel Hill: University of North Carolina Press, 2003), chapter 1.

recent examples of this phenomenon. Moreover, in addition to the long history of trade and contact between Europe and Asia through the ages, one cannot overlook the significance of the European expansion around the world since the time of Columbus, and particularly the high point of colonialism in the nineteenth century. The enormous economic and technical benefits that Europeans seized from their Oriental subjects, plus a fair amount of luck, undoubtedly played an enormous role in fashioning what we consider today the modern West, although there is an undeniable tendency for Europeans to claim superiority as a result of their own intrinsic civilizational virtue. But recent historians have begun to question "the Eurocentric discourse" that "implies a kind of intellectual apartheid regime in which the superior West is quarantined off from the inferior East."[4] The fact is that, both historically and in contemporary times, Muslims have played significant roles in relation to both America and Europe. In short, the opposition between "the West" and Islam is considerably overstated.

At the risk of sounding banal, I am forced to refer to a couple of well-known publications that have relentlessly and tendentiously hammered the theme of the opposition between the West and Islam. As anyone can predict, these are the writings of Samuel Huntington on *The Clash of Civilizations* and the fulminations of Bernard Lewis on "the roots of Muslim rage" along with his pontifications on *What went wrong?* with Islamic civilization. Both these books have been sharply criticized by professional historians for the shortcomings of their explanations and for the bias that characterizes their treatment of Islamic civilization in particular.[5] Yet an amazing popularity was guaranteed for their publications by the way in which these books capitalized upon fears and prejudices that have a long history in Europe and America. I would venture to say that Muslim readers

---

[4] John M. Hobson, *The Eastern Origins of Western Civilization* (Cambridge: Cambridge University Press, 2004), p. 283.

[5] For a review of Lewis, see Juan Cole, *Global Dialogue*, 27 January 2003 <http://www.juancole.com/essays/revlew.htm>; see also "What Is Wrong with What Went Wrong?" by Adam Sabra, in *Middle East Report Online* <http://www.merip.org/mero/interventions/sabra_interv.html>.

around the world were shocked and horrified by the picture of Islam that was drawn by these supremely ideological writers. Yet it is striking that few of these readers have bothered to question the matching concepts that form the basis of the projects of Huntington and Lewis, i.e., the notion that there is something called "the West", and that it can be clearly identified as a cultural unity. It is my feeling that implicit in the concept of "the West" is the colonial self-image of a superior civilization that is destined to rule over the rest of the world, whether in overt political domination or through the more subtle forms of globalizing economies. As long as Muslims and non-Europeans in general continue to allow imperialist Europeans and Americans to set the terms of debate, in other words, as long as they accept that there is such a thing as the "the West," they will have no way to win this argument; its outcome is implicit in the words themselves. As Mohammed Arkoun has observed regarding Bernard Lewis's book *What Went Wrong*, "It will suffice to point out that both its title and its contents betray the intellectual impasse born of a frame of mind intent on thinking in terms of the polarity of an imaginary 'Islam' and its equally imaginary counterpart of the 'West'. So long as this fictional dualism remains in place, the intellectual impasse which is thereby engendered is destined to remain irresolvable."[6] So I am hoping to convince people to stop using the phrase "the West", and to employ instead more specific identifiers that have a less ambiguous and less ideological implication—to speak in terms of particular regions and countries, such as America and France, for example.[7] In a similar fashion, I think it is important to abandon the phrase "the Muslim world" despite the idealistic concept of the Muslim *umma*. The conflictual implications of a unitary Muslim world in opposition to "the West" are simply too strong to avoid.

---

[6] Mohammed Arkoun, *Islam: To Reform or to Subvert?* (London: Saqi Essentials, 2006), pp. 9–10.

[7] It seems ironic that at least two geographical regions associated with Arabic culture are known as variations of "the West" in Arabic; I am thinking of Morocco (derived from *al-maghrib*), and the Portuguese region of the Algarve (from *al-gharb*), which was once an Arab-Andalusian dominion.

One can argue in this fashion against the dichotomy between "the West" and Islam on ethical grounds, but there are also important historical precedents in relatively recent times that question the current division. The Ottoman reformers of the Tanzimat period in the early nineteenth century (1839) identified with the universalist principles of the Enlightenment, which they believed was or could be detached from Christian religious identity, and they were not troubled by European racism, since the Ottomans considered themselves to be Caucasians rather than Asians. They did not anticipate how fiercely Europeans would resist any consideration of equality for the "Asiatic races" or for Muslims. Cemil Aydin has analyzed at length the repercussions of the extraordinary impact of the speech by Ernst Renan on "Islam and science" delivered in Paris in 1883. Renan rejected the notion that Muslims could form part of modern civilization, both for racial and religious reasons. Semites (including both Jews and Arabs) were in his view an inferior race incapable of the synthetic reasoning necessary for science and philosophy. The scientific achievements of premodern Islamic civilization, he argued, were due either to Iranians or to Arab Christians. This racist diatribe called forth refutations from leading Muslim intellectuals such as Jamal al-Din "al-Afghani" as well as other figures from Turkey.[8] The disappointment of the Ottomans who found themselves rejected as candidates for membership in Western civilization does not alter the fact that they initially considered themselves to be part of this formation.

In more recent times, the influential Egyptian writer Taha Husayn wrote in *The Future of Culture in Egypt* (1938) that Egypt had far more contact with Greece than with Persia or other eastern countries, so therefore Egyptian culture "should thus be regarded as Western or Mediterranean, rather than Eastern."[9] This position was reflected in other Arab thinkers like the Egyptian-Lebanese writer and philosopher René Habachi, who identified

[8] Cemil Aydin, *The Politics of Anti-Westernism in Asia: Visions of World Order in Pan-Islamic and Pan-Asian Thought*, Columbia Studies in International and Global History (New York: Columbia University Press, 2007), chapter 3.

[9] Cited in Majid Fakhry, "The Search for Cultural Identity in Islam: Fundamentalism and Occidentalism," *Cultures* 4 (1977), pp. 97–107, quoting page 103.

the deepest traditions of Arabic thought with Mediterranean culture.[10] While these pronouncements in favor of a Western or Mediterranean identity for Egypt and Arabs might be contested, both in Europe and in the Middle East, nevertheless, as exceptions to stereotyped generalities they offer an important corrective. Since these counter-intuitive examples cannot be predicted or accounted for by essentialist notions of East and West, they point us towards locality and history as correctives to the distortions inherent in the binary model. I will accordingly give a number of specific examples from particular countries and time periods to demonstrate the problems in the East-West dichotomy.

The broader ideologies of Orientalism and Occidentalism certainly draw upon the basic concepts of East and West, since Orient and Occident are simply the Latin forms of these geographic markers. But their broader and more pervasive implications need to be drawn out analytically. The intellectual debate about Orientalism and its relation to colonial power is well known and has played out extensively in the past 30 years. Literary critic Edward Said in his 1979 essay *Orientalism* drew in broad strokes a portrait of European scholarship in the service of empire, based on the study of the languages and texts of Oriental peoples. Said pointed out the consistent way in which Orientalist scholarship reified and essentialized an imaginary and unchanging Orient as the polar opposite of Europe; where the West was scientific, rational, and powerful, and the East was superstitious, tyrannical, and effeminate. Racial theory was deployed to demonstrate the superiority of Europeans over Asians and Africans. The result of this dichotomy was the projection of opposing essentialized identities onto Europe and its Orient, generally identified with the area we now call the Middle East. "This identification with a unified Islamic essence also led to an enduring interpretation of the region through dichotomous notions of East and West."[11] Subsequent commentators have pointed out the extent to which Said himself

---

[10] Fakhry, p. 105.

[11] S. Shami, "Middle East and North Africa: Socio-Cultural Aspects," *International Encyclopedia of the Social and Behavioral Sciences*, ed. Neil J. Smelser and Paul B. Baltes (Amsterdam: Elsevier, 2001; hereafter cited as IESBS) 14:9793.

oversimplified and indeed essentialized Orientalism, as if it were itself an unchanging characteristic. He left out of his argument any serious discussion of Orientalism in countries such as Germany that did not have colonies in the Middle East or Asia. He also glossed over the presence of prominent Orientalist scholars who were vigorous opponents of imperialist policies, such as the British scholar of Persian literature, E. G. Browne, or the leading American Islamic studies specialist of the twentieth century, Marshall Hodgson. While it is true that many Europeans believed that Orientals were naturally disposed toward despotism, there were critics of these positions even in the 18th century, such as Anquetil-Duperron, who pointed out the importance of legal systems in the East.[12] Postcolonial critiques have gone on to describe the history of the changing features of Orientalist scholarship in different regions and time periods, which have been characterized by differential ratios in the relationship between knowledge and power. Ashis Nandy has explored the psychological effects of the colonial mentality on the Europeans themselves, including the accentuation of aggression and hyper-masculine postures. Thus the entire project of Orientalism is not only vast and complex, but also extremely ambiguous; only a very superficial reading of Said would permit the conclusion that all Orientalist scholars have acted in bad faith in a sort of conspiracy.[13] One cannot deny that some of the scholarly achievements of 19th-century Orientalist scholars, such as the dictionaries and grammars of Middle Eastern and Asian languages, are still indispensable tools for research today. And while some Oriental scholarship (e.g., the work of Snouck Hurgronje for the Dutch in Indonesia) may have had a strong link to the support of colonial power, at the same time the colonial experience and its intellectual articulation is now an unavoidable and integral part of modern global history.

---

[12] Lucette Valensi, *The Birth of the Despot: Venice and the Sublime Porte* (Ithaca: Cornell University Press, 1993); M. Anquetil-Duperron, *Législation orientale: ouvrage dans lequel, en montrant quels sont en Turquie, en Perse et dans l'Indoustan, les principes fondamentaux du gouvernement* (Amsterdam: Chez Marc-Michel Rey, 1778).

[13] R. G. Fox, "Orientalism," IESBS, 16:10976–8.

In many cases, we do not have access to much that is precious in non-European culture independently of the Orientalist scholarship that catalogued all that was Asian in its museum. Therefore, as Alijah Gordon has remarked in connection with the study of the Islamization of Southeast Asia, "To understand the dynamics of what is happening today, we must look to yesterday when the Western colonial powers—Portugal, Spain, the Netherlands and Great Britain—laid the framework for the splits we inherited. Our task is to recognize these fractured realities and to work towards a devolution of power where each of our peoples can live their lives in their own way."[14]

A comparable level of ambiguity is also present in the concept of Occidentalism.[15] This can stand for on the one hand, a triumphal sense of inevitable European hegemony, which has indeed been linked with Christianity during various phases of colonialism. In this sense, Occidentalism would be a belief in the superiority of the West. It should be acknowledged that over a century ago there were many Muslim intellectuals who implicitly accepted this postulate of European superiority, in the movements we call modernist. Thus the Persian liberal thinker Taqizadeh could speak positively and even enthusiastically of "surrender to Western civilization."[16]

On the other hand, this symbolism of East and West can be easily inverted, so that Occidentalism can also be a critique of the West as negative in every sense. Iam Buruma and Avisahai Margalit have traced this type of negative Occidentalism to Japan in the 1940s, after which it became fairly widespread throughout the Third World during the period of the Cold War.[17] In some formulations, the West is so essentialized that one can speak of "ethno-Occidentalism", a kind of reverse racism that attributes unwavering qualities of negativity as almost

[14] Alijah Gordon, "Editor's Note," in *The Propagation of Islam in the Indonesian-Malay Archipelago* (Kuala Lumpur: Malaysian Sociological Research Institute, 2001), pp. xviii–xix.

[15] F. Coronil, "Occidentalism," IESBS 16:10822–26.

[16] Mehrzad Boroujerdi, "'The West' in the Eyes of the Iranian Intellectuals of the Interwar Years (1919–39)," in *Comparative Studies of South Asia, Africa and the Middle East* 26/3 (2006), p. 194 (this journal is here cited as CSSAAME).

[17] Ian Buruma and Avishai Margalit, *Occidentalism: The West in the Eyes of Its Enemies* (New York: Penguin Books, 2004).

a genetic identity for the West. A notable example is Egyptian thinker Hasan Hanafi, who has articulated his position in a book entitled *Introduction to the Science of Occidentalism* (*Muqaddima fi `ilm al-istighrab*). Hanafi begins from the assumption that Arabs need to make a critical study of Orientalism rather than using it as a factual source of self-knowledge. But from this promising critical beginning, he moves on to more ambitious attempts to rescue the Oriental self from its alienation by "reinforcing its own positive self image." This is largely to be attempted by simply reversing negative Orientalist stereotypes and projecting the negativity onto the West, a proposal that has been severely criticized by other Arab thinkers who have accused him of racism. Hanafi's ahistorical concept of Arab Islamic identity is remarkably similar to the approach of Samuel Huntington, as he "reduces the reading of both Islamic and Western awareness to religious and cultural perspectives."[18] Hanafi's project appears to be a sort of mirror image of Orientalism, and it is hard to see how he can avoid dehumanizing forms of alienation by adopting the methods of his opponent. Nevertheless, it should be emphasized that Orientalism and Occidentalism do not exist on the same level. There is a hierarchical and asymmetrical power relation between the two. Occidentalists do not have colonies in Europe and America. "Thus while European Orientalism was the result of buoyancy of spirits, prowess and offensiveness, Islamist Occidentalist modes of discourse are the product of flagging spirits, weakness and defensiveness."[19]

One of the most interesting aspects about negative Occidentalism is the extent to which it draws upon a long tradition of counter-Enlightenment critiques of "the West" by European thinkers. While these critics certainly existed in the nineteenth century (de Maistre, Herder, Nietzsche), some of the most important ones found their pessimistic expression at the time of the catastrophe of the First World War, particularly Oswald Spengler in his monumental *Decline of the West*. One of the most trenchant Occidentalist and anticolonial manifestos

18 Yudian Wahyudi, "Arab Responses to Hasan Hanafi's *Muqaddima fi `ilm al-istighrab*," *Muslim World* 93, no. 2 (2003), pp. 233–48, quoting pp. 236, 238.

19 Larbi Sadiki, "Occidentalism: The 'West' and 'Democracy' as Islamist constructs," *Orient* 39/1 (1998), pp. 103–20, quoting p. 116.

to emerge from Iran is of course the classic work of Jalal Al-e Ahmad (d. 1969), *Westoxication* (*Gharbzadegi*). This book posed the dilemma of modern Iranian intellectuals as a choice between cultural authenticity or a rootless and alienated subservience to the West. Al-e Ahmad diagnosed Westoxication as "the aggregate of events in the life, culture, civilization and mode of thought of the people having no supporting tradition, no historical continuity, no gradient of transformation."[20] Yet what is most striking about this formulation is the extent to which it depends upon a reading of the philosophy of Martin Heidegger as interpreted by Iranian scholar Ahmad Fardid, who essentially recast the colonially-inspired opposition between East and West around Heidegger's notion of historical truth. By shifting the critique of the European Enlightenment and German culture into an idealization of Islam and the Orient, Fardid and later Al-e Ahmad proposed a new path to authenticity. "In this construction of West and orient as bearing opposing essences, with the Orient harboring the ontologically legitimate truth capable of overcoming the technological nihilism engendered by the West, Fardid's *Gharbzadegi* (Westoxification) is the interlude between the self and being on the path to renewed Islamic self-realization."[21] It seems highly ironic that projects of redemption from alienation that focus on Islamic and Asian identity employ conceptual strategies and arguments derived from the heart of European culture (although admittedly deriving from its internal critics). But similar observations might be made of other Iranian thinkers, such as Ali Shari`ati, whose concept of revolutionary Shi`ism admittedly depended on Marxist categories while simply redefining them as Islamic.[22] It is also striking to see the extent to which Egyptian Islamist thinker Sayyid Qutb drew upon European and American authors in the very negative diagnosis of the West proposed in his *Islam and the Problems of Civilization* (1962); the tragic situation of modernity, in his view, had to be solved by Islam rather than liberal democracy or Marxism.[23] In the case of

---

[20] Ali Mirsepassi, "Religious Intellectuals and Western Critiques of Secular Modernity," CSSAAME 26/3 (2006), p. 418.

[21] Ibid., p. 420.

[22] Ibid., p. 427.

[23] Fakhry, p. 100.

these Muslim Occidentalists drawing upon European thinkers, the true lesson we should draw is the extent to which it is impossible to separate Islam from "the West" in the modern era.

While noting these intellectual linkages between anti-western ideas and their Western origins, it is also important for us not to over-read this as a case of derivative thinking. Cemil Aydin has observed in a critique of Buruma and Margalit that it is nevertheless important to recognize "the distinction between the 'dehumanizing' Occidentalist discourse on the west and the otherwise authentic Muslim critiques of modernity, international order, and colonialism. Should Muslims, whether Islamists or secular, not criticize the West at all? In the absence of a distinction between dehumanizing and progressive critiques, the Occidentalism paradigm can reduce all critiques of the West by Muslims either to an 'underdeveloped' copy of German romanticism or to a contagious Eurocentric disease of critique without any humanistic irredeemable content."[24] Aydin has shown how Islamist thinkers in Republican Turkey used Occidentalist rhetoric "about the decadent, materialist, positivist, soulless, immoral, communist, individualistic, and 'Masonic' West" to attack the secular regime of Mustafa Kemal in Turkey.[25] It is of course striking to see that in recent years Islamist parties in Turkey have become pragmatic advocates of Turkish accession to the European Union, so evidently modifications can be made in the previously negative forms of Occidentalism.

At this point I would like to focus more closely on the category of religion in the representation of East and West. This plays out in the dialectic of struggle between secular regimes and Islamist movements, for instance in Arab countries where "The Orientalists here are not Westerners but rather Westernizers.... French *laïcisme* informs political behavior in the Tunisian and Algerian centers of power."[26] Just as European-style secularism informs governmental concepts of Islamists as anti-democratic and extremist, so too do Islamists have their own vocabulary

[24] Cemil Aydin, "Between Occidentalism and the Global Left: Islamist Critiques of the West in Turkey," CSSAAME 26/3 (2006), p. 447.

[25] Ibid., p. 453.

[26] Sadiki, pp. 108–9.

for describing their opponents. Interviews with Islamists in a variety of countries have indicated that the vocabulary of Islamic ethics (*akhlaq*) forms the basis for the most important critiques of the West and its democracy, in terms of sexual perversity, imperialism, and materialism.[27] Despite the intrinsic interest of these observations, however, the stark difference between these opposing secularist and Islamist positions furnishes the opportunity for taking up an analysis that does not necessarily echo either formulation.

In a similar fashion, it is worth examining the term secular and its derivatives, which are the subject of much debate not only in the countries which enshrine secularism as a national principle (France, Indonesia, Turkey), but in other places as well. The early articulation of Orientalism postulated Europe as the abode of science and progressive thinking, with the official Enlightenment doctrine of secularism as a close corollary. This entailed as its opposite the projection of the Orient as the realm of retrograde superstition, with religion as the chief obstacle to progress. Occidentalist reversals were not slow to appear. Tagore, to give one example, argued that India was a civilization that enshrined spirituality while the West had abandoned its religion for a crass materialism. The problem with this assertion is its lack of historical evidence. It may certainly be a satisfying assertion to claim that the West is a soulless land where people watch music videos endlessly in a corrupt abandonment of spirituality. But this hardly corresponds with the picture that emerges from any sociological study of religion and its current role in American and European societies.

Some commentators have argued the issue of secularism in a more serious fashion. Malaysian thinker Syed Muhamad Naquib al-Attas argued, two decades ago, that secularization was a critical problem for the West, which would ultimately prove its downfall.[28] As a protective gesture against this danger, he was one of the proponents of "the Islamization of knowledge,"

---

[27] Ibid.

[28] Syed Muhamad Naquib al-Attas, *Islam, Secularism and the Philosophy of the Future*, Islamic Futures and Policy Studies (London: Mansell Publishing Ltd., 1985).

conceived as a way to ensure Islamic authenticity without any taint of Western secularism. The ideological character of this argument is apparent from the way in which it enshrines a particular alleged characteristic of "the West" as a timeless defining feature. Some Muslims argue from a position of scriptural essentialism that the American doctrine of separation of church and state is inherent in the teachings of the New Testament as we know it, but that this privatized notion of religion is foreign to Islam. This is interesting as a critique of the modern Euro-American concept of religion, although it frequently glosses over the way in which Islam formed one feature of premodern societies alongside of empire, local custom, and administrative decree without being the defining or overriding characteristic. To be sure, it is noteworthy that al-Attas did a close reading of a number of modern Christian theologians and European philosophers who addressed the issue of secularism during the 1960s and 1970s. Unfortunately, this limited sample is not actually definitive either of the past or future of Europe and America. This is one example where the collapse of Europe and America into an entity known as "the West" is clearly mistaken. Predictions of the disappearance of religion and the dominance of a secular mentality proved to be far off the mark after the Iranian revolution of 1978–79 and the rise of the religious right in America. Just to give one example, public opinion surveys in America indicate that the one issue that would cause the most voters to reject a presidential candidate would be a lack of belief in God. There are numerous indices that indicate that America is a country where religion is extraordinarily important. A number of commentators argue that the religious factor is so strong that America is in danger of becoming a theocracy.[29] Reputedly only a third of Americans acknowledge their confidence in the Darwinian theory of biological evolution, the rest presumably favoring a creationist approach or some other alternative. A series of apocalyptic novels entitled *Left Behind*, describing the events of the Day of Judgment and the resurrection according to the Book of

---

[29] Kevin Phillips, *American Theocracy: The Peril and Politics of Radical Religion, Oil, and Borrowed Money in the 21st Century* (New York: Penguin, 2007).

Revelation, has sold over 65 million copies in America. Abundant information on these and other issues touching the extraordinary role of religion in American life are available from the Pew Forum on Religion in Public Life (http://pewforum.org/). It is evidently necessary to do some more up-to-date investigation of the concept of secularization in Europe and America to understand the fortunes of this concept today.

Contemporary scholars like José Casanova, in conversation with anthropologist Talal Asad, have pointed out how the European critique of religion in the Enlightenment became a kind of self-fulfilling prophecy, a teleological theory of secularization that sufficed as its own proof.[30] The data alleged in support of this thesis as it applied to Europe included the increased differentiation of society, the reduction of the public role of religion in the state, science, and economy, plus a decreased percentage of active religious participation (despite the persistence of high religious belief). The secularization thesis was probably overstated, however, for nineteenth century Europe, which like the modern Middle East "in fact, saw a return to militant, literal, old-fashioned religion as processes of economic expansion began to threaten traditional structures."[31] In contrast, the American situation was seen as a reversal, based on the postulate that official disestablishment of religion correlated with a high degree of individual religiosity, as observed by Tocqueville and Marx. This classic divergence between Europe and America in the expectation of secularization has also been paralleled by different results in effects of secularization upon Catholic and Protestant communities. For Catholics, the conflict with modernity eventually led to a progressive secularism including social activism (e.g., liberation theology); Protestants saw instead the development of a collusion between the religious and the secular. An interesting case study is the example of human rights

---

[30] José Casanova, "A Reply to Talal Asad," in *Powers of the Secular Modern: Talal Asad And His Interlocutors*, ed. David Scott and Charles Hirschkind, Cultural Memory in the Present (Stanford, CA: Stanford University Press, 2006), pp. 12–30.

[31] Sandra Halperin, "Europe in the Mirror of the Contemporary Middle East: Aspects of Modern European History Reconsidered," in *Islam and the West: Critical Perspectives on Modernity*, ed. Michael J. Thompson (New York: Rowman & Littlefield Publishers, Inc., 2003), pp. 75–105, quoting p. 98.

and religious dissent. The Catholic Church was slow to warm to this issue during the nineteenth century, but there have been notable recent examples of Catholic Bishops demanding that the secular sphere be connected to public morality, in issues ranging from economics to birth control. The secularization theory according to Harvey Cox and others presupposed that modernity would inevitably mean a gradual abandonment of institutional religion, but this has proven to be spectacularly wrong for the late twentieth century and the emerging twenty-first century. There are also significant differences between concepts of secularism in different countries such as France, America, Turkey, and Indonesia. The inability of the secularization theories of the 1960s and 1970s to account for recent events or different countries indicates their unsuitability as an index of timeless features of the Western civilization.

What, then, are the alternatives to continuing with the familiar opposition of "the West" and Islam? This essay is certainly one such alternative: a presentation in English originally delivered in Malaysia with key members of the audience being graduates of a distinguished American university. How can the division between "the West" and Islam describe this kind of conversation? More substantively, I would suggest a number of directions that can be pursued so as to avoid what I have described as the inherently conflictual basis of the concept of "the West". One such agenda would be to encourage the equivalent of area studies in Malaysian universities and in other academic institutions in Southeast Asia and related regions for the study of the societies of North America and Europe. Rather than an ideological Occidentalism, this would be a kind of academic study that would concentrate on expertise in the culture, history, institutions, and practices of particular countries and regions such as America, Britain, France, etc. While area studies have their limitations, their virtue is to encourage multidisciplinary approaches to a particular region, which enables specialists from different fields of study to communicate and to broaden their own expertise with a view to creating more holistic and comprehensive analyses. Another prospect is to identify ethical communities that go beyond national and religious boundaries, as philosopher Alisdair McIntyre has put it, though there will admittedly have to be negotiations about multiple historical traditions. Tariq Ramadan has proposed in a similar fashion that Muslims should seek united fronts of interests between countries of the global South, regardless of their religious background. His point is that "an authentic dialogue between Jews, Christians, humanists and Muslims cannot but lead to a formidable common action of resistance to human folly, injustice and exploitation."[32] It is noteworthy that Ramadan's use of the economic language of industrialized North and developing South, while it remains contrastive, still avoids the ideological model inherent in the concepts of East and West. And my colleague at Duke University, Omid Safi, building on the Progressive Muslim project, argues the following: "It is mandatory to visit, challenge, critique, and deconstruct the powerful and seductive paradigm of 'Islam versus the West' (and the twin 'clash of civilizations') before we can offer a more holistic alternative. To do so, we will first deal with Muslim Westernophobes and then with Western Islamophobes."[33] In short, the language of "the West" and Islam shackles us to a past that is defined by colonial expansion and its contrary, anti-colonial resistance. If we are to forge a world where we can see beyond limited identities and seriously think about our shared humanity, it is time to move beyond these limited conceptions.

[32] Tariq Ramadan, *Islam, the West and the Challenges of Modernity* (Markfield, Leicester: The Islamic Foundation, 2001), p. 185.

[33] Omid Safi, "I and Thou in a Fluid World: Beyond 'Islam Versus the West,'" in *Voices of Islam*, ed. Vincent J. Cornell, volume 5, *Voices of Change*, ed. Omid Safi (Westport, CT: Prager, 2007), pp. 199–222, quoting p. 199.

4

Muḥammad as the Pole of Existence

It is difficult to question the importance of the Prophet Muḥammad for Islamic history, and indeed for world history. Yet the peculiar concerns of modern society tend to furnish the lenses through which figures like Muḥammad are viewed today. That is, modern biographies of the Prophet tend to see him chiefly as a leader responsible for establishing a movement, the significance of which is to be gauged mainly in terms of its social and political impact. His prophetic role is often understood primarily in terms of the establishment of ritual and legal norms that in principle governed the habits of an emerging Islamic civilization. The modern European concept of multiple religions carries with it assumptions about a contest between major religions for establishing a dominant position in the world today. Thus a prophet who is viewed as the founder of one of the world's major religions is inevitably seen in retrospect mostly as a key player in this historic struggle. This observation holds both for non-Muslim Euro-Americans alarmed about the very existence of Islam, and for Muslim triumphalists who take refuge in Islam as an anti-colonial identity. Modern reformist Muslims tend to downplay suggestions that the Prophet could have had any extraordinary status beyond ordinary human beings, and the Protestant inclinations that characterize much of the contemporary climate of opinion on religion (for Christians and non-Christians alike) reinforce the notion that Islam is a faith that lacks the supernatural baggage to be found, for instance, in Catholic Christianity. The legacy of anti-Islamic polemics among Christians since medieval times has also helped focus attention (mostly negative) on Muḥammad as a political and military leader.

From such a socio-political perspective, it therefore might seem surprising that Muḥammad has also been seen for centuries in a quite different light, as the prophet whose spiritual and cosmic role is the most important aspect of his career. Far from being viewed as a mere postman who delivered a message that happened to be of divine origin, for a considerable portion of pre-modern Muslims, Muḥammad was the primordial light through which God created world, viewed in semi-philosophical terms as the "Muḥammadan reality". The ascension of Muḥammad into the heavens and the divine presence, possibly alluded to in a couple of passages in the Qur'an, became a major theme defining his spiritual supremacy as "the seal of the prophets". Muḥammad was described as a human being of perfect beauty, immune from sin, whose life was marked by miracles testifying to his extraordinary status. He became the focus of a speculative prophetology, which, particularly in the hands of mystical thinkers of the Sufi tradition, drew upon the metaphysical concepts of philosophers like Ibn Sīnā to formulate a cosmic understanding of Muḥammad's role in relation to the emerging notion of sainthood (*walāya*). Concomitantly, the Prophet became increasingly invested with the power of intercession for the souls of the faithful on Judgment Day, a concept that would have wide repercussions on popular religious practice. This salvific power of Muḥammad became tangible in the form of devotional performances of literary texts in different languages, as well as the dreams and visions through which both elite mystics and ordinary believers could have direct access to the spirit of the Prophet. For these mystical understandings of the Prophet Muḥammad, we are particularly indebted to the research of Annemarie Schimmel, whose work is the standard reference on this subject.[1]

[1] Annemarie Schimmel, *And Muhammad Is His Messenger: The Veneration of the Prophet in Islamic Piety* (Chapel Hill: The University of North Carolina Press, 1985).

Since the literature on the Prophet's mystical qualities is vast, it will be convenient to begin with a short text that illustrates a number of important themes occurring in later Muslim piety. This is one of the short essays in rhyming Arabic prose composed by the early Sufi and martyr, al-Hallaj (d. 922), entitled *Ṭā-Sīn of the Lamp*. Without dwelling on the esoteric letter symbolism alluded to in the first words of the title, one can quickly recognize the powerful imagery of light that occurs throughout this passage, presenting Muhammad as the vessel through which the light of God is communicated to humanity. Moreover, Hallaj makes it clear that Muḥammad not only is foremost among humanity's elite, the prophets, but also has a transcendental status beyond the confines of space and time. While Hallaj securely anchors the career of Muḥammad to the Sanctuary of Mecca and the historical context of his companions such as Abū Bakr, he nevertheless identifies the actions of the Prophet as transparent reflections of the will of God and even as an indication of his unity with God:

> A lamp appeared from the light of the hidden realm; it returned, and surpassed the other lamps, and prevailed. A moon manifested itself among the other moons, a star whose constellation is in the heaven of secrets. God called Muḥammad "illiterate" (Qur'an 7:157) to concentrate his inspiration, "man of the Sanctuary" to increase of his fortune, and "Meccan" to reinforce his nearness to Him. God "opened his breast" (Qur'an 6:125), raised his rank, enforced his command, and revealed his full moon. His full moon arose from the cloud of Yamama, his sun dawned in the environs of Tahama, and his lamp radiated a mine of generosity. He only taught from his own insight, and he only commanded his example by the beauty of his life. He was present before God and made God present, he saw and informed, he cautioned and warned.
>
> No one has seen him in reality except his companion, (Abu Bakr) the Confirmer. For he was in agreement with him, and then he was his companion, so that no division would occur between them. No one really knew him, for all were ignorant of his true description. "Those to whom We gave the Book know Muḥammad as they know their own sons, but there is a division among them, who conceal the truth although they know it" (Qur'an 2:146). The lights of prophecy emerged from his light, and his lights appeared from the light of the Hidden. None of their lights is brighter, more splendid, or takes greater precedence in eternity, than the light of the Master of the Sanctuary.

His aspiration preceded all other aspirations, his existence preceded nothingness, and his name preceded the Pen, because he existed before all peoples. There is not in the horizons, beyond the horizons, or below the horizons, anyone more elegant, more noble, more knowing, more just, more fearsome, or more compassionate, than the subject of this tale. He is the leader of created beings, the one "whose name is glorious (Aḥmad)" (Qur'an 61:6). His nature is unique, his command is most certain, his essence is most excellent, his attribute is most illustrious, and his aspiration is most distinctive. How wonderful! How splendid, clear and pure, how magnificent and famous, how illuminated, capable, and patient he is! His fame was unceasing, before all created beings existed, and his renown was unceasing before there was any "before" and after any "after," when no substance or colors existed. His substance is pure, his word is prophetic, his knowledge is lofty, his expression is Arabic, his direction of prayer is "neither of the East nor the West" (Qur'an 24:35), his descent is paternal, his peer (Gabriel) is lordly, and his companion (Abu Bakr) is of his people.

Eyes have insight by his guidance, and inner minds and hearts attain their knowledge through him. God made him speak, the proof confirmed him, and God dispatched him. He is the proof and he is the proven. He is the one who polished the rust from the mirror of the suffering breast. He is the one who brought an eternal Word, timeless, unspoken, and uncreated, which is united with God without separation, and which passes beyond the understanding. He is the one who told of the ends, and the end of the end. He lifted the clouds and pointed to "the house of the Sanctuary" (Qur'an 5:97). He is the perfect one, he is the magnanimous one, he is the one who ordered the idols to be smashed, he is the one who tore away the clouds, he is the one sent to all humanity, and he is the one who distinguishes between favor and prohibition.

Above him, a cloud flashed lightning, and beneath him, lightning flashed and sparkled. It rained and brought forth fruit. All sciences are but a drop from his ocean, all wisdom but a spoonful from his sea, and all times are but an hour from his duration. Truth exists through him, and through him reality exists; sincerity exists through him, and companionship exists through him. Chaos exists through him, and order exists through him (cf. Qur'an 21:30). He is "the first" in attaining union and "the last" in prophecy, "the outward" in knowledge "and the inward" in reality (Qur'an 57:3). No learned man has attained to his knowledge, and no sage is aware of his understanding. God did not give him up to His creation, for he is He, as I am He, and "He is He."

Never has anyone departed from the M of Muḥammad, and no one has entered the H. (As for) his H, the second M, the D, and the M at the beginning: the D is his permanence (*dawām*), the M is his rank (*maḥall*),

> the H is his spiritual state (*ḥāl*), and the second M is his speech (*maqāl*). (God) revealed his proclamation, He displayed his proof, "He caused the Criterion (the Qur'an) to descend" (Qur'an 3:4), He made his tongue speak, He illuminated his paradises, He reduced his opponents to impotence, He confirmed his explanation, He raised his dignity. If you fled from his field, then where would be the path when there is no guide, you suffering one? For the wisdom of the sages, next to his wisdom, is "shifting sand" (Qur'an 73:14).[2]

The density of the Qur'anic allusions that Hallaj summons to evoke his mystical portrait points to what was already in his time a tradition of deep interiorization of scripture combined with speculation about the text's relationship with the messenger who delivered it.

The theme of Muḥammad as light seems to be anticipated in the Qur'an, where the Prophet is called "a shining lamp" (*sirāj munīr*, 33:46), a phrase to which Hallaj clearly refers by the title of his treatise. Several other Qur'anic texts dealing with light have also been frequently understood as symbols for the Prophet Muḥammad, particularly the famous "light verse" (24:35), where the eighth-century interpreter Muqātil understood the "lamp" (*miṣbāḥ*) mentioned there to be once again a symbol for the Prophet as the vessel of the divine light. Likewise, sura 93, "The Morning Light" (*al-ḍuḥā*), was convincingly interpreted as an address to the Prophet.

The stage had been set for the interpretation of Muḥammad as the light of the world by Hallaj's teacher and predecessor, Sahl al-Tustarī (d. 896), who explicitly states that Adam was created from the light of Muḥammad:

> When God willed to create Muḥammad, he displayed from his own light a light that he spread through the entire kingdom. And when it came before (God's) Majesty it prostrated itself, and God created from its prostration a column of dense light like a vessel of glass, the inside being visible from the outside and the outside being visible from the

---

[2] This translation of Hallaj's *Ṭā-Sīn al-sirāj* has been modified from an earlier version, trans. Carl W. Ernst, *Teachings of Sufism* (Boston: Shambhala Publications, 1999), pp. 15–20, by comparison with the new edition by Stéphane Ruspoli, *Le Livre Tâwasîn de Hallâj* (Beirut: Dar Albouraq, 2007), pp. 319–23, along with Rūzbihān al-Baqlī, *Manṭiq al-asrār* (MS Tashkent), fols. 132–36.

> inside. In this column of light Muḥammad worshiped before the Lord of the Worlds a thousand thousand years with the primordial faith, being in the revealed presence of the invisible within the invisible realm a thousand thousand years before the beginning of creation. And God created Adam from the light of Muḥammad, and then Muḥammad from the clay of Adam; and the clay is created from the column in which Muḥammad worshiped.[3]

The key to this striking image of the light of Muḥammad is clearly his emanation from the divine light and his priority over Adam as the beginning of the sequence of prophecy.

As Schimmel has observed, the subsequent elaboration of the symbolism of the light of Muḥammad owes a great deal to the Andalusian Sufi master Ibn `Arabi (d. 1240) and his interpreter `Abd al-Karīm al-Jīlī (d. ca. 1408), and there are numerous reflections of this doctrine in poetry composed in Arabic, Persian, and other languages.[4] On a more abstract level, this light symbolism merges into the notion of the "Muḥammadan reality" (*al-ḥaqīqa al-Muḥammadiyya*), which in turn is interpreted in terms of the "perfect human being" (*al-insān al-kāmil*), combining both a cosmic and a revelatory function that is inherited by the prophets and, eventually, the Sufi saints.

In dramatic terms, the most striking aspect of the spiritual itinerary of the Prophet is undoubtedly his ascension (*mi`rāj*) into the heavens, and that voyage is commonly merged into the account of his night journey (*isrā`*) from Mecca to Jerusalem, which becomes the point of departure for the heavenly journey. Muslim interpreters have typically seen two Qur'ānic texts (17:1–2, 53:1–18) as the locations for these events. A large narrative tradition has emerged on this topic, beginning with stories found in the standard hadith collections, but expanding beyond that to encompass a broad range of texts in various languages, which may be fruitfully compared with the heavenly journeys found in other religious traditions of the Near East. Some of

---

[3] Abū 'l-Ḥasan `Alī b. Muḥammad al-Daylamī, *A Treatise on Mystical Love*, trans. Joseph Norment Bell and Hassan Mahmood Abdul Latif Al Shafie, Journal of Arabic and Islamic Studies Monograph Series 1 (Edinburgh: Edinburgh University Press, 2005), p. 54.

[4] Schimmel, pp. 123–43.

these texts are accompanied by extraordinary miniature paintings depicting the story's celestial landscapes and encounters with angels and prophets.[5] The complicated history of these ascension narratives has recently been traced by Frederick Colby.[6] As an example of this literature, one may take the important Arabic collection of Sufi sayings on the topic of the ascension, which was compiled by the noted Sufi scholar, al-Sulamī (d. 1021), under the title *The Subtleties of the Ascension*. As Colby points out, there are several separate emphases to be found in this text: first, the night journey and ascension "as proof for the unique status and favor that Muḥammad enjoyed"; second, the notion that Muḥammad was "clothed with the lights of the divine attributes", which links up with the theme of the light of Muḥammad; third, Muḥammad's direct vision of God, something that is not typically found in the standard hadith collections; and fourth, the stipulation that this experience of ascension was an esoteric one that could not be fully revealed to the public.[7] In this distinctively Sufi approach to the ascension of the Prophet, one may see an increasing refinement in the notion of his distinctive status and unique proximity to God.

The special ontological status of the Prophet Muḥammad found more direct expression in the widespread literature devoted to Muḥammad as the physical and spiritual model of beauty.[8] This emphasis on his beauty goes beyond formal obedience to the Prophet, which is enjoined in several passages from the Qur'an: "Whoever obeys the messenger obeys God" (4:80); "Those who swear allegiance to you swear allegiance to God" (48:10). While texts like those might have established a model of his legal and political authority, the Qur'an also conveys a much

[5] Marie Rose Séguy, *The Miraculous Journey of Mahomet: Mirâj nâmeh* (New York: G. Braziller, 1977); *The Prophet's Ascension: Cross-Cultural Encounters with the Islamic Mi'raj Tales*, ed. Frederick Colby and Christiane Gruber (Bloomington: Indiana University Press, 2010).

[6] Frederick Colby, *Narrating Muhammad's Night Journey: Tracing the Development of the Ibn 'Abbas Ascension Discourse* (Albany: State University of New York Press, 2008).

[7] Abū `Abd al-Raḥmān Sulamī, *The Subtleties of the Ascension: Early Mystical Sayings on Muhammad's Heavenly Journey*, ed. and trans. Frederick Colby (Louisville, KY: Fons Vitae, 2006), pp. 16–19.

[8] Schimmel, pp. 24–55.

loftier and more attractive status for him by calling Muḥammad "a mercy for creation" (21:107), "of noble character" (68:4), and "a beautiful model" (33:21). This combination of obedience and admiration as attitudes towards Muḥammad helps to explain the profound emotional attachment that many Muslims have had for the Prophet. While this personal connection to the Prophet is by no means restricted to Sufi adepts, devotion directed towards him is an exceptionally strong characteristic of Sufi practice. An example of this kind of devotion is found in the description of the physical appearance of the Prophet by a woman named Umm Ma`bad, who entertained the Prophet and his companion Abū Bakr on their way from Mecca to Medina:

> I saw a man, pure and clean, with a handsome face and a fine figure. He was not marred by a skinny body, nor was he overly small in the head and neck. He was graceful and elegant, with intensely black eyes and thick eyelashes. There was a huskiness in his voice, and his neck was long. His beard was thick, and his eyebrows were finely arched and joined together. When silent, he was grave and dignified, and when he spoke, glory rose up and overcame him. He was from afar the most beautiful of men and the most glorious, and close up he was the sweetest and the loveliest. He was sweet of speech and articulate, but not petty or trifling. His speech was a string of cascading pearls, measured so that none despaired of its length, and no eye challenged him because of brevity. In company he is like a branch between two other branches, but he is the most flourishing of the three in appearance, and the loveliest in power. He has friends surrounding him, who listen to his words. If he commands, they obey implicitly, with eagerness and haste, without frown or complaint.

This description, with its laconic Bedouin eloquence, found its way into artistic representation in the calligraphic pieces known as "the adornment of the Prophet" (*ḥilyat al-nabī*), an art form that was highly developed in the Ottoman realms. Surrounded by medallions bearing the names of the four "rightly-guided" caliphs, and prominent quotations of the Qur'anic passages on the cosmic and ethical centrality of the Prophet, these descriptions of Muḥammad's physical beauty, whether by Umm Ma`bad or `Alī, formed a kind of verbal icon to create the imaginative picture of the Prophet in one's mind, while avoiding the idolatry of visual representation.[9] Short texts like this were complemented by extensive works on the virtues of the Prophet, such as the extraordinarily popular *Guides to Blessings* (*Dalā'il al-khayrāt*) of al-Jazūlī (d. 1465), a collection of prayers for the Prophet which included descriptions of his tomb in Medina, and commonly featured facing pages of illustrations of that shrine, or else showed both Medina and Mecca.[10]

The admiration for the Prophet that is evident in the examples just mentioned found further devotional expressions that increasingly stressed his perfection, his charisma, and his ability to intercede with God for the forgiveness of others. All of these tendencies admittedly move away from those passages of the Qur'an that repeatedly remind Muḥammad he is only a human being.[11] Scholars began to enunciate the doctrine of his immunity from sin, a stipulation that included all other prophets as well.[12] Despite the well-known doctrine that the Prophet's only miracle was the Qur'an, it was not long before the story of this life was embroidered with tales of miracles.[13] Some of these stories could take the form of exegetical elaborations of enigmatic passages in the Qur'an. Thus, a modern dictionary of the Qur'an takes the opening lines of sura 94, literally, "Did We not open your breast?", as a figure of speech meaning, "Did We not prepare you to receive something spiritual?"[14] Traditional commentators took it in a different direction, providing a detailed narrative of an initiatic experience, in which angelic visitors removed from Muḥammad's heart the black spot of sin deposited in all other humans by Satan. Likewise, the eschatological

---

[9] Carl W. Ernst, *Following Muhammad: Rethinking Islam in the Contemporary World* (Chapel Hill: The University of North Carolina Press, 2003), pp. 76–79.

[10] Muḥammad ibn Sulaymān Jazūlī, *Guide to Goodness (Dalā'il al-khayrāt)*, trans. Hassan Rosowsky (Chicago, IL: Great Books of the Islamic World, n.d. [2001?]); Jan Just Witkam, "The Battle of the Images: Mekka vs. Medina in the Iconography of the Manuscripts of al-Jazūlī's *Dalā'il al-Khayrāt*," in *Theoretical Approaches to the Transmission and Edition of Oriental Manuscripts*, Proceedings of a Symposium Held in Istanbul 28–30 March 2001, ed. Judith Pfeiffer and Manfred Kropp (Beirut: Ergon Verlag Würzburg, 2007), pp. 67–84.

[11] Schimmel, p. 25.

[12] Schimmel, pp. 53–66.

[13] Schimmel, pp. 67–80.

[14] Arne A. Ambros with Stephan Procházka, *A Concise Dictionary of Koranic Arabic* (Wiesbaden: Reichert Verlag, 2004), p. 146.

sign mentioned in sura 54, where "the moon was split", was understood as a miracle by which the Prophet split the moon into two halves to demonstrate his authority to the pagans of Mecca. The growth of these miraculous accounts of Muḥammad in literature was considerable. Alongside these tendencies was an increasing focus on Muḥammad as the intercessor who could act to obtain God's forgiveness for the sins of others. On this important question of intercession, the Qur'an has a number of ambiguous passages, sometimes rejecting the possibility, yet at other times conceding that God may permit others to intercede with Him at the time of resurrection.[15] This theme is enlarged in hadith, where the standard collections of the Sunnis emphasize Muḥammad's ability to obtain God's forgiveness for his community, and indeed humanity at large.

The classic expression of devotional piety towards the Prophet, in terms of these themes of sinlessness, miraculous deeds, and intercession, is unquestionably the Arabic "Poem of the Cloak" (*Qaṣīdat al-Burda*) of the Egyptian poet al-Būṣīrī (d. 1298).[16] Written to celebrate the author's miraculous recovery from illness, which he attributed to the intervention of the Prophet, the *Burda* encapsulates all these key features of popular Islamic prophetology. One passage will suffice as an example of this text's insistence on Muḥammad's pre-eminence:

> Leave aside what Christians claim about their prophet,
>
> But award to him [Muḥammad] whatever you want in terms of praise, and stand by it,
>
> And ascribe to his person whatever you want in terms of nobility
>
> And ascribe to his power every greatness you want,
>
> For the excellence of the Messenger of God has no limit
>
> So that anyone who speaks with his mouth could express it completely.[17]

---

[15] Schimmel, pp. 80–104; A.J. Wensinck, Annemarie Schimmel, "Shafā`a," in *Encyclopaedia of Islam, Second Edition*, ed. P. Bearman, Th. Bianquis, C.E. Bosworth, E. van Donzel and W.P. Heinrichs (Brill, 2009, Brill Online, University of North Carolina at Chapel Hill, 18 January 2009 <http://www.brillonline.nl/subscriber/entry?entry=islam_COM-1019>).

[16] Schimmel, pp. 183–89.

[17] Schimmel, p. 187.

It is especially noteworthy that this Arabic poem was itself credited with miraculous and healing abilities, something that doubtless contributed to its widespread popularity in different regions from North Africa to Indonesia.

At this point we may pause for a moment to consider a fundamental problem that Henry Corbin has summarized under the phrase "the paradox of monotheism". While his exposition of this issue is complex, it may be simplified as follows: if the God of Revelation is indeed beyond intellect and explanation, the need of humanity decrees that there must be an intermediary to provide a connection to that transcendent source. In the case of a human prophet, after his demise there is a crisis, when the community of believers must decide how to proceed in his absence. While one formulation historically has moved towards scriptural codification of legal and authoritarian systems as ways to preserve the legacy of a prophet, there has always been a constituency that demands continuous access to the sources of inspiration. In the case of Shi`ism, the Imams step in to provide that continuing access to divine authority, at least for a few generations, and thereafter the religious class as a whole stands as the intermediary. In the broader stream of spirituality called Sufism, it is through the Sufi saints that God continues to manifest on an ongoing basis. In either instance, there is an insistence on the notion of proximity to God, inadequately translated in English as "sainthood", and summarized under the Arabic term *walāya*.[18] It is especially noteworthy that the insistence on the intermediate authority of the Prophet Muḥammad also entails working out the roles of later saintly figures who continue to relay the divine message to humanity, but whose own authority is closely linked to and dependent on that of the Prophet.

Speculative understanding of prophecy and sainthood therefore went hand-in-hand, and in some respects it was difficult to disentangle the two concepts. As the Persian Sufi Rūzbihān Baqlī (d. 1209) put it, "The oceans of sainthood and prophethood

---

[18] Vincent Cornell, *Realm of the Saint: Power and Authority in Moroccan Sufism* (Austin, TX: University of Texas Press, 1998); Carl W. Ernst, "Introduction," in *Manifestations of Sainthood in Islam*, ed. Grace Martin Smith with Carl W. Ernst, (Istanbul: The Isis Press, 1993), pp. xi–xxviii.

interpenetrate each other."[19] While the devotional approach to the Prophet elevated his status to a cosmic principle comparable to the Christian logos doctrine, the mystical knowledge of the Sufi saint who could announce such a discovery also in effect came close to claiming an authority equivalent to that of prophecy. This tension between sainthood and prophecy is prefigured in the Qur'anic account (in sura 18) of the encounter of Moses with the "servant of God", identified as the immortal prophet Khiḍr, who has a divine knowledge that is not available to the prophet, and the same theme recurs regularly in the history of Sufism. One famous example is the first encounter between the great Persian Sufi Jalāl al-Dīn Rūmī (d. 1273) and his master Shams-i Tabrīz; according to one account, Shams announced that the Prophet Muḥammad had said he could not praise God adequately, while the Sufi saint Bāyazīd Bisṭāmī had proclaimed, "Glory be to me! How great is my majesty!"—so which had the higher state? This question was so shocking that it reportedly caused Rūmī to faint.[20] While most Sufi theorists insisted on the supremacy of the Prophet Muḥammad, the issue of the relationship between prophecy and sainthood remained volatile, since the mystical knowledge of sainthood was in effect necessary for the validation of prophecy.

The most extensive formulation of mystical prophetology in Sufism is found in the works of Ibn `Arabi and his successors.[21] Building on the theories of al-Ḥakīm al-Tirmidhī (d. ca. 936), he developed the concept of "the seal of the saints" (*khatm al-awliyā'*) as an esoteric and eschatological parallel to the status of Muḥammad as "the seal of the prophets".[22] While Ibn `Arabi was scrupulous in stating the supremacy of the Prophet, yet it cannot be denied that his claims about his own status were spectacular,

---

[19] Ruzbihan Baqli, *The Unveiling of Secrets: Diary of a Sufi Master*, trans. Carl W. Ernst (Chapel Hill: Parvardigar Press, 1997), p. 7.

[20] Annemarie Schimmel, *The Triumphal Sun: A Study of the Works of Jalāloddin Rumi* (Albany: State University of New York Press, 1993), pp. xvii–xviii.

[21] Michel Chodkiewicz, *Seal of the Saints: Prophethood and Sainthood in the Doctrine of Ibn `Arabi*, trans. Liadain Sherrard (Oxford: Islamic Texts Society, 1993); Naṣr Ḥāmid Abū Zayd, *Hakādhā takallama Ibn `Arabī* (Cairo: al-Hay'ah al-Miṣriyya al-`Āmma lil-Kitāb, 2002; 2nd ed., Casablanca: al-Markaz al-Thiqāfī al-`Arabī, 2004), pp. 62–72.

[22] *The Concept of Sainthood in Early Islamic Mysticism: Two Works by Al-Ḥakīm Al-Tirmidhī*, trans. Bernd Radtke and John O'Kane (London: Routledge, 1996).

though the boldest of his declarations were circumspectly concealed in books that were esoteric to the point of creating secret alphabets.[23] In any case, the cosmic role of the Prophet was accompanied by an impressively detailed portrait of the invisible hierarchy of the saints, who form an extensive retinue, as it were, for the supreme spiritual figure of Muḥammad. From a historical and ritual perspective, the centrality of the Prophet for the mystical tradition was evident in the formulation of the spiritual genealogies of the Sufi orders, which in every case were traced back to the Prophet as the source of spiritual knowledge. The oath of allegiance (*bay`a*) that the Arabs gave to the Prophet, sealed by a handshake, became the rite of initiation that was transmitted through the chain (*silsila*) of Sufi masters and disciples, constituting the authentic path of knowledge because of its prophetic source.

Yet there is certainly an overlap between the spiritual and cosmic status of the Prophet and the saint. An illustration is provided by the following poem addressed to the Prophet by al-Jīlī, known as a theorist of the doctrine of the perfect human:

> O Center of the compass! O inmost ground of the truth!
>
> O pivot of necessity and contingency!
>
> O eye of the entire circle of existence! O point of the Koran and the Furqan!
>
> O perfect one, and perfecter of the most perfect, who has been beautified by the majesty of God the Merciful!
>
> Thou art the Pole (*quṭb*) of the most wondrous things. The sphere of perfection in its solitude turns on thee.
>
> Thou art transcendent, nay thou art immanent, nay thine is all that is known and unknown, everlasting and imperishable.
>
> Thine in reality is Being and not-being; nadir and zenith are thy two garments.
>
> Thou art both the light and its opposite, nay but thou art only darkness to a gnostic who is dazed.[24]

---

[23] Gerald Elmore, *Islamic Sainthood in the Fullness of Time: Ibn Al-`Arabī's Book of the Fabulous Gryphon* (Leiden: E. J. Brill, 1999).

[24] Translated by R. A. Nicholson, *Studies in Islamic Mysticism*, pp. 86–87, cited in Schimmel, *And Muhammad Is His Messenger: The Veneration of the Prophet in Islamic Piety*, pp. 137–38.

The key term here is the pole or axis (*quṭb*), a symbol invoking the centrality of the Pole Star as the pivot around which the cosmos turns. While al-Jīlī applies this epithet to the Prophet Muḥammad, it is most commonly addressed to eminent mystics considered to perform the central role of sustaining the universe in their own day. And while from an ordinary geometrical view it might seem superfluous or contradictory to have more than one center, the mystical imagination has no problem with multiple centers of the world, so that the phrase "pole of poles" (*quṭb al-aqṭāb*) frequently occurs as a hyperbolic expression for the spiritual supremacy of a particularly favored saint. It is, moreover, on the basis of the applicability of that term, pole (*quṭb*), both to the Prophet and to the saints, that it can be used in the title for this chapter.

The horizontal transmission of prophetic blessing through the Sufi lineages was certainly an important manifestation of the ongoing role of the Prophet Muḥammad in Muslim religious life, but this institutional framework was far from exhausting the possibility of connecting to his spiritual essence. From an early date, it was recognized that dreams were a less intense version of the divine communication of prophecy, and dreams of the Prophet were accorded a special status; it was, after all, recorded in a hadith that Satan could never insinuate himself into a dream in the Prophet's form, so dreams featuring Muḥammad had the distinction of being true.[25] Thus even for ordinary people, it was possible to have direct vertical contact with the Prophet through a dream without being dependent on a Sufi initiation. But for elite mystics, waking visions also offered direct access to encounters with prophets and angels, sometimes on a daily basis.[26] A number of Sufis are reported to have made regular visits to the tomb of the Prophet in Medina, by miraculous means,

---

[25] Nile Green, "The Religious and Cultural Roles of Dreams and Visions in Islam," *Journal of the Royal Asiatic Society* 13 (2003), pp. 287–313; Jonathan G. Katz, *Dreams, Sufism and Sainthood: The Visionary Career of Muhammad al-Zawâwî* (Leiden: E. J. Brill, 1996); Pierre Lory, *Le rêve et ses interprétations en Islam* (Paris, Albin Michel, 2003); and Annemarie Schimmel *Die Träume des Kalifen : Träume und ihre Deutung in der islamischen Kultur* (München: C. H. Beck, 1998).

[26] Carl W. Ernst, *Ruzbihan Baqli: Mystical Experience and the Rhetoric of Sainthood in Persian Sufism* (London: Curzon Press, 1996); Ruzbihan Baqli, *The Unveiling of Secrets: Diary of a Sufi Master*, trans. Carl W. Ernst (Chapel Hill: Parvardigar Press, 1997).

where they received hadith directly from his spirit without any intermediary. There were even some Sufis who specialized in the talent of producing dreams of the Prophet for others, in this way democratizing access to the source of spirituality.[27]

If anything, it may be said that the focus on the Prophet Muḥammad in Sufi circles has continued to increase, regardless of whether the means of transmission was extraordinary, as in dreams or visions, or through the normal course of the study of hadith. Scholars have sometimes observed that the seventeenth and eighteenth centuries were a time of considerable activity, focused in Arabia, for the study of hadith, and that the principal networks fostering this scholarship were articulated through Sufi orders, prior to the rise of the Wahhābī movement with its strongly anti-Sufi attitude.[28] It was a highly mystical form of devotion to the Prophet Muḥammad that sustained the work of eminent Sufi scholars such as `Alī al-Muttaqī, `Abd al-Ḥaqq Muḥaddith Dihlawī, Ibrāhīm Kūrānī, and others. Indeed, it may be said that the forms of devotion sometimes referred to as the "Muḥammadan path" (*ṭarīqa Muḥammadiyya*) were not any kind of new ideology or institutional structure of Sufism, but simply a marked emphasis on the centrality of the Prophet.[29] In modern Egypt, for example, classical Sufi concepts such as the "annihilation" (*fanā'*) of the self have been redefined in effect as intense devotional absorption in the Prophet and his family.[30]

The major changes in Islamic thought signaled by the emergence of the Wahhābī movement in the late eighteenth century are still being felt today, but this is particularly the case with respect to its radical critique of the entire worldview associated with the notion of spiritual intercession. Recalling the view of Ibn Taymiyya that an intention to visit the tomb of the

---

[27] Meenakshi Khanna, "Dreams, and Visions in North Indian Sufic Traditions ca. (1500–1800) A.D.," PhD thesis, Jawaharlal Nehru University, New Delhi, 2001.

[28] John O. Voll, "Hadith Scholars and Tariqahs: An Ulama Group in the 18th-Century Haramayn and their Impact in the Islamic World," *Journal of Asian and African Studies* 15.3–4 (1980), pp. 264–72.

[29] Schimmel, *And Muhammad Is His Messenger: The Veneration of the Prophet in Islamic Piety*, pp. 216–38, where the political unity of this tendency is perhaps overstated.

[30] Valerie Hoffman, *Sufism, Mystics, and Saints in Modern Egypt* (Columbia, SC: University of South Carolina Press, 1995).

Prophet invalidates the performance of the ḥajj to Mecca, his successors in Wahhābī and Salafī circles have rejected many pious practices involving the visitation of the tombs of saints, imams, and indeed the Prophet himself, where police officials today severely discourage any undue expression of emotion that might be construed as an idolatrous reverence of the Prophet as more than human. Thus celebrating the Prophet's birthday is unlawful in Saudi Arabia today, and it is striking to see how many historical sites associated with the Prophet Muḥammad and his family (particularly the Jannat al-Baqī` cemetery in Medina) have been demolished or, more recently, removed in the name of urban development. This debate is not confined to Arab circles, either. Nineteenth-century reformist thinkers in India engaged in intense debates over questions such as standing or making other gestures of respect when the Prophet's name was mentioned. The controversies between the two major schools of the Barelwis and the Deobandis in South Asia swirl around the practices of intercessory piety, which the former defend and the latter reject, and the same issue applies whether it is the Prophet or the Sufi saints whose status is under discussion.[31] Examples of this debate among contemporary Muslims over the Prophet's status could be multiplied indefinitely. But the strength of the emotional and spiritual attachments to the Prophet Muḥammad among a significant proportion of Muslims today must be considered to demonstrate the ongoing importance of this tradition that reveres his central place in the cosmos. It can still be summarized in the memorable Arabic verses of the poet Sa`dī (d. 1292):

> He reached the acme (peak) of grandeur by his perfections,
> He dispersed the tenebrous clouds of darkness through his beauty.
> Excellent were all his character traits;
> Then shower your blessings upon him and his family![32]

[31] Usha Sanyal, *Devotional Islam and Politics in British India: Ahmad Riza Khan Barelwi and His Movement, 1870–1920* (New Delhi: Oxford University Press, 1999).

[32] Gholamreza Aavani, "Glorification of the Prophet Muhammad in the Poems of Sa'adi" <http://www.irip.ir/userfiles/Archive/Papers/English/R&M/Glorification%20of%20the%20Prophet%20Muhammad%20in%20the%20Poems%20of%20Sa'adi.pdf>.

5

It's Not Just Academic: Writing Public Scholarship in Middle Eastern and Islamic Studies[1]

Everyone knows that the work of scholars in America is often considered to be irrelevant to the real issues of life. According to the mild anti-intellectualism that seems to be an endemic feature of American culture, anything that is "academic" is automatically impractical, complex, and impenetrable—in short, it is bad. This is a little hard for professors to live with; no one likes being called a pointy-headed intellectual or an egghead. The very skills and specializations that are the keys to academic success can be seen by the public as defects that remove scholars from the sphere of ordinary existence and disqualify their pronouncements. Here I would like to argue that the gap between academics and an unappreciative public is in good part a function of the language and style of communication that scholars commonly practice in all fields. But if in fact there are large segments of the public who are keenly interested

[1] I would like to thank Fatemeh Keshavarz and Ahmet Karamustafa, of the University of Maryland, and Shafique Virani of the University of Toronto, for encouraging my initial public reflections on this topic.

in issues relating to subjects like Middle Eastern studies, or the study of Islam, it should be possible for academics to communicate the results of their labor in clear and meaningful ways. If qualified scholars do not respond to the demands of the public, we know what the alternative is: the public will remain content with the standard media sources of information—and disinformation. In response to this problem, I would like to sketch out some of the barriers preventing academics from communicating to the public, and to propose some ways to make scholarly research on these topics more accessible and available to a public that genuinely wants to understand them. While some of these observations apply to the academy at large, I will also reflect on some of the particular problems—and publics—that face scholars in Middle Eastern and Islamic studies.

The task of making scholarship accessible to public audiences, no matter the subject, is complicated by one of the central features of graduate education today, the doctoral dissertation. This is a literary work aimed at just about the smallest possible audience, the five members of the doctoral committee. Frequently, dissertation writers feel compelled to write in contorted ways, sometimes inserting incompatible items in order to satisfy the well-known prejudices of Professor X, or making sure to quote approvingly from the lesser-known articles of Professor Y. Excessive use of the passive voice, coy polemics buried in footnotes, insider jargon, and obsession with bibliographical minutiae are several of the less attractive aspects of dissertation style. The exercise of researching and eventually writing the dissertation, which can stretch over several years, is a powerful experience, creating in the scholar a sort of academic conscience that tends to be perfectionist and unforgiving. Some people never get over it. There are scholars who over the course of an academic career seem to be unable to write in any other way than in the arcane style they learned in the dissertation.

On the face of it, the compulsion to continue to write in the dissertation style is odd. After all, everyone uses a different register and language for addressing different audiences, such as family members, children, or friends. There is a time and place for different styles of communication, including creative forms such as poetry, which some academics are rumored to compose.

Nevertheless, dissertation-style writing permeates academic writing to an alarming degree. It is ironic that the very time when graduate students should be preparing for entering into a profession in which they will need to communicate with a wide range of colleagues (not to mention students) is the same time that they are moving into ever-narrower areas of expertise.

Another aspect of academic life that militates against public scholarship is an open scorn and derision directed at writing that might be considered "popular". I vividly recall, while in graduate school in the late 1970s, hearing both graduate students and faculty members speak scathingly about someone who had written a book that had moderately successful sales and was even mentioned in newspapers. The basic idea seemed to be that it was a kind of treason to write in a style that departed from the esoteric forms and conventions of what may be called *The Journal of Obscure Studies*. I have known more than a few people who freely confessed that their ultimate goal was to publish a book with a certain European press that will remain unnamed, which they imagined would confer upon them the academic status and dignity that they sought. The notion that such a publication would be priced out of the range any fellow scholar could afford, or that it would get little distribution outside of a few libraries, was not something that they considered relevant. Now it is true that many scholars feel the need, from time to time, to write specialized pieces aimed at the most serious of readers. But isn't it possible to entertain writing for a larger public as well?

One of the key markers of specialization is technical terminology, the use of which automatically divides readers into insiders and outsiders. Those who are in the know recognize familiar signals, while the uninitiated feel frustration on seeing strange and baffling terms. For graduate students, learning the jargon of the field (including the study of Middle Eastern languages) is part of their entry into scholarship, but too often they fail to appreciate the cost such language incurs by excluding a good portion of their potential audience. It is common to hear students using hard-core technical terms, or even worse, sprinkling their conversation liberally with Arabic words, to demonstrate their status as insiders. They may not recognize the extent to which this coded language gets them off the hook in terms of their responsibility to explain what they mean. But assuming that one's audience is the perfect reader is almost like asking for a mind-reader; in such a case, one is absolved of the duty to take a stand in interpretation, since one assumes that the reader should divine one's inner thoughts. For this reason, I demand that research papers should be written clearly and entirely in English, and I have outlawed the use of Arabic broken plurals in conversation. Technical terms can accomplish legitimate work for readers, of course, but one needs to weigh the benefits and costs of using them. The same principle applies to diacritical marks, which are generally useless for those who do not know the original languages and superfluous for those who do.

Well over a decade after receiving the PhD, I had several writing experiences that led me to question the idea of remaining stuck in dissertation style forever. Over several years, I went through a process almost akin to deprogramming, in which I deliberately began to set aside certain kinds of writing habits and cultivate new ones. This happened first as a matter of style, with my translation of an Arabic Sufi text, which was a very challenging project.[2] After struggling with the powerful metaphorical style of the author, and his intricate vocabulary, I produced a draft translation which was reasonably satisfactory, in my view. But then, with the publisher's encouragement, I located an editor who was not only experienced in editing university press publications, but was also herself a published poet and critic, and even a judge in poetry competitions. Her approach to editing the translation can only be described as ruthless. I was amazed to see the manuscript come back with at least ten yellow slips on every page, taking me to task for indulging in a vocabulary that automatically excluded many potential readers. "There is a literary style in English," she remarked to me, "that is appropriate for a mystical text, and it goes back to the 14th century and *The Cloud of Unknowing*. It does not," she added sternly, "include a lot of Latinate and Greek-derived words." In addition, she cautioned me that, in general, any readable book should employ no more

[2] This translation was published as Ruzbihan Baqli, *The Unveiling of Secrets: Diary of a Sufi Master* (Chapel Hill: Parvardigar Press, 1997).

than a dozen foreign words, and those need to be clearly and carefully explained. On reflection, I realized that I had imbibed a highly technical vocabulary from reading specialized works of scholarship, including works in French which tend to habituate one towards using a Latin-based terminology. Moreover, the habits I had picked up were flagrantly opposed to the principles of clear writing that I increasingly was requiring of students, since teaching writing has become an essential part of nearly all courses in humanities disciplines. My writing, in other words, was not up to the mark of Strunk & White's *Elements of Style*, nor did it adhere to the standards of George Orwell's 1946 essay on "Politics and the English Language", in terms of economy of expression, vigorous word choice, and clarity of meaning.[3] In practice, this harsh editing experience provided me with several liberating realizations, and I deliberately embraced the notion that clarity should triumph over insider language.

The second step took place on the level of argument, when I undertook to write a couple of introductory books for general audiences. One was commissioned by a trade publisher who asked me to write a survey of Islamic mysticism.[4] The other, which took this process a step further, was an introduction to Islam, something I had previously resisted due to my discomfort with the standard notion of a textbook.[5] That is, the textbook approach employs an authoritative mode of discourse that can be easily reduced to a list of bullet points. It proclaims statements about the way things are, and it is welcomed particularly by younger students who want to know mainly what questions will be asked on the final exam. The textbook mode is simplistic and prone to the bald assertion of ahistorical truths that can drive scholars

---

[3] William Strunk, Jr. and E.B. White, *The Elements of Style* (New York: Penguin Press, 2007); George Orwell, "Politics and the English Language," *Horizon* (April 1946), available online at <http://www.resort.com/~prime8/Orwell/patee.html>.

[4] Carl W. Ernst, *Guide to Sufism* (Boston: Shambhala Publications, 1997); reprint ed., under the title *Sufism: An Introduction to the Mystical Tradition of Islam* (Boston: Shambhala Publications, 2011).

[5] This book eventually became *Following Muhammad: Rethinking Islam in the Contemporary World* (Chapel Hill: The University of North Carolina Press, 2003; New Delhi: Yoda Press, 2005).

crazy; too often it represents a condescending dumbing down of scholarship. What is the alternative?

I propose the model of "stealth analysis". This is a method of presenting to the reader an argument and accompanying evidence that enable the reader to understand the critical issues and consequences that are at stake in any particular issue. It is most effectively done by providing a compelling example that demands engagement by the reader, effectively providing a reason for the reader to entertain a new narrative, and to construct a path to the explanation of that example, in a way that goes beyond received opinions. This style of presentation needs to be done without jargon, since jargon both reduces the size of the possible audience and short-circuits critical thought by inviting the reader to employ slogans. It need not sacrifice any of the subtlety or ambiguity that scholars find in their research; it presents a reasonable amount of references to the best of current university press publications and summarizes the main issues and debates. Ideally, one can present a subject fully enough so that it also achieves what I call "dismediation", displacing the media images that stand in for face-to-face encounter. This form of communication is one of the best ways to begin to break down stereotypes, which rely heavily on the language of overworked clichés.

To my mind, the "stealth analysis" approach is far superior to the authoritative textbook, insofar as it respects and empowers the reader rather than dictating a conclusion. Many readers have responded to this kind of argument with such vehement approval that it is clear they resent the patronizing attitude that characterizes far too many scholarly books and textbooks. It consequently became clear to me that there is a great need for books that employ a mode of argumentation that readers can more readily engage with and which furnishes them with materials of substance. And while I deliberately avoided the textbook style in writing the books in question, I have been delighted by the extent to which my academic colleagues have found them useful in their courses; I have been even more delighted, however, by students who tell me that they recommend the books to their relatives, and by appreciative non-academic readers who write to me out of the blue.

It is not that difficult to practice writing in a clear and open style for a non-specialist audience. Many scholars hone their arguments in discussions with students, who are after all an ideal audience in this respect: they are generally intelligent, but they know nothing of the subject. Thus the strategies that one develops in the classroom can often be refined into arguments and examples that will prove effective with others. Public lectures for local civic or religious groups are another kind of forum that can provide a useful laboratory for experimenting with different kinds of presentation.

Against such observations, one may point out that it is easy to propose writing in a style and argumentation that is publicly accessible, but that one then runs into the professional requirements of tenure, which don't tend to recognize the value of these public-oriented goals. This is admittedly an important objection. It is still the case that tenure reviews generally require the achievement of specialized scholarship that is recognized by one's peers, rather than explication of a subject to a wider public, and sometimes promotion and tenure committees only consider publications in certain journals or presses to be worthwhile. Indeed, writing "textbooks" or introductory works is generally considered to be a waste of time as far as tenure is concerned. Given that situation, it may be most practical to suggest that scholars who are past the bar of achieving tenure should be tasked with the job of making their scholarship public. Regardless, giving more value to what the French call "un livre de diffusion" would fit well within the national trend toward "engaged scholarship" as a way of connecting universities to the constituencies whose support makes their existence possible; this movement is already resulting in several initiatives aiming to give greater support to valuing public scholarship in the tenure process.[6] One should also keep in mind that it is much easier to place a manuscript with a publisher if one can argue

---

[6] See for instance the reports of the Imagining America Consortium, available online at <http://www.imaginingamerica.org/>, which aims to integrate "all the missions of higher education: research, teaching, service, and public engagement." A similar effort is under way at the National Center for the Study of University Engagement (NCSUE), as seen on its web site at <http://ncsue.msu.edu/default.aspx>.

that there are likely to be general readers interested in buying the book. In any case, I feel that it is definitely worthwhile to urge doctoral students to write their dissertations with a view to creating successful publications that will open their subjects up to much wider audiences than their doctoral committees. Without adding any more burdens to degree requirements, one might also encourage graduate students to consider writing in a more accessible way, by offering prizes for the best essays that could be considered publishable in a journal like *Harpers'* or *The Atlantic Monthly*, on subjects relating to Middle Eastern or Islamic studies.

There is, of course, a particular political climate for Middle Eastern and Islamic studies in the US today, relating both to longtime security concerns in the region and to anxieties over terrorism after the attacks on American targets in September 2001. In terms of public discourse and debate, this means that the Middle East and Islam are the subjects of heated disputes similar to controversies over evolution and global warming. Academics can find themselves the targets of attacks from right-wing news media and ideological think tanks.[7] This started to happen to me after the University of North Carolina at Chapel Hill, at my innocent suggestion, adopted an anthology of literary translations from the Qur'an as its summer reading program (required for all incoming first-year students) in 2002. The university was attacked as unpatriotic by Fox News (whose anchor Bill O'Reilly compared the Qur'an to Adolf-Hitler's *Mein Kampf*), it was sued by an evangelical Christian group who claimed that UNC was trying to convert students to Islam, and it was accused in the North Carolina state legislature of assisting terrorism. Eventually the discussions went forward, with full support from UNC, but the controversy demonstrated how many people were convinced that Islam remains the enemy of the

[7] I have discussed some of these issues in "Changing Approaches to Islamic Studies in North American Universities," in *Islamic Studies and Civilisational Dialogue: A Transdisciplinary Approach for Sustainability*, ed. Azizan Baharuddin (Kuala Lumpur: Centre for Civilisational Dialogue, University of Malaya, 2013), pp. 75–92.

American people.[8] Fortunately, the administration at UNC was strongly committed to defending academic freedom, and in my opinion the exercise was a resounding success in demonstrating the importance of books and ideas, which is the principal goal of such summer reading programs, after all.

Beyond the controversy over the summer reading program, the publicity surrounding this event provided me another lesson in how to communicate with a public audience. Along with UNC's provost, I underwent a brief training session with a media consultant, in which we were coached on how to provide sound bites to the news media, which had become a necessity due to the hordes of reporters descending on the campus. The consultant told us, by way of example, that the answers of presidential candidates to TV journalists' questions had been as long as 85 words in length in 1960, but that they had been reduced to about 17 words by 2000. Moreover, he advised us that it was perfectly appropriate to ignore the question and say what one wished, since only the answer would be shown on the TV news. I began to consider the sound bite in a new light, as almost a genre of literature (like haiku poems). It was a challenge to present meaningful answers in the briefest possible compass, but with some concentration and a little luck, I found that one could provide something reasonably concise and satisfactory without wandering off into complicated and overly qualified evasions. In this way, even brief interactions with the media can be made into positive experiences at times.

The demand for responsible information on Middle Eastern and Islamic studies has increased decisively in recent years, as can be seen in the increases in enrollments in classes on Arabic, Middle Eastern studies, and Islam around the country. No doubt that increased demand is directly to be correlated to the political shifts caused by 9/11. In any case, I believe this sea change is more than a passing fad, and that it mirrors a decisive change of perspective that includes the Middle East and Islam as immediate realities that are no longer foreign and exotic topics. Given the

---

[8] For a dossier on the 2002 UNC Summer Reading Program controversy, including several articles plus press coverage, see <http://www.unc.edu/~cernst/quran.htm>.

relative dearth of expertise on these subjects in the US, I believe that at least some academics[9] should take on the responsibility of trying to provide explanations to appropriate audiences of the important issues they have studied. Clarity of expression and a willingness to engage with audiences are the chief prerequisites for this activity. I hope that our professional organizations and the academy at large will support public scholarship and provide incentives for scholars to address this important task, so that it becomes more practical and normal for both graduate students and faculty members to communicate easily and effectively with the public.

[9] In this respect, I am calling for a recognition of the importance of public scholarship as similar to the doctrine of *fard kifaya* in Islamic law, i.e., a duty that needs to be fulfilled by some but not all members of the community.

6

The Global Significance of the Arabic Language

What has been the cultural significance of Arabic language and literature for the world? Obviously Arabic is central for language and literature in countries where it is the dominant language, and Arabic also has a unique role for Muslims worldwide due to the religious importance of the Qur'an. But in this age of globalization, how can we understand the role of Arabic language and literature as it relates to the rest of the world? This is an important question, because, as Sir Hamilton Gibb remarked, "Classical Arabic literature is the enduring monument of a civilization, not of a people."[1] In other words, the Arabic language is not the exclusive property of the people known today as the Arabs, nor, indeed, is it the exclusive property of the Muslims; it is, instead, a civilization's legacy for the world. In this discussion I offer a brief commentary on aspects of Arabic language and literature that go beyond the standard curriculum of Islamic culture to embrace a global and even a cosmopolitan perspective.

According to some estimates, in the year 2000 there were roughly 220 million native speakers of Arabic, but as many as 450 million could be counted as Arabic speakers, when one includes

---

[1] H. A. R. Gibb, *Arabic Literature: An Introduction* (2nd ed., Oxford: Clarendon Press, 1963), p. 1.

non-Arabs who have learned the language. In addition, Arabic is the language of religious practice for a billion and a half Muslims around the world. Arabic literature is the repository of a vast number of literary compositions covering all fields of culture, religion, history, and science.

Arabic is considered a West Semitic language, and it belongs to the family of languages with alphabetic scripts (such as Hebrew, Aramaic and Ethiopic) that all ultimately descend from ancient Phoenician. Old written forms of the Arabic language are found in rock inscriptions throughout the Arabian Peninsula, which employ several different scripts ultimately derived from South Arabia. Arabic speakers also used the Nabatean script from the second century B.C.E., notably in the city of Petra (in modern Jordan), and that became the basis for the distinctive Arabic script that emerged in Syria and northwest Arabia in the sixth century C.E., sometimes in multilingual inscriptions that included Greek or Syriac.[2]

The two major monuments of early Arabic literature are undoubtedly pre-Islamic poetry and the Qur'an, which was delivered during the career of the Prophet Muhammad, roughly 610–632 C.E. A tremendous shift in ethical and religious consciousness separates these two textual sources. On the one hand, the odes (*qasida*s) of the pre-Islamic poets were formidable creations that summarized and expressed the joys and sorrows of Arab society during the time of paganism. It is the poet who stands at the center of this structure, using the conventions of verse and the story of his life to comment on the limits that frame human existence. On the other hand, the Qur'an, framed as a divine revelation to a human messenger, recounted the tragic history of humanity's failure to heed the warnings delivered by the prophets, and it called upon its audience to repent and rely only upon God.[3] Despite the dramatic differences between the perspectives of pre-Islamic poetry and the Qur'an, there is a sense in which the *qasida*s function as a kind of classical literature for Arabic, in

---

[2] Beatrice Gruendler, "Arabic Script," *Encyclopaedia of the Qur'an*, 1:135–44.

[3] For a literary and historical introduction to the Qur'an, see Carl W. Ernst, *How to Read the Qur'an: A New Guide with Select Translations* (Chapel Hill: University of North Carolina Press, 2011).

which the Qur'an both abrogates the poetry of paganism while it also fulfills and continues the aesthetic space that the *qasida* had defined.[4] The subsequent development of Arabic literature during the Islamic era looks back both to the creations of the poets and to the Qur'an as literary models, although the Qur'an obviously has a much wider impact through the daily religious practice of Muslims.

From its birthplace in the Arabian Peninsula, Arabic spread through the early empire of the caliphate. The adoption of Arabic as the official language of governance was decreed by the Caliph `Abd al-Malik in the year 691. Before that time, the bureaucratic officials employed by the early Islamic empire had continued to use the local languages of administration—Greek, Syriac, Persian, etc.—for the collection of taxes and local affairs. Making Arabic the standard language of administration and coinage required many non-Arabs (and non-Muslims) to learn Arabic in order to function in the new political and cultural environment. The new prominence of Arabic as an administrative language created the conditions for a cultural flowering of Arabic as a literary tradition among a wide range of peoples.

The vast extent of the empire of the caliphate required civil servants to combine a knowledge of literary Arabic with a wide range of other subjects. As Marshall Hodgson has observed concerning Arabic literary culture (*adab*), "Knowledge of *fiqh* [Islamic law] was practical both for a private individual and for a state clerk, for it was the officially recognized basis of social order; knowledge of it also implied piety. At the same time, he should have a wider acquaintance with history (and geography); and he should know the famous tales and sayings to which allusions might be made. Naturally, he should be familiar especially with courtly precedents. Finally, he should command something of the natural sciences. But always he should have a good knowledge of poetry."[5] In practice, this meant knowledge of Persian historical traditions as well as biblical narratives, combined

---

[4] Suzanne Stetkevych, *The Mute Immortals Speak: Pre-Islamic Poetry and the Poetics of Ritual* (Ithaca, New York: Cornell University Press, 1993), p. 51.

[5] Marshall G. S. Hodgson, *The Venture of Islam: Conscience and History in a World Civilization* (Chicago: University Of Chicago Press, 1972), Vol. 1, p. 453.

with selections from the knowledge of the Greeks. The particular importance of Arabic poetry in courtly culture is evident in the portrayals of poets, singers, and musicians displayed by Abu al-Faraj al-Isfahani's vast compilation, *The Book of Songs* (*Kitab al-Aghani*).[6] The remarkable range of subjects available in Arabic at the end of the tenth century can be judged by the *Fihrist* ("Index") of al-Nadim, a comprehensive bookseller's list of all the titles that could be found in Baghdad at the time. Arranged by subject in 10 different categories, this catalog includes writings on scriptural religions (Jewish, Christian, and Islamic), grammar and philology, history and biography, poetry, theology, law and hadith, as well as secular intellectual topics such as philosophy and the sciences, legends and magic, the religions of India and China, and alchemy. From this broad catalog one gets a sense of the cosmopolitan perspective available to those who were educated in Arabic in the classical age.[7]

The spread of Arabic language and literature among the non-Arabs was thus a natural byproduct of the Arab conquests. The need to master Arabic literature was obvious to anyone who hoped to achieve social or political prominence. An interesting example of this tendency is the autobiographical account of the philosopher Ibn Sina (d. 1040), where we learn that, despite his remarkable accomplishments in science and philosophy, this Persian intellectual was once criticized by an Arab scholar for his lack of knowledge of Arabic grammar and philology. In response, Ibn Sina spent three years studying Arabic literature, and in the end he composed several poetic odes (*qasidas*) and literary epistles (*risalas*) in the most complicated styles of the great masters, Ibn al-`Amid, al-Sahib, and al-Sabi. He bound these writings into a book and made it look old, and then showed it to his Arab critic, pretending that he had found it in the desert while hunting. The Arab scholar was astounded at the difficult words and compositions in this volume, which rivaled the writings of the early

---

6 Hilary Kilpatrick, *Making the Great Book of Songs: Compilation and the Author's Craft in Abu l-Faraj al-Isbahani's* Kitab al-aghani (London: Routledge Curzon, 2003).

7 Rudolf Sellheim, Mohsen Zakeri, François de Blois, and Werner Sundermann, "Fehrest," *Encyclopaedia Iranica*, <http://www.iranica.com/articles/fehrest>. A complete translation is available in *The Fihrist of al-Nadīm, A Tenth-Century Survey of Muslim Culture*, ed. and trans. Bayard Dodge (New York: Columbia University Press, 1970).

masters of Arabic; he ended up apologizing to Ibn Sina, when he realized that the philosopher had attained a superior knowledge of Arabic literature despite his Persian origins.[8] For centuries the Arabic literary tradition continued to play a key role not only among Persians but also other dominant groups such as the Ottomans. The monumental record of Ottoman Arabic literature is the *Kashf al-zunun* (*Unveiling of Opinions*) by Hajji Khalifa (also known as Katib Chelebi, 1609–57), a compendium of such authority that the early Orientalist, Gustav Fluegel, produced a complete Latin translation to go along with his edition of the Arabic text.[9]

The story of Ibn Sina belongs to the well-established tradition of ethnic contestation known as the Shu`ubiyya, which includes numerous literary efforts to demonstrate the virtues of non-Arab peoples (in Arabic, singular *sha`b*, plural *shu`ub*) over Arabs, by using the medium of classical Arabic.[10] It is no secret that there were many non-Arabs who became among the most prominent scholars of all the different sciences found in Arabic. This phenomenon is perhaps explainable by the fact that non-Arabs had to make extraordinary efforts in order to master literary Arabic when it was not their mother tongue. Thus in history as well as in Qur'an commentary, there is perhaps no more famous name than the Persian scholar al-Tabari, whose monumental works are landmarks of scholarship in both those fields. Non-Arabs have likewise been prominent in the development of Islamic law (al-Marghinani), theology (al-Maturidi), the study of Prophetic sayings or hadith (al-Bukhari), and Arabic grammar (Sibawayh). It is perhaps less widely known that non-Muslim religious groups had an extensive Arabic literature as well. There is much to be learned from the massive German history of Christian Arabic literature that was compiled by the

---

[8] W. E. Gohlman, ed., *The Life of Ibn Sina* (Albany: State University of New York Press, 1974); A. J. Arberry, *Aspects of Islamic Civilization as Depicted in the Original Texts* (Ann Arbor: University of Michigan Press, 1965), pp. 142–43.

[9] Kâtip Çelebi, *Lexicon bibliographicum et encyclopaedicum . . . ad codicum Vindobonensium Parisiensium et Berolinensis fidem primum edidit Latine vertit et commentario indicibusque instruxit Gustavus Fluegel* (7 vols., Leipzig: Published for the Oriental Translation Fund of Great Britain and Ireland, 1835–58).

[10] S. Enderwitz, "Shu`ubiyya," *Encyclopaedia of Islam*, IX:513b–516a.

scholar Georg Graf over 50 years ago. This five-volume work describes Arabic translations of the Bible and the writings of the Greek, Syriac, and Coptic church fathers, as well as hundreds of Arabic writings by scholars of the different Christian churches (Melchites, Maronites, Nestorians, Jacobites, Copts, etc.) up to the end of the nineteenth century.[11] Likewise, there has been over the centuries an extensive literary production in Arabic by Arabic-speaking Jews.[12] This includes the remarkable development of Judeo-Arabic literature, which was classical Arabic written in Hebrew script. Major works in this category include the biblical commentary known as *Kitab al-Amanat wal-i`tiqadat* (*Book of Beliefs and Doctrines*) by the Baghdadian scholar, Saadiah Gaon (d. 942), as well as the monumental philosophical treatise, *The Guide of the Perplexed* (*Dalalat al-ha'irin*) by the Andalusian thinker, Moses Maimonides (d. 1204).[13] Judeo-Arabic was also the medium chosen by another Andalusian writer, Judah Ha-Levi (d. 1141), in his defense of Judaism known as *al-Kuzari*; in many respects, this was another example of the Shu`ubiyya movement that used the Arabic language to proclaim the supremacy of non-Arab peoples.[14]

One of the means by which the Arabic language became so extensive in its coverage of different cultures and sciences was undoubtedly the massive translation movement, which beginning around 800 C.E. transmitted a remarkable amount of scientific and philosophical literature from Greek into Arabic. This movement, which was largely facilitated by highly educated Syriac Christians, frequently involved an initial translation from Greek into Syriac, followed by another translation from Syriac into Arabic. It was only somewhat later that Arab scholars such as the

[11] Georg Graf, *Geschichte der christlichen arabischen Literatur* (5 vols., Città del Vaticano: Bibliotheca Apostolica Vaticana, 1944–1953). For a brief overview, see <http://www.mela.us/MELANotes//MELANotes6970/graf.html>.

[12] Moritz Steinschneider, *Jewish Arabic Literature: An Introduction* (Gorgias Press, 2008).

[13] Hava Lazarus-Yafeh, "Judeo-Arabic Literature," *Encyclopaedia Judaica*<http://www.jewishvirtuallibrary.org/jsource/judaica/ejud_0002_0011_0_10460.html>. Maimonides' philosophical treatise was published for the first time in Arabic script by a Turkish scholar, Hüseyin Atay, under the title *Delâlet'ü l-hâirîn* (Ankara: Ankara Universitesi Basimevi, 1974).

[14] Judah ha-Levi, *The Kuzari: In Defense of the Despised Faith*, trans. N. Daniel Korobkin (Northvale, N.J.: J. Aronson, 1998).

Christian physician Hunayn ibn Ishaq mastered Greek sufficiently to translate scientific and medical works directly into Arabic. The curriculum of Greek sciences that entered Arabic included the medical works of Galen and Hippocrates, the mathematics of Euclid, and the logic, physics, and metaphysics of Aristotle. Prominent translators also included the Sabian pagan, Thabit ibn Qurra', renowned for his mathematical studies; he was one of a number of Hellenistic pagans from the city of Harran who avoided theological criticism by claiming to be the monotheistic Sabians mentioned in the Qur'an. Later on, Andalusian scholars translated the Arabic philosophical writings of Aristotle and Ibn Rushd into Latin, at a time when the writings of the Greek philosophers were mostly unavailable in Europe. Thus it was that Christian theologians such as St. Thomas Aquinas studied Aristotle (and his Arabic commentator Ibn Rushd) in versions that were made available from Arabic sources. In addition, there were astronomical and medical texts translated into Arabic from Indian languages (presumably Sanskrit), including the famous astronomical tables known as the *Zij al-Sindhind*. Outside of the scientific realm, one of the most popular compositions in the history of world literature, the collection of Indian stories known as the *Panchatantra*, was translated into Arabic from the middle Persian version by the `Abbasid minister Ibn al-Muqaffa` under the title *Kalila wa Dimna*; this Arabic work was in turn translated into many of the world's languages (a dozen of the stories from this tradition found their way into the *Aesop's Fables* published in English by the pioneering English printer William Caxton in 1484).

On the level of geography, Arabic became the medium for describing the world much more comprehensively than was possible in other languages before the European expansion of the sixteenth century. Building on the knowledge of Greek scientists like Ptolemy, Arab geographers combined personal travel research with administrative reports to gain much more extensive knowledge of the regions of the world than their predecessors. Here I will just mention a couple of prominent examples out of many. As far as northern Europe was concerned, there is the example of Ibn Fadlan, who in 921 led an embassy from the `Abbasid caliph al-Muqtadir to the Bulgar king on the Volga River in southern Russia. His Arabic travel narrative, rediscovered in the twentieth century from a manuscript in Iran, describes his travels through central Asia and his encounters with Nordic peoples who were apparently Vikings (this travel account appears in a Hollywood version in the 1999 film *The 13th Warrior*). On a much more extensive level, the famous *Rihla* of Ibn Battuta (d. 1369) is the Arabic account of his travels from Morocco to China and back, as well as his visits to Spain and West Africa. This account was actually composed by a literary scholar named Abu Juzayy, to whom Ibn Battuta dictated his recollections, and it includes passages that seem to have been copied from the writings of other travelers such as Ibn Jubayr and al-Abdari. And there are questions about whether he actually visited all the places that he mentions in his travels. Nevertheless, Ibn Battuta's travel narrative is a remarkably detailed and richly informative work that provides important information about the holy places of Mecca and Medina, Cairo under the Mamluks, Anatolia at the time of the rise of the Ottomans, Delhi under the Tughluq dynasty, the Maldives, Sri Lanka, Bengal, Malacca, and Quanzhou in China. Having traveled far more extensively than the European traveler Marco Polo, Ibn Battuta was able to take advantage of his status as a scholar of Islamic law to find employment and patronage practically everywhere he went. He took advantage of the openness of the Eurasian continent after the Mongol conquests, and the result was an unmatched depiction of a wide range of Muslim and non-Muslim societies across the world.[15]

Arabic also became a medium by which Arabic scholars studied the cultures and religions of other peoples of the world. One of the most remarkable examples is the scholar al-Biruni (d. 1048), who studied Sanskrit texts on science and religion while in the service of the Turkish conqueror Mahmud of Ghazna (d. 1030); al-Biruni's study of Indian religion and culture seems to have been nearly forgotten until his great work on India was rediscovered by European Orientalists in the nineteenth century. Al-Biruni is of interest in this discussion, not because he

[15] Ross E. Dunn, *The Adventures of Ibn Battuta : A Muslim Traveler of the 14th Century* (Berkeley : University of California Press, 2005).

extended a universalizing recognition to Indian religions as such, but because of his typical method of using categories of Islamic thought as templates for understanding the Indian data.

Al-Biruni translated a number of Sanskrit works into Arabic (including selections from Patañjali's *Yogasutras* and the *Bhagavad Gita*) in connection with his encyclopedic treatise on India.[16] Although authors of Arabic books on sects and heresies, such as al-Shahrastani (d. 1153), generally devoted a section or a few pages to the religions of India, no other Arabic writer followed in al-Biruni's footsteps as a specialist on Indian religion and philosophy.[17] His translation of Patañjali's *Yogasutras* was based on a combination of the original text plus a commentary that is still not identified, all rephrased by al-Biruni into a question-and-answer format. Like the translators of pre-Islamic Greek texts (e.g., Plotinus) into Arabic, al-Biruni rendered terms like the Sanskrit word for "gods" (*deva*) with the Arabic terms for "angels" (*mala'ikah*) or "spiritual beings" (*ruhaniyyat*). He was, moreover, convinced on a deep level that Sanskrit texts were saturated with recognizable philosophical doctrines of reincarnation and union with God, which required comparative treatment. As he remarked, "For this reason their [the Indians'] talk, when it is heard, has a flavour composed of the beliefs (*`aqa'id*) of the ancient Greeks, of the Christian sects, and of the Sufi leaders."[18] Consequently, al-Biruni made deliberate and selective use of terms derived from Greek philosophy, Islamic heresiography, and Sufism to render the Sanskrit technical terms of yoga.

Arabic continued to be an important language for the culture of India for centuries. It has been argued that, due to its association with the Qur'an and the Islamic religious sciences, Arabic was viewed in India essentially as a religious language,

---

[16] Eduard Sachau, trans., *Alberuni's India* (London, 1888; reprint ed., Delhi: S. Chand & Co., 1964); Hellmut Ritter, ed., "Al-Biruni's Übersetzung des Yoga-sutra des Patañjali," *Oriens* 9 (1956), pp. 165–200.

[17] Bruce B. Lawrence, *Shahrastani on the Indian Religions* (The Hague: Mouton, 1976); Bruce Lawrence, "Biruni, Abu Rayhan. viii. Indology," *Encyclopaedia Iranica* IV (1990), 285–87. <http://www.iranicaonline.org/articles/biruni-abu-rayhan-viii>.

[18] Ritter, p. 167.

regardless of the subject matter of any particular treatise.[19] While that observation might represent the popular attitude of Indian Muslims toward the prestige of Arabic, it overstates the case by subsuming all subjects under the category of religion, and it does not do justice to the hundreds of Arabic works composed by Indian scholars in the fields of rhetoric, linguistics, poetry, logic, philosophy, and the sciences, which can hardly be considered marginal.[20] In particular, the philosophical tradition in Arabic was strongly represented in India, though this field has yet to be explored in modern scholarship.[21] And even if Arabic was only occasionally used in India for historical chronicles, the surviving examples are of considerable importance, such as Hajji Dabir's history of Gujarat, or Zayn al-Din al-Malibari's Arabic account of Portuguese imperialism as seen from southern India.[22] For a survey of the full extent of Arabic learning in South Asia in the eighteenth century, it is hard to improve upon *The Coral Rosary of Indian Traditions*, a composite work by Ghulam `Ali Azad Bilgrami (d. 1786), written separately in four parts, later combined together.[23] The first part is devoted to the statements of the Prophet Muhammad (*hadith*) regarding the sanctity of India as the place where Adam landed on Earth after his expulsion from Paradise.[24] The second part is a biographical dictionary

---

[19] Tahera Qutbuddin, "Arabic in India: A Survey and Classification of its Uses, Compared with Persian," *Journal of the American Oriental Society* 127/3 (2007), pp. 315–38.

[20] For a general survey, see Jamil Ahmad, *Harakat al-ta'lif bi-al-lughah al-`Arabiyah fi al-iqlim al-Shimali al-Hindi fi al-qarnayn al-thamin `ashar wa-al-tasi` `ashar (The Literary Movement in the Arabic Language in the North Indian Region in the 18th and 19th Centuries)* (Damascus: Wizarat al-Thaqifah wa-al-Irshad al-Qaumi, 1977).

[21] Sajjad Rizvi, "Mir Damad in India: Islamic Philosophical Traditions and the Problem of Creation," *Journal of the American Oriental Society* 131/1 (2011), pp. 9–23.

[22] Muhammad "Hajji al-Dabir" Ulughkhani, *Zafar al-walih bi-Muzaffar wa Alihi*, ed. E. Denison Ross (3 vols., London: John Murray Publishers, 1910–28); English trans. M. F. Lokhandwala, *An Arabic History of Gujarat* (2 vols., Baroda: Oriental Institute, 1970–74); Shaykh Zainuddin Makhdum, *Tuhfat al-Mujahidin, A Historical Epic of the Sixteenth Century*, trans. S. Muhammad Husayn Nainar (Kuala Lumpur: Islamic Book Trust, 2005), available online at <http://www.kalamullah.com/tuhfat-al-mujahidin.html>.

[23] Ghulam `Ali Azad al-Bilgrami, *Subhat al-marjan fi athar Hindustan*, ed. Muhammad Fadl al-Rahman al-Nadwi al-Siwani (2 vols., Aligarh: Jami`at `Aligarh al-Islamiyya, 1976–80).

[24] I have translated excerpts from this section in "India as a Sacred Islamic Land," *Refractions of Islam in India*, chapter 2. For comparable material from an early Islamic

containing accounts of 45 Indian Muslim scholars who wrote in Arabic, ranging from the eighth century to the author's own day.[25] The third and fourth parts are concerned with the rhetoric and the categories of lovers found in Indian literature, illustrated in part by Arabic verses of the author's own composition.[26] This work simultaneously finds a special place for India in the cosmology of Islam, while at the same time connecting the culture of India to Arabic literature through a kind of intertextual commentary.

Other regions beyond the historic Middle East welcomed the development of Arabic as a language of religion and culture. Since the seventeenth century, Arabic was used in Southeast Asia alongside Malay as a medium for the communication of Islamic teachings, particularly in a Sufi idiom.[27] Key Arabic texts for the dissemination of Islam were rendered into a variety of local languages around coastal areas ranging from the Arabian Sea to the Indonesian archipelago.[28] In more recent times, Arabic has been the medium for journalistic publications aimed at the Yemeni and Hadrami diaspora in Southeast Asia.[29]

Africa, too, has had a long engagement with Arabic, which became the principal language of culture and governance in much of North and East Africa, while in West Africa it was

---

source on Adam's descent to India, see *The History of al-Tabari: General Introduction and From the Creation to the Flood*, trans. Franz Rosenthal (Albany: State University of New York Press, 1989).

25 Carl W. Ernst, "Reconfiguring South Asian Islam: The 18th and 19th centuries," in *Refractions of Islam in India*, chapter 7.

26 The fourth section is described in Carl W. Ernst, "Indian Lovers in Arabic and Persian Guise: Āzād Bilgrāmī's Depiction of *nayikas*," in *Refractions of Islam in India*, chapter 21.

27 Karel Steenbrink, "Indonesia," *Encyclopedia of Arabic Language and Linguistics*, ed. Lutz Edzard, Rudolf de Jong (Brill Online, 2012; Reference. University of North Carolina at Chapel Hill (UNC). 26 December 2012 <http://referenceworks.brillonline.com.libproxy.lib.unc.edu/entries/encyclopedia-of-arabic-language-and-linguistics/indonesia-COM_vol2_0047>; Martin van Bruinessen, *al-Kitab al-`arabi fi andunisiya (The Arabic Book in Indonesia)*, trans. Qasim al-Samarra'i (Riyad: Maktabat al-Malik Fahd al-Wataniyya, 1415/1994–95).

28 Ronit Ricci, *Islam Translated: Literature, Conversion, and the Arabic Cosmopolis of South and Southeast Asia* (Chicago: University of Chicago Press, 2011).

29 `Abd Allah Yahya al-Zayn, *al-Nash'at al-thiqafi wal-sahafi lil-yamaniyyin fil-mahjar: Indunisiya, Malayziya, Singhafura (Cultural and Journalistic Development of the Yemenis in Diaspora: Indonesia, Malaysia, Singapore)* (Beirut: Dar al-Fikr al-Mu`asir, 1323/2003); Muhammad ibn `Abd al-Rahman al-Rabi`, *Adab al-mahjar al-sharqi (Literature of the Eastern Diaspora)* (Cairo: Markaz al-Darasat al-Sharqiyya, Jami`at al-Qahira, 1999).

a learned language that existed alongside local languages.[30] A recent comprehensive survey edited by John Hunwick and Rex S. O'Fahey and an international team of scholars has been undertaken under the title, *Arabic Literature of Africa*, and so far four volumes out of a projected six have appeared in print. The aim of this pioneering series is to provide an outline of the intellectual history of Muslim societies in all the areas it covers: the Nile valley, East Africa and the Horn of Africa, West Africa and the western Sahara, from earliest times to the present.[31] This African Arabic literature is particularly rich in history, religious teaching, devotional writings, and debates concerning the Sufi orders.

If we return to the notion of civilization itself, there is probably no greater name in premodern times than that of the North African scholar Ibn Khaldun (d. 1406) in terms of the quest to understand the forces that govern the rise and fall of all human societies and empires. Ibn Khaldun was a historian, but he wrote his famous Introduction (*al-Muqaddima*) as a philosophical analysis of society (*`umran*) in terms of the interplay between sedentary urban life (*hadara*) and pastoral nomadism (*badawa*). The range of examples that Ibn Khaldun used for his study included the ancient Greeks, Romans, Persians, and the Hebrews, and he paid special attention to nomadic peoples, particularly the Arabs, the Berbers, the Mongols, and the Turks. His observations about the role of religion in fostering group feeling (*`asabiyya*) have earned him the reputation of being the first sociologist. It is important to note that Ibn Khaldun was not primarily attempting to focus on an exclusively Islamic civilization—his work strove for universal application. He drew upon the rational categories of Greek science and philosophy in his understanding of prophecy and religion. His Arabic writings had a major impact on Ottoman thinkers of the eighteenth century, and they have reached new audiences in the nineteenth and twentieth centuries through scholarly French and English translations.[32]

---

[30] John O. Hunwick, "Africa, Arabic Literature," in *Encyclopedia of Arabic Literature*, ed. Julie Scott Meisami and Paul Starkey (London: Routledge, 1998), 1:60–63.

[31] John O. Hunwick and Rex S. O'Fahey, eds, *Arabic Literature of Africa* (4 vols., Leiden: E. J. Brill, 1994–).

[32] Ibn Khaldūn, *The Muqaddimah: An Introduction to History*, trans. Franz Rosenthal, ed. N. J. Dawood (Princeton, NJ: Princeton University Press, 2005).

Obviously there is much more that could be said about the significance of Arabic language and literature for many different subjects. The subject is immense, and it has only been touched by such massive surveys as Carl Brockelmann's five-volume German history of Arabic literature, or Fuat Sezgin's even more comprehensive German survey of Arabic literature, which in nine volumes only goes up to the year 430 hijri/1038 C.E.[33] Remarkably, the majority of the works described in these compilations have never been printed in any form, which means that many discoveries await the scholars who are willing to explore these manuscript treasures. And this is to say nothing of the enormous flowering of Arabic literature in modern times—with the appearance of new literary forms such as free verse, drama, and the novel—that is a subject in itself, which deserves separate treatment.

I will conclude with a few examples that indicate some of the new cultural possibilities created by the experience of globalization, from the early colonial era to the present, regarding the role of Arabic in the United States of America. In one of these cases, Arabic serves to document the important presence of Islam in America, through the African Muslims who were enslaved and brought to North America. One such instance was `Umar ibn Sayyid (d. 1864), who was born in the region of Senegal and sold into slavery in 1807. He ended up spending his life as a slave in North Carolina, but he claims our attention because he was a Muslim scholar. He wrote a short autobiography in Arabic in 1831, as well as several other documents, including portions of the Qur'an. This surprising presence of Islam in early America is only known to us because of the Arabic learning that was displayed by this remarkable individual.[34] Another important example is the famous Lebanese poet Khalil

---

[33] Carl Brockelmann, *Geschichte der Arabischen Litteratur* (5 vols., 2nd ed., Leiden: E. J. Brill, 1937–49). For a description of the contents, and a guide to using this comprehensive reference work, see <http://www.ghazali.org/articles/gal-howto.htm>. Fuat Sezgin, *Geschichte des arabischen Schrifttums* (9 vols., Leiden: E. J. Brill, 1974–96).

[34] "Oh ye Americans": *The Autobiography of Omar ibn Said*, National Humanities Center Resource Toolbox, <http://nationalhumanitiescenter.org/pds/maai/community/text3/religionomaribnsaid.pdf>; Ala A. Alryyes, *A Muslim American Slave: The Life of Omar Ibn Said* (University of Wisconsin Press, 2011). Although he is commonly known as Omar ibn Said, the Arabic spelling would normally be represented as `Umar ibn Sayyid.

Gibran (d. 1931), whose career took him from Mount Lebanon to New York at an early age, where he received support from American art patrons for his painting and literary abilities.[35] One of the most popular writers in English today, Gibran was also part of an important circle of New York Arabic poets in the 1920s, which included Mikha'il Na`imi; thus Arabic has become an American literary language, and interest in studying Arabic has increased dramatically in America in recent years. And from another point of view, there has been a long series of visits to America by Arabs, many of whom have recorded their observations in literary form. This tradition of Arabic writing about America has recently become the subject of an important book illustrating the important connections between the US and Arabic culture.[36]

In short, from its ancient origins Arabic has become a language of major significance, one of the six official languages of the United Nations, an enduring cultural property in the global heritage of civilization. The study and teaching of Arabic language and literature is therefore a subject of central importance that should be a top priority for the curriculum of humanistic studies; teachers and students of Arabic likewise deserve every encouragement from our universities.

---

[35] Robin Waterfield, *Prophet: The Life and Times of Kahlil Gibran* (New York: St. Martin's, 2000).

[36] Kamal Abdel-Malek and Mouna El Kahla, *America in an Arab Mirror: Images of America in Arabic Travel Literature, 1668 to 9/11 and Beyond* (New York: Palgrave Macmillan, 2011).

PART 2

EARLY SUFISM

7

Esoteric and Mystical Aspects of Religious Knowledge in Sufism

"He who knows himself knows his Lord." This saying, attributed to the Prophet Muhammad, illustrates some of the manifold resonances that religious knowledge acquired in medieval Islamic culture. The stress on self-knowledge is Socratic, with the impulse toward transcendence characteristic of Neoplatonic philosophy. Yet the context is prophetic; Sufis regarded this statement as a product of the revelation granted to Muhammad. The statement is also a gnostic one, insofar as knowledge of God is generally equated with salvation in this tradition.[1] In this essay, however, I would like to discuss two aspects of religious knowledge that are especially characteristic of Sufism, although they are sometimes expressed in philosophical terms. These are the esoteric, the restriction of knowledge to those who are by nature and by experience qualified to receive it, and the mystical, the negation and transcendence of ordinary knowing in unknowing.

[1] According to the philosopher Ibn Sina {Avicenna, d. 1037), this saying was accepted by both philosophers and saints; cf. Alexander Altmann, "The Delphic Maxim in Medieval Islam and Judaism", in *Studies in Religious Philosophy and Mysticism* (Plainview, NY: Books for Libraries Press, 1969), pp. 1–40, esp. pp. 1–2.

The kind of self-knowledge referred to in the statement above was in fact esoteric, in that the Sufis regarded it as a spiritual experience attainable by only the elect; it was also esoteric in practice, inasmuch as the saying itself was only given currency in restricted Sufi circles and specialized writings. Externalist Islamic scholars dismissed such sayings of Muhammad as lacking in canonical documentation (the above statement is first known to have been quoted by Yahya ibn Mu`adh, d. 871).[2]

The kind of self-knowledge that could lead to knowledge of God was not only esoteric but also mystical, in the sense of the Dionysian *Mystical Theology.* Self-knowledge could only be attained by self-naughting, emptying oneself; thus knowledge of God is the negation of limited concepts, and in the end can only be called unknowing.

One of the earliest authors to discuss the place of Sufism in the curriculum of Islamic sciences was Abu Nasr al-Sarraj (d. 988), a Sufi of Iranian origin, in his comprehensive *Book of Glimmerings on Sufism.* Sarraj articulates four kinds of religious knowledge: first, the knowledge of the sayings of the Prophet, which had been collected in several canonical works; second, the knowledge of religious law and ordinances; third, the knowledge of analogy, theory; and disputation, which can be termed dialectical theology; fourth, and highest of them all, is knowledge of spiritual realities, mystical stations, acts of piety, abstinence, and contemplation of God—in short, the knowledge sought by Sufis. Sufism is thus given a place as a science or form of knowledge (*`ilm*) alongside the traditional religious sciences. And just as with any other kind of knowledge, says Sarraj, one must always go to the experts in that particular field when there is a problem to be solved, so in questions of spiritual realities one must approach the appropriate experts, the Sufi masters. "It is inappropriate for anyone to think that he encompasses all knowledge, lest he err in his opinion of the sayings of the elect, and anathematize them and charge them with heresy, when he is devoid of experience

---

[2] Louis Massignon, *Essai sur les origines du lexique technique de la mystique musulmane,* Études musulmanes, II (2nd ed., Paris: Librairie Philosophique J. Vrin, 1968), p. 127.

in their states and the stations of their spiritual realities."[3] It is on the basis of spiritual experience that Sarraj formulates the relation of Sufism to the standard Islamic religious sciences. He further points out that the Sufis are frequently learned in the traditional fields of prophetic sayings, jurisprudence, and theology, in addition to their own specialty, while this is rarely true of experts in those other fields. Thus the knowledge of spiritual experience, for this author, is a kind of de facto esotericism. It happens to be the case that those who receive the special grace of God enjoy this knowledge, which is not attainable by study. This kind of religious knowledge is also the highest, since it alone is directly concerned with attaining salvation. The philosopher and theologian Fakhr al-Din al-Razi (d. 1209) asked the Sufi Najm al-Din al-Kubra (d. 1220) how he attained the knowledge of God. The reply was, "By certain events that occur in the heart, and which the soul is incapable of falsifying."[4]

In later centuries the place of this knowledge was enhanced by its expression in terms of metaphysics. Particularly in the vast synthesis of Ibn `Arabi (d. 1240), which exhibits strong Neoplatonic and Hermetic resonances, the doctrine of the universal theophany of divine attributes through creation made the knowledge of the Sufis essentially all-inclusive. As one seventeenth-century author in this tradition puts it,

> The knowledge of divine realities comprehends all the sciences that are customary among the religious scholars and philosophers. Why? Because the demonstration of this knowledge is dependent on the Essence and Attributes of the Transcendent, whose Essence and Attributes comprehend all things. Therefore the knowledge of divine realities comprehends all of the customary sciences.[5]

The knowledge of the Sufis is thus equivalent in scope to the special metaphysics of Aristotle, dealing with the divine being.

---

[3] Abu Nasr `Abdallah b. `Ali al-Sarraj al-Tusi, *The Kitab al-Luma` fi'l-Tasawwuf*, ed. Reynold Alleyne Nicholson, "E. J. W. Gibb Memorial" Series, vol. XXII (London: Luzac & Col, 1963), p. 378.

[4] Ibrahim-i Shattari, *A'ina-yi haqa'iq-numa, Sharh-i Jam-i Jahan-numa* (Hyderabad: Matba`-i Abu al-`Ala'i, 1313), pp. 7–8.

[5] Ibid.

It differs from the religious knowledge of theologians and philosophers in that it is concerned with the manner in which the individual attains union with God. From this Sufi point of view, the only purpose of creation is to know God and become one with Him. In one of the extra-Qur'anic revelations attributed to Muhammad, God says, "I was a hidden treasure, and I longed to be known; therefore I created the world."[6] Here creation is seen as a theophany designed to reveal the presence of God. Knowledge of God in this direct sense is considered the highest and most privileged form of knowledge.

The principle of esotericism in religious knowledge is more fully revealed in the issue of exegesis of the symbolic portions of scripture. Many traditional scholars insisted on a strictly literal interpretation of the Qur'an, or else, in the case of the verses that describe God in seemingly anthropomorphic terms (sitting on the throne, etc.), simply excluded any sort of interpretation or questioning. Certain Sufi writers, however, maintained that while it was appropriate for the common people to have faith in the Qur'an and not question the literal meanings, the elect were graced with a knowledge or gnosis that enabled them to perform symbolic exegesis. This is supported, they claim, by a verse from the Qur'an itself, which is, however, punctuated by them differently than in the standard commentaries. The verse in question (Qur'an 3:7) reads as follows in the usual reading: "And those with error in their hearts follow the symbolic part, desiring dissension and desiring its exegesis, but none knows the exegesis of it save God. And those who are firmly rooted in knowledge say, 'have faith in it…'." The reading supported by the Sufi writers (which has some traditional authority) gives, on the contrary: "… but none knows the exegesis of it save God *and* those who are firmly rooted in knowledge. (Others) say, 'We have faith in it… '."[7]

---

[6] Annemarie Schimmel, *Mystical Dimensions of Islam* (Chapel Hill: The University of North Carolina Press, 1976; New Delhi: Yoda Press, 2007), pp. 139, 189, 268, 291, 382.

[7] Ruzbihan Baqli Shirazi, *Sharh-i Shathiyyat*, ed. Henry Corbin, Bibliothèque Iranienne 12 (Tehran: Departement d'iranologie de 1'Institut franco-iranien; Paris: Institut d'études iraniennes de l'Université de Paris, 1966), pp. 57–58; this reading was supported by the early Qur'an scholar Mujahid (d. 722), cf. *The Glorious Qur'an*, trans. Abdullah Yusuf Ali (U.S.A.: The Muslim Students' Association of the United States & Canada, 1395/1975), p. 123, n. 348. The emphasis is mine.

The knowledge that enables the saint to interpret scripture is divine knowledge. According to Ruzbihan al-Baqli of Shiraz (d. 1206), it is identical with the knowledge that was one of God's qualities prior to the creation of the universe.[8] This same reading of the Qur'anic verse was in fact widely used to support the principle of esoteric knowledge. The Andalusian philosopher Ibn Rushd (Averroes, d. 1198) maintained that the common people must necessarily read this verse with the period in the middle, so that for them, only God knows the interpretation; from this point of view, the religious knowledge accessible to man is basically faith. The elect, on the other hand, must read this verse without the period; they have the right, even the duty, to interpret scripture, in accordance with their knowledge of the truth.[9] It should be noted, however, that Ibn Rushd is referring to the knowledge of the Aristotelian philosopher, gained by demonstration, not the gnosis given to the saint by God. In Ibn Rushd's systematic exposition of a dual interpretation we can see the seed of the theory of two truths, one for the masses and another for the elite, attributed to extreme Averroism. While the Sufis did not press the principle of esotericism this far, it is clear that they maintained that there is a special kind of religious knowledge which is only available through spiritual experience.

Moreover, this divine knowledge was not just limited in fact to those who were granted it; it was made esoteric in practice by being restricted to circles of initiates, and by being phrased in an ambiguous and deliberately difficult language to prevent hostile or immature inquirers from understanding it, should such writings chance to fall into their hands. But this esoteric knowledge did not stand in opposition to the exoteric tradition. It was conceived of, not as a substitute for the commonly available forms of religious knowledge, but as a complement. Most Sufis insisted, indeed, that the inner had to be approached through the outer; esoteric knowledge could only be attained by those who were

---

[8] Ruzbihan, p. 59.

[9] Averroes, "The Decisive Treatise, Determining what the Connection is between Religion and Philosophy," trans. George F. Hourani, in *Medieval Political Philosophy: A Sourcebook*, ed. Ralph Lerner and Muhsin Mahdi (New York: The Free Press of Glencoe, 1963), pp. 170, 172, 177.

already fully competent in the customary forms of learning.[10] Critics of Sufism have maintained that this esoteric knowledge has no organic and necessary relation to the external bases of revelation as found in the Qur'an and the sayings of Muhammad. It has also been a frequent accusation that preoccupation with esoteric truths has diverted the Sufis from observing the obligatory external rituals of Islam.[11] Regardless of the validity of any particular accusation, this very controversy points to the critical importance that was attached to the question of the proper relationship between esoteric and exoteric religious knowledge.

The principal of esotericism in religious knowledge was supported by the theory of mystical knowledge, which found expression in Sufism in almost the same form as in the *Mystical Theology* of Dionysius. From the position that the knowledge of the world is only a pale reflection of the esoteric knowledge of God, it is not difficult to make the transition to the view that real knowledge of God can only be described as a negation of worldly knowledge, as unknowing. We find this mystical theory in a saying attributed to the companion of Muhammad, Abu Bakr: "The inability to attain comprehension is (true) comprehension."[12] As interpreted by the Sufis, this saying is not merely the Socratic paradox, that the wisest man is he who knows that he knows nothing; it is now viewed as a description of the annihilation of the ego of the knower, through total acceptance of the incomprehension of the unattainable divine essence. This unknowing is true self-knowledge, in that the knower knows himself to be nothing. Annihilation of the self is the essential prerequisite for attaining divine knowledge. Once the knower is annihilated, the divine essence manifests itself without hindrance. The knower is effaced in the qualities of the known through this unknowing, and real knowledge then takes place.

Unknowing is a concept that is perhaps inevitably obscure. Although theoretical clarifications of this subject have been

---

[10] Marshall G. S. Hodgson, *The Venture of Islam, Conscience and History in a World Civilization, vol. II, The Expansion of Islam in the Middle Periods* (Chicago: The University of Chicago Press, 1974), pp. 195–200.

[11] Fazlur Rahman, *Islam* (2nd ed., Chicago: The University of Chicago Press, 1979), p. 143.

[12] Ruzbihan, ch. 21.

made in works such as *The Cloud of Unknowing* and Nicholas of Cues' *Of Learned Ignorance* in Christian Europe, it is a topic that lends itself more easily to aphoristic and paradoxical expression. Among the Sufis, unknowing was frequently mentioned in ecstatic utterances of a sometimes deliberately provocative character. In this vein we find abrupt denunciations of any form of positive and limited knowledge. Commenting on the dualistic nature of perception and thought, Shibli (d. 945) said, "Gazing is infidelity, thought is idolatry, and allusion is delusion."[13] Another early Sufi, Wasiti (d. ca. 932), boasted, "I sought God in clarity, but found Him in obscurity."[14] A synonym for unknowing is wonderment, which follows on the realization of the impotence of knowledge. Abu Yahya al-Shirazi describes it thus:

> Wonderment has a beginning and an end. Between the two wonderments knowledge appears. When men attain learning and tradition and authority, however, they do not enter into reality, because of the limitations of their understanding and the proofs of their sciences. Beyond that knowledge, wonderment within wonderment becomes manifest, and one never comes out of that wonderment.[15]

This alludes to the deadlock of positive knowledge that leads to a recognition of ignorance, and the subsequent opening up to greater realities that is described as intensified astonishment. The connection between unknowing and annihilation is evident in a stark saying of Jurayri (d. 981): "The knowledge with which we are concerned requires the denial of everything that is learned and habitual and the effacement of everything that is caused. Everything that is manifest is effaced."[16] Unknowing is also described as the result of the overwhelming of the perception by the sudden revelation of the divine being, which thus breaks down the normal structures of knowledge. As Ruzbihan says, "Unknowing is the obliteration of the eye of the inner

---

[13] Ibid., ch. 155. For the genre of ecstatic utterances (*shathiyyat*), see my *Words of Ecstasy in Sufism* (Albany: SUNY Press, 1985), chapter 1.

[14] Ruzbihan, ch. 175.

[15] Ibid., ch. 184.

[16] Ibid., ch. 465, reading *payda* for *bayda*.

consciousness, in the comprehension of the divine Essence and Attributes."[17]

The non-discursive nature of mystical unknowing is well illustrated also by metaphor, most notably the metaphor of being lost in the desert. Regarding those who are "firmly rooted in knowledge," Ruzbihan remarks that "the deserts on which their paths lie are too hot for conventional wayfarers."[18] Wonderment is thus equivalent to "desert upon desert".[19] Wandering alone in the desert amounts to a complete renunciation of the safe and structured world of the city-dweller. This goes back to the esoteric principle; real knowledge is distinct from the knowledge of the world, and can only be attained by going beyond outward knowledge. Yet in the end the relationship between knowledge and unknowing remains a mysterious dialectic. Husayn ibn Mansur al-Hallaj (d. 922) summed up this polarity by saying, "Knowledge is concealed in unknowing, and unknowing is concealed in knowledge."[20]

This brief account of the esoteric and mystical aspects of knowledge in Sufism only begins to touch upon the subject. There are many imperceptible degrees between traditional learning and mystical gnosis. Other important aspects of this subject are contemplative exercises, the role of grace, the use of speculative metaphysics and gnosticism, mystical experience as a datum for philosophy, and the gradation of knowledge and esotericism in Shi`i Islam. Still, at this point it is appropriate to ask what is really meant by knowledge of the divine reality. Can this refer to an actual attainment? It is a formulation of a relationship that is, strictly speaking, inconceivable. It is not possible to explain how a limited being can possess omniscience or be united with an Essence that is, by definition, independent and absolute. The Sufi expression posits knowledge of God as a limiting function, as an intuitive symbol for a relationship that

[17] Ruzbihan al-Baqli al-Shirazi, *Kitab Mashrab al-Arwah, wa-huwa Mashhur bi-Hazar-u-yak Maqam (bi-Alf Maqam wa-Maqam)*, ed. Nazif Muharram Khwaja, Istanbul Universitesi Edebiyat Fakultesi Yayinlari No. 1876 (Istanbul: Matba`at Kulliyat al-Adab, 1973), p. 199.

[18] Ruzbihan, *Sharh*, p. 59.

[19] Ja`far al-Hadhdha' (d. 922), in Ruzbihan, *Sharh*, ch. 183.

[20] Ibid., ch. 264.

is incapable of being symbolized. Hence the negative form of expression. The esoteric principle is primarily a way of reconciling spiritual insights with the fixed data of religious tradition; its practice became especially attractive in societies in which militant literal-mindedness frequently had official sanction. But ultimately, for the Sufis, knowledge of God was an ineffable mystery of participation. As Hallaj concluded in his critique of all theories of knowledge, *The Garden of Gnosis,* "God is Real, creation is created, and there is nothing to fear."[21]

---

[21] Abou al Moghith al Hosayn ibn Mansour al Hallaj al Baydhawi al Baghdadi, *Kitab al-Tawasin,* ed. Louis Massignon (Paris: Librairie Paul Geuthner, 1913), *Bustan al-Ma`rifa,* XI.26, p. 78.

8

Controversies over Ibn `Arabi's *Fusus*: The Faith of Pharaoh[1]

"I believe that there is no God but Him in whom the Children of Israel believe, and I am of those who submit to God."[2] These words of the Pharaoh of Egypt, spoken while the waters of the Red Sea were about to close over his head, appear in the Qur'anic account of the story of Moses, and they show the defiant opponent of the Prophet making one last effort to escape the doom that has befallen him. God's words do not appear encouraging, however: "Now? When before you rebelled, and were of the evildoers? But today We will save you in your body, so you may be a sign to those who come after…."[3] Commentators and storytellers have generally assumed that Pharaoh, though preserved bodily, was condemned to hell. As in Jewish legend, so in Muslim tales of the prophets, the angel Gabriel made Pharaoh wait until it was too late to make a valid confession of faith, by "cramming his mouth with slime."[4]

---

[1] An earlier version of this essay was read at the American Academy of Religion's conference at Chicago in 1984.

[2] Qur'an 10:90.

[3] Qur'an 10:91–92.

[4] A. J. Wensinck and G. Vajda, "Fir'awn," *Encyclopaedia of Islam*, new ed., vol. ii (1965), p. 917.

Yet in mystical circles, this common-sense interpretation has not always been upheld. A characteristic example of Sufistic interpretation of the Qur'an revolves around the case of the faith of Pharaoh, according to the analysis of Muhyi al-Din Ibn `Arabi's (d. 1240), probably the most prolific and influential of Sufi theorists. He himself was no stranger to controversy during his lifetime. His highly original views were provocative enough to rouse intense criticism also for many centuries after his death. Ibn `Arabi's thesis of the validity of Pharaoh's confession of faith, which occupies only a couple of pages in the *Fususal-Hikam,* has attracted a remarkable amount of comment from both his supporters and detractors. What were the issues at stake in this controversy, and what does it reveal of the method of scriptural exegesis practiced by Ibn `Arabi's and his school?

Many authors have written on Ibn `Arabi's theory of the faith of Pharaoh, in the dozens of commentaries that have been written on the *Fusus*, and in the many polemical works written for and against his theories.[5] Yet perhaps the most convenient example is a brief treatise on "The Faith of Pharaoh" that the fifteenth-century Iranian philosopher Jalal al-Din al-Davani[6] wrote in defense of Ibn `Arabi's view; this work was systematically

[5] *Cf.* Ibn Taymiyya (d.721/1328), *Risala fi iman Fir'awn,* and Badran ibn Ahmad al-Khalili (d. ca. 1103/169l), *Natijat al-tawfiq wal-`awn fi al-radd `ala al-qa'ilin bi-iman Fir`awn,* the eighth and ninth treatises in MS. 4644 Arabic, India Office Library, London (see A. J. Arberry, "Notes on Manuscripts Recently Acquired by the India Office Library," *Islamic Culture* 13/4 [Oct. 1939], pp. 446–49); see Muhammad ibn Muhammad al-Ghumri, also known as Sibt al-Marsafi (d. 970/1562), *Tanzih al-kawn `an i`tiqad iman Fir`awn, cf* Osman Yahya, *Histoire et classification de l'oeuvre d'Ibn al-`Arabi, Etude critique* (Damascus: Institute Français de Damas, 1964), 1:117; `Abd Allah al-Rumi al-Busnawi (d. 1054/1644), *Risalat al-Busnawi fi iman Fir`awn*, MS. Azhar 2794 (halim) 33397/27–28, cited by Yahya, 1:120. In the catalogue of the Yahuda MSS. by Rudolf Mach (*Catalogue of Arabic Manuscripts [Yahuda Section] in the Garrett Collection, Princeton University Library* (Princeton, NJ: Princeton University Press, 1977), there are five treatises on the subject: 2179, *Sharh qawl Ibn al-`Arabi fi haqq iman Fir`awn,* by Muhammad ibn Qutb al-Din al-Izniqi (d. 885/1480); 2182, *Risala fi bayan iman Fir`awn*, by Muhammad ibn `Ali al-Qarabaghi (d. 942/1535), shelflist 3091, fols. 44b–45a; 2183, *al-Muntakhab min al-ta'yid wal-`awn lil-qa'ilin bi-iman Fir`awn,* selections made by Nasri ibn Ahmad al-Husri from the *Ta'yid* of Muhammad ibn `Abd al-Rasul al-Barzanji (d. 1103/1691), Berlin 3399 (anon.), shelflist 518, fols. 60b–63a; 2184, *Risala fi iman Fir`awn*, by Akmal al-Din [al-Barbati?], shelflist 4129, fols. 53b–55b; 2185, *Risala fi `adm qabul iman Fir`awn*, anon.

[6] D. 907/1501, see Carl Brockelmann, *Geschichte Der Arabischen Litteratur,* (Leiden: E. J. Brill, 1943), 2:217.

refuted in a detailed commentary by the sixteenth-century jurist `Ali al-Qari al-Harawi,[7] who called his refutation, *The Flight for Relief from Those Who Claim Pharaoh's Belief.*[8] Davani follows Ibn `Arabi and his chief commentators in seeing the case of Pharaoh as the most extreme example of the divine mercy, which saves even this worst of sinners when he repents at the last minute. `Ali al-Qari, on the other hand, views Pharaoh's confession of faith as the most treacherous deception, but due to his respect for Ibn `Arabi's reputation, he regards the Shaykh's positive evaluation of Pharaoh as an unfortunate mistake. The underlying issue, though not stated directly, is that of scriptural exegesis. Ibn `Arabi's mystical interpretation of Pharaoh is so contrary to the Sunni consensus that even a sympathetic conservative Sufi like `Ali al-Qari only explains it away with difficulty.

Ibn `Arabi's discussion of the faith of Pharaoh is almost in the nature of an aside in the 25th chapter of the *Fusus,* which is devoted to Moses. When Pharaoh's daughter prophesies that the infant Moses will one day be a consolation both to her and to Pharaoh,[9] Ibn `Arabi comments that this refers to Pharaoh's eventual submission to God, which would render him sinless. Elsewhere, in the chapter on Solomon, Ibn `Arabi suggests that Pharaoh's conversion was inspired by the example of his magicians, who were convinced by the miraculous powers that God entrusted to Moses and Aaron. In any case, Pharaoh's confession of faith shows that he did not despair of the divine mercy.[10] After discussing at length the meaning of Moses' encounter with Pharaoh, Ibn `Arabi returns briefly to the subject of Pharaoh's confession of faith once more. He observes that Pharaoh was not certain of dying at that moment, and hence his confession was valid, unlike those who will belatedly protest their faith when

---

[7] D. 1014/ 1605 in Mecca, *cf. Brockelmann,* 2:394. He also wrote several treatises critical of Ibn al-`Arabi; *(ibid.,* 2:395/40–41).

[8] *Iman Fir`awn wal-radd `alayhi lil-`allama `Ali ibn Sultan Muhammad al-Qari wa ta'yid sayyidi Muhyi al-Din ibn al-`Arabi lil-iman,* ed. Ibn al-Khatib, Ghara'ib al-Musannafat (Cairo: al-Matba`a al-Misriyya wa-Maktabuh,1383/1964).

[9] Qur'an 28:9.

[10] Ibn `Arabi, *Fusus al-hikam,* ed. Abu al-`Ala' `Afifi (Beirut: Dar al-Kitab al`Arabi, 1365/1946), 1:201; *The Bezels of Wisdom,* trans. R. W. J. Austin, The Classics of Western Spirituality (New York: Paulist Press, 1980), pp. 195–255.

they see the punishments of hell before them. Thus God both saved him from the punishment of the afterlife and preserved his body from the flood. Ibn `Arabi acknowledges that most people consider Pharaoh among the damned, but points out that no verse of the Qur'an clearly states this, though the case is different with Pharaoh's people. Numerous Qur'anic passages refer to the punishment of Pharaoh's people in hellfire, but Pharaoh himself is never explicitly condemned in this way.[11]

Davani, writing some two and a half centuries after Ibn `Arabi, begins his short treatise as the response to an inquiry from an unnamed eminent person, and states that it is his purpose to clear Ibn `Arabi of the suspicion of heresy that has arisen as a result of this thesis. After asking his readers to cast aside any sectarian prejudice (*ta'assub*), he attempts to prove that Pharaoh's confession of faith was legally valid as an act of assent in the heart and confession with the tongue, without coercion. This submission erased his previous sins, and Pharaoh's bodily preservation is a sign for others of divine forgiveness. God's reply to Pharaoh, "Now? When before you rebelled, and were of the evildoers?"[12] is grammatically interpreted as God's courteous reproof to a no longer rebellious convert. Davani is particularly eager to show that Pharaoh's faith is not the "faith of despair" (*Iman al-ya's*) that is invalid because professed during the actual death throes or afterwards at the resurrection. In an ingenious deduction, Davani points out that Pharaoh confessed his faith in a fairly long sentence, so it is unlikely that the death-rattle had yet begun.[13]

Going further, Davani maintains that drowning in the flood that inundated the Egyptians was the only punishment that Pharaoh had to suffer for his oppression of the Israelites, and he supports this by citing the commentator Baydawi as maintaining this view. This is curious, since Baydawi held no such opinion. Kashani, incidentally, admits that Pharaoh will probably suffer some limited punishment in hell for his crimes against the Israelites. But Pharaoh's leading of his people into the floor of

[11] *Fusus*, 1:211–12; trans., p. 265.

[12] Qur'an 10:91.

[13] *Iman Fir'awn*, pp. 14–20.

the Red Sea, according to Davani, was a deliberate self-sacrifice, though he admits that there is no evidence regarding Pharaoh's ability to swim. In conclusion, Davani asserts that all of the Qur'anic references to the death of Pharaoh are liable to interpretation (*ihtimal*), with the exception of his confession of faith. Those who accuse Ibn `Arabi of heresy *(ilhad)* are ignoramuses incapable of understanding his thought. Such a one speaks ignorantly without knowing his technical terminology, for "he who does not know a thing denies it." Opposing the view of Ibn `Arabi on this question is therefore tantamount to restricting the divine mercy.[14] The main lines of Davani's interpretation agree with the conclusions of the principal commentators on the *Fusus,* such as Da'ud al Qaysari (d. 751/1350) and 'Abd al-Razzaq al-Kashani (d. 730/1330).[15]

`Ali al-Qari eagerly responded to Davani's treatise, a century after the latter's death. His initial reaction is that the whole idea of Pharaoh as a true believer is false according to the Qur'an and *Sunna,* and the consensus of the *'ulama'.* The main tenor of `Ali al-Qari's remarks is theological, but as a practiced polemicist he is not above casting satirical barbs at his opponent. For instance, his detailed commentary (which is over four times as long as the original text) begins with a tart remark about Davani's opening invocation in the *bism Allah*: Davani's use of the phrase "the straight path" (*al-siratal-mustaqim*) does not mean he is on it. `Ali al-Qari points out further that Davani's announced intention to proceed without "imitation"(*taqlid*) means that he arrogantly places himself in the rank of the masters of truth and subtlety. If he had been a follower of the traditional (*salaf wa khalaf*) commentators, he would not have fallen under the condemnation of the *hadith,* "He who speaks of the Qur'an from his opinion *(ra'y)* should mark out his place in hellfire." Finally, `Ali al-Qari can not resist pointing out the egotism that underlies Davani's use of phrases like, "from my praised Lord", instead of saying

---

[14] Ibid., pp. 23–24.

[15] Da'ud al-Qaysan, *Kitab Sharh fusus al-hikam* (Tehran, 1299), pp. 451–52; 'Abd al-Razzaq al-Kashani, *Sharh `ala fusus al-hikam* (2nd ed., Cairo: Shirkat Maktaba wa Matba`a Mustafa al-Babi al-Halabi, 1386/1966), pp. 310, 322.

"the praised Lord of all". In short, the position that `Ali al-Qari establishes at the beginning employs *ad hominem* arguments to question Davani's credentials.[16]

`Ali al-Qari next proceeds to question systematically nearly every one of Davani's assumptions. He strenuously objects to Davani calling the case of Pharaoh's faith an open question on which there are differences of opinion; this question is infact undisputed among the *'ulama'*, and the unlearned will be misled by such a brash assertion of a stupid heresy. Theologically, Davani's assertion of the sincerity of Pharaoh's confession of faith is unsupportable. Pharaoh's own pretension to divinity makes his confession of the divine unity impossible. Furthermore, he omitted to say the second half of the creed, certifying that he believed in Moses' prophethood, so his confession is legally invalid (as is that of the Jew or Christian who has faith in God but not in Muhammad's prophethood).`Ali al-Qari also refutes the notion that Pharaoh would be spared damnation, since his submission has already been proved invalid. As a sign of divine forgiveness, Pharaoh would make a poor example because of his ignominious death (here the modern editor balks and points out that many prophets have suffered terrible deaths also). In short, what Davani calls sincere,`Ali al-Qari calls a lie.[17]

Through many other arguments, `Ali al-Qari pursues his opponent, asserting again and again that no one can prove the sincerity of Pharaoh, that he in fact was a clever and duplicitous atheist who sought to avoid his impending doom by a ruse. At the end of the treatise, `Ali al-Qari returns to Davani's stated purpose of refuting the imputation of heresy to Ibn `Arabi. First of all, the charges against Ibn `Arabi are justified in this case. To Davani's charge that the critics do not understand the Sufi terminology, `Ali al-Qari coolly replies that externalist *`ulama'* may not know Sufi terminology, but esoteric *`ulama'* are ignorant of the basic points of Arabic grammar. In any case, this subject

[16] *Iman Fir'awn*, pp. 26–27, 32.

[17] Ibid., pp. 35, 38–39, 43–44.

concerns Qur'anic problems (*mabahith*) and theology, not Sufi terminology.[18]

`Ali al-Qari still has one formidable problem to deal with, and that is his basic respect for Ibn `Arabi as one of the classical masters of Sufism. Davani he can dispense with, but `Ali al-Qari's own master, Shaykh Shams al-Din Muhammad al-Bakri (d. A.D. 1547), frequently praised Ibn al-`Arabi in his assemblies. `Ali al-Qari then recounts the ambivalent feeling that many of the conservative modern Sufis have displayed toward Ibn `Arabi's theories. He quotes the Qur'an commentator Jalal al-Din al-Suyuti (d. 911/1505) on the dispute over Ibn al-`Arabi—among his supporters, his critics, and those who are totally confused. Suyuti's solution to the problem, based on a dubious remark attributed to Ibn `Arabi, is to recommend belief in his sainthood while forbidding the reading of his books. The Sufi terminology is too difficult for most people to read without falling into heresy, but one who without proof accuses lbn `Arabi of being a heretic runs the risk of incurring divine wrath by insulting one of God's saints. Therefore, it is simpler to forbid the reading of his books, since in any case spiritual experience cannot be produced by reading (this is essentially the situation current in Egypt today, where the works of Ibn `Arabi are periodically subjected to public condemnation). `Ali al-Qari then cites the interesting view of the *hadith* scholar Ibn Hajar al-'Asqalani (d. 852/1448) on Ibn `Arabi's thesis of the faith of Pharaoh. "God bereft this man [Ibn al-` Arabi] of his mind, and gave him no sense, and blinded him until that occurred .... That is the meaning of the saying of the Prophet, 'When God most high wishes to prosecute His decree, He deprives the intelligent of their intellects'"[19] (a saying that recalls the adage of Euripides, "Those whom God wishes to destroy, He first drives mad").

`Ali al-Qari has saved one scholarly shot with which to blast Davani. He states that Ibn `Arabi himself, in the 62nd chapter of the *Futuhat,* mentioned Pharaoh along with Nimrud as among the sinners who claimed divine lordship for themselves and are

[18] Ibid., pp. 80, 83.
[19] Ibid., pp. 85–90.

hence in hellfire eternally. It is `Ali al-Qari's opinion that Ibn al-`Arabi did not really contradict this correct view in the *Fusus*, but only meant that the proof of Pharaoh's infidelity appears less than decisive. Ibn `Arabi here suffered from a *lapsuscalami*, and a slip of the foot.`Ali al-Qari has inverted the usual argument about not interpreting Sufi technical terminology by ordinary standards; Ibn `Arabi's clear statement that Pharaoh was of the faithful was after all just a mistake—he really did not mean it.[20]

`Ali al-Qari's predicament was typical of later conservative Sufis, who actually disagreed with Ibn `Arabi's theories though they revered his name. His solution was to avoid the issue by condemning the doctrine while praising the man. The real issue was stated more forcibly by Da'ud al-Qaysari in his commentary on this passage. "There is no objection to the Shaykh [Ibn `Arabi] regarding his remarks on this subject, because he was ordered to say this, since everything that is in the book [*Fusus al-hikam*] was written at the order of the Prophet. Thus, he is excused, as the deluded objector is excused."[21] Qaysari is referring to Ibn `Arabi's own statement at the beginning of the *Fusus*, that the Prophet Muhammad gave him the book in Damascus in 627/1229, so the contents of this work are inspired. In effect, this constitutes license for mystical interpretation of the Qur'an, beyond the consensus of the traditional *'ulama'*, and this is where' Ibn `Arabi and Davani both differ radically from `Ali al-Qari. The faith of Pharaoh actually must be understood in the context of the *Fusus*, where it follows the startling interpretation of Moses and Pharaoh as manifestations of polar tensions in the Divine Being. By virtue of his lordship on earth, Pharaoh had the right to question Moses while inwardly recognizing Moses' mission as complementary to his own. Though we cannot pursue this context here, it is clear that the faith of Pharaoh is merely one aspect of Ibn `Arabi's reading of the Scripture. Like the Christian philosopher Origen (185?–254 C.E.), who foresaw even

20 Ibid., pp. 36, 91–92.

21 Qaysari, pp. 451–52.

the salvation of Satan when "God shall be all in all"[22] (I Cor. 15:28), Ibn `Arabi felt that the divine mercy would suffer no limitation. The variance of this mystical interpretation from the standard consensus constitutes a perennial tension within each religious tradition.

[22] Pierre Batiffol, "Apocatastasis," *Catholic Encyclopaedia,* (1907), 1:599–600, notes that this doctrine was condemned by the Council of Constantinople in A.D. 543.

9

Mystical Language and the Teaching Context in the Early Lexicons of Sufism

How does mystical language differ from other types of language? If one wishes to answer this question without relying on a priori definitions of mysticism, it would seem desirable to inquire how mystics have described their attitude toward language in general, and how they distinguish the characteristics of the special terminology and modes of discourse used in mystical writing. The literature of Islamic mysticism features a sub-genre that is particularly appropriate for such an inquiry: lexicons of the technical terminology of the Sufis. The Sufi lexicons have the appearance of the standard academic dictionaries that proliferated in all the fields of Arab-Islamic scholarship, yet the Sufis distinguished themselves from other lexicographers by consistently referring their technical terms to a manifold range of mystical experiences. Most of the early Sufi lexicons, written between the tenth and thirteenth centuries C.E., are designed for novices in the Sufi path, and amount to maps of the internal topography of Sufism. The mystical language of the Sufi lexicons expresses a wide range of experiences, not propositions, and it presupposes the authority of the master-disciple relationship as the basis for the intended experiences of transcendence. It is the special context of this teaching relationship that gives these Sufi lexicons importance for the concept of mystical language.

The construction of dictionaries was an activity that scholars of the Arab-Islamic world pursued diligently, to a degree perhaps only rivalled by the Chinese before modern times.[1] As an independent discipline, lexicography emerged slowly from the study of the Qur'an, as an attempt to deepen the understanding of the sacred book.[2] Arabic philological scholarship proceeded along the lines of the science of ḥadith, which studies the sayings and deeds of the Prophet Muhammad; transmitters of definitions, like ḥadith-transmitters, had to pass scrutiny of their ethical and religious character to gain full acceptance. Dictionaries were arranged in a number of ways, sometimes by subject or else by a variety of alphabetical orders.[3] A general dictionary such as the famous *Mafātīḥ al-`Ulūm* ("Keys of the Sciences") of al-Khwārazmī around 977 attempted to cover the terminology of both the traditional Islamic sciences and the intellectual sciences inherited from the Hellenistic world; this eclectic reference work was perfectly suited to the literary adab-culture of government secretaries in the late `Abbasid period.[4] The vast multi-volume Arabic dictionaries of Ibn Manẓūr (d. 1311) and al-Zabīdī (d. 1791) were models of literary scholarship, and used abundant specimens of pre-Islamic Arabic poetry as witnesses (*shawāhid*) to the usage of various words. While the study of the Arabic language thus enlarged its scope by absorbing secular literature, philology was never entirely separate from religious concerns; doctrinal considerations often precluded the conclusions that literary

---

[1] John A. Haywood, *Arabic Lexicography: Its History, and its Place in the General History of Lexicography* (2nd ed., Leiden: E. J. Brill, 1965), p. 1; Fuat Sezgin, *Geschichte des arabischen Schrifftums*, vol. VIII, Lexikographie (Leiden: E. J. Brill, 1982), p. 15, citing A. Fischer.

[2] Frithiof Rundgren, "La Lexicographie arabe," in *Studies on Semitic Lexicography*, ed. Pelio Fronzaroli, Quaderni de Semitistica 2 (Firenze: Università di Firenze, 1973), pp. 145–59.

[3] Cf. Haywood (passim) and Sezgin (pp. 7–16) for details of dictionary arrangements.

[4] Abu Abdallah Mohammed ibn Ahmed ibn Jusof al-Katib al-Khowarezmi, *Liber Mafatih al-Olum*, ed. G. van Vloten (Leiden, 1895; reprint ed., Leiden: E. J. Brill, 1968), pp. 3–4. For a list of translations of the different sections of this dictionary, see A. I. Sabra, "al-Khwārazmī, Abū `Abd Allāh," *Encyclopedia of Islam* (new ed.).

scholarship might have reached on its own, since the Qur'an could never be considered on the level of ordinary writings.[5]

Sufi dictionaries first appeared as appendices to the Arabic treatises on Sufism written in the tenth and eleventh centuries. Abū Naṣr al-Sarrāj (d. 988) included a chapter with definitions of 155 terms in his *Kitāb al-luma` fī al-taṣawwuf* ("Book of Glimmerings on Sufism").[6] Substantially the same list of terms, with significant development of the definitions, appeared two centuries later in the Persian work of Rūzbihān Baqlī (d. 1206), the *Sharḥ-i shaṭḥiyyāt* ("Commentary on Ecstatic Sayings").[7] Briefer lexicons were included in the *Risāla* ("Epistle") of Abū al-Qāsim al-Qushayrī (d. 1074) and the Persian *Kashf al-maḥjūb* ("Revelation of the Veiled") of `Alī al-Hujwīrī (d. 1072).[8] Of special interest are two dictionaries by the great Sufi master Muḥyī al-Dīn Ibn `Arabi (d. 1240), one a separate treatise written in 1218 and the other a section in his encyclopedic *al-Futūḥāt al-Makkiyya* ("Spiritual Conquests of Mecca").[9] These texts are

[5] Lother Kopf, "Religious Influences on Medieval Arabic Philology," in his *Studies in Arabic and Hebrew Lexicography*, ed. M. H. Goshen-Gottstein with the assistance of S. Assif (Jerusalem: The Magnes Press, The Hebrew University, 1976), pp. 19–45.

[6] Abú Naṣr `Abdallah B. `Alí al-Sarráj al-Ṭúsí, *The Kitáb al-Luma` fi 'l-Taṣawwuf*, ed. Reynold Alleyne Nicholson, "E. J. W. Gibb Memorial" Series, vol. XXII (London, 1914; reprint ed., London: Luzac & Company Ltd., 1963), pp. 333–75, listed on pp. 86–99 of the English summary; I count separately terms that Nicholson left grouped together to arrive at his total of 143 terms.

[7] Ruzbehan Baqli Shirazi, *Commentaire sur les paradoxes des Soufis* (*Sharh-e Shathîyât*), ed. Henry Corbin, Bibliothéque Iranienne, 12 (Tehran: Departement d'Iranologie de l'Institut Franco-Iranien, 1966), pp. 545–80, 613–32, giving 159 terms, plus a brief glossary of 47 additional terms on pp. 632–35. The *Sharḥ-i shaṭḥiyyāt* was Rūzbihān's own Persian translation of his earlier Arabic work *Manṭiq al-asrār*; in the dictionary section, the Persian text drops most of the specimens of Arabic Sufi poetry (originally given by Sarraj) and adds elaborations from Rūzbihān's own experience.

[8] Abū al-Qāsim `Abd al-Karīm al-Qushayrī, *al-Risāla al-Qushayriyya*, ed. `Abd al-Ḥalīm Maḥmūd and Maḥmūd ibn al-Sharīf (2 vols. continuously paginated, Cairo: Dār al-Kutub al-Ḥadītha, 1972–74), pp. 200–74, with 49 terms in the dictionary proper, followed by 51 chapters on various states; Abū al-Ḥasan `Alī ibn `Uthmān al-Jullābī al-Hujwīrī al-Ghaznawī al-Lāhawrī, *Kashf al-Maḥjūb*, ed. `Alī Qawīm (Islamabad: Markaz-i Taḥqīqāt-i Fārsī-i Irān wa Pākistān, 1398/1978), pp. 320–37, with 92 terms in four sections; cf. the English translation by Reynold A. Nicholson, *The Kashf al-Mahjúb, The Oldest Persian Treatise on Sufism*, "E. J. W. Gibb Memorial" Series, vol. XVII (new ed., London, 1936; reprinted, London: Messrs. Luzac and Company Ltd, 1976), pp. 367–92.

[9] Muḥyī al-Dīn Abī `Abd Allāh Muḥammad ibn `Alī ibn al-`Arabi, *Kitāb Iṣṭilāḥ al-Ṣūfiyya, in Rasā'il* (Hyderabad: Jāmi`at Dā'irat al-Ma`ārif al-`Uthmāniyya, 1367/1948), with 198

some of the most significant early Sufi lexical works.[10] Later works like the compendious Sufi dictionary of `Abd al-Razzāq al-Kāshānī (discussed below) adopted a different focus and arrangement to reach a wider audience, but in the process they departed from the original orientation toward Sufi novices. In more recent times, the publication of broadly-aimed dictionaries with significant amounts of Sufi terminology has continued, particularly in Persian.[11]

European scholars have devoted relatively little attention to the Sufi lexicons, although two of the earliest works of nineteenth-century scholarship on Sufism highlighted this genre. Tholuck cited excerpts from Kāshānī's dictionary in 1828, and Sprenger published Kāshānī's complete text in 1845.[12] Ibn `Arabi's separate lexicon, the *Iṣṭilāḥ al-Ṣūfiyya*, was the first of his writings to be published in Europe, appearing in 1845 in an edition by Flügel along with the general dictionary of Islamic subjects by Jurjānī (d. 1329).[13] These early efforts,

---

terms; idem, *al-Futūḥāt al-Makkiyya* (Beirut: Dār Ṣādir, n. d.) 2:127–34. I am indebted to Prof. William Chittick for calling the latter text to my attention.

[10] Other early Sufi writings, such as Anṣārī's *Manāzil al-sā'irīn*, and Abū Ṭālib al-Makkī's *Qūt al-qulūb*, are relevant to the development of mystical language in Sufism, but cannot be considered here for reasons of space.

[11] Much material from Kāshānī's lexicon appears in that of Jurjānī, and Kāshānī's work received a commentary by Shams al-Dīn Ghaffārī (d. 1430) as well as an abridgement by the Shi`i scholar Ḥaydar Amulī (d. 1385; cf. Ḥājjī Khalīfa, *Kashf al-zunūn*, ed. Flügel, 1:325, as cited by Sprenger, p. vi). The lengthy Arabic dictionary of the Indian scholar Muḥammad al-T'hānawī (ca. 1745), *Kashshāf iṣṭilāḥāt al-funūn*, Bibliotheca Indica 17 (Calcutta, 1853–62; reprint ed., Beirut: Khayyāṭ, al-Maktaba al-Islāmiyyah, 1966), added to the main entries a number of mystical definitions in Persian. Su`ād al-Ḥakīm's *al-Mu`jam al-Ṣūfī: al-ḥikma fī ḥudūd al-kalima* (Beirut: Dandala Publishers, 1981) is a comprehensive guide to Ibn `Arabi's terminology. Ja`far Sajjādī's Persian dictionary of technical terms, *Farhang-i muṣṭalaḥāt-i `urafā' wa mutaṣawwifa* (Tehran, 1339/1960), includes many excerpts from Sufi sources. Dr. Javad Nurbakhsh, the Ni`matullahi Sufi leader, published a multi-volume *Farhang-i Nurbakhsh* on Sufi terminology in Persian. The Pakistani Chishti leader Dhawqi Shah also compiled an excellent Urdu lexicon of Sufism, *Sirr-i Dilbarān* (Karachi: Maḥfil-i Dhawqiyya, 1405/1985), with many quotations from Arabic and Persian authorities.

[12] Tholuck, *Die Speculative Trinitätslehre des Späteren Orients* (1828), pp. 7, 11, 18, 26, 73, as cited by D. B. MacDonald, "`Abd al-Razzāk al-Kāshānī," *Encyclopedia of Islam* (new ed.) 1:88–89; `Abdu-r-Razzāq's *Dictionary of the Technical Terms of the Sufies [sic]*, ed. Aloys Sprenger (Calcutta: Asiatic Society of Bengal, 1845).

[13] `Ali Ben Mohammed Dschordschani, *Definitiones*, ed. Gustavus Flügel (Leipzig: Guil. Vogelii, Filii, 1845). Two translations of Ibn `Arabi's lexicon exist: A. Regnier,

however, did not inspire much further interest in the vocabulary and semantics of Sufism. Sprenger indeed called Sufi mysticism a "monomania" and a "disease" characteristic of civilizational decadence, though he conceded the importance of Sufism in poetry, "because the noblest feelings of man are morbidly exalted in this disease."[14] Reinhold Dozy, author of the *Supplement aux dictionnaires arabes*, spoke contemptuously of the recondite language of Sufism, observing, "I think that I would lose my mind if I submerged myself in the study of certain types of these words, in the alembical terminology of the Sufis, for example. This is a task that I voluntarily leave to others."[15] The principal work on Sufism that might have been expected to deal with the Sufi lexicons was the epochal study by Louis Massignon, *Essai sur la les origines du lexique technique de la mystique musulmane*. Massignon, despite his wide-ranging comments in this work, intended it to be specifically a study of the vocabulary of al-Hallaj, the Sufi martyr who exerted a consuming fascination over Massignon's researches. The early lexicons of Sufism, he observed, could be profitably compared with the terms used by al-Hallaj, but Massignon also left this inquiry to others.[16] The present essay is a brief survey of the early Sufi lexicons, with special reference to their explicit presentation of language as the expression of mystical experiences.

What was the purpose of a Sufi lexicon? As the authors of these texts explain, a lexicon is only necessary for a subject when a specialized technical vocabulary comes into existence, which only experts in that field properly understand. Unlike Khwarizmi's dictionary, however, the Sufi lexicons were not typically designed to assist outsiders to comprehend their vocabulary. On the contrary, the special terminology of Sufism was partially designed to conceal their meanings from outsiders who were not qualified to understand them. The Sufi authors

"La terminologie mystique des Ibn `Arabī," *La Museon* 48 (1935), pp. 145–62; Rabia Terri Harris, "Sufi Terminology: Ibn `Arabī's *Al-Iṣṭilāḥāt al-Ṣūfiyyah*," *Journal of the Muhyiddin Ibn `Arabi Society* III (1984), pp. 27–54.

[14] Sprenger, pp. v–vi.

[15] Reinhold Dozy, as cited by Louis Massignon, *Essai sur les origines du la lexique technique de la mystique musulmane* (2nd ed., Paris: Librairie Philosophique J. Vrin, 1968), p. 12.

[16] Massignon, pp. 19–20; the index of Hallajian terms is on pp. 19–36.

expound on this exclusive aspect of their terminology in the prefatory remarks to the lexicons. Qushayrī observes,

> Know, regarding the sciences, that every group among the scholars has words they employ on matters they share, by which they are distinguished from others, and they agree in this for the sake of their common goals: increasing understanding for those who discuss, or facilitating for the people of this art the comprehension of their meanings without restriction. This group [i.e., the Sufis] employs words on matters they share, through which they intend to reveal their meanings to themselves, and to summarize and conceal from those who oppose them in their path (*ṭarīqa*), so that the meanings of their words may be obscure to outsiders, out of jealousy toward them for their secrets. Thus they form a party against those who are unworthy . . . . By the commentary on these words we wish to facilitate the understanding of those among the wayfarers of these paths and the followers of their example (*sunna*) who wish to comprehend their meanings.[17]

So the vocabulary of Sufism is designed both to facilitate understanding among Sufis and to frustrate it for outsiders. It should not be surprising that some Muslim scholars, such as the Ḥanbalī jurist Ibn al-Jawzī, therefore severely criticized Qushayrī's Sufi terminology as a reprehensible innovation.[18] Hujwīrī is equally firm in maintaining the two functions of the mystical vocabulary, though he underlines the utility of the Sufi terminology as being more for novices than adepts:

> Know (may God make you happy) that the people of every art and the masters of every activity have expressions with each other in the issuing of their secrets, and words the meaning of which none knows but themselves. The purpose of setting up expressions is twofold: one is better instruction and simplification of intricacies to approximate the understanding of the aspirant, and the other is concealing the secret from those who are not worthy of that knowledge. The proofs of that are clear, for the philologists are distinguished by their own set expressions, such as "past tense," "future," "correct," [etc.; examples are given from jurists, ḥadith scholars, and theologians] . . . . Now this group also has set words to conceal and display their speech, so that they may act

---

[17] Qushayrī, p. 200.

[18] Abū al-Faraj `Abd al-Raḥmān ibn `Alī ibn al-Jawzī, *Talbīs Iblīs*, ed. Khayr al-Dīn `Alī (Beirut, 1970), p. 185.

> accordingly in their path; they show what they wish and hide what they wish.[19]

The terms of Sufism, then, are explicitly intended both to conceal and to display, to show and to hide. It might be supposed that the secretive "jealousy" of the Sufis (in Qushayrī's phrase) is not altogether different from the professional egotism that leads to jargon in every field. The Sufis have a different reasoning, however; their theory of meaning insists that the mystical language is esoteric in its essence, as we shall see.

It may not be easy to draw the line, however, between novices who can benefit from having technical terms defined and outsiders who should be prevented from learning the Sufi vocabulary. The difference between Ibn `Arabi's two lexicons illustrates this difficulty; the lexicon in the *Futūḥāt* occurs in the middle of an esoteric discussion of different types of divine knowledge, and it is aimed at the reader who has a deep acquaintance with Sufi teachings. This lexicon has the unusual feature, moreover, of chaining all the terms together so that the conclusion of each definition includes the next term, in this way introducing the next term's definition. This linkage of terms is certainly no accident; it suggests that they share an essential relationship beyond their purely lexical connotations.[20] The ingenious structuring of Ibn `Arabi's lexicon is based on the simultaneously experiential and transcendental nature of the Sufi vocabulary, as discussed below. It is, in addition, expressed in a teaching formula ("If you say . . then we say") characteristic of the Islamic religious sciences. Ibn `Arabi's lexicon by these formal characteristics perfectly illustrates the intentionality of mystical language in the teaching relationship. Ibn `Arabi noticed the difficulty of the Sufi vocabulary for "conventional scholars" when he replied to the request of the unnamed friend who inspired the separate lexicon, as he writes:

> You asked us to explain the words that the Sufi mystics, God's people, circulate among themselves, when you saw many of the conventional

---

19 Hujwīrī, p. 320.

20 Each definition concludes with a term (X), followed by the phrase, "And if you say, `What is X?' then we say, `X is . . . .'" Ibn `Arabi traces this "strange method (*ṭarīqa gharība*)" of chaining to the early Sufi Ibrāhīm ibn Adham (ca. 765; *Futūḥāt*, 2:134).

> scholars ask us about the meaning of our writings, and the writings of the people of our path, despite their lack of knowledge about the words which we have agreed upon, by which we understand one another. Just so is the custom of the people of every art among the sciences. So I answered you on that . . . .[21]

It appears that Ibn `Arabi's response to his friend's request is not really destined for a conventional audience, but for the friend, whom Ibn `Arabi calls a trusted intimate. Nonetheless, the separate lexicon is somewhat simpler than the excerpt in the *Futūḥāt*, although both contain substantially the same terms (in precisely the reverse order), and it seems to be aimed more at the Sufi novice.[22] The situation is different with Kāshānī, who in introducing his lengthy dictionary (516 terms in 167 pages) states that he wrote it for "the scholars of the traditional and intellectual sciences [who] did not recognize" the technical terms of Sufism.[23] As James Morris has pointed out, Kāshānī wrote on Sufism principally for mystically inclined intellectuals and scholars trained in the Avicennian philosophical tradition.[24] By adopting a philosophical approach, Kāshānī made his dictionary an intellectual commentary on Sufi vocabulary for non-Sufis.

What are the sources of the terms in the Sufi lexicons? The researches of Massignon, and more recently, Paul Nwyia, have shown the fundamental importance of the Qur'an in the formulation of the Sufi vocabulary.[25] This point should not

---

[21] Ibn `Arabi, *Iṣṭilāḥ*, p. 1.

[22] The lexicon in the *Rasā'il* contains mostly briefer versions of the definitions in the *Futūḥāt* lexicon, and it lacks the additional parts of the definitions that chain the terms one to another in the *Futūḥāt*. Thus in the *Rasā'il*, Ibn `Arabi avoids, on the surface, the complex problem of the interrelationship of the technical terms of Sufism.

[23] Kāshānī, p. 3; he states particularly that he wrote his lexicon to assist the comprehension of his commentaries on Anṣārī's *Manāzil al-sā'irīn*, Ibn `Arabi's *Fuṣūṣ al-ḥikam*, and on the Qur'an.

[24] James Winston Morris, "Ibn `Arabī and His Interpreters, Part II (Conclusion): Influences and Interpretations," *Journal of the American Oriental Society* 107 (1987), pp. 101–6. Many of the later Sufi dictionaries share more or less in Kāshānī's systematic tendencies.

[25] Massignon, pp. 45–47, cites 24 terms taken directly from the Qur'an and an equal number derived from roots occurring in the Qur'an. Paul Nwyia, in *Exégèse coranique et langage mystique, Nouvel essai sur le lexique technique des mystiques musulmans* (Beirut: Dar el-Machreq Éditeurs, 1970), has analyzed a series of early Sufi texts that illustrate the development of mystical exegesis of the Qur'an in Sufism.

be overstressed, however. Massignon's establishment of the Qur'anic and Islamic sources of Sufi language served the purpose of refuting the early Orientalist theories that sought extra-Islamic origins (Christian, Greek, or Indian) for Sufism. The Sufis' reliance on the Qur'an is unquestionably the starting point for understanding the language of Sufism, but the controversies over un-Qur'anic terms in Sufism are sufficient indication that the Sufis went outside Qur'anic language to formulate their insights.[26] Massignon himself pointed out three other sources of Sufi terminology: Arabic grammar and the Islamic religious sciences, the early schools of Islamic theology, and the vocabulary of the Hellenistic sciences.[27] Many of the terms that occur in the early Sufi lexicons are not to be found in the Qur'an at all; since our concern here is not linguistic but hermeneutic, for the moment it will suffice to make this general observation. Academic inquiries about literary sources, Quellenforschungen, are in any case inclined to fasten on minutiae to the neglect of authors' intentions. The Sufi authors are unanimous in agreeing that the real source of their terminology is mystical experience, a point that is examined more fully below. As far as the definitions themselves are concerned, poetic examples and quotations from authoritative Sufis appear frequently, particularly in the works of Sarrāj and Qushayrī. Occasionally, verses from the Qur'an are cited as illustrations.[28] There is sometimes a wide variation in the definitions themselves, from one author to another; each one seems to have felt a considerable freedom to add or subtract from the received definitions, in accordance with personal experience or the authoritative pronouncement of a teacher.

The loose arrangement of terms in the Sufi lexicons suggests, moreover, that small groupings of related but discrete mystical experiences form the basic units of terms that are defined.

---

[26] In addition to the critical remarks of Ibn al-Jawzī, cited above, see my *Words of Ecstasy in Sufism* (Albany: State University of New York Press, 1985), pp. 97–98 and 112, on the problem of non-Qur'anic language in the heresy trials of Sufis.

[27] Massignon, pp. 49–52.

[28] I count 13 Qur'anic citations of terms in Sarrāj's dictionary (*ḥaqq, mushāhada, shuhūd, qabḍ, basṭ, ru'ya, `aqd, maḥw, ṭamas, bādī, baḥr, iṣṭinā`, iṣṭifā', talbīs*), and Rūzbihān only cites 10 terms in Qur'anic contexts in his lexicon (*maqām, qabḍ, basṭ, faṣl, hamm, athar, bādī, iṣṭinā`, iṣṭifā', rūḥ*).

Most of the definitions are psychological, in terms of the soul's experience of different aspects of God; this is true even of poetic phrases and metaphysical terms usually given objectified and philosophical meanings in non-Sufi contexts.[29] Overall, there is no discernable order to the terms in these dictionaries, alphabetical or otherwise (here again, Kāshānī breaks the pattern of the early dictionaries by adopting a standard alphabetical arrangement). The lexicons instead group words into sets of two, three, or four, based on similarity of derivation (from a single root), semantic clusters, rhyme, grammatical form, semantic polarity, or parallel phraseology.[30] Comparison of the sequence of terms in the different lexicons shows a number of sections of terms that are repeated in roughly the same order, but with some variation. It is possible that a core list of Sufi mystical terms was widely used in oral teaching, and later became the basis for the similarity of sequence in the different texts; the similarities are not so great, though, as to suggest literary dependence in every case.

All the Sufi authors agree that their special terms designate mystical experiences, variously designated by such names as "realities (*ḥaqā'iq*)", "meanings (*ma'ānī*)", "states (*aḥwāl*)", "stations (*maqāmāt*)", and "unveiling (*kashf*)". Qushayrī, in his discussion of the esoteric nature of Sufi terminology, points out that mystical states are the result not of effort but divine grace: "Their [the Sufis'] realities are not collected by any sort of effort nor are gained by any kind of action; rather, they are meanings that God has promised to the hearts of a people, and by the realities of which he selects the consciences of a people."[31] Sufi esotericism, jealously guarding the secrets, is therefore designed to prevent wild misunderstandings on the part of people who have no access to the underlying experiences of encounter with God.

---

[29] The difference between Sufi definitions and philosophical definitions may be quickly verified by comparing terms such as *ḥāl, ḥaqīqa, fanā', faṣl, ishtibāh, rūḥ* in the Sufi lexicons and in Aristotelian usage; cf. Soheil M. Afnan, *A Philosophical Lexicon in Persian and Arabic* (Beirut: Dar el-Machreq Publishers, 1968), s.vv.

[30] Examples of lexical order taken from Sarrāj: root (*ḥaqq, ḥuqūq, taḥqīq, taḥaqquq, haqīqa*); semantic clusters (*ḥāl, maqām, makān*); rhyme (*kawn, bawn*); form (*lawā'iḥ, lawāmi'*); polarity (*qabḍ-basṭ, saḥw-sukr*); parallel phraseology (*anā bi-lā anā, naḥnu bi-lā naḥnu*).

[31] Qushayrī, p. 200.

Rūzbihān becomes rhapsodic in describing the mystical sources of Sufi language:

> Because there are certain words that are vessels for secrets and charged with lights, a subtle commentary will be spoken on that, God willing, so that the listener may recognize the understanding of the folk's expressions (*`ibārat*), and know their indication (*ishāra*). Those words hold the cyphers (*rumūz*) of the treasures of subtleties of [divine] commands, the stopping-places of the secrets of [mystical] states, the annunciations of [divine] commands, the desires of gnosis, and the radiance of the lights of unveilings, which are disclosed to the beginners in love in the journeying of spirits and consciences, from the revelation of the manifestation of eternity, the eternal speech, the unique [divine] actions, and the realities of the manifestation of the [divine] attributes. Since with one taste of the drink of the spirits' fonts,[32] in the unique and marvelous subtleties of the hidden world, they become masters of their momentary state (*waqt*), they make an indication of that sweetness with these words.[33]

The rushing torrent of words does not immediately reveal a pattern of interpretation, but on closer examination the sources expressed by mystical terms can be discerned again; the "expressions", "cyphers", and "indications" derive from the divine commands, mystical states, gnosis, and unveilings. Rūzbihān also gives a theological content to these experiences, consisting of eternity, the speech of God, and the divine actions and attributes (all terms familiar to Islamic dialectical theology). He insists, further, that mystical terminology has a firm relationship with states that are fully known to the adepts.

> Every cypher is connected to a station, every indication is the description of a state, and every expression is the discovery of an unveiling. None knows save the master of stations and the adept of indications. I shall repeat these points and names from the marvel of their states,

[32] This phrase "spirits' fonts (*mashārib al-arwāḥ*)" recalls the title of Rūzbihān's treatise "The Spirits' Font" or *Mashrab al-arwāḥ, wa huwa mashhūr bi-hazār u yak maqām*, ed. Naẓīf Muḥarram Khwāja (Istanbul: Maṭba`at Kulliyat al-Adab, 1973); this work describes the 1001 stations (*maqāmāt*) of the spiritual path from the creation of the universe to its end. Although the term *mashrab* has become conventionalized to mean "sect", for Rūzbihān it still holds something of the root meaning of "source of water" (or font); as his book on 1001 stations shows, the sources he has in mind are spiritual experiences.

[33] Rūzbihān, pp. 544–45.

> so that you may know how sweet and subtle is the elegance of their motions.[34]

In most of the entries of his dictionary, Rūzbihān therefore begins with the definition of Sarrāj or another clear description, and then follows with a characterization of the experiential basis of the term, which he introduces with the phrase, "Its reality is . . . ." Kāshānī also agrees with the experiential grounding of Sufi terminology, though he puts it in a typically intellectualist and systematic way: "I have indicated that the principles mentioned in the book are from the stations of the folk, which ramify into a thousand stations. I have pointed out the quality of their ramification and that which distinguishes the quality of their ramifications according to their type."[35] Whether poetic like Rūzbihān, or systematic like Kāshānī, the Sufis maintain that the essence of mystical terminology is the experience.

The experiential nature of the Sufi vocabulary is particularly evident in terms from grammatical categories. Even the terms for "word" and "name" have reference to mystical experience. To give some parallel examples: Sarrāj begins his definition of "name (*ism*)" prosaically, as "words put to give information about the named by a naming, to affirm the named; if the words fail, its meaning is not separated from the named."[36] In his view of language, meaning transcends the name. Rūzbihān partially translates and expands on this definition in a more overtly mystical way: "certain words by which they give information about the named. The name in reality is the attribute of the named. Know that the names [of God] manifest in the hearts of the faithful so that their certainty may increase."[37] In this definition, it becomes clear that in speaking of "name" and "the named", Sufis tend naturally to think of the names of God (the 99 names derived from the Qur'an) and how they experience God through those names, which are theologically the divine attributes. Since the names of God form a staple of Sufi meditation, it is

[34] Rūzbihān, p. 545.
[35] Kāshānī, p. 3.
[36] Sarrāj, p. 350.
[37] Rūzbihān, p. 570.

scarcely surprising that the divine names are assumed to be the main referents for the term "name". For Ibn `Arabi, names other than the names of God are not even included in the definition; he defines "name" as "that one of the divine names that governs the state of the devotee during his momentary state."[38] Likewise, Ibn `Arabi defines "word (*ḥarf*)" as "that expression by which God addresses you."[39] In the Sufi lexicon, all words and names function in the relationship of intimacy between the human soul and God.

The semantic categories of mystical language have an obviously experiential dimension, but their meaning is so transcendent that it is sometimes very difficult to pin down. Rūzbihān likes to use the word "cypher (*ramz*)", a term that occurs once in the Qur'an (3:41) to describe the signs by which the silent Zachariah communicated to his people. As Rūzbihān defines it, "cypher is the inner meaning (*ma`nā*) hidden beneath the external speech, which no one can grasp except those who are worthy of it. The cypher of the hidden realities pronounced by the tongue in the subtleties of knowledge is the secret in inverted letters."[40] The inner secret is so far beyond the outer speech that the letters of the word are described as "inverted" in comparison. An Arabic verse quoted by Sarrāj may have assumed silent Zachariah as the model of esoteric symbolism: "When they speak, may the goal of their cyphers incapacitate you, and when they are silent, how far you are from joining Him!"[41] Another favorite semantic category is "indication (ishāra)", which almost means "gesture", and implies a communication of so subtle a nature that it can scarcely be verbalized. As Sarrāj describes it, "The indication is that which is hidden from the speaker's revelation of it by verbal expression, because of the subtlety of its meaning. Abū `Alī al-Rūdhbārī said, 'This knowledge of ours is an indication which, when it become an expression, is hidden.'"[42]

---

[38] Ibn `Arabi, Rasā'il, p. 12. The topic of the different types of gnosis of the divine names introduces Ibn `Arabi's lexicon in the *Futūḥāt*.

[39] Ibn `Arabi, *Futūḥāt*, 2:130.

[40] Rūzbihān, p. 561.

[41] Sarrāj, p. 338, quoting Qannād.

[42] Sarrāj, p. 337.

Verbalization conceals reality; esotericism is inevitable. For Rūzbihān, "indication" is primarily the inner communication with God, and only derivatively is it the mystic's account of the experience to others.

> The reality of indication is the shining of the light of hidden subtle speech with God in the clothing of consciousness during the onslaught of finding God (*wujūd*) in the heart. The gnostic alludes to that from the mine of union with the tongue of reality for the people of the presence, so that he may thereby make an indication of that which is unveiled to him in the expansiveness of "the spirit of the spirit," which is present, witnessing, and speaking from God to God.[43]

The essence of mystical language is, again, the mystical experience, which the word attempts to convey; this is above all true of the controversial "ecstatic expressions (*shaṭḥiyyāt*)" of Sufism, which burst all conventional bounds in their intensity.[44]

What are the implications of the Sufi lexicons for the general concept of mystical language? The "contextual" studies of mysticism in the previous volumes edited by Steven Katz have stressed how mystical experiences are pre-conditioned by traditional concepts and metaphysical structures. Prof. Katz observes that "There is a clear causal connection between the religious and social structure one brings to experience and the nature of one's actual experience."[45] Without denying the importance of religious and social background as a background for mystical experience, I would not wish to reduce this complex phenomenon to pure immanence through psychologism; to state that mystical experience is a mediated, configured outcome of epistemological activity, as does Katz, might be interpreted as a one-sided relationship between language and experience, in which the built-in expectations of language have a "self-fulfilling prophetic aspect" for the experiential outcome.[46] Let us see how a broad contextual understanding of mystical language might

---

[43] Rūzbihān, p. 560.

[44] On shaṭḥiyyāt, see my *Words of Ecstasy*, esp. ch. 1.

[45] Steven T. Katz, "Language, Epistemology, and Mysticism," in *Mysticism and Philosophical Analysis* (New York: Oxford University Press, 1978), p. 40.

[46] Katz, p. 59.

apply to Sufism, and whether there are adequate reasons for resisting sociological and psychologistic reductionism. Sufis certainly use the theological and legal language of the Islamic tradition. Their special mystical teachings, too, constitute a tradition of consolidated wisdom and experience. Mystical teaching presupposes that there are certain goals which the teacher communicates to the student, towards which the student is guided; the student's attempts at understanding are corrected, shaped, and stimulated in the proper direction. Sufis were thus aware of the intentional function of language, above all as used in teaching, and this intentional function of mystical language is the basis of the Sufi lexicons. The terms used to indicate the master-disciple relationship put intentionality at the heart of this personal connection: the disciple is the *murīd* or seeker (aspirant), and the master is called the *murād* or object of search, that which is desired. Words are useful in the teaching to help shape the categories by which the student will approach experience, but since the Sufi terminology opens up unsuspected new possibilities of experience, the effect of absorbing them is broadening rather than narrowing. Yet the study of Sufi materials is not intended to be a solitary activity. The teaching is an interpersonal process, not an abstract doctrine. If it is correct to assume that the Sufi lexicons are an outgrowth of oral teaching, that suggests even more strongly the importance of the personal teaching factor. In Sufism as in the ḥadīth-based religious sciences generally, the focus upon the personal source of the teaching is an essential part of the disciple's ability to remember the teacher's words, to preserve them for himself and others.[47] The intentional language as used in the teaching relationship has two implications: first, it is language addressed to a specific audience for the sake of creating the conditions for the desired experience and understanding, not an independent body of philosophical propositions; and second, this language is a process implying the polar relationship of transcendence, in which the master and disciple

[47] See my "The Textual Formation of Oral Teachings in the Early Chishtī Order," in *Texts and Contexts: Traditional Hermeneutics in South Asia*, ed. Jeffrey Timm (Albany: State University of New York Press, 1991), pp. 271–97.

occupy roles analogous to those of divinity and humanity.[48] Each of those implications needs to be addressed separately.

The intentionality of mystical language in Sufism as a teaching points at certain experiential sources, but this is an enterprise that is distinct from instruction in abstract philosophical positions. Sufism needs to be understood in this kind of "contextual" fashion, for the master-disciple relationship decisively shapes the interpretive tradition. The views of W. T. Stace on mysticism would not in fact advance our understanding of Sufism appreciably.[49] The abstract monism of Stace, it has been rightly observed, destroys the meaning of the traditional religious language of mysticism, regarding it as mere camouflage retained to satisfy the orthodox and provide conventional means of communication. Such an approach would have been familiar to the Sufis, being reminiscent of the views of the Arab-Islamic philosophers like Ibn Sīnā (Avicenna, d. 1037), who regarded religion as an imitation of philosophy through the imagination. Although there was some overlap in the aims, epistemologies, and terminology of philosophy and Sufism, the intellectualism of the Aristotelian philosophers was fundamentally in contrast with the Sufis' insistence on attaining a state beyond reason.[50] Thus when the Andalusian philosopher Ibn Rushd (Averroes, d. 1198) asked Ibn `Arabi if the truths known to the philosophers and the Sufis were the same, the answer was, "Yes . . . and no."[51] The vital element of personal verification by experience (*taḥaqquq*) has for some philosophers given way to abstraction. Even so, let us remember that consistency for its own sake was not a goal of philosophy, either, to the degree that it also was a teaching tradition. The Jewish

---

[48] The Sufi master is not technically divinized, but there is a parallelism between the role of the master and that of God, reflected in the progression of mystical experience implicit in the formula, "annihilation in the master *(fanā' fī al-shaykh)*," "annihilation in the Prophet *(fanā' fī al-rasūl)*," "annihilation in God *(fanā' fī allāh)*."

[49] For these criticisms, see Katz, index, s.n. "Stace, W. T."

[50] This is the position of `Ayn al-Quḍāt al-Hamadānī; cf. *Words of Ecstasy*, p. 112.

[51] Henry Corbin, *Creative Imagination in the Sufism of Ibn `Arabī*, trans. Ralph Manheim, Bollingen Series XCI (Princeton, NJ: Princeton University Press, 1969), pp. 41–42. The issue of the relationship between Islamic philosophy and Sufism is highly complex, and can only be touched upon here; readers should refer to the studies of Corbin, S. H. Nasr, Fazlur Rahman, James Morris, and Parviz Morewedge (among others) for further details.

philosopher Maimonides spoke for the Arab-Islamic intellectual tradition as well when he pointed to the need to adapt knowledge to the capacities of particular audiences as one of the principal causes of authorial inconsistency.[52] This principle of esotericism in philosophic teaching is entirely parallel to that of Hujwīrī for Sufi teaching, which is "better instruction and simplification of intricacies to approximate the understanding of the aspirant."[53] Abstract propositions, whether those of Stace about "mysticism", or those of rationalist philosophers in general, are not the subject of Sufi teaching. The priority of teaching over reason received a comparable stress in Shi`ism. The Isma`ili theorist Ḥasan-i Sabbāḥ underlined the essential importance of the imam's teaching authority, by pointing out that reason alone cannot be a guide; if one refutes another's position by reason, one is acting as a teacher.[54] Even the doctrines of Islamic theology are not the subject of Sufi teaching, though it is impossible to separate the language of Sufism from its theological environment. Therefore to reduce Sufi teaching to the terms of its theology or "ontological structure" can be another form of de-contextualizing.[55]

The intentionality of mystical language in Sufism assumes the master-disciple relationship, as mentioned above, and within this language each term implies transcendence as both structure and experience. The role of the guide (whether master, Prophet, or God) is to act as a check on individual self-will and to open up the soul to what the Sufis call the "realities", "stations", and "names".

---

[52] Moses Maimonides, "Introduction to Guide of the Perplexed," trans. Shlomo Pines, in *A Maimonides Reader*, ed. Isadore Twersky (New York: Behrman House, Inc., 1972), pp. 244–45.

[53] Hujwīrī, p. 320. On esotericism as a principle of knowledge in the Islamic world, see Marshall G. S. Hodgson, *The Venture of Islam, Conscience and History in a World Civilization, Vol. II, The Expansion of Islam in the Middle Periods* (Chicago: The University of Chicago Press, 1974), pp. 195–200; and my "Esoteric and Mystical Aspects of Religious Knowledge in Sufism," chapter 7 in this volume.

[54] Ḥasan-i Sabbāḥ, "Four Chapters," in Marshall Hodgson, *The Order of Assassins* (reprint ed., New York: AMS Press, Inc., 1978), pp. 325–28.

[55] For a discussion of the "ontological schemata which shape the configuration of the [mystical] quest and its goal," see Steven T. Katz, "The `Conservative' Character of Mystical Experience," in *Mysticism and Religious Traditions* (Oxford: Oxford University Press, 1983), esp. pp. 32–43. A critique of doctrinal reductionism is found in Sallie B. King, "Two Epistemological Models for the Interpretation of Mysticism," *Journal of the American Academy of Religion* LVI (1988), pp. 257–79.

The technical terminology of Sufism, properly understood, has the same function. An example is Rūzbihān's definition of a "visitation (*wārid*)": "The source of `visitation' is the unveiling of the gnostic's object (*murād*), which enters spontaneously (*bī-qaṣd*), increasing his longing."[56] The intentionality of the "visitation" as the unveiling of the "object" coincides with the intentionality of focussing on the master; as we have seen, both the unveiling and the master are the "object (*murād*)". As Sarrāj defines the term, "the *murād* is the gnostic in whom there remains no seeking (*irāda*), who has attained the goals, and who has expressed the states, stations, aims, and seekings, for he is the sought object (*murād*) by which is sought that which is sought."[57] The one who has attained the goals, and who can express them, is not to be distinguished from them. The expression of the goals in the form of teaching indicates the transcendent experience to the student through a term or concept, just as the teaching personally mediates the attained experience. And just as transcendence is built into the teaching relationship, the Sufi sources agree that the language of Sufism has been articulated to express experiences that are transcendental. Though known and intended as object, the experience comes unasked, without reference to the aspirant's volition and beyond one's conscious control. It is for this reason that the Sufi authors define even semantic categories like "word" and "name" in terms of an experience of divine-human interaction. At the risk of repetition, let me stress that the Sufi vocabulary does not objectify the transcendent as a separate "object" but constitutes it as transcendent in consciousness. The transcendent is indicated by the various experiential modes that the Sufi tradition has defined.

If the experiential and transcendental orientation just outlined fairly corresponds to the self-understanding of the Sufis, can we generalize from this case to speak about mystical language more generally? If we call the Sufi tradition mystical, then mysticism is

---

[56] Rūzbihān, p. 549.

[57] Sarrāj, p. 342. Ibn `Arabi defines the *murād* as "an expression for the one who is ravished of his seeking while his affairs remain in readiness; he has passed all the customs and the stations without effort" (*Rasā'il*, p. 2).

not a particular doctrine or even a particular experience, and the term should not be used in an objectified way; it can, however, be useful as a term to describe the tendency to return to the experiential sources of philosophical and theological symbols. The very origin of the concept of experience in Western thought attests to a tension with rationalism, whether religious, philosophical, or scientific; it is experience that enlarges the field of thought.[58] In religion, it was primarily the Protestant reformers who invoked religious experience against the authority and doctrine of the Catholic church, and this non-doctrinal usage continued down to William James' use of the term in his classic study.[59] In the scientific field, along with Baconianism, alchemy was another source of our concept of experience in its struggle against Aristotelian orthodoxy; alchemy, of course, had religious implications as well. Here I would like to invoke an image from a seventeenth-century alchemical text, which allegorically depicts Experience as the Queen of Heaven, before whom Philosophy bows down and worships. The poem concludes,

> There with arose Phylosophy as one filled with grace,
> Whose looks did shew that she had byne in some Heavenly place;
> For oft she wipt her Eyes,
> And oft she bowd her knees.
> And oft she kist the Steps with dread,
> Whereon Experience did tread;
> And oft she cast her Head on high
> And oft full low she cast her Eye
> Experience for to espy.[60]

So, with apologies to Philo, I would like to suggest that we think of philosophy (and by extension language) as the handmaid of experience. This is not to suggest that language and prior

[58] André Lalande, *Vocabulaire technique et critique de la philosophie* (5th ed., Paris: Presses Universitaires de France, 1947), s.v. "experience," pp. 309 ff.

[59] H. Pinard, "La théorie de l'expérience religieuse. Son évolution, de Luther á W. James," *Revue d'histoire ecclesiastique* XVII (1921), pp. 63–83, 306–48, 547–74.

[60] "Experience and Philosophy," in Elias Ashmole, *Theatrum Chemicum Britannicum* (London: Nath. Brooke, MDCLII; reprint ed., Hildesheim: Georg Olms Verlags buchhandlung, 1968), p. 341.

conceptual formation have no role in mystical experience; their role is very real and significant, but it remains secondary to the experience itself.

It cannot be denied that mystical language is inextricably connected to religious and social contexts. Yet to assert that these religious and social contexts have a dominant causal relation to mystical experience and its interpretation is, in my view, unjustified, and it contradicts the very structure of mystical language as discussed above. If mysticism always has a religious and social aspect, then perhaps religion and society always have a mystical aspect. Here Ibn `Arabi might fundamentally agree with Nagarjuna, that there is no nirvana without samsara; transcendence and immanence are relational poles, not hypostatic entities.[61] Eric Voegelin, in his illuminating studies of the experiential sources of Western civilization, has convincingly argued that the interpretive symbol, the experience of reality, and consciousness itself, are inseparable aspects of a participatory whole. "A vision is not a dogma but an event in metaleptic reality . . . There is no `object' of the vision other than the vision as received; and there is no `subject' of the vision other than the response in a man's soul to divine presence."[62] Voegelin has also given an incisive analysis of the deformations that occur when philosophical propositions and theological doctrines are separated from the experiences to which they were originally tied.[63] The vocabulary of Sufism is one kind of source that can help us avoid this error; if we are right in generalizing about this mystical tendency, then mystical vocabularies in other religious traditions will have a similar experiential thrust.

The mystical language of Sufism as found in the Sufi lexicons is an expression of experiences of transcendence formulated according to the inner structure of the master-disciple relationship. In this sense there is no point in arguing that mystical

---

[61] Frederick J. Streng, "Language and Mystical Awareness," in *Mysticism and Philosophical Analysis*, pp. 141–69.

[62] Eric Voegelin, *Order and History*, vol. 4, *The Ecumenic Age* (Baton Rouge: Louisiana State University Press, 1974), p. 243, discussing "The Pauline Vision of the Resurrected"; cf. also Voegelin's *Anamnesis*, tr. Gerhart Niemeyer (Notre Dame: University of Notre Dame Press, 1978), esp. part III, "What is Political Reality?"

[63] See Voegelin, *Ecumenic Age*, Introduction, pp. 1–57.

experience is unmediated or "pure" experience. To the contrary, the teaching tradition is a powerful mediation that enables the individual to have symbolic access to experiences that may otherwise never be imagined. Yet the fundamentally transcendental orientation of the symbols and terms of mystical teaching is liberating rather than limiting. The model suggested by the Sufi lexicons condenses mystical experiences in terms designed to reveal the experiential possibilities to those who are prepared for them. At the same time these terms tend to shut out those who are not participants in the teaching process. Outsiders will naturally tend to analyse mystical terms by their externals, but mystical language retains the ability to indicate the transcendent by its own reverberation in the soul.

10

The Man without Attributes: Ibn `Arabi's Interpretation of Abū Yazīd al-Bisṭāmī[1]

One of the characteristic epithets of the great Sufi master Ibn `Arabi is Muḥyī al-Dīn, the "Revivifier of the Faith". When we ask what this means in practice, it raises the question of how a mystic interacts with the tradition. A Sufi of the stature of Ibn `Arabi does not simply recapitulate the experiences and commentaries of early generations of Sufis. The more comprehensive the vision of a thinker, the more important it is to examine how this vision integrates, or in this case revivifies, the insights of previous thinkers into a synthetic edifice. It has long been recognized that Ibn `Arabi paid close attention to his spiritual forebears, certainly the prophets but also of course the many Sufis who first elaborated the parameters of the Islamic mystical tradition. The interpretations that he has given to the sayings and experiences of earlier Sufis provide valuable indices of the ways in which the Shaykh constructed his relationship

[1] An earlier version of this article was originally presented at the conference of the Muhyiddin Ibn `Arabi Society, "The Revivifier of The Way," Berkeley CA, November 15, 1992.

with the Sufi tradition. As an example of Ibn `Arabi's treatment of his predecessors, I would like to examine his interpretation of Abū Yazīd al-Bisṭāmī (d. 848–49), the enigmatic Persian whose bold ecstatic sayings have posed a continuing challenge to subsequent generations. Especially when we contrast Ibn `Arabi's interpretation of Abū Yazīd with the Bistamian legacy as seen by other Sufis, we can come to understand the distinctiveness of Ibn `Arabi's approach to the tradition.

Ibn `Arabi has creatively appropriated the legacies of many other early Sufis, but the role of interpretation in the processes of oral and literary transmission has not yet been clarified. Probably his best known reflection on an earlier Sufi is his commentary on the 157 questions of al-Ḥakīm al-Tirmidhī on the subject of the "seal of the saints".[2] Ibn `Arabi also provided a critical commentary on a treatise by the Andalusian Ibn Qasyī (d. 1151).[3] Another notable example is Dhū al-Nūn the Egyptian (d. 860), to whom Ibn `Arabi dedicated a special monographic study, collecting over five hundred of his sayings. This text has been translated into French by Roger Deladrière from unpublished manuscripts.[4] In his valuable introduction, Deladrière has indicated the remarkable complexity of this text. Ibn `Arabi derived these sayings from both written and oral sources, with a good deal of overlapping. Some of Dhū al-Nūn's sayings come exclusively from written texts: 69 from Ibn Bākūya and 114 from Kharkūshī. Others, while found in standard Sufi texts, Ibn `Arabi received also by oral tradition: 190 from Abū Nu'aym al-Iṣfahānī, 153 from Ibn Khamīs, 75 from Ibn al-Jawzī, 21 from al-Qushayrī, and 21 from Ibn Jaḥḍam.[5] Deladrière has also shown that parallel texts from Dhū al-Nūn can be found in other Sufi sources

[2] Although the Cairo edition lists 155 questions (*al-Futūḥāt al-Makkiyya*, 2:39–139), Osman Yahia's critical edition lists 157; cf. Michel Chodkiewicz, ed., *Les Illuminations de La Mecque/The Meccan Illuminations* (Paris: Sindbad, 1988), p. 500, n. 178; id., *Le Sceau des saints: Prophétie et sainteté dans la doctrine d'Ibn Arabi*, Bibliothèque des Sciences humaines (Paris: Gallimard, 1986), pp. 146 ff.

[3] Claude Addas, *Ibn `Arabi ou La quête de Soufre Rouge*, Bibliothèque des Sciences humaines (Paris: Gallimard, 1989), pp. 77–78.

[4] Ibn `Arabi, *La vie merveilleuse de Dhû-l-Nûn l'Égyptien*, trans. Roger Deladrière (Paris: Sindbad, 1988).

[5] Deladrière, pp. 39–41.

and historical texts: 124 in Ibn 'Asākir's history of Damascus, 171 in 'Aṭṭār's Persian hagiography, 114 in al-Munāwī's Arabic hagiography, and a startling 402 in al-Suyūṭī's biography of Dhū al-Nūn.[6] A major problem looms in clarifying the role of interpretation in the selection of these sayings. How many of these sayings are found in a majority of later transmitters, and how many exist only in a single source? Which sayings does Ibn `Arabi exclude? Does the picture of Dhū al-Nūn that emerges in the works of other authors differ significantly from Ibn `Arabi's? Another problem occurs in the textual variations of these sayings. Quotations from early Sufi sources can often undergo major transformations in words and authorship.[7] A great deal of close textual work needs to be done before we can know the exact significance of Ibn `Arabi's interpretation of Dhū al-Nūn.

In terms of textual transmission, comparison with other sources indicates that the literal version of some of Dhū al-Nūn's sayings given by Ibn `Arabi differs significantly from versions known in other parts of the Islamic world. Persian and Indian Sufis quote a saying of Dhū al-Nūn on intimacy with God as a justification for listening to music (*samā'*). In the later sources, the authorship of the saying has shifted to one of its primary transmitters, so that it is now attributed to Rūzbihān Baqlī. Ibn `Arabi and other Arab Sufis, on the other hand, saw this saying (quoted in a significantly different form) as a description of the alternation between states of awe (*hayba*) and intimacy (*uns*).[8] The fact that Ibn `Arabi quoted different versions of Dhū al-Nūn's sayings than did other Sufi interpreters, or that he understood them differently, should not be a cause for suspicion, or for privileging one of these interpreters over another. It should rather be an opportunity to define Ibn `Arabi's unique position in terms of his relation to the rest of the tradition.

---

[6] Deladrière, pp. 42–44. al-Suyūṭī's work has a similar complexity, relying on extensive quotations from two works by Ibn Bākūya, from Abū Nu'aym, al-Sulamī, and Bayhaqī.

[7] I have explored an instance of this problem of transmission in "The Interpretation of Classical Sufi Texts in India: The *Sham'āil al-atqiyā'* of Rukn al-Dīn Kāshānī," in *Refractions of Islam in India*, chapter 3.

[8] For details, see my "Rūzbihān Baqlī on Love as 'Essential Desire,'" chapter 11 in this volume.

Returning to Abū Yazīd, it is apparent that Ibn `Arabi held the Persian in great regard, as a mystic of remarkable attainments. Ibn `Arabi probably makes more references to Abū Yazīd than to any other early Sufi.[9] He refers to him as one of "the people of blame" (*al-malāmiyya*), one of the highest categories of spiritual rank.[10] Abū Yazīd is one of the saints who have received every kind of divine manifestation in their breasts.[11] He is one of the "people of unveiling and finding" (*ahl al-kashf wal-wujūd*) who attains God through poverty.[12] Ibn `Arabi calls him "one of our companions" (*min aṣḥābinā*) who "has realized the truth" (*kāna muḥaqqiqan*).[13] To this category of "companions" belong others such as al-Ghazālī, "the companions of hearts, witnessings, and unveilings–not the devotees, ascetics, or Sufis in general, but the people of realities and realization among them."[14] As one of the "realizers of the truth" (*al-muḥaqqiqūn*), Abū Yazīd holds the same view as Ibn `Arabi on the relation between gnosis (*ma'rifa*) and knowledge (*'ilm*).[15] Abū Yazīd is one of the "substitutes" (*nā'ib*, pl. *nuwwāb*) who holds the degree of "interior succession" (*al-khilāfa al-bāṭina*), both terms referring to aspects of the office of the "pole" (*quṭb*), the supreme figure of the spiritual hierarchy.[16] Abū Yazīd's house, called "the house of the just" (*bayt al-abrār*), is one of the places where spiritual influences remain at such a high intensity that the sensitive heart can still perceive them; in this sense, like the retreats of Junayd and Ibrāhīm ibn Adham, it is comparable at a lesser level to the sacred precincts of Mecca.[17]

---

[9] William Chittick, *The Sufi Path of Knowledge: Ibn al-'Arabi's Metaphysics of Imagination* (Albany: SUNY Press, 1989), p. 387, n. 8 (hereafter cited as *SPK*).

[10] *al-Futūḥāt al-Makkiyya*, 3:34.11 (this category includes other figures such as Ḥamdūn al-Qaṣṣār and Abū Sa'īd al-Kharrāz).

[11] Ibid., 2:40.16–17 (citing also Sahl al-Tustarī); this occurs in response to the first of al-Ḥakīm al-Tirmidhī's 157 questions directed to "the seal of the saints," in the first *waṣl* of chapter 73 of *al-Futūḥāt al-Makkiyya*.

[12] *al-Futūḥāt al-Makkiyya*, 3:316.27; trans *SPK*, p. 40.

[13] *al-Futūḥāt al-Makkiyya*, 2:657.34; trans *SPK*, p. 392, n. 34.

[14] Ibid., 1.261.11; cf. trans. in *SPK*, p. 392, n. 34.

[15] *al-Futūḥāt al-Makkiyya*, 2:318.30–32 (citing also Sahl al-Tustarī, Ibn al-`Arīf, and Abū Madyan); trans. *SPK*, p. 149.

[16] *al-Futūḥāt al-Makkiyya*, 2:6.15, 30–31. For commentary on these terms, see Chodkiewicz, p. 120.

[17] al-Futūḥāt al-Makkiyya, 1:99.9–11.

Abū Yazīd is also described as one of the "solitaries" (*afrād*) who have attained to God, but who return to the world under divine compulsion.[18] In addition, Abū Yazīd continues to be active as an Uwaysī spiritual guide for later generations of Sufis (such as Abū al-Ḥasan al-Kharaqānī), and appears in visions to Ibn `Arabi himself as well as to other figures such as Abū Madyan.[19] In short, Abū Yazīd is clearly an authoritative representative of early Sufism, in the view of Ibn `Arabi.

In singling out Abū Yazīd as a Sufi authority, Ibn `Arabi was following the lead of many earlier biographers and commentators. The first we know of was Junayd of Baghdad (d. 910), who interrogated one of Abū Yazīd's relatives about his sayings, and then translated them from Persian into Arabic. Junayd's commentary (*tafsīr*) on these controversial sayings is partially preserved by Sarrāj.[20] Further commentary is occasionally found in the collection of Sahlagī, mentioned below.[21] Other important interpretations occur in the Persian commentary on ecstatic sayings by Rūzbihān Baqlī (d. 1209) and in 'Aṭṭār's (d. ca. 1220) famous Persian hagiography.[22]

Ibn `Arabi did not dedicate a single treatise to the sayings of Abū Yazīd, as he did with Dhū al-Nūn, so our task theoretically requires us to comb through the works of Ibn `Arabi, especially *al-Futūḥāt al-Makkiyya*, for significant references to Abū Yazīd. In the scope of this essay, it will only be possible to comment on a few examples, but these will suffice to frame the problem of how

---

18 *al-Futūḥāt al-Makkiyya*, 1:251.33, 252.10–15; cf. Chodkiewicz, *Le Sceau*, p. 141.

19 Chodkiewicz, *Le Sceau*, p. 179, n. 3; Addas, p. 87, n. 1; p. 89, citing *Mawāqi' al-nujūm*, p. 140; pp. 128–29, citing *Muḥāḍarāt al-abrār*.

20 Abú Naṣr 'Abdallah B. 'Alí al-Sarráj al-Ṭúsí, *The Kitáb al-Luma' fi 'l-Taṣawwuf*, ed. Reynold Alleyne Nicholson, "E. J. W. Gibb Memorial" Series, vol. XXII (London, 1914; reprint ed., London: Luzac & Company Ltd., 1963), pp. 380–95.

21 On Sahlagī (Arabicized as al-Sahlakī or al-Sahlajī), see Georges Vajda, "Une brève typologie du soufisme: K. Rūḥ al-Rūḥ, opuscule inédit de Muḥammad b. 'Alī al-Sahlakī al-Bisṭāmī," *Arabica* 29 (1982), pp. 307–14.

22 Rūzbihān Baqlī, *Sharḥ-i shaṭhiyyāt*, ed. Henry Corbin, Bibliothéque Iranienne, 12 (Tehran: Departement d'iranologie de l'Institut Franco-iranien, 1966), pp. 78–147, commenting on thirty-one sayings; Abū Ḥāmid Muḥammad ibn Abī Bakr Ibrāhīm Farīd al-Dīn 'Aṭṭār Nīshābūrī, *Kitāb-i tadhkirat al-awliyā'*, ed. R. A. Nicholson (5th ed., Tehran: Intishārāt-i Markaz, n.d.), I, 129–66.

Ibn `Arabi subtly interprets Abū Yazīd's sayings in terms of his own overall perspective. Our main check will be the largest and oldest independent collection of the sayings of Abū Yazīd, which was assembled in the eleventh century by al-Sahlagī (d. 1083) under the title *Kitāb al-nūr min kalimāt Abī Ṭayfūr* ("The Book of Light on the Sayings of Abū Ṭayfūr [Abū Yazīd]"). The archaic and faulty Arabic text, with full isnāds, was edited by 'Abd al-Raḥmān Badawī from two manuscripts in 1949, and a considerably abridged French translation by Abdelwahab Meddeb has also appeared.[23]

We may first consider cases where Ibn `Arabi has reported the sayings of Abū Yazīd with little or slight variation. An example is a saying on inspired exegesis. Ibn `Arabi reports the following:

> Abū Yazīd said to the exoteric scholars, "You take your knowledge dead from the dead, but we take our knowledge from the Living who does not die!"[24]

If we compare the version given by al-Sahlagī, we find an account with the isnād plus a slightly different context:

> Yūsuf ibn al-Ḥusayn said, "I heard Istanba (Ibrāhīm al-Harawī) say, 'I was attending the assembly of Abū Yazīd, and the people said, "So-and-so has met so-and-so." Abū Yazīd said, "Beggars! They have taken [their knowledge] from the dead, but I have taken our knowledge from the Living who does not die."[25]

The basic point is the same, although the nuances are different. Ibn `Arabi's version does not refer to the people praising scholars for their direct transmission of learning from other scholars–Abū Yazīd ridiculed this as a dead letter in comparison with the living God who is always accessible to the saint.

---

[23] 'Abd al-Raḥmān, *Shaṭaḥāt al-Ṣūfiyya*, Part One, *Abū Yazīd al-Bisṭāmī*, Darāsāt Islāmiyya 9 (Cairo: Maktaba al-Nahḍa al-Miṣriyya, 1949); Abdelwahab Meddeb, trans., *Les Dits de Bistami: Shatahât*, L'espace intérieur 38 (Paris: Fayard, 1989). Meddeb cites the Arabic text according to a reprint of Badawī's edition, published in Kuwait in 1978; this was not available to me.

[24] *al-Futūḥāt al-Makkiyya*, I 1:280.25; SPK, p. 249.

[25] Badawī, *Shaṭaḥāt*, p. 77; trans. Meddeb, p. 58, no. 71.

Rather than being a comment on exoteric learning occasioned by a chance remark, Ibn `Arabi's version is a direct address to exoteric scholars as a class. There are other slight differences of tense and person that make al-Sahlagī's version more circumstantial and Ibn `Arabi's more general. But none of this has major significance.

Another example is a saying which, shorn of context, becomes for Ibn `Arabi an opportunity to explain a general point about the relationship between the servant and the divine Lord. Ibn `Arabi's comment actually precedes and sets up the quotation from Abū Yazīd:

> At root the servant was created only to belong to God and to be a servant perpetually. He was not created to be a lord. So when God clothes him in the robe of mastership and commands him to appears in it, he appears as a servant in himself and a master in the view of the observer. This is the ornament of the Lord, the robe that He has placed upon him. Someone objected to Abū Yazīd that the people touched him with their hands and sought blessing from him (*fī tamassuḥ al-nās wa tabarrukihim*). He replied, "They are not touching me, they are only touching an adornment with which my Lord has adorned me. Should I forbid them from that, when it does not belong to me?"[26]

The earlier version is somewhat different. It gives a dramatic account of a meeting between the youthful Abū Yazīd and a condescending *ḥadīth* scholar, to whom Abū Yazīd replies with a stunning revelation of his level of mystical experience:

> A man from the Ḥadīth Folk said to Abū Yazīd, "Do you pray properly?" He said, "Yes, God willing." So he asked, "How do you pray?" He said, "I proclaim "God is Most Great" in obedience, I recite with modulation, I kneel in veneration, I prostrate with humility, and I give salutation full of peace." Then he said, "Boy, if you have this understanding, excellence, and knowledge, why do you permit the people to touch you seeking blessing?" He replied, "They are not touching me, they are only touching an adornment with which my Lord has adorned me. Should I forbid them from that, when it does not belong to me?"[27]

---

26 *al-Futūḥāt al-Makkiyya*, 3:136.8, trans. SPK, p. 323.

27 Badawī, *Shaṭaḥāt*, p. 76 (trans. Meddeb, p. 57, no. 68).

While Ibn `Arabi has quoted Abū Yazīd's words without significant variation, his omission of the context has displaced a story about the contrast between mystical experience and scholarly learning and transformed it into an instance of a metaphysical relationship.

Next are cases in which Ibn `Arabi has given a critical interpretation of Abū Yazīd's saying, in which there is a major textual difference between Ibn `Arabi's version and Sahlagī's. Here is an example:

> Abū Yazīd heard a Koran reciter reciting the verse, "On the day when We shall muster the godfearing to the All-merciful in droves" (19:85). He wept until his tears drummed upon the pulpit. It is also said that blood flowed from his eyes until it struck the pulpit. He cried out, saying, "How strange! Where will he who is sitting with Him be mustered?" When it came around to our time, I was asked about that. I replied: "There is nothing strange except the words of Abū Yazīd."[28]

Ibn `Arabi goes on to say that the "godfearing" are those souls who are related to the divine name "the Overbearing (*al-jabbār*)", not to the name "the All-merciful". He finds it peculiar that Abū Yazīd has not noticed that the Qur'an paradoxically connects the "godfearing" with what appears to be the wrong divine name. Ibn `Arabi explains this apparent anomaly by pointing out that each divine name by denoting the divine Essence implies all the other divine names. Elsewhere, Ibn `Arabi introduces the same anecdote with a long comment expanding on his doctrine of the divine names and Abū Yazīd's failure to understand them.

> Do you not see how Abū Yazīd (God have mercy on him) acted, when he was ignorant of the divine names and which realities are appropriate to them, on hearing [this verse?]. . . In this state, he was sitting with the Names, insofar as none of them indicates the Essence; [but] he was not with the name, insofar as . . . he experienced denial, or rather he experienced wonder in a special way, which is similar to denial but is not denial, so that if this saying had been from other than God, he would have commanded the speaker to be silent and restrained him from that. The man only showed wonder at the word of God in respect

[28] *al-Futūḥāt al-Makkiyya,* 1:210.7, 3:212.34, trans. in SPK, p. 37.

to the god-fearing who are sitting with God; how will they be mustered to Him?[29]

Ibn `Arabi notes that Abū Yazīd was amazed at the paradox of how God will summon those (the godfearing) who are already in His presence, but he discounts this explanation as a lack of metaphysical comprehension.

If we turn to Sahlagī's collection, it turns out that what Ibn `Arabi has reported is a conflation of separate accounts of Abū Yazīd's reactions to two Qur'anic verses. First, Sahlagī gives two versions of Abū Yazīd's response to the "mustering" verse (19:85):

1. "He got excited (*hāja*) and said, 'Whoever is with Him has no need to be mustered, because he is sitting with Him eternally.'"[30]
2. "He became ecstatic and enraptured (*tawājada wa hāma*), and started saying, 'Whoever is with Him has no need to be mustered, because he is sitting with Him eternally.'"[31]

These two versions only differ in the language used to describe Abū Yazīd's emotional state. The terms alluded to in each case indicate delighted ecstasy (*wajd*, *hayajān*, *hayamān*) rather than doubtful wonderment.[32] Abū Yazīd's remark belongs to the ecstatic critique of literal interpretations of the afterlife. In the context of early Sufism, this follows from the dissatisfaction with paradise as a final goal (Rābi'a, Shaqīq al-Balkhī), and it forms a part of the outrageous ecstatic sayings that Abū Yazīd and Shiblī delivered about hell and judgment.[33]

Second, the detail mentioned by Ibn `Arabi, that Abū Yazīd wept tears of blood onto the pulpit on hearing the verse, occurs

---

[29] *al-Futūḥāt al-Makkiyya*, 3:212.34–213.10.

[30] Badawī, *Shaṭaḥāt*, p. 23, no. 24 (citing *Ḥilya* X, 41), trans. Meddeb, p. 182, no. 453 (in n. 133, Meddeb mistakenly assumes that the source for this saying is Sarrāj).

[31] Badawī, *Shaṭaḥāt*, p. 119 (trans. Meddeb, p. 129, no. 302, in a truncated form that preserves only Abū Yazīd's response).

[32] For these terms, see my "The Stages of Love in Early Persian Sufism, from Rābi'a to Rūzbihān," chapter 13 in this volume.

[33] See Shiblī in my *Words of Ecstasy in Sufism* (Albany: State University of New York Press, 1985), p. 38.

in Sahlagī's report of his reaction to an altogether different Qur'ānic passage:

> Abū Yazīd one Friday sat above the pulpit, and the preacher sat on the pulpit and preached; when he reached this verse: "They did not truly measure the power of God" (6:91), Abū Yazīd heard, and blood fell from his eyes until it struck the pulpit.[34]

From the content of the verse, it appears that the emotional setting for Abū Yazīd's powerful reaction was overwhelming awe. The complex situations and different textual settings of Sahlagī's versions vary considerable from the portrayal of Ibn `Arabi.

In one of his most intriguing sayings, Abū Yazīd describes himself as the man without attributes. This saying has been commented on several times by Ibn `Arabi and others, with textual variants that permit us to distinguish divergent interpretations of the saying. Ibn `Arabi informs us that Abū Yazīd used to say, "I have no morning and no evening; morning and evening belong to him who becomes delimited by attributes, but I have no attributes."[35] He comments that God should be even less delimited by attributes: "The Real is more appropriately free from limitation (*taqyīd*) by attributes, due to his independence from the world, for attributes are only required by existing things. If there was in the Real that which the world requires, then it would not be correct that he be independent of that which seeks him."[36] In another place, Ibn `Arabi gives the text in a slightly different form, reading "Morning and evening only belong to one who becomes delimited by the attribute, but I have no attribute."[37] This citation occurs in the midst of Ibn `Arabi's lexicon of Sufi terminology (which comprises the answer to al-Tirmidhī's 153rd question), under the definition of the term "place" (*makān*):

> It is a station in "expansion" (*basṭ*) which only belongs to the perfect ones who have realized the stations and states, and who are permitted

[34] Badawī, *Shaṭaḥāt*, p. 110 (omitted by Meddeb, this follows the saying he numbers 253).

[35] SPK, p. 65, with note 9, giving a plural form "attributes".

[36] *al-Futūḥāt al-Makkiyya*, 4:319.32–33.

[37] The formula is *innamā al-ṣabāḥ wa al-masā' li-man taqayyada bil-ṣifa, wa lā ṣifata lī.*

> the station which is beyond majesty and beauty; they have no attribute or description. Abū Yazīd was asked, "How are you this morning?" He said, "Morning and evening only belong to one who is limited by the attribute, but I have no attribute."

After narrating Abū Yazīd's saying, Ibn `Arabi comments, "Our companions differ over whether or not this saying is an ecstatic utterance (*shaṭḥ*), but 'place' requires it of him."[38] We shall return to the question of ecstatic utterances below, but for the moment it suffices to notice that Ibn `Arabi's frequent references to this saying primarily indicate his interest in the problem of attributes and the concept of delimitation. This has theological ramifications for the divine attributes as well as mystical significance for those who have, like Abū Yazīd, gone beyond the attributes.[39]

Other Sufis give a different version of this saying with an interpretation that follows another line entirely. Rūzbihān Baqlī follows the version given by Sahlagī: "Morning and evening only belong to one who is held by the attribute, but as for me, I have no attribute."[40] This version preserves a much more archaic flavor than Ibn `Arabi's version, which uses a term from his own technical vocabulary; instead of saying that one is "held by (*ta'khudhuhu*)" the attribute, Ibn `Arabi's version has it that one is "limited by (*taqayyada bi-*)" the attribute.[41] In his

---

[38] *al-Futūḥāt al-Makkiyya,* 2:133.21–23.

[39] Other references to the "man without attributes" include *al-Futūḥāt al-Makkiyya,* 2:646.29 (trans. SPK, p. 376); 2:187.11; 3:106.16 (see SPK, p. 391, n. 9). The similar expression "no station" (Qur. 33:13) designates the rank of Abū Yazīd and other "Muḥammadans" who are heirs of the prophet (*al-Futūḥāt al-Makkiyya,* 1:223.2, trans. SPK, p. 377); place (*makān*) is a transcendent location for Idrīs (Qur. 19:57) and other perfect ones who have, like Abū Yazīd, passed beyond states and stations; cf. 2:386.19 (SPK, p. 379). Other citations occur in *al-Futūḥāt al-Makkiyya,* 3:177, 216, 500; 4:28. Chodkiewicz, *Le Sceau,* pp. 52–54, links the "no attributes" saying with Abū Yazīd's definitions of sainthood as reported by Sulamī and Qushayrī.

[40] Badawī, *Shaṭaḥāt,* p. 70, repeated on p. 111. Meddeb (p. 70, no. 47) translates, "Le matin et le soir sont pour celui sur qui l'attribut a prise; et moi, je'échappe à tout attribut."

[41] For the use of the term *taqyīd* and related terms, see SPK, index, s.v. "*qayd*". The term *ta'khudhuhu* recalls the Throne Verse (Qur. 2:256), "Slumber does not hold him (*lā ta'khudhuhu*), neither does he sleep." Curiously, Rūzbihān's Persian translation does not preserve the nuance, translating the saying as "Morning and evening belong to that person who has no attribute . . . " (*bāmdād u shabāngāh ān kas-rā bāshad kih ū-rā ṣifatī bāshad*); cf. *Sharḥ,* no. 77, p. 137.

original Arabic version of the commentary on ecstatic sayings, the *Manṭiq al-asrār* ("The Language of Consciences"), Rūzbihān Baqlī comments that Abū Yazīd's experience of witnessing God has taken him beyond time, to participate for a moment in eternity:

> By this saying he alludes to his being drowned in the vision of eternity, and none of his attributes remains in the vision of the might of the Real. "God has no morning or evening." Morning and evening are from the coursing of sun and moon in the heavens, and in the conscience of Abū Yazīd during the witnessing of the Real there was no existence of one who is less than "by the Real, with the Real, in the Real." He did not perceive time, place, the moment, or the seasons in this momentary state. I recall what the Master of the Gnostics [i.e., the Prophet] said, "I have a time with God."[42]

In his own later Persian translation of the same commentary on ecstatic sayings (*Sharḥ-i shaṭḥiyyāt*), Rūzbihān appears to have had new thoughts on the subject. He now begins by stressing passion, ecstasy, and annihilation as the main features of Abū Yazīd's experience:

> He alludes to ravishing (*walah*) and agitation (*hayajān*), and astonishment (*ḥayrat*) and bewilderment (*hayamān*), that is: "I am intoxicated and unconscious. From hearing the commands of creation without an ear, peace has been stripped from me. the bird of the elements and time has flown, my soul is lost in the hidden of the hidden, the form of existence has become changed for me, I remain in bewilderment without the attribute of wayfaring. Having recited the existence of the verse "Everything upon it is vanishing (*fān*^{in}, Qur. 11:26, alluding to *fanā'*), I am in the world without any trace, lifeless in love, and in the falsification of intellect and the confirmation of love, I cannot tell day from night.

Only after exhausting this theme does he return to the earlier interpretation of transcending time through witnessing God:

> It is also possible that he alludes to the drowning of the soul in the vision of eternity, and in this cypher he explains that in eternity, the

[42] Rūzbihān, *Manṭiq al-asrār*, MS Louis Massignon collection, Paris, fol. 83a/3 (*innamā al-ṣabāḥ wa al-masā' li-man ya'khudhuhu* [sic] *al-ṣifa, wa lā ṣifata lī*).

> soul has no traces of temporal existence. "There is no morning or evening for God" . . . .[43]

The saying "There is no morning or evening for God", also cited as *ḥadīth* by other Sufi writers,[44] brings Rūzbihān to invoke another Prophetic saying, "The time I have with God", the eternity that is the mode of relationship between God and the prophet. He concludes, "Abū Yazīd became qualified by the all in the essence of the all."

The variance between the views of Rūzbihān and Ibn `Arabi does not provide any grounds for privileging one line of interpretation over any other—Rūzbihān has felt free to elaborate new interpretations and relegate his own earlier thoughts to a secondary position. Divergent texts and interpretations indicate rather that these Sufis used the sayings of earlier mystics as a way to explore the possibilities of meaning and experience rather than search for a single authoritative teaching. If we wished, we might try to reconstruct Abū Yazīd's "doctrine" of divine attributes, on the basis of a number of passages in which he uses the term *ṣifa* or attribute.[45] Such an archeological purpose did not play a part in the projects of either Ibn `Arabi or Rūzbihān.

Another instance of Ibn `Arabi's reflection on Abū Yazīd contains a complex meditation on two different sayings about the all-encompassing nature of the heart.

> The heart of the gnostic is infinite and contains all. Abū Yazīd said, "If the Throne and all that surrounds it, multiplied a hundred million times, were to be in one of the many corners of the Heart of the gnostic, he would not be aware of it." This was the scope of Abū Yazīd in the realm of corporeal forms. I say, however, that, were limitless existence, if its limit could be imagined, together with the essence that brought it into existence, to be put into one of the corners of the Heart of the

---

43 Rūzbihān Baqlī, *Sharḥ*, no. 77, p. 137.

44 'Ayn al-Quḍāt Hamadānī, *Tamhīdāt*, ed. 'Afīf 'Usayrān, Intishārāt-i Dānishgāh-i Tihrān, 695 (Tehran: Chāpkhāna-i Dānishgāh, 1341/1962), p. 213.

45 E.g., Badawī, *Shaṭaḥāt*, pp. 78 (Meddeb, p. 60, no. 79), 79 (Meddeb, p. 62, no. 88), 82 (Meddeb, p. 67, no. 110), 111 (Meddeb, p. 116, no. 260). Similarly, one might contrast Ibn `Arabi's use of the "no attributes" saying to define *makān* with Abū Yazīd's long description of *makān*, in Badawī, *Shaṭaḥāt*, p. 75 (trans. Meddeb, p. 54, no. 63).

> gnostic, he would have no consciousness of it. It is established that the Heart encompasses the Reality, but though it be filled, it thirsts on, as Abū Yazīd said.[46]

Is this one-upmanship? It appears that Ibn `Arabi criticizes Abū Yazīd for merely using God's Throne as the measure of the heart, instead of all of existence and the divine essence too. Ibn `Arabi's commentator Qāshānī feels required to explain, "There is no criticism here, rather he means that Abū Yazīd, in his universal specification, gazed at the realm of corporeal forms through annihilation. But if he had gazed with the eye of God, he would have said something like [what Ibn `Arabi said]; it was [seen by] the eye of the realm of corporeal forms, however, which is related to the beloveds by existent things."[47] Thus the different comparisons used by the two mystics are merely a function of their different perspectives. The appearance of criticism is mitigated, too, by Ibn `Arabi's reference to the infinite thirst of the gnostic's heart, which Abū Yazīd has expressed in several sayings. It seems as though Ibn `Arabi uses the experiences and sayings of Abū Yazīd as points of departure for exploring his own experiences.[48]

In spite of his frequent reference to Abū Yazīd and the high regard in which he held him, Ibn `Arabi shows a certain ambivalence with regard to some of his sayings. We have already seen how Ibn `Arabi pointed to limitations in Abū Yazīd's comprehension of the divine names, and to certain mystical perceptions that Ibn `Arabi had surpassed. His ambivalence becomes most pronounced when it comes to the classification of Abū Yazīd's sayings as ecstatic utterances (*shaṭḥiyyāt*). As shown above, Ibn `Arabi resisted the suggestion that the "no attributes" saying was an ecstatic utterance, arguing instead that the

---

[46] *Fuṣūṣ al-ḥikam* ch.VI; Ibn al-`Arabi, *The Bezels of Wisdom*, trans. R. W. J. Austin, Classics of Western Spirituality (New York: Paulist Press, 1980), pp. 101–2. Cf. also ch. XII, trans. Austin, p. 148, for another brief citation of this saying.

[47] 'Abd al-Razzāq al-Qāshānī, *Sharḥ 'alā fuṣūṣ al-ḥikam* (2nd ed., Egypt: Muṣṭafā Bābī Ḥalabī wa Awlāduh, 1386/1966), p. 109.

[48] Another example is Ibn `Arabi's entry into the state of proximity or *qurba*, recalling the solitude that Abū Yazīd experienced on entering this state, but then reflecting that this state is his homeland and thus is no cause for loneliness. Cf. *al-Futūḥāt al-Makkiyya*, 2:261.2–4, trans. Denis Gril, in *Illuminations*, p. 340.

state of "place" required him (*iqtiḍāhu*) to speak. This comment needs to be placed in the context of Ibn `Arabi's attitude toward *shaṭḥiyyāt*.

In his lexicon of mystical terminology, Ibn `Arabi briefly defined *shaṭḥ* as "a verbal expression having a scent of thoughtlessness (*ru'ūna*) and a claim, which issues from an ecstasy (*tawajjud*) of the realizers of truth, the people of the religious law."[49] His unease with this category stems from its association with a lack of mental control and from the assertiveness of its claims, even though it may emerge as a result of a legitimate spiritual state. In a fuller account of *shaṭḥ* in chapter 195 of *al-Futūḥāt al-Makkiyya*, Ibn `Arabi elaborated further, describing it as a legitimate spiritual claim made without any divine command and by way of boasting (*fakhr*). Chittick conveys Ibn `Arabi's disapproval of *shaṭḥ* by translating the term as "unruly utterance".[50] Ibn `Arabi contrasted this irrepressible form of speaking with the self-control of prophets such as Jesus, who only speak by God's command and never boast. Indulging in *shaṭḥ* is thus a result of heedlessness that never befalls the true knower of God except by accident. Falsely claiming a spiritual state is of course nothing better than a contemptible lie. Ibn `Arabi rightly isolates boasting as a characteristic element in *shaṭḥ*, for its cultural antecedents go back to the boasting contest (*mufākhara*) of pre-Islamic Arabia.[51] Ibn `Arabi's distinctiveness lies in his rejecting the boast as an improper assertion of self, while other Sufis view it as a rhetorical form that is an acceptable genre for the expression of ecstasy.

It is curious that in his discussion of *shaṭḥ*, Ibn `Arabi does not refer to any particular ecstatic utterances of the Sufis, preferring instead to give examples of the sayings of Jesus from the Qur'an by way of contrast. This is odd because on numerous occasions, Ibn `Arabi cites famous examples of *shaṭḥiyyāt* (often without mentioning the names of their authors), in the context of other discussions, sometimes interpreting the same *shaṭḥ* in radically different ways depending on the context. For

---

[49] *al-Futūḥāt al-Makkiyya*, 2:133.23–24.

[50] *al-Futūḥāt al-Makkiyya*, 2:387.8–388.26, trans. Chittick, *Illuminations*, pp. 265–74.

[51] *Words of Ecstasy*, pp. 36–40.

instance, he continues his critical attitude toward spiritual arrogance, pointing out that those who say "I am God" or "Glory be to Me" are like Pharaoh; this condition is only possible when one is overcome by a state such as heedlessness, and it is not possible with a prophet or perfect saint.[52] Although this remark does not mention Abū Yazīd by name, he is clearly intended, although we have no evidence of Abū Yazīd using the phrase "I am God (*anā allāh*)".[53] Elsewhere, in contrast, Ibn `Arabi cites this very saying favorably, to illustrate the state of "the proximity of supererogatory works" (*qurb al-nawāfil*). He says (in allusion to a *ḥadīth qudsī*) that the only ones who can say "I am God" are God and the perfect servant whose tongue, hearing, sight, faculties, and organs are God—an example of this is Abū Yazīd.[54] In another context, Ibn `Arabi again refers to Abū Yazīd as one who loves God so passionately that he does not see God as different from him, and God loves him to the point of being his hearing, sight, and tongue.[55] Ambiguously, he comments on this state by quoting anonymously the first distich of a famous verse of Hallaj: "I am the one whom I desire, whom I desire is I" (*anā man ahwā wa man ahwā anā*).[56] As in the case of Abū Yazīd, Hallaj was someone whose spiritual status Ibn `Arabi respected, though he expressed reservations about Hallaj's unrestrained speech.[57] A comprehensive analysis of Ibn `Arabi's comments on the ecstatic sayings of Ibn `Arabi and al-Hallaj would certainly be desirable, but from these few examples it is clear that Ibn `Arabi sometimes

---

[52] *al-Futūḥāt al-Makkiyya,* 1:276.2, trans. SPK, p. 320.

[53] Abū Yazīd regards *allāh* as the only divine name that cannot be applied to a creature; Badawī, *Shaṭaḥāt*, p. 82 (trans. Meddeb, p. 67, no. 110). Abū Yazīd did actually use the claim of Pharaoh as reported in the Qur'an, "I am your highest lord," (*Words of Ecstasy*, p. 51), but this may be another case in which Ibn `Arabi treats the quotation in a flexible fashion.

[54] *al-Futūḥāt al-Makkiyya,* 4:11.16, in SPK, p. 410, n. 12. For the *ḥadīth al-nawāfil*, see Annemarie Schimmel, *Mystical Dimensions of Islam* (Chapel Hill: University of North Carolina Press, 1975), pp. 43, 133, 144, 277.

[55] *al-Futūḥāt al-Makkiyya,* 2:361.9–11; cf. the translation of Maurice Gloton, *Traité de l'amour*, Spiritualités vivantes, 60 (Paris: Albin Michel), pp. 257–58.

[56] Louis Massignon, ed., *Le Dîwân d'ál-Hallâj* (new ed., Paris: Librairie Orientaliste Paul Geuthner, 1955), no. 57, p. 93.

[57] On Ibn `Arabi's ambivalent attitude toward Hallaj, see Louis Massignon, *La Passion de Husayn Ibn Mansûr Hallâj* (new ed., Paris: Gallimard, 1975), II, 414–19.

dismisses ecstatic sayings as improper behavior, but that at other times he gives them a positive value in terms of recognized mystical knowledge. In fact, Ibn `Arabi makes it clear that the words of the saints do not have any independent meaning aside from the spiritual state (*ḥāl*) of the saint, as he understands it. Regarding the interpretation of two sayings on the subject of "gathering" (*jam'*) by an anonymous Sufi and by al-Daqqāq, Ibn `Arabi remarks,

> He may mean this, which is the position that we maintain and that the realities bestow. If we knew who is the author of this saying, we would judge it by his state, as we judged al-Daqqāq through our knowledge of his station and state.[58] The same words could have another meaning if uttered by someone else in a different state.

To return to the "man without qualities" saying, it appears that Ibn `Arabi regarded it as distinct from *shaṭḥ* or ecstatic utterance, on the grounds that the spiritual state required (*iqtiḍā*) its expression by Abū Yazīd. In other words, Abū Yazīd did not say it of his own volition, as a boast, but he was in effect ordered to do so by God. In this way it remains a valid source of spiritual knowledge rather than the willful result of thoughtlessness or frivolity. Rūzbihān Baqlī, on the other hand, classified this saying as *shaṭḥ* without qualification; in his view that classification, far from discrediting the saying, raised it to a level of lofty spiritual experience. The difference lies in the varying attitudes of the two authors toward ecstatic expressions. Yet there is a rhetorical tone in some of Ibn `Arabi's sayings about his own experiences that suggests *shaṭḥ*, especially when he contrasts the experiences of others unfavorably with his own. In terms of his own theory as just discussed, however, Ibn `Arabi's descriptions of his spiritual attainments do not constitute boasting, because he has not expressed them of his own will. On numerous occasions, Ibn `Arabi maintains that his books and teachings have been the direct products of the divine will: "I swear by God, I say nothing, I announce no judgment that does not proceed

---

[58] *al-Futūḥāt al-Makkiyya,* 2:517.15, trans. Chittick, *Illuminations*, p. 284.

from an inbreathing of the divine spirit in my heart."[59] Although technically this escapes from the reproach of boasting, since it is under divine command, it nonetheless has the appearance of a rhetoric of transcendental hyperbole that shares important characteristics with *shaṭḥ*. When he says that none of his teachings derive from his own will, Ibn `Arabi is making the boast that he makes no boast.

To continue this line of thinking, one might view, for instance, the claims of later Naqshbandī Sufis such as Aḥmad Sirhindī as a continual raising of the stakes vis-à-vis earlier Sufis (such as Ibn `Arabi!) in a sort of spiritual one-upmanship, and it is worth noting that some of Sirhindī's statements were also characterized as ecstatic utterances.[60] If Ibn `Arabi's statements are not simply taken at face value as irrefutable guides to his spiritual status, then his critical attitude toward *shaṭḥ* should be taken with a grain of salt. Ibn `Arabi's dramatic statements about his own status as the "seal of the saints", for example, place him in a position beyond that of any other saint and only just below the prophets. To regard this as devoid of boasting while rejecting the ecstatic sayings of Abū Yazīd or Hallaj amounts to special privilege. Unless an argument is to be made for extending this special privilege to Ibn `Arabi, then his interpretations of earlier Sufis should be treated as exactly that. I suggest that analysis of this kind of rhetoric of transcendental hyperbole, as an extension of

[59] *al-Futūḥāt al-Makkiyya,* 3:101.6–7; trans. Chodkiewicz, *Illuminations*, p. 24. Cf. *al-Futūḥāt al-Makkiyya,* 2:456, trans. Chodkiewicz, ibid.: "I have not written a single letter of this book except under the effect of a divine dictation, of a lordly projection, of a spiritual inbreathing at the heart of my being." The introduction to *Fuṣūṣ al-ḥikam* describes the Prophet Muḥammad handing the book to Ibn `Arabi and ordering him to disseminate its teachings, and commentators sometimes fall back on that to defend controversial positions.

[60] Yohanan Friedmann, *Shaykh Aḥmad Sirhindī: An Outline of His Thought and a Study of His Image in the Eyes of Posterity* (Montreal: McGill-Queen's University Press, 1971), pp. 94–96. Sirhindī explicitly claimed a spiritual status that exceeded both Abū Yazīd and Ibn `Arabi, observing that their claims were based on improperly interpreted experiences that his own teachings clarified; his critics in turn charged him with arrogance. See Ghulām 'Alī Āzād Bilgrāmī, *Ṣubḥat al-marjān fī āthār Hindūstān*, ed. Muḥammad Faḍl al-Raḥmān al-Nadwī al-Siwānī (Aligarh: Jāmi'at Alīgarh al-Islāmiyya, 1972), I, 131–37, and Friedmann, pp. 28, 60, 88, 62–68.

the boasting factor of *shaṭḥ*, would be a fruitful way to approach the self-descriptions of a number of later Sufis.

How should we understand the distinctive interpretation that Ibn `Arabi gives to the sayings of Abū Yazīd? On the issue of selection, judgment must be deferred until a comprehensive study can be made of all the references that Ibn `Arabi makes to his predecessor. In terms of textual transmission and variants we can say more, based on the examples reviewed above. It would be trivial and idiotic to complain that Ibn `Arabi has forgotten or willfully altered an existing text, just because the versions that he gives sometimes differ from those found in Sahlagī and others. The textual variants have greater significance than that. As Chittick remarks, "In his usual manner, Ibn `Arabi has in mind the sayings of earlier masters as the background for what he wants to explain, but then he takes the concept . . . back to its deepest meaning in the divine realities."[61] Some of the textual variants described above certainly permit Ibn `Arabi to expound upon his characteristic teachings on the divine attributes and the relation between God and humanity. It is in this doctrinal level of interpretation that we find the distinctive position of Ibn `Arabi, in contrast with the positions of other interpreters such as Rūzbihān Baqlī. Ibn `Arabi is also selective in how he categorizes the genre of the sayings of his predecessors. Sayings classified as ecstatic utterances, even though proceeding from a genuine spiritual state, cannot be accepted as sources of doctrine. Sayings that emerge by divine necessity, untainted by the boasting of *shaṭḥ*, may be treated as authoritative. Ibn `Arabi does not make clear what criteria he uses to describe a statement as ecstatic boasting rather than authoritative inspiration; he at different times considers the same statement as falling under both categories. If Ibn `Arabi's treatment of *shaṭḥ* partakes, however lightly, of the rhetoric of boasting, then his interpretation of the sayings and states of earlier Sufis also subordinates them to his own immediate doctrinal and experiential concerns.

Beyond the question of doctrinalization, we must also attempt to understand his use of quotations in terms of the function of

[61] Chittick, in *Illuminations*, p. 256.

texts, both written and oral, in Sufism; Ibn `Arabi is certainly not unique in this respect, but he has worked out his method in marvelously complete detail. If it is true that words, like people, find their meaning in contexts, it is really only through the re-voicing of a word, through its quotation from the mouth of another human being, that words receive life so a quotation approached in this way is not a fixed external text that is "dead from the dead", but is instead inspired (in the words of Abū Yazīd) "by the Living who does not die." Abū Yazīd's status as an Uwaysī guide, appearing directly like Khiḍr to inspire later generations of Sufis, may also have contributed to the flexibility with which Ibn `Arabi invokes him via quotation.[62]

We should recall that Ibn `Arabi's model for a text is the Qur'an, a text that is fully personalized, for it is inseparable from the Messenger who brings it. It is also deeply enmeshed in the being of the perfect saint who actualizes the scripture; as Ibn `Arabi puts it, "the universal man is the Qur'an."[63] Ibn `Arabi himself is a person who is fully textualized; he maintains that "everything about which we speak, both in (my) teaching sessions and in my writings, comes only from the presence of the Qur'ân and Its treasures."[64] For him, the Qur'an, ḥadīth, and the sayings and visions of the saints who are the inheritors of the prophets are not separate elements to be stitched together by laborious allegoresis. They are rather a seamless whole apprehended in a single intuition. The Qur'an (and by extension the sayings of the saints) is for Ibn `Arabi no dead letter, but perpetually renewed for every reciter.[65]

Quotation and interpretation, when viewed in this light, are not merely literary enterprises. The metaphor of giving life recalls another story that Ibn `Arabi relates about Abū Yazīd. It seems that Abū Yazīd blew on an ant he had killed, and it revived; Ibn `Arabi comments that God blew when he blew, and

---

[62] I owe this insight to John Mercer.

[63] Ibn `Arabi, *Kitāb al-isfār* (Hyderabad, 1948), p. 17, trans. Chodkiewicz, *Illuminations*, pp. 42–43. From another point of view, the universe as a whole is a great Qur'an; ibid., pp. 38, 428.

[64] *al-Futūḥāt al-Makkiyya*, 3:.334.30, trans. Morris, *Illuminations*, p. 135; cf. p. 521, n. 64.

[65] Cf. *al-Futūḥāt al-Makkiyya*, 3:93, trans. Chodkiewicz, *Illuminations*, pp. 56–57.

it was like Jesus' miracles as recorded in the Qur'an.[66] Despite its bizarre appearance, this story commends itself as a metaphor for quotation. As with the ant killed by Abū Yazīd, the words of the saints have undergone some violence in the course of textual transmission, but their death is necessary before they can be inspired and revived. Quotation, textual variation, and classification cannot be separated from interpretation. Ibn `Arabi explained his teachings by reciting and interpreting the words of Sufi saints, so that he could become the revivifier of the faith.

[66] *Fuṣūṣ al-ḥikam* ch. XV (trans. Austin, p. 179).

11

Rūzbihān Baqlī on Love as "Essential Desire"

From the beginning of her career as an Islamicist, Annemarie Schimmel devoted her energies particularly to the elucidation of the nuances of mystical love in the Sufi tradition. As early as her Inaugural-Dissertation, she pointed out the importance of the fact that the Sufis "see love as the central quality, even directly as the Essence, of God."[1] This position, which is associated above all with the Sufi martyr Ḥusayn ibn Manṣūr al-Hallaj (d. 922), is one of the boldest formulations of Islamic mysticism.[2] To equate God's essence with love means, paradoxically, that the absolute divinity is essentially related to the limited creature in some unfathomable way; love implies both a lover and a beloved. The idea of God as love constitutes a problem for conservative Islamic thinkers, since it conflicts with their abstract theological categories and does not have an obvious scriptural basis in the Qur'an. Islamic philosophers and Sufis, however, welcomed this concept, since it accorded with their own theories and experiences.[3] Hallaj's originality in this respect, and his proximity to philosophical positions,

---

[1] Annemarie Schimmel, "Studien zum Begriff der mystischen Liebe in der frühislamischen Mystik," Dr. sc. rel. dissertation, University of Marburg, 1954, p. xv.

[2] Annemarie Schimmel, *Mystical Dimensions of Islam* (Chapel Hill: University of North Carolina Press, 1975), p. 72 (Hallaj), 284 (Rūmī).

[3] See now Joseph Norment Bell, "Avicenna's *Treatise on Love* and the Nonphilosophical Muslim Tradition," *Der Islam* (1986), pp. 73–89.

were first set forth in a memorable essay by Louis Massignon.[4] Here I would like to reexamine the concept of God's essence as love according to one of Hallaj's followers, the great Persian Sufi of Shiraz, Rūzbihān Baqlī (d. 1209). Massignon, in his care to emphasize the uniqueness of Hallaj's spirituality, failed adequately to appreciate the centrality of the notion of God's essence as love in the thought of Rūzbihān. This is not surprising, since medieval Sufis in Persianate Central Asia and India also failed to comprehend Rūzbihān's position on occasion. But the availability of Rūzbihān's remarkable treatise on love, the *'Abhar al-`āshiqīn*, enables us to see more clearly how love as the divine essence functioned as a dominating motif for Rūzbihān.

Massignon regarded Hallaj's doctrine of divine love as an important step that brought Sufism in contact with Hellenistic philosophy. The tenth-century philosopher and Sufi al-Daylamī had pointed out that Hallaj was virtually alone among early Sufis in saying that love was the divine essence. Nonetheless, as al-Daylamī mentioned, there were definite precedents for this view, for instance, the pre-Socratic Greek philosopher, Heraclitus of Ephesus. Islamic philosophers like Ibn Sīnā (d. 1037) clearly followed suit in calling love part of the divine essence. Hallaj's step had been fundamental, however, as "a radical decentering of human desire, for a metaphysical reorientation."[5] The key term here was *`ishq* or passionate love, of non-Qur'anic origin and similar in connotation to the Greek *eros*. Scriptural purists were unhappy with this disturbing term and preferred the word *maḥabba* or compassionate love. This word had the advantage of Qur'anic origin and relatively milder associations than with *'ishq*. Hallaj had expounded on *`ishq* in a long fragment preserved by al-Daylamī.[6] Massignon was disturbed to find that in the version of this text preserved by Rūzbihān, in nine out of ten places the word *`ishq* had been replaced by the less controversial

[4] Louis Massignon, "Interférences philosophiques et percées métaphysiques dans la mystique hallagienne: Notion de 'essential désir,'" *Mélanges Joseph Maréchal*, vol. 2, *Hommages* (Brussels: L'Édition Universelle, S.A., 1950), pp. 263–96.

[5] Massignon, "Essential Désir," p. 289.

[6] Abū l Ḥasan 'Alī b. Muḥammad al Daylamī, *Kitāb 'aṭf al alif al mā'lūf 'alā l-lām al ma'ṭūf*, ed. J. C. Vadet, Textes et Traductions d'Auteurs Orientaux, vol. 20 (Cairo: Institut Français d'Archéologie Orientale, 1962), p. 25.

maḥabba.[7] Writing in 1950, Massignon exhibited a real irritation with Rūzbihān for changing the text in a way that had previously blocked him (in the 1922 *Passion de Hallaj*) from appreciating the uniqueness of the position of Hallaj.[8] *Maḥabba* is static, he argued, while *`ishq* is dynamic; *`ishq* removes anthropomorphism and leads to the divine presence.[9] In retrospect, it seems that Louis Massignon's views were in this case molded by his own theology. Hallaj was identified both with personal mysticism and with philosophy, and anything that detracts from his uniqueness was to be challenged.

Rūzbihān was well known as a lover of beauty, and he set his own seal in this style on the sayings of earlier mystics. Jāmī (d. 1492) attributes to him the saying, "Whoever becomes the intimate of God (*ista'nasa billāh*) becomes intimate with every beautiful thing (*shay' malīḥ*), every fair face (*wajh ṣabīḥ*), every pretty voice (*ṣawt ṭayyib*), and every sweet fragrance (*rā'iḥa ṭayyiba*)."[10] This saying is not actually Rūzbihān's, but is attributed by him to the early Egyptian Sufi Dhū al-Nūn (d. 859). Although this saying of Dhū al-Nūn has also been quoted as early as the tenth century by Abū al-Ḥasan al-Daylamī, Rūzbihān had evidently become the chief transmitter of it in the eastern Islamic world.[11] This might explain the confusion over the attribution of this saying to Rūzbihān by Persian and Indian Sufis.

---

[7] Rūzbihān Baqlī, *Manṭiq al-asrār*, MS Louis Massignon, fols. 56b-57b. I am extremely grateful to Daniel Massignon for making a photocopy of this important manuscript available to me.

[8] Massignon, "Essential désir," p. 270.

[9] Massignon, "Essential désir," pp. 295–96.

[10] In the text as quoted by Simnānī (below, n. 15), fol. 145b, marginal glosses in Persian translate the phrase *ista'nasa billāh* ("becomes the intimate of") by *dūst mī-dārad*, "likes" or "loves".

[11] Daylamī, *'Aṭf*, p. 69, no. 244, gives a short version: "Dhū al-Nūn was questioned about the gnostics' becoming intimate (*isti'nās*) [with God], and he said, 'He [the gnostic] likes (*ya'nas*) every fair face, every pretty voice, every beautiful form (*ṣūra malīḥa*), and every sweet fragrance.'" Rūzbihān quotes the saying in Arabic in his *Manṭiq al-asrār*, fol. 13b, and in his *'Abhar al-'āshiqīn*, ed. Henry Corbin and Muḥammad Mu'īn, Bibliothéque Iranienne, 8 (Tehran: Institut Français d'Iranologie de Téhéran, 1958; reprint ed., Tehran: Intishārāt-i Manūchihrī, 1365/1981), p. 9 (two slightly differing versions); Rūzbihān gives a Persian translation of the saying in *Sharḥ-i shaṭḥiyyāt*, ed. Henry Corbin, Bibliothéque Iranienne, 12 (Tehran: Departement d'iranologie de l'Institut Franco-iranien, 1966), p. 150, no. 86.

This saying of Dhū al-Nūn was controversial, and to some it evidently suggested anthropomorphic heresy. Rūzbihān regarded it as one of Dhū al-Nūn's *shaṭḥiyyāt* or ecstatic sayings. At this point in the manuscript of Rūzbihān's *Manṭiq al-asrār*, a marginal note by an unknown writer says, "Everything that this imbecile writer says regarding the divine unity could be found in the sayings of Pharoah, may God's curse be on both of them!"[12] In their enthusiasm for music and ecstasy, Indian Chishtīs of the fourteenth century understood Rūzbihān to refer, not to divine love in general, but to the recitation of poetry in *i`sama`*; what beautiful singers need to sooth the hearts of the gnostics in all auditions is "sweet fragrances, a fair face, and beautiful voices (*rawā'iḥ-i ṭayyiba wa ruy-i ṣabīḥa wa aṣwāt-i malīḥa*)."[13] It seems that, following al-Daylamī and Rūzbihān, the Persian and Indian Sufis located this saying in the lore of love and intoxication. Rūzbihān's emphasis on Dhū al-Nūn's saying in the context of love and ecstasy meshed with his own vocation as a lover. Other versions of Dhū al-Nūn's saying found in Arabic sources (Abū Nu`aym al-Iṣfahānī, Ibn al-`Arabī, al-Suyūṭī) do not connect it to love at all. They see it in terms of the dialectic between awe (*hayba*) and intimacy (*uns*), and they transmit it as follows: "Whoever becomes the intimate of God then becomes intimate with all that he sees, hears, or feels in the realm (*mulk*) of his Lord; he becomes intimate with the smallest atom, all the while experiencing awe (*hayba*)."[14]

A little-known text from India furnishes a testimony of mixed value about Rūzbihān's theory of love. Ashraf Jahāngīr Simnānī (d. 1425), originally from Central Asia, settled in northern India

---

[12] Rūzbihān, *Manṭiq al-asrār*, fol. 13b.

[13] Rukn al-Dīn ibn 'Imād al-Dīn Dabīr Kāshānī Khuldābādī, *Shamā'il al-atqiyā'*, ed. Sayyid 'Aṭā' Ḥusayn, Silsila-i Ishā'at al-'Ulūm, no. 85 (Hyderabad: Maṭbū'a Ashraf Press, 1347/1928–9), p. 359, quoting Shaykh Rūzbihān's *Kashf al-asrār*. Given the Chishtīs' application of this saying to *samā'*, it is noteworthy that Daylamī's version of the saying (the oldest one known to us) makes no mention of the voice.

[14] Ibn `Arabi, *La vie merveilleuse de Dhû-l-Nûn l'Égyptien*, trans. Roger Deladrière (Paris: Sindbad, 1988), p. 145, loosely rendering Deladrière's French; the Arabic original is not given. Deladrière comments that Ibn al-`Arabi locates this experience in the sensory world (*mulk*), while the version given by Abū Nu'aym and Suyūṭī refers it to the angelic realm (*malakūt*).

and joined the Chishtī order. He devoted one of his letters (no. 49 in the Aligarh collection) to elucidating Rūzbihān's views on love, ostensibly to clarify how his position differed from that of others. Simnānī's exposition is, however, troubling. Most of it consists of a lengthy quotation from Rūzbihān's preface to the *`Abhar al-`āshiqīn*, although with some gaps large enough to interfere with the argument.[15] More problematic is the way in which Simnānī appears to misrepresent Rūzbihān's position, precisely on the question of love as the essence of God. In his preface, Rūzbihān had introduced the questions of whether passionate love or desire (*`ishq*) was an appropriate term to use with respect to God, whether one can claim this love, and whether this name is shared by God and humanity. Rūzbihān acknowledged that there were differences on these points, but (in a passage skipped by Simnānī) he maintains that those who appeared to deny divine love were really merely concealing it from the gaze of the vulgar. Rūzbihān then listed an impressive number of early Sufis who upheld the legitimacy of speaking of God in terms of *`ishq*: 'Abd al-Wāḥid ibn Zayd, Abū Yazīd, Junayd, Nūrī, Dhū al-Nūn, Yūsuf ibn Ḥusayn Rāzī, Abū Bakr Wāsiṭī, Ḥuṣrī, Hallaj, and Shiblī (this would argue against the uniqueness of Hallaj's position as represented by al-Daylamī). Simnānī reproduced this list, but surprisingly, he went on to interpolate a second list of Sufis who restrict love to a human beloved: Abū al-Qāsim Gurgānī, Rūzbihān Baqlī, Muḥammad Ḥusayn Abū Ṭālib Dimashqī, and Abū al-Qāsim Tirmidhī.[16] Whatever may be said about the three obscure figures on this list (none of whom is even mentioned by Rūzbihān), Simnānī's report about Rūzbihān's position is simply false (see below). Why indulge in this distortion? One might speculate that the controversial character of this point led Simnānī (or perhaps a copyist of Rūzbihān's work) to invent a spurious retraction for Rūzbihān, so that the exposition of love as the divine essence is simply being described, not actually advocated. In this way Simnānī could discuss it without getting

[15] Ashraf Jahāngīr Simnānī, *Maktūbāt-i ashrafiyya*, MS History Department, Aligarh Muslim University, letter no. 49, fols. 145a–47a, quoting Rūzbihān Baqlī Shīrāzī, *'Abhar al-'āshiqīn*, p. 9, lines 2–14; p. 10, lines 2–15; p. 11, lines 4–17.

[16] Ibid., fol. 146a. In the first list, the MS omits Ḥusrī and calls the first figure 'Abd Allāh instead of 'Abd al-Wāḥid.

himself or his source, Rūzbihān, involved in charges of innovation or anthropomorphism.

Part of the problem can be explained from the flexibility with which Rūzbihān uses the terms *maḥabba* and *`ishq*. He is not confined to textbook definitions.[17] Sometimes in the *`Abhar al-`āshiqīn* he identifies them totally, speaking of "the *maḥabba* that is an essential attribute [of God], by which the lover (*`āshiq*) and beloved (*ma`shūq*) are described."[18] He refers to *maḥabba* as the inner reality (*ḥaqīqa*) of *`ishq*, but on the same page calls it *`ishq* when one has been submerged in the divine reality; these references occur in the chapter on "*maḥabba* as the introduction to *`ishq*."[19] Presumably this lack of rigor should be called unphilosophical, and Rūzbihān was certainly not a philosopher. Curiously, though, in his technical treatise on one thousand names of spiritual states, he goes so far as to quote the very same definition of love by Heraclitus that had been cited by al-Daylamī. Rūzbihān's praise of the pagan philosopher is unbounded: "Heraclitus the wise, from the divine ancients."[20] In any case, the concluding chapter of Rūzbihān's *`Abhar al-`āshiqīn*, "On the Perfection of Love", is worth quoting:

> Know, my brother–may God nourish you and ennoble you with the *`ishq* of the perfect ones–that the Lord–who is transcendent and sublime–in pre- and post-eternity is qualified with His primordial essence, with His primordial attributes. *`Ishq* is one of the attributes of the Real; He Himself is His own lover (*`āshiq*). Therefore love, lover, and beloved are one. From that love there is a single color, for the Attribute is He, and He is above the changing of temporality. *`Ishq* is the perfection of *maḥabba* and *maḥabba* is the attribute of the Real. Do not be tricked by words, for *`ishq* and *maḥabba* are one.[21]

Ultimately, for Rūzbihān, both *`ishq* and *maḥabba* described the essence of divine love. It may be that there are different

[17] For some classical attempts to relate *maḥabba* to *'ishq*, see Schimmel, "Begriff," pp. 40–42.

[18] Rūzbihān, *'Abhar al-āshiqīn*, p. 22.

[19] Ibid., p. 15.

[20] Abū Muḥammad Rūzbihān al-Baqlī al-Shīrāzī, *Kitāb mashrab al-arwāḥ*, ed. Nażīf Muḥarram Khwāja (Istanbul: Maṭba'at Kulliyat al-Ādāb, 1973), p. 135.

[21] Rūzbihān, *Mashrab*, p. 138.

tonalities of the two words that are more appropriate for different audiences. When Rūzbihān translated his own *Manṭiq al-asrār* from Arabic into Persian as the *Sharḥ-i shaṭḥiyyāt* for the use of his disciples, as Massignon points out, certain sensitive passages were not translated.[22] To me it seems more likely that they were omitted with regard to the nature of the intended audience rather than as an index of changing views or fears of repression on Rūzbihān's part.

One other use of the word *`ishq* does suggest a controversial aura when it was first introduced; this was the saying of Nūrī, "I love (*a`shaqu*) God and He loves (*ya`shaqu*) me."[23] This is alleged to be the reason why Nūrī was charged in the caliphal court with heresy, since *maḥabba* is Qur'anic but *`ishq* is an innovation suggestive of eroticism and anthropomorphism.[24] The versions of Nūrī's saying quoted by Sarrāj and Rūzbihān do show a certain defensiveness, as for instance when Nūrī (perhaps disingenuously) amplifies his saying by emphasizing that *`ishq* is restrained, while *maḥabba* implies enjoyment of the beloved.[25] In commenting on this saying, Rūzbihān shows no signs of shyness about the term *`ishq*, however; it becomes here the divine quality that underlies the creation of the world and humanity. Nor does he distinguish it from *maḥabba*; the two words are nearly synonymous.

> *`Ishq* and *maḥabba* are two streams from the ocean of eternity, which run into the confluence of the soul. They are the special attributes of the Real, and He is described by them. When He gazes at *`ishq*, He creates the world with His will; this is universal *`ishq*. When He produces the lover with this *`ishq*, He gazes upon him with the primordial Essence (*dhāt*); that is the elite *`ishq*. He knows this from Himself with primordial knowledge. That is affection (*dūstī*) for God among the prophets and saints. Know that "He loves (*yuḥibbu*) them and they love (*yuḥibbūna*) Him" [Qur. 5:59] is purely primordial attributes. It is beyond the

[22] Louis Massignon, *La Passion de Husayn Ibn Mansûr Hallâj* (new ed., 4 vols., Paris: Gallimard, 1975), II, 407; II, 498.

[23] *Manṭiq*, fol. 14a; *Sharḥ*, p. 165, no. 95, in the form "I am the lover of God (*man ba-khudāy 'āshiq-am*)."

[24] See my *Words of Ecstasy in Sufism* (Albany: State University of New York Press, 1985), part III.

[25] Cf. Schimmel, *Dimensions*, p. 137.

> slightness of nature and the variation of the temporal. He became the lover of His own beauty in eternity. Necessarily, love (*`ishq*), lover, and beloved became one. Because this was a [divine] Attribute, no temporal cause affected it. Since He became His own lover, He wanted to create humanity, so that there should be a place of love and His glance would be undisturbed, and His own intimacy and eternality created the spirits of the lovers. He made their eyes see by His beauty. He taught them that "I was your lover before you were." "I was a hidden treasure and I wanted to be known."[26]

Thus *`ishq* still retains some of the cosmic and philosophical associations it had with Hallaj. If *`ishq* had controversial implications in the tenth century, this appears to have no longer been the case for Rūzbihān in the twelfth century.

The use of a term like "essence" (*dhāt*) in Arabic is indeed an "interference" of Greek philosophy in Islam. Yet despite his acknowledgement of Heraclitus, Rūzbihān finds his authority for understanding God as love in traditional rather than in rational materials. *Ḥadīth* sayings of the Prophet Muḥammad and a whole array of early Sufis stand in evidence for the primacy of *`ishq*. It may be that Rūzbihān reinterpreted certain of his predecessors, like Dhū al-Nūn, in order to fit better with his own position. But Rūzbihān, in contrast to Louis Massignon, did not see Hallaj as a single lonely figure rising beyond philosophy and mysticism to forge a synthesis of the two. Nor did Rūzbihān find that the terms of mysticism are "fixed stars in the linguistic heaven of humanity."[27] Our fuller access to the writings of Rūzbihān allows us to correct some aspects of this early, brilliant analysis by Massignon. There remains, however, the paradox of a perfect God whose essence it is to love an imperfect world. This goes beyond philosophy.

---

26 i, pp. 165–66.

27 Massignon, "Essential désir,", p. 294.

12

An Indo-Persian Guide to Sufi Shrine Pilgrimage

Pilgrimage is a ritual that orients the cosmos around a holy place and provides ways for participants to integrate themselves around symbols of transcendence. In the Islamic tradition the *hajj* pilgrimage to Mecca is of paramount importance, but local and sectarian forms of pilgrimage are also practiced. Pilgrimage to the tombs of the Shi`i martyrs is an important feature of Shi`i piety, and across the Islamic world, from Morocco to Chinese Turkestan, the tombs of the saints are the resort of Muslims of many varying backgrounds. Reformers from Ibn Taymiyya down to the Wahhabis of Sa`udi Arabia have tended to denounce the veneration of both imams and saints as the idolatrous worship of fallible human beings.[1] In the Indian subcontinent, where pilgrimage (Arabic *ziyara*, Persian *ziyarat*) to Sufi shrines is particularly common, Protestant British civil

---

[1] A. J. Wensinck, "Ziyara," *Shorter Encyclopedia of Islam*, ed. H. A. R. Gibb and J. M. Kramers (Leiden, 1953; reprint ed., Leiden: E. J. Brill, 1974), p. 660. A modern example of juristic opposition to *ziyarat* is the collection of legal responsa by Rashid Ahmad Gangohi (d. 1323/1905), *Fatawa-i Rashidiyya* (Karachi: H. M. Sa`id Company, 1985), p. 59 (impropriety of petitioning the dead), p. 69 (condemnation of kissing tombs), p. 134 (condemnation of attending annual death anniversary festivals). The learned author, a scholar of the Deoband school and a member of the Sabiri Chishti order, does not deny that spiritual grace (*fayd*) emanates from tombs, but maintains that the common people must not be permitted to have access to it because of the danger of idolatry (p. 104). His main objection to these practices is their similarity to non-Muslim religious practices.

servants and modern Muslim reformers alike have often seen in this ritual the insidious influence of Indian paganism. From the frequent denunciations of ziyarat as "*pir*-worship" (worship of the master), one might suppose that it was a transparent case of the corruption of Islam by Hindu polytheism, but a closer look reveals that the case is not so simple. Hindu practices undoubtedly occur at some Muslim shrines, such as the shrine of the warrior-saint Salar Mas`ud at Bahraich.[2] The presence of Hindu practices cannot, however, explain the participation of educated Sufi masters in pilgrimage, for they found ziyarat to be an authentic expression of Islamic piety, Qur'anic in spirit and firmly based on the model of the Prophet Muhammad.[3] The purpose of this essay is to illustrate the Sufi interpretation of ziyarat, by presenting in translation a small treatise by a learned Indian Sufi of the eighteenth century that explains and justifies the practice of pilgrimage to saints' tombs according to the traditions of the Chishti Sufi order.

The treatise translated here is a guide to observance of Sufi saints' *`urs* (pl. *a`ras*) festivals, written as a preface to the *Makhzan-i a`ras* ("Treasury of Death Anniversaries") in 1742–43 by Muhammad Najib Qadiri Nagawri Ajmeri, a Sufi of the Chishti order who lived in the Deccan city of Awrangabad. The main body of the book is a calendar of saints, which, like the Roman Catholic calendars, lists for each day of the year the Sufi saints whose festivals are to be celebrated then according to the Islamic lunar calendar. Like the Catholic calendars, this Muslim

[2] Kerrin Gräfin Schwerin, "Saint Worship in Indian Islam: The Legend of the Martyr Salar Masud Ghazi," in *Ritual and Religion among Muslims in India*, ed. Imtiaz Ahmed (Delhi: Manohar, 1981), pp. 143–61. The festival of Salar Mas`ud is celebrated according to the Hindu solar-lunar calendar, unlike the Sufi death anniversaries discussed below, which follow the Islamic lunar calendar. The participation of both Muslims and non-Muslims in such festivals suggests that widely differing interpretations of this ceremony coexist at the same time. I have observed Hindu villagers performing rituals at the tomb of one of the Turkish Ghurid sultans (locally known as "Sultan Ghari") outside Delhi, with no inkling of the historical identity of the "saint" buried there. This problem of cross-cultural understanding calls for further investigation.

[3] For a modern example of the literary expression of Sufi attitudes toward pilgrimage, see the Persian poem in the classical style by the late Dr. Ishrat Hasan "Anwar", former head of the Department of Philosophy at Aligarh Muslim University, addressed to Khwaja Mu`in al-Din Chishti, in *Masnavi-i sarud-i bi-khudi* (Agra: Akbar Press, 1954), pp. 105–106.

calendar lists saints' festivals by the death anniversary or *`urs*, literally "wedding", which records the date when the saint's soul was "wedded", that is, united with God.[4] The celebration of saints' death anniversaries seems to be peculiar to the Islamic East, since in Mediterranean countries celebrations commonly occur on the birthday (*mawlid*) of the saint.[5] It is not clear when the term `urs first came into use, though it was common among the Chishtis in the early fourteenth century.[6] The later Sufi and scholar Hajji Imdad Allah (d. 1899) traced the term to a saying of the Prophet Muhammad, directed at the saints as they prepare for death: "Sleep with the sleep of a bridegroom (*`arus*)"; this saying suggests that the physical death of the saint is in fact the moment of joyous reunion with the beloved.[7] To make a pilgrimage or ziyarat to the tomb of a saint is considered beneficial at any time, but at the time of the `urs special blessings are available, since Paradise rejoices at the return of that supremely happy moment when a human soul is united with God. A comprehensive pilgrim's guide to these holy days, the lithographed edition of the *Makhzan-i a`ras* gives the death anniversaries of hundreds of saints in well over 200 pages. In the twelve-page introduction, the author describes the reasons for making pilgrimages to the tombs of Sufi saints, and how to perform the requisite ceremonies. It is this introduction that is translated here.

The *Makhzan-i a`ras* was not a novelty, but was based on an earlier calendar of saints and a number of other literary

---

[4] Conversely, the Catholic commemorations of martyrs' and saints' death anniversaries were called birthdays (*natalitia*) as a sign of rebirth into eternal life (*The Oxford Dictionary of the Christian Church*, ed. F. L. Cross [2nd ed., Oxford: Oxford University Press, 1983], pp. 954–55).

[5] Ignaz Goldziher, "Veneration of Saints in Islam," in *Muslim Studies (Muhammedanische Studien)*, ed. S. M. Stern, trans. C. R. Barber and S. M. Stern (2 vols.; London: George Allen & Unwin Ltd, 1971) II, 284–85.

[6] Nizam al-Din Awliya' Bada'oni (d. 725/1325), *Fawa'id al-fu'ad*, comp. Hasan `Ala Sijzi, ed. Muhammad Latif Malik (Lahore: Malik Siraj al-Din and Sons, 1386/1966), p. 209, gives the etymology of *`urs* as "getting married", but also mentions another meaning, "the alighting of a caravan at night". Jurists such as the Baghdadian Ibn al-Jawzi (d. 1201) criticized Sufi `urs festivities, and the Mevlevi Sufis in Anatolia used the term `urs in the thirteenth century; see Fritz Meier, *Abu Sa`id-i Abu l-Hayr (357–440/967–1049), Wirklichkeit und Legende*, Acta Iranica 11 (Leiden: E. J. Brill, 1976), pp. 250, 261.

[7] Wahid Bakhsh Sial, *Maqam-i Ganj-i Shakkar* (Lahore: Sufi Foundation, 1403/1983), p. 38.

sources. Muhammad Najib explained that the calendar was an expanded critical edition of the *A`ras namah* or "Book of Death Anniversaries" completed several decades earlier by one of Muhammad Najib's fellow disciples in Sufism, Sheikh Sharaf al-Din ibn Qadi Sheikh Muhammad Nahrawali. The introduction to the calendar is, however, quite unusual as an extended monograph on pilgrimage as a Sufi practice. While the introduction to the *Makhzan-i a`ras* cites by name or quotes from more than two dozen Persian and Arabic Sufi texts, it quotes most extensively from two texts, each of which makes up about one-fifth of the introduction. One of these sources is the *Lata'if-i ashrafi*, the discourses of Sayyid Ashraf Jahangir Simnani (d. 1425); though initially a disciple of the Central Asian Sufi master `Ala' al-Dawla Simnani (d. 1336), he made his way to India and joined the Chishti order, settling in eastern Bihar. His voluminous discourses reflect the Central Asian teachings of the Kubrawi order as well as the traditions of the Chishtis.[8] The other source is a manual on religious practices called *Adab al-talibin* ("Rules for Aspirants"), by Muhammad Chishti Ahmadabadi (d. 1630). This treatise, which lays heavy stress on Islamic law and ritual, codifies in a few pages current Chishti practices associated with pilgrimages to Sufi tombs.[9] An additional passage from *Adab*

---

[8] Ashraf Jahangir Simnani, *Lata'if-i ashrafi*, comp. Nizam Gharib Yamani (2 vols.; Delhi: Nusrat al-Matabi`, 1295/1878) II, 28–30, quoted in sections 13–17 of the text, below. On Simnani's life and works, see Bruce B. Lawrence, *Notes from a Distant Flute: The Extant Literature of Pre-Mughal Indian Sufism* (Tehran: Imperial Iranian Academy of Philosophy, 1978), pp. 53–55.

[9] Muhammad Chishti, *Adab al-talibin* (MS copied in Tawnsah, probably after 1790, personal collection of Carl Ernst), fols. 21b–22b (rules), 22b–24a (here later scribes have inserted a brief calendar of saints, including the `urs of Kalim Allah Shahjahanabadi [d. 1729]), 24a–b (concluding rules), quoted in sections 2–5 of the text; cf. Muhammad Chishti Gujarati, *Adab al-talibin, ma`a rafiq al-tullab wa albab thulatha*, Urdu trans. Muhammad Bashir Husayn, ed. Muhammad Aslam Rana (Lahore: Progressive Books, 1984), pp. 61–64, based on the Punjab University MS, which has no calendar of saints. The Persian text of *Adab al-talibin* was published in Delhi in 1311/1893–94 by Matba`-i Mujtaba'i, and there are a dozen copies of the MS in Pakistan alone; cf. Ahmad Munzawi, *Fihrist-i mushtarak-i nuskhah-ha-yi khatti-i farsi-i Pakistan*, vol. III (Islamabad: Markaz-i Tahqiqat-i Farsi-i Iran u Pakistan, 1363/1405/1984), p. 1213, no. 2140. K. A. Nizami has summarized some of the contents of this work in his *Tarikh-i mashayikh-i Chisht*, vol. I (2nd ed.; Delhi: Idarah-i Adabiyyat-i Delli, 1980), p. 446; for details of Muhammad Chishti's life, see the introduction to *Adab al-talibin*, Urdu trans., pp. 7–15. The manuscript of *Adab al-talibin* came into

al-talibin on the rites of pilgrimage, which was not included in the *Makhzan-i a`ras*, has also been translated here as Appendix A.

Muhammad Najib's own version of the calendar was also a scholarly work, quoting extensively from standard works of Sufi biography and history to complement the records of shrines and oral tradition.[10] He compiled this work as an act of piety, to enable Muslims to celebrate saints' death anniversaries and perform pilgrimage to their tombs. The intended audience of the *Makhzan-i a`ras* was the elite group of Sufi disciples educated in Persian and dedicated to the practices and piety of the Chishti order. References to problems of presenting food offerings during times of poverty indicate that the author had in mind the religious devotee lacking worldly resources. Yet the rich and powerful were also interested in observing the death anniversaries of the saints, to judge from the dedication of the work to a powerful noble of the time. The popularity of the calendar of saints among the ruling class is indicated by its appearance in another recension, compiled by Muhammad Sharif at the request of Tipu Sultan of Mysore (r. 1783–99), which eliminated the scholarly apparatus (including the year of death), thus becoming a purely devotional calendar.[11] A number of other works of this type have been written in Persian, and today one can still acquire current Urdu almanacs printed in Bombay and Lahore

my hands by good fortune; I would like to express my thanks to Mr. Khalil al-Rahman Dawoodi of Lahore for presenting me his copy.

[10] For a survey of Sufi biographical sources, see my "From Hagiography to Martyrology: Conflicting Testimonies to a Sufi Martyr of the Delhi Sultanate," in *Refractions of Islam in India*, chapter 1; see also Marcia K. Hermansen, "Survey Article: Interdisciplinary Approaches to Islamic Biographical Materials," *Religion* 18 (1988), pp. 163–82.

[11] *Tarikh-i wafat-i buzurgan* or *A`ras-i buzurgan*, cited in Hermann Ethé, *Catalogue of Persian Manuscripts in the India Office Library* (Oxford, 1903; reprint ed., London: India Office Library & Records, 1980), no. 2733, col. 1482; also called *Sahifat al-a`ras*, in Wladimir Ivanow, *Concise Descriptive Catalogue of the Persian Manuscripts in the Collection of the Asiatic Society of Bengal* (Calcutta: The Asiatic Society, 1924; reprint ed., 1985), p. 755, no. 1634. The relationship of this work with Muhammad Najib's collection is evident from its commencing with the same four names. Muhammad Sharif's treatise is apparently identical with the *A`ras-i buzurgan* attributed to one Sayyid `Alawi, edited by W. Nassau Lees and Mawlawi Kabir al-Din Ahmad and published at Calcutta in 1855, as cited by C. A. Storey, *Persian Literature, A Bio-Bibliographical Survey* (2 vols.; London: Luzac & Co., 1927–71), I, 1054.

which prominently feature the death anniversaries of Sufi saints of the Indian subcontinent.[12]

The most widespread of all Sufi orders in India is the Chishti order, established by Mu`in al-Din Chishti (d. 1236) late in the twelfth century. The early Chishtis were notable for both their avoidance of royal patronage and their fondness for music. In Muhammad Najib's treatise, the authorities cited most often are the Chishti masters of the thirteenth and fourteenth centuries, such as Qutb al-Din Bakhtiyar Kaki (d. 1235), Nizam al-Din Awliya' (d. 1325), Nasir al-Din Mahmud "Chiragh-i Dihli" (d. 1356), and Muhammad al-Husayni "Gisu Daraz" (d. 1422). By the early fourteenth century, pilgrimage to tombs such as Qutb al-Din's in Delhi was an established practice among the Chishtis, though authorities for this practice are cited from other orders as well, such as the Suhrawardis and Naqshbandis.[13] The famous Moroccan traveler Ibn Battuta made such a pilgrimage to the tomb of Farid al-Din Ganj-i Shakkar (d. 1265) at Ajodhan (modern Pakpattan) around the year 1340.[14] Historical literature from the Sultanate period also attests to the popularity of pilgrimage, and the visits of various sultans to major tombs are frequently mentioned.[15]

---

[12] A devotional work that arranges brief biographies of saints with their death anniversaries, in chronological order from the time of Adam, is `Abd al-Fattah ibn Muhammad Nu`man's *Miftah al-`arifin* (MS 4263/1613 Sherani, Punjab University, Lahore), an autograph written in 1096/1684–85 in Sirhind. Examples of modern Urdu calendars of saints include Muhammad `Abd al-Hayy Siddiqi's *Tadhkirat al-sulaha'* (Badaun: Matba`-i Nizami, 1330/1911–12); Kalam al-Din Banarsi and Ibrahim `Imadi Nadwi's *Islami Muhammadi ba'i taqwim Bombay 1402* (Bombay: `Ali Bha'i Sharaf `Ali and Company Private Limited, 1402/1981–82), pp. 18–38; and Hakim Mawlawi Muhammad Barakat `Ali's *Asrar-i `alam jantri 1987* (Lahore: Maktaba-i Rafiq-i Ruzgar, 1986), pp. 19–24.

[13] Nizam al-Din Awliya' told of his mother's visits to the tombs of martyrs and saints in Bada'on (*Fawa'id al-fu'ad*, p. 100), and mentioned the many tombs worth visiting in Lahore (p. 57). Simon Digby has briefly described pilgrimages to major Chishti shrines in "*Tabarrukat* and Succession among the Great Chishti Shaykhs," in *Delhi Through the Ages: Essays in Urban History, Culture and Society*, ed. R. E. Frykenberg (Delhi: Oxford University Press, 1986), esp. pp. 91–96.

[14] Ibn Battutah, *Travels in Asia and Africa 1325–1354*, trans. H. A. R. Gibb, ed. E. Denison Ross and Eileen Power (London, 1926; reprint ed., Karachi: Indus Publications, 1986), p. 191, where the translator understands this as a visit (*ziyarat*) to a living person.

[15] Sultan Firuz Shah ibn Tughluq (r. 1356–87) chronicled his own rebuilding of major Sufi shrines in his lengthy inscription, known as the *Futuhat-i Firuz Shahi*, ed. Shaikh Abdur Rashid (Aligarh: Muslim University, Department of History, 1954), pp. 14–15, translated

[Note: the following paragraph is based on a no longer justifiable "decline and revival" interpretation of the history of the Chishti Sufi order; see Ernst & Lawrence, *Sufi Martyrs of Love: Chishti Sufism in South Asia and Beyond* (New York: Palgrave Macmillan, 2002), esp. Chapter 5.] Muhammad Najib's calendar of saints was a product of the renaissance of the Chishti order in the eighteenth century, when leading Chishtis revived the traditions of their great predecessors. After Timur's destruction of the Delhi Sultanate in 1398, the Chishti order had been dispersed to all parts of India. Although this diaspora consolidated the order's popularity in many different regions, the new leaders did not measure up to the stature of their predecessors, and many of them accepted the patronage of kings or established hereditary successions. The leading modern authority on the Chishtis, K. A. Nizami, has argued that this period of decline was eventually followed by a renaissance of the order in the seventeenth and eighteenth centuries, led by such men as Kalim Allah Shahjahanabadi (d. 1729) and his disciple Nizam al-Din Awrangabadi (d. 1729). These masters not only raised the standards of Islamic scholarship in the order but also revived the intense spiritual discipline characteristic of the early Chishtis.[16] Their strong emphasis on hadith scholarship, concerned with the sayings and deeds of the Prophet Muhammad, was typical of the pan-Islamic phenomenon of that time, which John Voll has called "neo-Sufism".[17] Our author Muhammad Najib was clearly a part of the Chishti renaissance, as his scholarship attests, and he explicitly informs us that the basic text by Sharaf al-Din Nahrawali that he expanded

in Sir H. M. Elliot, *The History of India as Told by Its Own Historians*, ed. John Dowson (8 vols.; Allahabad: Kitab Mahal, n.d.), 3:384–85. The popularity of shrine festivals may be judged from the fact that Firuz Shah also forbade ladies from attending them, on the grounds that evil characters also frequented these occasions (*Futuhat-i Firuz Shahi*, p. 9; trans. Elliot and Dowson, 3:380).

[16] K. A. Nizami, "Čishtiyya," in *Encyclopaedia of Islam, Second Edition*, ed. P. Bearman, Th. Bianquis, C. E. Bosworth, E. van Donzel, W. P. Heinrichs, consulted online on 08 November 2016 http://dx.doi.org/10.1163/1573-3912_islam_COM_0141; idem, *Some Aspects of Religion and Politics in India in the Thirteenth Century* (2nd ed., Delhi: Idarah-i Adabiyat-i Delli, 1978 [1963]); idem, *Tarikh-i mashayikh-i Chisht*, vol. I, pp. 290 ff.; vol. V (1985), pp. 81–181.

[17] John Voll, *Islam: Continuity and Change in the Modern World* (Boulder, CO: Westview Press, 1982), index, s.vv. "neo-Sufism," "hadiths."

had been originally written at the order of their master Nizam al-Din Awrangabadi.[18] Moreover, the rules of pilgrimage that Muhammad Najib incorporated from Muhammad Chishti's Adab al-talibin also form part of the heritage of the Chishti renaissance; Muhammad Chishti had been the grandfather and teacher of Yahya Madani (d. 1689), the Medina-based teacher of the Chishti reformer Kalim Allah Shahjahanabadi.[19]

The times during which Muhammad Najib wrote were troubled ones, when, it may be supposed, the revival of religious traditions might serve as a source of order amid political chaos. India in the eighteenth century was a shambles, in which Afghans, Marathas and Sikhs fought over the wreckage of the Mughal empire. The British and French were eyeing opportunities for their own imperial expansion in India. The Deccan was nominally an appendage of the Mughals, but was increasingly independent under the powerful Nizam, who initially made Awrangabad his capital. The first Nizam (Nizam al-Mulk Asaf Jah, d. 1748) was closely attached to the Chishtis, and even wrote a biography of Nizam al-Din Awrangabadi.[20] Both the first Nizam and his successor, Nizam al-Dawla Nasir Jang (d. 1164/1750), were buried next to one of the principal Chishti places of pilgrimage in the Deccan, the tomb of Burhan al-Din Gharib (d. 1338) in Khuldabad, near Awrangabad.[21] In what appears to be a dedication at the end of his introduction, Muhammad Najib mentions as a friend of the Sufis Anwar al-Din Khan Bahadur (d. 1749), a noble of the Carnatic who was allied militarily with the Nizam against the French and British.[22] Evidently Sufis like Muhammad Najib still needed the support of powerful protectors. This had

---

[18] Neither Muhammad Najib nor Sharaf al-Din Nahrawali appears among the list of Nizam al-Din Awrangabadi's chief disciples; cf. Nizami, *Tarikh*, V, 178–79.

[19] *Adab al-talibin*, Urdu trans., p. 13; Nizami, *Tarikh*, 5:92–94.

[20] Nizami, *Tarikh*, 5:173, 175–76, notes that this book is no longer extant.

[21] P. Setu Madhava Rao, *Eighteenth Century Deccan* (Bombay: Popular Prakashan, 1963), p. 61. The first Nizam considered patronage of Sufi saints an important state duty, and stressed this point in his testament to his successor (ibid., pp. 62, 66–67).

[22] Samsam-ud-Daula Shah Nawaz Khan and his son `Abdul Hayy, *The Maathir-ul-Umara*, trans. H. Beveridge, rev. Baini Prashad (reprint ed., 2 vols.; New Delhi: Janaki Prakashan, 1979), II, 1065–1066 (where he is praised for his knowledge of Sufism); Elliot and Dowson, VIII, 391 (his death fighting the French); Ethé, II, col. 1011, Index, s.n. "(Nawwâb) Anwâr-aldînkhân."

also been true for his master Nizam al-Din Awrangabadi, who had to travel in the company of the royal army.[23] Although the revival of early Chishti practices implied the refusal of financial support from secular rulers, it was evidently impossible for the Chishtis to avoid political relationships; the exact nature of these relationships still has to be examined by the study of financial records in shrines and archives.[24] The internal reorganization of the Chishti order was, in any case, combined with highly uncertain political conditions. This makes it all the more understandable that a calendar of saints, recording and memorializing the religious heroes of the past and present, should have been considered an important enterprise. The eighteenth and nineteenth centuries witnessed a considerable growth in the literature of Islamic hagiography and martyrology in India, as I have shown elsewhere.[25] The invocation of the spirits of the great Chishti masters at the propitious time of the `urs, and attention to the classical pilgrimage rituals of these same masters, were equally important in the revival of tradition during a period of decadence.

Many of Muhammad Najib's allusions to the rituals of pilgrimage are casual, presupposing that the reader is familiar with them already, and they touch on observances concerned not only with saints' tombs but also with the tombs of one's relatives and other ordinary persons. Nevertheless, we can summarize here the most important rituals that he mentions.[26] There is an emphasis on determining the exact hour and day of death for commemoration, though this is not indispensable. Food and drink also play an important role, and are to be offered to the spirits of the dead and then distributed on whatever scale the pilgrim can afford. Offering food to the spirits of the saints brings good fortune in this life, and pilgrims may also present

---

[23] Nizami, *Tarikh*, 5:157–58.

[24] Nizami, *Tarikh*, 5:167, records Nizam al-Din Awrangabadi's regular distribution of gifts to the poor, which must have required substantial donations from lay followers.

[25] See Ernst, "From Hagiography to Martyrology."

[26] It would be desirable to collect information from gazetteers, travelers' reports, and modern anthropological studies on the different practices that have arisen at the major Sufi shrines in India and Pakistan, but such an investigation is beyond the scope of the present article.

petitions to the saints (section 19, below). The pilgrim is also urged to offer "sweets, roses, and flowers" at the tomb (section 17), or a bit of money, and this is still expected of the visitor today. Performance of music on these anniversaries is a characteristically Chishti practice. Yet the ziyarat is not a terribly rigid ritual, as can be seen from the frequent statement that one should perform only what can be done in accordance with one's ability, especially in case of poverty. Muhammad Chishti summarized this relaxed attitude toward pilgrimage by saying that one should perform it "as much as possible without objection [being attached to it] (*bi-la haraj*)."[27] The ritual is possible and permissible, but not blameworthy. This ritual flexibility is bolstered by a saying of the Prophet Muhammad, that one is to be judged by one's intentions. Another interesting feature is the mention of the superior nights and days of the year, according to the encyclopedic *Revival of Religious Sciences* of Muhammad al-Ghazali (d. 1111); this listing of holy days is tied in with the development of Sufi piety and stipulates the most propitious times for supererogatory prayer. Although the holy days have nothing intrinsically to do with saints' death anniversaries, their inclusion by Muhammad Najib is natural in a book that organizes the year into a series of daily sacred remembrances. In addition, repetition of sections from the Qur'an and of various Arabic prayers forms a major part of the pilgrimage procedure. An index of the Qur'anic passages mentioned in the text is attached at the end of the translation as Appendix B, and shows at a glance which were most popular for pilgrimage to tombs. To tie all the anniversaries together, there is a Muslim equivalent for the Christian All Saints' Day, on the first Thursday in the month of Rajab, when one may commemorate all the saints' festivals at once (sec. 5). Muhammad Najib also included instructions for prayers of intercession on behalf of deceased sinners who are undergoing pre-resurrection torments in the grave; one may willingly give to another the reward for years of prayer, as is shown by the story of Abu al-Rabi` and his 70,000 repetitions of the Islamic creed

[27] Muhammad Chishti, *Adab al-talibin*, fol. 22b, 24b. The text frequently uses the Arabic phrase *bi-la haraj*, meaning "there is no harm or crime in it" from an objective legal point of view; the pilgrimage rituals are harmless but not required.

(section 11). While no Islamic equivalent of the Christian All Souls' Day arose, celebration of the salvation of the saint is similarly distinguished from penitential remembrance of the sinner in both traditions.[28]

Other pilgrimage practices described by Muhammad Najib raise interesting questions about the status of ziyarat as an Islamic ritual and the psychological dimensions associated with its external performance. Like the hajj, ziyarat calls for circumambulation (section 12), in this case of the tomb rather than the Ka`ba.[29] Some enthusiastic pilgrims actually found ziyarat to be superior to the hajj (section 12). These comparisons were evidently designed to emphasize the acceptability of ziyarat as an Islamic ritual. That some questioned the pilgrimage to saints' tombs we may suppose from the response of the learned Nasir al-Din Chiragh-i Dihli, who discovered a hadith of the Prophet in support of ziyarat (section 12).[30] Muhammad Najib accepted this canonical approval of ziyarat wholeheartedly, and concluded his treatise by describing these practices as good *sunna*, that is, exemplary behavior based on the Prophet's word or deed (section 23). Muhammad Najib frequently reminds the reader to observe proper manners (*adab*) and reverentially correct behavior; otherwise one risks offending the saints, who are consciously present and not averse to correcting the offender. One should especially avoid turning one's back on the saint's tomb or turning one's feet disrespectfully in that direction. The pilgrim is also instructed to perform a deep psychological self-examination while visiting tombs, for receptivity to supernatural communications is then greatly increased and one may hope for spiritual guidance by this means.

One of the most interesting extended accounts in the treatise is `Ala' al-Dawla Simnani's lengthy and somewhat obscure reply (section 13) to an extreme idealist who scorned the spirit's need

[28] George Every, *Christian Mythology* (London: Hamlyn, 1970), p. 114. The Maliki jurist Ibn al-Hajj (d. 1336) refers to a candle festival for all the saints on 15 Sha`ban (Fritz Meier, *Abu Sa`id*, p. 264).

[29] Cf. Goldziher, "Veneration," II, 288, on circumambulation (*tawaf*).

[30] Cf. Goldziher, "Veneration," II, 335, n. 3, on hadith in favor of pilgrimage. For an early example of preferring pilgrimage to saints' tombs over the hajj, see Fritz Meier, *Abu Sa`id*, pp. 202–203.

for a body and so doubted the efficacy of pilgrimage to tombs. `Ala' al-Dawla pointed out that pilgrimage to tombs increases one's spiritual concentration (*tawajjuh*) through contact with the earthly remains of a saint. Simnani said further that, along with the subtle body that will appear at the resurrection, the place of bodily entombment is more closely connected with the spirit than is any other material phenomenon. Citing the example of the Prophet Muhammad's tomb in Medina, he argued that while meditation on the Prophet at any time is beneficial, physically visiting the Prophet's tomb is better, since the spirit of the Prophet senses the extra effort and hardship of the journey and assists the pilgrim in attaining the full realization of the inner meaning of the pilgrimage. The eminent scholar `Abd al-Haqq Dihlawi (d. 1642–43) also stressed the spiritual nature of the vision sought by pilgrims (section 18).

Muhammad Najib concedes that there is controversy over honoring the dead, and he argues that objections to this practice simply misunderstand its true nature. He maintains that those souls who received honors while living are still worthy of those honors after their death. This leads him to consider those honors that were controversial in Islamic law, such as prostration before the master. It is common for pilgrims to express their love and respect for the saints by kissing and touching their eyes to the tombs. Prostration, though customary in the courts of kings, is technically permissible only before God, as in ritual prayer; many jurists draw the inference that prostration before a mortal is therefore idolatrous, although some permit a distinction between the prostration of respect and the prostration of worship. The Chishti master Nizam al-Din Awliya' was uncomfortable with the practice, but permitted it since it was an established custom with his predecessors.[31] `Ala' al-Dawla Simnani mentioned an occasion when people bowed down before his own master, and a jurist forbade them to do so. Yet he made it clear that this prostration is not worship (*`ibadat*) of the person but spontaneous respect (*ta`zim*), which is paid to the spiritual reality that is manifest in the form of the sheikh.

---

31 *Fawa'id al-fu'ad*, pp. 267, 364.

Supporters of ziyarat pilgrimage reject the suspicion that it is the result of Hindu influence, and they find the Wahhabi iconoclasm extreme, pointing to passages in both the Qur'an (e.g., *al-Kahf*, 18:21) and the hadith reports which approved graves as memorials and allowed the visiting of saintly people's tombs as a pious and beneficial act. The tomb was in fact an untypical form of architecture in Hindu India, where cremation was the preferred method of disposal of the dead. From a purely architectural perspective, it might be more correct to describe Sufi shrines as mosques with funerary functions, since the tombs invariably have an orientation to the direction of Mecca, and large mausolea almost always feature a *qibla* niche in the appropriate wall.[32] From this functional perspective, tombs of Sufi saints are developments within the Islamic tradition that do not rely on any Hindu example.

Muhammad Najib's introduction to the *Makhzan-i a`ras* shows a learned Sufi's understanding of ziyarat pilgrimage to Sufi shrines as a religious practice comparable to the hajj pilgrimage and generally permissible according to Islamic law. Though some disputed the legitimacy of ziyarat, Sufi scholars almost unanimously accepted it as a practice founded on the example of the Prophet Muhammad, and in this view it was thoroughly Islamic in intention. The use of the Islamic lunar calendar and a ritual atmosphere saturated with recitation of the Qur'an reinforced the Islamic character of pilgrimages to saints' tombs. The Sufis' own understanding of the encounter with a saint's spirit derived from their intense cultivation of the master-disciple relationship, which for them reached beyond the limits of life and death. The ziyarat pilgrimage is not merely a journey to a place of burial, but is literally a visit to a living saint; one of the most common Persian terms for a saint's shrine is *mazar*, a place that is visited, indicating that the act of personal encounter takes priority over the structure's reliquary function. Pilgrimage to Sufi saints' shrines is, temporally, a search for union with God through synchronicity with the saint's death anniversary;

[32] James Dickie, "Allah and Eternity: Mosques, Madrasas and Tombs," in *Architecture of the Islamic World: Its History and Social Meaning*, ed. George Michell (London: Thames and Hudson, 1978), pp. 43–44.

physically it is an approach to the divine presence over the threshold of the saint's tomb. The traditional Sufi attitude to pilgrimage, as shown in Muhammad Najib's introduction, resulted from centuries of reflection on an extremely widespread ritual. Despite the theological and legal controversies that have raged around pilgrimage to Sufi tombs, the practice is rooted in the hearts of many Muslims and remains a vital part of the Islamic tradition.

Introduction to the Treasury of *Death Anniversaries* (*Makhzan al-a`ras*)[33]

1. Praise be to God, Lord of Creation, and blessings and peace on the chief of messengers and seal of the prophets Muhammad the Chosen, and on his family, and all his companions. Now, this special treatise is [taken] from the collection of death anniversaries of the prophets, companions, imams of guidance, and noble sheikhs (God be pleased with them) that was assembled previously by Sheikh Sharaf al-Din ibn Qadi Sheikh Muhammad Nahrawali. Since the names of the saints who were joined to the mercy of God after the compilation of the aforesaid treatise were lacking, as well as some names of the ancients, therefore a selection was made from biographical works in the year 1155 [1741–42] by this slave of dervishes, Muhammad Najib Qadiri Nagawri Ajmeri, who is one of the intimates and disciples of the threshold of all creation and the resort and exemplar of those united with God, the revered Sheikh Nizam al-Din Chishti Awrangabadi [d. 1142/1729] (disciple of the exemplar of the saints Sheikh Kalim Allah Chishti Shahjahanabadi [d. 1142/1729], disciple of the axis[34] of those united with God, Sheikh Muhammad Yahya Chishti al-Gujarati

al-Madani [d. 1101/1689], grandson and disciple of the axis of axes Sheikh Muhammad Chishti al-Gujarati [d. 1040/1630], God

[33] Muhammad Najib Qadiri Nagawri, *Kitab al-a'ras* (Agra, 1300/1883).

[34] "Axis (*qutb*)" is the Sufi term for the perfect one who, like the pole star, is an immovable axis around which all else revolves.

sanctify their consciences!). These works include *Nafahat al-uns*, *Mir'at al-janan*, the history of Imam Yafi`i, *Rashahat*, *Matlub al-talibin*, *Siyar al-awliya'*, *Siyar al-`arifin*, *Akhbar al-akhyar*, *Khizanat al-jalali*, *Fada'il al-awliya'*, *Khawariqat*, *Tabaqat-i nasiri*, *Rawdat al-shuhada'*, *Gulzar-i abrar*, *Safinat al-awliya'*, *Mukhbir al-wasilin*, *Tabaqat-i Shahjahani*, and other authentic texts. He found that for some [saints], the year and date and tomb and Sufi order were in books, and the dates of others, both ancient and modern, were not to be seen in books. At the tombs of those where a death anniversary is observed at a place where pilgrimage is possible, there were some papers that were there verified by the descendant (*sahib-i sajjada*) and the attendants of the tomb. In the places where it was impossible to go, verification was conveyed and confirmed by disciples of the order of that saint or by residents of the place who were well-known and trustworthy men. Dates contained in the aforementioned *Book of Death Anniversaries* were retained without change or substitution. If something has been found to contradict that in the biographical books, it has been added, and displayed, as a means of salvation in both worlds. May God (glory be to Him who is exalted!), in respect of the holy ones who are mentioned in this noble text, keep this rebellious and poorly armored sinner in the love of this lofty company, and make [me] die in their love, and resurrect [me] in the troop of their lovers and in the sanctuary of the Prophet and his noble family.

On Fixing Death Anniversaries

2. The axis of the saints, Sheikh Muhammad Chishti (son of Sheikh Muhammad Hasan ibn Ahmad ibn Sheikh Nasir al-Din-i Thani ibn Sheikh Badr al-Din ibn Kamal al-Din, disciple and true nephew of the axis of axes, Sheikh Nasir al-Din Mahmud Chiragh-i Dihli [d. 757/1356]) has said in his writings,[35] "Seeker of God, my dear, my beloved! You ought to observe the death anniversaries of the saints of God Most High, for help comes to you from them. God Most High gives the capacity for this work to their descendants,

---

[35] The following passage occurs in *Ādab al-talibin*, fol. 24a-b; Urdu trans., pp. 63–64.

from His own generosity. The author of the *Majmu` al-riwayat*[36] has said, 'If one wishes to select the [time of the saint's] feast, let him select it with awareness of the day of his death, and take care for the hour in which his spirit departed. For the spirits of the dead come every year in the days of the death anniversaries, in that place and in that hour. And it is fitting that one take food and drink in that hour, for that makes the spirits glad. Indeed, there is an extraordinary [spiritual] influence in this. And if one wants edibles and beverages, they [the spirits] will be glad, and wish one well and not ill.' Thus if the aspirant, in pilgrimage to that place, regardless of conditions, regardless of where it is, regardless of anything whatever, makes an offering to the best of his ability—and if that hour is not known, then if the spirit has passed on during the day, he does this during the day, and if it has passed on during the night, he does it during the night. The holy master of the secret, Gisu Daraz,[37] used to make a great offering to the spirit of the axis of axes, Sheikh Nasir al-Din Mahmud Chiragh-i Dihli (God be pleased with him!) during the night of the 18th of Ramadan, (p. 4) since the passing of his spirit had been on this night. But he also performed this during the day. And if it is not known with certainty whether it was by day or night, then one should perform it during the day, and also do something at night." Such was the practice of the axis of the saints.

Offerings to the Spirits of the Dead[38]

3. "Know, seeker of God (glory be to Him who is exalted), that the perfectly guided ones, sincere disciples, and trustworthy adherents ought to present food to the spirits of their elders, their masters, and their guides, as much as possible without objection. Thus by their [the spirits'] blessing, the benefits (*futuhat*) and good fortune of both worlds are increased, and their [the disciples'] life and wealth grow, and they attain their desire and stand in need of nothing created; might and fortune become

[36] Not traced; the quotation is all in Arabic.

[37] Sayyid Muhammad al-Husayni "Gisu Daraz" (d. 826/1422); cf. Lawrence, pp. 32–35.

[38] *Adab al-talibin*, fol. 24b–25a; Urdu trans., pp. 64–65.

great, and since 'The [real] man is he who loves,' by their blessing, their final state becomes good if God Most High wills. This having become clear by experience, there is no success, unless [for] the possessor of fortune and happiness." If [celebrating] all of the death anniversaries causes difficulty, let him only do some, and make an offering without sin to the spirits of all the prophets and saints and all the people of the heart, in the month of Rajab.

Flexibility in Observing the Death Anniversary

4. Know that, if one does not perform it on the day and night of the death anniversary, but performs it on another day on account of business, it is good. "The perfection of deeds is in intentions." He [Muhammad Chishti] has also said,[39] "One observes the death anniversaries of one's masters, as much as possible without objection, and in observing this, if one obtains the permission of the master both formally and spiritually, it is best. And if it is hard to give to anyone, let him give that which he owes to his family and children and people, and that which he eats [himself]; this shall be his intention.[40] And if the death anniversary is on a day when it is hard [to perform all customary practices], he performs it on whatever day is easy. On the day of incurring expenses for the death anniversary, he does not become extravagant, but does whatever is without extravagance."

Distributing Food Offerings at the Death Anniversary

5. In the *Khizanat al-jalali*[41] it is written, "One of the conditions of the sincere is that, for the spirit of one to whom one wishes to offer food, he should distribute food for the dervishes at that subtle time in which that saint has departed, for three days in succession. Whatever time he wishes is best." In the above-mentioned *Book of Death Anniversaries* it is written,[42]

---

[39] *Ādab al-talibin,* fols. 22a-b; Urdu trans., p. 63.

[40] Even if one can only distribute food to oneself and one's family, it shall serve the same purpose as if it were distributed to many.

[41] The *Khizanat al-jalali* of Jalal al-Din Bukhari (d. 785/1384).

[42] *Adab al-talibin,* fol. 24b; Urdu trans., p. 64.

"Making offerings on the day and night is a complete cycle (*bar-i tamam*), and the day of the death anniversary and the following night and the following day is the order of making offerings on the day of the death anniversary.[43] And if the day is not known, nor the night, then it is performed in the [appropriate] month, but if the month is not known, it should be performed in the month of Rajab, especially on 'the night of wishes (*laylat al-ragha'ib*)' or that day, the first Thursday that comes in the month of Rajab, which is called [the day of] 'the night of wishes.'[44] They say that in this night or day, [or on the night of the Prophet's ascension], if one performs it as much as possible for the souls of all the saints and the people of faith, what happiness is [then] in the breasts of all! If one is a faqir or dervish, whatever cooked food is in the house (p. 5) he dedicates to their spirits and eats it. And if it is a time of poverty, let him not forget the *Fatiha* [Qur. 1]."

6. One of the offspring of the disciples of the axis of axes, Sheikh Muhammad Chishti (God sanctify his conscience) writes,[45] "On the day of the death anniversary, or the night, one recites the *Fatiha* to his spirit and makes an offering of food. If one recites the *Fatiha* during the hour of the passing away of his spirit, it is better; otherwise [one does it] at whatever hour and whatever day is easiest without objection. Let him recite the *Fatiha* over the food and drink. If he cannot [distribute food], indeed let him recite the *Fatiha* for their spirits and eat the food that has been cooked for his own meal and for his family." In attempting to observe one, two, or three death anniversaries of one's own masters, one ought to engage in music sessions, complete Qur'an recitations, [distributing] food, and similar

---

[43] The Urdu translation here reads differently: "Having made offerings for three days and two nights on the death anniversary, if one intends to make an offering also on the next night and day, it will be continuous with the offering on the day of the death anniversary" (p. 64).

[44] The nature of the observance of "the night of wishes (laylat al-raghā'ib)" is not clear from the text. Niẓām al-Din Awliya' said that one who prayed on this night would not die during the year (Fawa'id al-fuæad, p. 37). The translator of Ādāb al-ṭālibin explains it as another term for the night of the Prophet's ascension (p. 64, n. 1), but Muḥammad Chishti regards the two holidays as separate.

[45] This passage does not occur in Ādāb al-ṭālibin.

things, and one ought to abstain from unlawful things. And if, in Rajab on "the night of wishes," until "the day of conquering," which is the 15th of Rajab, or the [27th] of the month, one distributes food dedicated to the spirits of the prophets, saints, martyrs, and pious ones, they say that one will obtain much benefit.

Prayers for Deceased Relatives

7. In the *Dalil al-`arifin*[46] it is written that the sheikh of sheikhs, Sheikh Husam al-Din Manikpuri [d. 852/1448], the disciple and successor of the axis of the world, Sheikh Nur al-Haqq [d. 813/1410] (God sanctify their consciences), used to make a pilgrimage to [the tomb of] his parents after every Friday's prayers, and he did this without fail. Once he went [instead] to speak with his master's son after the Friday prayers. When he returned, the tomb was in the road. He, riding in his palanquin, stood and recited the *Fatiha*, and came home. On Saturday, after the morning prayers, he went out on pilgrimage. He said, "On Friday, and the first hours on Saturday, the spirits are present in the tombs, and one should perform pilgrimage." He also said, "If one recites eleven times the *surat Ikhlas* [Qur. 112], and the *Mu`awwadhatayn* [Qur. 113–14] at the same time, and the Throne Verse [Qur. 2:256], the people in the tombs are absolved." When he went to the tombs, he was near the tomb of his father. He greeted them, standing at the head [of the tomb], and recited the *Fatiha* and the Throne Verse, up to [the word] "eternally." Eleven times he recited the *surat Ikhlas*, and at the same time the *Mu`awwadhatayn*, and once *Ilahukum al-takathur* [Qur. 102]. He went to the foot, and kissed the top of the tomb. He performed the same pilgrimage to his mother, also kissing the top of the foot [of the tomb], and at the time of departure recited *A-lam nashrah* [Qur. 94]. He said, "If one holds one's hands on top of the tomb and ten times recites the word of unity and praise, the dead are absolved." He also said, "One should perform pilgrimage every day, though it is not easy. One should do it on Friday, for the dead expect it. It is of the

[46] *Dalil al-'arifin,* the discourses of Mu'in al-Din Chishti, mentioned here by mistake; the correct title of the discourses of Husam al-Din Manikpuri is *Rafiq al-'ashiqin*.

same use to the mother and father." He also said, "My master, the axis of the world, Sheikh Nur al-Haqq, every day after morning prayers used to perform pilgrimage to his father, Sheikh `Ala' al-Haqq wa-al-Din (God sanctify his conscience)." He also said, "If someone once recites the *Fatiha* in a tomb, (p.6) for forty days, the punishment will be removed from that tomb." The axis of axes, Sheikh Nasir al-Din Chiragh-i Dihli (God be pleased with him), says, "While standing at the head of someone's grave, one says the *Fatiha* once, the Throne Verse three times, *al-Takathur* [Qur. 102] three times, and *Ikhlas* many times."

The Best Days for Pilgrimage and Prayer

8. In the *Khizanat al-jalali* it is written, "'Pilgrimage to graves every week is [legally] approved,' and the best days for pilgrimage are four: Saturday, Monday, Thursday, and Friday. It is the same with the blessed and superior nights, such as 'the night of orders,'[47] and with blessed times, such as 10 Dhu al-Hijja, the two `Ids,[48] and `Ashura."[49] In the *Ihya' al-`ulum*, written by Imam Muhammad Ghazali [d. 505/1111] (God's mercy upon him), he writes, "The superior days are seventeen: the first day is `Arafa;[50] the second day is `Ashura; the third day is 27 Rajab; the fourth day is 27 Ramadan; the fifth day is 15 Sha`ban; the sixth day is Friday; the seventh and eighth days are the two `Ids; and the nine days of Dhu al-Hijja, from the first night of the moon until the ninth. The superior nights are fifteen: In the month of Ramadan, the 21st, 23rd, 25th, 27th, 29th, and 7th; the first night of the month of Muharram; the night of `Ashura; the first night of the month of Rajab, and the 15th and 27th nights in Rajab; the 15th of Sha`ban; the night of `Arafa; and the nights of the two `Ids."[51]

---

47 The "night of orders (Ar. laylat al-bara'a, Pers. shab-i barat)" is the night of the 14th of Sha'ban, when a lengthy prayer may be followed by wishes that will be fulfilled.

48 `Id al-Adha is the Abrahamic sacrifice during hajj, and `Id al-Fitr is the breaking of the Ramadan fast.

49 'Ashura, the 10th of Muharram, is for Sunni Muslims the general day of repentance, while for Shi'is it commemorates the martyrdom of the imam Husayn.

50 Standing on Mt. 'Arafa near Mecca on the 9th of Dhu al-Hijja and addressing God.

51 Muhammad al-Ghazali, *Ihya' 'ulum al-din* (Cairo: Dar al-Shu'ab, n.d.), pp. 645–46.

Efficacy of Prayer for the Dead

9. At the time when one is standing, facing the deceased, one says, "Peace be unto you, people of the houses, among those who submit and are faithful! May He have mercy on those who have come before us, and those who come after; God willing, we shall be joined with you. I shall ask God for you, and forgiveness will be yours." The Messenger of God (God's blessings and peace upon him) spoke thus, then sat and said, "In the name of God, and for the community of the Messenger of God." One finds in hadith that whenever one recites this by the tomb of someone, the inhabitant of the tomb will be spared the punishment, darkness, and straitness [of the tomb] for forty years. Then one says, "There is no god but God, He alone, Who has no partner; His is the kingdom, His is the praise; He gives life and death, while He is living and does not die; good comes by His hand, and He has power over everything." Then one recites the *suratal-Fatiha*, the Throne Verse, and gives the reward of that to the inhabitants of the tombs. After that, one recites the *surat Ikhlas* seven times, but if one recites it ten times, it is better.

10. In the *Jawami` al-kalim*,[52] the discourses of Sayyid Gisu Daraz (God sanctify his conscience), it is written that he said, "One day (p. 7) a great man passed through a graveyard, and he saw a commotion in the cemetery. He asked, 'What is this commotion?' In the midst of this, they [the dead] replied, 'It is a week since Habib `Ajami [d. 156/773] (God's peace be upon him) passed by us, and he had recited one *Fatiha* intended for us. The abundance and reward produced from that is being divided among us.'"

11. In the *Nafahat al-uns*,[53] in the account of Abu al-Rabi` Malaqi, the disciple of Sheikh Abu al-`Abbas, it is written that it has come down in the hadith of the Prophet (God's blessings

[52] Sayyid Muhammad Akbar Husayni, *Jawami' al-kalim*, ed. Hafiz Muhammad Hamid Siddiqi (Cawnpore: Intizami Press, 1356/1937–38), p. 288.

[53] 'Abd al-Rahman Jami, *Nafahat al-uns*, ed. Mahdi Tawhidipur (Tehran, 1336 solar/1957), pp. 531–32.

and peace be upon him) with this meaning, that saying the phrase, "There is no god but God"[54] 70,000 times for the salvation of the speaker or for the salvation of that person whom the speaker intends, is completely efficacious. Sheikh Abu al-Rabi` has said, "I had said this *dhikr*[55] 70,000 times, but had not done it in the name of any particular person, until one day I was present with a group at someone's feast-table. With them was a youth who had experienced [spiritual] unveilings. At the moment when that youth laid a hand on the food to eat, suddenly he wept. They asked him, 'Why do you weep?' He said, 'Right here I am witnessing hell, and I see my mother in it undergoing punishment.'" Sheikh Abu al-Rabi` said, "Secretly I prayed, 'God! You know that I have said "There is no god but God" 70,000 times. I have offered that [reward] for the sake of freeing the mother of this particular youth from hellfire.' When I had completed forming this intention internally, that youth laughed and became cheerful, saying, 'I see my mother freed from hellfire! Praise be to God!' Then he joined in eating food with the group."

Legitimacy of Pilgrimage

12. In the discourses of Sayyid Gisu Daraz (God be pleased with him) it is written that he said, "They asked Khwajah Nasir al-Din Chiragh-i Dihli (God be pleased with him), 'Do you perform circumambulation around the tomb of Sheikh al-Islam Qutb al-Din [d. 634/1236] (God sanctify his conscience)? What is the [prophetic] basis of that?' He said, 'On "Pilgrimage to tombs," it is written, "Circumambulation around the tomb of a pious man is lawful."'" The collector of the above-mentioned discourses says, "He is a sincere lover who, at every new moon, circumambulates the hospice of his revered master with bare head and bare feet, saying, 'In this I find more than in pilgrimage to Mecca!'"

[54] This is the first half of the Muslim confession of faith (*shahada*), "There is no god but God, and Muhammad is the Messenger of God."

[55] The term dhikr among Sufis meant chanting prayers and the names of God as worship.

Spiritual Effects of Pilgrimage

13. In the *Lata'if-i ashrafi*,[56] the discourses of Sayyid Ashraf Jahangir Simnani Chishti [d. 829/1425] (God sanctify his conscience), it is written that he said, "After making pilgrimage to the saints who are seated on the seat of guidance and the chair of dignity, one makes pilgrimage to the tombs of the saints." He said, "One day I had sat in attendance on Sheikh Rukn al-Din `Ala' al-Dawla Simnani [d. 736/1336] (God sanctify his conscience) (p. 8) A dervish asked, 'Since in the tomb this body has no perception, and the acquired body (*badan-i muktasab*), is detached from it, together with the spirit, and since there is no veil in the world of spirits, what need is there to visit tombs? Concentrating on the spirit of a saint should be just as useful in any other place as at his tomb.' The sheikh said, 'It has many uses. One is that when one makes a pilgrimage to someone['s tomb], one's concentration increases as often as one goes. When one reaches the tomb and beholds it by sense-perception, one's sense-perception also becomes engaged with the tomb. He then becomes totally concentrated, and this has many uses. Another is that however much spirits lack a veil, and though the whole world is one to them, it keeps an eye on the body with which it [the spirit] has been connected for 70 years and on its resurrection body that it will become after the resurrection, for ever and ever. Its [the spirit's] connection is greater here than in any other place.[57] The benefits of making pilgrimage are great. If one concentrates here on the spirituality of that revered Mustafa [that is, the Prophet Muhammad] (God's blessing and peace upon him), one obtains benefit. But if one goes to Medina, the spirituality of Mustafa (God's blessing and peace upon him) is aware of one's traveling and the suffering of the road. When one reaches there, one sees by sense-perception the pure shrine (*rawda*) of that revered one. One becomes totally concentrated. How can the latter benefit be compared to the former? The people of vision (*mushahada*) realize this internal meaning (*ma`na*).'"

---

[56] *Lata'if-i ashrafi*, II, 28; translated by Hartwig Cordt, *Die sitzungen des 'Ala' addawla as-Simnani* (Zurich: Juris Druck + Verlag, 1977), pp. 201–02.

[57] *Lata'if-i ashrafi*, II, 28.

The Saints are Conscious

14. He [Ashraf Jahangir Simnani] also said,[58] "The dead are aware of the coming of a pilgrim and his concentration, for the spiritual world has a subtlety, specifically, that the spirits of the saints take notice of even a little concentration of the pilgrim." He said that Sultan al-Mashayikh, Sheikh Nizam al-Din Awliya' [d. 726/1325] (God sanctify his conscience) had gone to make pilgrimage to the blessed tomb of the axis of axes, Khwajah Qutb al-Din (God sanctify his conscience). In the midst of circumambulation, it occurred to him, "Is his spirituality yet aware of my concentration?" This incipient thought was not yet complete when from the luminous tomb a voice sprang up, with an eloquent expression, reciting this verse: "Think of me as living like yourself; I will come in spirit if you come in body. Do not think me lacking in companionship, for I see you even if you don't see me." He said, "Whenever one comes to a town, the first thing one ought to accomplish is to kiss the feet of the saints who are full of life, and after that, the honor of pilgrimage to the tombs of saints found there. If one's master's tomb is in that city, one first carries out the pilgrimage to him; otherwise one visits the tomb of every saint shown him."

Controversy over Prostration[59]

15. There is a debate among the legal scholars about placing the forehead (*jabha*) on the tombs of saints, and they have not permitted it, though among the sheikhs there are differences of opinion. (p.9) According to this faqir [that is, Ashraf Jahangir Simnani], just as in the world of travel many saints are seen, who while living have been looked upon with respect (*ta`zim*), so after death people look on them with the same respect. In the same way, the father and teacher and master and the like are worthy of respect.[60] When my revered master [`Ala' al-Dawla Simnani] returned from congregational prayer, people placed their heads

[58] Ibid., II, 29.

[59] Ibid., II, 29.

[60] Here (II, 29) a sentence has been omitted, on a minority position approving prostration.

at his feet, and the heads that were not honored by his blessed feet they put on the ground and so prostrated themselves. One of the *mullas* asked about the meaning of this, for it is unlawful that they should put their heads on the ground. He said, "I have often forbidden them and restrained them, so that they do not come back."

16. In the *Siyar al-awliya'*[61] it is written that one day in the assembly of Sultan al-Mashayikh, Sheikh Nizam al-Din Awliya' (God sanctify his conscience), there was talk about disciples coming to the revered master and placing their heads on the ground. Sultan al-Mashayikh said, "I wanted to forbid people, but since they have done this before my sheikh, I have not forbidden them." In sum, sincere friends and trustworthy aspirants, because of the form that they call vision in the mirror of the sheikh and the inner meaning (*ma`na*) that they witness in the form of the sheikh, involuntarily place their heads on the ground.[62] In the *Mirsad*[63] it is said that to place the head on the ground before the sheikh is not prostration; this is respect and honor for the light of the essence and attributes of the real object of worship [that is, God], for the sheikhs and saints are illuminated with that light.

Rules and Prayers of Pilgrimage[64]

17. He [Ashraf Jahangir Simnani] also says that when one comes to make pilgrimage to tombs, from modesty (*haya'*) he enters the tombs and circumambulates three or seven times. Then he puts his head at the foot of the grave, and turning his face toward the deceased, stands to the right of the grave and says, "Peace be unto you, people of 'There is no god but God,' from the people of 'There is no god but God'! How did you find his saying, 'There is no god but God'? God! [It was] by the truth of 'There is no god but God'! Resurrect us in the multitude of those who say, 'There is no

---

[61] *Fawa'id al-fu'ad*, pp. 267, 364.

[62] Here a passage supporting prostration has been omitted from *Lata'if-i ashrafi* (II, 29).

[63] Hamid Algar, trans., *The Path of God's Bondsmen from Origin to Return*, Persian Heritage Series No. 35 (Delmar, NY: Caravan Books, 1982).

[64] *Lata'if-i ashrafi*, II, 30.

god but God.' Forgive him who says, 'There is no god but God,' and do not deprive us of saying 'There is no god but God and Muhammad is the Messenger of God.'" Then he strews a rose or plant on the tomb and sitting or standing recites the *Fatiha*, the Throne verse, *Idha zulzilat al-ard* [Qur. 99], *ilahukum al-takathur* [Qur. 102] once, *Ikhlas* seven or ten times and once recites this prayer: "There is no god but God, He alone, He has no partner; His is the kingdom and the praise; He gives life and death. He is the Living who never dies, full of beauty and generous with his right hand. He has power over everything. In the name of God, for the nation of the Messenger of God." After that he says, "O God, I have recited this recitation, and I have made the reward for it as a gift for the spirit of so-and-so son of so-and-so" (p. 10) One should not go to make pilgrimage to the sheikhs without sweets, roses, and flowers. If it is the tomb of his master, he makes an offering of gold there, and then conveys [something] to the descendants of the master and also some alms—a bit of gold—to the people residing there.[65]

Benefits of Pilgrimage on Friday

18. In the commentary on the *Sirat al-mustaqim*[66] it is written, "On Friday the spirits of the faithful are near their tombs, near in a real sense. The attachment is a spiritual connection; vision and contact are a connection that they have with their bodies. The pilgrims who come near the tombs realize (*shinasand*) this, though they always realize this, but on this day they realize it with a realization greater than the realization of the other days, from the point of view of being near the tombs. Undoubtedly the realization through nearness is better and stronger than the realization through distance." In some accounts it is said that realization at the beginning of the day is better than at the end, and therefore for this reason pilgrimage to tombs at this time is preferred and customary in the holy shrines.

---

[65] *Lata'if-i ashrafi* provides another half page (II, 30) on the benefits of pilgrimage.

[66] This is probably a work by 'Abd al-Haqq Dihlawi; cf. Ethé, no. 2656, cols. 1441–45.

Rules and Prayers of Pilgrimage, Continued

19. In the *Jawami` al-kalim* it is written that if someone goes to make pilgrimage to the tombs of the sheikhs, when he reaches the door he should say once or seven times, "Glory be to God," etc., and kissing the ground recite the *Fatiha* once pronouncing the name of God, the Throne Verse three times, *Idha zulzilat al-ard* once, *ilahukum al-takathur* seven times, *Ikhlas* ten times, and praise of the Prophet (*durud*) three times. According to the revered master Nizam al-Din (God sanctify his conscience), [one recites] the *Fatiha* and the Throne Verse once, *Ikhlas* twelve times, and praise of the Prophet ten times. After that one sits and recites what one has memorized from the Qur'an. Rising, one circumambulates the tomb seven times and makes a petition for whatever concern one has; otherwise one kisses the ground. The feet are turned away and one never shows one's back toward the revered one. At the time of pilgrimage, in coming and going one is vigilant and expectant regarding who enters and leaves one's thoughts and who remains and what they did. From left and right, from before and behind, [one watches for] what they said, and what voice called out. In the *Lata'if-i shami*[67] it is written, "When from the garden one passes into the realm of the graves, the group who are honored by the happiness of [divine] protection, one faces them and says once, 'Peace be unto the people of the region, the faithful and submitting; may God have mercy on those who came before us and those who follow; God willing, I am with you who are attached [to God],' and once 'O God, make a reward for all these who are visited, O Most Merciful one!'"

Spiritual Presence of the Saints

20. In the *Makhzan al-fawa'id*[68] it is written, "However much the spirit of the saint departs from the body both in expressions and relations, yet its influences nonetheless leave their mark on a place. Just as when musk is removed from a letter or tray, even so his [the saint's] perfume (p. 11) continues to linger in the place

[67] Not traced.

[68] Not traced.

to which he was related. Thus they have said, (verse): 'When someone becomes dust after reaching perfection,/the dust of his feet replaces the elixir.'" In this manner, therefore, when the pilgrim presents himself in pilgrimage to the shrine with its miraculous influences, with firm faith, trustworthy belief, necessary good conduct, manners of sanctity, and good behavior, the beneficent spirit of the master of the tomb is present. It is not in accord with purity (*dar khwar-i safa'i*), but sincere belief in terms of the pilgrim's state obtains aid and assistance, and brings about the production of happy fortune and the attainment of favors. If sometimes a kind of discrepancy appears in the order of necessary conduct, the pilgrim will be caught by the occasion for reproach. Such was the case when Sayyid `Ala' al-Din Jiwari one day went to make pilgrimage to Sheikh al-Islam, Khwajah Qutb al-Din. He sat down near the tomb of the sheikh, and from within a voice cried out, saying "Sayyid, you see me as dead; if I were living, could you sit in this way?" After only hearing these words, he arose from that place and sat down far away in good conduct.

21. It is written that when you walk over the graves of the saints, ask their help and seek resolution (*himmat*), entrust [yourself] to the Lord (*mawla bar gumari*) by the force of maintaining your conduct, so that you will never be able to recall the world's desire. A dervish walked on the earth over [the grave of] Abu al-Hasan Fushanji and prayed to God Most High for the world. That night he saw Abu al-Hasan in a dream, saying, "Dervish, when you come upon the earth over us, completely free yourself from both worlds, but if you want the world's goods, walk upon the ground over kings."

Respect for All the Dead

22. In the *Mir'at al-Asrar*[69] it is written, "Since the state of the dead is concealed and hidden, thus it is not known who among them is wretched (*shaqi*) and which is happy, nor whether the deceased was learned, an ignoramus, or perfect. But it may be that his name is from the names of God and His Messenger.[70]

[69] 'Abd al-Rahman Chishti, *Mir'at al-asrar,* MS 676, H. L. 204A-B, Khudabakhsh Oriental Public Library, Patna.

[70] Muslim names connected to God or the Prophet call forth blessings.

Thus maintaining good conduct and respect for the deceased is necessary and required in all times for all people; so it is conveyed, and the rewards and benefits of the *Fatiha* are many and uncounted. May God aid us and you."

Conclusion

23. The goal of this arrangement and the purpose of the book contained here [is to show] each of the dates of the months of the whole year, for perpetually enduring are the death anniversaries of these revered ones of lofty rank whose aid is sought, as also the generality of spirits of the noble saints and great sheikhs. If one [wishes to know] the date of the passing away and death anniversary of one of God's saints that is in accordance with past report (p. 12), or is verified now or in the future, whether from a book or from a trustworthy tongue, and is authenticated by the agreement of books or transmitters, he should test it in this *Book of Death Anniversaries* known as *The Treasury of Death Anniversaries.* Then by the blessing of the prophetic report (God bless him and give him peace), "whoso prescribes a good exemplary deed (*sanna sunna hasana*) has his reward and the reward of the one who performs it," may the author of this book also find a pleasure and share of the Last Day and its reward, with the help of God Most High. This noble and blessed text was collected and reached completion by the expansion of several authenticated texts, such as *The Book of Death Anniversaries* by the previously mentioned Sheikh Sharaf al-Din, which is from the sublime library of the exemplar of those united with God, the revered Sheikh Nizam al-Din [Awrangabadi] (God sanctify his dear conscience), which was transcribed the 24th of Rabi` I, 1128 hijri [17 March 1716], according to the direction of the revered sheikh (God sanctify his conscience). I later compared two texts from the blessed port of Surat and another text from Awrangabad, in the days when the lover of dervishes, the believer in their believers, Anwar al-Din Khan Bahadur[71] (may God Most High strengthen him with the strength of His acceptance) was in the army of Nizam al-Mulk

[71] On Anwar al-Din Khan (d. 1162/1749), see above, n. 22.

Bahadur Asaf Jah, on the 5th of Shawwal, in the 1156th year since the prophetic emigration [18 November 1743]. Praise belongs to God, the Lord of creation, and blessings and peace be on our master and Prophet, Muhammad, the best of Messengers, and on the people of his house and all his companions.

Appendix A

Further Practices of Pilgrimage in the *Adab al-talibin* of Muhammad Chishti[72]

If the master commands concentration (*tawajjuh*) on one of his own masters, how fortunate! When he goes on pilgrimage to the tomb, when he gets close to the tomb he should not walk too quickly nor too slowly, but moderately. If there is no difficulty, he circumambulates it, but should he not do so, there is nothing to worry about. While circumambulating he says "God is great," then the *Fatiha* or "Master, help, for so-and-so, (that is, the master) is for our good!" He takes the master's name, or the name of the master that he has been told, or the name of the master whose grace he wishes to partake of. At the time of reciting the *Fatiha*, he turns away from the direction of prayer and turns toward him [that is, the saint]. If there is no difficulty, then he kisses the tomb, and touches his face to the tomb to kiss it, or places his hand on his breast and then touches it. At the time of return, he takes three paces backwards and then turns his back upon him [the saint]. If one recites the *Fatiha* in this manner, it is good. First one recites praise of the Prophet, then praise of God (*al-hamd*), then the Throne Verse three times, then *Ilahukum al-takathur* seven times, then *Ikhlas* eleven times [fol. 22a], then praise of the Prophet. Should he not do it in this way, there is nothing to worry about. Circumambulation is not required. If he does it, he does it; if he does not do it, he does not. But one should attempt to watch carefully one's going and coming in the manner described. Yet if inadvertently or by necessity this does not occur, there is nothing to worry about.

72 *Adab al-talibin*, fols. 21b–22a; Urdu trans., pp. 61–63.

When one performs pilgrimage to the tomb of one's master, or the tomb of a master on whom one has been told to concentrate, or pilgrimage to a tomb of [a master] whose grace one wishes to partake of, one should state one's object (*maqsud*), and request their help. One should state this slowly, and at the time of reciting the *Fatiha* look neither to the left nor the right. Without permission, one should not be involved with anything near the saint, unless elsewhere is difficult. He recalls the suppression of breath as much as possible, that is, when he breathes in, he conceives that he breathes in with the phrase "there is no god (*la ilaha*)," and when he breathes out, he conceives that he breathes out with the phrase "but God (*illa allah*)." He thinks that "There is none worshipped but God (*lama`bud illa allah*)," or he thinks that "There is no object but God (*la maqsud illa allah*)," or he thinks that "There is no existent but God (*la mawjud illa allah*)." In praying, he takes delight in the Qur'an if it is recited, or else he remains silent. He thinks, "Worship your lord as though you see him, for if you do not see him, he surely sees you," which necessarily applies to him.

Appendix B

Qur'anic Citations in the *Makhzan-i a`ras*

(suras cited according to section number of the translation in which they appear)

1 (*Fatiha*): 5, 6 (4 times), 7 (4 times), 9, 10, 17, 19, (2 times), 22, Appendix A (4 times).
2:256 (Throne Verse): 7 (2 times), 9, 17, 19, (2 times), Appendix A.
94 (*A-lam nashrah*): 7.
99 (*Idha zulzilat al-ard*): 17, 19.
102 (*Ilahukum al-takathur*): 7 (2 times), 17, 19, Appendix A.
112 (*Ikhlas*): 7 (3 times), 9, 17, 19 (2 times), Appendix A.
113–114 (*Mu`awwadhatayn*): 7 (2 times).

13

The Stages of Love in Early Persian Sufism, from Rabi`a to Ruzbihan

Everyone acknowledges that love is hard to classify, but that has not kept people from trying to do so. Especially in a tradition like Persian Sufism, in which love is the subject of innumerable tributes, it has been impossible to resist the attempt to describe the character of love. The panorama of early Sufism in Persia offers many testimonies to love and its many moods and degrees. Mystical classifications of the stages of love differed from secular, legal, and philosophical analyses of love in that the Sufis consistently placed love in the context of their mystical psychology of "states" and "stations", with an emphasis on love as the transcendence of the self.[1] Moreover, love in its various forms was of such importance that it generally was recognized

[1] For secular, mystical, and legal classifications of love, see the tables in Joseph Norment Bell, *Love Theory in Later Hanbalite Islam* (Albany: State University of New York Press, 1978), pp. 157–60. Surveys of the literature are found in Hellmut Ritter, "Philologika VII: Arabische und persische Schriften über die profane und die mystische Liebe," *Der Islam* 21 (1933); Hellmut Ritter, *Das Meer der Seele: Mensch, Welt und Gott in den Geschichten des Fariduddin `Attr* (Leiden: E. J. Brill, 1978), esp. pp. 504–74; Lois Anita Giffen, *The Theory of Profane Love Among the Arabs: The Development of the Genre* (New York: New York University Press, 1971); and `Abd al-Rahman ibn Muhammad al-Ansari al-ma`ruf bi-Ibn al-Dabbagh, *Kitab mashariq anwar al-qulub wa māftih asrar al-ghuyub*, ed. H. Ritter (Beirut: Dar Sadir, Dar Bayrut, 1379/1959), Introduction, pp. ii–vi (in Arabic).

as "the highest goal of the stations and the loftiest summit of the stages", in Abu Hamid al-Ghazali's phrase.[2] The classifications of the stages of love according to the early Sufis differed in detail, but the fundamental emphasis throughout was on love as the most important form of the human-divine relationship. We can trace the historical development of the classifications of love in Persian Sufism in an almost direct line from its origins through Rabi`a of Basra to the summa of love by the sixth/twelfth-century Sufi of Shiraz, Ruzbihan Baqli. Throughout this development, we can see the gradual elaboration of many refinements, and even the intrusion of vocabulary from the secular philosophical tradition, but the fundamental emphasis is on love aspiring to union with God.

The problem of the classification of love's stages is inseparable from the larger theme of the states (*ahwal*) and stations (*maqamat*) in Sufism. Ultimately, the impulse to categorize goes back to the Qur'an, with its differentiation of souls in the eschaton, and the term *maq̄m* is fairly frequent in the Qur'an.[3] In Sufism, many commentators have noticed that this type of classification goes back at least to Dhu al-Nun the Egyptian (d. 246/861), who is credited with lists of 19 or eight stages, while in Iran, Yahya ibn Mu'adh (d. 258/872) spoke of seven or four.[4] Paul Nwyia has traced the Sufi concern with the structure of mystical experience to the sixth imam of the Shi`a, Ja`far al-Sadiq (d. 148/765), whose Qur'an commentary formed the basis for the Sufi exegesis of Dhu al-Nun. Ja`far al-Sadiq compiled three lists of stages, which analysed the spiritual itinerary toward the vision of the

---

[2] Abu Hamid al-Ghazali, *Ihya' `ulum al-din* (16 parts in 4 vols., Cairo: Dar al-Shu`ab, n.d.), p. 2570. Cf. Zayn al-Din Hamid Muhammad Ghazali Tusi, *Kitab-i kimiya-yi sa`adat*, ed. Ahmad Aram (2nd ed., Tehran: Kitabkhana-i wa Chapkhana-i Markazi, 1333/1955; reprint ed., Istanbul: Waqf al-Ikhlas, 1408/1366/1988), p. 850, where he calls love (*mahabba*) "the greatest of the stages."

[3] The term *maqam* occurs 14 times in the Qur'an. It hardly seems necessary to suppose with Massignon that this concept is a "philosophical intrusion" of Stoic origin; cf. Louis Massignon, *La Passion de Husayn Ibn Mansur Hallaj, martyr mystique de l'Islam exécuté Baghdad le 26 mars 922* (new ed., 4 vols., Paris: Gallimard, 1975), I, 390, n. 3.

[4] Massignon, *Passion*, I, 390, nn. 3–4; idem, *Essai sur les origenes du lexique technique de la mystique musulmane*, Études Musulmanes, 2 (new ed., Paris: Librairie Philosophique J. Vrin, 1968), p. 41; Annemarie Schimmel, *Mystical Dimensions of Islam* (Chapel Hill: University of North Carolina, 1975; New Delhi: Yoda Press, 2009), p. 100.

face of God: the 12 springs of gnosis, the 12 constellations of the heart, and the 40 lights deriving from the light of God. As Nwyia pointed out, the order and selection of the terms included in the different lists vary considerably, indicating that the stages of the soul's progress were far from being fixed at this time.[5] Yet it is significant that stages of love occupied prominent positions in Ja`far al-Sadiq's lists: love (*mahabba*) and intimacy (*uns*) are the 11th and 12th of the 12 springs of gnosis, while love (*mahabba*), longing (*shawq*), and ravishing (*walah*) are the last three constellations of the heart. For the sake of illustration, Ja`far's second list reads as follows:

> Heaven is called "heaven" due to its loftiness. The heart is a heaven, since it ascends by faith and gnosis without limit or restriction. Just as "the known" [i.e., God] is unlimited, so the gnosis of it is unlimited. The zodiacal signs of heaven are the courses of the sun and moon, and they are Aries, Taurus, Gemini, Cancer, Leo, Virgo, Libra, Cancer, Sagittarius, Capricorn, Aquarius, and Pisces. In the heart there are zodiacal signs, and they are:
>
> 1. the sign of faith (*iman*);
> 2. the sign of gnosis (*ma`rifa*);
> 3. the sign of intellect (*`aql*);
> 4. the sign of certainty (*yaqin*);[6]
> 5. the sign of submission (*islam*);
> 6. the sign of beneficence (*ihsan*);
> 7. the sign of trust in God (*tawakkul*);
> 8. the sign of fear (*khawf*);
> 9. the sign of hope (*raja'*);
> 10. the sign of love (*mahabba*);
> 11. the sign of longing (*shawq*);
> 12. the sign of ravishing (*walah*).

It is by these 12 zodiacal signs that the heart remains good, just as it is by the 12 zodiacal signs, from Aries and Taurus to the end, that the evanescent world and its people are good.[7]

---

[5] Paul Nwyia, Exégèse *coranique et langage mystique, Nouvel essai sur le lexique technique des mystiques musulmanes*, Recherches publiées sous la direction de l'Institut de Lettres Orientales de Beyrouth, Série I: Pensée arabe et musulmane, vol. XLIX (Beirut: Dar el-Machreq Éditeurs, 1970), pp. 170–73.

[6] The Berlin MS has here instead "soul (*nafs*)," corresponding to no. 8 on the list of Hallaj, given below.

[7] Paul Nwyia, "Le Tafsir Mystique attribué à Ga'far Sadiq: Étion critique," *Méanges de l'université Saint-Joseph* XLIII/4 (1968), pp. 35–36, commenting on Qur. 25:61; Nwyia has summarized the text in his *Exégèse coranique*, pp. 171–72. The Arabic text is also given by

If it is correct to see a progression or ascent in this early classification, then the stages of love occupy an important, not to say pre-eminent, position in the spiritual experience of the soul.

The elevation of the love of God to a supreme level in Sufism has most often been connected to Rabi`a al-`Adawiyya (d. 185/801), the famous woman saint of Basra. An early Sufi ascetic of the so-called school of Basra, `Abd al-Wahid ibn Zayd in the seventh century, had introduced the non-Qur'anic term *`ishq* or "passionate love" to describe the divine-human relationship.[8] Another Basran, Rabah al-Qaysi, used the term *khulla* or "friendship".[9] But it is especially Rabi`a who has gained fame as the one who distinguished between the selfish lover of God who seeks paradise and the selfless lover who thinks only of the divine beloved. For her, love (*hubb* or *mahabba*) meant concentration on God to the exclusion of all else. When Sufyan al-Thawri asked Rabi`a what was the reality of her faith, she replied, "I have not worshipped Him from fear of His fire, nor for love of His garden, so that I should be like a lowly hireling; rather, I have worshipped Him for love of Him and longing for Him."[10] Her oft-quoted distinction between the "two loves", a selfish love seeking paradise and a selfless love seeking God's pleasure, is the fundamental beginning point in the understanding of the stages of love.[11] She wrote,

> I love You with two loves: a selfish love
> and a love of which You are worthy.
> That love which is a selfish love
> is my remembrance of You and nothing else.
> But as for the love of which You are worthy—
> Ah, then You've torn the veils for me so I see You.

Ruzbihan al-Baqli, *Tafsir `ara'is al-bayan* (Lucknow: Nawal Kishor, 1301/1883–4), II, 98; Ruzbihan al-Baqli, *`Ara'is al-bayan,* MS 864 Sprenger, Staatsbibliothek, Berlin, fol. 272a. I am indebted to Alan Godlas for supplying these references.

[8] Massignon, *Essai*, p. 214.

[9] Ibid., p. 217.

[10] Rabi`a, in Ghazali, Ihya, IV, 2598.

[11] Schimmel, *Dimensions*, pp. 38–40; Massignon, *Essai*, p. 216; Marijan Molé, *Les Mystiques Musulmans* (Paris: Les Deux Océans, 1982), p. 41; Roger Arnaldez, *Réflexions chrétiennes sur la mystique musulmane* (Paris: O.E.I.L., 1989), p. 233; G.-C. Anawati and Louis Gardet, *Mystique musulmane, Aspects et tendances - Expériences et techniques*, Études Musulmanes, VIII (4th ed., Paris: Librairie Philosophique J. Vrin, 1986), pp. 26–27, 162–70.

There is no praise for me in either love,
but praise is Yours in this love and in that.[12]

Although she did not go into detail regarding the analysis of love beyond this basic distinction, the great Andalusian Sufi Ibn `Arabi remarked of Rabi`a, that "she is the one who analyses and classes the categories of love to the point of being the most famous interpreter of love."[13] Although the poems and anecdotes that have come down to us concerning her are related by authors of later periods, it is striking that the Sufi tradition unanimously credits Rabi`a with these insights into love and regards her as the example of the pure lover of God.[14] Regardless of the difficulty of ascertaining her exact formulations, we may still invoke Rabi`a as the figure who stands for the first intensive meditations on the nature of mystical love in Islam.

The earliest Persian Sufis developed further the distinction between the selfish love of God that seeks paradise and the love of God for his own sake. Shaqiq al-Balkhi (d. 194/810), an early Sufi of Khurasan, was especially interested in psychological classification. Of him Sulami (d. 412/1021) remarked, "I believe that he was the first to speak of the sciences of the states (*ahwal*) in the districts of Khurasan."[15] In a small treatise on worship, *Adab al-`ibadat* ("The Manners of Worship"), Shaqiq gave one of the earliest descriptions in Sufi literature

---

[12] Rabi`a, in Ghazali, Ihya', IV, 2598. Gardet, p. 165, n. 20, cites Kalabadhi (d. 385/995) and Abu Talib al-Makki (d. 386/996) as transmitters of this poem with a variant reading in the second half of the third line: "Would that I see no more creatures, but see You!"

[13] Ibn `Arabi, *Traité de l'amour*, trans. Maurice Gloton (Paris: Albin Michel, 1986), p. 247 (from *al-Futuhat al-makkiyya*, chapter 115).

[14] Rabi`a was the subject of a biography by the Hanbali scholar Ibn al-Jawzi (d. 597/1200) (Massignon, *Essai*, p. 239), and her story was told by European Christians in the thirteenth and seventeenth centuries as a model of true charity (Gardet, p. 167, nn. 25–26; Schimmel, p. 8). Modern tributes to her include the well-known monograph by Margaret Smith, *Rabi`ah the Mystic and Her Fellow-Saints in Islam* (Cambridge: Cambridge University Press, 1928); `Abd al-Rahman al-Badawi, *Shahidat al-`ishq al-ilahi, Rabi`a al-`Adawiyya*, Darasat Islamiyya, no. 8 (Cairo: al-Nahda, 1946); a hagiography by Widad el Sakkakini, *First Among Sufis, The Life and Thought of Rabia al-Adawiyya, the Woman Saint of Basra*, trans. Nabil Safwat (London: The Octagon Press, 1982); and re-workings of English translations of her poetry by Charles Upton, *Doorkeeper of the Heart, Versions of Rabi`a* (Putney, VT: Threshold Books, 1988).

[15] Abu `Abd al-Rahman al-Sulami, *Tabaqat al-Sufiyya*, ed. Nur al-Din Shariba (Cairo: Maktabat al-Khanji, 1406/1986), p. 61.

of the progress of the soul through different abodes (*mañzil*). These abodes are four: asceticism (*zuhd*), fear (*khawf*), longing for paradise (*shawq ila al-janna*), and love of God (*mahabba lillah*). This classification is evidently very archaic. Shaqiq describes each stage in terms of a forty-day retreat, and for the first two abodes he gives details of the discipline of appetite and emotion, and of the illuminations of divine grace bestowed on the aspirant. The third abode calls for meditation on the delights of paradise to such an extent that by the 40th day one has forgotten about the previous stages and possesses a happiness that no misfortune can disturb.[16]

Although many enter the abodes of asceticism, fear, and longing for paradise, according to Shaqiq, not all enter the abode of love, which is the highest station. Those purified ones whom God brings to this abode have their hearts filled with the light of love and forget the previous stations; the light of divine love eclipses the other experiences, as the rising sun makes the moon and stars invisible. The essence of the experience of the love of God is that it is absolute and exclusive devotion, leaving room for nothing else in the heart.[17] It is especially noteworthy that in this classification, the term longing (*shawq*) is here reserved for longing for paradise, while in later discussions of love it is another mode of the soul's desire for God. It seems that the early Sufis' concern with establishing the primacy of the love of God succeeded in excluding the desire for paradise as a legitimate goal of mysticism; henceforth, longing can only be directed toward God.

It is difficult to trace out the precise development of Sufi teachings about love's stages from this point, but it is clear that the Baghdadian Sufis in the third/ninth century devoted much attention to this topic. As we can tell by his nickname, "the lover," Sumnun al-Muhibb (d. 287/900) is reported to have

---

[16] Shaqiq al-Balkhi, *Adab al-`ibadat*, in *Trois œuvres inédites de mystiques musulmans: Shaqiq al-Balkhi, Ibn `Ata, Niffari*, ed. Paul Nwyia, Recherches, Collection publiée sous la direction de la Faculté des Lettres et des Sciences Humaines de l'Université Saint-Joseph, Beyrouth, Série I: Pensée arabe et musulmane, vol. VII (2nd ed., Beirut: Dar el-Machreq Éditeurs SARL, 1982), pp. 17–20. Nwyia has analysed this passage at length in his *Exégèse*, pp. 213–31.

[17] Ibid., pp. 20–21.

raised love to the highest position in his teaching. In a testimony preserved by the Ghaznavid master `Ali Hujwiri (d. 465/1072), Sumnun described love as the highest and most comprehensive of spiritual states. "Love is the principle and foundation of the path to God Most High. The states and stations are abodes [all related to love]; in whichever abode the seeker resides, it is appropriate that it should end, except for the stage of love. In no way is it appropriate that this should come to an end, as long as the path exists."[18] Hujwiri comments that all other shaykhs agree with Sumnun in this matter, though they may use a different terminology out of prudence.

Among the Baghdadian Sufis, Hallaj (d. 309/922) also placed a particular emphasis on love as a quality of God, with what some have perceived as a philosophical emphasis.[19] Louis Massignon pointed out that Hallaj, in a passage recorded by Sulami, had described a list of psychological states and stages in which the final items are clearly related to love; this list is closely related to Ja`far al-Sadiq's list of "constellations of the heart," described above. In this passage, Hallaj proposes a test for the sincerity of spiritual claims, juxtaposing each moment (*waqt*) of inner experience with the practices and qualities that are required of one who claims it:

> And among their manners is striving in the gnosis of claims (*da'awi*)[20] and seeking [to attain] every moment with the manners [of the state] announced by the one who claims that moment. Husayn ibn Masur said,

---

[18] Sumnun al-Muhibb, in Abu al-Hasan `Ali ibn `Uthman al-Jullabi al-Hujwiri al-Ghaznawi al-Lahawri, *Kashf al-mahjub*, ed. `Ali Qawim (Islamabad: Markaz-i Tahqiqat-i Farsi-i Iran o Pakistan, 1398/1978), pp. 269–70. The phrase in brackets is missing from the Islamabad edition, but an old lithograph edition reads "the states and stages are abodes equally related to it [i.e., love]; cf. *Kashf al-mahjub-i farsi*, ed. Ahmad `Ali Shah (Lahore: Ilahi Bakhsh Muhammad Jalal al-Din, 1342/1923), p. 240. `Attar preserves a similar reading of this saying: "The states and stages all are related to love-play"; cf. Abu Hamid Muhammad ibn Abi Bakr Ibrahim Farid al-Din `Attar Nishapuri, *Kitab tadhkirat al-awliya'*, ed. Muhammad Khan Qazwini (2 vols., 5th ed., Tehran: Intisharat-i Markazi, n.d.), II, 69.

[19] I have briefly discussed this problem in "Ruzbihan Baqli on Love as 'Essential Desire,'" in *God is Beautiful and Loves Beauty: Essays presented to Annemarie Schimmel*, ed. J.-C. Burgel and Alma Giese (Leiden: Peter Lang, forthcoming).

[20] The term *da`wa* has been defined as follows: "The claim (*da`wa*) is the relationship of the soul with something that is not its station. But in reality, it is the manifestation

1. One who claims (da'i) faith (*iman*) needs (yad' u ila) guidance (*rushd*).
2. One who claims submission (*islam*) needs morals (*akhlaq*).
3. One who claims beneficence (*ihsan*) needs witnessing (*mushahada*).
4. One who claims understanding (*fahm*) needs abundance (*ziyada*).
5. One who claims intellect (`*aql*) needs taste (*madhaq*).
6. One who claims learning (`*ilm*) needs audition (*sama*`).
7. One who claims gnosis (*ma`rifa*) needs spirit, peace, and fragrance (*al-ruh wa al-raha wa al-ra'iha*).
8. One who claims the soul (*nafs*) needs worship (`*ibada*).
9. One who claims trust in God (*tawakkul*) needs confidence (*thiqa*).
10. One who claims fear (*khawf*) needs agitation (*inzi'aj*).
11. One who claims hope (*raja*) needs quietude (*tama'nina*).
12. One who claims love (*mahabba*) needs longing (*shawq*).
13. One who claims longing (*shawq*) needs ravishing (*walah*).
14. One who claims ravishing (*walah*) needs God (*allah*).

And one who has nothing remaining (*da`iyya*) from these claims will fail; he is among those who roam in the deserts of astonishment. And God is with the one who does not worry."[21]

Massignon rightly observed that Ja`far al-Sadiq's list partially duplicates that of Sadiq; the last six terms in both lists are identical, and the first six terms in Ja`far's list are (with one exception) duplicated in a different order in Hallaj's list.[22]

In comparing the lists of Ja`far's constellations and Hallaj's spiritual claims, one may ask how similar their purposes are. In terms of Sufi terminology, both lists belong largely to the category of states (*ahwal*) rather than stations (*maqamat*).[23] Hallaj's

---

of boldness (*jur'at*) with the quality of discovering reality" (Ruzbihan Baqli Shirazi, *Sharh-i shathiyyat*, ed. Henry Corbin, Bibliothèque Iranienne 12 [Tehran: Departement d'iranologie de l'Institut Franco-iranien, 1966], p. 572).

[21] Hallaj, in Abu `Abd al-Rahman al-Sulami, *Jawami adab al-sufiyya*, ed. Etan Kohlberg, Max Schloessinger Memorial Series, Texts 1 (Jerusalem: Jerusalem Academic Press, 1976), p. 61, para. 156; also reproduced from an Istanbul MS by Massignon, *Essai*, pp. 428–49, no. 8, omitting the eighth category and miscopying some words. Oddly, Massignon hastily described the remaining 13 terms as 12, stating that they are identical to the list of 12 psychological constellations enumerated by Ja`far al-Sadiq. Massignon speculated (*Passion*, I, 394, n. 4) that this text was transmitted by Ibn `Ata'.

[22] If the Berlin variant is followed, all of the first six terms in Ja`far's list occur in that of Hallaj.

[23] E.g., Sarraj lists four of these terms (*mahabba, khawf, raja', shawq*) as nos. 2–5 of the nine *ahwal* that he enumerates, while only one (*tawakkul*) occurs in his list of stages. Cf. Abu Nasr `Abdallah B. `Al al- Sarraj al-Tusi, *The Kitab al-Luma` fi 'l-Tasawwuf*, ed. Reynold

list seems more clearly to represent an ascending series, since it culminates in God. It complicates the basic list of states by making each state that one claims dependent on other attainments. The last terms in the series link up, so that the 12th, *mahabba*, depends on the 13th, *shawq*, which in turn depends on the 14th, *walah*. In contrast, Ja`far's list of states is structured in a simpler form in terms of the zodiacal signs. Each of these states is a constellation in the heaven of the heart, and forms a mode of relation to God. The states are essentially unlimited, since the object to which they are related (God) is unlimited. Like the zodiacal constellations in heaven, the states of the heart are the means of regulating order, in this case in the psychic microcosm, conceived of as orbiting around God. Hallaj's 14 spiritual claims appear to be a kind of commentary and expansion on the earlier list, explaining the human efforts or divine gifts that are prerequisites for these spiritual states. The two categories that he added to Ja`far al-Sadiq's list are *`ilm* and *fahm*, religious knowledge and understanding, both of which pertain to the realm of knowledge. But Hallaj recognized the extraordinary character of the last three stages relating to love; they are linked together, and the last stage, ravishing (*walah*), depends only on God. In this articulation of the stages of love, Hallaj adapted the scripturally based formulation of Ja`far al-Sadiq to illustrate and further emphasize the supreme position that love holds among the spiritual degrees.

Chronologically the next well-known analysis of love that pertains to Persian Sufism is that of Abu al-Hasan al-Daylami, a scholar of the late fourth/tenth century who followed the tradition of the Sufi shaykh Ibn al-Khafif of Shiraz (d. 371/981).[24] At the same time, however, Daylami participated in the Greco-Arabic philosophical tradition, probably through the circle of the philosopher Abu Hayyan al-Tawhidi. Daylami is the author

---

Alleyne Nicholson, "E. J. W. Gibb Memorial" Series, vol. XXII (London, 1914; reprint ed., London: Luzac & Company Ltd., 1963), pp. 41–71, esp. pp. 51–52, 57–64.

[24] Ibn al-Khafif evidently wrote two treatises on love, a *Kitab al-wudd* and a *Kitab al-mahabba*, but these are lost; see Abu al-Hasan Daylami, *Sirat-i shaykh-i kabir Abu `Abd Allah ibn Khafif Shirazi*, Persian trans. Rukn al-Din Yahya ibn Junayd Shirazi, ed. Annemarie Schimmel (Ankara, 1955; reprint ed., Tehran: Intisharat-i Babak, 1363/1984), Introduction, p. 28.

of the *Kitab `atf al-alif al-ma'luf `ala al-lam al-ma`tuf* ("The Book of the Inclination of the Familiar *Alif* toward the Inclined *Lam*"), a treatise on love, known from a unique manuscript, that draws on Sufism, philosophy, and Arabic court culture (*adab*). In the course of this treatise, Daylami has produced a list devoted exclusively to the stages of love, using the distinctive Sufi term "station (*maqam*)" to describe them. He describes these stages as 10, as follows:

1. *ulfa* or familiarity;
2. *uns* or intimacy;
3. *wudd* or affection
4. *mahabba haqiqiyya duna al-majaziyya* or real love without metaphorical (i.e., physical) love;
5. *khulla* or friendship;
6. *sha`af* or excessive love;
7. *shaghaf* or infatuation;
8. *istihtar* or recklessness;
9. *walah* or ravishing;
10. *hayaman* or bewilderment

These 10 categories are completed by an 11th, *`ishq* or passionate love, as a comprehensive term for exclusive devotion to the beloved.[25] Daylami succeeds in fine-tuning the gradations of love with an unmistakeable increase in energy and intensity in the progression of 10 stages. He preserves terms central to the Sufi vocabulary of love, such as *mahabba*, *uns*, and *walah*, and he has also put the hitherto controversial term *`ishq* at the heart of the discussion. Daylami in fact credits Hallaj with being the Sufi who was closest to the philosophers in speaking of *`ishq* as being the essence of God.[26] Another spirit breathes through this classification, however, recalling the court poetry of the `Abbasid age; not only are some of the terms unfamiliar in Sufi contexts, but in every instance, Daylami also gives learned etymologies and specimens from classical Arabic poetry, including several

[25] Abu l Hasan `Ali b. Muhammad al Daylami, *Kitab `atf al alif al ma'luf `ala l-lam al ma`luf [sic]*, ed. J. C. Vadet, Textes et Traductions d'Auteurs Orientaux, vol. 20 (Cairo: Institut Français d'Archéologie Orientale, 1962), pp. 20–24.

[26] Daylami, p. 25. See my previously cited article (above, n. 19) for more on this topic.

attributed to Majnun, to illustrate the overtones of each of the 10 terms. The title of his treatise, with its learned reference to the calligraphic properties of the letters *alif* and *lam*, further indicates the literary character of his approach. In addition, by separating the stations of love from the rest of the spiritual stations, Daylami has removed love from its Sufi context. His list of definitions and categorizations of love resembles instead the learned discussions that commonly took place in philosophical circles.[27] While this admittedly eclectic and partially secular work does not appear at first sight central to Persian Sufism, its sections on Sufi attitudes to love preserve some important testimonies, and it survived in the Shiraz tradition and was appropriated by Ruzbihan Baqli, as we shall see.[28] The significance of Daylami's arrangement is as a systematic classification of love uniting the tendencies of Sufism, philosophy, and court culture.

The important apologetic works and instruction manuals of Iranian Sufis in the fifth/eleventh century continued to elaborate on love in terms of the states and stations. Abu al-Qasim al-Qushayri (d. 465/1072), in his famous handbook on Sufism, listed love (*mahabba*) and longing (*shawq*) as the 49th and 50th of his 50 stations.[29] Qushayri's understanding of longing was complex; it was not simply a deprivation from the presence of the beloved. Longing for the vision of the divine countenance, in his view, was so intense that it could only continue in the encounter with God.[30] `Abd Allah Ansari (d. 481/1089), in his early Persian work *Sad maydan* ("One Hundred Fields"), regarded love as the comprehensive principle of spiritual progress. He concluded that "These one hundred 'fields' are all submerged in the field of love (*mahabba*)." Love itself he divided into the three degrees of

---

[27] Joel L. Kraemer, *Philosophy in the Renaissance of Islam: Abu Sulayman al-Sijistani and his Circle* (Leiden: E. J. Brill, 1986), pp. 52–53.

[28] See especially Daylami, pp. 32–36, 42–45, 68–71, 84–88 for quotations from Sufi authorities on love.

[29] Abu al-Qasim `Abd al-Karim al-Qushayri, *al-Risala al-Qushayriyya*, ed. `Abd al-Halim Mahmud and Mahmud ibn al-Sharif, 2 vols. continuously paginated (Cairo: Dar al-Kutub al-Haditha, 1972–74), II, 610–33.

[30] Ibid., II, 627.

uprightness (*rasti*), intoxication (*masti*), and nothingness (*nisti*).[31] In his later treatise on one hundred stations, *Manazil al-sa'irin* ("Abodes of the Wayfarers"), he downgraded the stations of love somewhat, for the purposes of instruction; love (*mahabba*) was now number 61, longing (*shawq*) was number 63, and bewilderment (*hayaman*) number 68. This shift of emphasis has been convincingly explained as a result of Ansari's strong insistence that the beginner focus on the annihilation (*fana'*) of the ego and the incomparability of the divine unity (*tawhid*). Love and longing are stages which still imply the existence of the lover, at least as far as the novice is concerned.[32] For the elite, however, "their love is their annihilation in the love of the Real, because all loves become invisible in the love of God, by His loving (*ihbab*)."[33]

The Seljuk era also saw the emergence of treatises especially devoted to love or placing great emphasis on it, although these works were often poetic and diffuse, in contrast to the more systematic Sufi handbooks. The best-known of these is the *Sawanih* of Ahmad Ghazali (d. 517/1123), brother of the famous theologian. Ritter described this as one of the most original writings on love produced in the Islamic world, yet he also confessed that its content was remarkably obscure.[34] Pourjavady, who recently translated and commented on this text, remarked with some understatement that Ghazali "does not express his ideas in a very systematic fashion."[35] *Sawanih* is in fact of a highly refined and allusive character, intended for a restricted audience, and it

---

[31] `Abd Allah Ansari, *Manazil al-sa'irin*, Arabic text ed. with Persian trans. by Ravan Farhadi (Tehran: Intisharat-i Mawlī, 1361/1982), p. 413.

[32] Ansari clarified this point in his *`Ilal al-maqamat* ("The Flaws of the Stations"), a text written in response to questions concerning the *Manazil al-sa'irin*; cf. *`Ilal al-maqamat*, quoted in *Manazil al-sa'irin*, pp. 413–14, and Bell, pp. 171–72.

[33] Farhadi describes this passage as "from the end of the treatise about love"; cf. *Manazil al-sa'irin*, p. 415, remark no. 4 (appended to the Persian translation of the section on *mahabba* from *`Ilal al-maqamat*).

[34] *Ahmad Ghazzali's Aphorismen uber die Liebe*, ed. Hellmut Ritter, Bibliotheca Islamica 15 (Istanbul: Staatsdruckerei, 1942), Introduction, pp. i–ii.

[35] Ahmad Ghazzali, *Sawanih, Inspirations from the World of Pure Spirits, The Oldest Persian Sufi Treatise on Love*, trans. Nasrollah Pourjavady (London: KPI, 1986), p. 6. One may note that a number of Indian Sufis wrote commentaries on the *Sawanih*, including Husayn Nagawri, as cited in `Abd al-Haqq Muhaddith Dihlawi al-Bukhari, *Akhbar al-akhyar fi asrar al-abrar*, ed. Muhammad `Abd al-Ahad, (Delhi: Matba`-i Mujtaba'i, 1332/1913–14) p. 177; and `Abd al-Karim Lahawri, *Sharh-i Sawanih*, MS 218 Persian, Jamia Millia Islamia, New Delhi.

makes no attempt to analyze love in terms of a system of stages. It is, rather, a kind of phenomenology and psychology of the human-divine love relationship, expressing that love with a rich symbolism; it presupposes the density of the Sufi literary and mystical tradition, but without ostentation.

Ghazali's disciple `Ayn al-Qudat Hamadani (d. 525/1131), the Sufi martyr, devoted several memorable passages in the sixth chapter of his *Tamhidat* to meditations on love, which are worth noting as an example of this freer style of expression. He identifies love as a religious requirement (*far*), since it brings humanity to God.[36] Like earlier Sufis, he makes a distinction between seeking heaven and seeking the love of God. He maintains that heaven as a separate state is a prison for the spiritual elite; properly speaking, God is himself the highest heaven.[37] Not a systematizer, `Ayn al-Qudat divides love (*`ishq*) into only three categories:[38]

1. the lesser love (*`ishq-i saghir*), which is our love for God;
2. the greater love, (*`ishq-i kabir*)which is God's love for Himself—it has no trace by which it can be recognized, and because of its surpassing beauty it is describable only by cypher and parable (*ba-ramzi o mithali*);[39]
3. the in-between or mutual love (*`ishq-i miyana*), which he also despairs of describing—in it one at first finds a difference between witnesser and witnessed, until it reaches the limit, when they become one.[40]

The various manifestations of the beloved's face, symbolized by Qur'anic passages, should be considered as many stations, not one.[41] But `Ayn al-Qudat is not interested in giving a detailed account of these stations. He only mentions that the first station

36 Abu al-Ma'ali `Abd Allah ibn Muhammad ibn `Ali ibn al-Hasan ibn `Ali al-Miyanji al-Hamadani mulaqqab ba-`Ayn al-Qudat, *Tamhidat*, ed. `Afif `Usayran, Intisharat-i Danishgah-i Tihran, 695 (Tehran: Chapkhana-i Danishgah, 1341/1962), pp. 96–97.

37 `Ayn al-Qudat, pp. 111, 135–37.

38 `Ayn al-Qudat, p. 101.

39 `Ayn al-Qudat, pp. 123–25.

40 `Ayn al-Qudat, p. 115.

41 `Ayn al-Qudat, p. 127.

of love is astonishment (*tahayyur*).[42] `Ayn al-Qudat's main concern is the state of mutual love between God and human, when the Qur'anic phrase "He loves them and they love Him" (*yuhibbuhum wa yuhibbunahu*, Qur. 5:54) becomes fulfilled. Experiencing this mutuality of love is like basking in the splendor of the cosmic sun, which is revealed in Qur'anic phrases that become seclusion retreats for the meditating soul.[43] At that point the essence of the intimate relationship between God and the soul is revealed to be love: "Did you know that the unique Essence of Might has a characteristic, and that characteristic (*`arad*) is nothing but passionate love? . . . God's love becomes the substance (*jawhar*) of the [human] soul, and our love becomes the characteristic of His existence."[44]

But it is with Ruzbihan Baqli (d. 606/1209) that we meet perhaps the most striking articulation of the stages of love in early Persian Sufism. Ruzbihan composed his Persian treatise *`Abhar al-ashiqin* ("The Jasmine of the Lovers") at the request of a female interlocutor, to decide the question of whether it is legitimate to describe God in terms of passionate love (*`ishq*); modern scholars like Corbin have speculated that this woman may have been the beautiful singer with whom Ruzbihan is supposed to have fallen in love during a sojourn in Mecca.[45] There are many aspects of this treatise deserving of comment and analysis, but for purposes of this discussion, two passages stand out. The first is Ruzbihan's brief recapitulation of Daylami's list of the stages of love, with some alterations; the second section is the lengthy description of Ruzbihan's own list of the stations of love. As Takeshita has shown, Ruzbihan incorporated a little less than one-sixth of

---

[42] `Ayn al-Qudat, p. 109.

[43] `Ayn al-Qudat, p. 128, where the following verse summarizes this state:

> Last night my idol placed his hand upon my breast,
> seized me hard and put a slave-ring in my ear.
> I said, "My beloved, I am crying from your love!"
> He pressed his lips on mine and silenced me.

[44] `Ayn al-Qudat, p. 112.

[45] Ruzbihan Baqli Shirazi, *`Abhar al-ashiqin*, ed. Henry Corbin and Muhammad Mu`in, Bibliothéque Iranienne, 8 (Tehran: Institut Français d'Iranologie de Téhéran, 1958; reprint ed., Tehran: Intisharat-i Manuchihri, 1365/1981), Introduction, p. 109, citing the report of Ibn al-`Arabi, *Kitab al-futuhat al-Makkiyya* (Cairo, 1329), II, 315.

Daylami's *`Atf al-alif* into the *`Abhar al-ashiqin*, and this list of 10 stations occupies a couple of pages in Ruzbihan's sixth chapter, on the nature of human love.[46] Actually Ruzbihan has abridged Daylami's list considerably, leaving out the samples of Arabic poetry for six of the 10 terms, and omitting one term (*istihtar*) altogether. Then, almost as an afterthought, he has added, with minimal explanation, three extra terms not employed by Daylami: *hayajan* or agitation, *`atsh* or thirst, and *shawq* or longing. As we have already seen, Daylami's list of 10 terms belongs more to the philosophical and courtly tradition than to Sufism. What is the significance of its presence here, in this form? The context indicates that Ruzbihan is using Daylami's list to illustrate the character of mundane human love.

The list of the stages of love follows on a somewhat obscure cosmological discussion, in which Ruzbihan describes four principles of love analogous to the four elements of nature. These principles appear to be: 1) the natural capacity of the body to receive spiritual influence; 2) uniting with the spiritual light; 3) love being constituted as the capacity of the lover to perceive beauty; and 4) beauty coming into actual relation with the lover's eye to create the unity of love, differentiated into lover and beloved.[47] The result of these four principles is that the lover seeks the beloved through the senses and then slowly ascends through the stations of love until reaching perfection. Now, the 11 stations of love that Ruzbihan has elaborated on the basis of Daylami's are only the beginning of the lover's progress; Ruzbihan describes them as rivulets leading to the sea of love. Then comes presence and absence, sobriety and intoxication, and a multitude of qualities for which love is the overarching rubric. But all this is still in the realm of human love, contemplating the works of the Creator, in the beginning of love. The philosophical categories of love borrowed from Daylami are still unpurified and contain the flaws (*`ilal*) of the carnal self. Natural

---

[46] *`Abhar*, pp. 40–41; cf. Masataka Takeshita, "Continuity and Change in the Tradition of Shirazi Love Mysticism—A Comparison between Daylami's *`Atf al-Alif* and Ruzbihan Baqli's *`Abhar al-ashiqin*," *Orient* XXIII (1987), pp. 113–31, esp. pp. 118–19.

[47] *`Abhar*, pp. 38–39. Although Takeshita remarks that Ruzbihan does not name these four "elements" in this admittedly obscure passage, the anonymous Persian commentary (*`Abhar*, p. 154) helps to clarify it along the lines suggested here.

love, the lowest form, can nonetheless be first spiritualized and then divinized.[48] The context indicates that Ruzbihan has reinserted Daylami's philosophical categories into a Sufi teaching.[49] Like Platonic *eros*, philosophical *`ishq* provides the energy that can be transformed and purified by the spiritual path. But that will come later.

In the last quarter of the *`Abhar al-ashiqin*, from chapters 19 to 32, Ruzbihan describes the mystical ascent to perfect love. This progress consists of 12 stations:

1. *`ubudiyyat* or servanthood
2. *wilayat* or sainthood
3. *muraqabat* or meditation
4. *khawf* or fear
5. *raja'* or hope
6. *wajd* or finding
7. *yaqin* or certainty
8. *qurbat* or nearness
9. *mukashafa* or unveiling
10. *mushahada* or witnessing
11. *mahabbat* or love
12. *shawq* or longing

These 12 stations are followed by "the highest rank, universal love (*`ishq-i kulli*), which is the goal of the spirit."[50] Ruzbihan has elaborated on the meaning of each station in a comprehensive and even practical way, although he often complicates his points with his distinctive style of metaphoric overflow. His explanations invoke specific Qur'anic verses that are seen as the loci

---

[48] *`Abhar*, pp. 42–43.

[49] Ruzbihan has appropriated philosophic views on love from Daylami into another of his writings. In his treatise on one thousand and one spiritual states, Ruzbihan quoted the pre-Socratic philosopher Heraclitus (via Daylami) on the nature of *`ishq*: "The Creator makes space for the souls in all creation so that they gaze on His pure light, which emerges from the substance of the Real. And at that time their passionate love (*`ishq*) and longing becomes intense and does not ever cease." Cf. Abu Muhammad Ruzbihan al-Baqli al-Shirazi, *Kitab mashrab al-arwah*, ed. Nazif Muharram Khwaja (Istanbul: Matba'at Kulliyat al-Adab, 1973), p. 135, corrected according to Daylami, *`Atf*, p. 25.

[50] *`Abhar*, p. 100. The stations are described on pp. 101–48.

of particular spiritual experiences. We may briefly summarize his descriptions of these stations as follows. Servanthood consists of the practices of spiritual discipline such as *dhikr* prayer, silence, and fasting, in order to purify one's character. Sainthood includes such qualities as repentance (*tawba*), piety (*wara`*), and asceticism (*zuhd*). Meditation is based on the control of random thoughts and seeing one's true nature. Fear is a kind of purifying fire that instills the manners of the prophets, although it is a deception if it alienates one from the beloved. Then hope is the cure, leading to the springtime of the soul. "Finding" is encountering the nearness of the beloved (Ruzbihan notes that he has explained its varieties in a work for novices, the *Risalat al-quds* or "Treatise on the Holy"). The certainty of the elite is something beyond the unshakeable faith that is the certainty of the ordinary person; it is a direct perception of divine attributes in the heart. Nearness is an ascent to the divine presence in an increasingly intensive transcendence, which Ruzbihan describes in a characteristic image as the burning of the wings of a bird in flight.[51] Unveiling operates on the levels of intellect, heart, and spirit to reveal the different forms of love; it joins love and beauty in the soul and reveals divine lordship as the wine of love. Witnessing is a category that Ruzbihan divides into two parts corresponding to sobriety and intoxication (a division that can be made in every station); the sober part of witnessing is clothing with divinity (*iltbas*), a trait of Abraham, while the intoxicated part is effacement (*mahw*), a characteristic of Moses—yet Muhammad united both experiences in his witnessing.[52]

After the 10 stations just described, Ruzbihan expands on the nature of the 11th, love (*mahabba*). This love can naturally be

[51] I have translated a section of this passage in "The Symbolism of Birds and Flight in the Writings of Ruzbihan Baqli," chapter 17 in this volume.

[52] At the beginning phase of witnessing, Ruzbihan invokes some terms from Daylami's list of the stations of love: "In the beginning, in witnessing the soul experiences no duration, because the assaults of the Essence violently cast it into universal intoxication from the vision [of God]. In that ravishing (*walah*), the eye has no power to see. When it reaches the witnessing of knowledge and union, it remains long in witnessing, but the bewilderment (*hayaman*) and agitation (*hayajan*) of its ecstasy (*wajd*) disturb it from the sweetness of beauty" (*`Abhar*, p. 130).

divided into two phases corresponding to the ordinary and the elite. The love of the ordinary is based on the manifestation of beauty in creation, and while it is indeed miraculous, its degrees are those of faith rather than direct witnessing. The elite love is based on three kinds of witnessing. The first of these occurred in the pre-creational state, when the disembodied spirits of humanity made a covenant with God by acknowledging him as their lord (Qur. 7:171).

They asked the Real for beauty, so that gnosis would be perfect. The Real removed the veil of might, and showed them the beauty of majesty's essence. The spirits of the prophets and saints became intoxicated from the influence of hearing [the divine speech and seeing] the beauty of majesty. They fell in love with the eternal beloved, with no trace of temporality. From that stage, their love began to increase with degrees of divine improvement, because when the holy spirits entered earthly form, from their prior melancholy they all began to say "Show me!" (Qur. 7:143). They found the locus of delight, so that whatever they saw in this world, they saw all as Him.[53]

This is followed by a second stage of witnessing in which the substance of the spirit is not veiled at all by human characteristics, and the divine beloved is encountered without any intervening medium. The third stage of witnessing perfects the second, as the unimpeded vision of God takes place in eternity. Each attribute of the beloved inspires a different kind of love, and the lover is transformed into a mirror of God, so that whoever looks upon the lover becomes in turn a lover of God. Even at this level of love, there are additional distinctions, depending on the degree of knowledge of the divine unity.

With the 12th stage, longing (*shawq*), Ruzbihan brings us so close to the divine unity that the distinctions implied by love and longing become paradoxical. He connects longing to prayers of Muhammad that ask for "the pleasure of gazing on your face, and the longing for meeting with you." He describes longing as a fire that burns away all thoughts, desires, and veils from the heart. Yet when the lover is united with the beloved, "for whom

[53] Ibid., p. 132. The Qur'anic reference (7:143) is to Moses' demand to see God face to face.

is there longing, for whom is there love if not oneself?"[54] The language of love still implies duality. If love and longing reach unity, they will no longer exist.

In the 13th and final section on the perfection of love, Ruzbihan resumes his theme by equating God with love. Since passionate love (*`ishq*) is a divine attribute, God loves himself; God is love, lover, and beloved. The perfection of *`ishq* is identical with divine *mahabba*. This does not imply any distinction within the divine essence; God's multiple attributes are simply aspects of his beauty that he revealed to the spirits of humanity. Love remains an eternal quality. Ruzbihan calls it "the ivy of the ground of eternity, which has twined around the tree of the lover's soul. It is a sword that cuts off the head of temporality from the lover. It is the peak of the mountains of the attributes, where the soul of the lover who arrives there becomes the prisoner of love."[55] When lover and beloved become one, there is a complete transformation: "Then the lover becomes the ruler in the kingdom of the Real. When the Real overpowers him, his bodily form becomes heavenly, his soul becomes spiritual, his life becomes divine. He becomes the beloved of the beloved, the desired of the desired."[56] Many paradoxes follow. From one point of view, love cannot be perfect, since the beloved has no limit. Yet the perfection of love is the essence of perfection. Love is also annihilation (*fana'*); when beauty is fully revealed, neither lover nor beloved remains. Lovers who find their life in the love of God cannot be said to die; they are like martyrs, always alive in God. Lovers become like angelic spirits, flying in the highest heaven with peacock angels, like Khidr, Ilyas, Idris, and Jesus. The world becomes subjugated by them, and they reveal themselves wherever they wish; this was the case with Abraham, Moses, Aaron, and Muhammad. Some take earthly form, like the Sufi saints, or discard their bodies like veils. Ultimately, the limit of love is defined by the two stations of gnosis (*ma`rifat*) and unity

---

[54] Ibid., p. 136.
[55] Ibid., p. 139.
[56] Ibid.

(*tawhid*).[57] It is characterized by the final stages of annihilation and subsistence. But the perfection of love is the end of love; at its highest stage it no longer exists. It is at this point that it becomes appropriate to speak in terms of ecstatic expressions (*shathiyyat*), such as Abu Yazid's "Glory be to me," or Hallaj's "I am the Real." The lover's experience of unity with God goes beyond all other modes of expression.[58]

In their meditations on the nature of love, Persian Sufis showed a remarkable consistency. The terms of the analysis multiplied over time, which is the natural tendency in the development of a tradition. Each generation refined on the insights it inherited, as individuals contributed their own nuances to the collective understanding. But the fundamental framework was the same. Love, together with its allied states, was conceived of as the ultimate form of the divine-human relationship. The principal factor that elevated this love above the mundane was recognized as early as Rabi`a: divinized love goes beyond the desires of the ego (it is precisely on the point that the Sufis differed most profoundly from the profane love theorists, who rejected any possibility of selfless or mystical love). The Sufis conveyed this understanding of love through the characteristic analysis of inner experience into spiritual states and stations, and the richness of their psychological analysis is what distinguishes their view of love. The number and sequence of these stations might differ from one author to another, or might show different emphases in separate works by the same author, according to the requirements of the audience. Yet the comparison of the lists of

[57] Ibid., p. 145. It may be asked why Ruzbihan, in his treatise on 1001 stations, places the stations of love in a relatively low position; out of the 20 chapters of 50 stations each, the stations of the lovers (*muhibbin*), those filled with longing (*mushtaqin*), and the passionate lovers (*ashiqin*) occupy the sixth, seventh, and eighth chapters, while the later chapters are reserved for the higher ranks of the spiritual hierarchy. The apparent discrepancy between this arrangement and the thrust of the *`Abhar al-ashiqin* may be explained by the fact that the description of 1001 stations is intended for spiritual novices (*Mashrab al-arwah*, pp. 3–4), while the *`Abhar al-ashiqin* (like other treatises dedicated to love) is reserved for the elite. The same difference of emphasis can be observed in the works of Ansari, mentioned above.

[58] See my *Words of Ecstasy in Sufism* (Albany: State University of New York Press, 1984), esp. Part I.

the stations of love has shown significant consistencies throughout. The impulse to categorize and define love at times took on a rationalistic character, as in the semi-philosophical presentation of Daylami. Sufis such as Ruzbihan, however, were able to reconnect their classifications to the mystical understanding of love and the annihilation of the ego. In the end, however, even the most ingenious explanations of the nuances of love were less than satisfactory. If writing on the stations of love was connected to a mystical teaching, its purpose seems to have been to indicate the sense of progression towards a goal of union with God. Yet as so many authors insisted, attainment of that goal makes the language of love an unacceptable dualism. It was the genius of these Sufi writers to express all the delicate shades of spiritual progress while at same time indicating the inadequacy of their explanations, thus pointing to what lay beyond. As Sumnun "the lover" put it, "Nothing explains a thing except something that is subtler, and there is nothing subtler than love, so what can explain it?"[59]

[59] Sumnun al-Muhibb, in Sulami, p. 196.

14

Sufism and Philosophy in Mulla Sadra[1]

What is the relationship between Sufism and philosophy? A question so general needs to be addressed in terms of specific examples, examining the way in which particular thinkers appropriate the legacies of others. So for instance, the concept of the "school of Shiraz" might lead one to assume some continuities between two prominent figures from that city, such as the early Sufi, Ruzbihan Baqli, and the later philosopher, Mulla Sadra, Yet Mulla Sadra never refers directly to Ruzbihan in any of his writings. Aside from the fact that they both lived in Shiraz, they appear to have had little in common. Mulla Sadra (1571–1640) was the most prominent philosopher of the Safavid era, while Ruzbihan Baqli (d. 1209) was one of the outstanding mystics of the pre-Mongol age. Each viewed reality from his own distinct perspective. Mulla Sadra, though he drew upon the insights of mysticism, was critical of institutional Sufism and held philosophical reason to be the ultimate standard. In contrast, Ruzbihan held that mystical knowledge is a gift of divine grace that is not based upon any human accomplishment; he expressed his feelings about the arrogance of philosophers in this passage from his autobiography: "Praise be to God who

[1] Paper presented at World Congress on the Philosophy of Mulla Sadra, Tehran, 23–27 May 1999.

ennobles by these stations his saints and his prophets without cause or reason, not because of their striving or discipline, not as the philosophers say—may God purify the earth of them!"[2] Although Ruzbihan did occasionally quote from philosophers, he was highly critical of their objectives.[3]

While this particular comparison goes nowhere, the larger question of the relationship between Sufism and philosophy in Mulla Sadra's writings is an important one that has occasioned significant debate. Recent scholarship on this question has divided into two opposing camps. On the one hand, S. H. Nasr, Henry Corbin, and James Winston Morris have argued that Sadra is basically an esoteric and mystically inclined thinker. Nasr translates the central symbol of Sadra's philosophy, *al-hikma al-muta`aliyya*, as "transcendent theosophy", accenting the notion of wisdom as divine knowledge. On the other hand, interpreters such as Fazlur Rahman, Hossein Ziai, and John Walbridge maintain that Sadra must be understood entirely within the technical framework of philosophy, preferably in a manner close to the contemporary presentation of analytical philosophy. Ziai translates *al-hikma al-muta`aliyya* simply as "metaphysical philosophy"; in his view, use of terms like "theosophy" (too often associated with the Theosophical Society of Madame Blavatsky) is misleading mystification.

This debate over the role of mysticism and philosophy in Mulla Sadra has often been carried out in an absolute and non-historical fashion. I would like to recast the question, not in terms of assigning an absolute characterization to Sadra and

---

2 Ruzbihan Baqli, *The Unveiling of Secrets: Diary of a Sufi Master*, trans. Carl W. Ernst (Chapel Hill: Parvardigar Press, 1997), p. 37, no. 56. For a general study of Ruzbihan, see my *Ruzbihan Baqli: Mysticism and the Rhetoric of Sainthood in Persian Sufism*, Curzon Sufi Series, 4 (London: Curzon Press, 1996); Persian translation by Majdoddin Keyvani, *Ruzbihan Baqli, `irfan va shath-i awliya' dar tasavvuf-i islami* (Tehran: Nashr-i Markaz, 1999).

3 Ruzbihan's treatment of philosophical views of love is discussed in my essay "The Stages of Love in Persian Sufism, from Rabi`a to Ruzbihan," in *Classical Persian Sufism from its Origins to Rumi*, ed. Leonard Lewisohn (London: Khaniqahi Nimatullahi, 1994), pp. 435–55; reprinted as *The Heritage of Sufism*, Volume 1, *Classical Persian Sufism from its Origins to Rumi (700–1300)*, ed. Leonard Lewisohn (Oxford: One World, 1999), pp. 435–55; Persian translation by Mojde-i Bayat, "Marahil-i `ishq dar nakhustin advar-i tasavvuf-i Iran, az Rabi`a ta Ruzbihan," in the Persian language edition of the Ni`matullahi magazine, *Sufi* 16 (1371/1992), pp. 6–17.

his philosophy, but instead examining his self-conscious use of earlier Sufi tradition through deliberate quotation. This task is facilitated by the recent publication of Sadra's masterwork *The Four Journeys* (and a number of other philosophical texts) in the form of a CD-ROM with a powerful search engine, which permits the location of names and terms at any point in the Arabic text.[4] On the basis of this material, I would then like to evaluate Sadra's philosophy in terms of the historical conditions of Safavid Iran, especially in terms of the contested status of wisdom (*hikma*), philosophical mysticism (*`irfan*), and institutional Sufism. Following this demonstration, I will conclude with a brief comparison of the approaches of Ruzbihan and Mulla Sadra to the question of mystical vision.

Before examining Mulla Sadra's treatment of Sufi texts, it would be well to rehearse the main outlines of his intellectual genealogy and his distinctive doctrines. It has been often pointed out that the most important sources for Mulla Sadra are five. First, and perhaps most important, was Aristotle, or rather a combination of Aristotle and Plotinus, inasmuch as the latter was known through the so-called *Theology of Aristotle* (a paraphrase of the last three books of the *Enneads* of Plotinus). Second was Ibn Sina, who was after al-Farabi the major interpreter of Aristotle in Islamicate culture. Third was Suhrawardi, the philosopher of Illumination, who insisted on combining the demonstrative proof of the philosopher with the spiritual experience of the mystic. Fourth was Ibn `Arabi, the premier Sufi metaphysician and exponent of the view of God as pure existence. Fifth is the comprehensive category of the scriptural resources of Shi`i Islam, including the Qur'an, the sayings of the Prophet Muhammad, and the sayings of the imams. As far as Sufism is concerned, it may be observed that both Ibn Sina and Suhrawardi (to varying degrees) considered the pronouncements and experiences articulated by Sufis to be important data to be analyzed by philosophical reason, although neither of them can be said to be predominantly a Sufi. In the case of Ibn `Arabi, however, it is

---

[4] *Nur al-Hekma*, CD-ROM published by the Computer Research Center for Islamic Sciences, P.O. Box 37158-3857, Qom, Islamic Republic of Iran, available from book distributors such as M. G. Noura in Tehran.

clear that we are dealing with someone who was situated centrally in the Sufi tradition.[5] Nevertheless, it is important to point out that, despite Ibn `Arabi's clear predilection for the experiential and scriptural basis of Sufism, philosophically-minded intellectuals commonly treated his writings as theoretical expositions comparable to the writings of Ibn Sina. Particularly as seen through the commentary tradition of authors like Qaysari and Kashani, Ibn `Arabi had become a thinker someone could approach primarily on a philosophical basis.[6]

As far as Mulla Sadra's principal doctrines are concerned, they are set forth in a number of treatises, among which the most important is of course *The Sublime Wisdom in the Four Intellectual Journeys*. It will be noted here that, in translating this title, I have avoided the tendentious phrases of both Nasr and Ziai, which suggest either a purely mystical or purely rationalist emphasis. Instead, I have translated *al-hikma al-muta`aliyya* in a more neutral fashion as "sublime wisdom", using this generic equivalent as a way to signal the widest possible applicability of the term. It is my contention (discussed below) that by this phrase Mulla Sadra and his colleagues intended a discourse meant to be dominant in every possible context, so that it would ultimately include and supersede everything from the mystical to the rational. Even the title of this philosophical treatise illustrates what I take to be Sadra's typical approach to Sufism. "The four journeys" is a theme that has been elaborated in Sufi writings at least since the time of Ibn `Arabi. These journeys are said to be as follows: (1) the journey from the creation to God; (2) the journey in God; (3) the journey from God to the creation; (4) the journey that brings God to the creation. Characteristically, Mulla Sadra has shifted this symbolism from its mystical origin to a philosophical application. In his masterwork, these journeys are stipulated to be "intellectual", and

---

5 On the relationship between Mulla Sadra and Ibn `Arabi, see Muhammad Reza Juzi, "The Influence of Ibn `Arabi's Doctrine of the Unity of Being on the Transcendental Theosophy of Sadr al-Din Shirazi," in *The Heritage of Sufism*, Volume 3, *Late Classical Persian Sufism (1501–1750)*, ed. Leonard Lewisohn and David Morgan (Oxford: Oneworld Publications, 1999), pp. 266–72.

6 James Winston Morris, "Ibn `Arabi and his Interpreters, Part II (Conclusion): Influences and Interpretations," *Journal of the American Oriental Society* 107 (1987), pp. 101–6.

they consist of the four basic divisions of philosophy: (1) ontology; (2) physics; (3) metaphysics; (4) psychology. In any case, the distinctive doctrines of Mulla Sadra can be summarized under the following four headings:

1. The primacy of existence over essence (quiddity), and the ambiguity of existence.
2. The unity of the intellect and the intelligible (a teaching strongly reminiscent of Plotinus).
3. "Substantial motion" as a category.
4. The world of the imagination as an independent entity.

Just to comment briefly on these themes, I would suggest that only perhaps in the last of these four items can we find something that resonates strongly with Sufi teachings. Insofar as the world of the imagination is the locus of eschatology according to Sadra, it also can be said to be the site of mystical vision. While one might attempt a comparison between Mulla Sadra and Sufi thinkers on subjects such as the nature of love (though Sadra is probably closer to Ibn Sina here), my feeling is that there will be greater degree of approximation between Mulla Sadra and Sufism on the question of mystical vision.

When we examine Mulla Sadra's quotations of Sufi texts, there is first of all a quantitative aspect that must be pointed out (and here I rely upon the indices provided in the CD-ROM version of *The Four Journeys*). With the single major exception of Ibn `Arabi, whom he quotes more than 200 times, Mulla Sadra only mentions the names of early Sufis rarely, and he does not mention later Sufis at all. I will propose an explanation for this later on, but for the time being it may suffice to examine in tabular form (and in order of increasing frequency) the actual number of citations of early Sufis (Table 1), ancient Greek philosophers (Table 2), and later Islamic philosophers (Table 3) in *The Four Journeys*.

It is quite striking to see that many of the Sufis who are quoted by Mulla Sadra are only mentioned a single time. Those who occur more frequently either have a more explicit engagement with philosophy (Ghazali, `Ayn al-Qudat) or have been in dialogue with speculative metaphysics, particularly in the tradition of Ibn `Arabi (Simnani, Qunawi, Qaysari). Most surprisingly,

Table 1
Sufis cited in The Four Journeys

Name	*Number of citations*
`Abd Allah Ansari	1
Abu Sa`id Kharraz	1
Hallaj	1
Ibn `Ata'	1
Junayd	1
Abu `Abd al-Rahman al-Sulami	1
Abu Bakr al-Wasiti	1
Abu Yazid Bistami	2
`Ala' al-Dawla Simnani	9
Abu Talib Makki	9
`Ayn al-Qudat Hamadani	10
Sadr al-Din al-Qunawi	13
Da'ud al-Qaysari	14
Abu Hamid Ghazali	38
Ibn `Arabi	227

there is an almost complete lack of reference to any Sufis after the thirteenth century. Sadra does not even once refer, for instance, to the numerous writings on practical and devotional Sufism by his fellow-townsman of the fifteenth century, Shah Da`i of Shiraz.

A quite different picture emerges when we consider the extensive quotations from ancient Greek philosophers whose opinions are cited by Mulla Sadra.

Here, too, the numbers are somewhat surprising. Both in number of individuals and in frequency of reference, Mulla Sadra refers to ancient Greek philosophers in significantly higher numbers than Sufis.

When one considers the later Islamic philosophers who appear in the pages of *The Four Journeys*, it becomes abundantly clear that they occupy a much more prominent place than the Sufis.

It is apparent just from these totals that the real dialog partners of Mulla Sadra are the major Islamic philosophers. They are

Table 2
Ancient Greek philosophers cited in The Four Journeys

Name	*Number of citations*
Epicurus	1
Ptolemy	1
Pythagoreans	1
Themistius	2
Hermes	3
Proclus	5
Anaximenes	6
Plotinus	6
Timaeus	7
Hippocrates	9
Anaxagoras	10
Platonists	10
Thales	10
Zeno	16
Socrates	17
Democritus	20
Porphyry	21
Galen	24
Stoics	24
Pythagoras	27
Empedocles	40
Aristotle	55
Alexander of Aphrodisias	67
Plato	133
Theology of Aristotle	188

the ones whom he cites most frequently; of that there is no question. So how in fact does Mulla Sadra treat the Sufis whom he quotes?

In some cases, Sadra treats an early Sufi as a mystical authority whose opinion is acknowledged as significant on a major issue.

Table 3
Later Islamic philosophers in The Four Journeys

Name	*Number of citations*
Kindi	2
Qushaji	5
Qutb al-Din Shirazi	14
Illuminationists	25
Bahmanyar	41
Farabi	49
Mir Damad	73
Davani	153
Tusi	160
Fakhr Razi	195
Suhrawardi	253
Ibn Sina	767

Thus, for example, after a lengthy discussion of divine truth as existence, he reaches the third level of unity, citing (2:338) `Abd Allah Ansari on "the divine unity of the elite" (*tawhid al-khawass*), which is defined as the unity that God has reserved for himself. Some of it radiates onto the consciences of the elect, "but the allusion is restricted to the tongues of the masters of this path." Sadra here acknowledges that this level of awareness belongs to ascetics and mystics (*ahl al-riyada wa-arbab al-ahwal*).

Likewise, there are passages where Sadra provides a gloss and commentary on the saying of an early Sufi, thus providing an interpretation of the relation between mysticism and philosophy. In this way, he discusses a statement by Junayd on the nature of spirit. Sadra states (8:310) that the world is necessarily a living being endowed with intellect. But in order for it to be perfect, God sent souls to this world, causing them to dwell in bodies. Then he introduces the Sufis:

> The ascetics (*mutamassikun*) have spoken in this true path about the substance of the spirit, some by demonstration and theory, others by experience (*dhawq*) and ecstasy (*wajdan*), without employing reflective

thought (*fikr*). That is how the Sufi masters speak, modeling themselves on the ethics of the Prophet. They only unveil the secret of the soul by way of symbol and allusion (*al-ramza wal-ishara*). We also only speak from certain stations of the divine spirit and its potencies and its intellectual and psychic stages, but not from its core, because that is impossible. Junayd said, "The spirit is something that God has reserved for his own knowledge." It is not legitimate to refer this expression to anything more than an existing thing, although perhaps he meant a merely existing thing and pure existence.

Notice how Sadra draws upon and refines a Sufi saying in terms of his own comprehensive philosophical outlook, rather than working within a framework determined by Sufism. Particularly when discussing concepts (like spirit) based in revelation, he feels free to draw upon Sufi sayings as glosses that can be further clarified in terms of his immediate argument.[7] In a similar way, Sadra quotes (9:287–88) Abu Talib al-Makki on the different ranks of prophets and saints, the symbolic forms they will take while crossing the bridge on Resurrection Day, and their differing capacities for experiencing the lights of the next world. Again, he interprets this symbolism through his own eschatological perspective.

Sometimes Sadra will use a poetic quotation from a Sufi as a way to seal a more complicated argument. This occurs in his discussion (1:115) of the view presented by Shahrazuri (in his *al-Shajara al-Ilahiyya*):

The necessary existence is the most beautiful and perfect of things – all beauty is a drop, a shadow, and a gleam of its beauty and perfection. It has the highest beauty, and the most beautiful light, but it is veiled by the perfection of its luminosity and the strength of its manifestation. The divine sages who know it testify to it but not to its core, because of the strength of its manifestation and the power of its radiance, and the weakness of our separate human essences, which prevent us from witnessing its core, as the strength of the sun's manifestation and the power of its light prevents our sight from penetrating it . . . .

The meaning of luminous intensity (intellectual or sensible) is a veil over comprehension for the intellect or the senses. It refers to the lack

[7] Sadra also quotes Sufi authorities when discussing technical terms (e.g., *ism, irada, sifa, wajib*) that overlap the vocabularies of philosophy and mysticism.

> of one of these things and the separation from attaining one's desire. It is possible that its identity can be raised up beyond the vision of witnessing it, but the situation is permanent, as Hallaj said:
>
> Between you and me is an I that fights with me,
> So raise up, by your grace, this I from in between.

In this context, the quotation from Hallaj serves mainly to underscore the metaphysical argument that the divine essence transcends human knowledge. Here Sadra is close to Plotinus in his use of the metaphor of excess light to suggest the inability of the mind to perceive the divine radiance.

In other cases, one can find passages in which Sadra makes a partial compliment to Sufism, at least in comparison with people who badly misunderstand philosophy. At one point (1:78), Sadra follows the example of Suhrawardi in presenting an elaborate excuse for presenting and refuting an argument that he regards as self-contradictory and wrong at face value. Suhrawardi had similarly apologized (*al-Mutaharat*, 1:209) for even discussing the absurd view of those who hold that non-existence is a thing (*shay'iyyat al-ma`dum*). Sadra reflected that it was just that kind of thinker who gave philosophy a bad name.

> These are the people who dwell in the Islamic community, who have an inclination to intellectual subjects, without much firm thinking, but who have not attained the experiences attained by the Sufis. What happened to them is like what transpired in the age of the Umayyad dynasty, with books by people whose names resemble those of the philosophers. These people imagine that every Greek name was the name of a philosopher. In these books they found sayings they approved of, which they carried and spread in their enthusiasm for philosophy. These books were publicized, people enjoyed them, and they were followed by some of the moderns (though they differed from them on some things), but they all were in error on account of [following] the Greek names they had heard, and because of those who wrote these books in which they imagined there was philosophy, though it was nothing of the sort. They had predecessors before them, and successors after them. But philosophy did not emerge until after the dissemination of the sayings of the vulgar Greeks, their discourses, and their popular acceptance.

While this brief positive reference cannot be called a detailed account of Sufism, it points again to Sadra's tendency to treat

Sufism in relation to the primary categories of philosophy, just as it signals his implicit willingness to assume for the sake of argument that the mystical experiences of the Sufis are real.

But in other cases, Sadra reveals a readiness to reject the anti-philosophical habits of Sufis. In discussing a passage from Ibn Sina's *De Anima* (6.5.6), Sadra confesses (3:323) his puzzlement at the notion that the essence of the soul can become the categories, i.e., that a thing can become another thing. After working out the contradictions in this proposition, Sadra reflects that most people unfortunately think in this way, as noted in the *Isagoge* (of Porphyry), and that this is like "talking in the imaginative poetic sayings of the Sufis." So Sadra is certainly capable of making negative passing references to Sufism as well. There are in fact a number of passages in which Sadra refers to "vulgar Sufis" and condemns their defects. His is a critical position in which everything depends on the precise issue at hand. Sufism as such does not have an unquestioned value for Sadra.

Beyond the particular passages in which Mulla Sadra refers to Sufism, there lies the larger issue of the relation between philosophy and mysticism in the Safavid age. There is an historical context for Sadra's philosophy, and it is framed by the rise of the Safavid dynasty and the institutionalization of Twelver Shi`ism as the dominant religion in Iran. As mentioned above, there has been a sharp divergence between those who regard Sadra's philosophy as an esoteric philosophical mysticism and those who see it as a rational and analytical philosophy. Nowhere is this tension more sharply exhibited than in a recent multi-authored handbook entitled *History of Islamic Philosophy*.[8] Articles in this collection by Seyyed Hossein Nasr and Hossein Ziai, in particular, present diametrically opposed interpretations of figures such as Suhrawardi and Mulla Sadra, and there are other contributors such as Hamid Dabashi who have their own distinctive perspectives. I find this debate fascinating, not least because it is being carried out by expatriate Iranian intellectuals in an English-language publication printed in London. It might be said that,

---

[8] Seyyed Hossein Nasr and Oliver Leaman, eds, *History of Islamic Philosophy*, Routledge History of World Philosophies (2 vols., London: Routledge, 1996).

in some respects, pre-modern philosophers have become a contested ground for resolving the major issues of cultural identity for modern Iran; why else, indeed, are academic conferences on philosophy being convened with the support of the Iranian government? In any case, I would like to draw here in part on the "discourse analysis" of Dabashi, which he develops in his study of the philosophy of Sadra's teacher Mir Damad; although I do not subscribe to all of the epistemological presuppositions of Dabashi's presentation, it has the virtue of including the political and ideological aspects of Safavid Iran in the study of philosophy.[9]

The rise of an authoritarian Safavid dynasty in Iran after 1504 had serious consequences for the intellectual disciplines. What Dabashi calls the "nomocentric" character of Safavid Shi`ism took the form of a revival of Shi`i legalism.[10] There was a consequent disruption of the activities of Sunni thinkers and a significant exodus from Iran, particularly to India. Dogmatism and sectarianism with state support was aimed against Sunnis, philosophers, and Sufis. The seriousness of the new mood was demonstrated by the murder of the philosopher Maybudi in 1504, and by the systematic extermination of the dervish orders. Dabashi argues that a furious struggle was taking place between anti-intellectual clerics and philosophers, whose very existence was now challenged in a society where theological institutions were the main objects of patronage and charitable trusts. Indeed, patronage by rulers like Shah `Abbas became critical to the support of philosophy. A staple theme in the rhetoric of Shi`i mujtahids was the ridicule of the pretensions to knowledge of classical philosophers in comparison with the divinely sanctioned Imams. To be sure, Ziai points to evidence that the study of philosophy was pursued fairly widely in the madrasas that were the training grounds for Shi`i theologians, since there were over 400 philosophers in Safavid Iran who were educated in such

---

[9] Hamid Dabashi, "Mir Damad and the founding of the 'School of Isfahan,'" in Nasr and Leaman, 1:597–635.

[10] Dabashi, 1:598–602.

academies.[11] Nevertheless, it is not difficult to see that overall, there was a challenging environment for philosophy.

The response among philosophers was the creation of what has generally been called "the school of Isfahan". This was a synthesizing response to Shi`i legal criticism. Wisdom (*hikma*) was the unifying symbol that cut across all intellectual disciplines, including philosophy, mysticism, and Shi`i theology. As Dabashi puts it, this wisdom teaching emerged in "the context of the Safavid state and the self-assuring confidence it engendered and sustained in the Shi`i intellectual disposition . . . [These intellectual disciplines were] the supreme cultural products of a confident, prosperous, and self-assertive Safavid state."[12] As an institution, this school (if it may be so called) was probably at its peak in the time of Mir Damad (d. 1631), who received significant court patronage. Mulla Sadra, in contrast, was persecuted by jurists, and he was for a time exiled to the village of Kahak. His own frustration is evident from his frequent criticism of both hidebound jurists and wild Sufis.

As far as mysticism was concerned, the new "wisdom" synthesis accompanied the decisive separation of theoretical mysticism (*`irfan*) from practical Sufism in its institutional form (*tasawwuf, darvishi*). The Safavid dynasty found Sufi orders to be unacceptable rivals, despite its own origins in a dervish order, and so the Sufi orders were suppressed; sainthood (*wilaya*) was reserved for the Imams. The extensive tradition of disciplined mystical philosophy developed in Sufi circles over centuries was in effect cut off. Philosophers in this age returned to the kind of intellectual analysis of mystical experiences pioneered by Ibn Sina in his *Isharat*. They recognized the necessity for meditation and even a certain amount of philosophical asceticism; as Dabashi puts it, for both the Peripatetic and the Illuminationist, "separation from the physical body, in this meta-epistemology, becomes the necessary precondition of conceptual cognitions."[13] But this

---

[11] Ziai, "The Illuminationist Tradition," in Nasr and Leaman, 1:482, citing Manuchehr-Sadugh Soha, *A Bio-bibliography of Post Sadr-ul-Muta'alihin Mystics and Philosophers* (Tehran, 1980).

[12] Dabashi, 1:625; see also 1:621–28.

[13] Dabashi, 1:627.

was a privatization of mysticism, and the end of a tradition of organized spiritual training. In this context, it is not surprising that Sadra does not cite any Sufis later than Ibn `Arabi and his immediate commentators. For Safavid thinkers, speculative Sufism was no more than a classical intellectual and spiritual repertoire of the distant past, and Sufi poetry was assimilated into the category of classical literature.

If we now turn to the way that Mulla Sadra approaches the nature of mystical vision, perhaps the best example is in the short Persian text *The Three Principles.* This work is formulated as an ethical treatise along philosophical lines. According to Sadra, the three principles of the title are the three obstacles to attaining knowledge: (1) ignorance of psychology and philosophical anthropology; (2) love of wealth, power, desire, and pleasure; and (3) the lust for domination, which, combined with demonic deception, confuses the distinction between right and wrong. Here is the relevant section, an extended passage on mystical vision:[14]

> Now you should know that the wayfarer sometimes treats the creation as the God-revealing mirror and the means for gazing at the divine attributes and names, and sometimes he makes God the mirror for gazing at things, the world-revealing mirror. The first journey is "from creation to God," and the second journey is "from God to creation." The allusion to the first is found in "We shall show them our signs on the horizons and in their souls, so that it shall be clear to them that he is the Truth" (Qur. 41:53).
>
> Go and look carefully, for every grain of dust
> Is a world-revealing cup when you gaze upon it.
>
> The allusion to the second journey is: "Is it not sufficient for your lord that he witnesses everything?"
>
> One who sees with knowledge from the light of purity,
> Sees God first in everything he sees.
>
> "I never saw anything without seeing God before it."[15] Both of these sciences are sciences of reality. The first one is called "the science of unity" in the language of the Sufis, and "theology and universal knowledge" in the language of the scholars of divinity. The second is called

[14] Sadr al-Din Shirazi, *Risala-i sih asl*, ed. S. H. Nasr (Tehran: Intisharat-i Mawla, 1997), pp. 153–56.

[15] An early Sufi saying. See Annemarie Schimmel, *Mystical Dimensions of Islam* (Chapel Hill: University Of North Carolina Press, 1975), p. 147.

"the science of horizons and souls" among the Sufis, and among the natural scientists it is divided into two sciences, one being astronomy and cosmology, and the other being psychology. Both of these, in their goal and result, refer back to the science of unity.

My dear, people at this time know nothing of the science of unity and the divine science, I myself in my whole life have seen no one who exuded even a fragrance of this knowledge. And regarding the second science (the science of horizons and the science of souls), the activity of intellectuals has not been productive enough to help anyone else. Most people believe in nothing but the senses. "They know the outer aspect of the life of this world, but of the next they are heedless" (Qur. 30:7). They are heedless of divine wonders and the angelic realm of the heavens and the earth.

> You who are happy with this life are like a cow or donkey with its fodder
> Heedless of this turquoise circle, unconnected to this center, the turning sun.
> Those who have insight have responsibility; fools have no regrets about the day.

Those who are in sympathy with heaven and earth see with this eye; they think there is nothing more than this, which anyone could see or know as roof or floor, with the same eyes that cows and donkeys share. "We made heaven a roof preserved, but they turn away from our signs." (Qur. 21:32).

This passage is rich in allusion to the Qur'an and tags of Persian poetry. It evokes the theme of the four journeys, and it marks equivalences between Sufi and philosophic terminologies. It is mystical in tone, but even in this small Persian text, far from the austere scholastic argumentation of the *Asfar*, Sadra remains a philosopher.

In contrast, I will close with a comparison from an Arabic text by Ruzbihan Baqli (*Sayr al-arwah*), in which he sets forth his own understanding of mystical vision.[16] This occurs in a fairly analytical passage, in which he has refuted the theological school of the Mu`tazila, which rationalistically concluded that the beatific vision of God in the afterlife could not possibly be seen with the

[16] Ruzbihan, *Sayr al-arwah*, ed. Paul Ballanfat, *Quatre traités inédits de Rûzbehân Baqlî Shîrâzî* (Tehran: Institut Français de Recherche en Iran, 1998), para. 37, pp. 36–37 of the Arabic text.

physical eye, but must be internal or psychological metaphor; thus they maintain that it is all the more impossible to see God in this world.

> The existence of the believer, in paradise, is all vision, because spirit and body here are a single thing, like the sun and its heat. One sees God most high with all the limbs. Just as it is possible for the heart to see the emanation of God most high without spatial dimension, it is possible for the eye to see God most high without spatial dimension. For the eye and the heart are both created, and there is no difference between them in terms of createdness. The aim of these theologians, in connecting vision to the heart, is to deny vision altogether, for they define the vision of the heart as increase of certainty. Their knowledge of God is not real vision; this is a great error and a false analogy.

There is, perhaps, a real affinity between Mulla Sadra and Ruzbihan on questions like mystical vision. It is not so much an exact verbal correspondence, or a precise conceptual equivalence, as it is a kind of underlying tone, which is similar to the positive attitude toward mystical experience that characterizes the philosopher Plotinus and many of his philosophical successors. But for Safavid Iran, Sufism in its institutional form was no longer an active component of philosophy; mysticism had become deprived of its public and social expressions. The question of the relation between philosophy and Sufism in Mulla Sadra's writings can only be meaningfully discussed if we rephrase it as the relation between philosophy and private intellectual mysticism.

15

Shams-i Tabriz and the Audacity of Bayazid Bistami

One of the most memorable encounters in the history of Sufism is surely the first meeting of Shams-i Tabriz and Maulana Jalal al-Din Rumi. Although there are numerous versions of the story of this encounter, probably the most important account is the one that Shams himself recorded in his discourses (*Maqalat*), where he says that he spoke as follows to Rumi:

> The first thing I spoke about with him was this: "How is it that Bayazid did not need to follow [the example of the Prophet], and did not say 'Glory be to Thee' or 'We worship Thee?'"
>
> And Rumi completely understood the full implications of the problem and where it came from and where it was leading to. It made him inebriated on account of his purity of spirit, for his spirit was pure and cleansed and it shone within him. I realized the sweetness of this question from his inebriation, though I had been previously unaware of its sweetness.[1]

---

[1] *Maqalat*, p. 685 (2:87), in Franklin D. Lewis, *Rumi: Past and Present, East and West* (Oxford: Oneworld 2000), p. 155. All references are to *Maqalat-i Shams-i Tabriz*, ed. Muhammad `Ali Movahhed (Tehran: Khwarizmi, 1369/1990), citing the volume and page number at the top of each page.

Franklin Lewis, who has analyzed this passage at length, has provided a persuasive interpretation of the way that

> both Shams and Rumi followed the Prophet, unlike Bayazid Bistami… Shams returns again and again to this question of following the Prophet, and the case of Bayazid apparently provided the touchstone by which Shams could gauge the inner orientation of others and test whether a fancy for mystical speculation or indulgence in antinomian behavior outweighed a person's love and respect for the spiritual attainment of the Prophet.[2]

Lewis is certainly correct in pointing to the central importance of the concept of "following the Prophet" (*mutaba`at*) in the mystical thought of Shams-i Tabriz; Omid Safi has discussed the likelihood that Shams even criticized Muhyi al-Din ibn `Arabi for insufficiently demonstrating this quality.[3] Yet I must confess that it has always seemed to me that there was something more to say about this episode. Perhaps it is the occurrence of the word inebriation or drunkenness (*sukr*), which Shams uses twice to describe the reaction of Rumi to the example of Bayazid; this intoxication in turn allowed Shams to appreciate something delightful about these sayings that had previously escaped him.[4] The appearance of this kind of intoxication suggests that there is some excess or overplus of meaning that does not quite fit into the conventional notion of devotion to the model of the Prophet. Despite the fact that Shams criticizes Bayazid on a number of occasions, one retains a lingering suspicion that there was something about the boldness of Bayazid's ecstatic claims, and the

---

[2] Ibid., p. 156.

[3] Omid Safi, "Did the Two Oceans Meet? Historical Connections and Disconnections between Ibn `Arabi and Rumi," *Journal of Muhyiddin Ibn `Arabi Society* XXVI (1999), pp. 55–88.

[4] As Movahhed notes, Rumi does not preserve Shams' critique of Bayazid, but generally treats him in a much more positive fashion, as we see in *Masnavi*, book 4 (*Maqalat*, 1:500). It may be that the literary genre of the Masnavi was more suited to portraying ecstatic figures like Bayazid as heroic exemplars of self-annihilation; the more didactic context of oral discourses, which also depends upon the audience that is present, could have been responsible for Shams's more critical remarks about Bayazid. Nevertheless, it is interesting to see that in Rumi's own oral discourses, he makes a number of extremely positive references to Bayazid in his ecstatic expressions. See Mawlana Jalal al-Din Muhammad Balkhi, *Fihi ma fihi*, ed. Tawfiq H. Subhani (Tehran: Kitab-i Parsa, 2009), pp. 139, 316, 323, 348.

audacity of his statements, that called forth a response of equal audacity from Shams-i Tabriz himself.

Lewis is quite aware that most Sufis would have been able to explain the sayings of Bayazid as ecstatic sayings or *shathiyyat*, which should not necessarily be taken at face value or condemned as blasphemous insults against God or the Prophet. He adds that other Sufi scholars were critical of the ecstatic expressions of Bayazid and Hallaj, which they explained away as the products of intoxication that could be safely disregarded. Yet, as previously mentioned, it is striking that Shams described Rumi's reaction to this question as also being a kind of intoxication. Does that mean Rumi's reaction was also invalid? Or was he responding to some deeper meaning in Bayazid's expressions? These questions require further exploration.

It is well known that outrageous expressions like Bayazid's "Glory be to Me" or Hallaj's even more startling phrase, "I am the Truth (*ana al-haqq*)", have often been classified as *shathiyyat* or ecstatic sayings.[5] It is important to point out that these sayings are not necessarily to be dismissed as the ravings of lunatics, though there are undoubtedly some who hold that opinion. But to the contrary, there is abundant evidence to indicate that these ecstatic sayings have often been considered to be deep and genuine mystical insights, which unfortunately cannot be understood by the ordinary person. It is noteworthy that an authority of the stature of Junayd composed a commentary on the ecstatic expressions of Bayazid, which fortunately was preserved by the early Sufi scholar Abu Nasr al-Sarraj in his *Book of Glimmerings on Sufism (Kitab al-luma` fil-tasawwuf)*. Notice the title that Sarraj gave to this section: "The Commentary on Ecstatic Expressions, and Words that are Externally Found Repulsive, though they are Internally Correct and Well-founded." While it is true that Sarraj had to debate with the theologian Ibn Salim, who objected to Bayazid's sayings, Sarraj argued that his opponent had understood the words of Bayazid in an overly literal manner; but these ecstatic expressions require that one know the inner knowledge and experience that gave depth and substance to these otherwise

---

[5] For a survey of the problem of *shathiyyat*, see Carl W. Ernst, *Words of Ecstasy in Sufism* (Albany: SUNY Press, 1984).

strange expressions. Indeed, Sarraj refers to Junayd's commentary as a *tafsir*, a word normally reserved for commentaries on the Qur'an.[6]

Other interpreters, like Abu Hamid al-Ghazali, basically accepted the validity of the insights expressed in ecstatic sayings, though Ghazali was seriously concerned about the possibility of misinterpretation by the less informed listener. Ghazali distinguishes two kinds of *shath*. The first kind consists of

> broad, extravagant claims (made) in passionate love of God Most High, in the union that is independent of outward actions, so that some go to the extent of claiming unification, rending of the veil, contemplative vision (of God), and oral conversation (with God). Then they say, "We were told such-and-such, and we said such-and-such." In this they resemble al-Husayn ibn Mansur al-Ḥallāj, who was crucified for uttering words of this kind, and they quote his saying, "I am the Truth."

Ghazali goes on to say that this kind of talk is very dangerous to the common people, because they lose their chance for salvation, if they think that a purified soul that has attained spiritual states can dispense with religious duties. The consequences of such an antinomian interpretation are so severe that Ghazali concludes that "the killing of him who utters something of this kind is better in the religion of God than the resurrection of ten others." The second kind of *shath* is that which is unintelligible to the listener, regardless of whether it is merely confused babbling or something which the speaker comprehends but cannot articulate properly. Since this is bound to be interpreted arbitrarily, it is not permissible to express such things publicly. In this exposition, Ghazali's main concern is to prevent ordinary people from being misled by difficult or strange sayings, even though he implicitly regards the genuine kind of *shathiyyat* as valid for those who can understand. In the most mystical sayings, however, he sees a real danger of antinomianism.[7] Other Sufi writers, such as Ruzbihan al-Baqli, have given much more extensive positive interpretations of *shathiyyat*, as we can see from the latter's

---

[6] Movvahed (*Maqalat*, 1:499), in citing Ibn Salim's condemnation of Bayazid as an infidel (*kafir*), does not fully indicate Sarraj's defense of the sayings of Bayazid.

[7] Abu Hamid al-Ghazali, *Ihya' `ulum al-din* (Cairo, n.d.), 1:60–62.

important commentary on ecstatic sayings, which is available in Arabic and Persian.[8] And it is well to remember that Farid al-Din `Attar, among others, has also given a spirited defense of the sayings of Bayazid.[9]

Now it is true that there are numerous passages in the discourses of Shams-i Tabriz where he criticizes Bayazid's saying, "Glory be to me", for various reasons. As indicated in the first example given above, one reason was that Bayazid appeared to be claiming a station beyond that of the Prophet Muhammad, which would be a form of blasphemy; even if this is a form of intoxication, Shams remarks that it is incompatible with the true following of the Prophet.[10] But this is not the only reason that Shams gives for criticizing Bayazid. Shams on other occasions observed that Bayazid did not have the capacity to keep secrets, and he could not contain within himself the revelation of divine speech. This is the well-known criticism of having a "shallow cup" (*tang-zarfi*), which certain Sufis had used to indicate the limited spiritual capacity of their predecessors or contemporary rivals. Thus Shams remarks as follows:

> These saints and perfect ones, to whom the world pays respect, also have a veil. And that is that sometimes they relate their secrets with God, in order not to be destroyed. At other times they do not have this veil. I tell secrets, but I do not have [divine] speech. It is a wonder of these saints, when [divine] speech appears. Bayazid does not belong to the tribe of these saints. They are the Prophets and messengers. Perhaps if they became intoxicated from the [divine] speech, they would be unable to drink. Not even 100,000 barrels of wine can do what the speech of the Lord of the worlds can do.[11]

So "revealing the secret" is also a charge that could be laid against Bayazid, precisely because it was unlike the behavior of the Prophet.[12]

---

[8] Carl W. Ernst, *Ruzbihan Baqli: Mystical Experience and the Rhetoric of Sainthood in Persian Sufism* (Richmond: Curzon Press, 1996), Appendix B, "Ruzbihan's Two Commentaries on the 'Ascension' of Abu Yazid al-Bistami."

[9] Movahhed, in *Maqalat*, 1:483.

[10] *Maqalat*, 2:92.

[11] *Maqalat*, 1:94.

[12] See also *Maqalat*, 2:130.

Shams does not stop here, however. On a number of occasions he goes out of his way to say negative things about the spiritual status of Bayazid. Shams even uses the story of Bayazid's prediction of the future appearance of the great Sufi Abu al-Hasan Kharaqani to point out his imperfections:

> Finally, they do not hold Bayazid to be one of the perfect saints. One sincere dervish went to his tomb [i.e., Bayazid], placed his finger on his mouth [in astonishment], and said, "Ah! Between this dervish and God a veil has remained." This Bayazid passed by the village of Kharaqan, and he said: "After 150 years, a man will come out of this village who will be five degrees beyond me." And so it was, at that very time Abu al-Hasan Kharaqani became a disciple and put on a dervish cloak by his tomb.[13]

The point is not only that a sensitive visitor to Bayazid's tomb could still detect the presence of his spiritual veil, but also that Bayazid would be surpassed by Kharaqani. More substantially, Shams responds to a well-known story, according to which Bayazid refused to eat melons, because he has seen no evidence about how the Prophet ate melons; this was often taken to be a sign of Bayazid's deep devotion to the Prophet. Shams, however, poured scorn upon this story:

> They say that Bayazid did not eat melons. He claimed, "I have never found out in what manner the Prophet, peace be upon him, ate melon." But following [of the Prophet] is both superficial and meaningful. You have observed the superficial aspect of following, but how is it that you failed to observe the truth and meaning of following?
>
> As the Chosen One [Muhammad], God's blessings upon him, says: "Glory to Thee, we have not worshiped Thee as it befits Thee." As he [Bayazid] says, "Glory to me, how great is my station." If someone supposed his station to be greater than the station of the Chosen One, he is a real idiot and ignoramus.[14]

So it would seem that there is good reason to think that Shams was focused upon the problem of Bayazid failing to follow the Prophet adequately.

---

[13] *Maqalat*, 1:117; also 2:228.

[14] *Maqalat*, 1:741, trans. Lewis, p. 158.

Nevertheless, there is a whole other class of remarks by Shams-i Tabriz concerning Bayazid, which is harder to explain. Many of these statements have a bold and audacious character that clearly falls into the category of acts of boasting and one-upmanship, which are indeed important characteristics of ecstatic sayings or *shathiyyat*. These audacious and aggressive sayings are not without precedent in Near Eastern culture. We can find the rhetorical basis for this audacity in the ancient boasting contest (*mufakhara*) of the pre-Islamic Arabs. In fact, the early Sufi author Abu al-Najib al-Suhrawardi (d. 563/1168) corroborates this connection in his widely used manual of conduct for Sufi novices, *Adab al-Muridin*. In the lengthy section on the dispensations (*rukhas*) or permissible deviations from the rules, Suhrawardi says the following:

> Among the (dispensations) are boasting and publicizing one's claim (to spiritual states). In this matter, their standard is that one should intend to publicize the bounties of God, who is exalted above it. "Indeed speak of the bounty of your Lord" (Qur. 93:11). That is (permissible) in the raptures of a spiritual state or in a boasting-contest (*mufakhara*) with an adversary.[15]

This is precisely the same sort of phenomenon that we see in the *shathiyat* contests of the saints, when one outrageous statement is outdone by the next. Ruzbihan concludes, "This action is from the jealousy of gnosis, and jealousy is an attribute of God. . . . This wrangling (*munaqara*) of the prophets and saints is exemplary (*sunna*)."[16]

Shams-i Tabriz was in fact familiar with this type of boasting contest, as he indicates in the following account:

> Two mystics were having a boasting contest (*mufakhara*) and a debate with each other, about secrets of mystical knowledge and the stations of

[15] `Abd al-Qahir ibn `Abd Allah al-Suhrawardi, *Adab al-Muridin*, ed. Menahem Milson, typescript, Widener Library, Harvard University, p. 88, no. 193. Cf. Abu al-Najib al-Suhrawardi, *A Sufi Rule for Novices: Kitab Adab al-Muridin*, trans. Menahem Milson (Cambridge, 1975), p. 81, no. 205.

[16] *Words of Ecstasy*, p. 38.

> the mystics. One said, "A person who comes along sitting on a donkey, to me that one is God." The other one said, "To me, the donkey is God." In short, they tried to outdo each other by force. With Bayazid and others, in their words it is clear that it is not like this. But to spend time on their sayings is a veil, for this reason, that it is something else. Someone said, "What is that something else?" I said, "For example, you heard these words of mine, they became cold in your heart. That veil became something like this. They are near to incarnationism; the words of the spirituals are, 'we dwelled in a single body.' How will you comprehend that you are full of desire?"[17]

Although the example that Shams gives of dervishes in a boasting contest is a ridiculous one, it nevertheless provides him with an opportunity to imply that there are others, like Bayazid, who are different from the foolish pair depicted here. One may conclude from this that Shams considered the sayings of Bayazid to be serious and important consequences of a spiritual state, but at the same time, he was concerned about how words can be misinterpreted and become a veil. His concluding remarks in this passage quote an excerpt from a famous poem by Hallaj ("we dwelled in a single body"), arguing that it could be the source of an antinomian misinterpretation by those who consider themselves to be "spirituals".

But there is something else hidden in the criticism of Bayazid by Shams. The fact is that Bayazid held a singular position as the pre-eminent early Sufi known for *shathiyyat*. From an early date, Sufis who were contemporary with Bayazid engaged in boasting contests with him in the form of their own ecstatic expressions. Wasiti said, "They all died in delusion, up to Bayazid, and he also died in delusion." Likewise Shibli said, "If Abu Yazid were here, he could become Muslim with the aid of our children."[18] At a later date, Muhyi al-Din ibn `Arabi also engaged in extensive interpretation of the sayings of Bayazid, including both praise of Bayazid and a subtle kind of one-upmanship to indicate his own superiority; Ibn `Arabi considered the sayings of Bayazid as boasting (*fakhr*), but he maintained that his own statements were not boasting but commanded by God—so he made the boast that

---

[17] *Maqalat*, 1:103.

[18] These and further examples are provided in *Words of Ecstasy*, pp. 36–40.

he made no boast. Subsequently, Sufi thinkers such as Ahmad Sirhindi engaged in the same kind of "rhetoric of transcendental hyperbole" to claim a spiritual state that went beyond both Bayazid and Ibn `Arabi.[19] So from this point of view, dramatic criticism of Bayazid in the form of *shath* is perfectly compatible with the recognition of his spiritual eminence—indeed, such spiritual critique in the form of a boasting contest could only be justified in relation to a spiritual master of very high degree.[20]

Shams-i Tabriz in some of his remarks actually insists that Bayazid must be recognized as a saint of the highest status. Thus, he maintains that even if the famous theologian Fakhr Razi were multiplied 100,000 times, he would not come close to the path of Bayazid.[21] Shams repeatedly cites examples of Bayazid's spiritual attainments, including his ability to perceive the true condition of inhabitants of the graveyard; he also refers to Bayazid's selfless actions, such as exchanging the merit of 17 pilgrimages to Mecca in order to give water to a dog, and performing pilgrimage by circumambulating his shaykh seven times.[22] Yet in other observations, Shams is willing to make theatrical denunciations, not only of the supposedly intoxicated Bayazid, but even of his sober counterpart, Junayd. Thus, Shams says, "They all speak about Junayd and Bayazid, let me say Junayd and Bayazid and their words are cold on the heart and appear cool."[23] And in the same breath, he can say, "That discussion that occurred yesterday—what place do Bayazid and Junayd have here? And that Hallaj, who was also the shame of his master, has fallen—and it has wiped him out! They are not even a hair on the body of [the Prophet]!"[24] Shams portrays Bayazid as giving a pretentious speech in a mosque, only to be silenced by a woman who denounces him for making a false spiritual claim.[25] In this way,

---

19 Carl W. Ernst, "The Man without Attributes: Ibn `Arabi's Interpretation of Abu Yazid al-Bistami," chapter 10 in this volume.

20 Further on the topic of spiritual boast, see Carl W. Ernst, "On Losing One's Head: Hallajian themes in works attributed to `Attar," chapter 18 in this volume.

21 *Maqalat*, 1:128.

22 *Maqalat*, 1:194; 1:229; 1:264.

23 *Maqalat*, 1:275.

24 *Maqalat*, 2:86.

25 *Maqalat*, 2:104.

Shams concludes, "Bayazid could not endure my presence, for five days, one day, or none."[26]

There is no question that Shams-i Tabriz was deeply devoted to following the example of the Prophet in a profound manner, and that did lead Shams to find fault with Bayazid Bistami for claiming a spiritual status that seemed to infringe upon the supremacy of the Prophet Muhammad. Yet the attitude of Shams towards Bayazid was complicated by the rhetoric of boasting that forms part of the tradition of *shathiyyat* or ecstatic expressions. In this respect, Shams also made boasts in the form of criticisms that included not only Bayazid but also the scrupulous and sober Junayd. The audacity of Shams-i Tabriz was born of the heat of his own spiritual experience, in comparison to which the words of previous mystics were simply cold texts. In short, the audacity of Bayazid Bistami was outmatched by the sayings that demonstrate the audacity of Shams-i Tabriz.

[26] *Maqalat*, 2:125.

PART 3

SUFISM, ART, AND LITERATURE

16

The Spirit of Islamic Calligraphy: Baba Shah Isfahani's *Adab al-mashq*

An eloquent description of the spiritual basis of Islamic calligraphy is contained in an old and beautiful Persian manuscript in the Punjab University Library, Lahore. Entitled *Adab al-mashq* ("Manners of Practice"), this book is an autograph written in the seventeenth century by the Iranian calligrapher Baba Shah Isfahani.[1] Despite stains and wear, it is still clear and legible, and the first two pages have fine gold illumination. Mawlavi Muhammad Shafi` *marhum* edited this work and published it, with a valuable introduction in Urdu, in the first

[1] Manuscripts of *Adab al-mashq* are evidently common in Iran, but are generally attributed to Mir `Imad, and the text has been printed in Iran with this attribution (*Adab al-mashq, ba-risala-i nasa'ih al-muluk* [Tehran: Karkhana-i Mashhadi-yi Khudadad, 1317/1938]). Nonetheless, Mahdi Bayani has pronounced the Lahore copy to be an authentic and undeniable example of Baba Shah's handwriting, and he has shown that unscrupulous book dealers falsely ascribed the work to Mir `Imad because of the great demand for specimens of the latter's work. Cf. Mahdi Bayani, *Ahwal u asar-i khwush-nivisan-i nasta`liq-niwisan*, Intisharat-i Danishgah-i Tihran, No. 1045/1 (Tehran: Danishgah-i Tihran, 1345/[1967]) I, 87. Another copy of *Adab al-mashq*, correctly attributed to Baba Shah but with the title *Risala dar khatt*, is preserved in the library of the Asiatic Society of Bengal, Calcutta, in MS 1623, fols. 73–86; its being the same as *Adab al-mashq* is certain from the opening words.

volume of his collected papers.[2] The present article is a discussion of Baba Shah's explanation of the secrets of his art. *Adab al-mashq* is an unusually complete presentation of the aesthetic and religious basis of Islamic calligraphy, and it reveals in particular a visionary method of concentration strongly influenced by Sufism. Baba Shah's treatise also comprehensively illustrates the stages in the development of a master calligrapher. It is no exaggeration to say that *Adab al-mashq* is one of the most revealing documents of the later development of Islamic calligraphy.

Baba Shah Isfahani was famed as a master of the *nasta`liq* style of calligraphy, the beautiful Persian hand developed primarily at the Timuri and Uzbek ateliers in Herat and Bukhara. A modern authority on calligraphy has remarked, "By general agreement of historians contemporary with and later than Baba Shah, no calligrapher had reached his level in writing *nasta`liq* before Baba Shah appeared. He was adorned with an elegant style and a sweet hand, and even the great calligraphers recognized his mastery."[3] The dates and details of his life have been subject to some dispute.[4] According to modern authorities like the Turkish scholar Habib Effendi, Baba Shah Isfahani had begun the study of calligraphy from the age of eight, and studied night and day for eight years with the celebrated Mir `Ali Haravi (d. 951/1544–45), who perfected the *nasta`liq* style in Herat and Bukhara. Habib Effendi further states that Mir `Imad (d. 1012/1603), perhaps the most admired master of *nasta`liq*, derived his style from Baba Shah.[5] If correct, this information would put Baba Shah's birth at least 16 years before Mir `Ali's death, or no later than 940/1533–34.[6] On the other hand, Muhammad Qutb al-Din Yazdi

[2] "Risala-i adab al-mashq az Baba Shah Isfahani," in *Maqalat-i Mawlavi Muhammad Shafi`*, ed. Ahmad Rabbani (Lahore: Majlis-i Taraqqi-i Adab, n.d. [1967]) I, 247–75; the article originally appeared in the *Oriental College Magazine* 101 (1950).

[3] Bayani, I, 85.

[4] The confusion over Baba Shah's dates has been noticed already by Annemarie Schimmel, *Calligraphy and Islamic Culture* (New York: New York University Press, 1984), p. 174, n. 99.

[5] Habib Effendi, *Khatt wa Khattatan* (Constantinople, 1305), in Shafi`, p. 239.

[6] Although Baba Shah Isfahani quotes the poetry of Mir `Ali Haravi (*Adab al-mashq*, p. 268), we cannot be certain that he was a student of the latter. Mir `Ali Haravi's date of death has been put anywhere from 924/1518 to 976/1568, but the date of 951/1544 is found in a contemporary tazkira written in Herat, *Muzakkir-i Ahbab* by Hasan "Nisari";

wrote that he had met Baba Shah Isfahani in 995/1586–87, when the latter was still a young man, and he was amazed to see that he had already surpassed most of the calligraphers of the day. Qutb al-Din said that if he had lived longer, Baba Shah would have surpassed Sultan `Ali Mashhadi and Mir `Ali Haravi, and to achieve so much he must have had a divine gift.[7] This information obviously conflicts with the statement of Habib Effendi, according to whom Baba Shah would have been over 50 at the very time when Qutb al-Din commented on his youth; Qutb al-Din's statement also implies that Baba Shah died young, before realizing his full potential. Following the researches of the modern Iranian scholar Mahdi Bayani, we should accept the eyewitness account of Qutb al-Din, so that Baba Shah must have died in Baghdad in 996/1587–88; the modern attempt to link Baba Shah into the chain of the two greatest masters of *nasta`liq* cannot be demonstrated.[8] Arthur Pope has maintained that Baba Shah was a painter as well as a calligrapher, and has referred to a fine specimen of his work, an illustrated manuscript of Jami's *Silsilat al-Zahab* dated to 977/1569–70 and preserved in the former royal library in Tehran.[9] This appears to be an error, however, for the colophon to the manuscript, the earliest known with Baba Shah's signature, only states that Baba Shah was the copyist.[10] Regardless of the confusion about dates, the sources are all agreed that in addition to his natural ability, Baba Shah

---

cf. Muhammad Bakhtavar Khan, *Mir'at al-`alam, tarikh-i Awrangzib*, ed. Sajida S. Alvi, Publication of the Research Society of Pakistan, No. 55 (Lahore: Research Society of Pakistan, 1979), II, 477, n. 1.

[7] Muhammad Qutb al-Din Yazdi, *Risala-i Qutbiyya*, in Shafi`, p. 249.

[8] Bayani, I, 86. `Ali Effendi's report that Baba Shah was the student of Mir `Ali's best pupil, Sayyid Ahmad Mashhadi (d. 986/1578–79), also appears unlikely, since Baba Shah seems never to have left Isfahan (ibid., 46).

[9] The date of this manuscript makes it hard to place Baba Shah's birth much later than 960/1553, so that he would have been around 35 at the time of his death; it is possible that he could still at this age have appeared to be a young man cut off in his prime.

[10] Bayani, I, 90. Bayani refers to three page specimens of Baba Shah's calligraphy in Istanbul, and mentions several manuscripts in Baba Shah's hand: a copy of Nasa'ih al-muluk dated 980/1572–73, a manuscript with the Khamsas of Nizami and Khusraw (994/1585–86), *Chihil kalima-i nabavi* (Ramazan 978/Jan. 1571), and *Tuhfat al-abrar* (982/1574–75), all in the former royal library in Tehran. Cf. Arthur Upham Pope and Phyllis Ackerman, eds, *A Survey of Persian Art from Prehistoric Times to the Present* (London: Oxford University Press; reprint ed., New York: Oxford University Press), II, 1738 (Shafi`, p. 250, mistakenly gives II, 1378), citing the illustrated Jami manuscript according to

had received supernatural assistance in his art. One authority wrote,

> The subtlety of his writing was of a miraculous order. . . . He had an inborn talent for calligraphy, but the beauty of his writing was a divine gift. The enthusiasm of the people of Isfahan for his writing is on such a level that they firmly believe that Mother Time has never brought forth a famous calligrapher child like Baba Shah.[11]

Iskandar Beg, the historian of the Safavi court, maintains that Baba Shah was without rival in Iraq and Khurasan. He devoted all his hours to penmanship, from which he made his living, and he left many examples of his work in books, albums, and individual pieces. Although many people in Iraq had specimens of his work, it became difficult to find any that were still available, because demand had driven the price very high.[12] His formal title in the court of Shah Tahmasp was Ra'is al-Ru'asa, "Chief of Chiefs".[13]

The autograph copy of *Adab al-mashq* now preserved in the Punjab University Library was once the property of the royal library in Bijapur. The `Adil Shahi kings were noted connoisseurs of calligraphy, and had enticed talented calligraphers to the Deccan from the Safavi court in Iran.[14] Baba Shah undoubtedly would have approved of the presence of his book in Bijapur, since he maintained that the finest and most expensive paper for calligraphy, "which the craftsman calls a rose without a thorn", was made in the `Adil Shahi kingdom.[15] It is worth noticing in passing that Baba Shah found another Deccan paper, the Sultani of Daulatabad, to be next best after the `Adil Shahi; the ancient paper factory at Kaghazipura, between Daulatabad and Khuldabad, has maintained a tradition of producing fine paper

---

L. Binyon, J. V. S. Wilkinson, and B. Gray, Persian Miniature Painting (London, 1933), p. 143.

11 `Ali Effendi, *Munaqib-i hunarvaran*, in Bayani, I, 85.

12 Iskandar Beg Munshi, *Tarikh-i `alam-ara-yi `Abbasi* (Tehran, 1314), p. 125, in Shafi`, p. 248.

13 Habib Effendi, in Shafi`, p. 249.

14 Schimmel, p. 70.

15 *Adab al-mashq*, p. 272.

from the Tughluq period to the present day.[16] From Bijapur Baba Shah's book fell into the hands of Awrangzib when he conquered the city in 1097/1686 and took over the royal library.[17]

Baba Shah wrote several works on calligraphy. One was a *masnavi* poem of a thousand lines on the method of writing the *nasta`liq* style, for the use of beginners. Here is a sample, explaining the formation of individual letters:

> Listen to a word gained from experience on the placement of the *nasta`liq* script.
>
> The height of *alif* should be three dots, but with the same pen with which it came.
>
> One dot is enough for the width of *ba*; six dots is the length of the body of *ba*.

Some of Baba Shah's verses, written under the pen-name "Hali", showed his dexterity in using the poetic conceits of calligraphy to endow the art with a religious meaning. In a lyric (*ghazal*) verse quoted by Razi, Baba Shah made the standard pun on the double meaning of *khatt*as both "writing" and the "down" of a young man's new beard; in this way spiritual lovers who contemplate the loops of Arabic script (*khatt*) are in effect gazing upon the curly down (*khatt*) on the beloved's face:

> "The pupil of the eye became all light in body as in soul,
> to look upon the sweet curls of his down (writing)."[18]

Although not unusual in itself, this verse in fact sums up Baba Shah's attitude toward calligraphy as a highly concentrated

[16] Rawnaq `Ali, *Rawzat al-aqtab al-ma`ruf ba-mazhar-i Asafiyya* (Lucknow: Dil-gudaz Press, 1349/1931), pp. 282–83; Syed Badshah Hussain, "Hand made paper industry in H. E. H. the Nizam's Dominions in the 18th and 19th Centuries," in Proceedings of the Deccan History Conference (Hyderabad, 1945), pp. 350–52; *Inksmith Artists' News* (Seattle: Daniel Smith Inc.) vol. II, no. 2, pp. 1, 3–4. Daniel Smith currently markets this paper as "Indian Village Watercolor Paper", but it does not seem to match the medieval standards.

[17] Shafi`, pp. 251–52.

[18] Ahmad Razi, *Haft iqlim*, MS Punjab University Library copied in 1045/1635–6 in Isfahan, fol. 354b, in Shafi`, pp. 247–48. For the script/down pun, see Schimmel, pp. 130 ff.

practice of contemplating the divine beauty, which he explained in further detail in *Adab al-mashq*.

Adab al-mashq belongs to a special class of writings by calligraphers about calligraphy, but it stands out by its relatively greater emphasis on the internal aspects of the art.[19] Even philosophers and aestheticians seem generally to have placed more importance on the formal aspects of calligraphy than on the act of concentration.[20] Baba Shah's originality in this respect is evident from his distinction, discussed below, between the acquired and the unacquired "parts of script"; the acquired aspects begin with stylistic features, but culminate in intellectual mastery, purification of the heart, and intense love. Baba Shah deliberately distinguishes these qualities from the formal categories of the classical Arab calligraphers. We can also get an idea of Baba Shah's originality by comparing his work to Sultan `Ali Mashhadi's poem on calligraphy, which Baba Shah admired and used as a model for *Adab al-mashq*, in which he quotes or refers to Sultan `Ali by name over a dozen times.[21] Sultan `Ali's poem,

---

[19] Other works by calligraphers include Siraj al-Din Ya`qub ibn Hasan, *Tuhfat al-muhibbin* (ca. 858/1454), MS 386 suppl. pers., Bibliotheque Nationale, Paris (Blochet, Catalogue, II, no. 1113), cited in Pope and Ackermann, p. 1737, and discussed in chapter 17 of this volume [the author, a native of Shiraz who went to India, was a disciple of a descendant of the Sufi master Ruzbihan al-Baqli (d. 606/1209]; Majnun ibn Kamal al-Din Mahmud Rafiqi Haravi, *Risala-i khatt u sawad*, ed. Yasin Niyazi, *Oriental College Magazine*, 11(1935), also ed. Riza Mayil (Kabul: Anjuman-i Tarikh-i Afghanistan, 1355/1976); idem, *Risala-i rasm al-khatt* (dated 909/1503–4) in 400 couplets, MS 2449 Raza Library, Rampur, also MS 2277, Khudabakhsh Oriental Public Library, Patna. The last two references are given by Nazir Ahmad, "Timurid Manuscripts of Artistic and historical value in Indian Collections," paper delivered at the International Symposium on the Art of Central Asia During the Timurid Period, held in Samarkand, 1969. Schimmel (p. 184, n. 233) also mentions a work on calligraphy written for Akbar, Khalifa Shaykh Ghulam Muhammad's *Haft iqlim-i Akbarshahi*, MS Or. 1861, British Museum.

[20] Edward Robertson, "Muhammad ibn `Abd al-Rahman on Calligraphy," *Studia Semitica et Orientalia* (Glasgow, 1920), pp. 57–83; Franz Rosenthal, "Abu Haiyan al-Tawhidi on Penmanship," *Ars Islamica* 13–14 (1948):1–30; Tashkuprizada, in Hajji Khalifa, *Kashf al-zunun*, p. 153, as cited in Pope and Ackermann, p. 1740.

[21] Sultan `Ali Mashhadi's poem, which is known by several titles (cf. Schimmel, p. 37), has become well-known through the English translation by Vladimir Minorsky, in Qazi Ahmad, *Calligraphers and Painters*, trans. V. Minorsky (Washington, D.C., 1959), pp. 120 ff.; this translation has not been available to me. Bayani (I, 253–54, with a list of the poem's headings) mentions that the Persian text has been published in Mirza Sanglakh, *Imtihan al-fuzala'* (Tabriz, 1291), and that Galina Kostinova published a facsimile edition of the autograph MS in Leningrad, with an introduction in Russian, in *Studies of the National Public Library*, vol. 52 (Leningrad, 1957). I have used the manuscript in the Punjab

in some two hundred-odd verses, begins with a brief invocation and some autobiographical observations, and proceeds to discuss various aspects of calligraphy, mostly regarding preparation of materials (pen, ink, paper) and stylistic formation of letters. Sultan `Ali only makes a few comments on the development of inner concentration, and on the nature of calligraphic practice (*mashq*), perhaps feeling that these subjects should be reserved for oral teaching.[22] By comparison, Baba Shah's extensive commentary on the ethics, internal discipline, and levels of mastery of calligraphy amounts to a major disclosure of the master-calligrapher's practice.

Here we may review the contents of the treatise. As in the *masnavi* poem mentioned above, Baba Shah apparently wrote *Adab al-mashq* with the novice calligrapher in mind. The author says in his introduction that in his youth he, "*in faqir-i haqir-i fani* (this humble insignificant faqir), Baba Shah-i Isfahani," once happened to be studying the nasta`liq script. "In searching for the light of the true beloved's beauty, he trod the path of the representation of script."[23] Then he happened to see some verses in the superb hand of Sultan `Ali Mashhadi, perhaps the calligraphic treatise mentioned above; the formation of the letters in this sample illustrated the *nasta`liq* style in a most enchanting way.

> His *alifs* were like the tall sapling-figures that give peace to the soul, and the eye of his *sad* was like the eye of the youthful sweethearts. His *dal* and *lam* were like the tresses of heart-ravishing beloveds, and the circles of the *nun* were like the eyebrows of devastating beauties. Every one of his dots was like the pupil of the dark-eyed, and every one of his strokes was like the water of life in the darkness of running ink.[24]

In short, seeing these lines inspired Baba Shah with the desire to achieve perfection in the art of writing, so he apprenticed

---

University Library (P i VII 46), which curiously bears the same title as Baba Shah's work, *Adab al-mashq*.

[22] The last heading in the Lahore manuscript is "on the beauty of script, which is [by] oral instruction" (*an ta`lim ast zabanan*).

[23] *Adab al-mashq*, p. 256.

[24] Ibid., p. 256. The last phrase, an allusion to Dhu al-Qarnayn and the search for the water of life in the land of darkness (cf. Qur. 18), is based on a line in Sultan `Ali's poem.

himself to masters of the profession. Now in writing this treatise he wished to communicate the fruit of his experience and practice, so that the beginner should be made happy and pray for the welfare of the author. The book comprises six parts: first, on avoiding blameworthy qualities; second, on the parts of script; third, on the excellence and duties of copying; fourth, on cutting the pen; fifth, on the manner of composition; and sixth, on the preparation of paper.

Although the technical and stylistic parts of *Adab al-mashq* are certainly valuable, I wish to concentrate here on Baba Shah's expression of the spiritual aspects of calligraphy. His concern for the symbolic aspect of the penman's art is evident from the opening invocations of the treatise. Here the faculty of reading and writing is God's gift to humanity through Adam. The ability to comprehend the divine message is not merely intellectual, however, but involves the heart as well. The merest reflection of God's writing on Adam's heart has inspired the world's greatest lovers:

> Recollection and praise be to the lord who created the simples and compounds of the world and chose Adam out of all beings for the nobility of his capacity for knowledge, and who inscribed some letters with the pen of might on the page of his fortunate mind. The gleam of the sparks of that writing's light cast a glimmer of the sun of Joseph's beauty into the heart of Zulaykha, and made her famous throughout the world as a lover. And a scent from the bower of that writing found its way from the rose of Layla's face and was scented by Majnun, so that he fled in amazement to the desert of disgrace. And a letter from the notebook of that writing's beauty came from Shirin's lip to the ear of Farhad, who tore the clothes of life in the mountains of madness.

Baba Shah reserves special praise for the Prophet Muhammad, whom he describes in traditional Islamic terms as the meaning of the book of existence, and as the source of the cosmological principles known as the Tablet and the Pen; thus the Prophet is that intelligible essence without which the world would have no meaning or existence:

> And blessings without end be on the luminous shrine of the Prophet, for if [he,] the object of the appearance of the book of existence, had not come from the hidden world to the world of appearance, the Tablet and the Pen would not have arisen, and were it not for [him,] the reason

> for the production of the parts of the script of that book, neither the form of length in heaven nor the form of width on earth would have appeared.[25]

Baba Shah reminds us of the calligraphic art with all the terms he uses to describe the intelligibility of the world; the Pen and Tablet are the metaphysical principles to which Islamic theologians ascribe the working out of creation and destiny, while the "length (*dur*)" and "width (*sath*)" of letters are two of the 12 "parts of the script" mentioned later in the text, which he says "must be copied from the script of the master."[26]

The treatise's brief first section summarizes the ethical aspect of calligraphic practice. Baba Shah's main point is practical; the practice of the calligraphic art requires moderation and balance in the soul, without which the expression of the divine beauty with pen and ink becomes flawed.

> Because blameable qualities in the soul are the sign of imbalance, God forbid that work proceed from an imbalanced soul, for there will be no balance in it.
>
> (Verse:) The same thing that is in the jug pours out of it.
>
> So the scribe should completely shun the blameable qualities and acquire the praiseworthy qualities, so that the luminous effects of these blessed qualities appear on the beauty's cheek of his writing, and it becomes sought after by the connoisseurs' temperament.[27]

Baba Shah's stress on the ethical requirements of his art is undoubtedly an example of Sufi practice at work.

In the second section, "on the explanation of the parts of script", Baba Shah Isfahani describes the stylistic and psychological basis of calligraphy, first making a distinction between the parts that are acquired (*tahsili*) and those that are not. The acquired parts may be gained by persistence, application, and maturity, while the unacquired parts come without any effort.

---

[25] *Adab al-mashq*, pp. 255–56. Baba Shah, who was a Shi`i, also included a blessing on the family of `Ali and Fatima, "who are the center of the circle of sainthood."

[26] Ibid., p. 261. For the symbolism of the Pen and Tablet, see Schimmel, p. 79; the world as a book, p. 146.

[27] *Adab al-mashq*, pp. 257–58.

The unacquired parts of script are in fact nothing but the five elements of writing according to the famous calligrapher Yaqut (d. 1298), namely inking (*sawad*), fair copying (*bayad*), preparation (*tashmir*), real rise (*su`ud-i haqiqi*), and real fall (*nuzul-i haqiqi*). Baba Shah does not think these worthy of much comment, since everyone who picks up a pen to write must employ these "parts", so he mentions them only for the sake of good manners towards past masters.[28] Of the 12 acquired parts of script, the first nine have to do with style. This is true of composition (*tarkib*), equal height of similar letters (*kursi*), proportion (*nisbat*), "weakness (*za`f*)" in round strokes, "strength (*quwwat*)" in long strokes, width (*sath*), length (*dur*), apparent rise (*su`ud-i majazi*), and apparent fall (*nuzul-i majazi*).[29]

Yet the last three "parts of script" go beyond style and clearly indicate attainment of mastery. The 10th part, "principles (*usul*)", is based on a skilful control of the nine stylistic parts:

> "Principles" is a characteristic which is gained from the balance in composition of the previously mentioned nine parts. All writing that contains even a little of this quality is precious, and easily will be held dearer than jewels. When this quality becomes conspicuous in writing, it is appropriate if it is loved more than life itself. It is no secret that the [first] nine parts of script are in the position of the body, and "principles" are in the position of the soul.
>
> (Verse:) By God, you will not know the flavor of this wine until you taste it!

The 11th part, "purity (*safa'*)", is primarily a quality of the heart that is the inner source of beauty.

> "Purity" is that condition which makes the temperament happy and refreshed, and makes the eye luminous. One cannot attain it without cleansing the heart. As the Mawlana [Sultan `Ali] said,
>
> (Verse:) Purity of writing is from purity of heart.
>
> Through this quality there is complete possession of [the art of] writing. Just so the human face, no matter how proportionate, is not attractive

[28] Ibid., pp. 264–65.
[29] Ibid., pp. 260–62.

> if it lacks purity. It is no secret that if principles and purity are joined with "authority (*sha'n*)," some call it "taste (*maza*)," and some also call it "effect (*asar*)."

"Authority (*sha'n*)," the last of the 12 parts of script, is the step that makes calligraphy into a part of mysticism, and this vocabulary is actually part of the Sufi terminology for the specification of divine manifestations into form.[30] The very act of writing, at this stage, is contemplation of the divine beauty.

> "Authority" is that condition in which the scribe becomes enraptured from its display when it is found in writing, and he has done with egotism. When the scribe's pen possesses "authority," heedless of the pleasures of the world, he turns his heart toward practice (*mashq*), and the luminous sparks of the real beloved's beauty appear in his vision.
>
> (Verse:) Everywhere the sparks of the beloved's face are found.
>
> And it is fitting, when such a scribe sets his hand to a white page and writes a letter on it in his practice, that he reddens that paper with bloody tears from the extremity of his love for that letter. This characteristic, with the aid of the praiseworthy attributes, becomes the face (*`arid*) of the human soul (*nafs*), and by the power of the pen its form is drawn on the paper page. Not everyone can comprehend this quality in writing, although he may be looking at it. Likewise, even if everyone saw Layla, Majnun saw something that others did not see.[31]

At this point, the calligrapher goes beyond his art to a perception of the invisible inner nature that is only partially revealed in script. Only those endowed with "eyes to see" have the ability to see this inner beauty.

The third section contains Baba Shah's original analysis of the three levels of competence in calligraphic practice (*mashq*), corresponding to the progress from discipleship to mastery. In the first stage of "visual practice (*mashq-i nazari*)", the apprentice studies the master's writing and benefits from learning its spiritual characteristics. This also has the effect of eliminating

---

[30] "When God manifests himself to the human, from the point of view of God the name of that manifestation is `divine authority (*sha'n ilahi*)', and from the point of view of the human it is called `[mystical] state (*hal*)'"–Shah Sayyid Muhammad Zawqi, *Sirr-i Dilbaran* (Karachi: Mahfil-i Zawqiyya, 1405), p. 81.

[31] *Adab al-mashq*, pp. 262–64.

bad habits in weak scribes. "The beginner should be told to do this practice for a while, so that his nature becomes attached to spiritual pleasures. After that, he is told to do pen practice, but even during the days of pen practice he should do this prac tice." The second stage of apprenticeship is pen practice (*mashq-i qalami*), "which is copying (*naql*) from the master's writing." Here the student begins by copying large specimens of isolated letters in the master's hand, so that he understands the form of every letter in the style in which it was written. Even if the copying is not easy, the student will derive considerable educational benefit from studying the large letters. After that, short compositions (less than one hundred lines) may be given to the student. Before doing anything else, the apprentice must contemplate the 17 acquired and unacquired parts of script in the master's model, seeking help in concentration (*himmat*) from the departed spirits of the masters of calligraphy. It goes without saying that the proper techniques of trimming the pen, making ink, and preparing paper will be followed. In pen practice it is of utmost importance that the student pay no attention to writing that is in conflict with the model to be copied, since that would be very harmful. Nor should he do any other exercise until his writing is thoroughly in the traditional style; to reach this point, no less than a full year is necessary. When the apprentice's pen practice has been accomplished to this degree, it is possible to attempt the third stage of "imaginative practice (*mashq-i khayali*)" for a day or two at a time, after preparing by doing several days of pen practice. "Imaginative practice" is not based on copying, but means that the calligrapher uses his purified imagination as the stage on which the forms of beauty appear. Ordinary thinking, which is necessary for pen practice, becomes an obstacle to the spontaneous power of conception of the calligraphic imagination.

> "Imaginative practice" is when the scribe writes not according to a model but with reference to the power of his own nature, and he writes every composition that appears [to him]. The benefit of this practice is that it makes the scribe a master of spontaneity (*tasarruf*),[32] and

[32] *Tasarruf* in Persian normally in this kind of context means "power, control; influence, art, cunning" (Steingass); but here I translate it as "spontaneity" to emphasize that it is

> when this practice mostly takes the place of pen practice, one's writing becomes non-reflective (*bi-maghz*). If someone makes a habit of pen practice and avoids imaginative practice, he lacks spontaneity, and is like the reader who grasps the writing of others but himself cannot write. Spontaneity is not permitted in pen practice.[33]

Through the discipline of total adherence to the models of tradition, and the spiritual influence of the great masters, the student moves towards the pinnacle of the calligraphic art. Here, the meditative contemplation of the divine beauty overflows into the intricate forms of ink on paper. Baba Shah ends his treatise abruptly after giving three more technical sections on cutting the pen, composition of letters, and the preparation of paper, so any conclusion about the inner aspect of calligraphy is now up to us to formulate.

Baba Shah's whole intent in describing calligraphic concentration is to focus on the visual contemplation of God's beauty as conveyed by the intricate shapes of black letters on white paper, and the aesthetic basis for this contemplation appears to be closely bound with Sufi mysticism. It is well known that Islamic calligraphy has been closely involved with the development of Sufism, and that many calligraphers were trained as disciples by Sufi masters.[34] Baba Shah himself was known for his inclination toward mysticism, and it has even been suggested that he belonged to an esoteric order known as the Nuqtaviyya, a little-known group that was strongly influenced by letter-mysticism.[35] With this background in mind, we can review some of the religious sources of Islamic calligraphy, and then recapitulate the main features of Baba Shah's treatise, in order to determine the points of impact of Sufism on his vision of the calligraphic art.

---

a talent without external cause or deliberation, since it is "non-reflective (*bi-maghz*)", literally "without brain", in contrast with the intellectual discipline of pen practice.

[33] *Adab al-mashq*, pp. 265–68.

[34] Pope and Ackerman, p. 1733; Schimmel, p. 47, and chapter III on calligraphy and Sufism in general.

[35] Bayani I, 86, citing Taqi al-Din Kashani, *Khulasat al-ash`ar*, MS partly in his collection and partly in the National Parliament Library, Tehran. The *nuqta* is the rhomboid dot or point made by the tip of the pen, which is the measure for construction of all the letters of the alphabet. A study of the Nuqtavi movement, which is evidently still active, has been promised by N. Mudarrisi Chahardihi, *Sayri dar tasawwuf, sharh-i hal-i haftad tan az mashayikh wa aqtab-i sufiyya* (Tehran, 1980).

The religious aspect of.Islamic calligraphy springs from the Qur'an, the word of God as expressed to Muhammad, which of necessity had a strongly visual component. The Qur'an itself frequently alludes to the pen and writing, generally in contexts that emphasize writing as a medium for conveying the divine message to humanity. The earliest Qur'ans exhibit large letters on parchment in the austere yet graceful Kufic style, so that the relatively small number of words on the page appear more like a visual icon than an ordinary book. Visualization of the actual form of the Arabic script in the Qur'an seems to have played an important role in Muslim religious experience from an early date, centered as it was on recitation from the holy book.[36] The controversies that raged over whether the Qur'an was co-eternal with God are an indication of the extraordinary position that the scripture assumed for the Muslim community. As Anthony Welch has written, "The written form of the *Qur'an* is the visual equivalent of the eternal *Qur'an* and is humanity's perceptual glimpse of the divine."[37] Visual concentration on the Qur'an as the word of God was the closest possible approximation on earth to seeing God face to face.

The mystical aesthetic of Islamic calligraphy derives in particular from what Schimmel calls "the tendency to equate human figures to letters," a symbolism that links the human to the divine through the medium of writing.[38] Regardless of its precise origin, the depiction of the human face or form as comprised of letters is a fascinating artistic phenomenon. The cabalistic faces comprising the names of `Ali, Muhammad, and Allah testify to a fundamental conviction that the human being is essentially composed of spiritual elements. This seemingly abstract concept is a graphic representation of an intuition of the intelligibility of the world. Everything is made of the word. The equation of the human face with the Qur'an itself is both a scriptural understanding of human nature and a calligraphic illustration of the hadith of the Prophet, "Do not disfigure the face,

---

[36] Martin Lings, in Schimmel, p. 82.

[37] Anthony Welch, *Calligraphy in the Arts of the Muslim World,* (Folkestone, Kent: Dawson, 1979), p. 22.

[38] Schimmel, p. 110, cf. 134.

for God created Adam in his own image (*la taqabbahu al-wajha, fa-inna allaha khalaqa adama `ala suratihi*)."[39] Not only can the human face be understood as scripture, but also the form of the sacred writing is a manifestation of the divine essence. To save a symbol like the "face of God (*wajhallah*)" from anthropomorphism, the Sufis understood it symbolically, as the theophany of positive divine attributes that sustains the world in existence.[40] In this symbolic configuration, the "face" of the divine being's positive or gracious attributes is framed by the black tresses of the negative or wrathful attributes, a contrast that immediately suggests white paper covered with black letters. When punning poets constantly compare the writing (*khatt*) on the page with the dark down (*khatt*) on the white cheek of the beloved, they surely intend this metaphor of the book as the manifestation of the divine countenance.[41] But metaphor is not anthropomorphism. The Sufis clearly understand the image of the written divine face to mean both the intelligible factor in human nature and the revelation of the divine nature. Thus the modern Sufi Shah Zawqi writes, "the divine face . . . comprehends the totality of manifestations of the essence and unlimited knowledge, gnosis, and secrets."[42] Like gazing at beautiful human faces, contemplating the beautiful faces of calligraphy is a metaphorical love (*`ishq-i majazi*) that can lead to real love (*`ishq-i haqiqi*).[43]

Baba Shah Isfahani's description of calligraphy in *Adab al-mashq* clearly stands in this tradition of mystical appreciation of calligraphy. When Baba Shah recalled his rapture on seeing Sultan `Ali's calligraphy, with letters like heart-ravishing beauties, it was not merely a figure of speech, but a passionate recognition of the divine manifestations in writing. In the primordial encounter of God and Adam, God "taught by the pen, taught

---

[39] Badi` al-Zaman Furuzanfarr, *Ahadis-i masnavi* (Tehran: Danishgah, 1334), p. 115, no. 346.

[40] `Ayn al-Quzat Hamadani's theory of the "face of God" is discussed in my *Words of Ecstasy in Sufism*, SUNY Series in Islam (Albany: State University of New York Press, 1984), pp. 76 ff.

[41] "This script on the face of the beloved so attracts with loveliness and grace that it has formed the totality of all subtleties and points of comeliness and beauty, and no loveliness of face or sweetness could surpass it" (Zawqi Shah, p. 155).

[42] Zawqi Shah, p. 177.

[43] Cf. Schimmel, p. 133.

man what he did not know" (Qur. 96:4–5). The letters inscribed on Adam's heart, according to Baba Shah, are the source of Zulaykha's love for Joseph, Majnun's love for Layla, and Farhad's love for Shirin. Beyond the ethical balance required of the calligrapher are the "principles" that form the soul of the lifeless mechanics of writing, and the "purity" of heart without which mere external proportion lacks beauty, whether in the human face or in the letter on the page. Mystical experience of the divine manifestations occurs in the state of "authority", in which the beloved's face is directly transformed into letters on the page. Even in the training of the apprentice, contemplation of the master's letters leads directly to the spiritual world, as geometry did according to Plato. Calligraphic practice, for those who have mastered its "imaginative" level, is the spontaneous result of non-reflective contemplation. This Sufi training in calligraphy unites the intellect with the heart in contemplating beauty. Where gnosis is tied to love, the very intelligibility of writing becomes passionate.

For the calligrapher of the spirit, then, the world is a book, and the writing in that book, that is, the intelligibility that is inscribed upon matter, is the manifestation of the divine essence. To understand this writing is to know God, and knowing God is love's passionate recognition of the features of the beloved. Baba Shah described his exposure to *nasta`liq* calligraphy as beginning with intellectual recognition, but culminating in a longing that overwhelmed him. "When my heart found out the news of the existence of that water of life, and its savor took root in my palate, it realized that it was overcome with thirst, and the cry of `thirst, thirst!' reverberated in the chamber of my breast."[44] Baba Shah Isfahani was by no means the first in the Islamic tradition to experience the rapture of calligraphic beauty, but he has given us one of its finest descriptions.

---

[44] *Adab al-mashq*, p. 256. With reference to the ink of the "water of life" (above, n. 24), Zawqi's observation underlines the Sufi associations of this imagery: "The specifications of the spirits (*ta`ayyunat-i arwah*) are that darkness in which the water of life is concealed. In this very darkness there is a hint of the signless sign, or the absolute essence; thus it is called 'the water of life'" (p. 155).

17

The Symbolism of Birds and Flight in the Writings of Rūzbihān Baqlī

The imagery of birds and flight has long been a universal symbol of the ascension of the human soul to a higher reality.[1] From the winged deities of the ancient Near East to the angels of the Bible and the winged souls of Plato's *Phaedrus*, poets and prophets have depicted the power of the wing to lift the soul through flight to paradise. Among non-scriptural peoples, it is especially in the complex of Central Asian and Siberian religious practices called "shamanistic" that the symbolism of flight is powerfully displayed.[2] In the Islamic tradition, notable early explorations of the symbolism of birds and flight can be found in the writings of philosophers, Sufis, and poets such as Ibn Sīnā (d. 1037), al-Ghāzālī (d. 1111), Suhrawardī (d. 1191), Khāqānī (d. 1199), and above all in the great mystical epic of Farīd al-Dīn `Aṭṭār (d. ca. 1220), *Manṭiq al-ṭayr* or *The Language of the Birds*.[3] But

---

[1] Manabu Waida, "Birds," *Encyclopedia of Religion* (New York: Macmillan Publishing Company, 1987), 2:224–27; William K. Mahony, "Flight," ibid., 5:349–53.

[2] Mircea Eliade, *Shamanism, Archaic Techniques of Ecstasy*, trans. Willard R. Trask, Bollingen Series LXXVI (Princeton, NJ: Princeton University Press, 1974), pp. 477–82. "Magical flight is the expression both of the soul's autonomy and of ecstasy" (ibid., p. 479).

[3] For Ibn Sīnā, al-Ghazālī, and the philosopher Suhrawardī, see Henry Corbin, *Avicenna and the Visionary Recital*, trans. Willard R. Trask, Bollingen Series LXVI (Princeton, NJ: Princeton

if we think in terms of Persian Sufism, one author in particular claims our attention for his extensive use of the symbolism of birds and flight. This is Rūzbihān Baqlī (d. 1206), the Sufi master of Shiraz, a prolific and powerful writer of works on Sufism in both Persian and Arabic. Rūzbihān's characteristically poetic style employs the full range of metaphors of birds and flight to express the different modes of mystical experience. Rūzbihān's concentration on the experiential dimension of Sufism makes his work especially valuable for revealing the mystical understanding of literary tropes.[4] Although he frequently strains symbols to the breaking point, his constant clarification of their mystical significations makes him one of the most revealing authors in the Persian Sufi tradition.

Rūzbihān lived in Shiraz when it was a small island of prosperity and culture under the rule of the Salghurid atabegs, after the decline of the Seljuks and before the storm of the Mongol conquest.[5] He continued the line of Sufi tradition in Shiraz that went back to Ibn al-Khafīf (d. 982) and through him to Baghdadian Sufis such as the martyr al-Hallaj (d. 922). One may ask, however, from a purely literary point of view, how significant the works of Rūzbihān are for the understanding of later Sufism through the fifteenth century. Direct references to Rūzbihān in later Persian Sufi literature are not terribly common, and they tend to focus on his reputation as a lover of beauty.[6] He is known for his prescription of the three things which the gnostics require

University Press, 1960; reprint ed., Dallas, TX: Spring Publications, Inc., 1980), pp. 165–203, and Farīd al-Dīn `Aṭṭār Nīshābūrī, *Manṭiq al-ṭayr*, ed. Muḥammad Jawād Mashkūr (3rd ed., Tehran: Nāṣir-i Khusraw, 1968), Introduction, pp. xxxi–xlii. The poem by Khāqānī called *manṭiq al-ṭayr* is found in *Dīvān-i Khāqānī-i Shīrvānī* (Tehran: Intishārāt-i Arisṭū, 1362), pp. 31–34; trans. Peter L. Wilson and Nasrollah Pourjavady, *The Drunken Universe: An Anthology of Persian Sufi Poetry* (Grand Rapids, MI: Phanes Press, 1988), pp. 119–29.

[4] Similar analyses could yield useful insights into Rūzbihān's use of other prominent symbols and metaphors, such as desert, ocean, mirror, vision, tongue, bride, veil, light, mine, clothes, and sun.

[5] Cf. C. E. Bosworth, "The Political and Dynastic History of the Iranian World (A.D. 1000–1217),", in *The Cambridge History of Iran*, vol. 5, *The Saljuq and Mongol Periods*, ed. J. A. Boyle (Cambridge: Cambridge University Press, 1968), pp. 172–73.

[6] See, e.g., Fakhr al-Dīn `Irāqī [attr.], *The Song of Lovers*, ed. and trans. A. J. Arberry (Calcutta: Islamic Research Association, 1939), pp. 88–90 (text), 57–58 (trans.). See also Arthur J. Arberry, *Shiraz: Persian City of Saints and Poets* (Norman: University of Oklahoma Press, 1960), pp. 86–111, for a brief sketch of Rūzbihān's life and works.

of a singer when listening to music (*samā`*): fine fragrances, a beautiful face, and a sweet voice (*rawā'iḥ-i ṭayyiba wa wajh-i ṣabīḥ wa ṣawt-i malīḥ*). Frequently one also finds mention of the well-known episode in which he forbade a young woman to veil her face, on the grounds that separating beauty and love would be a crime.[7]

Rūzbihān's writings were difficult, however, and there are not many explicit responses to his works by later authors. Some commentaries on his writings do exist, however; an Anatolian Naqshbandī Sufi named `Abd Allāh Ilāhī Sīmābī (d. 1491) commented on the *Risālat al-quds* (*Treatise on the Sacred*), a work on Sufism addressed to novices,[8] and an anonymous writer also glossed Rūzbihān's treatise on love, the *`Abhar al-`āshiqīn* (*Jasmine of the Lovers*).[9] We know that Rūzbihān's works were studied by authors such as Jāmī (d. 1492) in fifteenth-century Herat, and that they attracted the interest of the Mughal prince Dārā Shikūh (d. 1659) in the seventeenth century.[10] All these later figures testified to the difficulty of Rūzbihān's style, which at times is admittedly convoluted and obscure. Jāmī remarked that "he has sayings that have poured forth from him in the state

---

[7] Jāmī, *Tuḥfat al-aḥrār* (Lucknow: Tēj Kumār, 1966), pp. 61–62. Jāmī also tells the story in *Nafaḥāt al-uns wa ḥaḍarāt al-quds*, ed. Mahdī Tawḥīdīpūr (Tehran: Kitāb-furūshī-yi Maḥmūdī, 1337/1957), p. 256.

[8] This commentary, entitled *Manāzil al-qulūb*, is printed in Muḥammad Taqī Dānish-puzhūh, ed., *Rūzbihān nāma*, Silsila-yi Intishārāt-i Anjuman-i Āthār-i Millī, 60 (Tehran: Chāp-khāna-yi Bahman, 1347/1969), pp. 387–420, from a manuscript from Yugoslavia. Two other manuscripts of this text are in Egypt, and another is reported to be in Manisa, Turkey; cf. Abū Muḥammed Rūzbihān al-Baḳlī al-Şīrāzī, *Kitāb Maşrab al-arvāḥ*, ed. Nazif Hoca, İstanbul Üniversitesi Edebiyat Fakültesi Yayınları No. 1876 (Istanbul: Edebiyat Fakültesi Matbaası, 1974), Introduction, p. 1. On Ilāhī Sīmābī, who studied in Samarqand, met Jāmī in Herat, and died in Rumelia, see *Rūzbihān nāma*, pp. 64–66. See also Rūzbihān Baqlī Shīrāzī, *Risālat al-quds wa ghalaṭāt al-sālikīn*, ed. Jawād Nūrbakhsh (Tehran: Chāp-khāna-yi Firdawsī, 1351/1972).

[9] Rūzbihān Baqlī Shīrāzī, *`Abhar al-`āshiqīn*, eds Henry Corbin and Muḥammad Mu'īn, Ganjīna-yi Nivishtahā-yi Īrānī, 8 (Tehran: Anjuman-i Īrān-shināsī-yi Farānsa dar Tihrān, 1360/1981), pp. 149–202. These glosses appear to date from the early Safavid period (ibid., Persian Introduction, p. 108).

[10] Dārā Shikūh had Rūzbihān's *tafsīr*, *`Arā'is al-bayān*, translated into Persian, and he wrote an abridgement and update of Rūzbihān's commentary on the ecstatic sayings of the early Sufis (*Sharḥ-i shaṭḥiyyāt*) under the title *Ḥasanāt al-`ārifīn* (below, n. 12). For the original text, see Rūzbihān Baqlī Shīrāzī, *Sharḥ-i shaṭḥiyyāt*, ed. Henry Corbin, Bibliothéque Iranienne 12 (Tehran: Departement d'iranologie de l'Institut Franco-iranien, 1966).

of overpowering ecstasy, which not everyone can understand."[11] Dārā Shikūh found his style "fatiguing."[12] Despite the preservation of Rūzbihān's legacy by his son and grandson in Shiraz, and for all that Louis Massignon has traced the existence of the *ṭarīqa-i Rūzbihāniyya* as far as Timbuktu, it must be admitted that none of his physical or spiritual descendants has been able to reach Rūzbihān's level of mystical attainment or to match him as a stylist in Persian or Arabic.[13] It is not, however, the frequency of references to Rūzbihān that makes him relevant to the study of Persian Sufism; it is, rather, the penetration of his existential insight that makes his writing significant. It is only in recent decades that the rediscovery and publication of his writings has led to a renewed appreciation of his importance for the understanding of Sufism. Muḥammad Mu`īn, the pioneering editor of the *`Abhar al-`āshiqīn*, remarked about this text, that "to understand the works of mystics such as `Aṭṭār, Rūmī, `Irāqī, Awḥadī-i Kirmānī, and Ḥāfiẓ, researches on this book are quite necessary."[14] I would enlarge upon this statement and say that the various writings of Rūzbihān Baqlī form a vital resource for understanding the experiential basis of Persian Sufi literature.

Rūzbihān regards the symbol of the bird as multivalent, capable of standing for a wide variety of spirits, persons, and experiences. The importance of this image in Rūzbihān's writings may be gauged by the frequency with which he uses it in the beginnings of his treatises, immediately following the praise of

---

[11] Jāmī, *Nafaḥāt*, p. 255.

[12] Dārā Shikūh, *Ḥasanāt al-`ārifīn*, ed. Makhdūm Rahīn (Tehran, 1352/1973), p. 3.

[13] Louis Massignon, "La Vie et les œuvres de Ruzbehan Baqli," in *Opera Minora*, ed. Y. Moubarac (Beirut: Dar al-Maaref, 1963), II, 451–65, esp. 455–56 for the *ṭarīqa*. As far as the subject of this essay is concerned, Rūzbihān's descendants have very little to say; there are no references to the symbolism of flight in their biographies of Rūzbihān, and the only mention of birds is an incident in which Rūzbihān detected that a chicken offered to him as food was not lawful (*Rūzbihān nāma*, pp. 45, 220–21).

[14] Mu`īn, Introduction to *`Abhar*, p. 84. In this respect, Mu`īn shared the view of Dr. Qāsim Ghanī, that "from the point of view of the greatness of his mystical station, and from the perspective of ecstasy and spiritual state, Shaykh Rūzbihān is on the level of Shaykh Abu'l-Ḥasan Kharaqānī and Shaykh Abū Sa`īd-i Abu'l-Khayr"; Ghanī also placed Rūzbihān prominently in his list of 28 major Sufi authors. See his *Baḥth dar āthār wa afkār wa aḥwāl-i Ḥāfiẓ*, vol. 2, *Tārīkh-i taṣawwuf dar islām wa taṭawwurāt wa taḥawwulāt-i mukhtalifa-yi ān az ṣadr-i islām tā `aṣr-i Ḥāfiẓ* (Tehran: Kitābfurūshī Zawwār, 1340/1961), p. 395, n. 2; p. 545.

God and the Prophet.[15] When commenting on a phrase used by Hallaj, "the fortunate bird", Rūzbihān offered a startling number of possible interpretations:

> The "fortunate bird"[16] is the hoopoe of Solomon, on whom be peace, or the phoenix of the west, or the royal *humā*, or the bird of success, or the bird of inspiration, or the bird of the spirit, or lucky augury, or the bird of light who circumambulates the throne, or white cock that is beneath the throne, or Gabriel, or the chosen one [Muḥammad], blessings of God upon him.

Frequently, also, Rūzbihān speaks of the Prophet Muḥammad using bird symbolism, calling him "the nightingale of the love of pre-eternities, the *sīmurgh* of the nest of post-eternities."[17] The two birds, the *sīmurgh* and the nightingale, have sharply differing qualities as symbols of the divine beloved and the human lover (discussed below), but the dynamic role of the Prophet mediates between these two poles. Likewise the Sufi saint Bāyazīd Bisṭāmī (d. 874) is called "the bird of the nest of isolation", alluding to the spiritual state (*ifrād*) with which Bāyazīd is associated.[18] Sufis who have been persecuted and killed are called "the birds of sanctity" who have returned to their nests.[19] In a little-known text on theology, Rūzbihān calls upon the imagery of birds flying in acelestial garden to indicate the role of prophets, angels, and saints: "He manifested the gardens of intimacy and called them 'the enclosure of sanctity,' and in it flew the spirits of the elect, among the prophets, messengers, cherubs, spirituals, gnostics, and unitarians."[20] Somewhat more abstractly, Rūzbihān uses

---

[15] Extensive passages with bird imagery are found at the beginning in Rūzbihān's Qur'an commentary, *`Arā'is al-bayān* (below, at n. 52), in his letter to `Imad al-Dīn Kirmānī (below, at n. 41), and in the *Risālat al-quds* (below, at n. 43), and phrases with bird imagery are frequent in the exordia of other texts as well (e.g., *Sharḥ-i shaṭḥiyyāt*, p. 4, bottom).

[16] *Sharḥ-i shaṭḥiyyāt*, p. 365. This passage is a commentary on Hallaj's *Riwāya* 21, in which the "fortunate bird" is one of the symbolic transmitters of a *ḥadīth*.

[17] *`Abhar al-`āshiqīn*, p. 120; cf. also p. 20.

[18] *Sharḥ-i shaṭḥiyyāt*, p. 35.

[19] Ibid., p. 33.

[20] Rūzbihān Baqlī, *Lawāmi` al-tawḥīd*, MS 1460 Ahmet Salis, Topkapı Library, Istanbul, fol. 4b. This fine manuscript, which was not noticed by previous researchers (Mu`īn, Introduction to *Rūzbihān nāma*, p. 71; Dānish-puzhūh, *Rūzbihān nāma*, pp. 264–66 [extract], 341, no. 8), seems to be the sole existing complete copy of this work by Rūzbihān. It is

birds and their songs to symbolize particular spiritual experiences that have been revealed by the ecstatic expressions (*shaṭḥiyyāt*) of Sufis such as Bāyazīd and Hallaj:

> The bird of isolation sang "*allāh, allāh,*" the bird of uniting (*tawḥīd*) said, "I am the Real (*anā al-ḥaqq*)", the bird of sanctification said "Glory be to me (*subḥānī*)." When they arose from the New Year's garden of witnessing, they flew with the wings of pre-eternities in the post-eternities of post-eternities. Those birds of divinity brought the secret of divinity to the palace of humanity, and spoke with the soul of divinity in the tongue of humanity.[21]

Similarly, when the divine essence retracts and the soul is cut off from spiritual experience, we are told that "the bird of manifestation has gone to the nest of eternity."[22] Rūzbihān has been followed by his commentator Ilāhī Sīmābī in this tendency to use birds to symbolize spiritual experiences, in this case regarding the primacy of the experience of "opening (*futūḥ*)" as a prerequisite for receiving "unveiling (*kashf*)" of the divine sanctity: "From the atmosphere in which the spirit's *sīmurgh* [flies], before this, the bird of 'opening (*futūḥ*)' has been seen."[23] In other words, before the spirit can soar like the *sīmurgh*, it must first take flight with the experience of "opening". The anonymous commentator on the *`Abhar al-`āshiqīn* has also seen that Rūzbihān's use of bird imagery is meant to recall spiritual experiences. This can be seen in a passage in which Rūzbihān speaks of the trapped bird as an image of the soul trapped in the body: "See what bird is in your trap, that the nest of the *sīmurgh* of the throne cannot bear its grain!" The commentator remarks that "the universal

an elementary treatise on theology in 35 fols., accompanied by another short text previously not found, *Maslak al-tawḥīd*, in 21 fols. (cf. Mu`īn, p. 71, and *Rūzbihān nāma*, p. 342, no. 23).

[21] *Sharḥ-i shaṭḥiyyāt*, p. 22. On the subject of *shaṭḥiyyāt*, see my *Words of Ecstasy in Sufism* (Albany: State University of New York Press, 1985).

[22] *Sharḥ-i shaṭḥiyyāt*, p. 187.

[23] Sīmābī, *Manāzil al-qulūb*, in *Rūzbihān nāma*, p. 402 (verse), commenting on the phrase "unveiling of the sanctity of sanctity" in *Risālat al-quds*, ed. Nūrbakhsh, p. 44.

intellect is incapable of comprehending [the soul's] emanation, which is love."[24]

The particular birds most frequently invoked by Rūzbihān are the nightingale and the phoenix-like bird called *sīmurgh* or *`anqā*. Unlike Rūmī or `Aṭṭār, Rūzbihān is not too interested in describing other varieties of birds and the qualities they represent.[25] The nightingale, of course, is a staple of Persian poetry, as the figure of the impassioned human lover addressing the unattainable beauty of the divine rose.[26] The *sīmurgh*, at first a supernatural bird and helper of humanity in ancient Iranian mythology, has become a symbol of the divine in Persian literature.[27] Because Rūzbihān so often stresses the ascension from human attributes to divine ones, he frequently blurs the distinction between the nightingale and the *sīmurgh*. Thus he urges his reader to ascend to the true home, the heavenly nest:

> Remove the belongings of the *sīmurgh* from this narrow hut, for the orient of the throne is the nest of your eternal soul. Take the power of Jesus' soul from the heaven of pre-eternity, so that with the birds of angelicity you complete a house for this nightingale of power.[28]

Sometimes he combines the *sīmurgh* with the *humā*, the royal bird whose shadow designates a king. "Cast off the shadow of temporality's veil from existence, so that the *humā* of the Attributes opens the wings of pre-eternity, and the *sīmurgh* of

[24] *`Abhar al-`āshiqīn*, p. 190, commenting on text, p. 62. In a similar fashion, this commentator identifies the "birds of silence" (text, p. 60) as "the people of concentration and meditation" (p. 187).

[25] Occasionally Rūzbihān speaks of the peacock (*Sharḥ-i shaṭḥiyyāt*, pp. 226, 236; *`Abhar al-`āshiqīn*, p. 142), the hoopoe (*Sharḥ-i shaṭḥiyyāt*, pp. 365, 370), or the crow (ibid, p. 257; *Rūzbihān nāma*, p. 322).

[26] Annemarie Schimmel, "Rose und Nachtigall," *Numen* V (1958), pp. 85–109. For a survey of references to birds in early classical Persian poetry, see C.-H. de Fouchécour, *La Description de la nature dans la poésie lyrique persane du XIe siècle: Inventaire et analyse des thèmes* (Paris: Librairie C. Klincksieck, 1969), pp. 138–50.

[27] Cf. Alessandro Bausani, "Letteratura Neopersiana," in Antonino Pagliaro and Alessandro Bausani, *Storia della letteratura persiana* (Milan: Nuova Accademia Editrice, 1960), pp. 290–93; Johann Christoph Bürgel, *The Feather of Simurgh: The "Licit Magic" of the Arts in Medieval Islam* (New York: New York University Press, 1988), pp. 5–7.

[28] *Sharḥ-i shaṭḥiyyāt*, p. 283.

majesty comes from the orient of eternity."[29] But always the injunction is the same: the soul ascends like a heavenly bird to find its identity, and like the birds in `Aṭṭār's tale, it finds God as its true self. "When the *sīmurgh* of the soul flies from the realm of humanity to the world of divinity, the growing soul speaks to itself in the rose-bower of Adam's clay; those seeking the reflection of that shadowing `*anqā* become the shadow of God."[30] At times the `*anqā* as the transcendent God becomes overwhelming: "Existence in relation to His might is less than an atom, and all the angels of the heaven of power are lowly locusts in the beak of the `*anqā* of his eternal wrath."[31] Yet at other times, the soul overwhelmed by the ecstasy of *shaṭḥ* shifts from the self-effacement of the nightingale to the audacity of the hoopoe, who did not hesitate to show off his knowledge before Solomon.

> The lily of beauty reached the stage of the nightingale of perfection. The shadow of the blessed tree of eternity became the illumination of the spring of the nightingales who chant "I am the Real." At the confluence of the sources of pre-eternity the hoopoes of the spirits drank the water of life of "Glory be to me." Thus in the feast of the Solomon of unity, from intoxication they became the sovereigns of existence. With hidden tongue of the human intellect in the sanctified nest beyond canopy and throne, they said "I learned something which you did not."[32]

The plasticity of the nightingale and the *sīmurgh* in Rūzbihān's imagery is a direct result of the sudden and precipitous outbursts of his spiritual experiences, which he has chronicled in moredirect terms in his autobiographical *Kashf al-asrār*.[33]

---

[29] Ibid., p. 143. The "foolish" *humā* as image of the human soul appears in `*Abhar al-`āshiqīn*, p. 62, while in a verse by Rūzbihān the *humā* is the divinity which cannot fit into the nest of the human heart (*Rūzbihān nāma*, p. 355).

[30] *Sharḥ-i shaṭḥiyyāt*, p. 331.

[31] Ibid., p. 96.

[32] Ibid., p. 20, quoting Qur. 27:22, the speech of the hoopoe to Solomon (also cited at ibid., p. 370).

[33] For this text, see Henry Corbin, *En Islam iranien: Aspects spirituels et philosophiques*, vol. 3, *Les Fidèles d'amour, Shi'isme et soufisme* (Paris: Éditions Gallimard, Bibliothèque des Idées, 1972). Portions of the Arabic text have been published by Paul Nwyia, S.J., "Waqā'i` al-Shaykh Rūzbihān al-Baqlī al-Shīrāzī muqtaṭafāt min kitāb *Kashf al-asrār wa mukāshafat al-anwār*," *al-Mashriq* LXIV/4–5 (1970), pp. 385–406, and by Nazif Hoca, ed., *Rūzbihān al-Baḳlī ve Kitāb Kaşf al-asrār'ı ile Farsça bāzi şiirleri*, Istanbul Üniversitesi Edebiyat Fakültesi

Keeping in mind the freshness of these images in Rūzbihān's hands may help to counter the impression one frequently gets in later Persian poetry, that images such as the nightingale and the rose have been deprived of all life and loveliness at the hands of mediocre poets. Rūzbihān's use of these symbols to indicate the ascendant experiences of the soul can help remind us of what a mystical interpretion of Persian poetry can be.

Rūzbihān makes use of an extended complex of imagery related to birds to express various mystical insights. When combined, these images provide a more comprehensive picture of the celestial habitat of the soul-bird.[34] As we have already seen, the nest of the bird is a symbol of transcendence that reveals that the bird's true home is not earth but heaven. The nest must inevitably be located in a tree that is in the heavenly garden, such as the lotus or *ṭūbā* tree, as the bird discovers when it finally gains admission: "Since I saw that rose of the rose garden and the dark narcissus, the lotus and the *ṭūbā* trees are in my garden."[35] But getting to that heavenly garden is not so simple. Because of the rebellious nature of the soul, it must be trapped with bait of grain or sugar. Sometimes it is only the hope of that grain that holds the bird in the trap: "Such a sweet-singing nightingale with so many thousands of songs suddenly fell in the hunter's trap of persecution, and in hope of the grain of seeing the visage of that moon-faced beauty in the thorny rose garden, it remained an attendant at the feast of his pain."[36] Rūmī also writes of love trapping the bird of the soul with sugar.[37] This is a reversal of the pessimistic view of the bird's entrapment as a metaphor for the

---

Yayınları No. 1678 (Istanbul: Edebiyat Fakültesi Matbaası, 1971), pp. 103–18. For a complete translation, see Ruzbihan Baqli, *The Unveiling of Secrets: Diary of a Sufi Master*, trans. Carl W. Ernst (Chapel Hill: Parvardigar Press, 1997).

[34] For the motif of the soul-bird in general, see Annemarie Schimmel, *As Through a Veil: Mystical Poetry in Islam* (New York: Columbia University Press, 1982), pp. 75–76; id., *The Triumphal Sun: A Study of the Works of Jalāloddin Rumi* (London: Fine Books, 1978), pp. 113–124. To the standard stock of images, Rūzbihān does not hesitate to add even the ordinarily disgusting picture of a bird disgorging stones from its crop: "The annotations of those seas belong to the soul-killing birds, who from time to time cast forth the pearl of 'I am the Real' from the shells of their crops" (*Sharḥ-i shaṭḥiyyāt*, p. 501).

[35] Verse, in *Rūzbihān nāma*, p. 344. On the motifs of heavenly trees, see Bausani, pp. 286–90.

[36] *`Abhar al-`āshiqīn*, p. 60.

[37] Annemarie Schimmel, *As Through a Veil*, p. 112, with notes 207 and 208.

fall of the soul into matter, as Adam fell, also snared by a grain of wheat.[38] In a complex extended passage, Rūzbihān speaks of the entrapment of the bird as the soul's imprisonment in the body, but he optimistically predicts that the soul will free itself and ultimately attain the status of being the hawk on the wrist of the divine hunter:

> Know that when the spirit of humanity was placed in the clay of Adam, and the brides of the spirits were imprisoned in those mines, and the gates of the heart were barred with the obstacles of desires, it was for the sake of testing, so that cage-breaking bird would break out of the prison of temporality with the existence-holding beak, and fly in the atmosphere of divinity, and sit in the gardens of witnessing on the branches of the rose of sufficiency, and with a tongueless tongue tell to the beloved the pain of separation from the face of the beloved. But if it acquires a taste for the reins of desires, it will be imprisoned in the four walls of nature, and will be restrained from flight in the atmosphere of pre-eternity.
>
> Yes, if the secret of longing enters upon him, and he rattles the chain of eternal love, and he brings up that rational spirit from the cage of the body, and makes it fly in the garden of lordship, that hawk (*bāsha*) will wheel about in the existence of angelicity, and overlook the seraglio of might, and will find himself at no other place than the wrist of the hunter of pre-eternity, who catches the birds of the mountains of love with the love-charm of fate.[39]

The soul must make constant effort to practice discipline and avoid bad company, says Rūzbihān: "Start removing yourself from this flock of foolish sparrows, for in the flight of the Western *`anqā*, your soul will not fly with a broken wing."[40] But the divine mercy will also help to bring the hapless bird out of its imprisonment into the heavenly garden, calling it as God called to Moses on Sinai:

> Praise to that lord who brought the bird of felicity from the cage of persecution to the rosebower of purity and trust, with the ringing cry of 'We called him from the right side of the mountain' (Qur. 19:52), who

---

[38] For this theme in Rūmī, see Schimmel, *Triumphal Sun*, pp. 113–14.

[39] *Risālat al-quds*, p. 29.

[40] *Sharḥ-i shaṭḥiyyāt*, p. 599.

> expelled the crows of nature from the gardens of reality, and who called the nightingale of the most holy spirit with speech.[41]

Breaking out of the cage of the body will involve a death, whether physical or spiritual, before the soul can return to its home.[42] But when it does finally return to the garden, Rūzbihān is sure that the bird of the soul will perch on the branches of the rose and sing, recalling and fulfilling the primordial covenant it made by saying yes to God's question, "Am I not your lord?" (Qur. 7:171). "Let the rose of beauty grow before those nightingales of everlastingness on the branches of majesty, let the nightingale of 'Am I not [your lord] (*alast*)' speak the secrets of love with those birds of the throne."[43] According to Rūzbihān, the epiphany of God as the red rose is the supreme moment of this reunion.

There are times when Rūzbihān abandons the notion of the bird as symbolic of the soul, taking it instead as a symbol of creation. He is led to do this especially when considering Hallaj's exegesis of an enigmatic verse of the Qur'an addressed to Abraham, "'Take four birds and sacrifice them' [2:260], for the Real does not fly." Rūzbihān in this way treats the birds as representing the unstable four elements of matter, which must be annihilated and abolished from consciousness, so that the ego can be destroyed and the Real can be revealed:

> If you wish to know our allusion in reality, and to understand knowledge in oneness, and to arrive to that which we described of the annihilation of the creature in the creator, . . . call the four birds of the elements near to you, and with the sword of intoxication, love, and desire, cut them to pieces. . . . Cut the throat of each bird in the court of the spirit's jealousy, because the elements fly [away] and become unsteady; the knowledge of that does not fly [away]. . . . When you have killed and annihilated the birds of the elements, and torn off from them the wings of spatial dimensions, and loosened yourself from those weights of creation, then no duration, time, place, or witness remains; you reach the world of

[41] Letter to `Imād al-Dīn Kirmānī, in *Rūzbihān nāma*, p. 322.

[42] Some of the last verses that Rūmī wrote for his friends treated "the soul bird's flight from the cage of the body" (Schimmel, *As Through a Veil*, p. 94).

[43] *Risālat al-quds*, p. 3. The nightingale singing on the rose branch recurs in *Sharḥ-i shaṭḥiyyāt*, pp. 92, 225, 230, and *`Abhar al-`āshiqīn*, p. 124.

> utter nonexistence, and are astonished in it, so that you do not know who you are. . . .[44]

In a similar vein, Ilāhī Sīmābī on occasion deals with birds as symbols of earthly life, the physicality of which must be transcended: "Every pigeon flies in a certain way, but this pigeon [flies] in a directionless direction. We are not kin to the birds of the air, and our grain is a grainless grain."[45]

So at times the bird-symbolism is used to denote the limitations of physical existence. Most typically, however, Rūzbihān sees the bird as an image of the "rational spirit (*rūḥ-i nāṭiqa*)", the inner essence of humanity, which is forever seeking its divine counterpart even while trapped in the body. "The bird of intimacy, which is the rational spirit, flies in the lesser existence, which is the human body, in conversation with love in the cage of the heart."[46] In a surprising shift of images, Rūzbihān stretches the symbol of the soul-bird to the limit, by showing how the soul's wings are consumed by the experiences of nearness and unveiling; the bird has now been transformed into a moth, burning up in the flame of love:

> When the sacred birds of the spirits fly from the rose branches of witnessing temporality, and traverse the atmosphere of the heaven of certainty, their nests are nowhere but in the gardens of nearness. . . . The fire of witnessing reached from the light of unveiling to the wings of their souls. From the wrath of this fire, the wings of their souls are burned, and they remained wingless outside the door of the hidden of the hidden. . . . Since no wing remained, in that station of theirs another wing appeared from pure love. With that wing, like moths, they flew again; round the candle of beauty, on the basin of nearness, the light of their union flamed. When every wing, from spirit in spirit, had burned,

---

[44] *Sharḥ-i shaṭhiyyāt*, pp. 484–485, commenting on al-Hallaj's *Ṭawāsīn* 4.2, which contains the quotation of Qur. 2:260. Rūzbihān also offers the interpretation that the four birds are soul, heart, intellect, and spirit, which must be humbled to acknowledge the greatness of God; ibid., pp. 485–86. The symbolism of birds as the four elements recurs in ibid., p. 152. Rūmī identifies the four birds allegorically as representations of different lowly desires; cf. Schimmel, *Triumphal Sun*, p. 113.

[45] Ilāhī Sīmābī, *Manāzil al-qulūb*, in *Rūzbihān nāma*, p. 403 (*masnavī* verse).

[46] *`Abhar al-`āshiqīn*, pp. 70–71. For the use of this characteristic phrase *rūḥ-i nāṭiqa*, which derives from the vocabulary of al-Hallaj, see *Risālat al-quds*, p. 29 (quoted above, at n. 39); *Sharḥ-i shaṭhiyyāt*, pp. 245, 336, 340–41, 363, 408, 414, 603, 632.

> they collected the knowledge of realities in the palace of pre-eternity. That knowledge became their wings of love and longing, and they flew in the atmosphere of utter nearness.[47]

The successive destruction of each pair of wings at every level as the soul flies higher effectively conveys the devastating power of this experience of transcendence.

Perhaps the most remarkable guise in which birds appear in Rūzbihān's writings is as personifications of Qur'anic verses and *ḥadīth* sayings. Many poets relied on the Qur'an's statement, that "There is nothing that does not glorify him with praise" (17:44), to show how all creatures praise God; the beautiful songs of birds were natural examples to use as a metaphor for creation's testimony to the creator (cf. Qur. 21:79; 24:41). Rūzbihān has, in a way, inverted the process of the metaphor. The symbol of the soul-bird had given an externalized form to a psychological reality, the process and experience of transcendence. Now Rūzbihān re-psychologizes the image of the bird, reducing its image content to a minimum and making the symbol as transparent as possible to the underlying experience. Qur'anic verses, to Rūzbihān, are not mere words, but verbal theophanies, which act as catalysts for the transformation of the listening soul. The power of the Qur'an to bring about such a transformation is such that certain verses, for Rūzbihān, announce themselves like birds proclaiming the identity of the divine beloved. Thus we find that it is frequently "the bird of 'Am I not'" (cf. Qur. 7:171) who reminds us of the primordial covenant by which humanity was sealed to God in pre-eternity.[48] The bird of Qur'anic theophany does not only speak of the primordial covenant, but also recites the epiphanies to Moses on Sinai. "Have you not heard from Sinai's tree the *`anqā*'s cry of 'Truly I am God (28:30)'?"[49] The bird's Qur'anic proclamation of divinity does not concern some distant king, but is a reminder of intimate presence. "If from the

---

[47] *`Abhar al-`āshiqīn*, p. 124; cf. also pp. 48 and 88 for moth imagery.

[48] *Sharḥ-i shaṭḥiyyāt*, pp. 225, 230–31, 257 (where God gives the pearl of "Am I not" to the crows of creation), 316; *Risālat al-quds*, p. 3 (quoted above, at n. 43).

[49] *Sharḥ-i shaṭḥiyyāt*, p. 318; cf. p. 175, "the birds of manifestation strike the bell of 'Truly I am God' (28:30) from the tree of Moses."

suffering of love I heard the call of the birds of the morning, the birds of the morning of 'God spoke [to Moses]' (4:164), I would be the partner and companion of the Sinai of 'There is no conspiracy [of three but I am the fourth]' (58:7)."[50] Finally, Rūzbihān puts the prophetic seal on this bird-manifestation of scripture, through birds that recall the ascension of the soul, modeled on the Prophet Muḥammad's night journey (*isrā'*) to paradise and his confession of his inability to praise the infinity of God.

> Do you not know that knowledge is the wings of nearness, up to the gateway of eternity? Beyond that, one can fly no further with these. . . . Whoever does not come out from the twilight of nature, and does not travel the journey of "Glory to him who brought [his servant] by night" (17:1) in the night of the soul's ascension, does not know the cry of the nightingale of "I cannot count [your] praise" in the garden of the throne.[51]

In this way, Qur'anic verses become birds that fly like messengers from God and humanity, proclaiming divine lordship. Moreover, not only the Qur'anic revelation, but also the act of exegesis itself, becomes another bird-flight, in response to the divine word. In a revealing passage located at the very beginning of his massive Qur'an commentary, the *`Arā'is al-bayān* or *Brides of Explanation*, Rūzbihān describes his approach to scriptural interpretation as one long flight in bird form to the paradisal garden of the Qur'an.

> When the birds of my mysteries (*asrār*) had finished flying in the states and stations, rising beyond the battlefields of spiritual combat and self-observation, reaching the gardens of unveiling and witnessing, alighting on the branches of the flowers of nearness, and imbibing the wine of union, they became intoxicated by the seeing the divine beauty, love-stricken in the lights of divine splendor, and they recovered from [their intoxication] with the station of sanctity by the taste of intimacy. From the dawn of the Unmanifest they seized the blossoms of the subtleties of the Qur'an and the refinements of the truths of the Criterion. They

---

[50] *Sharḥ-i shaṭḥiyyāt*, p. 229.

[51] Ibid., p. 316. For the well-known *ḥadīth*, "I cannot count your praise," see Annemarie Schimmel, *Mystical Dimensions of Islam* (Chapel Hill: The University of North Carolina Press), pp. 126, 162, 222; Badī` al-Zamān Furūzānfarr, *Aḥādith-i mathnawī*, Intishārāt-i Dānishgāh-i Tihrān, 283 (Tehran: Chāp-khāna-yi Dānishgāh, 1334/1956), p. 2, no. 3.

> soared on wings of gnosis, and warbled the best elucidation by means of the melodies of paradise, [intoning] the mysteries (*rumūz*) of God (al-Ḥaqq) by means of this tongue, mysteries that He has hidden from the understanding of the people of forms.[52]

The bird of the spirit ascends, then, in response to the call of the bird of revelation.

Flight is a primary metaphor for spiritual experience. Rūzbihān states this boldly in his lexicon of Sufi terminology, when he defines the term "overwhelmings (*ghalabāt*)" as "the flight of the spirit in angelicity."[53] In his commentary on 1001 spiritual stations, he describes flight (*ṭayrān*) as station number 924, and he removes any suggestion of merely physical levitation from the term: "In the station of flight, it is the *khalīfas* who fly with the angels in spirit and body, for they are spirituals, in whom is the likeness of the angels. . . . I have not flown in the air because of my knowledge, but I found that meaning by which they fly in me."[54] Thus he knows the flight of the exalted figures called "successors (*khalīfas*)" not by external flight but by perceiving them in the atmosphere of his soul. One begins practising this kind of flight by meditation, which Rūzbihān describes in a chapter entitled "On the Meditation which is the Wing for the Bird of Intimacy in the Station of Love." In this section, all the metaphors of trapping birds in the desert are used to convey the approach to the beloved through the meditation of love.[55] At its highest, the experience of love brings the lover to a state of utter nearness to the beloved, and then "he may fly like the spirituals of angelicity in the highest of the high with

---

[52] *`Arā'is al-bayān fī ḥaqā'iq al-Qur'an* (Calcutta, 1883), I, 3, trans. Alan Godlas, "The Qur'ānic Hermeneutics of Rūzbihān al-Baqlī," Ph.D. dissertation, University of California at Berkeley, 1991. I would like to express my thanks to Alan Godlas for bringing this passage to my attention.

[53] *Sharḥ-i shaṭḥiyyāt*, p. 553.

[54] *Mashrab al-arwāḥ*, p. 284.

[55] *`Abhar al-`āshiqīn*, p. 106: "When the caravans of intellects pick up the burdens of the spirit's practice, flight in the atmosphere of the heaven of eternity becomes easy. The soul reaches the beloved's place of visitation, the bird of love joins the cage of the bird of intimacy in the station of meditation, and the hunters' trap catches the birds of manifestation in the desert of the heart."

the peacocks of the angels, like Khiżr, Ilyās, Idrīs and Jesus."[56] Spiritual experience as flight in this way encompasses the highest realms of the angels and prophets.

From the viewpoint of mystical experience, ascension to divinity is the key to the symbolism of birds and flight. Many of Rūzbihān's allusions to flight explicitly invoke the most famous account of mystical ascension in Sufi literature, the ascension of Bāyazīd Bisṭāmī. Rūzbihān himself commented extensively on Bāyazīd's ascension in his *Sharḥ-i shaṭḥiyyāt.*[57] Bāyazīd had described himself as becoming a bird with a body of oneness, and wings of everlastingness, flying in an atmosphere without quality until he reached an eternal tree, of which he ate the fruit; he then realized that all of this vision was a deceit, a trick of his own imagination.[58] Rūzbihān in his commentary amplified on the imagery of wings and flight, introducing, for example, the moth-like burning of the wings of the soul in the flame of divine majesty. The entire sequence of Bāyazīd's vision, if understood as a return of the soul-bird to the heavenly garden, fits very well with Rūzbihān's symbolic picture of the bird's flight to its nest on the branch of the celestial tree, where it will sing to its beloved the song of its pain. In one variation on this theme, Rūzbihān says,

> The pigeon of temporality escaped the beak of the falcon of love. It spread its wings in the atmosphere of identity, near the *sīmurgh* of the orient of eternity, and it flew at the edge of union. Then, with the tongueless tongue of 'I cannot count your praise,' it began to tell secrets

---

[56] Ibid., p. 142.

[57] *Sharḥ-i shaṭḥiyyāt*, pp. 80–82. See my *Words of Ecstasy*, Appendix, pp. 167–69, for a translation of this passage. The last sentence of the commentary on p. 169 is to be corrected as follows: "That which he said concerns the eclipse of the Attributes; otherwise, he who is of the Essence—Alas!" For another mystical use of the term "eclipse (*kusūf*)," cf. *Sharḥ-i shaṭḥiyyāt*, p. 92, line 2.

[58] It is surprising that R. C. Zaehner's fanciful theory of the Upanishadic origin of this symbolism has once again been revived, even if in a limited form, by Julian Baldick, in *Mystical Islam: An Introduction to Sufism* (London: I. B. Tauris, 1989). The imagery of wings, birds, and trees is abundantly present in the ascension literature of the Near East from ancient times onwards, and it hardly seems necessary or meaningful to suppose that Bāyazīd could only have learned of such an image from Indian sources, which in any case have altogether different structures.

> to the bird of pre-eternity. When it was finished with the hidden secret, it thought that there was no one else but itself.[59]

In the end, the images of birds, wings, and ascensions are only images, figures through which the soul attempts to comprehend its own nature. Therefore Bāyazīd ultimately denounced them as a deceit.

The fundamental experiences of the soul in tension toward the divine needs to find expression, however. Sometimes this can be done verbally, through the abstract technical terms of Sufism, through the ecstatic expressions of the mystics, or through scriptural passages that can act as the locus for the human-divine encounter. But it is also necessary for these experiences to take form, to be refracted in the medium of consciousness and assume the density of symbols taken from the natural world. Then, as Rūmī put it, the secret of the beloved can be revealed through stories about others. The poetic imagination uses imagery to express experience. If the poet is successful, the images will continue to function transparently; if the poet is less successful, the images will still work on the level of abstract allegory. But from the point of view of the mystic, the images become false when they solidify to the point of blocking out vision altogether, and take on an importance in themselves. The symbolism of birds and flight always remained, for Rūzbihān, a pliant and dynamic one, in which the lover's nightingale at any moment might be transformed into the beloved's *sīmurgh*. The alienation of existence was felt as a cage, from which the soul sought escape by flight, at last to find the heavenly garden, or even to perch on the wrist of the celestial hunter. The soul's ascent through self-transcendence was symbolized by the burning or ripping away of its wings, which were ever replaced by new ones. Birds and flight imagery thus formed an extensive complex of images from the natural world, one which was particularly well adapted for the expression of the realities of the soul. Rūzbihān reminds us that the flight of the bird covers the distance between heaven and

---

[59] *Sharḥ-i shaṭḥiyyāt*, p. 401. For other allusions to Bāyazīd's ascension, cf. ibid., pp. 22, 129, 167, 214; *Risālat al-quds*, pp. 29 (quoted above, at n. 39), 31, *`Abhar al-`āshiqīn*, pp. 3, 124.

earth; its arrival on earth and its departure to heaven imitate and embody the journey of the soul from its origin to its end, just as the bird's song can praise God or deliver a scriptural epiphany to humanity. When, therefore, we read Persian poets telling for the thousandth time of the nightingale's song to the rose, or the bird who nests in eternity, we should not be lulled into dullness, anaesthetized by mere repetition. Mystical authors like Rūzbihān can help us recover the experiential power of a symbol even when it becomes threadbare in the hands of lesser writers. Then, perhaps, when we encounter these symbols, we will follow the advice of one of Rūzbihān's followers, and recall that "These are the places of the descent of the *sīmurgh* of the spirit . . . [and] the ascent of the *`anqā* of the heart."[60]

[60] Ilāhī Sīmābī, *Manāzil al-qulūb*, in *Rūzbihān nāma*, p. 404.

18

On Losing One's Head: Hallajian Motifs and Authorial Identity in Poems Ascribed to ʿAṭṭār

In the concluding lines of his celebrated mystical epic, the *Manṭiq al-ṭayr*, Farīd al-Dīn ʿAṭṭār made the following declaration:

> This book is the adornment of time, offering a portion to both elite and common.
>
> If a frozen piece of ice saw this book, it would happily emerge from the veil like the sun.
>
> My poetry has a marvelous property, since it gives more results every time.
>
> If it's easy for you to read a lot, it will certainly be sweeter for you every time.
>
> This veiled bride in a teasing mood only gradually lets the veil fall open.
>
> *Till the resurrection, no one as selfless as I will ever write verse with pen on paper.*
>
> I am casting forth pearls from the ocean of reality. My words are finished, and this is the sign.

> If I praise myself a lot, how can that praise please anyone else? But the expert himself knows my value, because the light of my moon is not hidden.[1]

This passage is remarkable for the boast it contains, in which ʿAṭṭār claims that no one has ever annihilated his ego as successfully as he. Conjoined as it is with a bold advertisement of the quality of ʿAṭṭār's literary works, this paradoxical boast of ego-annihilation raises a difficult question regarding the nature of the authorship of Sufi writings. If the goal of the Sufi is the annihilation of the self, what sort of self may be ascribed to the authors of the central writings of Sufism? In principle, this question is an extension of the fundamental paradox of sainthood in Sufism: if sainthood means the extinction of the ego, how can the saint know that he is a saint? The concept of divinely inspired writings also parallels the ecstatic sayings (*shaṭḥiyyāt*) of the Sufis, which are in theory overflowings of inspiration that occur in the absence of the ego. As ʿAṭṭār himself remarked in comparing Hallaj's utterances with Moses' encounter with the burning bush on Sinai, it was not the bush that spoke, but God. Aṭṭār's declaration is a specimen of the rhetoric of sainthood, which permitted the spiritual elite to engage in a boasting contest (*mufākhara*) to demonstrate the extent of God's favours to them.[2] The debates of literary historians over the authenticity of the literary works ascribed to ʿAṭṭār collide with this paradoxical notion of selfless sainthood. Who is the real ʿAṭṭār? The differing understandings of this question depend entirely on the basic presuppositions that interpreters bring to it.

Helmut Ritter memorably presented the issues surrounding ʿAṭṭār's authorial identity in the article he devoted to ʿAṭṭār in the second edition of the *Encyclopaedia of Islam*. Here Ritter candidly admitted that he had completely revised his original understanding of ʿAṭṭār's writings. The problem, as Ritter saw

---

[1] Farīd al-Dīn ʿAṭṭār Nīshābūrī, *Manṭiq al-ṭayr*, ed. Muḥammad Javīd Mashkūr (3rd ed., Tehran, 1968), p. 288, lines 1–9 (emphasis mine).

[2] I have explored the topic of the rhetoric of sainthood in several places: *Words of Ecstasy in Sufism* (Albany, 1984); "The Man without Attributes: Ibn ʿArabi's Interpretation of Abu Yazid al-Bistami", chapter 10 in this volume; *Ruzbihan Baqli: Mysticism and the Rhetoric of Sainthood in Persian Sufism* (London, 1996).

it, was that "the works attributed to him [ʿAṭṭār] fall into three groups which differ so considerably in content and style that it is difficult to ascribe all three to the same person."[3] Briefly, these three groups of writings are: (1) *mathnawī* poetic compositions (*Manṭiq al-ṭayr, Ilāhī-nāma, Asrār-nāma*), usually characterized by clear frame stories, containing a rich variety of narrative material; (2) mystical epics (*Ushtur-nāma, Jawhar al-dhāt*) focused more narrowly on the identity of God and the world, with frequent reference to Hallaj; and (3) other writings (*Lisān al-ghayb, Maẓhar al-ʿajāʾib*) characterized by a strongly Shiʿite devotion to ʿAlī. Ritter himself had initially entertained the possibility that ʿAṭṭār had undergone an evolution of both thought and style, in which he had ultimately converted to Shiʿism in his old age. Saʿīd Nafīsī, following the earlier researches of Maḥmūd Sherānī, had then demonstrated that a separate individual named ʿAṭṭār Tūnī had in the fifteenth century composed the Shiʿite writings of the third group. Nafīsī supposed that it was conceivable that the same person had authored the writings of the first and second groups but, while admitting this possibility, Ritter on the whole considered it unlikely. He went on to describe a fourth category of clearly spurious writings that had been falsely ascribed to ʿAṭṭār.[4] More recently, François de Blois has concluded that seven works are authentic compositions of ʿAṭṭār (five *mathnawī* narrative poems, plus a *Dīwān* of *ghazal*s and the collection of *rubāʿī*s known as *Mukhtār-nāma*), and he has enumerated a total of 25 other works that may be considered apocryphal. Nevertheless, de Blois is willing to consider the possibility that three of these doubtful works (*Ushtur-nāma, Jawhar al-dhāt, Lisān al-ghayb*) may be in fact by ʿAṭṭār, though this question requires further research.[5]

There are in fact several diverse criteria that scholars have used to determine the authenticity of the works attributed to ʿAṭṭār. In the area of style, for instance, one may consider that

---

[3] Helmut Ritter, "ʿAṭṭār, Farīd al-Dīn Muḥammad ibn Ibrāhīm", *Encyclopaedia of Islam*, vol. 1, pp. 752b– 755a.

[4] See also B. Reinert, "ʿAṭṭār, Shaykh Farīd al-Dīn", *Encyclopaedia Iranica*, vol. 2, pp. 20–25.

[5] François de Blois, *Persian Literature: A Bio-bibliographical Survey* (London, 1994), vol. 5, part 2, *Poetry ca. A.D. 1100 to 1225*, pp. 270–313.

narrative is a typical component in ʿAṭṭār's writings, and the relative prominence or lack of narrative could be one index by which to accept or reject a particular work. Likewise, the stylistic device of repetition or anaphora, which is used at great length in several doubtful works, has been cited as evidence for rejecting them, although it should be noted that the accepted works of ʿAṭṭār display a certain taste for anaphora from time to time.[6] The age of particular manuscripts has been used as a criterion for judging certain works (or portions of works) as authentic or not. Meter could also be a factor, especially since some of the works which are considered apocryphal display surprising variations in metrical form, suggesting the possibility of different hands at work. From a thematic perspective, a focus on ʿAlī and Shiʿism, an obsession with Hallaj, and excessive boasting have all served as indications for considering a work of ʿAṭṭār as apocryphal. Another approach is to use autobiographical references in ʿAṭṭār's writings as a way of compiling an authentic canon of his works. But since the most detailed autobiographical information occurs in works (*Lisān al-ghayb, Maẓhar al-ʿajāʾib*) already judged to be doubtful, little actually remains that would allow us to fix ʿAṭṭār or his evolution as a writer with any confidence.

Much depends, though, on how one is disposed to understand in particular the themes of ʿAṭṭār's poetry and his character as an author, and scholars differ in how they evaluate these questions. The lines quoted above from the conclusion to the *Manṭiq al-ṭayr* were omitted from the excellent English translation by Afkham Darbandi and Dick Davis, on the grounds that this conclusion "consists largely of self-praise and is a distinct anticlimax after a poem devoted to the notion of passing beyond the Self."[7] Although an argument against the authenticity of this passage might be made on the basis of the absence of the conclusion

---

[6] As is demonstrated by J.C. Bürgel, "Some Remarks on Forms and Functions of Repetitive Structures in the Epic Poetry of `Aṭṭār," in Leonard Lewisohn and Christopher Shackle, eds., *Attar and the Persian Sufi Tradition: The Art of Spiritual Flight* (London: I. B. Tauris In Association With The Institute Of Ismaili Studies, 2007), pp. 197–214.

[7] Farīd al-Dīn ʿAṭṭār, *The Conference of the Birds*, tr. Afkham Darbandi and Dick Davis (Harmondsworth, NY, 1984), Introduction, p. 25. The translators also omitted the proemium, on the grounds that the lengthy praise of God contained there is irrelevant to the main thrust of the book.

from some early manuscripts of the text,[8] Darbandi and Davis reject the conclusion as being thematically and dramatically at odds with the rest of the poem. Yet there are difficulties with applying an overly strict construction of authorial consistency. One still has to face the fact that, up until the dawn of modern criticism, the chief expositors of the tradition of Persian Sufism, such as Jāmī, have accepted even the dubious works as authentic compositions of ʿAṭṭār. Even in recent times, there have been regular publications of the doubtful works, produced either in blissful ignorance of the controversy or decidedly in opposition to scholarly orthodoxy, although these editions are not always easy to find.[9] How have the various defenders of the dubious works understood their themes and their author?

In the generally accepted works of ʿAṭṭār (*Manṭiq al-ṭayr, Ilāhī-nāma, Asrār- nāma, Muṣībat-nāma*), for example, the Sufi martyr Hallaj frequently appears with brief references to his mystical state and dramatic end, which ʿAṭṭār portrayed so eloquently in his hagiographical anthology, the *Tadhkirat al-awliyāʾ*.[10] At the

[8] De Blois, *Persian Literature*, p. 281, notes that certain old MSS of *Manṭiq al-ṭayr* lack this *khātima*.

[9] The works of ʿAṭṭār, both accepted and doubtful, were frequently published in lithographed editions in British India, often in the form of large anthologies. For a comprehensive description of editions, commentaries, and translations into Indian languages, plus detailed accounts of manuscripts in Indian libraries, see Riḍā Muṣṭafawī Sabzawīrī, "ʿAṭṭār dar shibh-qārra-yi Hind (Puzhūhishī dar nuskhahā-yi khāṭṭī va chāpī va sharḥhā-yi āthār-i ʿAṭṭār)," *Qand-i Pārsī* (New Delhi, 1373 Sh./1994), no. 8, pp. 1–126. Modern Iranian editions of the works of ʿAṭṭār not mentioned by de Blois include the following: *Haylāj-nāma*, ed. Aḥmad Khwushnivīs (Tehran, n.d.); *Jawhar al-dhāt*, ed. Muḥammad Mīr Kamīlī (Tehran, 1936); *Jawhar al-dhāt* (Tehran, n.d.; repr., Tehran, 2001); *Majmūʿayi az āthār-i Farīd al-Dīn Muḥammad ibn Ibrāhīm ʿAṭṭār Nīshābūrī: Bīsar-nāma, Bulbul-nāma, Sī faṣl, Pand-nāma, Nuzʾhat al-aḥbāb, Bayān-i irshād*, ed. Aḥmad Khwushnivīs (Tehran, 1984); *Maẓhar al-ʿajāʾib*, ed. Taqī Ḥātimī Nīshābūrī (Tehran, 1966); *Maẓhar al-ʿajāʾib va Maẓhar al-asrār*, ed. Aḥmad Khwushnivīs (Tehran, 1991); *Ushtur-nāma*, ed. Mahdī Muḥaqqiq (Tehran, 1960; repr., Tehran, 1979); *Waṣlat-nāma* (Tehran, 1957). Recent studies on dubious works of ʿAṭṭār include Ḥusayn Ḥaydarkhīnī, *Andīshāha-yi ʿAṭṭār dar Lisān al-ghayb va Waṣlat-nāma va Miftāḥ al-irāda* (Tehran, 1997).

[10] Farīd al-Dīn ʿAṭṭār Nīshāpūri, *Ilāhī-nāma*, ed. Fūʾād Rūḥānī (Tehran, 1351 Sh./1972), pp. 86–87, 246; *Manṭiq al-ṭayr*, pp. 150, 276, 311. On Hallajian themes in ʿAṭṭār, see also *Meer*, index, s.n. 'Ḥallāc'; Riḍā Ashraf-zāda, *Tajallī-yi ramz va rivāyat dar shiʿr-i ʿAṭṭār-i Nīshābūrī* (Tehran, 1373 Sh./1994), pp. 239–45; Aḥmad Shawqī Nawbar, *Guft: Ān Yār… Shakhṣiyyāt-i Hallaj va bāztāb-i ān dar ashʿār-i panj shīʿir-i buzurg (Sanāʾī, ʿAṭṭār, Mawlawī, Ḥāfiẓ va Ṣāʾib)* (Tabrīz, 1377 Sh./1998), pp. 72–75; Marina Reisner, 'Maʿānī-yi qiṣṣa-i Hallaj

same time, however, these poems contain blatant examples of boasting, in which ʿAṭṭār claims to be the greatest poet of all time; sometimes this boasting includes a rejection of poetry, which has special reference to the role of court poet.[11] All this is combined with the mystical insistence that one annihilate the ego. In comparison, the doubtful works (*Lisān al-ghayb, Maẓhar al-ʿajāʾib, Pand-nāma*) may be said to contain the very same elements, but in sometimes greatly exaggerated form. In particular, the theme of headlessness—a universal theme per haps—becomes a Hallajian metaphor for transcending the self, particularly in the *Bīsar-nāma*, or The Headless Epic.[12] Thus the mere appearance of these themes would in itself not be a convincing reason for rejecting the texts completely, although one still would need to account for the different style and presentation of these themes and their author—such as the remarkable claim (found in the *Maẓhar al-ʿajāʾib* and *Pand-nāma*) of the ultimate unity of Hallaj, ʿAṭṭār, and ʿAlī.

In the examination which follows, I juxtapose a number of passages from both the accepted and doubtful writings of ʿAṭṭār with the interpretations that certain readers have brought to ʿAṭṭār. While it may be intrinsically impossible to reach an understanding of mystical authorship according to positivist standards, it is nevertheless useful to clarify the reading strategies employed by various interpreters to illuminate the conflicting concepts of authorship that they bring to the subject. But simple decisions on the nature of authorship ignore a series of difficult issues, including the question, "Is the human self infinite or finite?"[13] Even without a consideration of postmodern literary theory, it is by no means unproblematic to define authors by either stylistic or thematic consistency. As Maimonides pointed out, there are many reasons besides drunkenness and madness

---

dar ghazalīyyāt-i ʿAṭṭār,' *Kayhān-i Farhangī*, 12, (Adhar 1374 Sh./1995), pp. 32–33; Natalia Chalisova, 'Hallaj az nigāh-i ʿAṭṭār', ibid., pp. 34–35.

11 Reinert, "ʿAṭṭār", p. 22a.

12 For the theme of decapitation treated comparatively, see Ananda K. Coomaraswamy, "Headless Magicians; and an Act of Truth", *Journal of the American Oriental Society*, 64 (1944), pp. 215–17.

13 Donald E. Pease, "Author", in Frank Lentricchia and Thomas Mc Laughlin, eds., *Critical Terms for Literary Study* (Chicago and London, 1990), p. 105.

that may cause an author to be inconsistent in the treatment of a given subject. A good case in point from Islamicate culture would be Abū Ḥāmid al-Ghazālī, who was notorious for dealing with the same subject differently for diverse audiences; certain critics have consequently rejected some works ascribed to him on the grounds of inconsistency. By provisionally dealing with the doubtful works as part of the overall corpus of ʿAṭṭār's writings, we at least open up the possibility of understanding how he has been understood by generations of interpreters.

The headless Hallaj is the standard figure in such scenes as the following from ʿAṭṭār's *Asrār-nāma*:

> They saw Ḥallāj in a dream one night, his head cut off, but with cup in hand. They asked, 'How is it your head is cut off? Tell – how long you have chosen this cup?' He said, 'The king of blessed name gave this cup to the headless one. 'Those who forget their own heads can drink from this spiritual cup.'[14]

ʿAṭṭār indeed proclaims Hallaj as his teacher in several of his lyrical verses:

> That very fire that fell into Ḥallāj is the same that fell into my life.[15] The story of that sage Ḥallāj at this time is gladdening the hearts of the pious. Within the breast and the desert of the heart, his tale became the guide for ʿAṭṭār.[16]

In the Sufi tradition, authorities such as Jāmī accepted ʿAṭṭār as having had a mystical relationship with Hallaj that fell into the category of Uwaysī initiation; like the Prophet Muḥammad's contemporary, Uways al-Qaranī, ʿAṭṭār was considered a spiritual disciple who did not require physical or temporal proximity in order to obtain a genuine mystical initiation. Jāmī quoted with approval the remark of Jalāl al-Dīn Rūmī that "the light of Manṣūr [Hallaj] after one hundred fifty years manifested to the

---

[14] Farīd al-Dīn ʿAṭṭār Nīshābūrī, *Asrār-nāma*, ed. Muḥammad Ibrāhīmī (Tehran, 1376 Sh./1997), p. 42.

[15] Farīd al-Dīn ʿAṭṭār Nīshābūrī, *Dīwān*, ed. Saʿīd Nafīsī (Tehran, 1961), p. 127, v. 2215.

[16] Ibid., p. 228, vv. 4221–222.

spirit of Farīd al-Dīn ʿAṭṭār and became his spiritual authority."[17] Some stories even claim that, when the Mongols attacked Nishapur, ʿAṭṭār went to his death by decapitation, welcoming his executioner as a manifestation of his beloved.[18] That headless destiny would certainly be an extreme form of Hallajianism!

If ʿAṭṭār was indeed on the Hallajian path towards annihilating the self, this may explain in part his ambivalence toward writing. On one hand, he was not comfortable with the role of the poet as flatterer of kings. "I have not eaten the food of any tyrant, nor have I signed any book with my pen-name."[19] At times there is a discomfort with the role of the poet: "Don't count me any longer as one of the poets; don't see me any longer with the eye of the poets."[20] At the same time, ʿAṭṭār put the following words into the mouth of a nameless Sufi, who may be expressing ʿAṭṭār's own mixed attitude towards his poetry:

> My entire *Dīwān* is madness; intellect is a stranger to these words. I don't know what I'm saying – strange; how long will I seek what is not lost? – strange …But I am excused in what I say, even if I recite my own poetry…Since I saw no one trustworthy in the whole world, I spend time reciting my own poetry.[21]

The possibility that ʿAṭṭār's poetry is incomprehensible to others does not prevent him from making remarkable claims, however, including being "the seal of the poets".[22] All these remarks come from ʿAṭṭār's accepted writings.

Much in the same vein can be found in the apocryphal works. A sampling of Hallajian boasts from the *Maẓhar al-ʿajāʾib* includes the following:

---

[17] Nūr al-Dīn ʿAbd al-Raḥmīn Jāmī, *Nafaḥāt al-uns min ḥaḍarāt al-quds*, ed. Maḥmūd ʿĀbidī (Tehran, 1370 A.Hsh/1991), p. 597. See also Shams al-Dīn Aḥmad Aflākī, *The Feats of the Knowers of God (Manāqeb al-ʿarefīn)*, tr. John O'Kane, *Islamic History and Civilization: Studies and Texts*, 43 (Leiden, 2002), p. 399, para. 570.

[18] Muḥammad Ibrāhīmī, introduction to *Asrār-nāma*, pp. [ii–iv], citing Fakhr al-Dīn ʿAlī Ṣafī, *Laṭāʾif al-ṭawāʾif.*

[19] *Manṭiq al-ṭayr*, p. 293, line 16.

[20] *Asrār-nāma*, p. 23.

[21] *Manṭiq al-ṭayr*, p. 292, vv. 9–10, 16; p. 293, v. 1.

[22] *Muṣībat-nāma*, p. 364, bottom line.

> ʿAṭṭār, like Manṣūr, cries "I am the Truth", striking the entire world on fire.[23]
>
> The secrets of God are in my soul; my faith is the manifestation of the secret of God.[24]
>
> There is no bird like ʿAṭṭār in the world; he is the nightingale of this garden.[25]
>
> Your ʿAṭṭār came to know the meaning through God; he declared this in the way of Manṣūr.[26]

Here one also finds the repeated declarations of phrases, the anaphora referred to above, in which the poet begins 15 or 20 lines in the same words, "Go forth like Manṣūr, to the gallows of annihilation, till you see the light of God beyond encounter…."[27] In the *Haylaj-nāma*, extended passages ring variations on Hallaj's famous cry, "I am the Truth" (*anā al-Ḥaqq*), as in the following:

> From that wine, cry, "I am the Truth" like me; behold yourself in your body, through your body.
>
> From that wine, cry, "I am the Truth" at the lover's door, for you will see the grace of all—none but you is in the world.
>
> From that wine, cry, "I am the Truth" like Ḥallāj. Come out on top of heaven, wearing that crown.
>
> From that wine, I have drunk, my chosen shaykh; I have most certainly seen the beloved in reality.[28]

---

[23] Lacking access to independent editions of these titles, I have consulted the extensive subject concordances to the works of ʿAṭṭār compiled by Qādir Fāḍilī, *Farhang-i mawḍūʿī adab-i Pārsī, mawḍūʿ-bandī va naqd va barrasī, 1–2: Manṭiq al-ṭayr va Pand-nāma; 3–4: Asrār-nāma va Haylāj-nāma; 5–6: Muṣībat-nāma va Maẓhar al-ʿajīʾib* (Tehran, 1374 Sh./1995), who unfortunately does not provide exact information on the text editions he has used. This verse comes from *Maẓhar al-ʿajāʾib*, p. 25 (Fāḍilī, 3–4:414).

[24] *Maẓhar al-ʿajāʾib*, p. 45 (Fāḍilī, 3–4:416).

[25] Ibid., p. 61 (Fāḍilī, 3–4:416).

[26] Ibid., p. 152 (Fāḍilī, 3–4:418).

[27] Ibid., pp. 57–58 (Fāḍilī, 3–4:368). Several of these lines substitute Abū Dharr for Manṣūr. Other interesting anaphora passages use phrases like "I am not crazy, but…," in *Haylāj-nāma*, p. 112 (Fāḍilī, 5–6:338–39); 'I am the secret you have spoken…,' ibid., p. 159 (Fāḍilī, 5–6:339); "It is not Manṣūr…," ibid., p. 112 (Fāḍilī, 5–6:342).

[28] *Haylāj-nāma*, p. 82 (Fāḍilī, 5–6:187); see Fāḍilī, 5–6:184–93, for further examples on this topic.

Hallaj is described bluntly as the thief who has stolen and revealed reality: "Manṣūr, you have spoken the absolute secret: 'I am God,' you have stated, 'I am the Truth.'"[29] ʿAṭṭār focuses furiously on union with Hallaj:

> You are one with me, you rebel Manṣūr, and tomorrow I shall consume you with fire!
>
> You are one with me in heart and soul – you are I, and I am you, master of union![30]

In verses of stupefying grandiosity, ʿAṭṭār claims to be Hallaj, God, and the sun and the stars; all creation is seeking his mercy.[31]

In addition, we find in these apocryphal works a new emphasis on the role of ʿAlī, who somehow takes the leading role in an apotheosis in which ʿAṭṭār and Hallaj both merge.

> If you have faith, you become all light; you make the boast, "I am the Truth," like Manṣūr.
>
> "I am the Truth," says that enlightened pure one. He drank the wine of longing from the hand of ʿAlī.[32]

Elsewhere ʿAṭṭār's apostrophes are dedicated to ʿAlī alone:

> Who am I to describe you in speech? For you are hidden in all souls. Commander of the Faithful! I have spoken my soul, threading pearl of meaning upon meanings. Commander of the Faithful! Tell me the secret of God's secrets face to face, So my heart is clear and my soul complete, and I may recite your praises in full![33]

In long invocations addressed to ʿAlī, ʿAṭṭār himself becomes a second Manṣūr in search of the divine essence.[34] In turn ʿAlī has revealed to him all of his secrets.[35]

---

[29] Ibid., pp. 37–39 (Fāḍilī, 5–6:387–88).
[30] Ibid., p. 42 (Fāḍilī, 5–6:388).
[31] Ibid., p. 247 (Fāḍilī, 5–6:396).
[32] *Pand-nāma*, p. 115 (Fāḍilī, 1–2:243).
[33] *Maẓhar al-ʿajāʾib*, p. 181 (Fāḍilī, 3–4:412).
[34] Ibid., pp. 242–243 (Fāḍilī, 3–4:422–23).
[35] *Haylāj-nāma*, p. 203 (Fāḍilī, 5–6:343).

Despite the bold claims made in the apocryphal works, there is occasionally a delicate reflection on the phenomenon of ecstatic speech (*shaṭḥ*), in which we see the flickering of the authorial ego in the storm of divinity:

> What am I saying? What do I know? Who am I? In listening and speaking, who am I?
>
> He is speaking, like light in my body, for by his tongue I tell my story. I relate these words from him, giving guidance to the people of the world.[36]

Nevertheless, ʿAṭṭār occasionally shifts his authorial ego entirely to Hallaj: "All of the secret that lies in the essence of the book is from that Manṣūr, and is unveiled in him."[37] At other times, the shift to identification with God is complete: "It is not ʿAṭṭār, behold! It is the beloved who is in the text and the proof. Behold!"[38] Indeed, we find unadulterated boasts about annihilation of the self: "It was reality; I myself saw annihilation (*fanā'*). I saw annihilation and arrived at divine eternity (*baqā'*)."[39] Hyperbolic claims are made about the efficacy of these writings, and readers of the *Jawhar al-dhāt* and the *Maẓhar al-ʿajāʾib* are promised miraculous results.[40]

It would be easy to multiply examples of Hallajian headlessness, deification, and adoration of ʿAlī from the apocryphal writings, given how large all of these works are. It is difficult to deny that these works exhibit a much more extreme emphasis on these topics, and that at times they become monotonous in their relentless theophanic assertions. How have these works been understood by those who defend their authenticity?

The most prominent scholar to embrace these apocryphal works as genuine compositions by ʿAṭṭār was undoubtedly Louis Massignon who, in the course of decades of work devoted to the study of Hallaj, paid special attention to the role that ʿAṭṭār

36 *Maẓhar al-ʿajīʾib*, p. 42 (Fāḍilī, 3–4:415).
37 *Haylāj-nāma*, p. 70 (Fāḍilī, 5–6:389).
38 Ibid., p. 352 (Fāḍilī, 5–6:340).
39 Ibid., p. 181 (Fāḍilī, 5–6:355).
40 *Maẓhar al-ʿajīʾib*, p. 8 (Fāḍilī, 3–4:473); ibid., p. 45 (Fāḍilī, 3–4:474).

played in the dissemination of the Hallajian legend. Massignon maintained that "it was above all due to the literary works of ʿAṭṭār that the Hallajian theme became one of the most famous 'leitmotifs' in Iranian Muslim poetics, wherever Islam was propagated together with the love of Persian poetry."[41] The remarkable emphasis on Hallaj found in the apocryphal ʿAṭṭārian works required Massignon to deal with the issue of authenticity raised by Nafīsī and others. Massignon brushed aside the theory of pseudonymous authorship of these works, endorsing instead Jāmī's quotation from Rūmī, that the light of Manṣūr after many years had transfigured the spirit of ʿAṭṭār.[42] Massignon acknowledged that there had been tampering with the texts of works like the *Jawhar al-dhāt*, remarking that Attar's "extraordinary literary fecundity may perhaps also be explained by the flowering a century later of a cycle of pastiches," which seems to be a tacit admission of pseudonymous composition.[43] Massignon described the ʿAṭṭārian apocrypha as "amazing collections flowing with repeated outbursts, whose dimensions are as immense as the Hindu epics or the interior monologues of ... Joyce,... in which ʿAṭṭār tirelessly sings of the mystical drowning of the soul in divine totality, using Hallaj, 'the highway brigand' (*duzd-i rāh*), as the model and herald of this ardent annihilation."[44] Giving emphasis to the decapitation motif, Massignon provided numerous examples of Hallajian themes in these writings. It is notable that Massignon depicted ʿAṭṭār's intellectual lineage with considerable flexibility, linking him to the philosophers Suhrawardī and Avicenna as well as to the Ismāʿīlīs.[45] Massignon became almost rhapsodic in describing works like the *Haylaj-nāma*: "This esoteric book, in which ʿAṭṭār reveals to us all of his thoughts on Hallaj, is very important. It is not only a canonization, it is a

---

41 Louis Massignon, *The Passion of Al-Hallaj: Mystic and Martyr of Islām*, tr. and ed. Herbert Mason (Princeton, 1994), vol. 2, *The Survival of al-Hallaj*, pp. 361–62.

42 Ibid., p. 362.

43 Ibid., p. 363.

44 Ibid., p. 364.

45 Ibid., p. 382. Fritz Meier has also explored similarities between Ismaili thought and the accepted works of ʿAṭṭār in "Ismailiten und Mystik im 12. und 13. Jahrhundert," *Persica*, 16 (2000), pp. 9–29. See also Hermann Landolt, "ʿAṭṭār, Sufism, and Ismailism," in *ʿAṭṭār and the Persian Sufi Tradition*, pp. 3–27.

total and absolute divinization."[46] At the risk of appearing dismissive, one feels obliged here to point out that Massignon had a tendency to see Hallaj everywhere. What was frankly a life-long obsession with Hallaj impelled Massignon to accept as canonical those ʿAṭṭārian works that canonized Hallaj.

Yet as the ongoing publication of ʿAṭṭārian apocrypha reveals, there are evidently audiences, particularly in Iran, who continue to find reasons for accepting the validity of these works. One recent example is Qādir Fāḍilī, who has written on ʿAṭṭār as well as on contemporary religious thought in Iran.[47] Fāḍilī's large subject concordance to the writings of ʿAṭṭār furnishes a distinctively Shiʿite perspective on the ʿAṭṭārian apocrypha. Fāḍilī begins, however, from an unusual methodological position, arguing that the very concept of pseudonymous authorship and pseudepigrapha is illogical:

> Some believe that this book (*Maẓhar al-ʿajāʾib*) and the *Pand-nāma* are falsely attributed to ʿAṭṭār, and their proof is the weakness of metre in this book. Thus they say someone else published his own works in the name of ʿAṭṭār. This theory does not appear to be correct with such reasoning, because no one who is an author with ability attributes his work to another.[48]

Fāḍilī thus regards the ʿAṭṭār who wrote the *Manṭiq al-ṭayr, Ilāhī-nāma,* and *Muṣībat-nāma* as identical with the author of the *Maẓhar al-ʿajāʾib.* Acknowledging that there are problems with the rhyme and metre in certain writings, Fāḍilī pieces this together with autobiographical statements in the apocryphal *Maẓhar al-ʿajāʾib* (ʿAṭṭār's best work, in his opinion), in which ʿAṭṭār states his age as over 100 years; old age and weakness, he concludes, are responsible for any slips on ʿAṭṭār's part.[49]

---

[46] Massignon, *The Passion of Al-Hallaj,* p. 385.

[47] Qāḍir Fāḍilī, *Andīsha-i ʿAṭṭār: taḥlīl-i āfāq-i andīsha-i Shaykh Farīd al-Dīn ʿAṭṭār Nīshābūrī* (Tehran, 1995), to which I have unfortunately not had access; idem., *Khāṭṭ-i qirmiz: naqd va barrāsī-yi Kitāb-i Farbihtar az idiʾuluzhī* (Tehran, 1994), a critique of *Farbihtar az idiʾuluzhī* by ʿAbd al-Karīm Surūsh; idem., *Yād-i yār: 160 khāṭira az ʿallāma-yi ustād Muḥammad Taqī Jaʿfarī, va chand maqāla-yi dīgar dar khuṣūṣ-i vay* (Tehran, 1999).

[48] Fāḍilī, *Farhang* (see above, n. 22), 3–4:16.

[49] Ibid., 3–4:17.

Moving on to the question of Shiᶜite references, Fāḍilī maintains that the challenge to the apocryphal works is motivated by anti-Shiᶜite prejudice. It is only Sunni fanaticism that motivates the questioning or rejection of these works as being by ᶜAṭṭār, because his devotion to ᶜAlī and the Shīᶜite Imāms makes it clear that he is Shīᶜite. All true gnostics, even if they observe Sunni practice and the edicts of the four Sunni imāms, from the viewpoint of the mystics, their creed is Shīᶜite and they consider themselves Shīᶜite. Their *Dīvān*s and books are filled with poems in praise of the family of the Prophet and their role in the order of existence. This applies to many great past masters of mysticism and literature, such as Rūmī, Saᶜdī, Sanāʾī, Niẓāmī, Ibn ᶜArabī, Ibn al-Fāriḍ, Qayṣarī, etc.[50] The assumption that all true mystics are Shiᶜites handily eliminates any question of inconsistency about the move toward veneration of ᶜAlī in the apocryphal works.

Nevertheless, Fāḍilī is not able to overcome certain critical theological reservations about the radicalization of Hallaj in these ᶜAṭṭārian works, particularly the blatant tilt toward divinization that shifts from Hallaj's "I am the Truth" into an outright "I am God". This he sees as extremism, fundamentally in contradiction with the mystical teachings with which Hallaj inspired ᶜAṭṭār, as Rūmī and Jāmī have attested. Thus a certain suspicion attaches to these writings of ᶜAṭṭār insofar as he presents Hallaj in such a radical form.[51] Fāḍilī therefore takes ᶜAṭṭār to task for having written the verse, "I am God, I am God, I am God!" Fāḍilī views this as logically impossible, because the very use of the separate words "I" and "God" demonstrates an inescapable duality.[52]

In the end, Fāḍilī is deeply uncomfortable with the self-praise that appears in many ᶜAṭṭārian writings. For one thing, he considers this to involve implicit criticism and denigration of others, as when ᶜAṭṭār styles himself as the "seal of the poets", or "the unique pearl (Farīd) of the age". Fāḍilī concedes that there is an ambiguity in the Hallajian claim, "I am the Truth". It can mean the elimination of the ego and total submission to God through

---

[50] Ibid., 3–4:18.

[51] Ibid., 5–6:16.

[52] Ibid., 1–2:434–35, citing *Pand-nāma*, p. 55.

annihilation. Amazingly, Fāḍilī quotes a poem from Khomeini to this effect: "I abandoned my self and clashed the cymbals of 'I am the truth'; like Manṣūr, I became a customer of the gallows." In this manner Fāḍilī demonstrates at length what he sees as the difference between legitimate proximity to God and extreme claims to union with God that no genuine prophet or saint has ever made.[53] Throughout his interpretation of ʿAṭṭār, Fāḍilī has recourse to firm dogmatic principles that allow him, with a certain circularity of logic, both to claim as authentic the disputed works of ʿAṭṭār and to criticize them when they fall short of his standards.

The persistence of apocrypha and pseudepigraphic writing has been noted in many of the world's literary traditions. While it is perhaps easy to dismiss such works as forgeries, many questions remain, particularly when recent criticism runs into long-established traditions in which these writings have been accepted (this has been particularly true of the criticism of Biblical texts and other sacred writings). In part, the production of pseudepigrapha forms part of the reception history of texts, and it is particularly challenging to assign a motive for the production of such works. Is it vanity? A crude attempt to gain consideration for writings that would otherwise be dismissed? An innocent and admiring tribute? A confident submission of truths considered to be inspired? There are many possibilities.[54] One may assume that the works of ʿAṭṭār were initially in private circulation in Khurāsān, and that they began to attain more popularity in the course of the thirteenth and fourteenth centuries. This period coincides with an increase in ʿAlid piety in Persianate lands, as well as the popularization of monistic philosophies summarized under the heading of "the unity of existence" (*waḥdat al-wujūd*), particularly through the medium of Persian poetry. The annihilation of the authorial ego leaves open special opportunities for would-be imitators of the great masters of Sufi literature.

[53] Ibid., 5–6:440–45.

[54] For methodological reflections on pseudonymity in New Testament Studies, see Frank W. Hughes, "Pseudonymity as Rhetoric: A Prolegomenon to the Study of Pauline Pseudepigrapha", *Journal for the Study of Rhetorical Criticism of the New Testament*, available online at http://rhetjournal.net/Hughes.html, accessed 15 July 2003.

The boldness of Hallaj was so captivating, after all, precisely because he revealed the secret (*ifshāʾ al-sirr*), publicizing the intimacy of his relationship with God. Although some judged this revelation to be a crime, others clearly took it to be a licence and authorization for new authors to declare the same truth, that they too had become one with God. The very popularity of ʿAṭṭār's writings as manifestos of mysticism made them almost a *sui generis* category of literature: what we might call the poetry of annihilation (*fanāʾiyyāt*), in parallel with the poetry of wine (*khamriyyāt*) or unconventionality (*qalandariyyāt*). Thus ʿAṭṭār, like 'Umar Khayyām, may be said to have become "no longer a historical person but a genre".[55] From the frequently quoted testimony of Rūmī and Jāmī, we know that ʿAṭṭār has been considered to be particularly inspired by the spirit of Hallaj. It is less well known that ʿAṭṭār himself has performed similar initiatic functions in certain Sufi circles, particularly those associated with the Shaṭṭārī Sufi order. In the complicated lineages claimed by the sixteenth-century Shaṭṭārī master Shaykh Muḥammad Ghawth, Farīd al-Dīn ʿAṭṭār plays a central and inspiring role.[56] Both the annihilation of the ego and the expansion of ʿAṭṭār's popularity make it easier to understand how his literary oeuvre might miraculously expand as well.

The growth of a Shiʿite interpretation of or response to ʿAṭṭār should be no more surprising than the extension of the Hallajian message. According to Ivanow, ʿAṭṭār was particularly popular with Ismā'īlī readers, and we may assume that they brought their own hermeneutic to bear upon his writings.[57] At roughly the same time that the ʿAṭṭārian apocrypha may have been produced (i.e., the thirteenth and fourteenth centuries), the works of Rūzbihān Baqlī were likewise undergoing alteration in a Twelver Shiʿite direction. In their biographies of Ruzbihan, his descendants typically translated his Arabic writings into Persian with dramatic shifts of emphasis, in which ʿAlī takes over the

---

[55] De Blois, *Persian Literature,* p. 363.

[56] Muḥammad Salīm Akhtār, "Taʾthīr-i ʿAṭṭār-i Nīshābūrīdar shibh-qārra...," *Haft guftār dar bāra-yi Sanāʾī va ʿAṭṭār va ʿIrāqī* (Tehran, 1375 Sh./1996), pp. 129–42.

[57] See Farhad Daftary, *The Ismāʿīlīs: Their History and Doctrines* (Cambridge, 1990), p. 454, references cited in n. 38.

central role as dispenser of mystical knowledge.[58] While the blatant Shiᶜite partisanship of Fāḍilī may be overdone, it forms part of a long tradition of strongly Shiᶜite interpretation of Sufi texts.

The critical evaluation of the writings of ᶜAṭṭār is a fairly recent phenomenon. Before the twentieth century, it was normal to read all the epics ascribed to ᶜAṭṭār as part of a continuous whole. An eclectic and inclusive reading strategy was a characteristic aspect of the history of these texts. It is certainly legitimate for scholars to raise questions about these works in terms of their style and themes. But the changes in Ritter's views on this question, the Hallajian enthusiasm of Massignon, and the Shiᶜite rationalism of Fāḍilī demonstrate how differently readers continue to approach the ᶜAṭṭārian corpus, even after the introduction of modern criticism. In short, there is still no agreement about who ᶜAṭṭār really was. This debate would no doubt have been amusing to ᶜAṭṭār, who after all had so eloquently expressed this fundamental paradox, the boast of the author without ego: "Till the resurrection, no one as selfless as I will ever write verse with pen on paper."

---

[58] Ernst, *Ruzbihan Baqli*, esp. ch. 3.

19

Beauty and the Feminine Element of Spirituality[1]

The Prophet Muhammad once said, "God is beautiful, and He loves beauty." He also said, "Three things in your world have been made lovely to me: women, perfume, and prayer is the delight of my eyes." What is the significance of the love of beauty for spirituality? And how does gender enter into this delicate topic? Ultimately, the question of being male or female may fade in importance when compared to the aesthetic shock of the contemplation of divine beauty. Yet the fact that we are embedded in a particular social and historical moment makes it impossible for us to ignore the roles and expectations that society has placed upon men and women. The transformations of global economies over the past century have created a situation in which women's participation in education, culture, and religion has become public in an unprecedented fashion, in every corner of the world. Perhaps the greatest lesson to be learned from the changes we now experience is not that feminine spirituality is different from masculine spirituality; instead, listening to the voices of insightful women may allow us to step aside from the limitations of the egotistical patriarchy that has unjustly dismissed women as inferior to men.

---

[1] Presented at the Conference on "Women and Sufism: Centenary Celebration of the Birth of Samiha Ayverdi," Istanbul, Turkey, December 16, 2005

It must be acknowledged that all the major religious traditions of the world have experienced similar forms of social organization through male-dominated political structures. The fact remains that women have played important spiritual roles, and yet this is generally not acknowledged in official histories. One of the major achievements of scholarship in recent years has been the effort to recover the voices of women in all the major civilized regions of the world, from which on the whole they had been mysteriously excluded. History was once considered to consist exclusively of the actions of kings and great men, but increasingly it is being admitted that our understanding of the past will be incomplete and distorted unless we comprehend the parts that women have played.

In the history of religion, considerable attention has been paid to the contributions of women mystics to Christian spirituality, and there are numerous publications addressed to this important topic. If we turn to Islamic spirituality, the situation is more complicated, particularly due to the relative lack of writings by women before recent times. It is possible to get some access to the spiritual lives of Muslim women, yet we must rely primarily on writings by men. As an example, Jami concluded his Persian biographical work on Sufis, *Nafahat al-Uns* (*The Breezes of Intimacy*), with a brief appendix entitled, "On the Remembrance of the Women Knowers of God who have Attained the Levels of the Men of God." In it he writes,

> The author of *The Meccan Openings*, Muhyi al-Din ibn al-`Arabi (God have mercy on him), in the seventy-third chapter, after mentioning some of the generations of the men of God, says, "Everything that we have said regarding these men, as men, includes women, though there is more reference to men. Someone was asked, 'How many "Substitutes" (*abdal*) are there?' He replied, 'Forty souls.' He was asked, 'Why did you not say forty men?' He answered, 'Because there are women among them.'"
>
> The master Abu `Abd al-Rahman al-Sulami, author of *Generations of the Masters*, compiled a particular book, the *Memoir of the Spiritual States of Women Devotees and Knowers of God*, and he has clarified much in explanation of the spiritual states of many of them. The poet al-Mutanabbi has written a verse, alluding to the fact that "sun" (*shams*) is feminine and "moon" (*qamar*) is masculine in Arabic:

Were women as I have described,
    Women would be superior to men.
Femininity is no defect in the sun,
    Nor should the moon be proud of masculinity.

The lost treatise of al-Sulami has been rediscovered, and it has been translated into English by Rkia Laroui Cornell.[2] This text permits us to see with a little more detail the ambiguity and sensitivity of the issue of gender in Sufi hagiography (note that the verse by al-Mutanabbi is really a backhanded compliment to women, since it makes one exceptional woman appear to be a very strange phenomenon indeed). This ambiguous position is stated with peculiar force by one of the women who figures in that anthology, `A'isha bint Ahmad of Merv: "Concealment is more appropriate for women than unveiling, for women are not to be exposed."

This is a surprising answer that `A'isha gave to a question about the kind of mystical experience that the Sufis call unveiling (*kashf*). It is unexpected, because the text itself provides abundant evidence of such spiritual experiences among women. But in a sense, this answer illustrates one of the main problems confronting anyone who seeks to understand the subject we are addressing: how can we have access to the feminine dimension of Islamic culture without trespassing in the private sphere? On one level, this quotation explains why so few women are represented in biographical works in general and in biographies of Sufis in particular. That is, in most cases, biographies of women (when given at all) are included as an appendix to the biographies of men that are the "main" subject of the book. Certainly misogyny was one attitude to be found in Sufi texts. Still, on another level, the notion of concealment and privacy for women may help explain both the relatively small space granted to women in Sufi writings, and the brevity and lack of personal detail in these biographies. Where women do figure in Sufi biographies, one finds typical patterns of presentation that may well be explained by predictable male-female dynamics. How many

---

[2] Abū `Abd ar-Rahmān as-Sulamī, *Early Sufi women: Dhikr an-niswa al-muta`abbidāt as-Sūfiyyāt*, ed. and trans. Rkia Elaroui Cornell (Louisville, KY: Fons Vitae, 1999).

times has it been said of an impressive woman, that she was, as it were, a man in the form of a woman? This sort of negative compliment seems to be the last resort of the male hagiographer who is perplexed and bewildered (and struck with admiration) by the spiritual power of a woman.

Yet despite the common omission of women from the public record of religion and spirituality, it is striking to see how frequently and how inevitably women figure prominently in key discussions of the nature of love and beauty as avenues to the divine. Plato in the *Symposium* depicts Socrates as receiving instruction from the priestess Diotima on the philosophical teachings of love and beauty. When the Qur'an tells the story of Joseph and Zulaykha, it is called "the most beautiful of stories." Why is that? According to the Persian Sufi master Rūzbihān Baqli (d. 1209), it is because

> Worldly love is the beginning of that divine love. For both beginner and adept there is an unavoidable condition for reaching the intoxication of divine love–and that is to clothe the created with divinity. There is proof in support of chaste love in the religious law of Muhammad (God's prayers be upon him). The word of God (who is great and mighty): "We shall tell you the most beautiful of stories" (Qur'an 12:3), that is, we shall tell you the story of the lover and the beloved, Joseph and Zulaykha (peace be upon them), and also the love of Jacob and Joseph (peace be upon them), for the tale of love is the most beautiful of stories for those who have passion and love.[3]

In the biography of Ruzbihan, it is related that he caused a sensation when he returned to Shiraz and first preached in public. In the oldest version, the story goes like this:

> When the shaykh came from Pasā to Shiraz, the first day that he preached in the 'Atiq mosque, in the midst of his sermon, he said, "When I entered the mosque, in the corner of the herb sellers a woman was advising her daughter, saying, 'My dear, your mother advises you to cover your face, and don't show everyone your beauty from the window. This should not be, for by reason of your loveliness and beauty, someone may fall into temptation. Don't you hear my words and accept my advice?'"

---

[3] Ruzbihan Baqli, *`Abhar al-`ashiqin*, in *Teachings of Sufism*, trans. Carl W. Ernst (Boston: Shambhala, 1999), p. 90.

> When Rūzbihān heard these words, he wanted to tell that woman, "Although you advise her and forbid her, let her show herself! She should not listen to these words of yours or accept this advice, for she is beautiful, and beauty has no rest until love becomes joined to it."
>
> When the shaykh said this, one of the travelers on the path of God was present. The arrow of these words hit the target of his heart, so that he cried out and gave up his spirit. The cry went up in the town that "Shaykh Rūzbihān is cutting souls to bits with the sword of his words!" The people of the town turned toward him and became his disciples.

Later accounts add to Rūzbihān's advice to the mother the comment that "Love and beauty made a pact in pre-eternity never to be separate from one another."[4] Indeed, in his own major treatise on love, *The Jasmine of the Lovers*, Ruzbihan engages in a dialogue with an unnamed woman who challenges him to define the relationship between human love and divine love, so that she acted in a way as his teacher.

Another famous Sufi, Ibn `Arabi (d. 1240), comments on the divine beauty and takes as his point of departure the divine name al-Jamil, "the Beautiful," as attested in the Qur'an and hadith. In an introductory poem to a discussion of this divine name in *al-Futuhat al-Makkiya*, he sets forth the enigma of the divine beloved whose beauty is beyond the reach of the senses, and yet who is somehow witnessed by the lover's heart–and the love of this divine beauty is the model for all the great loves celebrated in Arabic poetry.

> Beautiful but not longing, luminous but not seen,
> yet hearts witness Him, just as they do not know.
> "Eyes do not encompass Him" except for one
> whom master intellects have left behind.
> If I call Him "beloved," I would not be a liar,
> and if I call Him "witnessed," that is what I know.
> There is no other beloved but He,
> and only Salmas, Laylas, and Zaynabs are for the veil.
> They are the curtains that veil, that are conveyed
> by the poetry of lovers, and their prose,

---

[4] For details, see my *Ruzbihan Baqli: Mysticism and the Rhetoric of Sainthood in Persian Sufism*, Curzon Sufi Series, 4 (London: Curzon Press, 1996).

> Like Majnun and Layla, and those who came before,
> like Bishr and Hind–my heart cannot bear their names.[5]

In this way Ibn `Arabi explains the relation of the creative and transcendent divine beauty to the beautiful things of this world, and this can only be done through the names of male and female lovers. It should be recalled that Ibn `Arabi himself studied with several prominent women Sufis, including Fatima of Cordova, whom he praised as a great mystic, and he also wrote poems in honor of 14 women to whom he gave authorization (*ijaza*) to be Sufi teachers.

Nevertheless, despite these striking references to women, it can be argued that the idealization of women has also served as a kind of symbolic or intellectual prison, particularly if this means defining women into an entirely separate role or metaphysical status distinct from men. But the reality is that women have been eminent spiritual teachers who have indeed earned the respect of men. Although shrouded in legend, and often used as the exception justifying the marginalization of other women, the stories of Rabi`a al-`Adawiyya (eighth century) clearly show her as the teacher (*mu'addiba*) of men.[6] The great master of the Indian Chishti order, Shaykh Nizam al-Din Awliya' (d. 1325), paid tribute to the charisma of Bibi Fatima Sam:

> When the lion has come out of the forest, nobody asks if it is male or female; the children of Adam must obey and show respect, whether it is male or female. Now, in the stories of Fatima Sam there has been much said regarding her extreme piety and old age. I have seen her. She was a great woman.[7]

Sayyida Zaynab bint al-Rifa`i (d. 1232), the daughter of Shaykh Ahmad al-Rifa`i, was described by a biographer as "the patient, humble lady, the one who recollected God, the perfect woman saint, the pure knower of God, the pious God-fearing one, the

---

[5] Ibn `Arabi, *al-Futuhat al-Makkiya,* II, 542 (ch. 142). The phrase "eyes do not encompass Him" recalls Qur'an 6:104.

[6] Rkia Elaroui Cornell, "Rabi`a, from Narrative to Myth: Tropics of Identity of a Muslim Woman Saint," Ph.D. dissertation, Free University of Amsterdam, 2013.

[7] `Abd al-Haqq Muhaddith Dihlawi, *Akhbar al-akhyar*, in *Teachings of Sufism*, p. 186.

hopeful luminous one, the one who took precedence over saintly men, through her lofty qualities and her illustrious spiritual states."[8]

These clear statements of admiration for women as spiritual teachers have been rare before modern times, but they are important historical indications that the spiritual equality of men and women was recognized in certain quarters, despite the common dismissal of women to the private sphere in many Muslim societies. Now, we are in an age when necessity decrees that both men and women need to seek education and participate in the modern workforce on a scale previously undreamt of. The spread of mass literacy through policies of universal education has made it possible for countless talented women to undertake careers that would have been unthinkable a century ago. This is no less true in the Middle East than it is in Europe and America. The reconfiguration of religion in secular states has opened up the possibility of women's public leadership in matters of religion and culture even while it has also increased the factor of conservative control of women's dress and behavior in other sectors.

In her memoirs, my former teacher Annemarie Schimmel has written the following:

> During my second stay (in Turkey), new friends helped me to gain access to another part of Turkish culture, to the best traditions of Turkish Sufism. There were successful businessmen who yet would spend night after night in silent meditation, and there was Samiha Ayverdi, the towering figure among mystics and writers, author of numerous books and articles in which she conjures up the traditional life. In her house I was introduced to the culture of Ottoman Turkey, and she and her family opened my eyes to the eternal beauty of Islamic fine arts, in particular calligraphy. I loved to listen to her discourses which went on in long, swinging sentences, while the sky over the Bosphorus seemed to be covered with clouds of roses. A few weeks ago, in March 1993, she passed away on the eve of the Feast of Fastbreaking, three days after I had kissed her frail hands for the last time.[9]

---

[8] Ahmad ibn Muhammad al-Witri, *Rawdat al-nazirin*, in *Teachings of Sufism*, p. 191.

[9] Annemarie Schimmel, "A Life of Learning," Charles Homer Haskins Lecture for 1993, American Council of Learned Societies, Occasional Paper No. 21 (available online at

From this deeply personal tribute, we can see the powerful effect that this Turkish teacher had on her German friend, who herself became an outstanding authority on Islamic art and spirituality. It is no accident that their relationship centered on the appreciation of beauty, and that both women became exemplary teachers. May we all be fortunate enough to know such outstanding individuals.

---

http://www.acls.org/op21.htm). See also Schimmel's article "Samiha Ayverdi - Eine istanbuler Schriftstellerin," in *Der Orient in der Forschung: Festschrift für Otto Spies zum 5. April 1966*, ed. Wilhelm Hoenerbach (Wiesbaden: Harrassowitz, 1967), pp. 569–585. Professor Schimmel dedicated to Samiha Ayverdi her book *My Soul Is a Woman: The Feminine in Islam*, trans. Susan H. Ray (New York: Continuum International Publishing Group, 2003).

20

Sufism and the Aesthetics of Penmanship in Sirāj al-Shīrāzī's *Tuḥfat al-Muḥibbīn* (1454)[1]

Arabic calligraphy has exerted its enchantment over many generations, both of writers and readers. Despite the existence of numerous treatises on the subject in Arabic and Persian on the techniques of penmanship, hearkening back to the methods developed by the great calligraphers of the `Abbasid era such as Ibn Muqla (d. 940) and Yāqūt (d. ca. 1297), few authors have attempted to explain the aesthetic and spiritual basis of the art of the pen.[2] A master calligrapher from Shiraz, Sirāj al-Shīrāzī, composed one such work under the title *Tuḥfat al-Muḥibbīn* ("The Bounty of the Lovers") in the Deccan kingdom of Bidar in 1454.[3] Although this work has not attracted much

---

[1] An earlier version of this paper was presented at the Dar al-Athar al-Islamiyya Museum in Kuwait on 12 May 2008.

[2] For one example, see Carl W. Ernst, "The Spirit of Islamic Calligraphy: Bābā Shāh Iṣfahānī's *Ādāb al-Mashq*," chapter 16 in this volume. For a comprehensive survey of Arabic penmanship, see Sheila S. Blair, *Islamic Calligraphy* (Edinburgh: Edinburgh University Press, 2006).

[3] Ya`qūb ibn Ḥasan Sirāj Shīrāzī, *Tuḥfat al-Muḥibbīn (dar ā'īn-i khushnivīsī va laṭā'if-i ma`nawī-i ān)*, eds Muḥammad Taqī Dānish-Puzhūh, Karāmat Ra`ná Ḥusaynī and Īraj

scholarly attention, it is a rich source on the early history and understanding of the cultural significance of the Arabic script.[4] In this work the author reveals the intimate relationship of his art to Sufism, as expounded by his teacher, a calligrapher descended from the famous Persian Sufi, Rūzbihān al-Baqlī (d. 1209). Here I would like briefly to describe the contents of this guide to the art of penmanship and analyze the extent to which Sufi teachings play a role in the aesthetics of this calligrapher, that is, the form of artistic judgment and interpretation that he brings to the understanding of the art of the Arabic script.

The author of this treatise gives his complete name as Abū al-Da`ī Ya`qūb ibn Ḥasan ibn Shaykh, known as Sirāj al-Ḥasanī al-Shīrāzī; for convenience, I refer to him as Sirāj. Unfortunately we do not have any detailed information about him from any other source than his own writing, *The Bounty of the Lovers*. There he states that this text was composed in 858/1454 in Muhammadabad (better known as Bidar), capital of the Indian kingdom of the Bahmanī Sultanate, where he had traveled from his homeland in Shiraz. The text itself was dedicated, not to any reigning monarch, but to his Sufi teacher in India, Amīr-zāda Muḥibb Allāh, son of Khalīl Allāh, and grandson of the well-known Persian Sufi master Shāh Ni`mat Allāh Walī. Moreover, he informs us that the title of his treatise was adopted from an identically named work by the famous Sufi of Shiraz, Shaykh Rūzbihān al-Baqlī (d. 1209).[5] Shīrāzī's master in the art

---

Afshār, Daftar-i Nashr-i Mīrāth-i Maktūb, `Ulūm o Funūn, 8 (Tehran: Nuqṭa, 1374/1997). In my translations from this Persian text, Arabic passages are printed in bold. The translation of Arabic *tuḥfa* as "bounty" in the title reflects Lane's definition: "a gratuitous gift, or favor; or a bounty, or benefit . . . a gift not given to any one before" (E. W. Lane, *Arabic-English Lexicon* [Cambridge: The Islamic Texts Society, 1984]), p. 208).

[4] Francis Richard, "Naṣr al-Solṭānī, Naṣīr al-Dīn Mozahheb et la bibliothèque d'Ebrāhīm Solṭānī à Shiraz," *Studia Iranica* 30 (2001): 87–104; Yves Porter, "La réglure (*masṭar*): de la 'formule d'atelier' aux jeux de l'esprit," *Studia Islamica* 96 (2003): 55–74, esp. 57–58; Ruqayya Abū al-Qāsimī, "Thulth," *Dānishnāma-i Jahān-i Islām* <http://www.encyclopaediaislamica.com/madkhal2.php?sid=4266>; more extensive references are found in Vlad Atanasiu, "Hypercalligraphie: Le phénomène calligraphique à l'époque du sultanat mamluk, Moyen-Orient, XIIIe–XVIe siècle," Ph.D. Diss., École pratique des Hautes Études / Section des Sciences historiques et philologiques, Paris, 2003 <http://www.atanasiu.freesurf.fr/thesis/atanasiu2003phd.pdf>.

[5] For a short Arabic excerpt from this lost work, see Muḥammad Taqī Dānish-Puzhūh, *Rūzbihān nāma* (Tehran: Anjuman-i Āthār-i Millī, 1969), 276, consisting of stories and sayings about great lovers.

of calligraphy, whom he mentions frequently (13 times in the text), was Ṣadr al-Dīn Rūzbihān Shīrāzī, a descendent of the Sufi master. Sirāj refers to his teacher with utmost reverence, calling him "the seal of the calligraphers" (*khātam al-khaṭṭāṭīn*).[6]

To judge from what we know about the family of Rūzbihān in Shiraz, Sirāj's master in calligraphy was probably a fifth-generation descendant. Rūzbihān's great-grandson Sharaf al-Dīn Ibrāhīm ibn Ṣadral-Dīn "Rūzbihān al-Thānī" (i.e., Rūzbihān II, active in 700/1300) had a son named Ṣadral-Dīn bin Sharaf al-Dīn Ibrāhīm "Rūzbihān al-Thālith" (Rūzbihān III), but the time interval is too long to make it possible for the latter to have been the teacher of Sirāj, who must have been educated at the latest by the beginning of the fifteenth century. Therefore it seems likely that it was one generation later (at least) that the calligrapher Ṣadral-Dīn Rūzbihān appeared, who would thus have been Rūzbihān IV, or conceivably, a generation later, Rūzbihān V (see Chart 1).[7]

Chart 1: The Descendants of Rūzbihān al-Baqlī
1. Rūzbihān al-Baqlī al-Shīrāzī (1128–1209)
2. Fakhr al-Dīn Aḥmad ibn Rūzbihān (ca. 1174–1247)
3. Ṣadral-DīnIbrāhīm ibn Fakhr al-Dīn Aḥmad Rūzbihān II (1218–86)
4. Sharaf al-Dīn Ibrāhīm ibn Ṣadr al-Dīn (ca. 1300)
5. Ṣadr al-Dīn ibn Sharaf al-Dīn Ibrāhīm Rūzbihān III
6. Ṣadr al-Dīn Rūzbihān al-Shīrāzī [IV? ca. 1400]

The vocabulary and style of Ya`qūb ibn Ḥasan's text frequently show strong resemblances to the writings of Rūzbihān, so there is no question about the affiliation of this calligraphic work with the mystical school of Shiraz.

Yet Sirāj also makes it clear that after his arrival in India he formed new attachments with a different Sufi lineage, the

[6] Sirāj also cites as one of his teachers Maulānā Sharaf al-Dīn Amīra, a calligrapher separated by one intermediary from the great Yāqūt, addressing him by the title "the master of the calligraphers" (*shaykh al-khaṭṭāṭīn*, 245); the closing lines of the treatise appear to refer (by the use of the same title) to the same individual's incipient departure on pilgrimage to Mecca and Medina (291).

[7] For further details see Carl W. Ernst, *Ruzbihan Baqli: Mystical Experience and the Rhetoric of Sainthood in Persian Sufism* (London: Curzon Press, 1996), chart 1, xxi.

Ni`matullāhī order, established by Shāh Ni`mat Allāh Walī (1330–1430). When the Bahmanī Sultan Aḥmad Shāh Walī (r. 1422–1436) acceded to the throne, one of his early gestures was to send a delegation to Kerman to invite Shāh Ni`mat Allāh to come to the Deccan to establish his spiritual influence there. While the shaykh (who would have been over 90 years old at this time) declined this invitation, he first sent a disciple to initiate the sultan into the order; Aḥmad Shāh, not satisfied, entrusted another delegation with a second invitation to the shaykh, who this time agreed to send his grandson Nūr Allāh (d. 1430) in his place. The latter was graciously received and married into the royal. Then Shāh Ni`mat Allāh, just prior to his death, appointed his son Khalīl Allāh (1373–1455) as his successor. Khalīl Allāh, after a brief sojourn in Herat at the invitation of Shāhrukh, made his way to the Deccan, probably arriving in Bidar by 1436, along with his two sons; the elder of these, Shāh Muḥibb al-Dīn (1427–1502), succeeded him as head of the Ni`matullāhīs in India.[8] Both Khalīl Allāh's sons followed Nur Allāh's example by marrying into the Bahmanī royal family. Sirāj pays tribute (pp. 51–52) to both Muhibb al-Dīn and his father Khalīl Allāh as his new spiritual guides in the Indian environment, and it is striking that he makes no reference to the ruling Sultan, `Alā' al-Dīn Aḥmad II (r. 1436–58).

Aside from these declarations of Sufi discipleship, Sirāj offers little by way of historical information about his times. Sirāj is said to have copied (presumably in Shiraz) a manuscript of the *Ẓafar nāma* of Sharaf al-Dīn Yazdī (d. 1454), a Persian biography of Timur, in a MS dated 1437.[9] The only other near-contemporary figure that he mentions is Ibrāhīm ibn Shāhrukh (1394–1435), a Timurid prince known for his patronage of art and architecture; Sirāj mentions him as both a connoisseur and practitioner

---

[8] Muhammad Suleman Siddiqi, *The Bahmani Sufis* (Delhi: Idarah-i Adabiyat-i Delli, 1989), 78–83.

[9] According to Mahdī Bayānī, this MS copied by Sirāj was in the Majlis library in Tehran, though Īraj Afshār was unable to locate it, leading him to speculate that it may have been in another library but mistakenly cited by Bayānī (*Tuḥfat*, 36). Sirāj refers to Yazdī (171) with language indicating that the latter was still living at the time of the book's composition. For an illustration from this manuscript, see Blair, 264, fig. 7.10.

of calligraphy, as well as being the sponsor of numerous building projects in Shiraz, including a mosque known as the Dār al-Ṣafā-yi Sulṭānī. From the Timurid author Qāḍī Aḥmad we know that this building was one of several in Shiraz (including the tomb of the poet Sa`dī) that featured the prince's own calligraphy; unfortunately, a rebellious governor destroyed Ibrāhīm's mosques at the end of the sixteenth century.[10] Sirāj also remarks that Ibrāhīm's court was adorned by a calligrapher such as his own teacher, Ṣadral-Dīn Rūzbihān.[11] His familiarity with a Timurid prince deceased two decades before the composition of his treatise, together with the dating of his *Ẓafarnāma* manuscript, suggests that Sirāj may have been in his youth when Ibrāhīm was active in Shiraz (1415–35); thus the *Tuḥfat al-Muḥibbīn* would have been the product of his maturity, though the chronology must admittedly remain speculative at this point.[12]

Sirāj was an example of the extraordinary movement of talent from Iran to India that formed a dominant cultural trend from the fifteenth to the eighteenth century. Particularly in the Deccan at an early stage, but later on in the Mughal regions of northern India as well, the wealthy courts of India proved an irresistible draw to numerous writers and intellectuals from Persia.[13] Schimmel describes the "influx of calligraphers" to the Bahmanī kingdom as a characteristic of this period.[14] The tomb of the Bahmanī Sultan Aḥmad Shāh I in his new capital of Bidar is particularly impressive, and it is noteworthy for its extensive inscriptions, including lengthy quotations from the Persian poetry of Shāh Ni`mat Allāh, as well as two spiritual genealogies

---

10 *Calligraphers and Painters: A Treatise by Qadi Ahmad, son of Mir Munshi (circa A.H. 1015/A. D1606)*, trans. V. Minorsky, Freer Gallery of Art Occasional Papers, 3 (Washington, DC: Smithsonian Institution, 1959), 28, 69–71.

11 *Tuḥfat*, 141. For a MS of Rūmī's *Mathnawī* commissioned by this prince in Shiraz in 1419, see Annemarie Schimmel, *The Triumphal Sun: A Study of the Works of Jalaloddin Rumi*, Persian Studies, No. 8 (Albany: State University of New York Press, 1993), 11.

12 Priscilla P. Soucek, "Ibrahim Sultan's Military Career," in *Iran and Iranian Studies: Essays in Honor of Iraj Afshar*, ed. Kambiz Eslami (Princeton, NJ: Zagros, 1998), 24–41.

13 Carl W. Ernst, "Deccan I. Political and Literary History," *Encyclopaedia Iranica* (Costa Mesa CA: Mazda Publishers), VII:181–85 (1995).

14 Annemarie Schimmel, *Calligraphy and Islamic Culture* (New York: New York University Press, 1984), 69.

of the shaykh's Sufi lineage in the central dome.[15] Schimmel considers the madrasa built in Bidar in 1472 by the minister Maḥmūd Gāwān (d. 1481, who had arrived in the Deccan only a year before Sirāj's treatise was written, in 1453) as one of the masterpieces of monumental calligraphy of that era; it included compositions by `Alī al-Sūfī, whose work also adorned edifices constructed by the Ottoman emperor Mehmet the Conqueror.[16] It is tempting to speculate that the work of a calligrapher like Sirāj, who was so closely connected to elite circles among the Bahmanīs, may have formed a part of the inscriptions found in the monuments of Bidar. It would have been natural, for example, for Sirāj to have been involved in the calligraphic program attached to the tomb of the reigning Bahmanī Sultan Aḥmad II, whose death took place only four years after the composition of the *Tuḥfat al-Muḥibbīn*.[17] Even more importantly, Sirāj would have had a keen interest, if not an active hand, in the calligraphic decoration on the four-storey (Hindi *ćau-khanḍī*) shrine of the father of his Sufi mentor, Shaykh Khalīl Allāh, who died in 1455.[18] This tomb features a remarkable monumental inscription in *thulth* style, signed by another calligrapher from Shiraz, one Mughīth al-Qārī. Begley calls this "one of the great masterpieces of monumental Islamic calligraphy in India", and Michell and Zebrowski concur that it is "among the greatest epigraphic inscriptions of Indian and Islamic art."[19] And one also wonders if the teachings of Sirāj would have had an impact on the Bahmanī sultan Maḥmūd Shāh (r. 1482–1518), a calligrapher whose work adorns the Sharza Gate of Bidar fort, in an inscription dated to 1503.[20]

---

[15] Khwaja Muhammad Ahmad, "Calligraphy," in *History of Medieval Deccan*, vol. 2, *Mainly Cultural Aspects*, eds H. K. Sherwani and P. M. Joshi (Hyderabad: Government of Andhra Pradesh, 1974), 411–22, esp. 415–17; G. Yazdani, *Bidar: Its History and Monuments* (Oxford: Oxford University Press, 1947), 114–29.

[16] Schimmel, 69.

[17] Yazdani, 129–31, with plates LXXVI–LXXVII. Unfortunately the tiles of this tomb have been largely destroyed by time.

[18] Yazdani, 141–43, with plates LXXXIII-LXXXV.

[19] W. E. Begley, *Monumental Islamic Calligraphy from India* (Villa Park, Illinois: Islamic Foundation, 1985), 58; George Michell and Mark Zebrowski, *Architecture and Art of the Deccan Sultanates* (Cambridge: Cambridge University Press, 1999), 121.

[20] Yazdani, 12, with plate III; Khwaja Muhammad Ahmad, "Two Inscriptions from Bidar," *Epigraphia Indo-Moslemica* (1925–26): 17–19.

The text of *Tuḥfat al-Muḥibbīn* exists in a unique manuscript, dated probably to the eighteenth century, which claims to be copied from the author's autograph, although it is written in an ordinary hand; the manuscript exhibits archaic orthographic practices that have been modernized by the editors in the printed edition. This document was acquired by the French Orientalist, Anquetil du Perron, in India in the 1790s, and it is preserved today in the Bibliothèque Nationale in Paris (suppl. persane 1086). It was first noticed among modern scholars by Muḥammad Taqī Dānish-Puzhūh, who enlisted the support of Karāmat Ra`ná Ḥusaynī and Īraj Afshār for its publication in a critical edition (with an introduction by Afshār) published in 1997, as part of a longstanding project to publish all available Persian texts on calligraphy. It is considered to be the second-oldest independent treatise on the Arabic script to be written in Persian, after the work of `Abd Allāh Ṣīrafī Tabrīzī (fourteenth century), which Sirāj quotes repeatedly.[21] The *Tuḥfat al-Muḥibbīn* was a product of the sophisticated calligraphic milieu of Shiraz, which was an important international center for the production of fine manuscripts; as Qāḍī Aḥmad remarked, in comparison to the calligraphers of Shiraz, "most of the renowned calligraphers in Fars, Khurasan, Kirman, and `Iraq 'are eaters of crumbs from their table.'"[22] Vlad Atanasiu has compared the *Tuḥfat al-Muḥibbīn*, as a wide-ranging manual of calligraphy, to the encyclopedic *Ṣubḥ al-a`shá* of the Mamluk author al-Qalqashandī: "Both distinguish themselves in calligraphic literature, as much Persian as Mamluk, by the variety and clarity of the information that they give, sometimes unpublished, as well as by a more personal and less rigid style."[23]

---

[21] *Tuḥfat*, 23. A handful of Persian works on calligraphy, none composed before the sixteenth century, are noticed by C. A. Storey, *Persian Literature: A Bio-bibliographical Survey* (London: Royal Asiatic Society, 1977), II.3:382–87. The text of Ṣīrafī's *Adab-i khaṭṭ* has been edited by Najīb Māyil Harawī, *Kitāb-ārāyī dar tamaddun-i islāmī* (Mashhad: Bunyād-i Pazhūhesh-hā-yi Islāmī, 1372/1993), xli–xliii, 13–32.

[22] Qāḍī Aḥmad, 67 (also mentioning as a leading calligrapher of Shiraz Maulānā Rūzbihān, most probably identical with Sirāj's teacher, Ṣadr al-Dīn Rūzbihān); Atanasiu, 64–65.

[23] Atanasiu, 54, with additional comments on calligraphic exchanges between Mamluk Egypt and the Indian sultanates.

Since this work is still not well-known, I provide here a brief description of its contents. The lengthy text of the *Tuḥfat al-Muḥibbīn* (over 250 pages in the published edition) is divided into the following sections:

Opening sermon (pp. 39–44)

Reasons for the composition of the book (pp. 45–53)

Adornment (*tawshīḥ*) "explaining the excellence of calligraphy and clarifying that it is the noblest of arts" (pp. 55–60)

Preface "explaining the placement of the script and the pens" (pp. 61–66)

Discourse 1, "explaining the conditions of the pen and its qualities, the trimming of the pen, and mention of the composition of inks, tools, and materials for writing, and the manners of the scribe, in five chapters" (pp. 67–112)

Discourse 2, "explaining the manner of placing the script, the names of the scripts, and the clarification of their principles and rules in isolation and in combination," in eight chapters (pp. 113–273)

Conclusion, "explaining certain forms of words and expressions that should be written in a [particular] style of writing," in two chapters (pp. 275–91).

Thus it can be seen that the text is wide-ranging, and covers a large variety of topics beyond the scope of this analysis.

The *Tuḥfat al-Muḥibbīn* is a learned and intensely intertextual work, with many quotations and references to sources in both Arabic and Persian. It contains 69 quotations from the Qur'an, 52 hadith, 72 Arabic sayings and proverbs, and over 50 Arabic poems. The bilingual sensibility of Sirāj is frequently evident, particularly in the more ornate sections, in long Persian sentences that employ as many as four separate Arabic phrases, plus perhaps a Persian verse or two, each of which operates as a noun in extended and elaborate metaphors that are exceedingly difficult to translate. There are many dozens of lines of Persian poetry, including 48 citations of the poetry of Ḥāfiẓ, making this one of the earliest sources to quote extensively from the work of the great Persian poet, who had died barely 60 years previously, perhaps within the author's lifetime. As was common, Sirāj only occasionally names the authors of the verses and sayings he quotes, though one can recognize certain well-known lines from figures such as Hallaj or Rūmī. Sirāj quotes liberally from the Arabic grammarian Ibn al-Ḥājib (d. 1249) and his work *al-Shāfiyya*, to establish basic linguistic concepts of the relationship between words and writing (pp. 118, 276). Sirāj also reproduces four extracts from separate biographies of calligraphers from Ibn Khallikān's (d. 1289) famous Arabic biographical dictionary *Wafāyāt al-a`yān*. The names of famous early Sufis and poets appear in the text, including Abū Sa`īd, Ruwaym, Wāsiṭī, Shibīi, Sa`dī, and Rūmī, with the most frequently quoted Persian poets being Qāsim-i Anvar (d. 1433–34) and Muḥammad Shīrīn Maghribī (d. 1408), both extremely popular in Sufi circles of the fifteenth century. But greater prominence is undoubtedly given to the masters of Arabic calligraphy, particularly Ibn Muqla, Ibn al-Bawwāb, and Yāqūt al-Musta`ṣimī.

In his review of the origins and history of the Arabic script, Sirāj covers well-known legendary territory, but his distinctive approach is well illustrated by his detailed account of the `Abbasid vizier Ibn Muqla and his role in the standardization of the geometrical basis of Arabic writing. Sirāj describes the early scripts known as Kufic and *ma`qilī*, which were understood to be composed entirely of straight lines (particularly the latter, associated with script composed of bricks).[24] Like many other authorities, Sirāj credits the fourth caliph, `Alī ibn Abī Ṭālib, with a major role in the development of the early Arabic script; he is said to have employed a style in Kufic that was 1/6 curved but predominantly straight. Drawing upon an otherwise unknown account which he attributes to Ṣīrafī,[25] Sirāj describes the role of Ibn Muqla in introducing the circular element as a major feature

[24] Wheeler M. Thackston, *Album Prefaces and Other Documents on the History of Calligraphers and Painters* (Leiden: Brill, 2001), 7, n. 4, reports that *ma`qilī* is "named after Nahr al-Ma`qil at Basra in southern Iraq."

[25] This narrative does not occur in the brief *Adab-i khaṭṭ* of Ṣīrafī, so perhaps another (lost) treatise is intended here.

of Arabic script, considering this as an innovation of truly cosmic significance.[26] I quote this passage at length, since it illustrates not only the concept of the circle as integral to the new form of Arabic script, but also because of its distinctive employment of Sufi-style quotations of Prophetic hadith with a strong cosmological flavor:

> And since by the principles of wisdom it is demonstrated that God (glory be to the Most High) created the world in a circular form, even so the explanation of this meaning has occurred in the words of the sages: **"The world is a circle, the earth is a dot, the heavens are bows, accidents are arrows, and man is a target; so where is one to flee?"** This is based on the judgment that **"The best of shapes is the shape of the circle."** The master Abū `Alī Muḥammad ibn `Alī ibn al-Ḥusayn ibn Muqla the scribe (may God have mercy on him) realized that writing could be made circular. He transmitted that method of [round] Kufic in this fashion that is now current, so that it would be related to the creation of the Earth, which is the principle of all principles.
>
> And Khwāja `Abd Allāh Ṣīrafī (may God refresh his spirit) has an epistle on the science of writing, and he maintains that the cause of the transfer of script from the [square] Kufic to the round was that on a certain day one of the children of the Caliph, to whom the master Abū`Alī [ibn Muqla] attended as a tutor, went out for a stroll. At the time of his return, the Caliph asked his child whether he had brought back any keepsake or gift as a companion from his outing.
>
> The son of the Caliph, after presenting his respects, observed, "I overheard a couple of verses from a lover, which I recall as follows:
>
> **My lover's teeth are in the form of the *sīn,***
> **And his mouth's shape is like a rounded *mīm.***
> **Together they spell poison (*samm*); amazing, by my life!**
> **After I tasted it, there was no doubt."**
>
> The Caliph considered these verses, and to one of his dear ones remarked, "The poet has compared the mouth of his beloved to a *mīm*, and now your mouth is round, but the Kufic *mīm* is not round at all, so the poet has foolishly said nothing."
>
> In the midst of this thought, he summoned Abū`Alī ibn Muḥammad [ibn Muqla] and he entered into discussion with him on this subject. The master replied that if the Caliph was so inclined, he would consider the subject further. Exerting his creativity in the manner that the poet had

[26] See also Blair, 157–60.

> versified and by the method that was in accord with the verses, he made his proposal, and sought a space of 40 days, according to the [Prophetic] saying, **"Anoint yourself with the qualities of God"** (*takhallaqū bi-akhlāq allāh*). He made use of the flashes of divine lights and sought the emanation from the contents filled with grace of [the divine saying,] **"I kneaded the clay of Adam with my hands for 40 days"** (*khammartu ṭīnata ādam bi-aydayya arbaʿīna ṣabāḥan*). He took a period of 40 days in retreat of meditation to imagine the kneading of the clay of letters possessing elegant forms, transferring them from the lines of Kufic to the heavenly form of round and circular lines (pp. 120–21).

Thus Ibn Muqla's development of the new forms of the Arabic script is depicted as a result of a meditative retreat that imitates divine creativity, which is invoked by the *ḥadīth qudsī*, an extra-Qur'anic saying of God related by the Prophet Muḥammad, in which God describes kneading the clay of Adam with his own hands for 40 days, as a preparation for the creation of humanity.

Sirāj's detailed discussions of later masters of calligraphy after Ibn Muqla (pp. 124–34), the different varieties of script (pp. 135–46), and the specific oral teachings of his masters (pp. 262–71) are certainly worthy of further study as part of the larger history of Arabic calligraphy. In any case, it is clear that he regards the `Abbasid vizier as in many respects the founding figure in this tradition. The role of Ibn Muqla, as transmitted by Ibn al-Bawwāb, is decisive in the third chapter of Discourse 2, which presents the principles of writing on the geometrical basis of the dot produced by the tip of the reed pen. Here (pp. 147–75) Sirāj proceeds through the Arabic alphabet, following the alphabetical order based upon the similarity of letter shapes that is still in common use today. In each case, he opens his discussion with a series of poetic and mystical remarks, frequently in rhyming prose with metaphors based on writing, employing words that begin with or contain the letter under consideration; he then moves on to technical considerations of the size and shape of the letters as measured by the dot. In each case, he includes an Arabic quotation describing the shape of the letter, using technical terms that are clearly derived from Ibn Muqla: *munkabb* or oblique, *mustalqī* or inclined, *munsaṭiḥ* or horizontal, and *muntaṣib* or upright. With minor variations, a nearly identical language is found in the description of letters according to the system of Ibn

Muqla as preserved in the monumental encyclopedia of Mamluk chancery practice, the *Ṣubḥ al-a`shá* of al-Qalqashandī.[27] Whether Sirāj had direct access to the work of al-Qalqashandī, or knew the writings of Ibn Muqla via other sources, cannot presently be established, but it is clear that both authors are referring to the very same principles. As an example of Sirāj's presentation, his description of the letter *fā'* will suffice:

> *Fā'* is the index (*fihrist*) of the collection of benefits (*fawā'id*) and the introduction to the collected poems of excellences and rarities (*faḍā'il wa farā'id*), like the inner heart (*fu'ād*) among trustworthy people (*ahl-i wafā'*) and the cardium in the body of the masters of purity (*arbāb-i ṣafā'*). [Persian verse:]
>
> Since revealing her head from the collar of thought (*fikr*),
> She has thrown a world into consternation.
>
> And in the deserts (*fayāfī*), there is desire for the cavalry captain of the knights (*fārisān*) of the field of gnosis, and the victors (*fā'izān*) of the plains of secrets.
>
> The manifestations of its rules and principles have been clarified by the explanation, **"the *fā'* is a shape composed of three lines: oblique, inclined, and horizontal (*munkabb, mustalq^in^, munsaṭiḥ*)."** Its head should be rounded, and the space in the head should resemble the grain of a pear seed. Its neck is one dot, and the measure of its height is equivalent to the height of the *bā'*, and the totality of this is no greater than 14 dots.[28]

---

[27] Aḥmad ibn `Alī al-Qalqashandī, *Ṣubḥ al-a`shá fī ṣanā`at al-inshā'*, ed. Muḥammad Ḥusayn Shams al-Dīn (15 vols., Beirut: Dār al-Kutub al-`Ilmiyya, 1987–1989), 2:30–37. I am greatly indebted to Dr. Ahmed Moustafa for drawing my attention to this important source and making it available to me. His monograph on Ibn Muqla (co-authored with Stefan Sperl), entitled *The Cosmic Script: Sacred Geometry and the Science of Arabic Penmanship* (Rochester, Vermont: Inner Traditions, 2014), is a major contribution to our understanding of the origins and significance of the Arabic script, and I am grateful to both authors for sharing their work with me and for commenting on an earlier draft of this essay. The editors of *Tuḥfat al-Muḥibbīn* have conveniently assembled Sirāj's Arabic quotations of Ibn Muqla's definitions in a separate index (350–51).

[28] *Tuḥfat al-Muḥibbīn*, 162, quoting *Ṣubḥ*, 2:34, with a minor variation: al-Qalqashandī says the composition of *fā'* has four lines, adding one that is upright (*muntaṣib*). Stefan Sperl comments, "*Munkabb* literally means 'falling on one's face' and hence refers to an oblique stroke extending between the upper left and the lower right. *Mustalqi* means 'falling on one's back' and hence refers to an inclined stroke pointing in the opposite direction, i.e., extending between the lower left and the upper right. *Munsaṭiḥ* means horizontal (lit. lying stretched out on the ground)" (letter of 8 May 2008). For these Arabic technical terms, see also the brief lexicon supplied by Sirāj (272), where the *maṣdar* verbal

So the basic catalog of letters in Sirāj's presentation is a combination of aesthetic associations, sharpened by a poetic and mystical vocabulary, along with technical descriptions of the formation of the letters in terms of dots, as well as sometimes picturesque descriptions of the shapes. While Sirāj is clearly indebted to Ibn Muqla's formulation of "proportional script" (*al-khaṭṭ al-manṣūb*), he does not systematically integrate its geometrical principles, but rather concentrates on what Ahmed Moustafa and Stefan Sperl have called "measurements reflecting the actual appearance of letter shapes in different script styles."[29]

At this point, I would like to turn to the longest section of the book, the fourth chapter of Discourse 2, which contains a lengthy section (pp. 176–232, amounting to one-fourth of the entire text) that describes all possible two-letter combinations of the letters of the Arabic alphabet and their symbolic meanings. It is here that we see Sirāj increasingly engaging his repertory of mystical interpretations as a demonstration of a Sufi approach to penmanship. After a brief discussion of the *alif*, which does not connect to succeeding letters, Sirāj undertakes a consideration of the different shapes and letter combinations with the *bā'* (and by implication its sisters *tā'* and *thā'*), and he follows a similar descriptive pattern with *jīm*, *dāl*, and *sīn*. Thus he informs us that one form of the *dāl* resembles the shape of a gourd or cup, leading to a recollection of some wine verses; then he points out that another form of the *dāl* is shaped like a sheep's lung, which only suggests the meat of good living. But the last form of the *dāl* is like the flint of a tinderbox, which is capable of igniting an internal heat from the fire that Moses

forms of the same terms are given short Persian definitions. Moustafa and Sperl offer an extensive discussion of these terms in their study. For a preliminary related study defining these pen strokes, see Ahmed Moustafa, *The Geometrical Cosmos of Arabic Numerals: Discovering the Archetypal Shapes of Arabic Numerals* (London: Fe-Noon Ahmed Moustafa, 1996), esp. 33–34. The unique manuscript of *Tuḥfat al-Muḥibbīn*, as the editors acknowledge, has many passages that are difficult to read, but some of these may be emended by comparison with parallel texts, including al-Qalqashandī. For instance, the anomalous reading *istiflā'* in the quotation from Ibn Muqla on 149, line 4, should be corrected to the regular term *istilqā'* or "inclination".

[29] Ahmed Moustafa and Stefan Sperl, letter of 27 April 2008.

saw on Mount Sinai, as recalled in the Qur'an (20:10). Similarly, with the letter *sīn*, Sirāj describes various letter combinations in different scripts; but when he reaches the combination of *sīn* plus *yā'*, he remarks, "The wise man who is the master of ecstasy becomes thoughtful about the inverse of the form of *sīn yā'*, with the sparks of the lights of blessings from its recitation as *yā' sīn*" (p. 182), which is of course the title of Sura 36 of the Qur'an. In this way Sirāj establishes the principle that a letter combination itself may lead to unsuspected meanings by its permutations or other hidden implications.

Sufi language starts to become more evident in the discussion of the letter *ṣād*, where Sirāj refers (p. 183) to "the clever and noble ones, who are in conformity with the exegesis (*istinbāṭ*) of subtle points and the extraction (*istikhrāj*) of hidden meanings from forms." He increasingly cites poetic references suggested by the letter at hand, using formulas such as "it comes to mind" (*ba-khāṭir āyad*) to introduce the free association. Sometimes a two-letter combination forms an actual word, such as *ṭā'* plus *yā'*, which yields the word *ṭayy* or "folding", recalling the miraculous ability of saints to translocate across space (*ṭayy al-makān*): "If *ṭā'* is written with *yā'*, from the concept of the translocation of the saints, one can be transported by folding up the carpet of one's own existence" (p. 185). But at other times, nonsense combinations can be deconstructed into meaningful numerological equivalents by substituting the arithmetic values of the Arabic alphabet in the *abjad* or *ḥisāb al-jummal* system. So when one sees the combination *ṭā'* plus *lām*, which produces the meaningless word *ṭal* (p. 187), one recognizes that its numerological total (9 plus 30 = 39) is equivalent to the numerological total of the two divine names *wāḥid wadūd* ("the One, the Loving"; 19 + 20 = 39). In a similar fashion, the meaningless combination *ṭā'* plus *jīm* has a numerological total of 12, which suggests the spiritual significance of the 12 imams of Shi`ism, to whom Sirāj expresses devotion on more than one occasion. The following intricate passage, written in a style suggestive of the writings of Rūzbihān al-Baqlī, illustrates the remarkable extent to which Sirāj can go in seeing deep significance suggested by letters which are not actually present on the page, but which come to mind from seeing a particular combination. With reference to the combination *fā'* plus *yā'*, Sirāj writes:

> For the wise man there are things he ought to know from this discussion. After [seeing] the picture of the *fā'* and *alif*, from the extremity of victory (*fawz*) he is led to the imagination of the letter *zā'*, so that from the fragrances of the breezes of **"he is victorious (*fāza*) who gains religion"** (*fāza man ẓafara bil-dīn*) the glad aromas of victory (*fawz*) and success are conveyed to the senses of the soul (p. 191).

So the significance of a letter combination is ultimately given by still invisible letters which one must imaginatively supply in order to yield the desired result. These are the basic patterns of free association that govern Sirāj's approach to letter combinations in the first third of this section.

But during the discussion of combinations involving the letter *kāf*, Sirāj begins to apply a new strategy that continues until the end of this section, where he begins to introduce Arabic passages, both short and long, based on unidentified mystical definitions, which are clearly from the well-known lexicon of Sufi terminology, the *Iṣṭilāḥāt al-Ṣūfiyya* of `Abd al-Razzāq al-Kāshānī (d. 1330), a prominent representative of the school of Ibn `Arabi.[30] Thus the combination of the letters *kāf* and *qāf* suggests two different words beginning with those letters, alchemy (*kīmīyā'*) and contentment (*qanā`a*); Sirāj quotes the last part of Kāshānī's definition of alchemy, which is **"contentment with the existent and abandoning longing for the perishable; and the Commander of the Faithful, `Alī (may God be pleased with him) said, 'contentment is an inexhaustible treasure.'"**[31] From this point onward, Sirāj quotes over 30 esoteric definitions from Kāshānī's Sufi dictionary, to define terms that are suggested (sometimes more than once) by letter combinations occurring in the latter parts of the alphabet (see Chart 2). As can be seen, these are often unusual terms that might be considered arbitrary identifications for the letter combinations with which they are associated.

30 *'Abdu-r-Razzaq's Dictionary of the Technical Terms of the Sufies*, ed. Aloys Sprenger (Calcutta: The Asiatic Society of Bengal, 1845).

31 *Tuḥfat al-Muḥibbīn*, 198, quoting Kāshānī, 44–45.

Chart 2

Quotations of definitions from Kāshānī's Iṣṭilāḥāt al-Ṣūfiyya in the Tuḥfat al-Muḥibbīn of Sirāj al-Shīrāzī

Sirāj	*letters*	*phrase*	*meaning*	*Kāshānī*
198	*kāf-qāf*	*kīmīyā'*	alchemy	44
199	*kāf-wāw*	*kawkab*	planet	43
201	*lām-dāl*	*al-durra al-bayḍā'*	white pearl	22
202	*lām-sīn*	*lawā'iḥ*	flashes	46–47
207	*lām-rā'*	*lubb, lubb al-lubb*	pith, pith of the pith	45
207	*lām-rā'*	*ridā'*	garment	148
207	*lām-ṣād*	*ṣabā'*	morning breeze	132–33
208	*lām-tā'*	*lā'iḥa*	flash	44
208	*lām-tā'*	*ṭawāli`*	sunrises	39
208	*lām-`ayn*	*al-laṭīfa al-insāniyya*	human subtle element	46
211	*mīm-bā'*	*mabādī*	beginnings	49
212	*mīm-dāl*	*shāhid*	witness	150
213	*mīm-kāf*	*kīmīyā'*	alchemy	44
213	*mīm-lām*	*mabná al-taṣawwuf*	basis of Sufism	49–50
213	*mīm-lām*	*al-laṭīfa al-insāniyya*	human subtle element	46
216	*mīm-sīn*	*majdhūb*	enraptured	50
217	*mīm-sīn*	*sirr al-ḥaqīqa*	secret of reality	84
217	*mīm-ṣād*	*mashāriq al-fatḥ*	dawnings of victory	61
218	*mīm-tā'*	*muṭṭala`*	point of ascent	63
218	*mīm-tā'*	*ṭāhir al-sirr*	purifier of the secret	40
219	*mīm-`ayn*	*mashāriq shams al-ḥaqīqa*	dawnings of the sun of reality	61
221	*mīm-fā'*	*al-fatḥ al-mubīn*	the clear victory	124
221	*mīm-qāf*	*musharrif al-ḍamā'ir*	ennobler of consciences	61–62

Sirāj	*letters*	*phrase*	*meaning*	*Kāshānī*
221	*mīm-qāf*	*al-quṭbiyya al-kubrá*	supreme axis-hood	141
225	*hā'-bā'*	*hibā'*	dust	23
227	*hā'-ṣād*	*ṣawāmi` al-dhikr*	monasteries of remembrance	137
227	*hā'-tā'*	*al-ṭabīb al-rūḥānī*	spiritual physician	40
228	*hā'-fā'*	*al-fatḥ al-qarīb*	near victory	129
229	*hā'-qāf*	*al-qiyām lillāh*	standing with God	138
231	*hā'-nūn*	*hawājim*	assaults	25
231	*hā'-yā'*	*al-hā'*	H	23
232	*hā'-yā'*	*yawm al-jum`a*	Friday	42

There are times when, as for instance in the description of combinations of the letter *lām*, Sirāj spends as much as five pages (201–6) demonstrating the metaphysical and symbolic properties of letters, before he returns to the formal aspect, announcing, "We have come back to the explanation of the principles of the letter forms." His is to a certain extent a bookish approach to Sufism, relying as it does upon a Sufi lexicon that was compiled from a particularly philosophical perspective, and which was even organized alphabetically to facilitate exactly the kind of systematic consultation that Sirāj brought to it.[32] In a way, it is not surprising that Sirāj was comfortable with this intellectualist approach to mysticism, given his willingness to quote at the same time (p. 58) from such philosophical works as the *Nasirean Ethics* of the philosopher Naṣīr al-Dīn Ṭūsī (d. 1272).

So how may we characterize the approach of Sirāj al-Shīrāzī to the art of penmanship in terms of Sufism? Let us return to a couple of passages where he cites the dictionary of Kāshānī. After describing the space separating the combined letters *kāf*

[32] See Carl W. Ernst, "Mystical Language and the Teaching Context in the Early Sufi Lexicons," chapter 9 in this volume.

and *lām* as being the distance of two dots, or just slightly greater than the width of a hair, he comments as follows:

> Among the appropriate conceptual and intellectual graces of these letters, according to the path of the lords of insight and gnosis—nay, the masters of ecstasy and unveiling—rather, the authorities of the experience of witnessing—in the form of writing the *lām* and *rā'*, with the proof of the illuminated intellect, one may comprehend the allusion to the *lām* of **"the pith (*lubb*) is the intellect that the sacred pure light illuminates from the shells of fancies and imaginations"**, and the *rā'* of the garment (*ridā'*) of **"divine majesty is my garment."**[33]

These repeated and emphatic invocations of mystical authority, as a series of increasingly exalted levels, serve as justifications for understanding the letters of the alphabet as ciphers for mysteries that are otherwise insoluble. This approach is presented as a possibility, by which mystical interpretations (in a characteristically Rūzbihānian phrase) "can take the lead so that the brides of the realities of these meanings mayreveal their faces beyond the veils of power" (p. 209). This is a series of possible interpretations that may be undertaken "in the technical vocabulary of the people of Sufism and gnosis" (p. 212). Sirāj never claims that these mystical meanings are inherent in the letters themselves as a kind of intrinsic property.

By treating the Sufi understanding of penmanship as an option available to a spiritual elite, Sirāj is quite consistent with the predominant Sufi approaches to the interpretation of other art forms, particularly poetry and music. As Rūzbihān al-Baqlī put it, "Listening to music is of three kinds: there is one kind for the common people, one kind for the elite, and one kind for the elite of the elite."[34] In this way, music may be appreciated by people on different levels of perception and understanding. It is noteworthy that the Sufis simply refer to the faculty of listening (*samā`*) rather than the production of sound. Likewise, with poetry, it is the capacity of the reader

---

[33] *Tuḥfat al-Muḥibbīn*, 207, quoting Kāshānī, 45, 148.

[34] Rūzbihān al-Baqlī, *Risālat al-quds*, trans. Carl W. Ernst, *Teachings of Sufism* (Boston: Shambhala Publications, 1999), 102.

that produces a mystical reading, rather than the text itself, as one can see from the popularity of the profane Arabic lyrics of Abū Nuwās in Sufi circles. The ultimate paradigm of Sufi aesthetics may be best expressed by the anecdotes of mystics who serendipitously discovered profound meaning in the most mundane encounters. One such example is recounted by Sirāj (p. 186), in an anecdote about the Baghdadian Sufi, Abū Bakr al-Shiblī. He was said one day to have been passing through the bazaar, when he chanced upon an ice-vendor, who was reciting the following verse in order to attract the attention of customers:

> **"Have mercy on one whose stock in trade is melting!"** (*arḥamū `alá man ra'su mālihi yadhūb*).On hearing these words, the fire of regret was so inflamed in his [Shibli's] blessed soul that he started sobbing. The situation was described by these verses from Mawlānā Jalāl al-Dīn Rūmī:
>
> The soul's love became Sinai, lover!
> Sinai was drunk and "Moses fell down fainting."[35]
>
> After some time, when he returned from this absorption, his disciples placed a foot on the carpet of explanation of the unveiling of that incident. The revered master stated, "from the words of that person, the capital of my life passed before my mind, so that I knew it was just like melted snow, and by means of him something was prepared of the provisions for the journey that lies ahead."

This very principle of sudden and unlooked-for inspiration has been frequently invoked by Sufi commentators, as for instance in the interpretation of the inner levels of the poetry of Hafiz written by Sirāj's contemporary in Shiraz, Jalāl al-Dīn Davānī.[36] In this respect, the approach of Sirāj is similar to the principle of "taking warning or example" (*i`tibār*, *`ibrat*), which Nasrollah

---

[35] These lines are from the opening of Rūmī's *Mathnawī* (I:26), and the words in quotation are an adaptation of Qur. 7:143, thus likening Shibli's experience to the astonishment of the Prophet Moses.

[36] Carl W. Ernst, "Davānī's Interpretation of Ḥāfiẓ," chapter 21 in this volume. It is noteworthy that Davānī follows the lead of Muhammad al-Ghazālī and Abu Naṣr al-Sarrāj, who cited the very same stories to explain the inspiration produced by listening to music. Thus Sufis have employed the very same principle to the aesthetic reception of various art forms.

Pourjavady has described as a kind of motion or reflection that transitions between one state and another. In Sufi circles, these terms described a mode of contemplating the divine beauty, whether in a visual or aural manner, no matter how unexpected the manifestation.[37]

For artists like Sirāj, the art of penmanship was a consuming passion, and they were surrounded throughout their lives by a tradition of discipline with strong debts to Sufism. They saw the letters of the alphabet as vehicles for the manifestation of God in beautiful forms, as part of the process of cosmic unfolding. As Sirāj remarks in the very opening lines of his invocation for the text (p. 39), "The shining of the ornaments of limitless praise radiate from the faces of the brides of the letters of those graceful arts of form and meaning in the insightful eyes of the possessors of power and vision. This is the largess of the royal court, which by the writing of the glorious canopy gives ornament and adornment to the beauty of the word of unity and the portrait of the name of the beloved who must be respected and honored." It was undoubtedly those whom the Qur'an calls "possessors of vision" that Sirāj intended as the proper audience for his treatise on penmanship, and it is in that sense that we can speak of his work as embodying a Sufi aesthetic for the appreciation of the written word.

[37] Nasrollah Pourjavady, *Bāda-i `ishq: puzhūhishī dar ma`nā-yi bāda dar shi`r-i `irfānī-yi fārsī* (Tehran: Nashr-i Kārnāma, 1387/2008), 149–60. For additional examples of ecstatic perception of the divine among early Sufis, see Carl W. Ernst, *Words of Ecstasy in Sufism* (Albany: State University of New York Press, 1985), 37.

21

Jalāl al-Dīn Davānī's Interpretation of Ḥāfiẓ

One of the perennial debates about the poetry of Ḥāfiẓ has revolved around the interpretation of his poetry, whether it should properly be considered part of the secular tradition of Persian court poetry, or whether it should be interpreted in some kind of mystical or allegorical sense in relation to Sufism. This question has been discussed since the very dawn of European Orientalist scholarship, having formed a significant part of the labors of Sir William Jones and his successors. Without attempting to summarize the details of this extensive debate, we can take a recent example as an indication of how hotly this question can be argued; I have in mind the overview to the multi-authored article on Ḥāfiẓ in the *Encyclopaedia Iranica*, penned by the distinguished scholar and editor of the *Encyclopaedia*, Dr. Ehsan Yarshater. He writes:

> It was only natural that a Sufistic interpretation should be applied to the poems of Hafez, ignoring in the process many indications to the contrary. Some commentators and even some Western translators of Hafez, notably Wilberforce Clarke, a translator of the *Divān* (London, 1974), satisfied themselves, to the point of utter absurdity, that every single word written by Hafez had a mystical meaning and no line of Hafez actually meant what it said. The reading of Hafez as codified poetry implying an esoteric meaning for each line or word propounded the view that his ghazals can be read at two levels, one apparent, the other hidden—the

> latter representing the intended meaning. Deciphering Hafez's underlying meaning grew into an esoteric art, not dissimilar to the explanations offered by the addicts of "conspiracy theories" (q.v.) in political affairs....

Then, acknowledging some ambiguity in the application of the term *'ārif* (gnostic) to Ḥāfiẓ, Dr. Yarshater makes it quite clear that he rejects any significant association of the poet with institutional Sufism:

> On the other hand, if by *'āref* is meant a "mystic," that is, a person who believes in the theory and practice of Sufism, is attached to a certain Order or the circle of a Sufi mentor (*pīr*) or a *kānaqāh*, or allows the clarity of his mind to be clouded by the irrational and obfuscated by the woolly thinking of some Sufis and their belief in miraculous deeds ascribed to their saints, then the epithet is a misnomer.[1]

The *Encyclopaedia* is not of one mind on this matter; the section by Franklin Lewis on the image of the rogue (*rind*) in Ḥāfiẓ is considerably more nuanced in balancing the denunciation of religious hypocrisy with the symbolism of spiritual authenticity.[2]

Be that as it may, in this essay I will not attempt to decide whether Ḥāfiẓ is by intention a secular or mystical poet, since the question as posed may in fact be badly framed. Instead, I would like to examine the case of one of the very earliest formal commentators on the poetry of Ḥāfiẓ, Jalāl al-Dīn Davānī (d. 908/1502), the eminent philosopher and scholar of Shiraz.[3] Davānī is credited with half a dozen short untitled texts commenting on various verses by Ḥāfiẓ. Although these are generally undated, in one of these writings the author refers to the near completion of another of his works (the *Shawākil al-ḥūr*, dated 872/1468); thus we can conclude that Davānī is certainly one of the earliest, if not the very first, to write a separate commentary on Ḥāfiẓ. The fact that Davānī lived in Shiraz not long

---

[1] Ehsan Yarshater, "Hafez. i. An Overview," *Encyclopaedia Iranica*.

[2] Franklin Lewis, "Hafez. viii. Hafez and Rendi," *Encyclopaedia Iranica*.

[3] A useful overview of the metaphysical views of Davani was provided in an early article by Mehmed Ali Ayni, "Note sur l'idéalisme de Djelaleddin Davani," *Revue Neo-scholastique de Philosophie*, new series, 8 (1931), pp. 236–40.

after the death of Ḥāfiẓ gives his interpretations a special significance for the likely reader reception of his poetry by at least some contemporary audiences.[4] Three of these commentaries by Davānī have been collected together in a convenient edition by Ḥusayn Mu`allim, entitled *Naqd-i niyāzī*, and as representative samples, these will constitute the basis for the following observations.[5]

The first of Davānī's commentaries on Ḥāfiẓ focuses on the well-known verse *dūsh dīdam ki malāyik dar-i maykhāna zadand/ gil-i Ādam bi-sirishtand u bi-paymānah zadand*, "Last night I saw the angels knocking on the tavern door; / they mixed the clay of Adam and threw it as a cup." In the opening pages, he describes his aim as follows:

> The purpose of this introduction is that certain of the sincere lovers, in the times of conversation and the hours of closeness, asked about the commentary on a verse by 'the tongue of the moment,' Master Shams al-Millat wal-Dīn Muḥammad Ḥāfiẓ.... After fulfilling that request, two or three words were speedily written down to the taste of the unitarians and the path of the Sufis. On completion, that document was lost. Once more they began to ask, and with the help of time, it was formed in our way with correct composition and written with a verified description. Its basis was established in the path of the unitarians, the Sufis, and the sages, since to each of these groups on this subject there is a perspective and a reflection, and in accordance with the grasp of every soul there is a condition of recollection. Beware not to get lost in "every tribe knew its drinking place (*mashrab*)" (Qur. 2:60). Every person in this knowledge is associated with a path. One may have achieved eternal happiness, while another is stuck at the beginning of the alphabet. One person takes pleasure in ecstasy and listening to music, while another finds peace in dancing. Most sought textual confirmation [for their path] from the verses of the poet referred to, so that their objectives would also become illuminated [by his poetry], and the sorrowful soul would find fresh fragrances from the breeze of that garden.[6]

---

[4] Reza Pourjavady, "Kitāb-shināsi-i āthār-i Jalāl al-Dīn Davānī," *Ma'ārif* 15/1-2 (1377/1998), pp. 81–139; see especially items numbered 8–14, pp. 90–94, and the author's remarks on p. 91. One of these commentaries (Pourjavady, no. 8) has also been discussed by Terry Graham, "Hafiz and His Master," *Sufi* 42 (Summer 1999), pp. 35–40.

[5] Jalāl al-Dīn Davānī Kāzarūnī, *Naqd-i niyāzī, dar sharḥ-i do bayt u yik ghazal az Khwājah Ḥāfiẓ*, ed. Ḥusayn Mu`allim (Tehran: Amīr Kabīr, 1373/1995).

[6] *Naqd*, p. 44.

It is important to underline the extent to which multiple interpretations of the verse of Ḥāfiẓ are assumed to be normal. Davānī's procedure in this particular text is, on the surface at least, systematic. He undertakes to explore the verse from three different perspectives: first, the unitarians; second, the Sufis; and third, the Peripatetic and Illuminationist sages (*ḥukamā*). Davānī does not precisely indicate who these groups are or how they differ from one another—there is certainly at this time a fair amount of overlap between the concerns of philosophers and Sufis, for example. His category of unitarians is similar to the use of that term by 'Azīz al-Dīn Nasafī, to describe a kind of philosophical mystic.[7] In any case, for Davānī it seems to be an important methodological principle to acknowledge these different perspectives, which he likens to the different "drinking places" found by each of the 12 Israelite tribes in the Qur'anic text, playing upon the alternate meaning of this word (*mashrab*) as a school or teaching. It is also noteworthy that Davānī applies an oracular epithet to Ḥāfiẓ, calling him "the tongue of the moment" (*lisān al-waqt*). His approach is not literary in the ordinary sense, but exegetical, even as it acknowledges that all readers are likely to find their own perspectives confirmed by the poetry of Ḥāfiẓ.

The discussion of the unitarians is the longest, and it is divided into six separate sections or "observations" (entitled *mashhad*), each devoted to the interpretation of a particular symbol or aspect of the verse: 1) last night; 2) the speaker of the verse; 3) the angels; 4) the tavern; 5) the clay of Adam; 6) the meaning of throwing the clay of Adam in the form of a cup. Davānī defends this focus on individual images with the following justification:

> The subtle *qalandars* and realized great ones are of the view that, in order that the brides of meaning should remained hidden from the unworthy and should not be pawed by the worldly, the realities of gnosis have been displayed in the cloak of similitudes, and spiritual meanings in the forms of perceptible things. They have taken their inspiration from this verse: "These are the similitudes that We coin for the people, and

[7] See the comments on the *ahl-e waḥdat* ("monists") in Herman Landolt, "Nasafī, 'Azīz b. Moḥammad," *Encyclopaedia Iranica* <http://www.iranica.com/newsite/articles/unicode/sup/Nasafi_Aziz.html>.

> none understands except the wise" (Qur. 29:43). Verse: "When you hear the name spoken, run towards the thing that is named; / otherwise the speech of ecstatics remains a riddle." Necessarily, whenever the people of the heart tell a secret, they reveal their aims by the method of metonymy (*kināyat*), so that the people of interpretation (*ta'wīl*) may understand the goals of those melodies through experiential proofs.[8]

So Davānī's method depends upon reading individual words and coded symbols that metaphorically represent unstated realities.[9] This is a robust hermeneutic that he applies without hesitation, while still locating the exercise aesthetically in the realm of poetry framed in performance with musical melody (*tarāna*).

When Davānī implements his interpretation of the symbols employed by Ḥāfiẓ, he does so in this section with a highly technical philosophical vocabulary that is presumed to furnish a categorical explanation. It is, moreover, framed in a highly ornate style drawing on arcane vocabulary and expressed with the artifices of rhyming prose. There are frequent citations of anonymous lines of Persian poetry (which I will skip for reasons of brevity), as well as Arabic verses from the Qur'an, and the occasional deployment of hadith. This may be seen in his exploration of the meaning of "last night" according to the unitarians:

> Know that existence has a substance and a determination. From the perspective of substance, this demands that in a purely absolute fashion it should be freed from every limitation and denuded of all relationships. Pure being, which does not set foot in manifestation, and transcendence, which is no companion to relationship, they call the absolutely hidden presence and the reality in truth.... Necessarily, from this degree, by a path that is absolutely required and by necessary volition, the nightingales of that garden [i.e., the unitarians] express the absolute substance with the phrase "clear day."... Likewise, the determination of existence, which is the source of the emanation of providence, from the perspective of the understanding of those who are near perceptible things, is expressed by the phrase "dark day," because the degrees of determination have hidden the beauty of reality. The people of spiritual meaning have called that the veil of the two worlds. And the tress is the allusion, and the lock of hair and the mole are the expression, for the same thing.... Thus according to those who are perfumed

---

8 *Naqd*, pp. 44–45.

9 See Ch. Pellat, "Kināya," *Encyclopaedia of Islam*, vol. 5, pp. 116–18.

> by this fresh breeze, the metonyms for the divine reality and the degree of determination are morning and night.... The first they call the hidden divine identity, and the second they say is the degree of unity; this is an example of the melody of the unitarians.

Then, observing that, in reality, there is no night and day for God, Davānī reverses the symbolism.

> Yes, but the times of pre-eternity and post-eternity are joined in the point of now, even if the intellect says that that situation is impossible. In short, the Muḥammadan faqirs call the period of the extension of reality "perpetual time" (*waqt-i sarmadī*) and by way of deceiving the unworthy and clouding the sight of those lost in the desert of ignorance, they call that "last night."... And the period of the extension of determination and existence, which requires manifestation and disclosure, in their parlance is called duration (*dahr*). By metonymy, they call that "today."[10]

The method employed in this interpretation is notable both for its assumption of the Neoplatonic-Avicennan cosmology and metaphysics typical of Davānī's age, and for the characteristic equivalency that he posits between philosophical concepts and poetic images. A notable expression of this way of reading symbols in Persian literature from a Sufi perspective was the *Gulshan-i rāz* of Maḥmūd Shabistarī (d. after 740/1340), a work doubtless known to Ḥāfiẓ as well as Davānī.[11] Moreover, the concept of an esoteric methodology is deeply rooted in Davānī's approach to symbolism both as an obstacle for the unworthy and a key for the initiate.

Skipping over the remainder of the section on the unitarians (which is the longest section in his treatise), we can contrast Davānī's treatment of the way that the Sufis understand the symbolism of "last night."

> Know that the chivalrous Sufi youths have an eternity from annihilation in God, and a progression from the ascensions of sanctity. From the contents of this verse, they understand a different secret, by reason of

---

[10] *Naqd*, pp. 45–47.

[11] Hâfez de Chiraz, *Le Divân*, trans. Charles-Henri de Fouchécour (Paris : Verdier, 2006), pp. 19–20, 113–4, 160.

> the fact that they are the world-revealing cup.... First, one should know what "last night" is in their parlance, and why the tress and mole are its likeness, since they are an expression for the grain and the trap. Yes, realizing that requires an introduction.[12]

Here too, Davānī provides a cosmology, but this time it is much more psychological and dramatic, as Sufi dervishes enact the cosmic unfoldment from divine latency to phenomenal reality in their response to the call of divine love. Sufi authorities such as 'Ayn al-Quḍāt, Hallaj, Ibn Khafīf, and Rūzbihān are invoked and quoted. On the symbolism of "last night," Davānī explains,

> altogether, the group of Sufis expresses the period of this travel from the realm of nonexistence [to] essential and compulsory possibility, with the help of spiritual love and the overpowering of spiritual longing, as "last night." In that situation, sobriety was produced from intoxication and attainment [from] the root of existence.[13]

Summarizing the sense of the first half of the verse, he writes,

> In the period of the travel of existing things, I turned around the folds and orbits, and I saw the degrees of each attainment. In their midst, however much the angels were praising the sea of divine isolation, and had no impurity within the veil of chastity, they still did not have the adornment of being wounded by love.[14]

In conclusion, he observes, "this was a sample of commentary on the verse by the experience of the Sufis, who annihilate multiplicity in unity, and at the time of intoxication speak in the manner of the people of sobriety."[15] So while there is some parallel between the views of the unitarians and the Sufis on this verse, insofar as both groups see it as symbolizing the cosmogonic process of God's creation of the world, they nevertheless express it in very different terms.

Davānī begins the section on the sages by commenting sarcastically that, while the philosophical sage is close to the Sufi,

---

[12] *Naqd*, p. 64.
[13] *Naqd*, p. 67.
[14] *Naqd*, p. 68.
[15] *Naqd*, p. 71.

his sight has been darkened by the overturning of intellect mixed with imagination. Intellect and logic, as Rūmī points out, are poor supports. Davānī continues,

> Altogether, "last night" in the technical language of the philosophical sages is the time of the release of the rational soul from the control of the body by contemplation of its superior origins, for the intellect, because of being veiled with the coverings of the body, has no portion either of the wine or of the cask, and it is excluded by the proximity of nature from witnessing the sources of emanation.[16]

Davānī then goes into an explanation of the union of the rational soul with the Active Intellect according to the theories of the Illuminationist and Peripatetic schools of philosophy. He explains that Ḥāfiẓ wishes to portray the ascending soul as saying something like the following:

> With the eye of realization I gazed upon the forms of existence from above and below, I saw the separate intellects, which transcend acceptance and rejection, who by contemplating their own perfection in the fields of possibility were knocking on the door of the tavern of universal creation and their own luminous perfection. This is an expression for the comprehensive Adamic presence.[17]

While the tone of this explanation has a mocking character, it is quite technical and thoroughly immersed in one of the chief academic discourses of premodern Islamic thought.

Finally, it may come as no surprise that some of Davānī's companions had requested that he provide a briefer commentary on this verse; evidently some of them had simply gotten lost in the intricate gyrations of the preceding three sections. Here is how he responded:

> Know that the gist of the verse is that when burning love—may it be ever fortunate and victorious—with the aid of the momentary inspiration (*waqt*) went forth in the form of its own display and became the mirror of the pure condition of every beauty in the clear moment during that journey of a victorious king, it brought the degrees of its

---

[16] *Naqd*, p. 72.
[17] *Naqd*, p. 74.

own perfection into view in the forms that are present. It witnessed its own essential and potential spiritual faculties, which went in search of the tavern and the wine-selling master with shouts and cries. If they were joined in presence with some of the active degrees which they call "immutable entities" (*a'yān-i thābita*) and were free from a general measure of spiritual suffering, yet since their power of longing was still in action, they searched for the most perfect of the lights of manifestation and the limit of adornment. Then with complete effort they knocked on the door the tavern of love, for they had the remainder of creation on their heads. If they had a crown of stability on the head of ambition and sought that universal existence, these degrees have a limit: it is the master of the merciful breath (*nafas-i raḥmānī*), Isrāfīl[18] and his trumpet. Necessarily from his mixed clay, which the dervishes say is the elemental human power and the upright body, they expressed it as a cup, and they trained him to the limits of all ways. Thus here they call the "immutable entities" persons. There, the first love sees itself as the last, and it finds its own beauty to be exceedingly glorious in the completeness of its perfection. This is on the principle that for anything to see itself in itself is like seeing itself in a mirror, but the latter form of seeing is superior and more perfect; therefore the first seeing [gazing at oneself] is [only] a likeness, and the second seeing [in a mirror] is [true] reflections of beauty.[19]

Whether Davānī's associates found any additional clarity in this concluding passage, with its dense language drawing upon the vocabulary of Ibn `Arabi, can best be imagined.

The second treatise on Ḥāfiẓ by Davānī has a much more literary bent than the first, focusing as it does upon an entire poem, the *ghazal* beginning *dar hama dayr-i mughān nīst chū man shaydā'ī*: "In all this temple of the Magi no one is as wild as me." The ostensibly literary character of this commentary is further enhanced by the quotation of numerous other verses by Ḥāfiẓ,

---

[18] In the Islamic tradition, Isrāfīl figures as an angel of death, and in particular, the angel who blows the trumpet on the Day of Resurrection.

[19] *Naqd*, p. 76. The last sentence paraphrases the famous opening lines of the first chapter of Ibn `Arabi's *Fuṣūṣ al-ḥikam*: "The Reality wanted to see the essence of His Most Beautiful Names or, to put it in another way, to see His own Essence, in an all-inclusive object encompassing the whole [divine] Command, which, qualified by existence, would reveal to Him His own mystery. For the seeing of a thing, itself by itself, is not the same as it seeing itself in another, as it were in a mirror; for it appears to itself in a form that is invested by the location of the vision by that which would only appear to it given the existence of the location and its [the location's] self-disclosure to it" (Ibn al-'Arabī, *The Bezels of Wisdom*, trans. R. W. J. Austin [Mahwah, NJ: Paulist Press, 1980], p. 50).

cited to substantiate a consistent point of view ascribed to the author. Nevertheless, Davānī maintains here a consistent hermeneutic that assumes a deep structure of concealing and revealing the divine mysteries as the operative principle behind all serious literature. Once again, he confers oracular titles upon Ḥāfiẓ, calling him this time "the tongue of the moment and the interpreter of time" (*lisān al-waqt, tarjumān al-zamān*). As before, Davānī is responding to the importunities of his friends who sought a solution to the mysteries of Ḥāfiẓ, and he apologizes for the delay in hopes that his work will be appreciated by connoisseurs. He begins the treatise with an introduction[20] in which he lays out his strategy of interpretation, drawing explicitly on images and figures associated with martyrdom for having revealed the secret, such as Hallaj and 'Ayn al-Quḍāt Hamadānī.

> The jealousy of love's power demands that the subtle secrets of its effects should be hidden in the privacy of inner sanctums and the retreats of the hidden essence. The loveliness of that holy beauty should not have its veil polluted by the gaze of impure worldlings, who are by no means cleansed of the abandonment of poverty and the impurities of connections to existing things.
>
> (Arabic verse): We, the men of the tribe, say the charms of Layla should be seen when the stars arise, / for how should Layla be seen with an eye that sees others and is not cleansed with tears?
>
> (Persian verse): I performed ablutions with tears, as the men of the path say; / first be pure yourself, and then cast your eyes on the pure one. [Ḥāfiẓ] [21]
>
> It is for this reason that the illustrious divine way (*sunnat*) has been ordered in this fashion, the fundamentals of the explanation of which are based upon the categorical principles of the sign that "you shall not find any change in the way (*sunnah*) of God" (Qur'an 33:62). This is because some of the people of realities are hidden from the eyes of ignorant formalists by the clothing of conventional forms, and they lose themselves in the midst of the generality of people by sharing their remaining customs. This is the path of the people of soundness.

---

[20] *Naqd*, pp. 172–75.

[21] This verse can be found in *Dīwān-i Ḥāfiẓ*, ed. Parvīz Nātil Khānlarī (Tehran: Khwārazmī 1362 A.Hsh./1983), ghazal 258, v. 7.

(Persian verse): I am a rogue, and the people call me a Sufi; / see this nice name that I have discovered!

And some, having fled from the affairs of the ignorant mob to the cave of the abiding darkness of nonexistence, have wagered the cash of the two worlds in the dice house of isolation and asceticism with a single throw, and have cast themselves beyond the sight of men, on account of being uprooted from the forms of customary conventions. This is the style of the audacious ones of the corner of blame.

(Persian verse): My heart's upset with the monastery and the stained cloak. /Where is the temple of the Magi, and where's the pure wine? [Ḥāfiẓ][22]

Even though in the path there may be a group between these two positions, the aim of both factions is the concealment of realities, for in the law of love, for the intoxicated lover revealing secrets is a crime. Even though gradually the wine-bearer of ecstasy gives them another swallow of the wine of realities in the goblet of time, and every moment from the arrival of the cups of satisfaction with the manifestations of majesty and glory they have another increase, continually the voice of divine power gives the cry that:

(Persian verse): It is the Sultan's feast, so don't get drunk; / have a cup of wine, and then shut up!

And if occasionally the hopeless lover gives off some smoke from the overwhelming flames of the fires of love, and like an incense-burner releases sighs from within, he keeps them concealed and imprisoned at the bottom of his skirt of infamy, for [as the hadith states] "My friends are underneath my domes; no one knows them except me." And if from the overwhelming force of intoxication he utters a word of the secrets of love, they take him to the gallows of blame.

(Arabic verse): By the secret, if they are effaced, their blood is shed; / thus it is that the blood of lovers may be shed. ['Ayn al-Quḍāt]

(Persian verse): For the helpless one who spills the secret of love, / tell him to scratch his face with the fingers of blame.

That friend by whom the gallows was ennobled – / his crime was this: he made the secrets public. [Ḥāfiẓ] [23]

It is for this reason that if any of the children of the path of longing has an appropriately delicate relationship with this group from his original

[22] *Dīwān-i Ḥāfiẓ*, ed. Khānlarī, ghazal 2, v. 3.
[23] *Dīwān-i Ḥāfiẓ*, ed. Khānlarī, ghazal 136, v. 6.

nature, he may be worthy of the inheritance of those great ones by reason of that spiritual proximity, by reason of "We joined to them their seed" (Qur'an 52:21). Or they may fall under the suspicion of belonging to the group of the mob who are "like beasts" (Qur'an 7:179). This is because the lustful ones of delicate temperament, whose intended prayer direction is the acceptance of the masses, are rebuffed by those ferocious attacks from concentrating on the sacred target of love.

(Persian verse): Sufi, pass us by in safety, for this red wine / steals heart and religion from you in a manner that—don't ask![24] [Ḥāfiẓ]

My friends, haul back your reins from the tavern road; / because Ḥāfiẓ traveled by this path, and now he's poor.[25]

And despite the fact that deceptive and fickle love demands the concealing of secrets from the perspective of God's essential power, from the perspective of the perfection of the beloved it demands manifestation and revealing. Every moment in a visual and visionary location she is displayed in a different way to the heart and eye of the astonished lover. With glances mixed with elegance and looks most exciting, she places the words describing her own beauty on the tongue of that silent one, and then with the tongue of the assault of divine wrath, she begins to reproach and interrogate that unfortunate wretch. It is here that the cry arises from the lovers' disposition:

(Persian verse): She showed her face, and herself described her face; / since things are so, why does it hurt my heart?

Throughout this introduction, Davānī assumes that these two perspectives—the concealment of the secret of love, and its revelation—frame the character of poetry around the interaction of the lover and the beloved. He adduces additional proof from the hadith of the Prophet, particularly the well-known saying "I was a hidden treasure, and I longed to be known," which makes the manifestation of the universe the result of the divine self-disclosure.

Davānī then inserts another digression which he calls a reminder (*tadhkira*), devoted to the concept of love as that which joins together extremes and unites opposites. Love achieves these goals both by concealing secrets and by giving indications

---

[24] *Dīwān-i Ḥāfiẓ*, ed. Khānlarī, ghazal 266, v. 4 (reading *zāhid* instead of *ṣūfī*).

[25] *Dīwān-i Ḥāfiẓ*, ed. Khānlarī, ghazal 163, v. 8.

that remove veils. He explains these ambiguities as usual with illustrative verses:

> (Persian verse): His eyebrow says no, but his eyes say yes!
>
> (Persian verse): That longing is worth a hundred souls when the lover / says "I don't want to," but wants to with a hundred souls.

Davānī goes on, in a passage dense with allusions to Sufi doctrines, to describe how this cosmic role of love encompasses the unfolding emanation of the different levels of existence, and their perfection which is attained through the Seal of the Prophets, that is, Muḥammad. This passage links the cosmic role of the Prophet Muḥammad with his experience of heavenly ascension described in the Qur'an (53:9) as approaching "two bows' lengths or nearer" to the divine presence. Davānī qualifies the two arcs (*qaws*) of the "bows' lengths" as comprising the prophetic role in cosmic manifestation (*ẓuhūr*) and the saintly degree of consciousness (*shu'ūr*). This permits him to connect the notion of gradual manifestation and unveiling with "the Seal of the Saints", the esoteric figure whose advent had been proclaimed by al-Ḥakīm al-Tirmidhī and whose role was claimed by Ibn `Arabi. Davānī is fully aware of the messianic implications of this linkage, citing in support the well-known prophetic hadith on the coming of one who shall "fill the earth with justice and equity as it is now filled with oppression and injustice." The approach of the apocalypse means that overflowing revelation is available everywhere, including in poetry.

> Since the time of the manifestation of that holy one draws near, the annunciation of those lights increase daily in display and manifestation, and the proofs of the truth of this claim are established on the page of time's conditions, if anyone with an insightful glance looks closely. For the grace of flowing geniuses and the close capacity of most of the children of the time is advanced in relation to their fathers, and their ambitions likewise by the same relation, again by the benefits of the approaching time of the revered inheritor and master of time [i.e., the expected messiah], as the saying goes (Arabic verse): "the Earth has a portion of the cup of generosity." The secrets of gnosis are pronounced on every tongue, and the shout is raised of the original aim of reality, in accordance with the voices of differing capabilities.

> The secret of God, which the gnostic traveler tells to no one –/ I am amazed where the wine sellers heard it from.[26] [Ḥāfiẓ]

> And since the perfection of consciousness [*ish'ār*, a pun on *ash'ār*, "verses"] is from the special characteristics of the creation of the Seal [of the Saints], those who resort to the deserts of annihilation in explanation of the realities of joy, having taken the path of poetic similitudes, express sublime intentions with the customary images of rogues with shameless cheeks.[27]

To demonstrate his point that poetry is the expression of mystical truths, Davānī then quotes in support two verses from the famous wine ode (*al-Khamriyya*) of the master of Arabic mystical poetry, Ibn al-Fāriḍ (d. 1235). As with his other quotations, Davānī does not bother to provide the author's name, assuming that the reader will be familiar with it.

At this point Davānī shifts into a quick allegorical exposition of the frequently appearing images of non-Muslim religious groups ("infidels") that appear so often in Persian poetry.[28]

> The wayfarer at the beginning of the path, who is concerned with the perfection of the soul, has both himself and God in view. From this perspective, whoever wants to bring himself to God in this way has a relationship with the Magi (*majūs*), who believe in light and darkness. Both himself and the light of God are his contemplation, and by the very same expression, they call the seeker a Zoroastrian (*gabr*), as is the case in the poetry of Mawlana Jalāl al-Dīn Rūmī. Like this expression, sometimes they call him a Christian, since he affirms the reality of himself, God, and his own seeking and concentration, just as the Christians believe in the Trinity. And they call the station of love the tavern, considering that in this degree the constraint of dividing into self and the other is removed from the character of the gnostic....[29]

---

[26] *Dīwān-i Ḥāfiẓ*, ed. Khānlarī, ghazal 238, v. 8.

[27] *Naqd*, p. 178.

[28] On which, see Alessandro Bausani, *Storia della letteratura persiana* (Milano: Nuova Accademia, 1960), pp. 247, 263–69; Leonard Lewisohn, "Sufi Symbolism and the Persian Hermeneutic Tradition: Reconstructing the Pagoda of Attar's Esoteric Poetics," in *'Aṭṭār and the Persian Sufi Tradition: The Art of Spiritual Flight*, eds. Leonard Lewisohn and Christopher Shackle (London: I. B. Tauris & the Institute for Ismaili Studies 2007), pp. 255–308.

[29] *Naqd*, p. 179.

Having established this principle of poetic symbolism, Davānī goes on to comment on the image of the cup that represents the heart, adding several other Persian verses by Ḥāfiẓ in support, and referring explicitly to the poetry of Fakhr al-Dīn 'Irāqī as an example of the same symbolic principle. This remark concludes the "reminder" passage, after which the commentary proper can begin.

It is apparent that this second treatise by Davānī is based on a more thoroughgoing hermeneutical framework than the first treatise, in which he had simply outlined the possibilities of three complementary perspectives on a particular verse by Ḥāfiẓ. To be sure, the first treatise is also firm in insisting on the principle of metonymy, in which a term used in a poem is considered to be a symbol for an underlying spiritual reality. The metaphysical assumptions underlying the second text are more technical and indeed esoteric, relying upon long traditions of philosophical and mystical reflection and inter-textual reference. It is noteworthy that Davānī here asserts that poetry must be read, not only in terms of the dialectic of secrecy and disclosure, but also in relation to mystical teachings about the consciousness of the Prophet Muḥammad, the esoteric figure of the Seal of the Saints, and the universal impact of the coming advent of the expected messiah. This is of course the very same hermeneutic that Davānī would bring to bear on any other text, including the Qur'an.

Enough has been said so far to make it clear how Davānī approaches the poetry of Ḥāfiẓ, and for reasons of space I will not attempt to go through his exposition of the details of the lyric that is explored in the second treatise, fascinating though these interpretations are. Nor will I linger on the third treatise in the anthology of Davānī's writings on Ḥāfiẓ, which is extremely short and basically uses a single verse as a springboard for arguing the doctrine of predestination.[30] Instead, I would like to turn briefly to an issue of historical or narrative interpretation that is also offered by Davānī, who clearly assumes that the verses of Ḥāfiẓ were written "in the form of describing his own state (*bi-ṣūrat-i vaṣf al-ḥāl-i khwud*)."

---

[30] *Naqd*, pp. 266–74.

While commenting on a variation of the saying attributed to Jesus, that one should not present wisdom before the unworthy, Davānī recalls the story that he heard from a dervish who maintained that Ḥāfiẓ was a disciple of a Sufi master. The name of the master is given as Shaykh Maḥmūd 'Aṭṭār, who is described as an outstanding Sufi of his time. The same source maintained that, during a visit to the shrine of Shaykh Ibn Khafīf in Shiraz, he encountered a master there who was deeply immersed in the teachings of Shaykh Rūzbihān Baqlī. When the narrator described Shaykh Maḥmūd 'Aṭṭār, his interlocutor replied that that was his own master. Davānī concludes that this is the justification for commentators to explain the poetry of Ḥāfiẓ in terms of his spiritual states. Most modern scholars have focused on this account as a piece of historical evidence to be considered in deciding upon the facticity of Ḥāfiẓ's connection to Sufism, or else its refutation.[31] Frequent attempts have been made to link the poetry of Ḥāfiẓ with the Sufi teachings of Rūzbihān.[32]

Yet it is interesting to see the accompanying hermeneutical argument that Davānī adds alongside this ostensibly historical account:

> Secondly, there is that which most of the literati say about some of the states of the author [Ḥāfiẓ], which are on the lips of the people. "And God has insight into the conditions of his servants." They have understood his words in the same external meanings that no intellectual would consider it legitimate to restrict to those suppositions. They have placed the finger of astonishment on the teeth of thought from the interpretation of [his verses] by the likes of these spiritual realities. They are completely ignorant of the contents of "Don't look at who speaks, look at what is spoken," and the meaning of "Know the man by the truth, not the truth by the man."[33] And if it is assumed that the intelligent person has in no way even a glimmering of truth in relation to this meaning, the derivation of these meanings from him is the ultimate manifestation and distinction, and the source of insight. The

[31] Akbar Sobūt, "Pīr-i Gol-rang," *Encyclopedia of the World of Islam*, 5:381, accessed online at <http://www.encyclopaediaislamica.com/>, 24 March 2007.

[32] For an attempt to link Hafiz to Ruzbihan, see the useful article by 'Alī Sharīat Kāshānī, "La prééternité et la pérennité de l'amour et de la beauté en literature mystique persane de Rūzbehān à Ḥāfeẓ," *Luqmān* 17/2 (2001), pp. 25–54.

[33] Two sayings commonly attributed to 'Alī ibn Abī Ṭālib.

> possessor of a spiritual state has spiritual states as a result of that. If someone charges himself, he knows without a hint of doubt or imagination that from [the vendor's cry of] "Country thyme!" (*sa'tar barrī*) he hears, "Open up and see my piety" (*as'a tara birrī*).[34] For that reason, he is overwhelmed with ecstasy, by the latter path, for which parallel meanings may be discovered for the likes of these sayings.[35]

While the argument is a trifle convoluted, I take this to mean that, first of all, ordinary people have understood the verses of Ḥāfiẓ in the most external and literal sense. Yet if someone knows nothing of the spiritual meanings of such expressions, and yet nevertheless discovers them through accidental similarity, this is in reality a genuine source of insight and indeed ecstasy. There are numerous examples of such "accidental" discoveries in Sufi lore. Yet the implication is that the legitimacy of the mystical interpretation of Ḥāfiẓ does not in fact rest upon the argument from authority, which asserts the historical connection of Ḥāfiẓ with the Sufi tradition through actual initiation. It rather rests upon the adventitious and even serendipitous discovery of inner meanings, which by their very nature point to the insight of the listener rather than being dependent upon the intention of the writer.

I have suggested elsewhere that Sufi poetry is not defined by the author so much as by the audience.[36] For a reader such as Davānī, the poetry of Ḥāfiẓ exists on a continuum that ranges from Sufis like Hallaj and 'Ayn al-Quḍāt to the philosopher Ibn

---

[34] For this celebrated example of the Sufi doctrine of listening (*samā'*), which befell Abū Ḥulmān in Baghdad, see Abū Naṣr al-Sarrāj al-Ṭūsī, *Kitāb al-luma' fi'l-taṣawwuf*, ed. R. A. Nicholson, E. J. W. Gibb Memorial series, 22 (London: Luzac & Company Ltd., 1914; reprint edition, 1963), p. 289, line 9; Abū Ḥāmid al-Ghazālī, *Iḥyā' 'ulūm al-dīn* (4 vols., Cairo: Dār al-Shu'ab, n.d.), Book 18.3, p. 1145 (in this edition, the second expression erroneously repeats the first); Duncan Black MacDonald, "Emotional Religion in Islam as affected by Music and Singing, being a translation of the *Ihya 'Ulum ad-Din* of al-Ghazzali with Analysis, Annotation, and Appendices," *Journal of the Royal Asiatic Society of Great Britain and Ireland* (1901), pp. 195–252, citing p. 238. Ghazālī states the underlying principle as follows: "meanings that predominate in the heart precede in the understanding, despite the words." Further on this theme see Leonard Lewisohn, "The Sacred Music of Islam: *Samā'* in the Persian Sufi Tradition," *British Journal of Ethnomusicology* 6 (1997), pp. 1–33, esp. pp. 18–19.

[35] *Naqd*, p. 193.

[36] Carl W. Ernst, *Guide to Sufism* (Boston: Shambhala Publications 1997), chapter 6.

Sīnā[37] and the profane Abbasid court poet Abu Nuwās.[38] For him, it was just as natural and inevitable to employ a Sufi hermeneutic for the poetry of Ḥāfiẓ as it was for Sa'īd al-Dīn Farghānī (d. 1301), Ṣadr al-Dīn Qunawī (d. 1351), or 'Abd al-Ghanī al-Nābulusī to write detailed mystical commentaries on the Arabic poems of Ibn al-Farid.[39] Davānī is clearly an advocate of the systematic interpretation of poetry by a metaphysical system of correspondences based on writers such as Ibn `Arabi and Suhrawardī, and for this he has been criticized for not respecting the clear sense of the text of Ḥāfiẓ.[40] Whether or not Ḥāfiẓ would have appreciated or approved the philosophical and mystical interpretations which have been brought to his verses, the testimony of Davānī makes it abundantly clear that such interpretations have been present among the readers of Ḥāfiẓ from a very early date.

---

[37] *Naqd*, pp. 216–17.

[38] *Naqd*, p. 81.

[39] Dāwūd ibn Maḥmūd Qayṣarī, *Sharḥ Ṭā'iyyat Ibn al-Fāriḍ al-kubrá*, ed. Aḥmad ibn Fāriḍ ibn Aḥmad Mazīdī (Beirut: Dār al-Kutub al-'Ilmiyyah, 2004); *Ṭā'iyyah-i 'Abd al-Raḥmān Jāmī: tarjumah-i Ṭā'iyyah-i Ibn Fāriḍ, bi-inḍimām-i sharḥ-i Maḥmūd Qayṣārī bar Ṭā'iyyah-i Ibn Fāriḍ* (Tehran: Nuqtah, 1997); Sa'īd al-Dīn ibn Aḥmad Farghānī, *Mashāriq al-ḍararī: sharḥ-i Ṭā'iyyah-i Ibn Fāriḍ*, ed. Jalāl al-Dīn Āshtiyānī ([Mashhad: s.n.], 1978); Emile Dermenghem, trans., *L'éloge du vin (Al khamriya): poème mystique de 'Omar ibn al Faridh, et son commentaire par 'Abd al Ghani an Nabolosi* (Paris, Les Éditions Véga, 1980). Davānī quotes Ibn al-Fāriḍ in *Naqd*, p. 71 (see note, p. 93), p. 178 (see note, p. 216).

[40] Fouchécour, *Le Divân*, p. 20.

22

"A Little Indicates Much": Structure and Meaning in the Prefaces to Rumi's *Masnavī*, Books 1–3

For over seven centuries, readers of Jalal al-Din Muhammad Rumi's *Masnavi* have been struck by his marvelous preface, written in Arabic, where he begins with the remarkable claim, that "This is the book of the *Masnavi*, which is the roots of the roots of the roots of religion." The language he uses actually claims the position of the principles of jurisprudence (*usul al-din*), except in an exaggerated form. He goes on to make other remarkable pronouncements about the character of this extraordinary poem, which he frequently and without reservation compares to the Qur'an itself.

Rumi has in fact written prose prefaces to each of the six books of the *Masnavi*. It is striking that most commentators have not really attempted to relate these introductions to the text that follows. The tendency of most commentators has been to consider these prefaces as extraneous to the poetry, which has typically been discussed on a line-by-line basis. The justification for this exclusion of the prefaces from consideration would seem to be that several of them (Books 1, 3, and 4) are in Arabic, and all six are prose; thus they could be technically separated from the Persian poems that follow. Yet it is striking to consider the extent to which these prefaces also relate to the introductory sections of each of the six books of this epic of mysticism, each of which contains an opening dialogue between Rumi and his chief disciple in later times, Husam al-Din Chalabi. In this presentation, I would like to propose that Rumi uses these prefaces to set up his primary goal as a teacher of Sufism. That is, he wants to clarify the way in which language functions as a way to bring about the understanding of a reality that is much larger than any concept. At the same time, he uses the dialog form to highlight the shortcomings of language, together with the longing of spiritual aspirants who seek a way to overcome those limitations. Each of these six prefaces plays variations on this theme of the adequacy of language and the transcendence of the divine reality. The point I wish to make here that is that Rumi is a very deliberate author whose introductory gestures are extremely important for understanding the purpose of his symbolic declarations.

In the preface to Book 1, the first theme that Rumi introduces is the extraordinary significance of the *Masnavi* itself. It reveals the secrets of union and certainty, and it is "the greatest understanding (*fiqh*) of God, and the most luminous law (*shar`*) of God", again invoking the language of the religious law. Rumi compares the *Masnavi* to the divine light described in the famous Light Verse of the Qur'an (24:35) and to the gardens and fountains of paradise. His variations on Qur'anic verses are characteristically infused with a Sufi vocabulary. Thus he invokes Qur. 25:24, "The companions of paradise are the best that day in their abode and the finest in repose," with these similar words: "Among the companions of stations (*maqamat*) and wonders (*karamat*), it is the best in its station and the finest in repose." He then compares it to the river Nile, which nourishes the patient ones but is a sorrow for Pharaoh and the infidels. Rumi then explicitly compares the *Masnavi* to the Qur'an, citing Qur. 2:26, "He misleads many by it, and guides many by it." Note that in its context that verse described the similitudes that God uses, which the unbelievers question. Then follow several other allusions to the *Masnavi* as the "revealer of the Qur'an" and as the book which only the pure may touch (see Qur. 56:79), a "revelation" (*tanzil*) from God. The *Masnavi* is watched over by God. Rumi maintains that it has other names given it by God, but "we have reduced it to this little amount, for a little indicates much, the mouthful indicates the lake, and the handful indicates the great storehouse." This is how Rumi introduces the *Masnavi*.

Next, Rumi proceeds to introduce himself by name, stating that he labored on this poem to produce rarities and expressions for ascetics and devotees, "brief in constructions but great in meanings." Again, the emphasis is on the brevity of the text and its enormous significance. But quickly he shifts to introduce the person who demanded the writing of the *Masnavi*, Husam al-Din Chalabi. In a hyperbole that approaches parody, he is described in the most eloquent of terms as the pinnacle of spirituality, the Abu Yazid and Junayd of his day, and a man of noble lineage. Most importantly, he is like a star that shines and becomes a refuge for the divine and spiritual ones possessing insight, who are undoubtedly the elite mystics. That universe of Sufis may be presumed to be the audience for the *Masnavi*.

The claims made in the preface for the religious authority of the *Masnavi* are thus matched by describing its efficacy with the briefest of hints, combined with a dedication of the text to the ideal listener, an advanced Sufi. The opening verses of the Persian text provide an elaboration of these basic principles announced in the preface, constructed around a dialogue with Husam al-Din. In all the subsequent books (2–6), the dialog is a clearly demarcated section that opens the book prior to the first story. In Book 1, perhaps because of the intensity of the beginning effort, the dialog not only comprises the opening, the song of the reed or *nay-namah* (1.1–18), but also recurs as an interruption of the first story. The beginning of the *Masnavi* is in some respects a break with the style of the Persian Sufi *masnavi*, as Dick Davis has pointed out.[1] While the epics of Sana'i and `Attar begin with powerful doctrinal statements about the omnipotence and creativity of God, Rumi begins instead with his own

[1] Dick Davis, "Narrative and doctrine in the first story of Rumi's *Mathnawi*," in *Studies in Islamic and Middle Eastern Texts and Traditions in Memory of Norman Calder*, ed. G. R. Hawting, J. A. Mojaddedi and A. Samely (Oxford: Oxford University Press, 2000), pp. 93–104, citing p. 96.

human voice, which merges with the persona of the humble reed that begins speaking in 1.2.[2] Throughout this brief and famously eloquent passage, Rumi seeks an audience capable of understanding a message that cannot possibly fit into words, stressing the need for a light (1.7) to illumine the listener. He inescapably turns to his memory of Shams-i Tabriz, who was the perfect listener, whom he calls "you the incomparably pure" (1.16). After the conclusion of the reed section, dialog with Husam al-Din begins, as Rumi urges him to throw of worldly bonds. He coins a classic phrase for the inability of language to render spiritual reality, when he warns against putting an ocean into a flask (1.20). At this point he invokes love as the only remedy for this situation, but the problem of receiving revelation remains as difficult as ever. It is just like the overpowering experience that Moses received when God manifested Himself to the mountain, which was destroyed, as Moses fell into a faint. Rumi closely models these lines (1.25–26) on this Qur'anic story (Qur. 7:143). His conclusion is that there is no communication without a true companion (1.28).

Then follows the first story of the *Masnavi*, a tale of a mysterious sickness caused by love. We should not linger here, except that there is an extraordinary interpolation in the story (1.109–144) on the nature of love, which takes the form once again of a dialog. Rumi starts this digression by complaining once again that he cannot explain love (1.112), observing that when he starts to write down its explanation, his pen breaks (1.114). Suddenly he has started to rhapsodize about the sun, which is the proof that indicates itself. Though he begins by using the Persian word for sun (*aftab*), he imperceptibly shifts to the Arabic term (*shams*), a move that had to be seen as a profound signal in Rumi's circle;[3] indeed, so powerful is the sun that, when it comes, the moon splits (a reference to the apocalyptic sign in Qur. 54:1). And Rumi specifies that this is the unique and eternal sun within. But a few verses later (1.123), he cannot hold back from naming Shams al-Din, whose secret must be explained (*sharh*, compare

[2] Muhammad Isti`lami agrees that the reed is Rumi's voice; see his edition of the *Masnavi* (Tehran: Intisharat-i Zavvar, 1371/1992), 1:124.

[3] Isti`lami, 1:206, on *Masnavi* 1.123.

1.3). Now there is an interruption; Husam al-Din, named only as "my soul" (*jan*, 1.125) plucks Rumi's skirt and begs to hear the story of Shams. The mood changes drastically; Rumi switches into Arabic, saying, "Don't bother me! I am in annihilation! My understandings fail, and 'I cannot count Your praise!'" (1.128). The formality and grandeur of this response are astonishing. Although Rumi has been hinting strongly that Shams is the missing figure needed for a real conversation, once Husam asks directly about him, Rumi is plunged into a mood of desperation and longing. Words are inadequate to express this longing, so Rumi recites the famous hadith of the Prophet, when he said to God, "I cannot count Your praise; You are as You have praised Yourself." The fact that Shams al-Din and not God is the subject of Rumi's adoration is typical of his state. The shift into Arabic is also an example of what Paul Nwyia referred to as the "Qur'anization of the heart", in which the register of scriptural language is resorted to for the most intense experiences. Rumi is first evasive, saying he can't speak now, but perhaps later. Then Husam al-Din responds on the same level of intensity, saying (in Arabic) that he is hungry and needs feeding (1.132). Rumi fends him off with teasing, telling him to be a true Sufi and not worry about time. But finally Rumi states the real point of this opening to the mystical epic: the beloved's secrets cannot be told directly, so the solution is to tell them in the form of stories about other people.

One more objection follows. In a quite outrageous fashion, the unsatisfied Husam al-Din says that he wants the story naked, since "I don't sleep with my lover in a shirt" (1.138). Recalling explicitly the image of Moses and the mountain, Rumi warns that speaking so nakedly would mean self-destruction; this sun will consume the world if it is unveiled, so nothing more will be said of Shams al-Din—instead, talk will turn to other stories, endlessly (1.143). Throughout these opening lines of verse, Rumi returns adroitly to the main themes he announced in the prose preface: the revelatory power of the *Masnavi*, the inadequacy of words, and the need for the perfect listener (which raised and then removed Shams from discussion). The interrupted dialog with Husam al-Din is interwoven with the first story of the *Masnavi*, to demonstrate that only through the cloak of such narratives can the revelation shine through.

The later books of the *Masnavi* employed a similar pattern, announcing important themes in the prose preface, and then developing them further in the poetic dialogue with Husam al-Din. For reasons of space, I will confine the following remarks to Books 2 and 3. Book 2 begins with a preface in Persian, in contrast to the Arabic preface to Book 1, commenting on the delay in the production of this volume. This delay was evidently caused by the fact that Husam al-Din's wife had died, plunging him into a profound sorrow for nearly two years. Rumi does not address this circumstance in the preface directly, but speaks instead about the impossibility of revealing the totality of the divine wisdom to an individual human; knowledge of the benefits of that wisdom would overwhelm the individual, leading to paralysis and inaction. It is for this reason that God uses the perfume of that infinite wisdom to guide humans, like the nose-ring guides the camel. The principle that Rumi seeks to apply is the proper proportion of divine wisdom that may be revealed, much like the proper proportion of water that is mixed with earth to make bricks. This principle of balance and proportion applies to everything except one who has transcended the world of creation. Rumi then pauses to entertain a question: what is love? He answers that love is limitless when it concerns God's love, although paradoxically there is no real proportion or reciprocity between human and divine love. The tension between the principle of balance and the incommensurability of the divine and the human creates a space in which Rumi can address the nature of the symbolic language used in the *Masnavi*.

The poetry of Book 2 opens with a reference to the two years' delay in its composition, treating it as a period of gestation, necessary "so that blood becomes milk" (2.1). Rumi then launches his narrative in a fluid dialogical form, almost one third of which in this opening section (2.1–110) is directly in conversation with Husam al-Din. This all concerns the spiritual rebirth (2.2) that produces the milk of Rumi's teaching.

In the first section (2.3–9), Rumi describes Husam al-Din, the Radiance of Truth (*ziya' al-haqq*), as making a spiritual ascension (his seclusion after his wife's death), but his return has released the poetry of the *Masnavi*. So significant is this moment that Rumi tells us the date (662). The return of the falcon opens the gate of spiritual knowledge. Then follows (2.10–18) a discourse on the obstacles to that door, in the form of desire and lust—these are infernal in character, in fact the reverse of the spiritual process of rebirth, so that through their action "your milk becomes blood" (2.13). The condition of desire is synonymous with the fall of Adam, who lost much to satisfy his lust.

To avoid the catastrophic failure of Adam, Rumi stresses the need to find good counsel (2.19–27). He reiterates the point (2.20, 26) that intellects guard each other against evil speech and action while illuminating the path; equally, carnal souls (2.2 1, 27) together produce idleness and darken the way. This is not merely general advice, but a connection to sainthood; the key symbol of the sun appears alongside the friend (*yar*), who is the friend of God (2.22–25).

What should be the relationship with that friend? Rumi explores this (2.28–34) with direct address, presumably to Husam al-Din. That friend, he informs him, is not outside, but is your very own eye, and it must be kept pure. Rumi here invokes the image of the mirror, quoting the Prophetic dictum that "the believer is the mirror of the believer", an image that will return as a powerful depiction of this pivotal mystical relationship. While being with a friend is like spring, bad companionship is like the fading autumn, and is best avoided entirely (2:35–41). When a tyrant like the Emperor Decian is present, one should emulate the Seven Sleepers (*ashab al-kahf*) and retreat from the world; nightingales cannot thrive without the sun.

As in Book 1, the mere mention of the sun is enough to trigger a chain of associations and reveries that implicitly invoke Shams-i Tabriz. This sun (2.42–47) is also connected to Husam al-Din, who is, at a somewhat lower level, the radiance of the sun. Rumi here seems to shift between addressing Shams and the transcendental sun of which Shams is an image, yet he swiftly turns to Husam al-Din to urge him to seek that sun, like Alexander. Pausing briefly once again to excoriate the vile attractions of the senses (2.48–51), Rumi turns irresistibly to make an encomium to the Sun (2.52–55), all addressed in the second person. This is a passionate exclamation, highly reminiscent of the lyrics on Shams in the *Divan-i Kabir*. He concludes, "you are neither this nor that in your essence, you who go beyond fancies, more than more!" (2.55).

Rumi then drops the dialogical style for an extended passage (2.56–84) in which he meditates on the nature of the similarity (*tashbih*) between God and humanity, criticizing the Mu`tazili doctrine for its reliance on the senses. This leads to reflections on the nature of vision, culminating in the vision of the self, and the attraction of like for like. But Rumi shifts from the discursive mode back to urgent dialog when he deals with the way one seeks that ideal likeness (2.84–89). He commands his interlocutor to open the eye of the heart, since it is always seeking "that incomparable radiance" (2.87).

Rumi interrupts the dialog in order to question himself repeatedly (2.90–100), whether he is indeed worthy of the beauty who attracts him. This in turn means asking what the real mirror is for, which turns out to be the reflection of the heart in the face of the friend. He tells his heart to seek that universal mirror, and the consequent spiritual rebirth (2.98). And who is that one whom he seeks? "You are the universal mirror I saw eternally; I saw my own image in your eye" (2.100). Finally, the beloved replies (2.103–110), confirming the reality of the vision and the futility of the lover seeking himself in the eyes of any others. The introductory dialog of Book 2 is now over. To illustrate the point further, Rumi will have to turn to "stories of other people."

The preface to Book 3 returns again to Arabic for its expression. It begins with an invocation of God's multiple forms of wisdom (*hikam*), by which He rescues knowledge from ignorance, justice from injustice, existence from hypocrisy, and forbearance from stupidity. These divine wisdoms bring faraway understandings near and make the difficult easy. That cosmic role has been explained by prophets, who announce the esoteric secrets of God. Rumi remarks that God's turning of the luminous and compassionate pearly heaven, which rules the smoky heaven of this world, is like the commanding role of intellect over the forms of earth and the inner and outer senses. The turning of that spiritual heaven commands all other existence, from the luminous stars to earth and water.

From this all-encompassing effect of the divine wisdom, Rumi turns to the question of the human capacity for knowledge. Every human type strives according to proper ability—the reciter of the Qur'an according to his wisdom, the ascetic according to his struggle, the jurist according to his opinion, the giver according to his capacity, and even the one who receives by the excellence that he recognizes.

Between the divine wisdoms and human ability there is obviously a gap, which does not invalidate the effect of seeking. Rumi says that one who lacks water in the desert does not by seeking it lose the knowledge of the content of the seas, but rather strives for the water of life before preoccupation with worldly things cuts him off from it, or before illness and need hold him back, or mental objectives interfere with the sought object toward which he hastens.

Rumi now characterizes the obstacles that prevent one from attaining this knowledge: desire, seeking one's ease, avoiding that object, fearing for oneself, or being concerned with a livelihood. Only those can attain this knowledge who in positive terms turned to God, imprint their faith upon the world, take great wealth from the never-failing treasury of wisdom along with illumination, thankful for those divine gifts. In negative terms, they are described as turning to God away from base desires and from the ignorance that magnifies one's meanness, and belittles the greatness of others, marveling at itself for things that God has not in fact permitted it.

This classic and even Platonic attraction to the divine combined with rejection of the ego has to be framed by an abandonment of pride in knowledge. For the wise seek to learn what they do not know, and to teach what they know, while being kind to those who are slower to understand. Rumi appropriately quotes the Qur'an (4:94): "You were like that before, but God was gracious to you." The ultimate reason for giving up human pretensions to wisdom is the infinite nature of God, which transcends the sayings of heretics, the idolatry of idolaters, the detraction of detractors, the misbegotten fancies of rationalists, and the caprices of the fanciful.

Rumi closes this preface with thanks and praise of God for the completion of this divine and lordly book of the *Masnavi*. He ends by quoting three passages from the Qur'an, which proclaim the protection and preservation of the Qur'anic revelation itself. One has the unmistakable impression that these allusions to the Qur'anic miracle, placed alongside praise of the *Masnavi*, are once again designed to underline the way in which the *Masnavi* itself functions as a sacred book.

After this formal and majestic preface, in Arabic prose marked by strongly balanced rhyming sequences, Rumi breaks into the opening lines of Persian verse with a sense of release and ease. He starts by addressing Ziya' al-Haqq Husam al-Din, his constant interlocutor and amanuensis, asking him to bring on this third book, like the sunnah of the Prophet, which is established by three repetitions of an act. In the first six lines, Rumi shows a teasing impatience to get started, as he tells Husam al-Din to stop making excuses, then praising him as one whose strength comes from divine sources, not from the body, and whose light comes from the sun (*shams*), not from a lamp.

In the next section (3.7–14), Rumi enumerates the ways in which Husam al-Din's strength is angelic and spiritual rather than physical in nature. Because of his glorious character, like Abraham, Husam al-Din can avoid the fires of disease. Worldly folk are too narrow to grasp his character, therefore it is up to Husam al-Din to give them a "mouth" (*halq*, literally "throat") by which to consume the mystical teachings of the *Masnavi*; this notion of a mouth becomes a major theme throughout this introductory dialog.

The next couple of lines (3.15–16) briefly digress on a theme familiar in the preface to Book 1 (1.25–26), namely the shattering of Mount Sinai under the full force of divine revelation, to the astonishment of Moses. The Qur'anic reference (7:143) is amplified by an Arabic half verse, likening the shifting mountain to a dancing camel. This is evidently the potential impact of the transcendental knowledge conveyed by the *Masnavi*.

Rumi then turns to develop the theme of the mouth, one of several very physical images used in this passage to convey transcendence while preserving the tension between the body and beyond. He initially employs the image of "giving a mouth" to creation (3.17–25) as a divine work of realization applicable to every limb of the body and to the spirit as well. It is the source of glorification for Husam al-Din, though he is cautioned not to reveal its secret to the public. Consumption is the action that transforms one realm of creation into another, from earth to vegetable to animal to human, until the earth finally consumes the expired human body. Rumi envisions (3.26–30) a cosmic process of consumption, from the most humble particle on up, so that all the world can be seen as eating or eaten.

Shifting to a transcendental perspective, Rumi proceeds to lay out the stark contrast between the scattered world and that enduring world, a dichotomy that naturally includes the inhabitants of both realms. The lovers of this world are cut off (Arabic *munqata`*) from the source, recalling, though in a negative mode, the restless reed flute that in Book 1 is cut off (Persian *burida*) from the read-bed. The dwellers of that world, in contrast, are eternally collected. Those who have obtained the water of life endure, freed from affliction, and though there may be thousands, they are one person in reality.

Returning to the motif of consumption (3.36–42), Rumi clarifies that both eater and eaten are more than material creations, possessing as they do an intellectual basis. His example is Moses' "staff of justice", which in the Qur'anic story became a serpent and ate the snakes of Pharaoh's magicians. But Moses' serpent did not increase by this consumption, because it was not a meal of animal flesh—it was instead the triumph of certainty (*yaqin*), which consumed all imaginations (*har khayali*). Inner spiritual meanings thus have mouths by which God nourishes them. Once again, Rumi sees consumption as a constant feature of creation, in anything that is attracted to another substance. The mouth of the soul is emphatically not physical, for its sustenance is glorification (already indicated as the goal for Husam al-Din, in 3.19).

The paradoxical use of such a physical image to describe the bodiless impels Rumi to explain further (3.43–45) the conditions by which the temperament can change so radically from its deadly preoccupation with this world. He compares that worldly desire to the pathological condition of people who perversely are drawn to eat earth. But when that temperament changes, the result is plain from the illuminated face.

Rumi calls upon another metaphor of the body when he introduces the weaning of the infant as an image of spiritual transformation (3.46-49). The wetnurse (*daya*), in a symbolism familiar in other Sufi contexts, stands for the spiritual master who gradually weans the disciple from the fascination to the world, leading instead to the solid food of the spiritual life.

If that imagery of weaning were not enough, Rumi adds one more layer of bodily symbolism in comparing the reluctant disciple to an embryo still content with the nourishment of the womb (3.50–61), though its destiny is to move on through birth to sustenance with milk and then solid food. This likewise recalls the symbolism of gestation developed in the preface to Book 2. Making that progression to a mouthful of food (*luqma*) brings one to the level of a sage like Luqman. This is despite the natural refusal of the embryo to listen to the talk of the wonders of the outside world, or to pay attention to unfavorable comments on its dark and narrow present location. Thus the incredulous embryo can become the model of the stubborn infidels who blindly refuse to believe the proclamations of the prophets.

Rumi's final remarks in his introductory dialog (3.62–68) build on the notion of blindness to point out the inability of worldly souls even to conceive images of the spiritual realm. If this world is a darkened well, those within cannot imagine the illumination of the world outside. Eyes and ears are blocked by preconceptions from perceiving the world of reality. Thus the incredulous embryo remains satisfied with its nourishment in the womb, forgoing its birth and new sources of sustenance. So ends the third preface and introductory dialog, leaving the way clear for the unfolding of further stories.

Turning back to consider the prefaces to Books 1-3, it is evident that Rumi employs them to set up the dynamic interaction that follows in each case in dialog with Husam al-Din. The encounter is framed by declarations of the status of the *Masnavi* as revelation, unfolding truths that would shatter the recipient if experienced directly. This message must be communicated to the perfect listener, who is explicitly named as Husam al-Din. The situation, then, is an overwhelming and limitless revelation with an ideal audience, who nevertheless must be given hints and guidance, since the full disclosure would destroy him.

Further elaborations relate to the spiritual sustenance that provides strength, the temptation of pride in one's knowledge, and perceptual obstacles blocking the transformation of the soul's temperament. Rumi uses imagery of the body with great skill to convey these spiritual meanings.

Similarly, the opening poetic sequences of Books 1–3 illustrate, in a much more fluid fashion, the basic problematic of mystical expression as outlined in the prefaces. Rumi constantly returns to the necessity of companionship with the perfect friend, who can hear the explanation of longing, and who can be a mirror for the soul. The dialog with Husam al-Din, by focusing on this ideal relationship, inevitably recalls the memory of Shams-i Tabriz, compared to whom Husam al-Din is a secondary "radiance". But the impossibility of rendering this truth of love in words requires as a substitute the endless invention of "stories about other people" that form the substance of this mystical epic. It is in the sense that, for Rumi, "a little indicates much."

23

Wakened by the Dove's Trill: Structure and Meaning in the Preface to Rūmī's *Masnavī*, Book 4

Beginnings are difficult, as all authors know. How should one start a complicated piece of writing, in such a way that alert readers know how to interpret the text correctly? Plato is said to have rewritten the opening to his *Republic* many times. When an expert writer prefaces his work with a formal introduction, it is especially important to take that opening seriously, as an announcement of the purpose, context, and audience envisioned for the work. The introduction may be explicit, or it may fall back on allusive and indirect references, but in either case it arguably forms an essential part of the literary structure of the work. Here I would like to investigate one particular example of such an introduction, the preface to Book 4 of Jalāl al-Dīn Rūmī's *Masnavī*. I am building on my analysis in the previous chapter of the prefaces to the first three books of the *Masnavī* and their relation to the opening dialogs with his disciple Ḥusām al-Dīn Chalabī, which are prominently featured at the beginning of each book.[1] There I argued that Rūmī uses these prefaces to set up his

[1] Carl W. Ernst, "A Little Indicates Much: Structure and Meaning in the Prefaces to Rūmī's *Masnavī*," chapter 22 in this volume.

primary goal as a teacher of Sufism. That is, he wants to clarify the way in which language functions as a way to bring about the comprehension of a reality that is much larger than any concept. At the same time, he uses the dialog form to highlight the shortcomings of language, together with the longing of spiritual aspirants who seek a way to overcome those limitations. Each of these prefaces plays variations on this theme of the adequacy of language and the transcendence of the divine reality, with powerful gestures towards the key roles played by both Rūmī's disciple Ḥusām al-Dīn and his spiritual mentor, Shams-i Tabrīz. The point is that Rūmī is a very deliberate author whose introductory gestures are extremely important for understanding the purpose of his symbolic declarations. Here I would like to argue that the same applies to the preface of Book 4 of the *Masnavī* as well, although it stands out by its citation of an Arabic poem of the Umayyad era that serves to evoke a passionate undertone that is crucial for understanding Rūmī's relationship with his Sufi associates. Book 4 is thus distinctive in calling upon a love poem from the secular Arabic tradition to frame the Sufi dialog in Persian that opens this section of the *Masnavī*.

In Book 1, Rūmī began with an extensive comparison between the *Masnavī* and the Qur'an, stressing how the brevity of its expression encompasses a world of meaning: "a little indicates much." He also praised Ḥusām al-Dīn, the instigator of the poem's composition, with an extravagance verging on parody, at the same time clarifying that the audience of the *Masnavī* is an advanced spiritual elite. The opening dialog with Ḥusām al-Dīn starts right after the song of the reed, and resumes after a break for the beginning of the first story. It contains powerful evocations of Shams-i Tabrīz as the ideal teacher and listener, who also demonstrates the inability of language to express reality directly, despite the unavoidable necessity of language. Stories of other people (*ḥadīth-i dīgarān*) emerge as the way to communicate spiritual truths indirectly. In a similar fashion, the preface to Book II dwells on the need for proportion and balance, which are paradoxically impossible in relation to the infinity of God and divine love. The opening dialog focuses on the issue of companionship, again with strong references to Shams-i Tabrīz as the solar exemplar of living truth, and the mysterious relationship between lover and beloved.

The preface to Book 3 opens with a portrayal of the forms of divine wisdom that rule the universe, and the corresponding incapacity of the human intellect to comprehend them. But this human defect is caused by distractions that can be eliminated in those who are intent on only God; Rūmī closes this section with additional comparisons between the Qur'an and the *Masnavī* as vehicles of guidance. In the opening lines of verse, Ḥusām al-Dīn is alternately teased and praised, increasingly in terms stressing his similarity to Shams, as the "radiance" (*ḍiyā'*) derived from the sun. Rūmī deploys extensive comparisons involving bodily life, using the imagery of consumption, weaning, and the embryo to indicate the human condition. So far the emphasis has been on the nature of spiritual communication itself, the need for a perfect listener, and the inadequacy of all representations, yet Ḥusām al-Dīn is fully aware of these issues.

Book 4 starts with a preface that (as with Books 1 and 3) is in Arabic, though it is brief. It announces itself as "the fourth journey to the best of abodes", but the *Masnavī* remains very much a book; reading it gives joy to the hearts of gnostics. The recitation of its virtues emphasizes its cosmic and salvific character; there are only indirect further allusions to its textual character, when it is called "the shout of the clouds" (*ṣawt al-ghimām*) that thunderously announces the rain, or when we are told that its breast (or introduction, *ṣadr*) contains adornments not seen on gorgeous singers. In chains of rhyming prose, Rūmī declaims the power of the *Masnavī* to heal, and he portrays it as the desire of seekers and the greatest gift, the renewer of affection and reliever of affliction, and the reward for those who know and act.

Rūmī quickly introduces the key symbols of the moon and sun, which seem to play directly on the identities of Ḥusām al-Dīn and Shams. Thus, the *Masnavī* is like a rising moon and a returning fortune, increasing hope for the hopeful. Rūmī reiterates the point that the *Masnavī* restores hope, utilizing the typical Sufi terms for the "expansion" (*basṭ*) of hope after its "contraction" (*inqibāḍ*, cf. *qabḍ*). Because now the *Masnavī* is like the sun (*shams*) dawning among clouds dispersed, a light (*nūr*) to our companions and a treasure to our followers. Rūmī closes the section with a prayer to God for thanks, since gratitude is the source of the increase of all things.

At this point Rūmī makes a striking shift, quoting four verses from the early Umayyad poet 'Adī ibn al-Riqā', a panegyrist of the Caliph al-Walīd (d. 715). This invocation of an early Arabic poem stands out as a dramatic gesture, building upon the elegant literary effect created by the balanced rhyming phrases that precede it. As Nargis Virani has shown, Rūmī was an attentive reader of Arabic poetry, and himself composed many verses in Arabic.[2] What is the nature of this poetic citation, and what is the effect of its quotation? First let me quote the lines in question:

Wa-mimmā shajānī anna-nī kuntu nā'iman
U'allilu min bardin bi-ṭībi al-tanassumi
ilá an da'at warqā'u fī ghuṣni aykatin
tugharridu mubkāhā bi-ḥusni al-tarannumi
fa-law qabla mubkāhā bakaytu ṣabātan
li-su'dá shafaytu al-nafsa qabla al-tanaddumi
wa-lakinna bakat qablī fa-hayyaja lī al-bukā
bukāhā fa-qultu al-faḍlu lil-mutaqaddimi

Something that bothered me was once, while sleeping,
I was struck with the cool of a fragrant breeze,
Until a dove called out to me from the thicket's branch,
trilling its lament with a lovely song.
If I had just cried for Su'dā's love from longing,
before it cried, I'd have healed my soul before I felt remorse.
But it cried before me, its tears provoking mine.
So I said: the glory goes to the one who's first.

As Nicholson points out, these verses have been anthologized, notably in *al-Kāmil* by Mubarrad in the fourth/tenth century, in what Nicholson calls "a more correct text."[3] It is not clear what classicizing impulse led Nicholson to make that judgment. A recent critical edition of that work cites only the last

[2] Nargis Virani, "Multilinguality: A Dynamic and Unique Strategy for Apophatic Discourse," unpublished paper given at conference on "Wondrous Words: The Poetic Mastery of Jalāl al-Din Rūmī," British Museum, 13–15 September 2007.

[3] *The Masnaví of Jalálu'ddín Rúmí*, ed. Reynold Alleyne Nicholson (London: Luzac & Co., 1925; reprint ed., 1971), commentary on Bk. 4, vol. 8, p. 125.

two verses that appear in Rūmī's preface, adding the first two verses in a footnote as marginal additions, with minor variants.[4] Surprisingly, these verses are still quite popular today, to judge from several versions found on the Internet containing the apparently complete *qaṣīda* of Ibn al-Riqā' (also known as Ibn Abī Maryam) from which it is taken, a poem otherwise attributed to Zayd ibn Mu'āwiya and others.[5] Nicholson rightly observed that the ordinary sense of the poem was the way that the dove's lament inspires the sleeping lover and kindles his longing by awakening him, but he pointed out that Rūmī allegorized this trope in a mystical sense; he further commented that the verses, however, have a particular application to the preceding passage in which the *Masnavī* is glorified. Rūmī hints, plainly enough for anyone familiar with his style, that under God all credit for the spiritual power and holy influence of the poem is due to its originator and inspirer, Ḥusām al-Dīn.

So far so good, but I would like to suggest that Rūmī had in mind more of the poem than the few verses that he quoted. Although Nicholson dismissed the poem of Ibn al-Riqā' as "an ordinary *nasīb*" (erotic ode), the complete ode contains distinctive features that could well have been attractive to Rūmī, in which the poet raises the metaphorical descriptions of lovers to quasi-prophetic descriptions of remarkable boldness. It begins with the enquiry of a lover's friend, who compares the lover to an ecstatic pilgrim at the *ḥajj* pilgrimage:

> Do I see you cheerful like one enthralled, circumambulating the sides of the sacred place?

---

[4] Abū al-`Abbās Muḥammad ibn Yazīd al-Mubarrad, *al-Kāmil*, ed. Muḥammad Aḥmad al-Dālī (Beirut: Mu'assasat al-Risāla, 1986), 3:1029. Line 1 reads, "I was struck by the breeze with the cool of sleep" (*min bard al-karā*) while line 2 has the dove "striking" (*turaddidu*) its lament.

[5] Cited on the Madrasat al-Mīzān lin-Naqd al-Adabī (The School of the Balance for Literary Criticism) website, http://www.1121.com/?LINK=Article&id=31, accessed 5 December 2007, where the verses cited by Rūmī are lines 16–19 out of 40; a copy of this file is also available at http://www.unc.edu/~cernst/research/adi.doc. This offers the variant in line 16: "I was struck with exceeding desire by the breeze" (*farṭ al-hawa bil-tanassum*), and it replaces the name of Su`dā with a pleonastic verb (*la-kuntu*). This poem is said to be from Ibn al-Riqā's *Dīwān*, published in Iraq; presumably this is *Dīwān shi`r `Adī ibn al-Riqā' al-`Āmilī*, ed. Abū al-`Abbās Aḥmad ibn Yaḥyā Tha`lab al-Shaybānī, Nūrī Ḥammūdī al-Qaysī, and Ḥātim Ṣāliḥ al-Ḍāmin (Baghdad: Maṭba`at Majma` al-`Ilmī al-`Irāqī, 1987).

> An arrow's struck you, or you've suffered a glance, and this is nothing but a lovelorn trait (lines 1–2).

This question elicits in answer the complaint of the lover, who claims that his beloved is responsible for his death from longing, though he pleads that she should not be held guilty. She is an enchanting creature, described in Arabian terms as "refined of speech, Meccan within, Ḥijāzī about the eyes, and Ṭā'ifī in the mouth" (line 6). After confessing his jealousy even of her toothbrush and her clothes, and whatever is close to her, the lover (line 10) notices that her fingertips are red as though stained with henna, which he interprets as a sign of the enmity and disdain that she shows towards him. She replies (lines 12–15) by saying that his departure, when she was depending upon him, caused her to cry so much that when she wiped away her tears, her fingers were red with blood.

The four lines quoted by Rūmī are the lover's response to this reproach, in which he shifts into a reflective mood and confesses that the kindling of his passion was sparked by the dove's call; he claims still to be a lover, though evidently he needed a reminder. After his invocation of the dove and its passion, the lover goes on to say that he wept for her, "whose face enhances beauty, and has no peer, Arab or Persian" (line 20). Not only that, but she has extraordinary qualities resembling the prophets, to which he contrasts his own suffering, also using prophetic examples:

> She has the wisdom of Luqman, the form of Joseph, the song of David, and the purity of Mary,
>
> The speech of Ishmael in every melody, and the kingdom of Solomon son of David; realize this!
>
> But I have Jacob's sadness, and the lowliness of Jonah, the sufferings of Job, and the wildness of Adam (lines 21–23).

The lover goes on to compare the houris of paradise unfavorably to her, and he proclaims that he will never leave her. Then he announces, just barely restraining the audacity of his boast:

> I then recalled in the Qur'an the sura of Joseph, and what the Merciful One told of Joseph the brave.

> So she was Zulaykha on the day I was like Joseph, although [Joseph] the Prophet of God was the best of the noble (lines 31–32).

The poet here evidently hopes that his beloved will attempt to seduce him, as Zulaykha tried to do with Joseph in the Qur'anic account. After further protestations of his love, the lover makes clear that the implicitly Arabian location is in fact the sacred territory of Mecca, in a daring boast: "By God! If it were not for God, and fear and hope, I would have embraced her right between Ḥaṭīm and Zamzam!" (line 35). Even covering her with kisses there may be alright, because "this is lawful (*ḥalāl*) to me, for I am no relation (*maḥram*)" (line 37). The poem then winds down in a conclusion where the lover sees once again a dove cooing its forlorn passion, and he realizes that he is afflicted with an incurable malady of love.

Reflecting on the sense and imagery of the ode of Ibn al-Riqā', it seems plausible that its use by Rūmī is another example of the Sufi appropriation of the secular court poetry of the Umayyad and 'Abbasid eras, in which the combination of near-blasphemy and intense emotional coloring provided just the right amount of aesthetic shock to satisfy the mystics.[6] The dove of the poem is no doubt a direct reference to Ḥusām al-Dīn, whose sympathetic presence powerfully incites the longing that Rūmī expresses here. The dove (*warqā'*) is indeed the turning point of the poem, as is appropriate with a bird that commonly served as a messenger, thus inevitably becoming an intermediary between lovers.[7] Indeed, Warqā' was the name of one of the lovers in the eleventh-century Persian *Masnavī* poem, *Warqā' u Gulshāh* by 'Ayyūqī (d. ca. 1030). The verses announcing the dove's appearance, moreover, take on a semi-prophetic tone, as the narrator sinks into sleep, so that his perception of what follows has the dream-like quality that Muslim thinkers viewed as a partial approximation of prophetic revelation. Thus for the

---

[6] For examples of Sufi use of secular Arabic poetry, see my *Guide to Sufism* (Boston: Shambhala, 1997), chapter 6, pp. 147–78.

[7] F. Viré, "Ḥamām," *Encyclopaedia of Islam*, Second Edition, edited by P. Bearman, Th. Bianquis, C. E. Bosworth, E. van Donzel and W. P. Heinrichs (Leiden: Brill, 2008), Brill Online, University of North Carolina at Chapel Hill, 30 November 2008, http://www.brillonline.nl/subscriber/entry?entry=islam_SIM-2656.

"full-knowing reader", the allusions packed into these Arabic verses would be enough to stimulate a line of thinking that would draw attention to spiritual tensions beyond what was explicitly contained in the few verses that appeared upon the page.[8]

On the formal level of Ibn al-Riqā's poem considered as a whole, the verses quoted by Rūmī serve as a central hinge between the standard repartee between lovers in the first half, and the strikingly audacious religious language of the second half (although the *ḥajj* imagery is anticipated by the opening line). And the dove returns to accompany the concluding coda, reflecting on the incurable character of love. But what rhetoricians call the unspoken "third persona",[9] who inevitably comes to mind although he is not expressly mentioned, is undoubtedly Shams-i Tabrīz; he is clearly evoked in Rūmī's mention of the sun (*shams*) just before quoting the Arabic verses. Shams, I would suggest, is the unspoken parallel to the prophetically described beloved in the Arabic poem, and the intensity of Rūmī's passion is aptly signaled by the imagined encounter in the precincts of the holy shrine of the Ka'ba. In short, the verses of Ibn al-Riqā' fit remarkably well as a subtle echo of the spiritual roles of both Ḥusām al-Dīn and Shams-i Tabrīz for the audience of the *Masnavī*. An audience accustomed to esoteric readings, and to seeking "the secret of beloveds" in stories about other people, would have the aptitude to make connections with the unquoted lines of the poem.

Rūmī concludes the preface with phrases that seem to continue the indirect invocation of Ḥusām al-Dīn and Shams: "God have mercy on those who are first, and those who are later; those who achieve, and those who make others achieve." The preface closes with a litany of divine names, including Jacob's words to his sons, "He is the best as protector, for He is the most merciful of the merciful ones" (Qur'an 12:64); the last lines focus on God as the one who cares for all humanity, followed by blessings on the Prophet.

---

[8] Joseph Michael Pucci, *The Full-knowing Reader: Allusion and the Power of the Reader in the Western Literary Tradition* (New Haven: Yale University Press, 1998).

[9] Philip Wander, "The Third Persona: An Ideological Turn in Rhetorical Theory," *Central States Speech Journal* 35 (1984), pp. 197–216.

The introductory Persian verses of Book 4, comprising a relatively short section of 36 lines, play on many of the themes announced in the Arabic preface, such as the gratitude that leads to increase, and particularly the lights representing the spiritual personalities of Ḥusām al-Dīn and Shams.[10] The opening section (4:1–9) is a direct address to Ḥusām al-Dīn, who is hailed by his epithet "radiance of truth", by whose light the *Masnavī* has surpassed the moon. It is his lofty concentration that takes the *Masnavī* to a destination that he alone knows; somewhat humorously, he is depicted as yanking the *Masnavī* along by the neck. Ḥusām al-Dīn is the invisible leader of the *Masnavī*, and since he is its origin (*mabda'*), he is told, "If it increases, you have increased it" (4:5); because of his proximity to God, it takes shape as he desires. Rūmī expresses the nexus between the classical Islamic virtue of gratitude for favor (*shukr al-ni'ma*) and the consequential increase of blessings, as stated for instance in Qur'an 14:7, "if you give thanks, you will indeed be increased." In this way Rūmī personifies the *Masnavī*:

> The *Masnavī* has a thousand thanks for you, raising its hands in prayer and thanks.
>
> By its lips and hands, God sought your thanks, gave you glory, and proclaimed increasing grace (4:8–9).

After further refinements on the theme of increase and thankfulness (4:10–12), Rūmī returns again to Ḥusām al-Dīn, who is urged to pull the caravan of the *Masnavī* towards its pilgrimage—but not just a pilgrimage to the house, rather to the Lord of the House (4:14–15). It is hard to know from these descriptions whether Ḥusām al-Dīn's role was primarily to stimulate Rūmī to keep writing the *Masnavī*, or whether these words signify that he had any active part in its planning and composition.

At this point Rūmī again recalls emphatically the names of light, as mentioned in the Qur'an (10:5): "He is the one who made the sun (*shams*) into radiance (Arabic *ḍiyā'*) and the moon into a light (*nūr*)." He also plays with the Persian equivalents of these

---

[10] All citations are to Jalāl al-Dīn Muḥammad Balkhī, *Masnavī*, ed. Muḥammad Isti`lāmī (Tehran: Zavvār, 1370./1991).

words. Since Ḥusām al-Dīn, the "radiance" of God, now also merits the title of being called the sun (*khvurshīd*), in principle this raises the question of his relation to Shams. Rūmī dwells on this theme at length (4:16–24), reflecting a certain tension between the Qur'anic identification of the terms and the very personal way he has used these names to distinguish his two very different spiritual interlocutors.

> Since the sun is higher than the moon, know that radiance outranks the light.
>
> Many have lost their way by moonlight, but when the sun came up, that was clear.
>
> The sun (*āftāb*) shows defects perfectly—that's why they have markets in the day,
>
> So that the heart and good cash become clear, so that they remain far from guile and tricks.

This last digression into market symbolism causes Rūmī to rank this truth-clarifying light with the Qur'anic epithet, "a mercy for creation" (21:107), from this perspective collapsing both Ḥusām al-Dīn and Shams into the providential function of the Prophet Muḥammad. He spends five more lines (4:25–29) musing on the cheats and thieves who are the enemy of the light.

Light and its origin, the sun, return once more to the center, as Rūmī approaches the final charge for this volume (4:30–31), assigning to Book 4 the celestial position held by the Sun in traditional cosmology:

> Pour brightness on Book IV, for the Sun (*āftāb*) has arisen from the fourth heaven!
>
> Here, Sun-like (*khvurshīdvār*), give light from the fourth [heaven], so it shines over lands and regions.

This command to Ḥusām al-Dīn, which is at the same time an invocation of the presence of Shams, metamorphoses these two spiritual lights into the text of the *Masnavī*, which like the sun shines on everyone. "It's fiction for those who read it as fiction, but for one who sees, it's cash is truly manly" (4:32). The imagery of light must take into account those who choose to see darkness. Rūmī lingers obsessively on those who are perverted in their perceptions, like the Egyptians who saw the Nile as blood. Thus he concludes by evoking the imaginal form (*mumaththal*) that is the suitable eschatological recompense for such deniers:

> The enemy of this discourse now appears in the mind's eye hanging upside down in hellfire.
>
> You've seen his state, Ḍiyā' al-Ḥaqq! God has shown you the answer to his deeds.
>
> Master, since the hidden vision is hidden, make this gift of sight increase in this world (4:34–36).

After this somber note, the introductory lines shift to recall the last story of Book 3, which needs now to be completed.

So how does the Arabic preface to Book 4 relate to the dialog in the opening Persian verses? I have argued that the introductions to each of the first three books simultaneously proclaim the power of the word, specifically the *Masnavī*, to create spiritual transformation, while at the same time reflecting on the limitations of those words, and the extensive parts of creation that try not to see the light. Moreover, this hide-and-seek quality of language is inseparable, in Rūmī's own experience, from the spiritual companions—Ḥusām al-Dīn and Shams-i Tabrīz—who personified that same energy that is manifest in the *Masnavī*. Book 4 seems to follow that pattern fairly closely. In this sense, Rūmī adhered to a certain extent to the model of the introduction in Arabic literature (*muqaddima*), which had evolved to constitute a three-part literary genre consisting of the invocation of the name of God (*basmala*), the statement for the reasons for composing the book, and the closing lines of praise.[11] Yet in other respects, Rūmī breaks out of the conventional mold for the literary introduction, which often features stereotyped

[11] P. Freimark, "Muḳaddima," *Encyclopaedia of Islam*, Second Edition, ed. P. Bearman, Th. Bianquis, C.E. Bosworth, E. van Donzel and W.P. Heinrichs (Leiden: Brill, 2008), Brill Online, University of North Carolina at Chapel Hill, 30 November 2008, http://www.brillonline.nl/subscriber/entry?entry=islam_SIM-5453.

expressions of modesty and praise for patrons. That is, the form of this introduction is highly personal, and it encodes symbols known to an elite audience of Sufis (particularly Ḥusām al-Dīn) who had intensely personal connections to Rūmī and Shams. The opening of the introduction presents the *Masnavī* itself as the supreme manifestation of spiritual power. The Arabic verses quoted from Ibn al-Riqā' most likely were well known in this circle, and they would have triggered associations with the complete ode from which they were drawn, further enhancing the role of Ḥusām al-Dīn as the inspiration for the text. The opening section of Persian verse that precedes the first story of Book 4 continues with the theme of gratitude for Ḥusām al-Dīn's role, and also juxtaposes Ḥusām al-Dīn and Shams as the two sources of light that can overcome the darkness in humanity.

Yet it is extraordinary to juxtapose the very different stylistic registers of these two sections. The Arabic preface has a coolly composed and elegant surface, yet the allusion buried in its refined quotation of a verse, which was already five centuries old in Rūmī's time, still beats with passionate emotion today. The intimate and even jocular tone of the Persian dialogue with Ḥusām al-Dīn carries with it a dark recognition of the negative aspects of creation. In the space marked out by these two formal gestures, Rūmī is able to present his spiritual teachings with remarkable freedom, so that his audience grasps their power despite the inadequacies of language.

PART 4

CONTEMPORARY SUFISM

24

Ideological and Technological Transformations of Contemporary Sufism

Islam, Ideology, and Sufism

One of the major trends in the development of Islamic religious culture over the past two centuries has been what one may call the Islamization of Islam. With the growing domination of European culture through colonialism, the modern western concept of religion was applied to categorize what we now familiarly call the religions of the world.

Islam, an Arabic term designating both the individual act of surrender to God and the corporate performance of ritual, became the accepted designation for one religion among many.[1] Nineteenth-century European Orientalist scholarship played

[1] The *Oxford English Dictionary* cites Edward Lane's 1842 *Manners and Customs of the Modern Egyptians* as the first use of the term "Islam" in English. Prior to that, "Mahometanism" was the common designation for this religion. Both terms conveyed the Enlightenment concept of religion as one of many competitive belief structures. For a fuller discussion, see my *Following Muhammad: Rethinking Islam in the Contemporary World* (Chapel Hill: University of North Carolina Press, 2003), especially chapter 2.

a key role in developing this "religionizing" concept of Islam, which excluded many of the intellectual and spiritual dimensions of the tradition; at the same time, colonial policy marginalized and privatized the institutions that had supported and transmitted these aspects of Islamic culture in Muslim countries. Curiously enough, nineteenth-century Muslim thinkers, in part responding to this colonial concept, articulated positions of reform and revivalism that mirrored the Orientalist concept of Islam. In the twentieth century, Islam has been increasingly used by fundamentalists as an ideological term for mobilizing mass activism against colonial interests or the secular postcolonial state, and this simple, hard-edged formula of opposition has been uncritically accepted and reproduced by Western media outlets.

Up till now, one major aspect of the contemporary Islamic tradition has been frequently omitted from public discussions: Sufism, or Islamic mysticism. In a survey of the topic, I have argued that Orientalist scholarship has, since its inception two centuries ago, systematically attempted to exclude Sufism from its definition of Islam.[2] In the nineteenth century and even well into the twentieth century, Sufism was almost invariably defined as the product of "foreign influences", which might be anything from Greek philosophy to Buddhism to yoga. This exclusion of Sufism from Islam was paralleled by the new concepts of Islam that were being introduced at the same time by Islamic reformists, forebears of today's fundamentalists. What both Orientalists and fundamentalists failed to acknowledge was the way in which Sufism, broadly defined, had characterized most of the leading Muslim religious thinkers of the premodern period. Certain tropes of hagiography, such as the execution of the Sufi martyr Hallaj (d. 922), were interpreted to mean that Sufism was totally opposed by "orthodox" Islam (however, or by whomever, that is to be defined). The fact that Muslim scholars from al-Ghazali (d. 1111) to Shah Wali Allah (d. 1762) were saturated with Sufi

---

[2] See the evidence discussed in my *Sufism: An Introduction to the Mystical Tradition of Islam* (Boston: Shambhala Publications, 2011), especially chapter 1; also in "Between Orientalism and Fundamentalism: Problematizing the Teaching of Sufism," chapter 1 in this volume.

teachings was an embarrassment to be left out of the history of Islam. Even those figures most often invoked by today's anti-Sufi ideologists, such as Ibn Taymiyya (d. 1328), were themselves members of Sufi orders, despite their critiques of particular Sufi doctrines and practices. Muslim modernists like Sir Muhammad Iqbal have also tended to reject Sufism as medieval superstition, contributing further to the notion that Sufism is irrelevant to Islam.

It was not possible to ignore Sufism completely, however. Again, in what conspiracy theorists might call a deep collusion, Orientalists and fundamentalists both conceded that Sufism was once legitimately Islamic, but this concession was tempered by being limited to a classical golden age in the distant past. One could confidently speak well of Sufi masters who were safely buried centuries ago; Europeans, particularly the Protestant British, agreed with the Wahhabi founders of the Sa`udi regime that dead saints are lifeless dust—this in contrast to the vehement pronouncements of Sufis, that the saints in their tombs are living conduits to the divine presence. In practice, this attitude had the added advantage that one could safely dismiss contemporary Sufis as the degenerate representatives of a once-great tradition. As far as the study of Sufism is concerned, the golden-age attitude translated into a direct correlation between the relative antiquity of a Sufi and the attention of which he was deemed worthy; consequently, studies of contemporary Sufism, except from a purely political perspective, have been rare until recent times.[3]

[3] The critique of "golden-age" approaches to Sufism has been fully developed in Carl W. Ernst and Bruce B. Lawrence, *Sufi Martyrs of Love: Chishti Sufism in South Asia and Beyond* (Palgrave Press, 2002). Although certain major scholars (Louis Massignon, Marshall Hodgson, Ira Lapidus) have recognized the centrality of Sufism in Muslim societies, there has been little attention to contemporary Sufism until fairly recently. For brief surveys of nineteenth- and twentieth-century Sufism, see the following articles listed under "Tasawwuf" in the *Encyclopaedia of Islam* (Leiden: E. J. Brill, 1999), X:313–340: "4. In 19th- and 20th-century Egypt" (F. de Jong); "5. In Persia from 1800 onwards" (L. Lewisohn); "6. Amongst the Turks (c) The Ottoman Turkish lands and Republican Turkey in the 19th and 20th centuries" (Th. Zarcone); "7. In Muslim India (b) In the 19th and 20th centuries" (C. Ernst); "8. In Chinese Islam" (J. Aubin); "9. In Africa south of the Maghrib during the 19th and 20th centuries" (J. O. Hunwick).

Nevertheless, upon closer examination, it turns out that Sufi leaders, Sufi institutions, and Sufi trends of thought have been surprisingly resilient and adaptive to the contested situations of modernity. Nineteenth-century Sufi leaders such as Emir `Abd al-Qadir of Algeria were not only active in anticolonial resistance, but were also connected with reformist circles. Much the same could be said of Indian Sufis such as the Naqshbandi leader Ahmad Barelwi and the Chishti master Hajji Imdad Allah, the North African shaykh Ahmad ibn Idris, and many others. Today, both in traditionally Muslim countries and in the West, a battle is being waged for control of the symbolic resources of Islam, and in this contest, both fundamentalists and modernists regarded Sufism as their chief opponent. In spite of appearances generated by the media, if Sufism is defined broadly to include a range of devotional practices including the intercession of saints and reverence for the Prophet Muhammad, it may fairly be said that the majority of Muslims today still adhere to a Sufi perspective on Islam. The aim of this essay is to illustrate how proponents of Sufism and admirers of its cultural products have expressed themselves through the communications media of modern technology, and to venture some speculations about the kind of community that is sustained by this technology. In making this analysis, I rely in particular on the insightful observations of Manuel Castells, in delineating varied cultural expressions found in the media of print, sound recording, broadcast media and film, and the interactive networking of the Internet.[4]

Sufism in Print

In European history, it has become a truism to state that the Protestant Reformation was to a certain extent the child of print; Gutenberg's invention of moveable type made possible the first modern bestseller, Martin Luther's German translation of the Bible. In a comparative extension of this topic, Sinologists are now examining the relationship between religion and print in

[4] Manuel Castells, *The Information Age: Economy, Society and Culture*, volume 1, *The Rise of the Network Society* (Oxford: Blackwell Publishers Ltd, 1996), pp. 327–75.

China, where the long history of printing is closely tied to religious texts. Anthropologists and historians of religion alike have focused on the question of the relation between the oral and written aspects of sacred texts. Yet for Islam, perhaps preeminently the "religion of the book", research on the relationship between religion and the technology of print is still in its infancy. Partly this is due to the relatively late introduction of print to Muslim countries; despite the existence of Arabic printing in Europe by 1500, there were only a few experiments with printing in Muslim countries by the eighteenth century, and it was not until the late nineteenth century that printing became a major factor in the dissemination of Islamic texts.

To date, much of the scholarship on the subject of Islam and print has focused on the phenomena most easily accessible to Europeans, such as the presses established by European Christian missionaries and by governments, whether native or colonial; many other aspects of printing in Muslim countries remain unexplored, however. Orientalists have speculated, often in a condescending way, on the possible causes that hindered the introduction of printing among Muslims until such a late date. Was it an economic threat to the thousands of calligraphers who made their livelihood from copying manuscripts? Was it a problem of capital formation and marketing, due to the difficulty of recouping the large sums required to invest in the machinery of a printing press? Or was it a profound attachment to the oral transmission of the divine word as embodied in the Qur'an? These questions, and many others, will remain highly debatable as long as the actual history of printing in Muslim countries remains relatively unknown. Clearly, even establishing the outlines of this history will require the labors of scholars working on many different regions and languages, so these large questions remain premature, and may not even be useful. What is most questionable, however, is the degree to which inquiries about Islam and print have been posed from a thoroughly Eurocentric perspective, rather than from a comprehensive inquiry as to the religious purposes to which Muslims turned the new technology.

To be sure, scholars such as Barbara Metcalf have recognized the important role of print in the Islamic religious academies of nineteenth-century colonial India. Since the *'ulama'* (religious scholars) have been the articulators and transmitters of Islamic religious texts, they are certainly a key element to examine for the relation between Islam and print. Yet they are not by any means the only actors to consider. In a provocative essay, Francis Robinson has argued that Islamic religious scholars in India accepted print because, under colonial rule, "without power, they were fearful for Islam".[5] He also points out that the adoption of print for religious texts had several unexpected results: 1) the rise of "Islamic protestantism", i.e., a scripturalist revivalism that rejected many aspects of traditional Islamic practice; 2) the internationalization of the Muslim community; and 3) the democratization of religious knowledge and the consequent erosion of the authority of the *`ulama'*. Robinson observes, "Print came to be the main forum in which religious debate was conducted", a generalization that works well even beyond the specific groups he describes.

Another aspect of this topic that has recently claimed the attention of scholars is the use of print (and other means of communication, like the cassette) by twentieth-century Islamist or fundamentalist groups to propagate their ideologies. Certainly the ability of print to fix a text without variants has contributed to the bibliolatry and scriptural literalism that characterizes these groups. But partly because of the way in which these groups have succeeded in monopolizing Islamic symbolism, both in the eyes of foreign journalists and in indigenous forums, those who raise the question of Islam and print have not been impelled to look past these highly visible phenomena. A cynic might call this the closed-feedback loop in which Western media and scholarship use and are used by twin agendas, that of the fundamentalists and that of the secular governments which they oppose. Once again, those topics of most interest to the West are most prominent in research.

Perhaps the most remarkable aspect of the emergence of Sufism as a topic in the nineteenth and twentieth centuries has been the publicizing of a previously esoteric system of teaching

[5] Francis Robinson, "Technology and religious change: Islam and the Impact of print," *Modern Asian Studies* 27/i (1993), pp. 229–51, quoting p. 240. Revised version: "Islam and the Impact of Print in South Asia," in Nigel Crook, ed., *The Transmission of Learning in South* Asia (Delhi: Oxford University Press, 1996), pp. 62–97.

through modern communications media. Today, Sufi orders and shrines in Muslim countries produce a stream of publications aimed at a variety of followers from the ordinary devotee to the scholar. Just as the recording industry democratized the private rituals of *sama'* (listening to music) for a mass audience (see below), the introduction of print and lithography technology made possible the distribution of Sufi teachings on a scale far beyond what manuscript production could attain. As has been noted in the case of Ibn `Arabi's Arabic works, when they first emerged into print early in the nineteenth century, suddenly a work that had existed in at most a hundred manuscripts around the world (and those difficult of access) was now made easily available at a corner bookstore through print runs of up to a thousand copies.[6]

Evidence is still far from complete, but it has been recently suggested, largely on the basis of Arab and Ottoman evidence, that the main patrons of publishing in Muslim countries in the nineteenth century, aside from governments, were Sufi orders.[7] What was the character and extent of publication by Sufi groups, or on Sufism in general?

The evidence is still very thin, and it is necessary to tease out Sufism from subject categories that are otherwise defined. What is available, however, is suggestive. For instance, a preliminary survey indicates that there were 112 native presses in various parts of India publishing books in Persian and Urdu during the first half of the nineteenth century, and that most of

---

[6] Martin Notcutt, "Ibn `Arabi in Print," in *Muhyiddin Ibn `Arabi, A Commemorative Volume*, ed. Stephen Hirtenstein (Rockport, MA: Element, 1993), pp. 328–39.

[7] Muhsin Mahdi, "From the Manuscript Age to the Age of Printed Books," in *The Book in the Islamic World: The Written Word and Communication in the Middle East*, ed. George N. Atiyeh (Albany: State University of New York Press/Library of Congress, 1995), pp. 6–7. Mahdi suggests that the large followings of mystical orders made such publishing economically feasible. Rich evidence from Morocco is supplied by Fawzi Abdulrazak, "The kingdom of the book: The history of printing as an agency of change in Morocco between 1865 and 1912," Ph.D. dissertation, Harvard University, 1990; translated into Arabic by Khalid Bin al-Saghir, *Mamlakat al-kitab: tarikh al-tiba'h fi al-Maghrib, 1865–1912* (Rabat: al-Mamlaka al-Maghribiyya, Jami'at Muhammad al-Khamis, Kulliyyat al-Adab wa-al-'Ulum al-Insaniyya, 1996).

their publications were on religion, poetry, and law.[8] It is quite likely that many books falling into the categories of religion and poetry could be described as connected to Sufism. Lists of books published in the early nineteenth century from Bengal include the philosophical encyclopedia of the Brethren of Purity (both in Arabic and in Urdu) and Persian literary classics by Sa`di, Jami, and others.[9] The prominence of Persian literary classics in the Indian native presses is also reflected in the presses operated by Europeans in Calcutta in the late eighteenth century.[10] Likewise, books published in Iran since the mid-nineteenth century fall primarily into the categories of classical Persian literature, religious writings, and romantic epics and popular narratives, all of which overlap to some extent with Sufism.[11] Similarly, in the press founded by the Egyptian ruler Muhammad `Ali in 1822, in addition to a large number of translations of European works on subjects like military science, there were significant works on religion, ethics, and poetry. Among these were a number of Arabic, Persian, and Turkish Sufi texts by authors such as Sa`di, Rumi, and Ibn `Arabi.[12]

---

[8] Syed Jalaluddin Haider, "Munshi Nawal Kishore (1836–1895): Mirror of Urdu Printing in British India," *Libri: International Journal of Libraries and Information Services* (Copenhagen, Denmark) 31 (1981), pp. 227–37, citing p. 230.

[9] B. S. Kesavan, *History of Printing and Publishing in India: A Story of Cultural Re-awakening* (New Delhi: National Book Trust, 1985), pp. 396, 398–402.

[10] Examples include *Layli-Majnun* by Hatifi, edited by Sir William Jones (1788); the text and translation of Sa`di's ethical treatise, *Pand nama*, ed. Francis Gladwin (1788); Sa`di's complete works (1791 and 1795); and the poems of Hafiz (1791). See Graham Shaw, *Printing in Calcutta to 1800: A Description and Checklist of Printing in Late 18th-century Calcutta* (London: The Bibliographical Society, 1981), nos. 111, 113, 181, 186, 277. See also C. A. Storey, "The Beginning of Persian printing in India," in *Oriental Studies in Honour of Cursetji Erachji Pavry* (London: Oxford University Press, 1933), pp. 457–61.

[11] Ulrich Marzolph, *Narrative Illustration in Persian Lithographed Books* (Leiden: Brill, 2001).

[12] Titles include the anonymous *Jawhar al-tawhid* (1241/1825); Sa`di's *Gulistan* (1244/1828 and 1287/1841); `Attar's *Pand nama* (1244/1828, 1253/1838, and 1257/1842); a Turkish commentary on Hafiz (1250/1835); *Ma`rifat nama*, a Turkish work on mysticism by Ibrahim Haqqi (1251/1836); a three-volume Turkish commentary on Rumi's *Masnavi* by Kefravi (1251/1836); Ibn `Arabi's *Fusus al-hikam* (1253/1838); the Ottoman poetry of Shaykh Ghalib (1253/1838); a Sufi Qur'an commentary by Isma`il Haqqi (1255/1840); the Persian poems of Hafiz (1256/1841); and several Turkish works on Sufism. See T. X. Bianchi, "Catalogue Général des livres arabes, persans et turcs, imprimés à Boulac en Egypte depuis l'introduction de l'imprimerie dans ce pays," *Journal Asiatique* (July-August

The publicization of Sufism occurred at precisely the time when Sufism was becoming an abstract subject, separated from Islam in Orientalist writings, and condemned by reformists as a non-Islamic innovation. Some of these publications in turn responded directly to presentations of Sufism by Orientalists, fundamentalists, and modernists. In this category one can find not only editions of "classical" Sufi texts in Arabic and Persian (and their Urdu translations), but also writings of contemporary Sufi leaders, including discourses, lectures and essays, biographies, prayer and meditation practices, and manuals for using talismans and charms bearing the names of God (*ta`widh*). Since all these books were available commercially, this new trend amounted to a mass marketing of Sufism on an unprecedented scale.

Through printed books, today one can also gain access to Sufism via scholarly publications from Western-style universities, learned societies, and cultural centers with government sponsorship. In format and style, these works are very much in the same tradition as European academic Orientalism; European-style punctuation, footnotes, and editorial techniques have been largely adopted in Arabic-script publishing. In contrast, non- academic Sufi writings tend to preserve the aesthetic form of the manuscript, particularly in lithographs created by trained calligraphers. As opposed to the elite monopoly on culture characteristic of the manuscript, book publication presupposes a mass audience created by public education and sustained by print capitalism. While access to manuscripts in the premodern period was rare and difficult, and scribal errors required the comparison of different manuscripts, print makes books easy to acquire and standardizes their texts.

Therefore, when a scholar today edits a classical Sufi text, it does not merely replicate the experience of an eleventh-century author for the modern reader. Carrying official authorization as part of "classical" Islamic literature, the printed text now functions in new ways to defend Sufism from the polemics of both fundamentalists and Westernized secularists. In countries

1843), pp. 24–61, citing nos. 19, 46, 47, 97, 109, 113, 137, 148, 149, 190, 199, 201, 202, 209, 217.

like Pakistan where Arabic and Persian both function as "classical" languages, there has been a concerted effort to translate much of the curriculum of Arabic and Persian Sufi literature into Urdu. Like the classical Greek works of Aristotle and Euripides at Oxford bookstores, the Arabic Sufi works of Sarraj, Qushayri, and Suhrawardi are now to be found in Urdu versions on bookshelves in Lahore. Their eminence and Islamic scholarship makes them powerful allies in the defense of Sufism against ideological opponents.

A striking evidence of the newly specialized situation of Sufism is the way Sufi leaders could focus on marketing to their disciples through the publication of serials, a topic that is only beginning to be explored. Probably the first leading Sufi involved in publication of serials in India was Hasan Nizami, a prolific author and publisher in Urdu from 1908.[13] Arthur Buehler has shown how the modern Naqshbandi teacher Jama`at `Ali Shah (d. 1951) directed his movement through *Anwar al-Sufiyya*, a periodical aimed at Sufi devotees.

Mandatory subscriptions for disciples combined with a rigorous train-travel program for Jama`at `Ali Shah enabled him to use modern technology to keep in touch with a far-flung network of followers.[14] The role of modern communications technology in Pakistani Sufism is also evident in the case of the Chishti master Zauqi Shah (d. 1951). Educated at Aligarh and trained as a journalist in both English and Urdu, he founded a Sufi magazine, *Anwar al- Quds* (The Lights of Holiness), which was published in Bombay from October 1925 to February 1927. He continued to publish in newspapers, including some pieces in *Dawn* (Karachi, 1945–46) and a weekly column in *The People's Voice* (1948–49). While he published some polemical articles on the superiority of Islam in the magazine of Abu'l `Ala' Mawdudi,

---

[13] Nithar Ahmad Faruqi, ed., *Khwaja Hasan Nizami* (New Delhi: Mahnama Kitab-numa, 1994), esp. pp. 89–107. See also Ernst and Lawrence, *Sufi Martyrs of Love: The Chishti Sufi Order in South Asia and Beyond*, chapter 6.

[14] Arthur F. Buehler, *Sufi Heirs of the Prophet: The Indian Naqshbandiyya and the Rise of the Mediating Sufi Shaykh* (Charleston SC: University of South Carolina Press, 1998). This periodical has recently been revived in English: *Sufi Illuminations* (*Risala-yi Anwar as-Sufiyya* 1/1–2 (1996), available from the Naqshbandiya Foundation for Islamic Education, PO Box 3526, Peoria, IL 61612-3526 (individual subscription $10/year).

Tarjuman al-Qur'an, he also wrote essays refuting the claims to authority by the fundamentalist leader of the Jama`at-i Islami. In recent years, his successors have published an intermittent English language journal called *The Sufi Path*. A number of other periodicals devoted to Sufism are published in India and Pakistan currently in Urdu and other languages.[15] There are likewise numerous other examples of Sufi periodicals in Egypt and Turkey. Periodicals have the effect of preserving a sense of community among individuals scattered far from the traditional local center.

Sufis were not without ambivalence regarding the use of print for these purposes. Early in the nineteenth century, the Naqshbandi master Shah Ghulam `Ali was enraged to hear that pictures of saints (evidently printed) were available at the great mosque of Delhi. In a conversation that took place in the 1890s, Haydar `Ali Shah (a prominent Chishti leader of the Punjab, d. 1908) denounced the production of printed prayer manuals. Affirming the supreme value of oral transmission, he stated that even if a master got the Arabic names of God wrong, and taught disciples to say the nonsense words *hajj qajjum* instead of *hayy qayyum* ("The Living, the Subsistent"), his instruction was to be preferred to an impersonal practice derived from a book. This prejudice did not, however, prevent his disciples from publishing his Persian discourses in 1909.[16] Yet it is striking to see that ritual could be adapted to the new technology, as in the case of constructing documents of initiation. Typically, initiation into a Sufi order in previous times had involved the disciple learning by heart and then transcribing by hand the family "tree" of the Sufi lineage, inscribing his own name at the end of a line traced back to the Prophet Muhammad. With the availability of

---

[15] The Khanqah Mujibiya in Phulwari Sharif, Bihar, published a journal called *Ma`arif* from the 1950s up to the 1980s; see Fozail Ahmad Qadri, *The Celebrated Garden: A Study of Phulwari Sharif Family of Muslim Divines* (Shillong: North-Eastern Hill University Publications, 1998), p. 68. American libraries have holdings of several Sufi periodicals from Pakistan published over the past two decades, including three from Karachi (*Darvish*, *Rumi Digest*, and *Sachal Sa'in*) and one from Quetta (*Dastgir*).

[16] Ghulam Haydar `Ali Shah of Jalalpur Sharif, *Nafahat al-mahbub* (Sadhura, Pakistan: Bilali Steam Press, 1327/1909); Urdu trans. from Persian by `Abd al-Ghani as *Malfuzat-i Haydari* (Lahore: al-Qamar Book Corporation, 1404/1983–4).

print for this ritual process (as in the mass production of *qawwali* recordings), some Sufi groups produced ready-made printed lineage documents, with the "tree" ending in blank spaces for the would-be initiate and the master to inscribe their own names.[17]

The publicizing of Sufism through print (and, more recently, electronic media) has brought about a remarkable shift in this tradition. Advocates of Sufism have defended their heritage by publishing refutations of fundamentalist or modernist attacks on Sufism. In this sense the media permit Sufism to be contested and defended in the public sphere as one ideology alongside others. This is very much the case, for instance, in the numerous publications of the Barelvi theological school in South Asia, which over the past century have defended the devotional practices of Sufism against the scripturalist attacks of the Deoband school.[18] Likewise, leaders of Egyptian Sufi groups have responded directly to reformist criticisms posed to them by newspaper editors, claiming that Sufism is at the core of Islam, refuting charges of its foreign origins, and defending Sufi rituals and the master-disciple relationship.[19] Traditional Sufi genres like biographies and discourses created an intimate relationship between readers and Sufi masters; through the wider distribution made possible by print, such publications both served local Sufi networks and at the same time functioned as proclamations that at least potentially formed part of the public legitimation of Sufism.

Through these modern public media, Sufism is no longer just an esoteric community constructed largely through direct contact, ritual interaction, and oral instruction.

---

[17] *Silsila-i `aliyya-i Chishtiyya Nizamiyya Fakhriyya Sulaymaniyya Lutfiyya*, ed. Hajji Makhdum Bakhsh (Lucknow: Nawal Kishor, 1913); a photograph of the signature page of this document may be seen at http://www.unc.edu/~cernst/chishti.htm. For other examples of printed *shajara* genealogies, see Qadri, p. 43, n. 16, and Liebeskind, p. 219.

[18] This controversy has been discussed at length by Usha Sanyal, *Devotional Islam and politics in British India: Ahmad Riza Khan Barelwi and His Movement, 1870–1920* (New York: Oxford University Press, 1996; New Delhi: Yoda Press, 2010). See also the extensive list of Barelvi publications offered for sale in the large (224-page) catalog *Kitabi Dunya* offered by the Nizami Book Agency of Budaun, UP (1988–89).

[19] Julian Johansen, *Sufism and Islamic Reform in Egypt: The Battle for Islamic Tradition* (Oxford: Clarendon Press, 1996), pp. 169–210.

Now that Sufism has been publicized through mass printing, what are the changes in personal relationships that the new media entail? As Dale Eickelman has observed, "The intellectual technologies of writing and printing create not only new forms of communication, they also engender new forms of community and authority."[20] Many questions remain about the number and kinds of books produced on Sufism, the number of copies printed, the kind of audience they were aimed at, the publishers themselves, etc., but it is possible to make a few preliminary observations here. Sometimes print is interactive and facilitates interaction of networks, or functions in defense against polemical opponents, but at other times it may be a symbolic or ritual gesture. Simply to publish the writings of a Sufi saint might be considered a pious act that brings blessings with it, and indeed the elaborate poems, dedications, and memorials that conclude many of these publications often have a decidedly ritualistic character. Print as the medium for debate about an imagined Muslim community had an ambiguous relation to the networks in Muslim societies. In the case of Sufism, the defense of strongly local lineages attempted to deflect criticism by claiming to embody the essential teachings of Islam. But there is an inescapably local element to any Sufi tradition or order, which is expressed by devotion to particular shaykhs, ritual at certain shrines, and writing in local languages. This very concreteness of local networks exists in tension with universal notions of community; indeed, we cannot speak of any empirical community of Sufis on a global basis. Sufis attempt to trump the systematic ideologies of reformist critics by staking a claim to the key symbolic capital enshrined in the Qur'an and the Prophet Muhammad. In polemical and academic publications, a universal Sufism aims at capturing "the mantle of the Prophet" in Roy Mottahedeh's apt phrase, but Sufi lineages still depend on face-to-face contact and real communities that are of necessity more limited. It is my assumption that the extent of publication by contemporary Sufi groups has been underestimated, partly

[20] Dale F. Eickelman, "Introduction: Print, Writing, and the Politics of Religious Identity in the Middle East," *Anthropological Quarterly* 68 iii (1995), pp. 133–38, quoting p. 133.

because of the reformist critique mentioned above. But this misreading is also a result of inadequate access to locally distributed publications, and the limited amount of historical research that has been done on printing in Muslim countries. For instance, a knowledgeable British scholar, Graham Shaw, estimated that Munshi Nawal Kishor, the Hindu founder of the most important Persian/Urdu press in nineteenth-century India, had published around 500 books by the time of his death in 1895.[21] But Prof. Mohamad Tavakoli-Targhi of the University of Toronto a few years ago acquired a complete collection of the publications of the Nawal Kishor Press, consisting of nearly 5000 volumes! No doubt some of these were printed by Nawal Kishor's successors, but less than one-fourth of these titles are listed in European or American libraries.[22] A great many of these publications were classical Persian poetry (including Sufi poetry), Sufism, and Islamic religious texts. The major libraries of Muslim countries doubtless hold a considerable number of volumes on Sufism still unknown in the West, so at the very least, the question of Sufism in print provides a charter for further research.

Audio and Film

After the late introduction of print in Muslim countries, the technological pace picked up quickly in the twentieth century with the introduction of mass media, including sound recordings, film, radio, and television. Sufi-related music, which may be found in many countries, soon began to become available in commercially available recordings. This was at first produced both for popular local audiences, as in the case of Indian *qawwali* recordings in the 1920s and 1930s, as well as for highbrow European ethnomusicologists some years later.[23] In neither case

[21] G. W. Shaw, "Matba`a [printing]. 4. In Muslim India," *Encyclopaedia of Islam* (new ed., 1991), 6:806.

[22] The Persian titles of this magnificent collection are in the private collection of Prof. Tavakoli-Targhi; the Urdu volumes (about 15% of the total) have been purchased by the University of Chicago.

[23] See *Sufism*, pp. 189–91, 195–96.

can this be said to be a product of traditional Sufi *tariqa* organizations; it is, instead, a reconfiguration of cultural products for resale on the mass distribution market (whether one calls it "pop culture" or not).

In recent years, Sufi music has been the subject of a new appropriation that may be called "remix". In World Music albums, international festivals, and fusion performances, Sufi music has been performed in contexts never before envisioned. To take but a single example, the *qawwali* music of Pakistani singer Nusrat Fateh `Ali Khan ("Must Must Qalandar") was remixed by the British trip-hop group Massive Attack in 1990 to become an international dance hit with a strong reggae flavor. At the same time, performers who were once low-status service professionals catering to the spiritual experience of elite listeners have made the shift to become box office superstars who are regarded as spiritual personalities in their own right. A glance of the top 25 recordings listed under Sufi music by online bookseller Amazon.com indicates the remarkable variety and profusion available to the world of consumers today. But this is best described as a cultural and commercial appropriation of Sufism rather than as the dissemination of Sufi teaching and authority.[24] Broadcast media in most formerly colonized countries are typically under the control of the state, and so it is not surprising to find that films prepared for television distribution in Muslim countries strongly reflect government interests. This political emphasis is obvious in the few documentary films on Sufism that have been produced in non-European countries, in contrast with the cultural focus of the ethnographic films on Sufism made by Western anthropologists. A notable example of the official documentary film on Sufism is *The Lamp in the Niche*, a two-part film directed by Girish R Karnad and produced in 1990 by the Ministry of Information of the Government of India. This film (winner of a national award for "Best non feature film on social issues") portrays Sufism as a broadly tolerant movement, Islamic in its origins to be sure, but more closely

[24] Regula Qureshi, "'Muslim Devotional': Popular Religious Music and Muslim Identity under British, Indian and Pakistani Hegemony," *Asian Music* 24 (1992-3), pp. 111-21.

akin to the devotional Bhakti currents of Hinduism than to anything else. Likewise, the secular government of Turkey has produced a film called *Tolerance*, devoted to the life and teachings of the thirteenth-century Sufi and poet Jalaluddin Rumi. Rumi is here portrayed as a universal polymath who foreshadows both Turkish nationalism and the secular values of post-Enlightenment modernity, an ironic configuration in a country where the practice of Sufism has been illegal since 1925.[25] The Foreign Trade Association of the City of Bokhara has also released *The Beaming One*, a film on the famous fourteenth-century saint, Baha'uddin Naqshband. The commercial slant of this film, evidently aimed at encouraging pilgrimage to Uzbekistan from South Asia and Turkey, reveals the curious indecisiveness of post-Soviet societies striving to recapture an Islamic identity; at a loss to explain the mystical charisma of the saint, the narrator ends by comparing him to Gandhi and Tolstoy.[26] Like the occasions when official television broadcasts the ceremonies at annual festivals held at saints' shrines, these official films show a clumsy approach in attempting to manipulate the symbolism of Sufism for the benefit of the state.

On the Internet

The apparent paradox of publicizing an esoteric tradition is nowhere more apparent than on the Internet, where the open secret of mysticism must be reconfigured in terms of what are basically advertising paradigms. There are today a host of Sufi websites that proclaim themselves to interested Internet

---

25 "Tolerance, dedicated to Mawlana Jalal-Al-Din Rumi," (Landmark Films, 1995).

26 "The Beaming One" (Ozma Productions, 1993). This latter film should definitely be viewed in conjunction with "Habiba: a Sufi saint from Uzbekistan," a New Age film distributed by Mystic Fire Video (1997) in their "Women of Power" series. While this female healer from Uzbekistan quotes the Qur'an, the Prophet Muhammad, and the Sufi saints, she also makes mysterious references to "the snakes" and to the Goddess, as she leads followers on pilgrimage both to the tomb of Baha'uddin Naqshband and to the tomb of his mother.

surfers, offering everything from detailed textual materials online to boutiques of unusual products. Some of these are related to traditional Sufi orders, such as the Nimatollahi, Naqshbandi, Rifa`i, and Chishti orders. Sometimes, they appear to prolong and perpetuate the authority of the printed text, as one can see from the extensive devotional and spiritual treatises available online, in English translation, in the elaborate websites of the American Naqshbandi order led by Shaikh Hisham Kabbani (http://www.sunnah.org/). This website also features extensive polemics directed against fundamentalist forms of Islam, and the name itself indicates an attempt to appropriate the key symbolic term of the Prophet's moral example (*sunnah*). Although many of the Sufi websites do have some interactive features, such as email addresses, in terms of their religious message they tend to be largely informational with a proselytizing touch.

In contrast, the websites associated with Hazrat Inayat Khan in North America play much more fully into the Internet sensibility. Pir Vilayat Khan, Sufi Sam, and other branches of this Sufi tradition have a massive presence that is ramified in a number of parallel but distinct organizations as well as individual websites. These sites feature numerous interactive features including discussion groups, travel schedules of leaders, online classes, daily inspirational messages, audio files, and massive collections of links to sites on Sufism and other religions. Discussion groups associated with these sites have free-ranging and sometimes combative debates on topics such as the relationship between Sufism and Islam.

This kind of website may truly be said to constitute a "virtual community", which has been defined as "a self-defined electronic network of interactive communication organized around a shared interest or purpose, although sometimes communication becomes the goal in itself."[27] I shall return to these groups below, in connection with the de-emphasis on Islam found in these popular forms of Sufism.

---

27 Castells, I:361.

The variation in the kind of Internet presence maintained by different Sufi groups can be understood in terms of some of the fundamental characteristics of modern communications media and technology. As Castells points out, "in a society organized around mass media, the existence of messages that are outside the media is restricted to interpersonal networks, thus disappearing from the collective mind."[28] This new situation constitutes a challenge for groups that were traditionally defined by granting access to esoteric teachings reserved for a spiritual elite. I once asked the leader of a South Asian Sufi group whether or not he was interested in setting up a website (I posed this question on email, since he has access to this technology in his professional capacity as an engineer). He responded by quoting the words of a twentieth-century Sufi master from his lineage: "We are not vendors who hawk our wares in the bazaar; we are like Mahajans (wholesale merchants)—people come to us." Nevertheless, he indicated that he did find the idea interesting, and it turns out that Malaysian disciples of this order have in fact set up a website where English-language publications of the leading masters of the order are offered for sale.

We should not imagine, however, that Internet representation is completely displacing earlier forms of communications and technology. The history of technology indicates that older cultural forms persist alongside newly introduced forms of communication. Well after the introduction of writing, and even after the invention of printing, oral forms of culture have persisted up to the present day. The vast majority of participants in the Sufi tradition in Muslim countries are still from social strata that have very little access to the most modern forms of electronic communication, and many are indeed illiterate. Lower class devotees who attend the festivals of Sufi saints in Egypt and Pakistan are not represented on the Web. The effect of the spread of Internet technologies is likely to be "the reinforcement of the culturally dominant social networks, as well as the increase of their cosmopolitanism and

[28] Ibid., I:336.

globalization."[29] As might be expected, the authors of Sufi websites tend to be members of such cosmopolitan and globalizing classes: either immigrant Sufi leaders establishing new bases in America and Europe, immigrant technocrats who happen to be connected to Sufi lineages, or Euro-American converts to Sufism in one form or other. Outside of America and Europe, the chief locations for hosting Sufi websites are predictably in high-tech areas like Australia, South Africa, and Malaysia. In this respect the networks of Sufism in the Internet age differ significantly from the locally centered Sufi networks of the time of Ibn Battuta. Now the diasporas based on international business are linked through electronic communications in multiple locations, although it is still possible for Sufi practitioners to return to sacred sites at key times for face-to-face meetings of master and disciple.

Changing Forms of Community

These new forms of communications technology have introduced a tension into the internal aspect of religious community associated with Sufism. There is, on the one hand, a continued need for personal mediation and interpretation by the Sufi master, and a focus on local shrines, combined with the ritual use of texts. On the other hand, texts are published for external audiences, both as printed books and increasingly on the Internet, as invitations to approach the inner teachings. This constitutes, in effect, a kind of Sufi preaching (*da`wa*) that has a self-consciously public posture far more extensive than in previous generations.

But the alternative would be a privatization amounting to complete obscurity. Some Sufi websites are tantalizing advertisements of spiritual authority, using sparing amounts of text, graphics, and occasionally photographs to convey the powerful mediating effect of Sufi masters and lineages; their primary

[29] Ibid., I:363.

interactive goal is to get the viewer into direct personal contact with the Sufi group. Other sites are comprehensive vehicles for virtual communities, loaded with extensive texts and links, where new forms of personal interaction are carried out and mediated by the technology itself. In contrast to the more limited circulation of print, the Internet makes possible the maintenance of networks in a more fluid fashion over any distance. The possibility of a virtual community facilitated by instant communications gives a new significance to the concept of Uwaysi initiation, by which Sufis could enter into contact with masters removed in time or space. Cyberspace becomes a reflection of the unseen spiritual world, though place and physicality are never abandoned.[30]

The spread of new communications media has also had unforeseen effects in allowing popular culture to trump ideology. Muslims who came to the United States after the liberalization of immigration laws in 1965 have tended to be middle-class technical and medical specialists who gravitated towards reformist and fundamentalist forms of Islam.

Their children, who are reaching college age today, have been unexpectedly enchanted by the world music phenomenon, and large numbers of them are discovering Sufism through the powerful music of Nusrat Fateh `Ali Khan and others. In view of the overwhelming anti-Muslim bias in the news media, the stunning popularity of the Sufi poetry of Rumi is another surprising embrace of a manifestation of Islamic culture—although, to be sure, Rumi's Muslim identity is frequently underplayed or elided in favor of a universalist spirituality.

Nevertheless, despite the anti-Sufi influence of Saudi-financed forms of fundamentalism, there are increasing signs of interest in Sufi devotionalism in American Muslim communities (particularly among those of South Asian origin, about 45 percent of immigrant Muslims).

Another consequence of the new media is the erosion of textual authority and the social hierarchies associated with religion. The multiple "translations" of poets like Rumi and Hafiz

[30] Letter of Jamiluddin Morris Zahuri, 19 March 2001.

illustrate a very postmodern concept of the poetic text. Almost none of these are by authors conversant with the original language, and while some like Coleman Barks are professional poets who work closely with translators and standard editions, there are "versions" of the Sufi poets that have no discernible relationship with any original text. This form of "Sufism in print" sometimes verges on total fantasy, in which the imagined words of the mystic poet become the protean mirror of desire.[31] It is striking, too, that the gender separation and stratification associated with traditional Muslim societies has been ignored in many new Sufi groups in the West. Not only are some groups actually headed by women, but women also join with men in performing ritual music and dance in public (like the *sema* of the Whirling Dervishes). It would be hard to find any precedent for this in traditional Sufi orders.

In addition, Sufism is no longer just for Muslims. The oldest modern presence of Sufism in Europe and America, dating from the early years of the twentieth century, derives from the Indian Sufi master Hazrat Inayat Khan. In view of the anti-Muslim feeling that still dominated the late colonial era, he presented Sufism as a universal form of spirituality beyond any particular religion or creed, despite its acknowledged Islamic roots. Other Sufi teachers who have come to the West, like the Sri Lankan teacher Bawa Muhaiyadeen, have followings comprised of both Muslims and non-Muslims, who dispute the ultimate religious identity of his teachings. While this erosion of Islamic identity fulfills the predictions of anti-Sufi fundamentalists, it is balanced by groups that insist upon Sufism as the true essence of Islam. Sufism has become a contested badge of identity, which is announced, performed, and disputed through all of the new forms of communication.

Sufism is a form of identity that was partially severed from Islam during the traumatic experience of European colonial domination over most of the rest of the world. It has been

---

[31] See the recording, "a gift of love: deepak & friends present music inspired by the love poems of rumi" (tommy boy music RCSD 3078), featuring readings by such celebrities as Deepak Chopra, Goldie Hawn, Madonna, Demi Moore, Rosa Parks, Martin Sheen, and Debra Winger.

defined by Orientalists, maligned by fundamentalists, and condemned as irrelevant by modernists. Yet it has proven to be a highly resilient symbolic system that has endured in local contexts even as it has been appropriated by cosmopolitan elites, both Muslim and non-Muslim. In private networks, publications, pop culture, and virtual communities, it may be expected to continue operating for the formation of identity and community in a variety of situations. And it is safe to say that Sufism will continue to be a formidable issue for Islamic identity in the foreseeable future.[32]

[32] For further reflections on this topic, see "Sufism, Islam, and Globalization in the Contemporary World: Methodological Reflections on a Changing Field of Study," chapter 25 in this volume.

25

Sufism, Islam, and Globalization in the Contemporary World: Methodological Reflections on a Changing Field of Study[1]

Sufism is often referred to as the mystical dimension of Islam; I prefer to describe it as a teaching of ethical and spiritual ideals, which has been historically embodied in lineages of teachers who held prominent positions in Muslim societies.[2] It was formerly understood in Orientalist scholarship as a spiritual movement that reached its apogee during the medieval period of Islamic history, with its crowning achievement being the brilliant literary productions in Arabic and Persian that became

[1] Earlier versions of this essay appeared as "Il sufismo nel mondo musulmano contemporaneo: la 'divulgazione del segreto,'" in *Sufismo e confraternite nell'islam contemporaneo: Il difficile equilibrio tra mistica e politica*, ed. Marietta Stepanyants, trans. Marco Cena (Turin, Italy: Edizioni della Fondazione Giovanni Agnelli, 2003), pp. 301–24; and in *Islamic Spirituality and the Contemporary World*, ed. Azizan Baharuddin (Kuala Lumpur: Centre for Civilisational Dialogue, University of Malaya, 2009).

[2] For a general survey, see my *Guide to Sufism* (Boston: Shambhala Publications, 2011).

the classics of the Sufi tradition. This "golden age" theory of Sufism, shared equally by modern reformist Muslim critics of Sufism, entailed as its corollary the inevitable degeneration of Sufism in more recent times. The study of Sufism also tended to privilege the "classical" sources in Arabic and Persian over the "folk" manifestations of Sufism in Turkish, Urdu, and other languages (the word "classic" has been imported into Persian and Urdu as *klasik*, while the Arabic word *turath*, or "heritage", serves the same purpose). It has only recently become possible to begin to locate this conceit in the historical conditions of modernity, in which academic discourse on Sufism and Islam forms part of a process involving European colonialism, the rise of Salafi reformism and fundamentalism, and secular modernism.[3]

In a study of the Chishti Sufi order, Bruce Lawrence and I have challenged the "golden age and decline" historiography of Sufism, which seems to be the result of a deep collusion between Orientalists and fundamentalists.[4] In particular, we have pointed to the realization among Sufi masters of the Chishti order that the ongoing challenges of each age must be met anew with spiritual resources and responses suitable to current needs. The following anecdote concerning the Chishti master Muhammad Chishti in the late sixteenth century (which today would be considered the period of decline) illustrates this problem, with reference to the central Chishti spiritual practice of listening to music (*sama`*):

> It is related of the revered Shaykh Hasan Muhammad that a man of Lahore came and said, "In this time there is no one worthy of listening to music (*sama`*)." [The master] replied, "If there were no one worthy of listening to music, the world would be destroyed." The man said, "In times past, there were men like Shaykh Nasir ad-Din [Chiragh-i Dihli], the Emperor of the Shaykhs [Nizam ad- Din Awliya'], and the revered [Farid ad-Din] Ganj-i Shakkar. Now there is no one like them." [The master] answered, "In their time, men said the very same thing."[5]

---

[3] Carl W. Ernst and Bruce B. Lawrence *Sufi Martyrs of Love: Chishti Sufism in South Asia and Beyond* (New York: Palgrave Press, 2002), esp. chapter 1; Carl W. Ernst, "Between Orientalism and Fundamentalism: Problematizing the Teaching of Sufism,"—chapter 1 in this volume; id., *Sufism*, esp. chapter 1.

[4] *Sufi Martyrs of Love.*

[5] Gul Muhammad Ahmadpuri, *Takmila-i siyar al-awliya'* (MS K. A. Nizami, Aligarh, India), fols. 43b-44a, cited in *Sufi Martyrs of Love*, p. 13.

The theme of decline is always with us, it seems. We caution our fellow scholars against the temptation to become Orientalist connoisseurs who praise the great Sufis of the past while looking disdainfully at contemporary Sufi leaders. If Ibn `Arabi or Rumi were alive today, would they simply replicate the powerful literary productions they designed for the thirteenth century, with its Mongol invasions, Crusades, and other catastrophes? For better or worse, Sufism as a spiritual repertoire today faces different challenges that undoubtedly call for different responses.

Modern Sufi groups have not, however, been passive observers of their fate. Like everyone else, they too have been caught up in the effects of what we now call globalization, the increasingly complex linkage of networks of every kind around the world. I begin from the premise that contemporary Sufis are no more immune to globalization than any other group; they too are affected by the commodification of religion in global capitalism, with its inevitable technological mediation of culture, communication, and personal relations.[6] Sufi groups have likewise participated in ecumenical consideration of inter-religious relations, though the necessarily local situation of each group dictates a wide variety of responses to religious pluralism. Sufis have actively contested the reformist claim to exclusive ownership of the symbolic capital of Islam. They have also refuted Orientalist scholarship that has typically viewed Sufism as a foreign doctrine grafted onto Islam.[7]

The most important local context for Sufism (as for religion in general) is the state, which everywhere is the ultimate authority that defines religion; whether the state attempts to outlaw Sufism or merely regulates its institutional centers, much of the energy of contemporary Sufi groups must go into negotiating the forms of their social existence within the limitations imposed by the state. Ideologically, Sufi groups like other subaltern traditions

---

[6] I presented an earlier analysis of this phenomenon in "Ideological and Technological Transformations of Contemporary Sufism," chapter 24 in this volume.

[7] Wahid Bakhsh Sial Rabbani, *Islamic Sufism: The Science of Flight in God, with God, by God and Union and Communion with God, Also showing the Tremendous Sufi Influence on Christian and Hindu Mystics and Mysticism* (Lahore: Sufi Foundation, 1984).

have had to negotiate a modus vivendi with respect to the intellectual basis of the European enlightenment and its sequels; this means that secularism, the prestige of modern science, and all the apparatus of modern societies (universities, the press, etc.) became contexts in which Sufism has had to find a place. In addition, Sufi groups have been involved in rethinking the politics of peace and war.

In addressing the main theme of this essay, however, it is important to raise several preliminary questions before proceeding with a brief and selective analysis of these factors. First, is it possible anymore to speak of a "Muslim world" as if it were an entity somehow separate from Europe and America (a.k.a. "the West")? I argue that this is no longer a meaningful concept, at least outside of neocolonial contexts.[8] Likewise, it is risky to make a diagnosis of the spiritual needs of the current age with an eye to Sufism as a potential cure. In this context, I would urge that considerable caution be taken to avoid making magisterial Orientalist pronouncements, which may have unforeseen effects of a political character. Scholarly study of religious movements like Sufism should have a descriptive character, rather than having the academy take it upon itself to issue prescriptive decrees on what is or is not an acceptable form of religion for other people. This being said, the following analysis will examine the interaction of global processes with local contexts, focusing on Sufism in both its traditional homelands and in its new Euro-American homes, and it will not be possible to make sweeping generalizations that apply in all cases. Although it may be said that all of the recent phenomena that have impacted Sufi groups are part of the larger process of globalization, that does not erase by any means the significance of locality. Indeed, the interaction between the local and the global always means that there are differential factors and outcomes, so that we cannot with any confidence predict uniformity among the Sufi responses to modernity.

---

[8] See my *Following Muhammad: Rethinking Islam in the Contemporary World* (Chapel Hill: University of North Carolina Press, 2003) for a critique of the notion of a "Muslim world".

Sufism and Globalization

For one of the most important aspects of globalization in relation to Sufism, we must look first, not to the traditional homelands of Sufism in the countries of Asia and Africa, but to the representation of Sufism in Europe and America; this example will help clarify how similar processes are also functioning in traditionally Muslim countries.[9] The most striking recent representation of Sufism has been the spectacular popularity of the poetry of the great Persian Sufi Jalaluddin Rumi, whose verse in modern English translation is said to be the best selling poetry in America. Through the efforts of gifted American poets like Robert Bly and Coleman Barks (followed by a host of less talented imitators), these new versions of Rumi have attracted the attention of some of the luminaries of American culture, ranging from journalist Bill Moyers to popular entertainers and actors such as Debra Winger, Martin Sheen, and even Madonna.[10] New Age guru Deepak Chopra has gotten into the act with his own "translation" of Rumi (with the aid of an Iranian associate) as well as a popular CD recording.[11] What is remarkable about these poems is the way that they present Rumi as an ecumenical figure who transcends any religion; both Islamic origins and Persian poetic conventions are downplayed, and the erotic and humorous aspects of his verse are emphasized.[12] Another distinctive feature of Rumi interpretation is the view that he and his teacher Shams-i Tabriz had a homosexual relationship.[13] This theory of "gay mysticism" plays into significant transformation of gender roles that are taking place in some modern societies,

---

[9] For a collection of studies on contemporary Sufism, see *Sufism in the West*, ed. Jamal Malik and John Hinnells (London: Routledge, 2006).

[10] For a critique of inferior translations of Rumi's poetry, see Ibrahim Gamard's website, http://www.dar-al-masnavi.org/.

[11] *The Love Poems of Rumi*, ed. Deepak Chopra, trans. Fereydoun Kia (New York: Harmony, 1998); *A Gift Of Love: Deepak & Friends Present Music Inspired by the Love Poems of Rumi* (Rasa Music CD 3078), containing recitations by Deepak Chopra, Madonna, Demi Moore, Martin Sheen, Blythe Danner, Goldie Hawn, Robert A. F. Thurman, and Rosa Parks.

[12] Olav Hammer, "Sufism for Westerners," in David Westerland, ed., *Sufism in Europe and North America* (London: Routledge Curzon, 2004), pp. 127–43.

[13] Although Andrew Harvey omits Rumi from his anthology, *The Essential Gay Mystics* (Book Sales, 1998), the Persian Sufi poets Sa`di, Hafiz, Attar, `Iraqi, and Jami are included.

which indeed it may be projecting onto the thirteenth-century mystic. In any case, what is striking is the way in which Rumi has become the touchstone for modern rethinking of identity in a non-authoritarian mode.

A parallel phenomenon is the widespread production and distribution of sound recordings of Sufi music, in a variety of formats ranging from sober and academic ethnomusicology to exuberant world-music recordings and fusion dance hits. The wildly popular crossover success of Pakistani vocalist Nusrat Fateh Ali Khan, who has appeared on Hollywood film scores, is a powerful testimony to the broad appeal of this particular tradition of Sufi music, based on the qawwali performance associated mainly with the Chishti order. Pakistani-American rock group Junoon is likewise determined to make the Punjabi lyrics of Sufi poet Bullhe Shah the basis for a message of liberation that can appeal to youth worldwide. Similar tendencies can be seen in Senegal, where the well-established Mouride Sufi brotherhood has had a powerful impact on music and popular culture over the past century. The influence of this Sufi tradition appears in musicians like Youssou N'dour, who has an enormous following in Europe, particularly France. Devotional performance of the Arabic and Wolof poems of Mouride founder Ahmadu Bamba is featured on fusion recordings made in Canada by Musa Dieng Kala.[14]

Both the print and audio dissemination of cultural products associated with Sufism illustrate a process that has been taking place in Muslim societies for at least a century and a half, which consists of the use of new technologies to publicize the previously esoteric teachings of Sufism; I call this process "the publication of the secret."[15] Another recent area of publicizing Sufism has occurred in relation to Sufi shrines and rituals, which governments increasingly view as sources of tourist revenue.

---

[14] Fiona McLaughlin, "Islam and Popular Music in Senegal: The Emergence of 'New Tradition,'" *Africa* 67 (1997), pp. 560–81; id., "'In the Name of God I will Sing Again, Mawdo Malik the Good': Popular Music and the Senegalese Sufi Tariqas," *Journal of Religion in Africa* 30 (2000), pp. 191–207; id., "Music for modern Muslims: Griots and Sufism in Senegal," *Africa* 67 (1997); Musa Dieng Kala, *Shakawtu - Faith* (Shanachie CD SHA-64072).

[15] See chapter 24 in this volume for further discussion of Sufism in print.

The revival of the whirling dervish dance in Turkey in 1954 was permitted only on condition that it be a purely aesthetic and cultural performance rather than a religious event. Visitors to Turkey today are greeted by innumerable cassettes, posters, and kitsch statuettes relating to Mevlana and the dervishes, with the annual festival of Rumi's death anniversary celebrated by the secular calendar on 17 December in Konya (for years held in a gymnasium rather than a Sufi lodge) as a major tourist draw. Music hall performances of the Whirling Dervishes in Turkey and in tours overseas are arranged by the Turkish Ministry of Culture, frequently in combination with concerts of classical Ottoman music. Yet the reception accorded the Whirling Dervishes is frequently at least as spiritual as it is aesthetic.[16] Uzbekistan, having recently rediscovered its Islamic past after decades of official Soviet atheism, has taken to promoting pious pilgrimage to sites like the tomb of Baha'uddin Naqshband in Bukhara, as seen in a film produced by the Foreign Trade Association of Bukhara.[17]

This commodification of Sufism needs to be juxtaposed with the similar objectification and reification of Islam.[18] This is a significant process that has all but escaped noticed in many Muslim countries, and it has certainly gone over the heads of Euro-American journalists (as W. C. Smith trenchantly observed, it used to be that Muslims believed in God, but now they believe in Islam). A striking instance is the constitution of the Islamic Republic of Iran, in which Islam is defined as ideology (using the Persian neologism *idiuluzhi*, a transliteration of the French idéologie). If this is not a radical transformation of the notion of Islam, it is hard to imagine what would be. But perhaps the most spectacular example comes from Pakistan, which since its founding in 1947 has struggled to define itself as an Islamic state. One of the most contentious issues among the many sectarian

---

16 See the memoirs of Turkish Mevlevi musician Kudsi Erguner, *La Fontaine de la Séparation: Voyages d'un musicien Soufi* (Paris: Le Bois d'Orion, 2001); English trans., *Journeys of a Sufi Musician* (London: Saqi Books, 2006).

17 "Beaming One," (Ozma Productions for the Foreign Trade Association, City of Bokhara, 1993). A copy is available in the Media Resource Center of the library of the University of North Carolina, catalog no. V4816.

18 On the objectification of Islam in recent times, see Dale F. Eickelman and James Piscatori, *Muslim Politics* (Princeton, NJ: Princeton University Press, 1996), especially chapter 2.

disputes that have troubled the state has been the status of the Ahmadi sect. This group has tested the boundaries of orthodoxy because of claims that the nineteenth-century founder, Mirza Ghulam Ahmad, could have been a prophet after Muhammad (many Muslims regard the prophethood of Muhammad as the final revelation, so that any claimant to prophecy is typically looked upon with great suspicion). In 1974, the government of President Z. A. Bhutto passed a law that declared Ahmadis (also called Qadianis) to be non-Muslims. Subsequent challenges to this law, on the basis of fundamental rights guaranteed by Pakistan's constitution, succeeded in calling it into question.

A major reversal of religious rights in Pakistan took place, however, in a 1993 decision that perhaps for the first time actually spelled out a detailed governmental definition of Islam. The presiding judge declared that the symbols and rites of Islam (such as the profession of faith, and buildings called mosques) were the equivalent of intellectual property that could be copyrighted by the rightful owners, although he never spelled out just how such claims of ownership could be established. Therefore anyone who improperly recited the profession of faith, or called their place of worship a mosque, was in effect using a copyrighted logo without permission, and was liable to legal penalties.[19] The implications of this decision are breathtaking. Not only is a religion being defined as a commodity or piece of property, which the judge actually compared to Coca-Cola, but also the courts—not religious communities—are entitled to decide what is essential to any religion. Moreover, in this decision the limits of Islam are being characterized in relation to a sectarian group. Current Pakistani passports now require professed Muslim citizens to sign a declaration that they adhere to the finality of the prophethood of Muhammad, i.e., that they are not Ahmadis. Such an outcome (reminiscent of oaths of orthodox interpretation of Holy Communion during the Protestant Reformation) can only be imagined as a result of very recent local history, especially

[19] Martin Lau, "Islam and Fundamental Rights in Pakistan: The case of Zaheer-ud-din v. The State and its impact on the fundamental right to freedom of religion," *Centre of Islamic and Middle Eastern Law Yearbook* 1 (1994), available online at http://www.soas.ac.uk/Centres/IslamicLaw/YB1Zaheer-uprintd-din.html.

when religion is reduced to the status of a brand name. It recalls the pontification of the Egyptian parliament in the 1980s on the question of whether the Sufi writings of Ibn `Arabi should be considered as contrary to Islam; this is another example of how the modern state defines religion, in this case banning the works of the Andalusian mystic as un-Islamic.[20]

The production of items like books and recordings is by no means the only form of technological change that has affected Sufism. While television remains under government control in Middle Eastern countries, and film has had only occasional use for purposes connected with Sufism, the Internet boasts a robust Sufi presence, with dozens if not hundreds of websites representing Sufi traditions from all over the world.[21] And in another sign of Sufi presence on the Internet, one can now take advantage of several Sufi blogs, including one (http://sufinews.blogspot.com/) maintained by an academic specialist on Sufism, Prof. Alan Godlas.

Whatever may be the social realities of those individuals and groups who profess the Sufi ideal, Sufism as an academic concept is undeniably a child of the Enlightenment, one more in the large series of ideological and religious "isms" given nominal existence by European encyclopedists. How have the actual participants in Sufi traditions responded to this type of scholarly categorization? One trend has been the wholesale rejection of the Enlightenment and modernity among circles of Sufi-influenced thinkers who advocate the notion of a Perennial Philosophy, or Tradition. These authors include Huston Smith, Sayyed Hossein Nasr, René Guenon, and Frithjof Schuon.[22] The origins of this philosophy may

---

[20] Th. Emil Homerin, "Ibn `Arabi in the People's Assembly: Religion, Press, and Politics in Sadat's Egypt." *Middle East Journal* 80:4 (Summer, 1986), pp. 462–77.

[21] In Indonesia, remarkably, a popular television program on Sufism ("Tasawuf") began appearing in May 2000, featuring interviews of Sufi laypeople plus commentary by academic experts on Sufism; see Julia Day Howell, "Sufism and the Indonesian Islamic Revival," *Journal of Asian Studies* 60 (2001), pp. 701–29, citing p. 720, n. 35. For Sufism on the Internet, see chapter 24 in this volume.

[22] Marcia Hermansen, "In the Garden of American Sufi Movements: Hybrids and Perennials," in *New Trends and Developments in the World of Islam*, ed. Peter Clarke (London: Luzac Oriental Press, 1997), pp. 155–78; Carl W. Ernst, "Traditionalism, the Perennial Philosophy, and Islamic Studies," *Middle East Studies Association Bulletin*, vol. 28, no. 2 (December 1994), pp. 176–81; Mark Sedgwick, *Against the Modern World: Traditionalism and*

be traced to the Traditionalist position developed by a number of ultramontane French Catholic thinkers of the nineteenth century, and it elevated tradition (particularly the Catholic Church) to a position of divine and absolute authority. What is especially relevant here is that, despite their theoretical respect for Catholicism, most of the adherents of the Perennial Philosophy were attracted to Islam. Disenchantment with the excesses of the European Enlightenment and modernism (particularly colonialism, racism, scientism, nationalism, and secularism) would seem to be the primary reason for this attraction. Against this promethean enterprise the Perennialists held out the more-than-human authority of primordial revelation, divine gnosis adapted providentially to different circumstances in the form of religions, and a devolutionistic view of history that sees modernity as a debased and demonic revolt against reality. With these premises in mind, one can see how Islam as a sacred tradition, and Sufi metaphysics as its exposition, would naturally occupy the central position. The Islamic theological emphasis on unity, the historiographic concept of Islam as final revelation in a sequence of prophetic dispensations, and the oppositional position of Islamic countries as the largest bloc undergoing European colonization, all make Islam a natural standpoint for Traditionalists seeking an authentic affiliation. The Traditionalist perspective is now shared principally by a small but influential number of mostly Muslim intellectuals in Europe and America, but increasingly also in other countries such as Pakistan and Malaysia.

There are other manifestations of Sufi-influenced criticism of the Enlightenment that are harder to classify. One is the Murabitun movement led by `Abd al-Qadir al-Murabit (formerly known as Ian Dallas, author of a popular Sufi-style autobiographical novel, *The Book of Strangers*).[23] In part a development of the Shadhili-Darqawi Sufi order of North Africa, combined with an insistence on the Maliki school of Islamic law, this movement has been active in Europe, the US, and Mexico. Members of this movement reject Hobbesian theories of politics and advocate a

---

the Secret Intellectual History of the Twentieth Century (New York: Oxford University Press, 2004).

[23] Ian Dallas, *The Book of Strangers* (Albany: State University of New York Press, 1989).

return to the principles of the Sokoto caliphate established in West Africa in the eighteenth century by Shaykh `Uthman dan Fodio.[24] The former website of this group (http://www.murabitun.org) was, remarkably, esoteric; in late 2002, only authorized members had permission to view the website. Even more individualistic Sufi-inspired critiques of the Enlightenment and globalization can be found in the anarchist manifestoes of Hakim Bey (Peter L. Wilson).[25] All these examples demonstrate the variety of ways in which Sufi themes are inflected with the accents of globalizing modernity.

Sufism and Ecumenism

As sociologist Bryan Turner has pointed out, globalization can engender two main kinds of ideological responses, one being a retrenchment to local and traditional identities, and the other being an embrace of universal tendencies already found in the tradition.[26] In modern Sufi movements, we can see many examples of the latter kind of universalistic response, particularly in the cluster of European and American movements associated with Hazrat Inayat Khan. An Indian master associated particularly with the Chishti order, Inayat Khan made the momentous decision to present Sufism to Europeans and Americans as a spiritual path that was not necessarily tied to Islam. More than most of his contemporaries, he grasped the depth of the enormous prejudice against Islam in Europe and America, and concluded that his message of spirituality would be far more effective if presented in a different way. With over a hundred centers in America, the Sufi Order in the West (now led by Pir Zia Inayat

---

[24] Aisha Abdurrahman Bewley, "The Natural State," available online at http://bewley.virtualave.net/Page2.html. This website also contains extensive excerpts from the writings of `Abd al-Qadir al-Murabit.

[25] Hakim Bey, *T. A. Z.: The Temporary Autonomous Zone, Ontological Anarchy, Poetic Terrorism* (Brooklyn, NY: Autonomedia, 1991); Peter Lamborn Wilson, *Scandal: Studies in Islamic Heresy* (New York: Autonomedia, 1988); id., *Sacred Drift: Essays on the Margins of Islam* (San Francisco, CA: City Lights Books, 1993).

[26] Bryan Turner, *Orientalism, Postmodernism, and Globalism* (London and New York: Routledge, 1994), esp. pp. 77–114.

Khan, grandson of the founder) is probably the largest single Sufi group in the USA, yet it is striking that neither shari`a practice nor distinctively Islamic beliefs play an important role for this movement.[27] A comparable emphasis on universality is found in the teachings of Mehmet Sherif Catalkaya er-Rifai, a Turkish Sufi master of the Rifai-Marufi Fellowship. True Sufism delves beyond religion, Sherif Baba said in a lecture at the University of Arkansas. "What brings people together, what allows the love of God to enter the hearts of people, is morality. . . . All religions are the same," Sherif Baba said. "Sufism isn't religion. It is the love of humanity." Nonetheless, this Rifa`i group places considerable importance on the veneration of the Prophet Muhammad and on the 99 beautiful names of God as the sources of ethics, and includes observation of Islamic rituals such as the fast of Ramadan, so its universalism is combined with a recognition of the primacy of Islamic themes. Another example of a Sufi group offering a universalist perspective is Muhammad Zuhri, an Indonesian master who has created a website (http://www.barzakh.net/) offering to contribute prayers on behalf of those suffering from HIV-AIDS, regardless of their religious affiliation. All one has to do is to contact the website, and then at an agreed upon time pray (in whatever manner one wishes) while the Indonesian Sufi master does the same. This is an interesting example of inter-religious engagement in the form of service by Sufis for a virtual cyber-community. While universalistic tendencies are quite noticeable in some Sufi movements in Europe and America, it should be acknowledged that others insist on shari`a practice, and even include the wearing of clothing from the order's country of origin as a normal feature of membership.[28]

An additional dimension of universalism is the relationship between Sufi orders, which is characterized both by rivalry and by collaboration. It has been observed that intra-order schisms

---

[27] Pirzade Zia Inayat Khan, ed., *A Pearl in Wine: Essays on the Life, Music and Sufism of Hazrat Inayat Khan* (New Lebanon, NY: Omega Press, 2001).

[28] Marcia Hermansen has also pointed to the phenomenon of gradualism in several American Sufi orders, in which complete conversion to Islam is not demanded all at once, but gradual adoption of Islamic practices is encouraged; see Hermansen, "What's American about American Sufi Movements?", in Westerlund, pp. 33–63, citing p. 43.

and competition between orders were in fact the order of the day in Iran during much of the nineteenth and twentieth centuries.[29] In this respect one of the new phenomena is a congress of Sufi orders that has taken place in North America annually over the past five years, under the auspices of the International Association for Sufism, a primarily Iranian group headed by Dr. Nahid Angha, a professional psychologist. This Sufi conference has brought together Sufi groups of all different perspectives from a variety of different national origins (Iranian, Turkish, Bangladeshi, Senegalese, etc.), with different degrees of emphasis on Islamic shari`a practice and customs. The focus of these conferences is not academic lectures but zikr performance and proclamations of universal brotherhood (and sisterhood, given the prominence of women in these meetings). This kind of eclectic meeting of different Sufi orders is repeated on a smaller scale in other gatherings taking place around America, as for instance at the tomb of Baba Muhaiyaddeen near Philadelphia, reflecting the dictum that ultimately all the different paths to God are one. At the same time, it should be noted that the sponsor organization of the Sufi conference, the International Association for Sufism, has been engaged in a legal dispute with the Maktab-e Tariqa-e Oveissi-e Shahmaghsoudi over the succession to the authority of the late Nader Angha, founder of that order; this dispute has ended up focusing on the issue of intellectual property and ownership of logos and trademarks, a further example of commodification of religion.[30] Leadership disputes thus remain a potential source of conflict within and among the Sufi orders.

Another aspect of the ideological adaptation of Sufism to globalization has been a strong interest in feminism and the

---

[29] Leonard Lewisohn, "Tasawwuf. 5. In Persia from 1800 onwards," *Encyclopaedia of Islam* (Leiden: E. J. Brill, 1999), X:326–32, esp. 330a. A fuller version of this article is available: Leonard Lewisohn, "An Introduction to the History of Modern Persian Sufism," *Bulletin of the School for Oriental and African Studies* 61 (1998), pp. 437–64; 62 (1999), pp. 36–59.

[30] Maktab Tarighe Oveyssi Shah Maghsoudi, Inc.; Nader Angha, Plaintiffs-Appellants, v. Ali Kianfar; Nahid Kianfar; International Association of Sufism, Inc., Defendants-Appellees (No. 96-15002, United States Court of Appeals for the Ninth Circuit, D.C. No. CV-95-02881-DLJ; Appeal from the United States District Court for the Northern District of California, Decided: June 17, 1999).

historic role of women in the Sufi orders.[31] One can point to the prominent positions of women in many Sufi groups in Europe and America, including positions of leadership with the title of *shaykha*, as examples of this trend. The dissemination of the practice of the Mevlevi turning dance now includes many women performers (*sema-zans*), who have been fully trained in the ritual according to traditional forms. American women in this Mevlevi tradition have recreated what is in effect a parallel female initiatic lineage that parallels the standard patriarchal *silsila* or chain of male teachers that constitutes the backbone of the Sufi order. By delving into the early history of the Mevlevi order, and reconstructing the role of women in the circle of Rumi himself, these modern women Sufis have produced an interesting new interpretation of gender roles in Sufism.[32] At the same time, it should be noticed that women in Turkish Sufi circles have also come into their own in recent years, as we see for example in the Halveti Cerrahi charitable foundation in Istanbul.[33] There is also a prominent circle of female Sufi teachers in the lineage of Turkish Sufi leader Kenan Rifai (d. 1950).[34] One such prominent teacher, Cemalnur Sargut, has brought groups of up to 40 disciples (mostly well-educated women) from Istanbul to the US to participate in the Rumi Festival in Chapel Hill NC on more than one occasion.[35] It is probably safe to say that the participation of women in Sufi orders is a subject that still remains relatively unexplored, but at the same time the changes in gender roles

---

[31] Camille Adams Helminski, "Women & Sufism," *Gnosis* #30 (Winter 1994); Lynn Wilcox, *Women and the holy Qur'an: a Sufi perspective* (Riverside, CA: M. T. O. Shahmaghsoudi, 1998); Muhammad ibn al-Husayn Sulami, *Early Sufi women: Dhikr an-niswa al-muta'abbidat as-Sufiyyat*, trans. Cornell, Rkia Elaroui (Louisville, KY: Fons Vitae, 1999); Shemeem Burney Abbas, *The Female Voice in Sufi Ritual: Devotional Practices of Pakistan and India* (Austin, TX: University of Texas Press, 2002); Karen Ask and Marit Tjomsland, ed., *Women and Islamization: Contemporary Dimensions of Discourse on Gender Relations* (Oxford: Berg, 1998); Carl W. Ernst, *Teachings of Sufism* (Boston: Shambhala Publications, 1999), pp. 179–99.

[32] Shakina Reinhertz, *Women Called to the Path of Rumi: The Way of the Whirling Dervish* (Prescott, AZ: Hohm Press, 2001), esp. pp. 15–28.

[33] Catharina Raudvere, *The Book and the Roses: Sufi Women, Visibility and Zikr in Contemporary Istanbul* (London: I. B. Tauris, 2003).

[34] See http://www.kenan-rifai.org.

[35] See the web site of Cemalnur Sargut at http://www.cemalnur.org, with extensive biographies of women connected to this Sufi group.

that are occurring worldwide are bound to have transformative effects on traditional Muslim societies where Sufism still flourishes.

Sufism and the State

One of the most notable aspects of the history of Sufism in the modern period was that of resistance to colonial invasions by foreign (largely European) powers. Prominent examples of this defensive militancy include the Sanusis in Libya until Qadhdhafi, the Mahdists in the Sudan, Shaykh Shamil in the Caucasus, `Abd al-Qadir al-Jaza'iri in Algeria, and many others. The elimination of local elites by superior European military power often left the Sufi orders as the only organizations capable of mounting resistance against invaders. While the memory of this kind of Sufi defensive jihad lives on most strongly perhaps in Chechnya and nearby territories, that day is for the most part now gone, as first the colonial, and then the postcolonial state assumed greater and greater power over the lives of their citizens. Part of this process has involved the bureaucratic control of Sufi orders by the centralized government, with special attention to regulation of shrine festivals and the revenue collected by the shrines. Without going into the administrative details of how the regulation of Sufism is handled in countries like Pakistan and Egypt, we can nevertheless point out that this means Sufism is necessarily defined in its social and bureaucratic form by local government policies.[36]

Both the colonial and postcolonial state have agreed in regarding Sufism with considerable ambivalence.[37] On the one

[36] Edward B Reeves, *The Hidden Government: Ritual, Clientelism, and Legitimation in Northern Egypt* (Salt Lake City: University of Utah Press, 1990); 'Ammar 'Ali Hasan, *al-Sufiyah wa-al-siyasah fi Misr* (al-Ma'adi [Cairo]: Markaz al-Mahrusah lil-Buhuth wa-al-Tadrib wa-al-Nashr, 1997); Taoufik Bachrouch, *Les élites tunisiennes du pouvoir et de la dévotion: contribution à l'étude des groupes sociaux dominants, 1782-1881* ([Tunis]: Université de Tunis, 1989); Leonardo Alfonso Villalón, *Islamic society and state power in Senegal: disciples and citizens in Fatick* (Cambridge; New York: Cambridge University Press, 1995).

[37] For the case of Sufism in Pakistan, see especially Katherine Pratt Ewing, *Arguing Sainthood: Modernity, Psychoanalysis, and Islam* (Durham, NC: Duke University Press, 1997).

hand, Sufism has been increasingly viewed from a modernist perspective as containing elements of irrational superstition and disorder that need to be restrained. Idiosyncratic traditions of local practice are also criticized as being foreign to the central canonical texts and teachings of Islam. Class enters into the picture, as middle- and upper-class Muslims increasingly partake of either European secular education or reformist interpretations of Islam; from either perspective, participants at large Sufi festivals appear to be misguided members of an uneducated lower class. For precisely the same reason, Sufism still functions as a symbol of resistance against dogmatic authority among small numbers of well-educated Muslims who see in it the possibility of a larger worldview than that proposed either by the `ulama' or the salafi reformists.

On a case-by-case local basis, one can lay out a program for research on contemporary Sufism and its role in particular countries, from colonial times through the present. There is, for example, the marginalization of Sufi leaders in Afghanistan by the Pakistani and American patrons of the anti-Soviet jihad in the 1980s.[38] There is also the example of the immensely popular Maijbhandari Sufi order in Bangladesh, which has had a major effect particularly on local government in relation to its seat in Chittagong, as well as influencing the national government.[39] Then there is the at-first-sight surprising emphasis on spiritual nationalism among the Sabiri Chishtis of Pakistan, who have predicted military supremacy for the Pakistan armed forces if they correctly follow the national destiny as charted out by modern Sufis, particularly Capt. Wahid Bakhsh Sial Rabbani.[40] This emphasis on politics among the Sabiri Chishtis goes back to

[38] Almut Wieland, *Islamische Mystik in Afghanistan: die strukturelle Einbindung der Sufik in die Gesellschaft* (Stuttgart: F. Steiner, 1998).

[39] Peter J. Bertocci, "Form and Variation in Maijbhandari Sufism," paper prepared for the conference on "The Work of the Imaginaire in South Asian Islam," North Carolina State University, 12–14 April, 2002; id., "A Sufi Movement in Modern Bangladesh," *Oakland Journal* (Fall 2001), available online at http://www2.oakland.edu/oujournal/files/Bertocci.pdf.

[40] Robert Rozehnal, "Faqir or Faker?: The Public Battle Over Sufism in Contemporary Pakistan," in *Visions of Community: The South Asian Muslim Imaginaire*, ed. David Gilmartin, Bruce B. Lawrence and Tony Stewart (Gainesville: University Press of Florida,

Sayyid Zauqi Shah (d. 1950), who carried on an extensive correspondence with Muhammad Ali Jinnah. His biography portrays him as the inner or spiritual founder of Pakistan, in parallel with Jinnah, who was the external founder.[41] A different example that has not yet been analyzed is the case of the Sufi-oriented Darul Arqam organization, banned in Malaysia since 1994.[42] There is much material available on relations between Sufism and the state in Senegal and Mauritania.[43] Iran, as usual, is a special case. The transformation of Persia into a Shi`i nation by the Sufi-based Safavi movement has left a deeply ambiguous situation, in which philosophical mysticism (*`irfan*) is valued, while institutional Sufism and dervish orders are considered highly questionable.[44] In an example of official enmity towards Sufism, in February 2006, Iranian government forces destroyed a center of the Gonabadi Sufi order in the holy city of Qom, and among the hundreds of dervishes arrested, many were reportedly forced to pronounce public abjurations of Sufism.[45] In India, heavy-handed political agendas can be detected in attempts to locate Sufism as a potential antidote to Muslim fundamentalism and communal violence.[46] At the same time, underprivileged Dalit

---

forthcoming); id., "Islamic Sufism Unbound: Tracing Contemporary Chishti Sabiri Identity," Ph.D. dissertation, Duke University, 2003.

[41] Shah Sayyid Muhammad Zauqi, *Tarbiyat al-`ushshaq*, comp. Shahid Allah Faridi, ed. Wahid Bakhsh Siyal (Karachi: Mahfil-i Zauqiyya, 1393/1974), pp. 76–78 (introduction); Syed Muhammad Zauqi Shah, *Letters of a Sufi Saint to Jinnah* (Lahore: Talifat-i Shaheedi, 1998).

[42] Ahmad Fauzi Abdul Hamid, "The Futuristic Thought of Ustaz Ashaari Muhammad of Malaysia," in *The Blackwell Companion to Contemporary Islamic Thought*, ed. Ibrahim Abu-Rabi (Oxford: Blackwell Publishers Ltd, 2006). In the 1980s, Darul Arqam was seen as one of the three most important independent Islamic organizations in Malaysia, along with ABIM and the Tablighi Jama`at; see Judith Nagata, *The Reflowering of Malaysian Islam: Modern Religious Radicals and Their Roots* (Vancouver: University of British Columbia Press, 1984), esp. pp. 104–16.

[43] David Robinson, *Paths of Accommodation: Muslim Societies and French Colonial Authorities in Senegal and Mauritania, 1880–1920* (Athens, OH: Ohio State University Press, 2000).

[44] Matthijs van den Bos, *Mystic Regimes: Sufism and the State in Iran, from the Late Qajar Era to the Islamic Republic* (Leiden: Brill, 2002).

[45] The Amnesty International report on this incident is available online at http://www.amnestyusa.org/news/document.do?id=ENGMDE130162006.

[46] Syeda Saiyidain Hameed, ed., *Contemporary Relevance of Sufism* (New Delhi: Indian Council for Cultural Relations, 1993); Asgharali Engineer, ed., *Sufism and Communal Harmony* (Jaipur: Printwell, 1991).

("untouchable") groups in the Indian Punjab have been seizing on the message of Punjabi Sufis to support a progressive socialist agenda to combat caste and gender discrimination in India.[47]

The problem of Sufism and politics was the subject of a wide-ranging discussion in an April 2000 workshop on "Muslim Intellectuals and Modern Challenges" held at the Institute for the Study of Islam in the Modern World in Leiden. In response to the proposal of Indonesian scholar Jalaluddin Rakhmat that Sufism could serve as a source for Islamic liberalism, thinkers like Abdolkarim Soroush argued that Sufism inevitably tends toward charismatic authoritarianism; in his view, the ascendancy of Khomeini's ideas in the current Iranian regime shows the danger of allowing Sufism to penetrate into politics.[48] I would argue, however, that local situations inevitably trump sociological generalizations about the political role of Sufism; scholars should suspend judgment until it is clear exactly how a given Sufi movement will function within its own local environment.

Sufism and the Politics of Peace

While the historical legacy of Sufism in the early colonial period included many examples of military resistance to foreign invaders, the shackling of Sufi groups by the modern nation-state has put an end to militant activities for the most part (although the Sabiri Chishtis in Pakistan provide an interesting example of a Sufi concept of nationalist military might). Islamic militancy, once linked to dervishes and marabouts, is now firmly ensconced in fundamentalist and salafi circles. Any consideration of Sufi involvement in issues of war and peace needs to take into account the wider debates about jihad in Muslim circles over the

[47] This phenomenon is described in "Kitte Mil Ve Mahi (Where the Twain Shall Meet)," a Punjabi film with English subtitles directed and produced by Ajay Bhardwaj (India Foundation for the Arts, 2005), reviewed by Arshia Sattar (http://indiadocu.blogspot.com/).

[48] A detailed summary of this conference is available online at http://files.meetup.com/218224/muslim_intellectuals_report.doc, in the discussion of paper no. 8, Jalaluddin Rakhmat, "The Revival of Sufism: Does it help? A glance at the Modern Sufi Associations in Indonesia."

past two centuries. In many cases, it would be fair to say that Sufi groups have tended toward liberal interpretations of jihad as defensive warfare, rejecting unprovoked military aggression against non-Muslims. There are important exceptions, however, and it would be a mistake to indulge in apologetics here.[49] Under the circumstances of late postcolonial globalization, then, what roles have Sufis taken in relation to international political conflict and peace activism?

One notable example was Bawa Muhaiyaddeen (d. 1986), the Sri Lankan Sufi master who spent the last years of his life in Philadelphia, and who is buried in a tomb on a Pennsylvania farm. He was disturbed by the interpretation of Islam that underlay the 1978–79 Iranian revolution, and he felt that this climactic event provided a confrontational and militant image of Islam that distorted what he saw as the universal Islamic emphasis on peace. While not engaging in a direct critique of the political thought of Khomeini and the ideologues of the Iranian revolution, Bawa Muhaiyaddeen wrote a treatise on Islam and peace that was in effect a defense of the peaceful vision of Islam.[50]

Another instance of Sufi involvement in politics was Shaykh Hisham Kabbani's establishment of the Islamic Supreme Council of America as yet another branch of his multi-pronged Naqshbandi organization. This organization is defined as follows:

> The Islamic Supreme Council of America (ISCA) is a non-profit, non-governmental religious organization dedicated to working for the cause of Islam. ISCA aims to provide practical solutions for American Muslims, based on the traditional Islamic legal rulings of an international advisory board, many of whom are recognized as the highest

---

[49] The similarities between the al-Qa'ida organization of Usama bin Laden and Sufi-style jihad have been discussed by James Howarth, "Al-Qaida, globalisation and Islam: a response to Faisal Devji" (http://www.opendemocracy.net/conflict-middle_east_politics/al-qaida_3200.jsp); and Juan Cole, "Al-Qaeda's Doomsday Document and Psychological Manipulation" (http://interlinkconsulting.com/Bonus_Info/Doomsday%20Document-Atta's%20Letter%20and%20Al%20Qaeda-Comment%20by%20Dr.%20Juan%20Cole.pdf), both internet sites accessed 17 December 2016.

[50] M. R. Bawa Muhaiyaddeen, *Islam & World Peace* (Philadelphia, PA: Fellowship Press, 2002).

> ranking Islamic scholars in the world. For the first time in America, we have tried to integrate traditional scholarship in resolving contemporary issues affecting the maintenance of Islamic beliefs in a modern, secular society.

Considered in the context of Shaykh Kabbani's extensive ongoing polemics against Wahhabi and salafi interpretations of Islam, and despite the bland language of its mission statement, the very name of this organization was a deliberate challenge to the authority of Saudi-financed Islamic institutions in America.[51] Early on after its formation, in an apparent bid for influence with the American government, ISCA was somehow invited to give a briefing on Islamic issues for the US State Department. This event aroused the ire of Kabbani's opponents, who charged him with being willing to sell out Muslim interests in order to become the pet of the American government. Attacks made against this group[52] have raised charges reminiscent of suspicions of the Ahmadi movement in Pakistan, whose ecumenical and spiritual understanding of jihad is still widely believed to have been inspired by the British in an effort to undermine Islam and any principled Islamic resistance against British colonial rule. In any case, there continues to be interest in certain US government circles on Sufism as a form of Islam that can be made compatible with American interests.[53]

In many countries of the Middle East, religion and politics since the colonial period have had explosive results, nowhere more vividly displayed than in multi-religious Lebanon during its murderous civil war of the 1980s. While the world is most familiar with the violent activities of groups like the Shi`i

---

[51] For a synthesis of this polemic against Wahhabis, see Muhammad Hisham Kabbani, *Encyclopedia of Islamic doctrine* (8 vols., Mountainview, CA: As-Sunna Foundation of America, 2nd ed., 1998); see also http://www.sunnah.org.

[52] Open Letter to Hisham Kabbani, circulated on alt.sufi newsgroup, 20 July 1998.

[53] Zeyno Baran, ed., "Understanding Sufism and its Potential Role in US Policy," a report on an October 2003 conference sponsored by the Nixon Center of Washington, D.C., which featured academic presentations plus a dialogue between Shaykh Kabbani and U.S. Middle East adviser Bernard Lewis (available online at http://www.hudson.org/research/3977-understanding-sufism-and-its-potential-role-in-us-policy, accessed 17 December 2016).

Hizbollah and the Christian Phalangists, it is instructive to see that one particular Lebanese Sufi group of African origin, the Ahbash movement, had a program of religious pluralism and peace within the framework of the secular state.

> Indeed, by positioning themselves as a non-militant alternative to the Islamists, the Ahbash have emerged as a Sunni middle-class movement that attracts intellectuals, professionals, and businessmen, particularly the traditional Sunni commercial families of the urban centers. Among these social groups, the Ahbash call for religious moderation, political civility, and peace has had a powerful resonance after fifteen years of civil war and bloodshed. Indeed, there has been a convergence between the values, aspirations, and socioeconomic interests of the Sunni middle classes and the contents of Shaykh Habashi's message-that is, intersectarian accord and political stability; an enlightened Islamic spiritualism within a modern secularist framework; a Lebanese identity wedded to Arab nationalism; and an accommodating attitude toward the Arab regimes, particularly the Syrian government.[54]

Of course, this remains one voice among many in a society as diverse as Lebanon.

A more recent example of Sufi peace efforts is Sheikh Abdoulaye Dieye of Senegal, a leader of the Mourides. He has been a prominent participant in ecumenical congresses of religious leaders of different faiths, and he is distinctive particularly for seeking out Jewish rabbis for discussions of common religious values, in search of a solution for the Palestine conflict. In a wide-ranging declaration made in California in February 2002, he touched on issues such as ecology, poverty, and the effects of globalization, before making these interesting remarks on the quest for peace:

> Many wars have been waged in the name of religions but the real reason for these armed conflicts and other acts of violence are only greed and the desire for power. This is true for Muslims and Islam, for the Jews and Judaism as well as for Christians and Christianity. . . . Let the Jewish and Muslim scholars meet in a part of the globe to ask for peace and reconciliation between these two nations. At the dawn of this millennium

---

[54] A. Nizar Hamzeh and R. Hrair Dekmejian, "A Sufi Response to Political Islamism: Al-Ahbash of Lebanon," *International Journal of Middle East Studies* 28 (1996), 217–29.

> when it has been proved that violence merely aggravates the conflict and politicians can only acknowledge their inadequacy, I appeal to Muslim Sufis and Jewish Rabbis to find common grounds for better relations. Let them pray together, so that God Who is Merciful and Gracious, extinguishes with the flow of His Mercy all the areas seething with conflicts in the Middle East and the fire of despair that is consuming the heart of so many women, children and men.[55]

It is noteworthy that Sheikh Dieye feels that it is the Sufi leaders who must step forward to represent Islam in this challenging encounter for the sake of peace. Based on an ecumenical recognition of the legitimacy of Jewish and Christian revelations and religious practice, this Sufi appeal completely bypasses the established `ulama' as well as the fundamentalists in an urgent effort to reach the heart of religion for the sake of all humanity.

Conclusion

The Enlightenment and its avatars, modernity and globalization, constructed Islam and Sufism as separate categories that it could confront or absorb as circumstances required. Its deep collusion with its conflictive partner, Salafi reformism, has led to a defensive incorporation of European ideologies in Muslim societies, principally Protestant scripturalism and rationalist fundamentalism. In this way, modern Islam fulfilled the Enlightenment definition of religion, even while resisting it. At the same time, the fixation on a medieval golden age of Sufism worked to the advantage both of colonial Orientalism and to anticolonial reformists and fundamentalists. In the contemporary situation, Sufism has been officially pushed into a dubious and marginal posture, while still providing spiritual and intellectual tools that

[55] "Declaration of La Jolla, California," document circulated on Internet by International Sufi School of the revered master Sheikh Abdoulaye Dieye. The latter is also author of a book, *Touba: Signs and Symbols* (1997), on the significance of the Mouride pilgrimage city in Touba, Senegal, plus several works on Mouride history: *Le centenaire du Jihad al-akbar, 1895–1995* ([Sénégal], 1979); *Sur les traces de Cheikh Ahmadou Bamba: l'exile au Gabon, période coloniale 1895–1902* (Paris: Ed. Ndigel, 1985); *L'histoire du Cheikh Ahmadou Bamba, "Serviteur du prophète"* [a children's book] (Paris: CDG Creations, 1990).

hold their appeal in many diverse and irreducibly local contexts related to religion and politics.

The study of contemporary Sufism requires scholars trained as traditional Orientalists to reappraise their ambiguous position vis-à-vis the subject of their research, as do other scholars in religious studies.[56] No longer is it possible for the scholar to claim an Olympian posture of detachment based on the study of ancient texts and foreign lands. As anthropologists are required to submit "human subjects" research proposals to Institutional Review Boards, so scholars in religious studies investigating contemporary movements need to scrutinize their ethical responsibilities.[57] Scholarly research on Sufism can have direct political effects on lineage disputes within orders, Sufi debates with reformists, inter-religious dialog, and state policies toward Sufis; Sufis themselves are quite aware of these potential political effects of scholarship.[58] All these factors call for self-critical thinking about the positioning of scholars.

If Euro-American scholars, as representatives of the Enlightenment, decide to promote their concept of Sufism as a tameable form of Islam, this risks the possibility of delegitimizing Sufism, both in its traditional homes and in its new immigrant abodes, making it seem fully a tool of neocolonialism or state policy.[59] Instead of following that script, we need to join

[56] Thomas Tweed, "Between the Living and the Dead: Fieldwork, History, and the Interpreter's Position," in *Personal Knowledge and Beyond: Reshaping the Ethnography of Religion*, eds James V. Spickard, J. Shawn Landres, and Meredith B. McGuire (New York: New York University Press, 2002), pp. 63–74. For a university policy statement on the ethics of human research ethics, see http://research.unc.edu/ohre/.

[57] Mustafa Draper, "Ethnicity, Politics and Transnational Islam: A Study of an International Sufi Order," in *Ethnology of Sufi Oders: Theory and Practice*, eds Antonina Zhelyazkova and Jorgen S Nielsen, The Fate of Muslim Communities in the Balkans (Sofia: IMIR, 2001), pp. 396–411.

[58] See as an example the appropriation of the academic concept of "neo-Sufism" (as proposed by Fazlur Rahman and John Voll) among Indonesian thinkers; this is discussed by Michael Laffan, "From Alternative Medicine to National Cure: A New Voice for the Sufi Orders in the Indonesian Media," *Archives de Sciences Sociales des Religions* 135–36 (2006), pp. 91–115, citing p. 97.

[59] Edward A. Alpers, "Islam in the Service of Colonialism? Portuguese Strategy During the Armed Liberation Struggle in Mozambique," *Lusotopie* (1999), pp. 165–84. See also, for the case of Tatarstan, Ravil Bukharaev, "Sufism in Russia: Nostalgia for Revelation," in Westerlund, pp. 64–94, esp. pp. 65–66.

consideration of Sufism in Muslim majority countries with the study of Sufism as a force in non-Muslim societies, recognizing it as one more phenomenon that is affecting and changing the character of the post-Enlightenment globalizing world of which it is a part. Sufism as a contemporary global activity is, in other words, a highly suitable subject for the study of religion, but it needs to be pursued in a manner suitable to the times. It is in this spirit that I propose engaging in the study of Sufism and Islam in the contemporary world.

PART 5

PERSIANATE THEMES

26

Persianate Islamic Studies in American Universities[1]

Islamic studies as an academic field has been pursued within American universities for over a century, initially within the framework of Orientalism and the philological study of Arabic texts. That tendency, still visible in departments of Near Eastern Languages and Civilizations, has been balanced since the 1950s by the more contemporary focus of area studies as found in centers for Middle East studies, many of them supported by the US Department of Education's Title VI Program. In more recent years, Islamic studies has increasingly found a place in academic departments of religious studies, which are extremely widespread in American colleges and universities.[2] Islamic studies as a field has outgrown its Orientalist roots and has embraced interdisciplinary perspectives on the humanities and social sciences to communicate its conclusions more widely.

---

[1] An earlier version of this essay was presented at a workshop of the American Institute of Iranian Studies. I would like to thank Charles Kurzman, Matthew Lynch, and Tehseen Thaver for their helpful comments on this article.

[2] For overviews of the field of Islamic studies, see Carl W. Ernst and Richard C. Martin, "Toward a Post-Orientalist Approach to Islamic Religious Studies," Introduction to *Rethinking Islamic Studies: From Orientalism to Cosmopolitanism* (Columbia, SC: University of South Carolina Press, 2010); Charles Kurzman and Carl W. Ernst, "Islamic Studies in U.S. Universities," in *At the Precipice: Middle East Studies and the American University*, eds Seteney Shami and Cynthia Miller-Idriss (New York: New York University Press, 2012).

How does Iran relate to the study of Islam? Given the prominence of the 1978–79 Iranian Revolution and the establishment of the Islamic Republic of Iran, it may seem obvious today that Iran must play a key role in Islamic studies. But that is not in fact always the case. In the approximately two dozen American PhD programs in religious studies that feature the study of Islam, only a couple have a major emphasis on Persian language or Islam in Iranian cultural regions; it is far more common for universities to focus exclusively on Arabic as the *sine qua non* of the study of Islam.[3] Indeed, from the perspective of religious studies, it could be problematic to assert that there is a field of Iranian Islamic studies. Iran, for one thing, is not an analytic category, but a cultural symbol which has been powerfully deployed in nationalist politics, particularly since the 1930s, although with quite different emphases under the Pahlavi dynasty and the Islamic Republic. While it may be the case that modern nation-states have been very effective in defining religion on their own terms (and contemporary Iran is no exception to this rule), adopting such a nationalist perspective would amount to essentialism by asserting the existence of an unchanging Iranian identity in all historical periods. From another perspective, Islam has been excluded from the purview of "Iranian religions" by scholars of ancient Iran, who restrict the category to ancient Iranian religions, especially Zoroastrianism.[4] From the 1960s through the 1980s, data indicates that Islamic studies, and religious studies in general, was the focus of fewer than 5 percent of American scholars in the field of Iranian studies.[5] And since the Iranian Revolution, modern scholarship on Iran has been disproportionately focused on contemporary history to the exclusion

[3] The two American PhD programs that emphasize Persian in Islamic studies are Yale University and the University of North Carolina at Chapel Hill. For a list of PhD programs in religious studies that include the study of Islam as a specialty, see http://www.unc.edu/~cernst/reliprograms.htm.

[4] Gherardo Gnoli, "Iranian Religions," *Encyclopedia of Religion*, ed. Mircea Eliade (New York: Macmillan Publishing Company, 1987; reprint ed., 2005), 7:277.

[5] Ahmad Ashraf, "Iranian Studies in North America: an Overview of the State of the Art," unpublished paper prepared for discussion at American Institute of Iranian Studies conference, "Iranian Studies in North America," 26–28 January 1989.

of premodern Islamic culture in Persia, even while the field of Iranian studies has seen a relative decline in strength overall.

Nevertheless, there is reason to say that American scholars have made important contributions to Islamic studies in relation to the larger sphere of what Marshall Hodgson (d. 1968) called "Persianate" culture. Hodgson, a professor of Islamic studies and world history at the University of Chicago in the 1950s and 1960s, introduced this neologism, a parallel to his famous coinage "Islamicate", to describe the "Persianate flowering" that took place in the Safavid, Mughal, and Ottoman empires.[6] He also offered strong readings of Persianate culture throughout the earlier periods of Islamic civilization, which still repay attention. Hodgson's early research included a brilliant study of Isma`ili Shi`ism, and his comprehensive history of Islamic civilization, *The Venture of Islam*, set a benchmark for the understanding of the role of Persian language and culture in terms of the Islamic framework.[7] It is a tribute to Hodgson that the Association for the Study of Persianate Societies, with its attendant *Journal of Persianate Studies*, was established as an international academic organization in 2002, drawing attention to Persianate culture not only in Iran but also in the Ottoman, Central Asian, and South Asian regions.[8] Another pioneer in this regard was the well-known American specialist in Iranian studies, Richard Frye, who was appointed Professor of Iranian history and languages at Harvard University in 1948. In his early signature publication

---

[6] Marshall G. S. Hodgson, *The Venture of Islam*, Volume 3, *The Gunpowder Empires and Modern Times* (Chicago: University of Chicago Press, 1968), pp. 46–52. See also Bruce B. Lawrence, "Islamicate Civilization: The View from Asia," in Brannon M. Wheeler, ed., *Teaching Islam*, American Academy of Religion Teaching Religious Studies Series (New York: Oxford University Press, 2003), pp. 61–74.

[7] Marshall G. S. Hodgson, *The Order of Assassins; The Struggle of the Early Nizârî Ismâ'îlîs against the Islamic World* ('s-Gravenhage: Mouton, 1955); reprint ed., *The Secret Order of Assassins* (Philadelphia: University of Pennsylvania Press, 2005). It is instructive to contrast this sophisticated and nuanced interpretation of Isma`ilism as a religious movement with the crude and conspiratorial sensationalism of Bernard Lewis, *The Assassins: A Radical Sect in Islam* (London: Weidenfeld and Nicholson, 1967); the 2002 reprint of this work by Basic Books advertises it as an "authoritative account of history's first terrorists… [which] sheds new light on the fanatic mind."

[8] Said Amir Arjomand, "From the Editor: Defining Persianate Studies," *Journal of Persianate Studies* 1 (2008), 1–4.

The Heritage of Persia (1962), Frye emphasized the critical role of Iran for early Islamic history by speaking, somewhat counter intuitively, of the "Persian conquest of Islam".[9] Frye also spoke of the "Iranicization of Islam" as a recognizable historical process, which he understood from a historical and philological perspective.[10] In particular, Frye drew attention to the importance of the city chronicles of Central Asia and Khurasan, which were essentially local histories of Muslim scholars, as important resources for understanding the cultural deployment of Islam in Iranian regions.

At roughly the same time, the work of French scholar Henry Corbin (1903–78) began to have an impact on American scholars, including Hodgson. Corbin seems to have been more influential in America than other Europeans, such as the Italian Iranist, Alessandro Bausani.[11] Drawn chiefly by his interest in philosophy, Corbin had become attracted to the Illuminationist philosopher Suhrawardi (d. 1191), whose Arabic and Persian writings he in fact introduced to European audiences for the first time. In an extensive series of publications, including numerous text editions published in the Bibliothèque Iranienne series for the Institut Français pour Recherches Iraniennes, Corbin explored numerous examples of esoteric and mystical thought, mostly from Iranian Sufi and Shi`i traditions; he cited these materials as incontrovertible evidence that Islam had to be understood from more than an Arabocentric perspective.[12] Indeed, he insisted that there were deep cultural continuities that connected the Mazdean legacy of ancient Persia with Iranian Islam, though Corbin made this argument as a phenomenologist rather than

---

[9] Richard Nelson Frye, *The Heritage of Persia* (London, 1962; Cleveland: World Publishing Company, 1963; reprint, Costa Mesa, CA: Mazda, 1993). For a complete bibliography, see Frye's website at http://www.richardfrye.org/.

[10] R. N. Frye, "The Iranicization of Islam," delivered at the University of Chicago (May 1978) as the annual Marshall Hodgson Memorial Lecture, reproduced in R. N. Frye, *Islamic Iran and Central Asia: 7th-12th centuries* (London: Variorum, 1979).

[11] Alessandro Bausani, *Religion in Iran: From Zoroaster to Baha'ullah*, Studies in the Bábí and Bahá'í Religions, 11 (New York: Bibliotheca Persica Press, 2000).

[12] An extensive website dedicated to Henry Corbin and his writings is available at http://henrycorbinproject.blogspot.com/.

as a historian.[13] In North America, a project headed by Charles Adams at McGill University aimed at producing an English translation of Corbin's four volume anthology, *En Islam iranien*, but it was never completed. In addition, Iranian-American scholar Seyyed Hossein Nasr, a specialist in Islamic philosophy, comparative religion, and the history of science, collaborated with Corbin in publications and in lectures at the University of Tehran over a number of years, before returning to the US after the 1979 revolution.[14] Despite the popularity of Corbin's writings in English translation, his work also drew criticism. One such expression was a 1980 critical review by Hamid Algar, a British-born scholar who taught at the University of California, Berkeley. Although Algar recognized Corbin's contributions, he faulted him for ignoring Islamic law and theology, and he dismissed Corbin's interest in ancient Persia, flatly declaring, "There is no substantial pre-Islamic substratum in the mainstream religious history of Islamic Iran."[15] Algar also derided Corbin's fascination with Suhrawardi (along with Louis Massignon's obsession with the Sufi martyr Hallaj) as an eccentric preoccupation with a figure whose marginality was demonstrated by the fact that he was executed—an assumption that rings oddly in light of the history of martyrdom in Shi`ism. Some years later, another American scholar, Stephen Wasserstrom, criticized Corbin in a study of modern esoteric interpretations of religion by scholars including Gershom Scholem and Mircea Eliade. Wasserstrom accused Corbin of fascist and anti-Semitic tendencies and, going farther than Algar, charged him with complicity in support of the regime of Muhammad Reza Shah, whose "Aryan" policies

[13] Henry Corbin, *Spiritual Body and Celestial Earth: From Mazdean Iran to Shi'ite Iran*, trans. Nancy Pearson, Bollingen Series XCI, (Princeton, NJ: Princeton University Press, 1977).

[14] For Seyyed Hossein Nasr's many scholarly publications, see the website devoted to his work at http://www.nasrfoundation.org/. On the Perennial Philosophy espoused by Nasr, and its background in the counter-enlightenment movement of Catholic traditionalism, see Carl W. Ernst, "Traditionalism, the Perennial Philosophy, and Islamic Studies (review article)," *Middle East Studies Association Bulletin*, vol. 28, no. 2 (December 1994), pp. 176–81, available at http://www.unc.edu/~cernst/Traditionalism.htm.

[15] Hamid Algar, "The Study of Islam: The Work of Henry Corbin," *Religious Studies Review* 6, no. 2 (1980), pp. 85–91, citing p. 89. The tone of this review may be gauged from its final comment: "His enterprise was a rarefied and idiosyncratic form of spiritual colonialism" (p. 91).

would have benefited from Corbin's theories regarding ancient Iran.[16] Corbin's defenders have pointed out serious flaws and distortions in both Algar's and Wasserstrom's critiques.[17] From the viewpoint of Islamic studies, it is striking that the debate over Corbin is colored both by the question of the Persian character of Islam (as an a priori given, rather than a historical conclusion) and by the politics of modern Iranian nationalism, both before and after the 1978–79 revolution.

In light of this dispute, it is instructive to see that Algar maintained the same argument in his erudite and detailed *Encyclopaedia Iranica* article (completed in 2006) on "Islam in Iran," which is divided into three sections: 1) the advent of Islam in Iran; 2) the Mongol-Timurid period; and 3) Shi`ism in Iran since the Safavids.[18] Here again, Algar specifically rejects Corbin's concept of "Iranian Islam" at any time before the Safavid era. His article generally treats the Iranian Revolution of 1978–79 as the genuine religious expression of the will of the Iranian people, and it features Ayatollah Ruh Allah Khomeini prominently as a protagonist (Algar has translated Khomeini's writings into English).[19] The prescriptive tone of the article, which treats established Twelver Shi`ism as authoritative, is evident from its regular description of competing religious movements as "fantastic and decadent" (Horufis), "deviant" (early Safavids), and "marginal" (Zaydis, Isma`ilis, Naqshbandis). Indeed, it appears that the editors of the *Encyclopaedia Iranica* felt the need for more diverse perspectives on this topic, since they have now commissioned an additional 14 sections of "Islam in Iran" under two separate headings: "Messianism and Millenarianism in Islam"

---

[16] Steven M. Wasserstrom, *Religion after Religion: Gershom Scholem, Mircea Eliade, and Henry Corbin at Eranos* (Princeton, NJ: Princeton University Press, 1999).

[17] Maria E. Subtelny, "History and Religion: The Fallacy of Metaphysical Questions (A Review Article)," *Iranian Studies* 36/1 (2003), pp. 91–101; Pierry Lory, review of Wasserstrom at http://www.amiscorbin.com/textes/francais/congr%E8s%20religion.htm.

[18] Hamid Algar, "Islam in Iran" (Iran, ix, Religions in Iran, 2.1–3), *Encyclopaedia Iranica*, online edition (2006), http://www.iranicaonline.org/articles/iran-ix2-islam-in-iran.

[19] Ruhollah Khomeini, *Islam and Revolution: Writings and Declarations of Imam Khomeini*, trans. Hamid Algar (Berkeley, CA: Mizan Press, 1981). See also Hamid Algar, *Roots of the Islamic Revolution in Iran: Four Lectures* (Oneonta, N.Y.: Islamic Publications International, 2001).

and "Islamic Political Movements."[20] These added materials both address sectarian manifestations of Islam (including some that drew upon pre-Islamic Persia) and problematize nationalistic framings of religion.

In a larger historical sense, the Iranian cultural region has never been separate from the prophetic and scriptural religions of the Near East. It was for this reason that Hodgson referred to "Irano-Semitic" cultural traditions. This complex interaction clearly continued in Islamic Iran, as recent publications by American scholars have shown. Travis Zadeh has demonstrated how pervasive was the use of the New Persian language (in Arabic script) for the dissemination of Islamic ritual praxis, religious conversion, and exegesis of the Qur'an.[21] Fine-grained historical research has demonstrated how Zoroastrian and Islamic apocalyptic literatures mutually reinforced each other, using the language of prophecy. As Jamsheed Choksy has argued, in the conversion of Iran to Islam, "the majority of Zoroastrians did not simply assimilate Islamic mores; upon entering the Muslim community, they embraced and then modified both Islam and its behavioral norms."[22] Likewise, Richard Bulliet has demonstrated, through close analysis of early biographies of Iranian Muslim scholars, how "Iran played a unique and crucial role in the origination and diffusion of institutions that eventually contributed to the centripetal tendency of later Islamic civilization."[23] In an important study of the Iranian messianic movements that led up to the establishment of the Safavid dynasty, Kathryn Babayan has persuasively argued for the persistence of Persianate themes of cyclical time and divine incarnation in the millenarian tendencies that were dismissed as heretical exaggerators (*ghulat*) by the guardians of both Sunni and Shi`i authority. What is especially remarkable is the way in which the triumphal Safavid clerical establishment erased as far

[20] Ibid., http://www.iranicaonline.org/articles/islam-in-iran-1#i.

[21] Travis Zadeh, *The Vernacular Qur'an: Translation and the Rise of Persian Exegesis*, Institute of Ismaili Studies Qur'anic Study Series, 7 (Oxford: Oxford University Press, 2012).

[22] Jamsheed K. Choksy, *Conflict and Cooperation: Zoroastrian Subalterns and Muslim Elites in Medieval Iranian Society* (New York: Columbia University Press, 1997), p. 141.

[23] Richard W. Bulliet, *Islam: the View from the Edge* (New York: Columbia University Press, 1994), p. 11.

as possible the historical traces of the Qizilbash and Nuqtavi cosmologies and histories, which had persistently sought to return to a pre-Islamic Iranian past. "Ironically," she observes, "just as the Safavis attempt a rationalization of religion, they come to reject the very language with which they led a successful revolution in early modern Iran."[24] In short, despite the theological and ideological claims of current orthodoxies, there are good historical reasons for regarding Persianate Islamic studies as a coherent subject for investigation.

With these preliminary remarks in mind, the remainder of this essay will be devoted to a brief sketch of some of the principal monographic contributions of American scholarship to Persianate Islamic studies, emphasizing religious studies approaches with additional attention to historical studies (the study of Islamic philosophy is beyond the scope of this sketch). This body of scholarship can be loosely divided into the following categories: 1) Islamic religious scholars in general; 2) Shi`ism; 3) Sufism; 4) Persianate sectarian movements; 5) Islam in contemporary Iran, including the 1978–79 revolution. This classification reflects the scholarly literature that is currently available on Persianate Islam, although one can imagine expanding the scope of research to other topics, particularly in the social sciences. It is unfortunate that we lack a significant body of ethnographic study of religious practice in Iran, because of the political barriers that prevent American anthropologists from conducting research there; the studies of women's religious practice in pre-revolutionary Shiraz by Anne Betteridge of the University of Arizona provide an example of the possibilities.[25] Likewise there

---

[24] Kathryn Babayan, *Mystics, Monarchs, and Messiahs: Cultural Landscapes of Early Modern Iran* (Cambridge: Harvard University Press, 2002), p. xix. Compare contemporary Iranian clerics' dismissal of the "fictions" of the martyrological text, *Rawzat al-shuhada'* by Husayn Wa`iz Kashifi, despite its centrality in Shi`i tradition; Karen G. Ruffle, *Gender, Sainthood, & Everyday Practice in South Asian Shi`ism* (Chapel Hill: University of North Carolina Press, 2011), pp. 147–49, 153, 156.

[25] Anne Betteridge, "Muslim Women and Shrines in Shiraz," in Donna Lee Bowen and Evelyn A. Early, ed., *Everyday Life in the Muslim Middle East* (2nd ed., Bloomington: Indiana University Press, 2002), pp. 276–91; id., "Specialists in Miraculous Action: Some Shrines in Shiraz," in *Sacred Journeys: The Anthropology of Pilgrimage*, ed. Alan Morinis (Westport, CT: Greenwood Press, 1992), pp. 189–210.

are excellent prospects for developing the topic of religion and visual culture in Persianate Islam, as one can see in the perceptive studies by Christiane Gruber of Indiana University, focusing on illustrated versions of the Prophet Muhammad's ascension narratives as well as on post-revolutionary poster art.[26] In terms of scope, while one could make a case for looking more broadly at Persianate Islam in South Asia (or even the Ottoman Empire), for reasons of space such efforts must be deferred to another occasion. Nevertheless, the prominence of Iran in all these themes of Islamic religion underlines how challenging it is to separate Iran from its historical connections with other regions.

1. Islamic religious scholars and the state. It is widely recognized that religious scholars (*'ulama'*) have played an important institutional role in Islamic intellectual and religious history. They have worked at times in collaboration with political power, and at other times in opposition. Giving a location to institutions of Islamic religious scholarship inevitably raises the question of the relationship of religious scholars to the state. Mention has already been made of Richard Bulliet's 1994 essay on Iran in the formation of early Islamic institutions. Bulliet, a professor of History at Columbia University since 1978, had earlier written an important analysis of biographies of Iranian Muslim scholars in the well-known study, *The Patricians of Nishapur* (1972), as well as a provocative interpretation of the process of conversion to Islam in Iran.[27] Bulliet's analysis explored the roles of elite

---

[26] Christiane Gruber, *The Ilkhanid Book of Ascension: A Persian-Sunni Devotional Tale* (London: I. B. Tauris, 2010); id., *The Timurid Book of Ascension (Mi'rajnama): A Study of Text and Image in a Pan-Asian Context* (Valencia, Spain: Patrimonio Ediciones, 2008); id., "Media/ting Conflict: Iranian Posters from the Iran-Iraq War (1980–88)," in *Crossing Cultures: Conflict, Migration. Convergence, Proceedings of the 32nd Congress of the International Committee of the History of Art*, ed. Jaynie Anderson (Melbourne: Melbourne University Press, 2009), pp. 710–15; id., "Jerusalem in the Visual Propaganda of Post-Revolutionary Iran," in *Jerusalem: Idea and Reality*, eds Suleiman Mourad and Tamar Mayer (London: Routledge, 2008), pp. 168–97.

[27] Richard W. Bulliet, *The Patricians of Nishapur; A Study in Medieval Islamic Social History*, Harvard Middle Eastern Studies, 16 (Cambridge: Harvard University Press, 1972); id., *Conversion to Islam in the Medieval Period: An Essay in Quantitative History* (Cambridge: Harvard University Press, 1979). Bulliet's other publications are listed on his website at http://www.columbia.edu/~rwb3/Bulliet/Richard_W._Bulliet.html.

families in Nishapur who supplied leading jurists for the competing Hanafi and Shafi`i legal schools, which came to dominate the politics of the region.

Other social and intellectual historians also explored the landscape of early Islamic religious history. Roy Mottahedeh, Professor of Islamic History at Harvard, made an important contribution to the understanding of the Buyid period in his *Loyalty and Leadership in an Early Islamic Society*, which explored the dynamics of social cohesion in post-caliphal Iran and Iraq, including some insightful comments on leadership among religious scholars.[28] Mottahedeh also wrote an evocative depiction of the religious and intellectual life of Iran over the centuries, in *The Mantle of the Prophet*.[29] This volume engagingly presented two different intertwined narratives in alternating chapters: the first narrative depicted the life of a contemporary Iranian religious intellectual (known under the pseudonym `Ali Hashemi) on the brink of the Iranian Revolution, while the second provided skillful historical summations of the major philosophical and religious tendencies that have been prevalent in Iran over the last millennium. The result was a highly readable presentation that was successful precisely because it interwove the personal biography of a believable Iranian scholar with the intellectual and religious history and the contemporary reality of Iran.

More recently, Omid Safi has contributed an important study of Islamic religious scholars during the Saljuq era, describing the creation of religious orthodoxy as the imposition of political loyalty. In the process, Safi explores in detail the religious and political perspectives of al-Ghazali and the nascent Sufi movement as exemplified by Abu Sa`id ibn Abi al-Khayr and `Ayn al-Qudat Hamadani, at a time when Persian

---

[28] Roy P. Mottahedeh, *Loyalty and Leadership in an Early Islamic Society*, Princeton Studies on the Near East (Princeton, NJ: Princeton University Press, 1980), esp. pp. 135–50.

[29] Roy P. Mottahedeh, *The Mantle of the Prophet* (New York: Simon & Schuster, 1985; reprint ed., Oxford: Oneworld, 2000). For a complete list of Mottahedeh's publications, see http://isites.harvard.edu/icb/icb.do?keyword=k86379&pageid=icb.page495469.

was emerging as a potent language of scholarship and poetry alongside Arabic.[30]

**2. Shi`ism.** Shi`ism, the movement or faction within Islam advocating the religious authority of `Ali ibn Abi Talib and his descendants, has played a dramatic part in Islamic history, though it remains a minority tradition today (except in Iraq, Iran, and Lebanon, where Shi`is constitute a majority of Muslims). Within the field of Islamic studies, it is probably safe to say that Shi`ism has been relatively downplayed, in part because early Orientalists tended to adopt the perspective of their mostly Sunni sources, according to which Shi`ism was to be rejected as a heresy. The remarks that follow refer to Twelver or Imami Shi`ism, on which a significant amount of research has been done by American scholars.

In terms of locations, it might be observed that Shi`ism is not that firmly connected to Iran, since the majority of the imams of Twelver Shi`ism are commemorated by shrines that lie outside Iran, and significant Shi`i populations reside elsewhere, for instance in Lebanon and South Asia. But it is also the case that important early narratives connected the Shi`i imams to Persia, by reporting the marriage of Shahbanu, daughter of the last Sasanian Shah, to Imam Husayn. And while only one Imam is represented by a tomb within the boundaries of modern Iran (the eighth, Imam Reza, in Mashhad), countless other Iranian shrines commemorate the descendants of the imams. Numerous messianic movements over the centuries have drawn upon both the symbolism of ancient Persia and the charisma of Shi`i Islam. And since the triumph of the Safavid movement in the early sixteenth century, Shi`ism has been more or less enforced as the state religion of Persia to the present day. Therefore, it is no surprise to see significant scholarly effort aimed at understanding the dynamics of Iranian Shi`ism, although it is striking to see how the impact of the recent Iranian Revolution tends to color the perception of earlier phases of Persian Shi`ism. A

---

[30] Omid Safi, *The Politics of Knowledge in Premodern Islam: Negotiating Ideology and Religious Inquiry*, Islamic Civilization and Muslim Networks (Chapel Hill: University of North Carolina Press, 2006).

useful corrective to those particular Orientalist blinkers is the comparative approach to sacred kingship, as demonstrated by A. Azfar Moin in his juxtaposition of messianic visions of empire in Mughal India and Safavid Iran.[31]

Some American scholars have devoted their attention to the formative period of Shi`ism, when Iran was host to an important center of Shi`i scholarship in the city of Qum. Hossein Modarressi, an Iranian scholar who taught for many years at Princeton University, explored the debates over the authority of the Imams, particularly in the crucial period following the death of the 11th Imam, Hasan al-`Askari, in 874.[32] Likewise, Andrew Newman (trained at UCLA though now teaching at the University of Edinburgh) investigated the formation of the Shi`i canonical collections of the hadith sayings of the Imams.[33] And Maria Dakake has focused on the development of religious identity and spiritual charisma in early Shi`ism.[34]

Other scholars have studied the history of Shi`ism in Iran in later historical periods and over the long term. Such is the case with Saïd Amir Arjomand, who has taught Sociology at Stony Brook University since 1978. His classic synthesis, *The Shadow of God and the Hidden Imam*, provides a persuasive and comprehensive overview of the interplay of religion and politics and the establishment of Shi`ism, particularly during the Safavid and Qajar periods.[35] Michel Mazzaoui, who taught history at the University of Utah, examined the process by which the Safavid

---

[31] A. Azfar Moin, *The Millennial Sovereign: Sacred Kingship and Sainthood in Islam* (New York: Columbia University press, 2012).

[32] Hossein Modarressi, *Crisis and Consolidation in the Formative Period of Shi`ite Islam: Abu Ja`far ibn Qiba al-Razi and His Contribution to Imamite Shi`ite Thought* (Princeton, NJ: Darwin Press, Inc., 1993). For a list of Modarressi's publications in English and Persian, see http://tazkereh.kateban.com/entry519.html.

[33] Newman, Andrew J. *The Formative Period of Twelver Shī'ism: Hadīth as Discourse between Qum and Baghdad*, Culture and Civilization in the Middle East (Richmond, Surrey: Curzon Press, 2000).

[34] Maria Massi Dakake, *The Charismatic Community: Shi'ite Identity in Early Islam* (Albany: State University of New York Press, 2007).

[35] Said Amir Arjomand, *The Shadow of God and the Hidden Imam: Religion, Political Order, and Societal Change in Shi'ite Iran from the Beginning to 1890*, Publications of the Center for Middle Eastern Studies, no. 17 (Chicago: University of Chicago Press, 1984). For a list of Arjomand's publications, see his website at http://www.stonybrook.edu/commcms/sociology/people/faculty/arjomand.html.

movement came to power in Iran.[36] Abbas Amanat, who teaches history at Yale University, in a series of articles has drawn attention to the long-term significance of apocalyptic and millennial thought in Iranian Shi`ism.[37] Hamid Algar's earlier contribution was his 1969 analysis of the role of Shi`i religious scholars in their relationship to the Qajar state, particularly during the nineteenth century.[38] Juan Cole, professor of history at the University of Michigan, has addressed the location of Shi`ism in terms of its early modern national and cultural contexts, ranging from India to Iraq, Iran, and Lebanon. His scholarship has been particularly rich in drawing upon the writings of Shi`i scholars of various theological schools, and in establishing the relationship between North Indian Shi`ism and the traditional scholarly centers in Iran and Iraq.[39] Another recent synthesis comes from the pen of Hamid Dabashi, professor of Iranian studies and comparative literature at Columbia University, who makes the argument that (particularly in Iran) Shi`ism "is morally triumphant when it is politically defiant, and that it morally fails when it politically succeeds".[40]

3. Sufism. The study of Sufism or Islamic mysticism has been well developed as a subfield in Islamic studies, having played a significant role in early Orientalist approaches to Islam since the late eighteenth century. The importance of Sufi studies as a field of academic research was recognized by the formation of the Islamic Mysticism Group in 2003 as an academic unit of the American Academy of Religion. Among US-based scholars, perhaps the most influential was German-born Islamicist Annemarie

---

[36] Michel M. Mazzaoui, *The Origins of the Ṣafawids: Šī`ism, Ṣūfism, and the Ġulāt*, Freiburger Islamstudien, 3 (Wiesbaden: Franz Steiner Verlag GMBH, 1972).

[37] Abbas Amanat, *Apocalyptic Islam and Iranian Shi`ism* (New York: I. B. Tauris, 2009).

[38] Hamid Algar, *Religion and State in Iran, 1785–1906: The Role of the Ulama in the Qajar Period* (Berkeley: University of California Press, 1969).

[39] Juan Ricardo Cole, *Sacred Space and Holy War: The Politics, Culture and History of Shi'ite Islam* (London: I. B. Tauris, 2002). Cole's publications can be consulted on his website at http://www-personal.umich.edu/~jrcole/index/indexa.htm.

[40] Hamid Dabashi, Shi'ism*: A Religion of Protest* (Cambridge, Mass.: The Belknap Press of Harvard University Press, 2011), p. xvi. Dabashi's publications are listed on his website at http://www.hamiddabashi.com/.

Schimmel (d. 2003), who taught at Harvard University for many years. Her *Mystical Dimensions of Islam* has been a standard handbook on the subject for decades.[41] Although she had broad interests in Arabic, Turkish, and South Asian sources of Sufism, she had a special focus on Sufism in Persian poetry, particularly the poetry of Rumi.[42] A number of American scholars have followed in Schimmel's footsteps in exploring the Persian Sufi tradition, often including new translations of Persian Sufi texts. William Chittick, professor at the State University of New York at Stony Brook, prepared an anthology of translations from Rumi, organized by subject, as well as translations of the mystical writings of Fakhr al-Din `Iraqi, `Abd al-Rahman Jami, and Shams-i Tabrizi.[43] Franklin Lewis, who teaches at the University of Chicago, has written a comprehensive biography of Rumi and his Sufi circle, and he has also translated selections of Rumi's poetry as well as a hagiography devoted to the early Sufi saint, Ahmad-i Jam.[44] Rumi's poetry is the subject of an important literary analysis by Fatemeh Keshavarz of the University of Maryland, and his teachings on prophecy have been studied by John Renard of St. Louis

---

[41] Annemarie Schimmel, *Mystical Dimensions of Islam* (Chapel Hill: University of North Carolina Press, 1975; reprint ed., with a Foreword by Carl W. Ernst, 2011). See also Burzine Waghmar and M. Ikram Chaghatai, *Bibliography of the Works of Scholar-hermit Dr Annemarie Schimmel: 1943 to 2003* (Lahore: Iqbal Academy, 2004).

[42] Annemarie Schimmel, *The Triumphal Sun: A Study of the Works of Jalaloddin Rumi* (London: Fine Books, 1978); id., *Rumi's World: The Life and Work of the Great Sufi Poet* (Boston: Shambhala, 2001); id., *As through a Veil: Mystical Poetry in Islam* (New York: Columbia University Press, 1982).

[43] William Chittick, *The Sufi Path of Love: The Spiritual Teachings of Rumi* (Albany: State University of New York Press, 1983); Fakhr al-Din `Iraqi, *Divine Flashes*, trans. William Chittick and Peter Lamborn Wilson (New York: Paulist Press, 1982); William Chittick, *Faith and Practice of Islam: Three Thirteenth Century Sufi Texts* (Albany: State University of New York Press, 1992); `Abd al-Rahman Jami, *Gleams*, trans. William Chittick, in Sachiko Murata, *Chinese Gleams of Sufi Light: Wang Tai-yu's Great Learning of the Pure and Real and Liu Chih's Displaying the Concealment of the Real Realm* (Albany: State University of New York Press, 2000); Shams al-Din Tabrizi, *Me and Rumi: The Autobiography of Shams-i Tabrizi*, trans. William Chittick (Louisville, KY: Fons Vitae, 2004).

[44] Franklin Lewis, *Rumi, Past and Present, East and West: The Life, Teaching and Poetry of Jalal al-Din Rumi* (Oxford: Oneworld, 2000); id., *Rumi: Swallowing the Sun – Poems Translated from the Persian* (Oxford: Oneworld, 2008); id., *The Colossal Elephant and his Spiritual Feats: Shaykh Ahmad-e Jām: The Life and Legend of a Popular Sufi Saint of 12th-Century Iran* (Costa Mesa, CA: Mazda Publishers, 2004).

University.[45] Paul Losensky, of Indiana University, has contributed an important translation of the classic Persian collection of Sufi biographies by `Attar.[46] Also noteworthy for their Sufi content are the elegant literary translations of the poetry of `Attar and Hafiz by Dick Davis, a British-born poet and professor of Persian at Ohio State University.[47] Several introductory works and anthologies include useful materials on Persian Sufism. These include introductions to Sufism by William Chittick and myself, and a series of textbooks and anthologies on Islamic spirituality and sainthood compiled by John Renard.[48]

Persian Sufism received special emphasis in a series of international conferences on the subject that resulted in the publication of a three-volume set entitled *The Heritage of Sufism*, edited by Leonard Lewisohn, an American scholar now at the University of Exeter.[49] This collection of richly researched articles, many by American scholars, opens up new perspectives on key topics and important figures in the history of Persian Sufism, although Lewisohn in introducing these studies enthusiastically

---

[45] Fatemeh Keshavarz, *Reading Mystical Lyric: The Case of Jalal al-Din Rumi* (Columbia, SC: University of South Carolina Press, 1998); John Renard, *All the King's Falcons: Rumi on Prophets and Revelation* (Albany: State University of New York Press, 1994).

[46] *Farid ad-Din 'Attār's Memorial of God's Friends: Lives and Sayings of Sufis*, trans. Paul Losensky (New York: Paulist Press, 2009).

[47] Farīd al-Dīn 'Aṭṭār, *The Conference of the Birds*, trans. Dick Davis and Afkham Darbandi (New York: Penguin Books, 1984); *Faces of Love: Hafez and the Poets of Shiraz*, trans. Dick Davis (Waldorf, Maryland: Mage Publishers, 2012).

[48] William Chittick, *Sufism: A Short Introduction* (Oxford: Oneworld, 2000); Carl W. Ernst, *The Shambhala Guide to Sufism* (Boston: Shambhala Publications, 1997), reprint ed., *Sufism: An Introduction to the Mystical Tradition of Islam* (Boston: Shambhala Publications, 2011); id., *Teachings of Sufism* (Boston: Shambhala Publications, 1999); John Renard, *Seven Doors to Islam: Spirituality and the Religious Life of Muslims* (Berkeley: University of California Press, 1996); id., *Windows on the House of Islam: Muslim Sources on Spirituality and Religious Life* (Berkeley: University of California Press, 1998); id., *Friends of God: Islamic Images of Piety, Commitment, and Servanthood* (Berkeley: University of California Press, 2008); id., *Tales of God's Friends: Islamic Hagiography in Translation* (Berkeley: University of California Press, 2009).

[49] *The Heritage of Sufism*: vol. 1, *Classical Persian Sufism from its Origins to Rumi (700–1300)*; vol. 2, *The Legacy of Medieval Persian Sufism (1150–1500)*; vol. 3, *Late Classical Persianate Sufism (1501–1750)*, ed. Leonard Lewisohn [and David Morgan for vol. 3] (Oxford: Oneworld, 1999). Volumes 1 and 2 of this collection were originally published in 1993 and 1992 by the diasporic Nimatollahi Sufi order (Khaniqahi Nimatullahi Publications) directed by Dr. Javad Nurbakhsh.

overstated the historic confrontation between Sufism and "fundamentalist Islam", to the extent of subscribing to "an innate predisposition to mysticism in the Persian psyche."[50] Lewisohn has added to this dossier by editing two subsequent volumes of essays on Sufism in connection with the writings of `Attar and Hafiz, as well as authoring a detailed analysis of the mysticism of Mahmud Shabistari, author of the *Gulshan-i Raz*.[51]

Other scholars have produced original research on neglected topics and figures in the early history of Sufism. This new work includes a study of the formation of early Sufism by Ahmet Karamustafa, a professor at the University of Maryland, as well as an analysis of Sufi biographical literature and a study of Rumi's teachings by Jawid Mojaddedi of Rutgers University; the latter is also producing a complete new translation of Rumi's *Masnavi* in rhyming couplets.[52] Firoozeh Papan-Matin has authored a recent reflective meditation on the Sufi teachings of `Ayn al-Qudat Hamadani (d. 1131), who is also the subject of a lengthy if idiosyncratic monograph by Hamid Dabashi.[53] I have examined the concept of sainthood in the writings of Ruzbihan Baqli (d. 1209) and translated his visionary autobiography.[54] A new biographical study of the Kubrawi master, `Ala al-Dawla Simnani (d. 1336),

---

[50] Lewisohn, "Overview: Iranian Islam and Persianate Sufism," in ibid., 2:11–43, quoting pp. 1, 37.

[51] *'Aṭṭār and the Persian Sufi Tradition: The Art of Spiritual Flight*, ed. Leonard Lewisohn (London: I. B. Tauris in association with The Institute of Ismaili Studies, 2006); *Hafiz and the Religion of Love in Classical Persian Poetry*, ed. Leonard Lewisohn (London: I. B. Tauris in association with Iran Heritage Foundation, 2010); Leonard Lewisohn, *Beyond Faith and Infidelity: The Sufi Poetry and Teachings of Mahmud Shabistari* (Richmond, Surrey: Curzon Press, 1995).

[52] Ahmet T. Karamustafa, *Sufism: The Formative Period* (Berkeley: University of California Press, 2007); Jawid Ahmad Mojaddedi, *The Biographical Tradition in Sufism: The Tabaqāt Genre from al-Sulamī to Jāmī* (Richmond, Surrey: Curzon Press, 2001); id., *Beyond Dogma: Rumi's Teachings on Friendship with God and Early Sufi Theories* (Oxford: Oxford University Press, 2012); Jalal al-Din Rumi, *The Masnavi*, trans. Jawid Mojaddedi, Oxford World's Classics (Oxford: Oxford University Press, 2004–8).

[53] Firoozeh Papan-Matin, *Beyond Death: The Mystical Teachings of 'Ayn al-Quḍāt al-Hamadhānī* (Leiden: Brill, 2010); Hamid Dabashi, *Truth and Narrative: The Untimely Thoughts of 'Ayn al-Quḍāt al-Hamadhānī* (Richmond, Surrey: Curzon, 1999).

[54] Carl W. Ernst, *Ruzbihan Baqli: Mystical Experience and the Rhetoric of Sainthood in Persian Sufism* (London: Curzon Press, 1996); Ruzbihan Baqli, *The Unveiling of Secrets: Diary of a Sufi Master*, trans. Carl W. Ernst (Chapel Hill: Parvardigar Press, 1997).

was produced by Jamal Elias of the University of Pennsylvania.[55] The topic of embodied religious practice in Persianate Sufism has been addressed by Shahzad Bashir of Stanford University.[56]

Despite the progress that has been made in this field through the studies just mentioned, it must be admitted that there are still major figures and topics in the history of Persian Sufism that have scarcely been discussed in modern American scholarship, so there are many topics awaiting investigation. This observation holds true particularly for later periods of history, especially with the suppression of many Sunni Sufi orders in Iran after the rise of the Safavids. But it is also remarkable how little scholarship there has been on the history of Persian Sufism since the nineteenth century. In this respect, the study of Persian Sufism has continued to reflect the classicist bias of Orientalist scholarship.[57]

4. Persianate sectarian movements. As previously mentioned, scholars such as Kathryn Babayan have made a persuasive case for the persistence of Persianate trends in the messianic and millenarian movements that have periodically resurfaced throughout Iranian history. Shahzad Bashir has devoted two studies to the analysis of the messianic career of Muhammad Nurbakhsh (d. 1464) as well as the Hurufi movement and its founder Fazl Allah Astarabadi (d. 1394).[58] After the end of the Safavid dynasty and under the Qajars, messianic hopes once again came to the fore in the Shaykhi school of thought, to emerge full-blown in

---

[55] Jamal J. Elias, *The Throne Carrier of God: The Life and Thought of 'Alā' ad-Dawla as-Simnānī* (Albany: State University of New York Press, 1995).

[56] Shahzad Bashir, *Sufi Bodies: Religion and Society in Medieval Islam* (New York: Columbia University Press, 2011).

[57] One of the few studies of modern Persian Sufism is the two-part study by Leonard Lewisohn, "An Introduction to the History of Modern Persian Sufism, I: The Ni'matullahi Order" BSOAS 61:3 (1998), pp. 437–64; and "Introduction to the History of Modern Persian Sufism, II: A Socio-Cultural Profile of Sufism from Dhahabi Revival to Present Day," BSOAS 62/1 (1999), pp. 36–59. A rare translation of a modern Persian mystical text is Nûr Alî-Shâh Elâhi, *Knowing the Spirit*, trans. James Winston Morris (Albany: State University of New York Press, 2007).

[58] Shahzad Bashir, *Messianic Hopes and Mystical Visions: The Nūrbakhshīya between Medieval and Modern Islam* (Columbia: University of South Carolina Press, 2003); id., *Fazlallah Astarabadi and the Hurufis* (Oxford: Oneworld, 2005).

the Babi movement and eventually the Baha'i faith, which went beyond the boundaries of nineteenth-century Shi`ism and is today a persecuted minority in Iran. Several American scholars, including Mangol Bayat, Abbas Amanat, and Juan Cole, have contributed important historical studies of the origins and historical development of these later messianic tendencies in the context of nineteenth-century Persia.[59]

5. Islam in modern Iran. Finally, one may return to the question of the role of religion in Iran since the turn of the twentieth century, a period that tends to be dominated by the revolution of 1978–79 and the establishment of the Islamic Republic of Iran. In a way, this subject represents the contemporary extension of the first topic outlined above, "Islamic religious scholars and the state". But the transformations that have occurred since the revolution, after the installation of an Islamic government under the supervision of Ayatollah Khomeini, have so drastically changed the basic structure of this relationship that it is arguably a completely different situation. There is an enormous amount of literature that has been published on religion in contemporary Iran, mostly from political and historical perspectives. One of the leading contributors to this field of study has been Nikki Keddie, for many years a professor of history at UCLA, who has published extensively on the religion and politics of modern Iran.[60] A number of scholars, such as Hamid Dabashi and Michael Fischer, have looked for the ideological roots of the Iranian Revolution in modern Sh`i religious thought.[61] Yet as Charles Kurzman has pointed out, there is an interesting fallacy in much

---

[59] Mangol Bayat, *Mysticism and Dissent: Socioreligious Thought in Qajar Iran* (Syracuse: Syracuse University Press, 1982); Abbas Amanat, *Resurrection and Renewal: The Making of the Babi Movement in Iran, 1844–1850* (Ithaca, NY: Cornell University Press, 1989); Juan Ricardo Cole, *Modernity and the Millennium: The Genesis of the Baha'i Faith in the Nineteenth-Century Middle East* (New York: Columbia University Press, 1998). See also the comparative study of Christopher Buck, *Paradise and Paradigm: Key Symbols in Persian Christianity and the Bahá'í Faith* (Albany: State University of New York, 1999).

[60] The publications of Nikki Keddie are listed on her website at http://www.sscnet.ucla.edu/history/keddie/.

[61] Hamid Dabashi, *Theology of Discontent: The Ideological Foundation of the Islamic Revolution in Iran* (New Brunswick, NJ: Transaction Publishers, 2006); Michael M. J. Fischer, *Iran: From Religious Dispute to Revolution* (Madison: University of Wisconsin Press, 2003).

of the literature that attempts to explain the causes of something as chaotic as a revolution, insofar as such explanations amount to retroactive predictions, although few social scientists would claim to be able to predict future events.[62] I will not attempt to describe here all of the American scholarly writing about the Iranian Revolution and its aftermath, which frequently focuses on the Iranian government's use of religious authority as the main locus of research, although one can point to a number of Iranian-American scholars who have recently made valuable social science contributions on the subject of Islam and modernity in Iran.[63] But a couple of final comments may be added at this point. First is the striking presence in American universities of dissenting Iranian religious thinkers such as Abdolkarim Soroush and Mohsen Kadivar, who have been forced to leave Iran by persecution there. Their articulation of a critique of the current Iranian regime draws upon key religious resources of Persianate Islam, but it is increasingly expressed in the language of the American academy.[64] Second is the religious debate in Iran today, which goes on in the seminaries and is easily viewed in their Internet publications. This is a debate that draws upon not only Shi`i authoritative tradition but also on contemporary critical thinkers from Europe and America.[65] The story of contemporary Persianate Islam is obviously still unfolding, and the complexity of its development deserves serious treatment.

* * *

The foregoing sketch of American scholarship on Persianate Islamic studies is only a broad outline, and it does not include the promising work of a number of emerging scholars who are

---

[62] Charles Kurzman, *The Unthinkable Revolution in Iran* (Cambridge: Harvard University Press, 2005).

[63] The writings of scholars such as Mehrzad Boroujerdi, Behrooz Ghamari-Tabrizi, Forough Jahanbaksh, Farzin Vahdat, Ali Mirsepassi, and Farhang Rajaee provide a range of analyses of Islam and modernity in Iran.

[64] See the website of Abdulkarim Soroush at http://www.drsoroush.com/English.htm, and that of Mohsen Kadivar at http://en.kadivar.com/.

[65] Kathleen M. Foody, "Thinking Islam: Islamic Scholars, Tradition, and the State in the Islamic Republic of Iran," Ph.D. dissertation, Religious Studies, UNC, 2012.

just beginning to publish on important themes in this field of study. But I hope that this summary provides sufficient evidence both that Persianate Islam is a coherent field of study, and that American scholars have made important contributions to its development. While it would be possible to make a case for many other regions of Islamic civilization as appropriate rubrics for separate investigation, nevertheless there is something compelling about the Persianate cultural sphere that makes it arguably a priority field for any comprehensive program in Islamic studies.

27

Concepts of Religion in the *Dabistan*[1]

The Project of *The School of Religious Teachings*

Your name is the title page for children of the school,
    Your memory is night's candle for wise elders.
Without your name, Persia has no taste for language,
    However much it knows the speech of Arabia.
With your name, the bodily heart of devotee and mystic
    Is the peaceful ruler of the throne of the kingdom of delight.
Every road I took connects to your address—
    You are the desire of existence, and you are the realm of desire.
Mobad comprehends comprehension, there's none other than this:
    God is your professor, and the world is your academy.[2]

So begins the *Dabistan-i mazahib* or *School of Religious Teachings*, an eclectic survey of the religious traditions known to intellectuals and spiritual seekers in seventeenth-century Mughal India. These verses carry the signature of Mobad, a term for a Zoroastrian priest, and it has now been established beyond doubt that this was the pen name of Mir Zul-fiqar Azar Sasani, the author of the *Dabistan*, completed in 1653. It is also clear that

[1] An earlier version of this essay was presented in the Dinshaw J. Irani Memorial Lectures at the K. R. Cama Oriental Institute in Mumbai, July 2016.

[2] Kayḫusraw Isfandiyar (attr.), *Dabistan-i mazahib*, ed. Rahim Rizazadah Malik (Tehran: Kitabkhana-i Tahuri, 1983), 1:3.

Mobad was a devout member of the esoteric Zoroastrian group of thinkers who were followers of Azar Kayvan (d. 1618), and who adopted the Persian Neoplatonism of the Illuminationist philosopher Suhrawardias the basis of their religious ideas. The recent discovery of a manuscript of the text dated 1650, personally corrected and annotated by the author, has decisively changed our understanding of the nature of this text.[3]

These very bookish lines at the opening of the *Dabistan* signal the didactic character of the text and its concept of religion. This passage occurs in the opening of the text, a place reserved in Islamicate literary culture for the invocation of God, who is the implied addressee; rhetorically, these lines present the prayer of the "devotee and mystic". Embedded in the second line is an intercultural tension between insurgent Iranism and hegemonic Arabism, an engine that drives much of the argument of the book. The comprehension that Mobad extols is the scholastic image of God (*haqq*) as a professor or literary scholar (*adib*) in the academy of the world.

Immediately following these lines comes a blessing studded with astral and royal images, expressed in a highly Persianized vocabulary:

> And limitless praises upon the lofty existent, the revered existence, whose steed is the sun, his witness heaven, his slave Saturn, his page Jupiter, his star Mars, his worshipper Venus—the throne adornment of the climes of religion, the royal crown of the kingdom of certainty:
>
> The essence who, in the words of holy God,
> "Were it not for you, I would not have created the world!"
> The first intellect, and the soul of the world,
> That Adam of spirit, and the spirit of Adam.[4]

Experienced readers know that the customary gesture in the second place of any Perso-Arabic literary composition is

---

[3] Karim Najafi Barzigar, "Sayr-i nazariyya pardazi dar bara-i Dabistan-i mazahib," *Shibh-qarra* (Special issue of *Nama-i Farhangistan*), 2 (1393/2015), pp. 77–88. This manuscript has now been published in a facsimile edition, *Dabistan-i mazahib: chap-i `aksi-yi nuskha-yi khatti-yi sal 1060/1650* (Tehran: Sazman-i asnad wa kitabkhana-yi milli-yi Jomhuri-i Islami-yi Iran, 1393/2015), but I have not yet had access to it.

[4] Dabistan, 1:3.

dedicated to the Prophet Muhammad, and indeed the poem quotes a statement in Arabic from the *hadith qudsi*, extra-Qur'anic revelations, in this case honoring the Prophet in his cosmic role, as the first creation, and the reason why God created the cosmos. The praises are then extended to "the rightly guided caliphs and revered imams of religion", a liberal inclusion of both Sunni and Shi`i Muslims, but the name of the historical prophet is omitted. This second prayer is addressed more to the first intellect than Muhammad. Then follows an even more bookish quatrain:

> The world is like a book, full of wisdom and justice.
> Fate's the bookbinder, creation and end-time are the covers,
> The binding's the shari`at, religious teachings are the pages,
> The community are the pupils, and the prophet is the teacher.

If anyone had missed this message at the beginning, it should by now be clear from this repetition that the *Dabistan*'s model of religion is deeply pedagogic.

This didactic impression is borne out by the brief announcement of the contents of the book, described as follows:

> In this book, known as the *Dabistan*, having mentioned a certain amount of ancient wisdom, practice, and faith, speech and action have been elicited concerning the groups of the knowers of the obvious and the seers of the hidden, the worshiper of form and the chooser of meaning, without lack or defect, enmity or envy, affirmation or rejection. And this text contains several subjects of instruction (*ta`lim*).[5]

These subjects are enumerated in 12 chapters of uneven length, each of which is called an "instruction" and describes the beliefs (*`aqa'id*) of a particular religious group. So from this close look at the short preface to the *Dabistan*, one can see how emphatically it concentrates on cognitive definitions of different religions. While particular religious practices do come up for discussion, the focus is really on what people think. The author's additional promise is to present this in an even-handed manner and without bias or preference. So ends the preface of the *Dabistan*.

---

[5] Ibid., 1:4.

In the very terms that it employs, the *Dabistan-i mazahib* by its title promises to introduce religious teachings, evoked by the second word in the title (*mazhab*, plural *mazahib*). In this respect it follows a literary usage established in Persian nearly five centuries earlier by Abu al-Ma`ali's *Bayan al-adyan* (1092), a survey of religions in which "the terms 'division' (*firqa*) and 'grouping' (*guruh*) are used interchangeably to describe social collectivities, while 'religious teaching' (*mazhab*) becomes the key word for doctrines."[6] Dihkhuda's Persian lexicon delineates three main meanings of *mazhab*: first, a special method of understanding questions of belief in Islamic theology; second, a particular technique of deriving Islamic legal applications from the Qur'an and the example of the Prophet Muhammad; and third, a philosophical or political perspective.[7] It is apparent from the contents of the *Dabistan* that the first meaning of the term is intended, so the title of the text might equally be translated as *The School of Theologies*.

The "Exact Classification" of Religious Beliefs

The mirror image of the brief opening of the *Dabistan* is its final remarks, which occur in a short passage appended to the 12th chapter, and just before the colophon. In these concluding pages, the author summarizes the methodological principles that have ostensibly guided his exploration of different religious teachings. This section has been egregiously mistranslated in the past, since it had escaped notice that Azar Sasani in this section was quoting, and drastically revising, a classification of religious teachings proposed by the early Muslim theologian Shahrastani (d. 1153). Accordingly, here I offer a new version, inserting numbered paragraphs and using bold for emphasis, to clarify the

[6] Carl W. Ernst, "Bayan Al-Adyan," *Perso-Indica*, accessed 9 August 2016, http://www.perso-indica.net/work/bayan_al-adyan.

[7] `Ali Akbar Dihkhuda, *Lughat namah*, accessed 9 August 2016, http://www.vajehyab.com/dehkhoda/مذهب.

argument of the *Dabistan* regarding the ideal types underlying all religious positions.[8]

The classification (*taqsim*) that can be exact (*zabit*) for all divisions is the following:

1. One group (*ta'ifa*) does not affirm the existence of perceptible and intelligible things (*mahsusat wa ma`qulat*), and they consider all existing things as imaginary. They are called **Sophists**, and Sumradi in Persian.
2. The community (*jama`at*) that considers existence to be limited to perceptible things and who absolutely deny intelligible things are called **Materialists** (*tabi`iyya*),[9] and Manasi in Persian. The belief of the Materialists is that the world is limited to perceptible things, and individual humans, animals, and plants are alike, for one becomes dry and another turns fresh, and this situation will never end. Pleasures are limited to drinking, eating, woman, horse, and the like, and beyond this world there is no other creation.
3. The portion (*barkh*) that affirms the perceptible and the intelligible but does not affirm divine punishments and commandments are called **Atheist Philosophers** (*falasifa-i dahriyya*), or Jaygari in Persian. This group proves the intelligible world but not from the perceptible world. Their belief is that the perfection sought by men is that which is from the proof of the Most High Creator. Having related their spiritual resurrection to the level of the world of intelligibles, they resort to the source of all emanating felicities [i.e., the Creator], having considered the precious pearl, the jewel of wisdom, to be essential for the

[8] See my article "The *Dabistan* and Orientalist views of Sufism," In *Sufism East and West: Reorientation and Dynamism of Mystical Islam in the Modern World*, ed. Jamal Malik and Saeed Zarrabi-Zadeh (Leiden: E. J. Brill, forthcoming).

[9] Although from a literal point of view, *tabi`i* would be translated as "naturalist", that term in English is normally applied to the student of the natural sciences, whereas the Persian term designates those who hold that worldly affairs have natural causes and who therefore do not believe in God (*Farhang-i Mu`in*, http://www.vajehyab.com/moein/%D8%B7%D8%A8%DB%8C%D8%B9%DB%8C). Hence "materialist" is a closer approximation to the meaning of this term.

attainment of this happiness. In spite of the existence of intellect, it [the Creator] has no need of any other human. Suffering is an expression for the avoidance of practices approved by intellect. Religious laws (*shara'i`*) are practices that benefit individuals from the mass of humanity in accordance with the governance of the intellectuals.

4. But there is another grouping (*guruh*) who, in spite of the proof of the perceptible and intelligible world, and the power of wisdom, [still] have faith in the prophets. They say that this class (*tabaqa*) established *shari`at* for the good of God's creatures and the order of the realm; for them knowledge of these matters is attained in the most complete and perfect manner. They are established on the basis of the Necessary Existent in the demonstration of the commandments and the distinction of lawful from forbidden. The information they provide about the states of the world of spirits, the angels, the canopy, the throne, the tablet, the pen, and the like, are all intelligible matters relating to the instruction of the masses, which they express in imaginative and bodily forms. Thus, they indicate the states of the bodily resurrection from paradise, the houris, castles, rivers, birds, and fruit, purely for the sake of encouragement, to seize the hearts of the masses who are "like cattle"[10]—for mostly their natures are inclined toward these matters. The awareness they create of chains, iron collars, and Hell is also part of the scare tactics of this group. This class—i.e., the **Philosophers** (or sages, *hukama`*)—also have this capacity for symbol and allusion. Their followers say, the goal of introducing symbols is to follow the prophets, who are perfect sages, who are considered **Divine Philosophers,** or Jansay in Persian.
5. The grouping that affirms the perceptible and the intelligible, and also affirms rational commandments, but does

[10] The expression is Qur'anic (7:179), "they are like cattle—no; they are more misguided."

not affirm the *shari`at* of the prophets. They are called **Sabeans.**[11]

6. The division that affirms the perceptible, the intelligible, and the rational religious commandments—who say one needs a rational *shari`at* of the prophets, since no prophet who has ever come has contradicted the first prophet or promulgated a self-indulgent *shari`at*—they are the **Yazdanis.**
7. Some, who affirm the traditional *shari`at*, which they present in words outwardly contrary to reason, are famous; they are found in five divisions: **Hindus, Jews, Magians, Christians,** and **Muslims.** All five divisions claim that their *shari`at* is sound, and on the basis of their own *shari`at*, they introduce a text according to their own belief.[12]

In short, this classification contains 1) Sophists, 2) Materialists, 3) Atheist Philosophers, 4) Divine Philosophers, 5) Sabeans, 6) Yazdanis, 7) upholders of the traditional *shari`at*, (in five divisions: Hindus, Jews, Magi, Christians, and Muslims). They are distinguished according to rule, depending on whether and how they affirm that perceptible and intelligible objects affect their understanding of existence and religious ethics. In short, this list offers a comprehensive summary of seven types of theology. The fact that the so-called major religions all fall into the final category, defined by irrationality, indicates how far the author is from actual approval of those religions.

On closer examination, this entire passage from the *Dabistan* turns out to be a revision of a key text in Arabic from Shahrastani, a systematic summary of religious beliefs found at the beginning of the second volume of his famous Arabic work, *The Book of Congregations and Cults*:

---

[11] On the Sabeans, see T. Fahd, "Ṣabiʾa", in *Encyclopaedia of Islam, Second Edition*, eds P. Bearman, Th. Bianquis, C. E. Bosworth, E. van Donzel, W. P. Heinrichs. Consulted online on 16 August 2016 <http://dx.doi.org.libproxy.lib.unc.edu/10.1163/1573-3912_islam_COM_0953>.

[12] *Dabistan*, 1:366–67.

The exact classification (*al-taqsim al-zabit*) is that we say of people:

1. There are those who do not affirm either the perceptible or the intelligible, and they are **Sophists.**
2. There are those who affirm the perceptible, but do not affirm the intelligible, and they are **Materialists.**
3. There are those who affirm the perceptible and the intelligible, and do not affirm divine punishments and commandments, and they are called **Atheist Philosophers.**
4. There are those who affirm the perceptible and the intelligible, and affirm divine punishments and commandments, but they do not affirm the shari`a and Islam (*al-shari`a wal-islam*); they are the **Sabeans.**
5. There are those who affirm all of this, and a certain kind of shari`a and submission (*shari`atu ma waislamun*), but they do not affirm the shari`a of our Prophet Muhammad; they are the **Magians**, the **Jews**, and the **Christians.**
6. There are those who affirm all of this, and they are the **Muslims.**[13]

It is immediately obvious that Azar Sasani had this passage from Shahrasani in mind when concluding the *Dabistan*, and it is also clear that he wanted to alter its structure and argument—though his tone is tentative when he declares that his classification "can be precise." There is a strong progressive movement in Shahrastani's original, which adds an affirmation at each step, culminating in the announcement of what the Muslims affirm. It is hard to see this as anything but a triumphant assertion of the supremacy of Islam over other faiths. Yet at the same time, Shahrastani's abstract classification remained something of a rhetorical gesture, since it did not really affect his detailed historical account of different religious teachings.[14] The revision of this text in the *Dabistan* performs a similar function, a parting salvo in a defiant manifesto.

What is new in the *Dabistan*'s version of this passage? A fifth group is inserted, the Divine Philosophers, which actually draws

[13] Muhammad ibn 'Abd al-Karim Shahrastani, *Kitab al-milalwa-al-nihal*, ed. Muhammad ibn Fath Allah Badran (Cairo: Maktabat al-Anjlu al-Missriyah, 1956), 2:4–5 (numbering added).

[14] Jacques Waardenburg, *Muslim Perceptions of Other Religions: A Historical Survey* (Oxford University Press, 1999), 200.

on a nearby passage from Shahrastani, presenting the philosophers' allegorical interpretations of scriptural symbols. There Shahrastani emphasizes that all of the philosophers are hostile to religion: "By them [the Atheist Philosophers] I only mean those from prior times, whether atheist, assassin, materialist, or divine."[15] For him there is no difference between atheist and divine philosophers, the latter being apparently an ironic reference. The entire second volume of Shahrastani's book is then devoted to "The people of fancies and cults (*nihal*)," keeping in mind the pejorative associations of *nihal*, as a term for pretentious claims. In practice, this category covers the Sabeans, philosophers, pagan Arabs, and Hindus, groups which Shahrastani described as "opposed to the monotheistic congregations with the opposition of contraries."[16]

The *Dabistan* alters this account, by asserting that the Divine Philosophers are a separate group who accept the prophets. It also elides the Divine Philosophers' dismissal of religious law and scriptural symbols as human conventions (a position that the *Dabistan*in fact strongly endorses). A sixth group is added, the Yazdanis, a mythical Parsi group from the opening chapter of the *Dabistan*, who never contradict previous prophets, an obvious corollary of universalism. Then the Magians, Jews, and Christians are combined with the Muslims (plus Hindus for good measure) in what is now the seventh category. The progressive structure of the systematic presentation is gone; the five scriptural religions languish under criticism for their anti-intellectual tendencies, so that the Sabeans, Yazdanis, and Divine Philosophers appear superior by comparison. By this alteration, Azar Sasani is able to present his accounts of religion as non-partisan, while simultaneously dislodging Islam (and other scriptural religions) from a privileged position. This is a good example of the way in which the *Dabistan* both draws upon Muslim categories of religion and at the same time transforms them, in order to create

---

[15] Shahrastani, 2:4.

[16] Shahrastani, 2:3.

space for a universalism that incidentally overthrows the hegemony of Islam.

The Problem of Translation and Universalism

The program announced by the author is extremely ambitious. Exactly how can such judiciousness and equanimity be maintained in the face of a host of conflicting religious beliefs? As we shall see, the grammar of religious belief in the *Dabistan* is based on two premises, translatability and universality, which offer the prospect of fair-minded treatment of diverse positions and doctrines. The sublime language of transcendence employed in the *Dabistan* conceals a revolutionary and millenarian perspective with a strongly Persianate inflection, which implicitly challenged the dominance of Islam and Arab culture. What is less obvious is the price to be paid, by rigidly imposing a singular philosophical and religious worldview as the ultimate explanation of everything. The Sufi-minded Persian Neoplatonism proposed by Suhrawardi has become a template to which all religious expressions could be made to conform (recall how the obligatory blessing on the Prophet Muhammad in the preface was imperceptibly turned into a generic salute to a cosmic principle). In what follows, I will explore several examples of Mobad's explanation of different religious groups in the *Dabistan*. Among other conclusions, one must acknowledge that the irenic and tolerant tone that the author projects is undercut by the systematic and indeed dogmatic insistence that his own worldview explains everything. Attractive though it may be to offer a universal explanation, the *Dabistan*'s project remains imperialistic.

The *Dabistan* was regarded by early European Orientalists as a potential key to the understanding of all the religions of the east. Those hopes, enshrined in the three-volume translation of the text published in 1843, were dashed by the stern positivistic standards to which its extravagant claims were subjected; it did not help that the translation was deeply flawed. The fantastically long mythic periods of time, which the text insists were dominated by the ancient Persian kings, do not fit into the modern scientific concept of history. Although Henry Corbin, the great

French scholar of Islamic philosophy, viewed the text as an imaginative symbolic construction, his article about the *Dabistan* for the *Encyclopaedia Iranica* was formally refuted by the editors of the encyclopedia, who viewed the text as basically a fraud and an imposture.[17] Likewise, while the initial publication of the Persian text of the *Dabistan*, and its translation into Gujarati, were enthusiastically supported by leading Parsi scholars of Bombay, it subsequently fell into disfavor, its esoteric teachings viewed as foreign to contemporary Zoroastrianism.

Here I am not concerned with adjudicating the authenticity of the *Dabistan*, or the lack thereof. Instead, I would like to interrogate the concepts of religion which are employed throughout the text. Recent scholarship, particularly in the field of the religions of India, has been once again attracted to the text, in part because of the quasi-ethnographic character of the author's reports of contemporary Hindu and Muslim religious movements in Mughal India.[18] Instead of regarding these accounts as transparent records of religious facts, I would like to consider them instead as part of a conceptual apparatus that draws heavily upon Islamic, Sufi, and philosophical views of religion, in the process constituting a distinctive worldview. Although the *Dabistan* covers a wide range of religious teachings in its 12 chapters, I will focus here mainly on intertextual connections between the first chapter on the ancient Persian prophetic kings and the second chapter on the religion of the Hindus.

One of the key aspects of the eclectic worldview of the *Dabistan* is a concept of universal translation that is powerfully illustrated by the following story, about the attempt of the Mughal emperor Akbar, and his minister Abu al-Fazl, to invite Azar Kayvan to India.

> They wrote a letter to Azar Kayvan, who had been made head of the Yazdanis and the Abadis (i.e., the followers of his teachings), and they invited him to India. Azar Kayvan excused himself from coming and

---

[17] Henry Corbin, "Dabestan-e Mazaheb," ed. Fath-Allah Mojtabaʾi, *Encyclopaedia Iranica*, accessed 12 July 2016, http://www.iranicaonline.org/articles/dabestan-e-madaheb.

[18] Aditya Behl, "An Ethnographer in Disguise: Comparing Self and Other in Mughal India," in Laurie Patton and David Haberman, eds, *Notes from a Mandala: Essays in Honour of Wendy Doniger* (University of Delaware Press, 2010), pp. 113–49.

> sent a letter of his own composition, in praise of the necessary existent, the intellects, the souls, the heavens, the planets, and the elements, including advice to the Emperor, containing 14 sections. Every first line of that was in pure Dari Persian, but when they read it backwards, it became Arabic; when they turned it upside down, it was Turkish, and when they read it backwards, it became Hindi. The minister Abu al-Fazl `Allami had complete faith in Azar Kayvan.[19]

This remarkable account contains several distinct elements. One is the detailed cosmological content of the letter, and another aspect is the distinct hint that the Mughal Emperor Akbar and his prime minister were keenly interested in this material. But the third and major point is the notion of translatability. The nimbleness with which the text could shift from Persian to Arabic to Turkish to Hindi is certainly amazing. This miraculous facility is a characteristic feature throughout the *Dabistan*, although Turkish is no longer required in India, so there is generally a bilingual or trilingual process. The first five pages of Chapter 1 contain more than two dozen such translations, always presented in a natural and easy style that assumes these translations are completely obvious and unsurprising.[20] Yet beneath this matter-of-fact presentation is the creation of an artificial language claiming to be pure Persian, containing many neologisms being smuggled into use by the innocent phrase "that is (*ya`ni*)." Thus we are told that among the noble attributes of God are "existence, unity, and *kasa'i*—that is, personhood (Arabic *tashakhkhus*)."[21] While a little reflection suggests that the abstract noun *kasa'i*, formed from Persian *kas* or "person", is a reasonable equivalent for the Arabic, this does not conceal the novelty of the terminology. Further Persian coinages are deployed to describe the first intellect, the empyrean sphere, the fixed and moving stars, the rational soul, religious knowledge and practice, and a host of other concepts. Although it appears that the new Persian vocabulary is basically formed on the extensive technical terminology of medieval

---

[19] Ibid., 1:300–301.

[20] See the glossary of Hindi and Persian terms in the first edition of the text, Muhsin Fani (attr.), *Dabistan-i Mazahib*, eds Nazir Ashraf and W. Butterworth Bayley (Calcutta, 1809), pp. 512–35.

[21] Ibid., 1:6.

Arabic, in the narrative of this chapter these terms describe the beliefs of the ancient Persian kings who lived countless ages in the past, so the Arabic words are presented as commentaries on ostensibly much more ancient Persian originals. The primary tension between Persian and Arab cultures that underlies much of the text is elided by the ease of translation in these descriptions. The gradual introduction of Hindi terminology enlarges the field of universalism, and makes it possible to project Indian ideas back on to the remote antiquity of Persia.

The Vision of Ancient Persian Wisdom

Iranocentrism might be considered the core idea of the *Dabistan*. In the opening section of Chapter 1, Iran is viewed as the ancient source of all civilization and culture. This is strikingly demonstrated in the account of the planetary temples of the ancient Persians, devoted to the seven planetary intelligences. In this connection, the author of the *Dabistan* observes that all the holy places of the Middle East were formerly temples in the Persian style of worship:

> The noble places, such as the Ka'ba, Jerusalem, the tomb of the Prophet Muhammad in Medina, the grave of the commander of the faithful, `Ali, in Najaf, the memorial of Imam Husayn in Kerbala, the tomb of Imam Musa in Baghdad, the shrine of Imam Reza in Tus (Mashhad), and the shrine of `Ali in Balkh (Mazar-i Sharif), were [originally] idol temples and planetary shrines (*haykalistan wa azarkada*).[22]

This sweeping statement is buttressed by the claim that, since worship of the moon was dominant among the pagans of Mecca, the original name of that shrine was "place of the moon" (*mahgah*), a name which the Arabs (*taziyan*) gradually corrupted into the word Mecca. This is further reinforced by the observation that the famous black stone found in the Ka'ba is an image of the planet Saturn preserved from the ancient times of the Abadi Persians. Likewise, the etymology of Medina is said to be

---

[22] *Dabistan*, 1:19–20.

"the moon is religion" (*mahdina*), but the Arabs changed it to Medina. In addition, the name of Najaf, the site of `Ali's tomb, is derived from a Persian word meaning "untroubled" (*nakaf*, *na akaft*). The same kind of exercise in creative etymology is carried out for the Muslim pilgrimage sites of Kerbala, Baghdad, Kufa, Tus, Balkh, and Ardabil. But why stop there? By the same logic, it turns out that the principal Hindu holy places were also originally planetary shrines established by the ancient Persians, in places like Dwarka (*dizkayvan*), Gaya (*gahkayvan*), and Mathura (*mihtara*). In this way, the apparent religious diversity of the world is explained by reference to the original Iranian sources.

The supremacy of Persian wisdom was described in several parallel narratives of a mythical character, in which the supreme wisemen of Greece and India humbled themselves as disciples of the Persian prophet Zarathustra. An example is the following:

> When the good religion [Zoroastrianism] was established in Iran, in India there was a wise sage named Changaranghacha, whose student Jamasp had been for many years, and he gloried in it. When he heard that Gushtasp was pledged to Zarathustra, he wrote a letter and forbade the king [Gushtasp] from joining the good religion. And at the bidding of the king, he came to Iran to have a disputation with Zarathustra. Zarathustra said to him, "Just listen to one nask of this Avesta which I have brought from God, and its translation in the chapter." Then at the order of the Prophet, a distinguished student read out one nask. And in this nask, God said to Zarathustra, "When the good religion becomes proclaimed, a wise man named Changaranghacha will come from India and ask you questions. His question is this, and the answer is that." In this manner all his questions were answered.... Changaranghacha from hearing this answer fell off his chair, and when he regained consciousness, he entered the good religion.[23]

This conversion to Zoroastrianism by a prominent Indian sage is indeed remarkable. Who could this have been? The name Changaranghacha sounds quite similar to that of the well-known Indian philosopher of the Vedanta school, Shankaracharya, whose name occurs elsewhere in the *Dabistan* with two different spellings (Šankaračaraja, Sankarajarya).[24] Since there is no

---

[23] *Dabistan*, 1:93.

[24] Ibid., 1:163–64; 1:151.

mention of Shankara in early Zoroastrian texts, one is strongly tempted to regard this episode as a parallel to the boasting stories of rivalry between Greek and Indian philosophy, in which scholars like al-Biruni and Shahrastani claimed that Pythagoras had been the teacher of all the Hindu thinkers. By way of retort, Hindu scholars writing in Persian argued that Plato became the humble student of Indian sages such as Vyasa, the transmitter of the Vedas.[25] But in the *Dabistan*, immediately after the story of Changaranghacha is related, we are told that Vyasa himself was so astounded by the conversion of Shankara to Zoroastrianism, that he went himself to Iran, where he too was overcome with admiration for Zarathustra and so became his disciple as well.[26] Similar accounts of the subservience of Greek and Indian sages to Zarathustra are found in other late Persian texts, furnishing a vigorous argument in support of the centrality of ancient Persian wisdom.[27]

The portrait that Azar Sasani paints of the ancient Persian kings in the opening pages of the *Dabistan* does not correspond to anything we know about Iranian history. Instead, he begins with a philosophical creed, stating that God is beyond rational knowledge, and quickly proceeds to describe a cosmology that is deeply indebted to the Persian-tinged Neoplatonism of Suhrawardi, the philosopher of Illumination (*shaykh al-ishraq*) who was executed in Aleppo in 1191. Suhrawardi treated the emanation of the levels of existence from the One-Good as the radiation of divine light, and he was notable for having joined Greek philosophy with the wisdom of the ancient Persian rulers. There are also strong indications of engagement with Illuminationist thought in various intellectual circles of Mughal India.[28] In presenting ancient Persia, at every stage the author

---

[25] Carl W. Ernst, "Fayzi's Illuminationist Interpretation of Vedanta: The *Shariq al-Ma'rifa*," in *Refractions of Islam in India*, chapter 16.

[26] Ibid., 1:93–94. A parallel story is told in Firuz ibn Kawus, *The Desatir, Or, Sacred Writings of the Ancient Persian Prophets, in the Original Tongue* (Bombay: J. F. de Jesus, 1818), 185–86, //catalog.hathitrust.org/Record/100580115.

[27] *Dabistan*, 2:154–68.

[28] Akbar Subut, "Suhrawardi Dar Hind," in *Majmu`a-i maqalat-i hamayish, `irfan, islam, Īran wa insan-i mu`asir, nikudasht-i Shaykh Shihab al-Din Suhrawardi*, ed. Shahram Pazuki (Tehran: Intisharat-i Ḥikmat, 1385/2007), 125–60.

leans heavily on Persian terminology, occasionally nodding to its Arabic equivalent; this Persianizing tendency is also visible in the writings of Abu al-Fazl. Azar Sasani briefly summarizes the emanation of the first intellect and the simultaneous emergence of the sphere of the fixed stars, and the process of unfoldment that sequentially produces the planetary spheres and their guiding intellects, concluding with the earthly elements and the rational soul. This is the metaphysical world picture developed earlier by the philosophers al-Farabi and Ibn Sina. It envisions a process by which the human soul may become detached from the body and united with the heavenly spirits. The stars have a dominating influence over earthly life, and the seven planets have particularly important roles. Here the author articulates the ancient astrological concept of 1000-year cycles of planetary revolutions, in which the planets and stars in sequence ruled over successive ages of history. The overriding concept is the great year, when all the planets return to their original position, signaling a momentous renewal of the entire world. While not exactly a Nietzschean eternal recurrence, there is definitely a cyclical aspect to this cosmology. The apocalyptic and millenarian tendencies visible in the court of Akbar, as well as in the messianic Nuqtawi and Rawshani movements (all of which feature prominently in the *Dabistan*) linked their expectations to the cosmic restoration promised by this doctrine.[29] Azar Sasani insists that "this belief is in accordance with the philosophical principles and beliefs of the Greek scholars."[30]

It is at this point that the *Dabistan* introduces Mahabad, the chief of humanity who became the first prophet by divine decree. Quoting esoteric texts that are now lost, the *Dabistan* portrays this primal religious figure as an ascetic noted for eating and drinking little. It is to him that the development of civilization, crafts, government, law, education, and philosophy are due. In this enterprise he was guided by the divine light and angelic spirits,

---

[29] Azfar Moin, *The Millennial Sovereign: Sacred Kingship and Sainthood in Islam* (New York: Columbia University Press, 2012); E. Kennedy, *The Astrological History of Masha'allah*, Harvard Monographs in the History of Science (Cambridge: Distributed by Oxford University Press, 1971).

[30] *Dabistan*, 1:9.

and he worked to ensure that human faculties were properly balanced, so in this way humanity prospered. People were organized in four classes: priests, rulers, farmers and craftsmen, and servants, corresponding to the four elements. Harmless animals were preserved and dangerous ones were killed. God provided a scripture for humanity, which was none other than the *Dasatir*, a text sacred to the Azar Kayvan movement, which purports to contain the revelations given to the ancient Persian kings. Mahabad gave languages to each community, which is the reason why the Persian, Hindi, and Greek languages exist. His revelation (Arabic *wahy*) affirmed what Suhrawardi called the imaginal world. A key point in this sacred history is the notion that many prophets were sent after Mahabad, but they never contradicted his sacred law (*shari`at*), an assumption that facilitates the assertion of universal truth in other discussions. It is perhaps a coincidence that the sequence of 14 prophets enumerated in the *Dabistan* mirrors the 14 immaculate persons of Shi`ism (i.e., the Prophet Muhammad, Fatima, and the 12 imams). This primeval society was known as the Mahabadians, and as a result of their true worship, they prospered in every way; it was a veritable utopia—"that which does not exist now, and in wealth and imperial power has never been heard of, existed [then]."[31] Eventually, humanity fell from this ideal condition, but that is another story.

Because of the strongly doctrinal and philosophical emphasis of the text, there is a marked tendency to treat narratives, such as the details of the Persian epic, in a completely allegorical fashion. Thus we are told that when the Persian hero Siamak kills a demon with his own hands, the real subject is the war between the self and the ignorant unconsciousness of God. Similarly, "whenever in the speech of this faction a demon is mentioned, they mean such types of men.... And they say that in certain places the expulsion of demons and their killing is an allusion to the subjugation of bodily faculties, and the subordination of blameworthy attributes."[32] In a similar fashion, the story of Khizr and Alexander lost in the darkness, and the discovery of the water

[31] *Dabistan*, 1:11.
[32] *Dabistan*, 1:13.

of life, is symbolic for the rational soul receiving intellectual knowledge.[33] These allegorical readings translate narratives to the level of moral and psychological instruction. But the text still insists upon a rich liturgy of rituals aimed at honoring "the Necessary Existence and the greatness of the intellects and the souls, and praise of bodies high and low."[34] Therefore the ritual calendar remains of considerable importance. It is also noteworthy that the *Dabistan* enjoins religious tolerance, in terms that would not be out of place at an interfaith meeting today:

> According to them, criticism of any religion and law (*din wa a'in*) is not right. One can reach God by any doctrine (*kish*), and there is not one of the religions that has been abrogated. They say that the multitude of prophets is because they show the path to God, and their followers know that the paths to God are many.[35]

Thus the posture of the *Dabistan* is, at least on the surface, irenic and nonconfrontational as far as different religions are concerned, although it implicitly rejects the hegemonic claim that Islam has abrogated previous revelations. Ethical allegories explain away any stories that ostensibly demonstrate violence.

The most surprising aspect of the depiction of the teachings of Mahabad is the emphasis on practices associated most often with Hinduism. Thus the text affirms that the path to God is blocked by the killing of harmless animals like the cow, the sheep, and the camel (which are typical elements in the diet of Muslims). This subject is treated with vehemence and at considerable length. Anyone who engages in such violence against animals will be hindered from achieving the ascension through the heavenly spheres that is the goal for these seekers. While carnivorous and predatory animals such as the lion are considered fair game for killing, this was not done in the golden age of Mahabad. It seems that wild animals were restrained by the spiritual power of the presumably vegetarian kings, though here too the author prefers to treat this as an allegory for the subjugation of one's desires.

---

33 *Dabistan*, 1:20–21.

34 *Dabistan*, 1:22.

35 *Dabistan*, 1:22–23.

Even more important than nonviolence is the regime of asceticism, purification, trust in God, and self-restraint, all virtues that are celebrated in the esoteric writings of Azar Kayvan's followers. In this way, a text entitled *The Cup of Kaykhusraw*, itself a commentary on the poetry of Azar Kayvvan, praises his ascetic virtues together with religious inclusiveness:

> The wayfarer should become knowledgeable about healing so that he may rectify imbalance and excess of the humors, and then he removes himself from all beliefs of religion and law, and the faiths and paths; he is at peace (*ssulh*) with all. He sits in a narrow and dark place, and gradually reduces his food.[36]

The language of this passage echoes the formula of "universal peace" (*sulh-i kull*) associated with the imperial project of Akbar and Abu al-Fazl. The *Dabistan* goes on to depict meditative practices that seem to draw up on Sufi examples, but even more so from the repertoire of yoga. One example is what is described as a four-beat or three-beat meditation, which has a particular name in the artificial technical language of the Azaris, as we have come to expect. The equivalents for these terms in Persian (three beat is *sehzarb*, four beat is *chaharzarb*) are well-known phrases for zikr performance in Sufi meditation manuals, the number indicating how many times a particular visualization or meditation is performed.

With no further transition, the author informs us that there are important seated postures among the Azaris, and the choicest among them are 84 in number, from which one may select smaller samples of 14, five, or finally two, which are especially efficacious. Such numbers as the 84 positions of meditation correspond to well-known accounts of yoga postures (*asanas*). When one of these postures receives its own technical name in Persian, from the description it is not at all surprising to learn that the yogis call it the lotus posture (*padma asana*). Breathing exercises are described in which one recites the words "is not" and "existence" as one inhales and exhales. This account turns out to be based upon the important formula, "there is no existence except

[36] *Dabistan*, 1:27.

God" (*nist hasti magar yazdan*), a phrase that appears to be identical in meaning with the Muslim confession of faith, "there is no god but God" (*la ilaha illah allah*), frequently recited aloud in Sufi circles. The difference of course is that the *Dabistan* concentrates on providing these formulas only in pure Persian to the extent possible. Yet it is clear that this meditation is understood in reference to Sufi terminology, as one sees in the distinction between the spoken recitation (*zikr-i jahr*) and the silent recitation (*zikr-i khafu*).

The next stage in the exposition of Mahabadian religion is control of the breath, known in Persian as the science of breath and imagination (`ilm-i dam wa wahm) and in Azari terminology as *samrad.* The Persian phrase denotes yogic practices that Sufis had been studying for several centuries by this time. It begins with crossing the eyes by gazing at the tip of the nose, a familiar feature of yoga. Then, according to esoteric texts like *The Companion of Zarathustra* (*Zardusht afshar*), instructions include reciting the name of God (*izad*) while inhaling through the right nostril to the count of 16, then repeating the name of God again 64 times with both nostrils, then 22 times more, finally releasing the breath from the right nostril. While counting, one draws the breath up and passes from the sixth station to the seventh station, where the abundant power of imagination is such that the breath pours over the top of one's head like a fountain of water. When one pauses to inquire about the "seven stations" just mentioned, one learns that this is a phrase from the legend of Rustam in the Persian epic, the *Shahnama*; like the 12 labors of Hercules, the seven tasks or stations (*khwan*) of Rustam are synonymous with the accomplishment of impossible challenges. Now, however, this epic phrase is being applied to describe seven different locations within the body, ranging from the seat to the genitals, the navel, the heart, the throat, the forehead, and the crown of the head—in short, it is impossible to distinguish this from the seven chakras of Indian yoga. We are informed that one who masters this effort and takes the breath to the top level "becomes the representative of God" (*khalifat-i khuday*). An alternative rule (the Dabistan uses the Persian word *a'in*, "law" or "rule", for these yogic practices) is to go into retreat, concentrate the heart on the world above, and silently repeat the name of God—"and it is correct to say it in every language, such as Arabic and Hindi."[37] The principle of translatability means that even sacred formulas can be turned into any language. Additional meditations include the rules for visualizing the spiritual master, the performance of breath control (*habs-i nafas*) until thought is suppressed, and the perception of the unlimited voice, which in Hindi is called *anahid* and in Arabic *ssawt-i muṭṭlaq* or the absolute sound. In a side comment, the author observes that some Muslim seekers interpret the Prophet Muhammad's reports of hearing bells during his experiences of revelation as an example of the same phenomenon. Similarly, some Muslims have compared the practice of crossing the eyes to the "two bows' lengths", a phrase from the Qur'anic description (53:9) of how close Muhammad approached God during his ascension into paradise; but now the focus is on the shape of the bows resembling the eyebrows of the cross-eyed yogi. This whole set of meditations has the appearance of being a Persianized version of well-known yoga techniques, which already were in the process of reinterpretation in Islamic terms. The conclusion of this meditation is the contemplation of the formless deity, known in Persian as *izad*, in Arabic as *allah*, and in Hindi as *pa[ra]brahma niranjan*, going beyond verbal expressions in different languages to transcend imagination and reach God.

Having offered a description of meditative practices strongly resembling yoga, the author pauses for a philosophical reflection on what it all means.

> They have stated that the goal of union with the origin, which the Sufis have expressed by "annihilation" (*fana'*) and "becoming eternal" (*baqa'*), according to the Illuminationist thinkers of Iran, does not mean mixing the possible with the necessary, nor that the possible becomes nonexistent—rather the meaning of that is when the sun necessarily manifests, in the eyes of possible beings the radiance of stars becomes veiled by that brightness. If at that level stillness befalls one, he realizes that he has become veiled in the overwhelming light of the sun. If not, he would think everything is nonexistent. Just so, the astonished Sufi types have reached the same distinction just mentioned, but they are precious and few, and not well known.[38]

[37] *Dabistan*, 1:28.

[38] *Dabistan*, 1:29.

Notice how easily the author slips into Sufi and philosophical language in order to describe these yoga experiences. Indeed, the *Dabistan* treats Sufism and Illuminationist philosophy as interchangeable, since Sufism is presented in the twelfth chapter as a generic form of mysticism, which is found in all religions. Thus one returns full-circle to the philosophy of Illumination as the key to all mysteries. The opening section of Chapter 1 concludes with further reflections on the nature of sleep, the withdrawal of the soul from the body to attain union with spiritual reality, and the seven levels of existence that constitute the unfolding of the divine being through the universe.

The synthetic character of the worldview of the *Dabistan* is firmly established by the beginning of the book as just described. These touches continue throughout, but it is worth pointing out that the account of the life of Azar Kayvan in the second section of Chapter 1 also emphasizes both the asceticism and the universalism that have already been highlighted. Azar Kayvan is portrayed as fasting from his earliest childhood. His mission is confirmed by powerful visions. As one source informs us,

> Azar Kayvan in his first spiritual practice possessed the art of learning the knowledge and beliefs of the masters. The great sages of Greece, India, and Persia appeared to him, and they entrusted to him the divisions of wisdom. One day he went to the Muslim academy (*madrasa*). Whatever they asked him he answered, and he solved their difficulties. Thus he was known as "the master of sciences."[39]

When a couple of Sufi disciples doubted the legitimacy of his reputation, their master had a dream in which the Prophet Muhammad himself appeared and informed him that Azar Kayvan was the perfect sage who had accomplished all of the levels of spiritual attainment that were conceivable. In this way, the authorities of all regions and religions were enrolled as witnesses to the truth of the Azari perspective.

Conversely, Sufi and Illuminationist concepts are the key for allegorical interpretations of any religious position, including the views of the various Hindu schools. In this way, a colleague of

---

[39] *Dabistan*, 1:29.

the author by the name of Shidush explained the Hindu concept of the avatar, with the following interpretation (*ta'wil*):

> Among the Sufis it is established that the first intellect is the knowledge of God, the universal soul is the life of God, and the attributes of God Most High are distinguished in this station.... They [the Hindus] claim love as the attribute of Vishnu, meaning the universal soul, and the spirit that emanates from the soul of the first heaven they call the avatar.[40]

It is evident that this kind of allegorical reading of Hindu theology sticks closely to the Neoplatonic principles of the school of Azar Kayvan. But the *Dabistan* assumes the correctness of this approach as a matter of principle. In introducing the teachings of the Hindus, the author comments about their leaders, that "the principles of this group are expressed in symbolism and allusion (*ramzwaisharat*), in the manner of Zarathustra and like the ancient philosophers."[41] Therefore anyone possessing the key to all these mysteries—i.e., the teachings of Azar Kayvan—has the means to comprehend the true significance of all religions. It would be easy to multiply examples of this compulsive effort at comparison and translation, since it is the pervasive theme of the book. One additional instance is worth quoting. The author states regarding the Vedas,

> ... whoever wants to prove his own religious teaching from the Veda may do so, to the extent that this is done for the demonstration of philosophy, Sufism, Nuqtawis, heretics, theism, Hinduism, Judaism, Christianity, Zoroastrianism, Sunni and Shi`i Islam, etc.; for they (the Vedas) are so full of symbolism and allusions that all seekers make use of them.[42]

Then immediately follows another ingenious comparison with the theories of Suhrawardi. This wisdom teaching, linked to ancient Persia, explains everything.

---

[40] *Dabistan*, 1:128.
[41] *Dabistan*, 1:122.
[42] *Dabistan*, 1:133.

Conclusions

The modern editor of the text of the *Dabistan*, Rahim Rezazada Malik, has located the text alongside a series of scholarly works in the Arabic and Persian that attempt to classify different schools of religious belief. These writings are epitomized by the great Arabic synthesis of Shahrastani (d. 1153), *The Book of Congregations and Cults (Kitab al-milal wal-nihal)*. While this text demonstrates a profound understanding of the different philosophical perspectives under discussion, its framework has an undeniably polemical aspect. It takes as its starting point a hadith saying attributed to the Prophet Muhammad, in which he predicted that after his death Muslims would be divided into 73 divisions (*firaq*), of which only one was destined for salvation.[43] The task of the heresiographer, to borrow a word from the history of Christianity, is then to construct a map of religious doctrines in which various teachings may be classified and evaluated; authors of such works commonly felt it necessary to fit these groups into the requisite number of 72.[44] Implicit in this approach is a partisan bias in which the author typically rejects every other group except his own; Malik describes these books as polemics (*kutub-i raddiyya*).[45]

That polemical approach is indeed widespread, and their catalogs of different schools of belief almost rival the encyclopedic classification of "isms" produced during the European Enlightenment.[46] Malik argues that the *Dabistan* is distinctive to the degree that the author demonstrates exceptional impartiality in his ability to relate the beliefs of the adherents of different religions.[47] In making this assessment, Malik is taking the author, Azar Sasani, at his own word, in a well-known declaration

[43] I hesitate to translate the Arabic term *firqa* (plural *firaq*) as "sect", because of the complicated history of the latter term in the sociology of Christianity, where it is contrasted with "church".

[44] David Thomas, "Milal Wa'l-Nihal, Al-," *Encyclopaedia of Islam*, ed. Ian Richard Netton (New York: Routledge, 2013).

[45] *Dabistan*, 2:78. To be sure, the case of Shahrastani is complicated by the fact that he was probably an Isma`ili who wrote with circumspection.

[46] See the list of different schools of thought in *Dabistan*, 2:80–120.

[47] *Dabistan*, 2:124–29.

occurring at the end of the text. It is worthwhile taking a closer look at this passage, in which the author attempts to defend himself against any comparison with such polemical works as Shahrastani's, or a similar work composed by a Shi`i author, Murtaza Razi. This final comment of Azar Sasani is in fact appended to his revision of Shahrastani's "exact classification" of religious view, discussed above. There he protests that he has done nothing except to transmit the beliefs of different religious groups as stated directly by the believers, whether orally or from written sources:

> After finishing this book, it became apparent that some important people have said that [books such as] *The Congregations and Cults* (*Kitab al-milal wal-nihal*) [of Shahrastani] and *Insight for the Public* (*Tabsirat al-`awamm*) [of Murtaza Razi], which have presented [various] beliefs and religious teachings, are not devoid of partisanship, so the reality of religion remains concealed.[48] Also, after them many groups have come together in this demand, and [so the author] performed the writing of this book. And in this realm of practice and city of creed (*kirdaristan-i `aqida-abad*, i.e., the *Dabistan*), whatever has been written of the beliefs of diverse groups is from the tongue of those who hold that belief and from their book, and it is established from encountering people in the present state of every group, even as the followers and devotees honor its name. This is in order that even the scent of fanaticism and partisanship should not appear, so the author has no other aim from this encounter save that of the translator.[49]

But let us pause here at the end of the book, and ask what the author is actually saying, particularly since this passage has itself been badly mistranslated in earlier scholarship.[50]

It is true that the author labored extensively to create this work, drawing upon numerous written sources for his portraits of a dozen major religious groups.[51] And it is also undeniable that

[48] Malik's edition here reads "the reality of religion (*haqiqat-i din*)", while the 1809 and 1877 editions simply read "the reality of this (*haqiqat-iin*)".

[49] *Dabistan*, 2:367.

[50] See Carl W. Ernst, "The *Dabistan* and Orientalist views of Sufism."

[51] Malik lists over 70 written sources; *Dabistan*, 2:122–24. When the facsimile edition of the newly discovered 1650 manuscript of Dabistan becomes available, it will be interesting to see what revisions the author made to the section on Hinduism in the final revision in 1653, when he asked a number of Indian scholars to advise him.

he provides a rich dossier of personal accounts of conversations with an amazing variety of colorful characters from different religious groups. Yet it is striking how often these conversations revolve around the same conclusions, and how frequently allegorical interpretation is applied triumphantly to produce the same result. Notice how the declaration of the author's impartiality ends with the affirmation that he is only a translator. Yet translation, for members of the Azari community, was not so much a neutral transmission as it was the deployment of a powerful hermeneutic, a universalism that discovered its own conclusions everywhere. It is therefore especially in those places where the *Dabistan* claims to provide a mere "translation" that one needs to read it with a critical eye. In those declarations of universal equivalents, the agonistic relationship between Azari mysticism and Islam is most intense; and that underlying ambiguity, ironically, is expressed in terms inseparable from the history of Islam.

28

Early Orientalist Concepts of Sufism[1]

One of the major issues in religious studies over the past few centuries has been how to conceptualize the diverse aspects of Islam, which has all too often been placed in an oppositional relationship with European Christianity and with "the West" in general. A key part of this effort was the understanding of what we now call Sufism, which can be called a tradition of ethical and spiritual practice found throughout Muslim societies and beyond. Some years ago, I drew attention to the formation of the term and concept of Sufism in the early phase of British orientalism in India, under the guidance of figures such as Sir William Jones and Sir John Malcolm.[2] Very much an example of Enlightenment classification of religious "isms", the identification of "Sufism" as a category was tied to a hostility toward Islam, and it demonstrated the conviction that all Oriental mysticism derived from India. In these studies produced at the end of the eighteenth and beginning of the nineteenth centuries, Sufism was defined as separate from Islam and was assumed to derive from some other source, generally Indian. This early scholarship tended to ignore the

[1] An earlier version of this essay was presented in the Dinshaw J. Irani Memorial Lectures, at the K. R. Cama Oriental Institute, Mumbai, in July 2016.

[2] Carl W. Ernst, *The Shambhala Guide to Sufism* (Boston: Shambhala, 1997), chapter 1.

self-understanding of Sufi authors who saw their tradition as emerging directly from the religious impact of the Qur'an and the Prophet Muhammad.

Yet there were previous European encounters with Sufis prior to the creation of the term "Sufism", and these too played a role in the conceptualization of this category of religion.[3] Early travelers who spent years in India and Persia had recourse to a vocabulary that explicitly compared the Sufis either to Christian monks or to marginal religious groups in contemporary Europe, particularly the quasi-heretical Quietist movement. At the same time, they anticipated British Orientalists in assuming the fundamental identity between Sufi doctrines and Hindu teachings, often equated with Greek philosophy as well. The Orientalist scholarly literature that emerged in the seventeenth and eighteenth centuries, in the form of dictionaries, encyclopedias, and manuscript catalogs, took much the same approach. A survey of these materials reveals the long extent of this attempt to categorize the Sufis, and it reveals a sharp ambivalence that was defined in terms of major debates taking place within Europe. Travelers, relying on their own experience combined with the writings of previous travelers, often expressed contempt and disgust for the unconventional dervishes that they encountered in public, and they were quick to announce the similarities they observed among Sufis, yogis, and other ascetics. Scholars who had access to writings in Arabic, Persian, and Turkish sometimes formulated more positive evaluations of Sufis in terms of Christian categories such as mystical theology, spirituality, and monasticism. But in all these cases, Europeans struggled to conceptualize Sufis as a religious group by applying to them European categories, which despite their limitations often persist until today in a remarkably resilient fashion.

[3] Europeans often also used the word Sufi (or Sophy) to refer, confusingly, to the Safavid dynasty that ruled Persia from the sixteenth to the eighteenth century. Particularly in view of the anti-Sufi attitudes of the Safavid dynasty and its clerical supporters, this usage is irrelevant to the discussion that follows.

Two Seventeenth-century Travelers' Accounts of Sufis: Bernier and Chardin

The first account of the Sufis that I would like to discuss comes from a French intellectual, François Bernier (1620–88), who spent over a decade in India (1658–69), serving the Mughal nobility as a physician.[4] Bernier was a student of the philosopher Gassendi, a now forgotten rival to Descartes, and Bernier in fact edited his teacher's writings; he claims in addition that he spent five years translating the works of Descartes and Gassendi into Persian, for the use of his employer Danishmand Khan. His descriptions of the war of succession to the Mughal throne, in which Aurangzeb triumphed over Dara Shikoh, were avidly read in Europe.

Bernier expressed his views on the Sufis in a lengthy letter to M. Chapelain, composed while in Shiraz on 4 October 1667, and first published in Paris in 1671.[5] It is remarkable that the main subject matter of this entire letter is described as "Touching on the superstitions, strange manners of acting, and doctrine of the Hindus (Indous) or Gentiles of Hindustan." In other words, not only are the Sufis placed among the exotic and bizarre sights of the Orient, but also they are unconnected to Islam; they only come to mind in connection with the group that seems inevitable to come to mind when Sufis are mentioned: the yogis. They are introduced, using the north Indian pronunciation "jogi", as "those who are believed to be true illuminated Saints and perfect Jauguis or perfectly united with God" (p. 57). Bernier uses language from Christian monasticism to describe the jogis: "many have convents, governed by superiors, where vows of chastity, poverty and submission are made." But he is horrified in general by the appearance of "these naked fakirs, hideous

---

[4] Bernier's medical training in France was a special three-month accelerated course, which included the requirement that the new physician should practice his profession in other countries than France.

[5] François Bernier, *Suite des mémoires du sieur Bernier sur l'empire du grand Mogol dédiez au roy* (Paris: Claude Barbin, 1671). This letter (137 pages) is separately paginated following the first letter in the volume, addressed to M. de la Mothe le Vayer (178 pages). An English translation is available in François Bernier, *Travels in the Mogul Empire*, trans. Irving Brook, vol. 2 (London: W. Pickering, 1826), pp. 1–58.

to behold." Bernier's disapproval of nakedness includes a brief contemptuous reference to Sarmad, the unconventional Sufi who was executed in 1661. He notes with skepticism the meditative practices of the jogis, and it is clearly in such techniques, and their esoteric character, that he locates the similarity with the Sufis: "The trance (French ravissement) and the means of enjoying it form the grand mystery of the cabal of the Jauguis, as well as of the Soufys. I call it mystery, because they keep these things secret among themselves."[6] Bernier acknowledged that his knowledge of this subject was due to "the aid of the pundit or Hindoo doctor" hired by Bernier's employer, the Mughal noble Danishmand Khan, who "also knew the mystery of the cabal of the Soufys."[7] The choice of language here is striking. The term "cabal" is derived from kabbalah, the name for the Jewish mystical tradition, and it has implications of esoteric secrecy, to be sure (oddly, the French term "Cabale" is completely missing from the English translation). At the same time, cabal in European circles carried the connotation of rebellion against authority, by implication revolutionary. For Bernier, the phrase "mystery and cabal" was dismissive; he elsewhere applied it to an astrologer whom Gassendi had refuted, so it may be taken to mean generally an irrational superstition.[8]

In any case, Bernier concludes his account of the Sufis, already colored by the views of a Hindu pandit, with a description of a lively debate over the immanence of God in the world, "inasmuch as certain pundits or pagan doctors, had instilled it into the minds of Dara and Sultan Sujah, the elder sons of Shah-Jehan."[9] Bernier observes that practically the entire Orient embraced the notion of God pervading all things.

> This is the almost universal doctrine of the pagan pundits of India, and it is this same doctrine which is still present in the Cabal of the Soufys and

[6] Bernier, *Mémoires*, p. 61; *Travels*, p. 27.

[7] Ibid.; the English translation simply says he "was already acquainted with the doctrines of the soofies." The Hindu pundit remains unidentified, despite the conjecture of P. K. Gode, "Bernier and Kavīndrācārya Sarasvatī at the Mughal Court," *Annals of S.V. Oriental Institute (Tirupati)* 1 (1940), pp. 1–16.

[8] Nicholas Dew, *Orientalism in Louis XIV's France* (Oxford; New York: Oxford University Press, 2009), p. 154.

[9] Bernier, *Mémoires*, pp. 127–34; *Travels*, pp. 54–56.

> most of the literary figures of Persia, and which is set forth in Persian poetry in very exalted and emphatic language, in their *goultchen-raz*, or garden of mysteries.[10]

The poetry that Bernier cites in this passage is the well-known Persian treatise by Mahmud Shabistari (d. 1340), the *Gulshan-i Raz* or *Rosegarden of Mystery*, an extremely popular Sufi text that is commonly viewed as expressing the metaphysics of Ibn `Arabi.[11] As part of a rising tide of Enlightenment philosophes, Bernier is dismissive of this doctrine, which he equates with "the opinion of [Robert] Fludd whom our great Gassendi has so ably refuted", and he finds it as worthless as alchemy. Bernier portrays this position as based only on empty figures of speech, devoid of logic. Although he presents the details of the argument in Hindu terms with Sanskrit vocabulary, Bernier appears to be unfamiliar with the genealogy of Sufi ideas that lies behind the *Gulshan-i Raz*, viewing it instead as interchangeable with Hindu teachings. He concludes with a grimly sardonic summary:

> I would ask, in allusion to all this, do you not think I have reason to take as a motto to this letter, the wretched fruit of so many voyages and so many reflections, a motto of which the modern satirist has so well known how to catch and convey the idea without so long a journey: "there are no opinions too extravagant and ridiculous to find reception in the mind of man."[12]

The foreignness of the Orient is reduced to proverbial folly.

A very similar account occurs in the travel narrative of Jean (Sir John) Chardin (1643–1713), a jewel merchant who spent years traveling in Persia and India (1664–70, 1672–80). His detailed accounts of Persia in particular (first published in 1686) are among the most extensive by any European traveler. His remarks on the Sufis clearly indicate familiarity with the writings of Bernier, whose language he repeats in describing the "cabal" of the Sufis. Indeed, Chardin had met Bernier in Surat in 1666, when

---

[10] Bernier, *Mémoires*, p. 128; *Travels*, p. 56, with modifications of some inaccuracies.

[11] Seyyed Hossein Nasr, "Mahmud Shabistari and Shams al-Din Muhammad Lahiji," in *Anthology of Philosophy in Persia*, vol. IV: *From the School of Illumination to Philosophical Mysticism* (London: I. B. Tauris, 2012).

[12] Bernier, *Mémoires*, p. 135 ; *Travels*, p. 57.

they joined other Europeans in witnessing a sati, the immolation of a young widow on her late husband's funeral pyre. Chardin's account of the Sufis is located in the brief chapter on philosophy in Persia.[13] It is noteworthy that Chardin placed the description here, rather than in the lengthy section on religion, much of which is an extended translation of a prescriptive text on the practices of Shi`i Islam.[14] While much of the writings of Chardin remains untranslated, curiously, this particular passage "On the Philosophy of the Soufies" appeared in 1821 in an American periodical devoted to Freemasonry.[15] From the beginning of this presentation, Chardin frames his discussion of "the Soufies" in a universalizing philosophical discourse that easily slips between ostensibly separate religious groups of the Orient. Thus the philosophy "of Pythagoras, is the great and universal philosophy of the Hindoos, and of all the idolatrous nations of the east." He regards the basis of this philosophy as the belief in the "great soul of the world", a phrase used by Bernier as well (though he attributes it to Aristotle and Plato instead of Pythagoras).[16] Chardin is confident that "That philosophy is taught amongst the Mahommedans, and more particularly amongst the Parsees, by a cabal of people called Soufies." Chardin asserts that this "ancient and celebrated sect . . . is nevertheless but little known, because its doctrine is all mysterious."

Echoing Bernier, Chardin is emphatic on the secrecy and mystery of the Sufis. Also following Bernier, he identifies Sufi teaching with the *Gulshan-i Raz*. Chardin explicitly identifies this text as a work of "mystical theology". While that category might

---

[13] John Chardin, *Voyages Du Chevalier Chardin En Perse, et Autres Lieux de l'Orient, Enrichis D'un Grand Nombre de Belles Figures En Taille-Douce, Représentant Les Antiquités et Les Choses Remarquables Du Pays*, Nouv. éd., Soigneusement conférée sur les 3 éditions originales, d'une Notice de la Perse, depuis les temps les plus reculés jusqu'à ce jour, de Notes (Paris: Le Normant, 1811), vol. 4, pp. 449–64, http://hdl.handle.net/2027/nyp.33433082406475.

[14] The section on religion (Chardin, vol. 6, pp. 165–496; vol. 7, pp. 1–270) is largely based on the *Jami`-i `Abbasi* of Baha' al-Din `Amili, a Shi`i theological treatise of the Safavid era. See John Emerson, "Chardin, Sir John," *Encyclopaedia Iranica*, accessed 12 June 2016, http://www.iranicaonline.org/articles/chardin-sir-john.

[15] Anonymous, "Philosophy of the Soufies. Translated From Chiv. Chardin's *Voyages en Perse*," *The American Masonic Register, and Ladies' and Gentlemen's Magazine* 1–2 (1821), pp. 74–75.

[16] Chardin, vol. 4, p. 455; Bernier, *Mémoires*, p. 127.

have provided an opportunity for reflection on formulations of God as beyond intellectual categories, Chardin reverts to calling the Sufis a cabal that practices impenetrable secrecy. He dwells at length on the extent to which Sufis will pretend to conform to officially recognized forms of religion. By this Chardin seems clearly to imply that at heart the Sufi is fundamentally critical of conventional faith. His lead example here, again identified as Pythagorean, is the Persian phrase *haqq man-am* (spelled *hack-menem*). Chardin glosses this as follows: "I am that is (the true-being;) what you see is as a garment which covers the eternal infinite essence, which is called God." It is worth pausing here to point out that the phrase in question is undoubtedly the Persian translation of the Arabic *anaal-haqq* or "I am the Truth", the ecstatic saying unforgettably associated with the early Sufi martyr, Hallaj (d. 922). While it is certainly plausible that the Hallajian declaration was still current among Persian dervishes, Chardin goes on to observe that "the Mohammedan devotees" (presumably members of the Shi`i hierarchy) despised the Sufis as unbelievers because of such claims to divinity.

Chardin further depicts the Sufis as shrugging off rational objections to their views, and as displaying remarkable tolerance of the religious views of others. After an offhand reference to the asceticism of Junayd (d. 910), Chardin concludes the passage with another comparative gesture, one which is laden with ambivalence. It is first of all proverbial in Persia that one can only with difficulty distinguish the heretic (*mulhid* or "atheist") from the followers of the Sufi path, whom Chardin inconsistently calls "contemplatists or fanatics". Here too Chardin seems to have imbibed the contemptuous attitude towards Sufis that was so common in post-Safavid Persia. His final remark places the Sufis alongside religious movements that had aroused immense controversy in the Catholic countries of seventeenth-century Europe: the Sufis, he claims, "resemble the illuminados of Spain, the molinistas of Italy, and the quietists of France." Indeed, so neatly does Chardin identify the Sufis with these heretical Christians, that he ends up blaming the Sufis for the spread of such doctrines. "It is probable that this mystical theology of the Soufies passed from east to west by way of Africa; and that it has thus infected first Spain, and then the rest of Europe."

Thus, at a stroke Chardin manages to describe Sufism as universal, as offensive to normative Islam, and as a movement to be understood in terms derived from marginal European religious groups. His multiple references to his precursor Bernier are standard practice in the popular genre of travel writing; as one scholar observes, "Chardin quotes almost all his predecessors."[17] Nonetheless, Chardin manages enough of his own observations, based on his experience of Persia, that he establishes a position with independent value. Still, it is striking that Chardin paid so much attention to the Shi`i scholars of Safavid Persia; like Sir John Malcolm, he received from those authorities a jaundiced view of the Sufis, regarding them as dangers to Islam.

The hints of Chardin regarding the resemblance of Sufi doctrines to Hinduism seem to have been accepted as axiomatic by his readers. In the standard 10-volume edition of Chardin's works published by Langlés in 1811, the editor confidently explained the quotation from Hallaj with a reference to the Bhagavad Gita, saying, "it is good to observe that the Indians also give the Supreme being the epithet *sat*, meaning at once existence and truth; and Vichnu in the Bhagavatgita, says, speaking of himself, *sadasmi*, which corresponds exactly to *haqq menem* or to *ego sum qui sum*", the latter being the phrase used by God to declare to Moses, "I am that I am", in the Latin Vulgate translation of Exodus 3:14. It also seems to Langlés "worthy of remark that 'I am the Alpha' [*ego sum alpha*, Revelations 1:8] is found literally in the mouth of Vichnu, when he says, *akcharânâmakaràsmi*, i.e., I am the vowel among the letters [*Litterarum (inter litteras) vocalis sum*]." It is amazing to see such displays of free association, on the basis of superficial similarities, serving as the basis for sweeping generalizations about inter-religious connections. Langlés persists in this approach with enthusiasm, commenting on a Persian verse quoted by Chardin that it has a "striking rapport" with another passage from the Bhagavad Gita, which portrays Brahma as the essence underlying all things.

[17] Anne-Marie Touzard, "France.vii. French Travelers In Persia, 1600–1730," *Encyclopaedia Iranica*, accessed 13 June 2016, http://www.iranicaonline.org/articles/france-vii-french-travelers-in-persia-1600–1730.

To return briefly to Bernier, it is a little surprising that he picked up Chardin's hostility to the quietist movement, an animus that he expressed in an essay that was published the year of his death in 1688. The quietists, associated initially with Spanish contemplatives like Molinos, advocated annihilation of the self and absorption in God. Their emphasis on passively awaiting a divine response to prayer was seen as corrosive to true religious responsibility, so much so that Pope Innocent XI condemned the teaching as a heresy. The French dictionary of the Académie Française in 1762 still defined quietism as "a kind of heresy of certain pretended mystics, which by a false spirituality, makes all of Christian perfection consist of complete repose and inactivity of the soul, and completely neglects external works."[18] So it was that Bernier drew upon his earlier writing on Oriental religions to provide a scathing critique of quietism.[19] Bernier's nineteenth-century commentator, H. Castonnet des Fosse, sketched out the particulars of the quietist movement, including the semi-reforms of a notable French religious figure, Mme. Guyon (d. 1717). Castonnet's admiration for Mme. Guyon was tempered by his description of her writings, as "all impressed with the error of Molinos, and one can say that quietism was taught with unparalleled audacity and a genius that never fails to surprise."[20] Evidently Bernier was troubled by his observation of quietist propaganda in Montpellier in 1688, and so he composed this brief but sharp critique drawing upon his observations in Mughal India.

Bernier in his polemic against quietism described the deep meditations of the Indian ascetics he had observed, and their conviction of having encountered the supreme being in the form of light. This he viewed as a massive error, remarking that long ago the idolatry of India passed to China, "where it rules still among the people and among the *bonzes* [Buddhist monks] who

---

[18] "Dictionnaires d'autrefois: French dictionaries of the 17th, 18th, 19th and 20th centuries," search on "quietisme," accessed June 14, 2016, http://artfl-project.uchicago.edu/content/dictionnaires-dautrefois.

[19] François Bernier, "Mémoire Sur Le Quiétisme Des Indes," *Histoire Des Ouvrages Des Savans*, (September 1688), pp. 447–48.

[20] H. Castonnet des Fosse, "Une Lettre de François Bernier Sur Le Quietisme," *Memoires de La Société Nationale D'agriculture, Sciences Et Arts d'Angers*, 4, no. 3 (1889), pp. 206–12.

are the same as the fakirs and the joguis of India." He refers derisively to the inactivity of the monk Tamo (Bodhidharma), who meditated nine years in front of a wall. He further comments, in language recalling his letter of 1671, that all talk of ecstasy and union with the supreme principle is, according to "the chief joguis who are entirely instructed and initiated in the secret of the cabal", nothing but an illusion to attract the admiration of the masses. "I know," he claims, "that they finally put everyone, like the Turkish and Persian cabalists, in that great soul of the world, of which our souls . . . are parts." This is nothing but atheism, in his view, since it is basically an expansion of the ego. Such evidence leaves Bernier suspicious of the value of the writings of Molinos and other quietists.

Bernier's preoccupation with the shortcomings of Christian quietists may seem at first glance tangential to the subject at hand. Yet Bernier's argument establishes several of the key strategies that later Orientalists would resort to again and again in approaching subjects like Sufism. First, all Oriental mysticisms are painted with the same brush; their separate histories are unimportant, and Sufis must be understood in terms of Hinduism. Second, these mystical teachings, insofar as they are universal, are fundamentally in conflict with a religion like Islam. Third, it is appropriate to describe groups like Sufis with terms derived from marginal European groups like quietists. In this way, Oriental mysticism serves as a cipher representing internal conflicts in European religious thought.[21]

Dictionary, Encyclopedia, and Catalog: Sufis in European Reference Works

The growth of European learning about the cultures of the Middle East was assisted by a long series of scholarly studies produced by missionaries and scholarly figures who took on the role of mediating this knowledge for European audiences.

[21] Richard King, *Orientalism and Religion: Post-Colonial Theory, India and "The Mystic East,"* First Paperback Edition (London; New York: Routledge, 1999).

One such figure was the French Carmelite monk Joseph Labrosse, whose ecclesiastical name was Ange de St. Joseph (1636–1697). He served as a Catholic missionary in Persia from 1664 to 1678, part of a large network of missionary activity that stretched from the New World to the far reaches of Asia. On his return to Europe, in 1681 he published a translation of a Persian pharmacopeia, and then in 1684, a voluminous dictionary from Italian, Latin, and French into Persian. Intended more for a European audience than a Persian one, the *Gazophy lacium Linguae Persarum Triplici Linguarum Clavi* (*Trilingual Key to the Treasury of the Persians' Language)* was an informative guide to numerous topics relating to Persia, and the earliest dictionary from European languages into Persian.[22] It was organized in parallel columns, with brief dictionary-style entries of European terms with definitions, accompanied by Persian translations of the terms and definitions, often with interesting inconsistencies between the different versions (e.g., opinions that would be offensive to the Persians were typically omitted from the Persian text).

Saint-Joseph cites the term Sufi under the definitions of the Latin words *religiose* and *religiosus*, meaning "religiously" and "religious", in the older sense of being a member of a monastic order.[23] The Persian definitions of these terms lean heavily on Christian terminology for monks and priests:

> Religiously: *ṣūfiyāna* (in a Sufi way), *bi-rahbāniyya* (monastic), *bi-solūk* (spiritually), *bi-ṭarīq-ipādriyān* (in the path of the priests)
>
> Religious: *du'ā'ī* (prayerful), *darvīsh-imustajāb al-da'wa* (dervish whose prayers are answered), *rāhib* (monk), *pārsā* (pure), *pādām* (snare)
>
> Persian religious: Sufi, *darvīsh*, *ahl-itaṣawwuf* (people of Sufi practice)[24]

---

[22] Ange de Saint-Joseph, *Souvenirs de La Perse Safavide et Autres Lieux de l'Orient, 1664–1678*, ed. Michel Bastiaensen (Bruxelles, Belgique: Editions de l'Université de Bruxelles, 1985), pp. 5–6, 12.

[23] The oldest meaning of the term "religious" in English is a person or group "belonging to a monastic order, especially in the Roman Catholic Church" (*Oxford English Dictionary*).

[24] Ange de Saint-Joseph, *Gazophylacium Linguae Persarum Triplici Linguarum Clavi, Italice, Latine, Gallice, Nec Non Specialibus Praeceptis Ejusdem Linguae Reseratum* (Amstelodami: ex officina Jansonio-Waesbergiana, 1684), p. 333.

Saint-Joseph then offers the following observation on the etymology of the word Sufi:

> The Persian religious are called Sufi, but regarding the etymology of this term there is considerable argument. On this topic Hafiz the Arab has intelligently and elegantly said, "People dispute regarding the Sufi and differ on this, thinking it is derived from wool (*ṣūf*), but I do not ascribe this name except to a pure (*ṣāfī*) youth, and he is called Sufi because he is pure."

The quotation from "Hafiz the Arab" is elsewhere known to have been cited by the scientist and philosopher al-Biruni in his Arabic treatise on philosophy and religion in India (ca. 1030), where it is ascribed to a certain Abu al-Fath al-Busti.[25]

Saint-Joseph also presents a slightly longer account of dervishes, presenting Sufis as failed imitators of Christian monks, a judgment that is omitted from the Persian translation. His description (listed under the Italian term for beggar, mendico) is contemptuous:

> These beggars in Turkey, Persia, and India pass for bad Mahometans among the scholarly interpreters of the Qur'an, but they are bad copies of excellent originals, that is, early Christian monks (Persian: they are not Mahometans, but people without religion). In their monasteries, with hypocrisy and extravagance they profess poverty, austerity, and obedience to their superior. They belong to different orders, among which some are solitaries or cenobites… while others, vagabonds and epicureans, are called Kalandars, and others who are military are known as Bektassi, etc.
>
> Practically all are so singular and extravagant that they use opium in quantity and feign enthusiasms, revelations, and ecstatic expressions; they turn about themselves, nearly every day, with extraordinary speed. Any longer account on the subject would be tasteless and hardly consistent.[26]

---

[25] Muḥammad Bīrūnī, *Taḥqīq mā lil-Hind min maqūlah maqbūlah fī al-ʿaql aw mardhūlah* (Hyderabad: Da'irat al-Maʿārifal-ʿUṯmānīya, 1958), p. 25; Muḥammad Bīrūnī, *Alberuni's India: An Account of the Religion, Philosophy, Literature, Geography, Chronology, Astronomy, Customs, Laws, and Astrology of India about A.D. 1030*, trans. Eduard Sachau (New Delhi: S. Chand, 1964), 1:34. It is possible that Saint-Joseph is quoting the verse from another source, in view of the different author to whom it is attributed.

[26] Saint-Joseph, pp. 224–25; Bastiaensen, pp. 152–53.

Saint-Joseph's caustic tone in describing Persian dervishes, like Chardin's account, echoes the hostility towards the social manifestations of Sufism that was so entrenched in the Shi`i religious establishment ("the scholarly interpreters of the Qur'an" is rendered simply by *`ulama'* in the Persian).

Saint-Joseph provides further details on the Sufis, in an unexpected article on Mt. Carmel, optimistically expressing the missionary hope that they are ripe for conversion. Quoting a Sufi leader from Isfahan named Mukhlis, he maintains, improbably, that the Sufis are secret Christians:

> Among them [the Sufis], the Alcoran is hated, and the divinity of Christ is a mystery of faith that is not communicated to novices, but reserved to experienced veterans of their sect. "Before the people," he says, "we have the custom of only professing this in concealed terms."[27]

Even more surprising is Saint-Joseph's statement that Mukhlis claimed that the origin of his Sufi order (*ta'ifa*) was actually Mt. Carmel, the origin of the Carmelite monks, and that their master (*pir*) was the prophet Elias (Ilya). To find a Sufi order in seventeenth-century Persia who were not only crypto-Christians but also connected to the Carmelite monks seems most unlikely. Was this assertion perhaps an ecumenic gesture by the Persian Sufi? Or did Saint-Joseph over-interpret the situation, in his enthusiasm to find a candidate for conversion? The monastic background and missionary focus of Saint-Joseph explain why he resorts to familiar Catholic terminology to describe the Sufis. His highly critical description of their practices, combined with an unrealistic expectation of their prospects for conversion to Christianity, say more about his own hopes and frustrations than they do about the Sufis themselves.

A more extensive scholarly presentation in truly encyclopedic form was the *Bibliothéque Orientale* of Barthélemy d'Herbelot (1625–95), a reference work published in 1697 in French with ambitious objectives. As its title page proclaimed, this work contained generally everything regarding the knowledge of the

---

[27] Saint-Joseph, pp. 235–236; Bastiaensen, pp. 152–154.

peoples of the Orient, their histories and traditions both veritable and fabulous, their religions, sects and poetics, their government, laws, customs, manners, wars, and the revolutions of their empires, their sciences, and their arts, their theology, mythology, magic, physics, morality, medicine, mathematics, natural history, chronology, geography, astronomical observations, grammar, rhetoric, and the list went on from there.[28] Herbelot was a scholar of Oriental languages who benefited from his association with Jewish and Maronite Christian scholars. He was supported by the patronage of the king of France, and while on a trip to Italy in 1666, he was given an immense library of Oriental manuscripts by the Duke of Tuscany. The dominant style of scholarship in those days was classical and antiquarian, and the study of the Orient (what we call today the Middle East) had the same attitude of studying remote and different people that was applied to the study of Greco-Roman antiquity.[29] The *Bibliothéque Orientale* was based mainly on Eastern sources, and did not include materials from contemporary European voyagers.

Herbelot was doubtless inspired to compile this encyclopedia when he received the gift of the Oriental library, and he took as a model the extensive Arabic bibliographical reference work, the *Kashf al-zunun* by the Ottoman polymath Hajji Khalifa, a.k.a. Katip Çelebi (1609–57). Indeed, over half of the *Bibliothéque Orientale* is basically bibliographic listing of texts and authors following its Ottoman model.[30] That voluminous work would later be published in the mid-nineteenth century in a bilingual Arabic and Latin edition by the German scholar Gustav Flügel.[31] Herbelot

---

[28] Barthélemy d'Herbelot de Molainville, *Bibliothèque Orientale, Ou Dictionnaire Universel Contenant Généralement Tout Ce Qui Regarde La Connaissance Des Peuples de l'Orient; Leurs Histoires & Traditions, Tant Fabuleuses Que Véritables; Leurs Religions & Leurs Sectes; Leurs Gouvernements, Loix, Politique, Moeurs, Coutumes; & Les Révolutions de Leurs Empires, &c.* (Paris: La Compagnie des Libraires, 1697), http://gallica.bnf.fr/ark:/12148/bpt6k82422h.

[29] Henry Laurens, *Aux Sources de L'orientalisme: La Bibliothèque Orientale de Barthélemi D'Herbelot* (Paris: G. P. Maisonneuve et Larose, 1978), p. 7.

[30] Laurens, p. 63.

[31] Kâtip Çelebi, *Lexicon a Mustafa Ben Abdallach Katib Jelebi, Dicto et Nomine Haji Khalfa, Celebrato Compositum Ad Codicum Vindobonensium Parisiensium et Berolinensis Fidem Primum*, ed. Gustav Lebrecht Fluegel, 7 vols. (Leipzig: Oriental Translation Fund of Great Britain and Ireland, 1835–1858), //catalog.hathitrust.org/Record/009737676.

drew on his extensive knowledge of Arabic, Persian, and Turkish literature to expand the coverage of his encyclopedia, which was reprinted several times in the late eighteenth century.

To investigate the Islamic civilization on a large scale attempted by this work was a sensitive enterprise in Catholic France during the eighteenth century. Religion was a very important part of the *Bibliothéque Orientale*, so it was not only expected, but demanded, that the errors and falsity of Islam should be demonstrated in any published book; as might be expected, Herbelot made the usual critical remarks about the Prophet Muhammad and the Qur'an. Moreover, as a product of the Catholic counter reformation, he was eager to denounce superstition, and he could only approve of a faith that was interiorized and not corrupted by popular practices.[32]

Herbelot offered a separate article with the thumbnail description of the Sufi (spelled Sofi), declaring his preference for the Greek origin of the term as many Orientalists would do. His choice of terminology focuses on philosophy and the religious orders of Christendom as the most obvious models.

> Sofi: This word signifies in Arabic a man wearing wool, and who does not wear silk, according to the origin that some give it of *sof* or *souf*, which means wool: but there is more likelihood that this word comes from the Greek Sophos; because it is used among Muslims for a Sage or Philosopher who lives apart & removed from things of the world, by a kind of religious profession.
>
> The word Sofi is used in Persia for a Muslim religious, who is also called Dervish, that is to say, Poor, as in Turkey & Persia: the Arabs use the word Fakir in same meaning. This is the nickname that Sofis or Dervishes receive in India.
>
> However, the Sofis seem to be distinguished as a special Order of the Muslim Religious, who profess a more regular and more contemplative life than ordinary Dervishes. Indeed, many of these people who have written books on spirituality, devotion and contemplation, which usually bear the title of Tessaouf (*tasawwuf*), that is to say the spiritual life.[33]

---

[32] Laurens, p. 77.

[33] Herbelot, s.v. "Sofi."

European scholars debated, but generally accepted, the etymology that proposed the Greek word sophos, "wise", as the origin for the word Sufi. In making this move, they followed the unconvincing attempt of the Persian philosopher al-Biruni to connect the Arabic word Sufi to the Greek sophos, "wise", a comparative move that required the assumption that Arab authors misspelled a perfectly clear Greek word.[34] It is linguistically improbable for the Greek letter sigma to turn into the "emphatic" Arabic letter *ṣād* (ص), and indeed there is no parallel among the Greek terms adapted into Arabic.[35] Early Sufism had developed largely without connection to the scientific and philosophical circles interested in translating works of the Greek philosophers. So the persistence of the attempt to see Greek philosophy as the origin of Sufism, despite a lack of historical evidence, betrays a deeper conviction that Sufism had to be explained in extra-Islamic terms.

Herbelot presented biographies of a number of prominent Sufis such as Junayd ("Giuneid") and Hallaj ("Hallage", in a surprisingly detailed account), and he regularly quoted from Rumi ("Gelaladdin Mohammed"), whose Masnavi received a separate article ("Mathnaoui, Methnevi"). He also provided a separate article on the Arabic term *tasawwuf*, viewing it as spiritual practice rather than a philosophy or "ism":

> Tassaouf: Exercises of devotion, or spirituality. The Musulmans call the science of tasawwuf the science which raises a man from the purely human state to that of felicity, making him pass from one degree to another up to the highest perfection that is possible for his nature. It is from this science or art, which those who profess it take the name Sufis.... The Musulmans have a great number of books on this material.[36]

What is new in Herbelot is the concept of spirituality as a description of Sufi practice, evidently signaling his recognition

---

[34] See above, note 25.

[35] The Greek term *sophistike* (sophistical), derived from the same word *sophos*, is used in the title of a work by Aristotle, and it is always spelled with the Arabic letter *sīn*, as *sūfisṭiqā*. See Soheil M. Afnan, *A Philosophical Lexicon in Persian and Arabic* (Beirut, Lebanon: Dar El-Mashreq, 1968), p. 210.

[36] Herbelot, s.v. "Tassaouf."

raised by scholars, and Casiri has been described as the founder of Oriental studies in Spain.[40] Because of the noticeable presence of books by Sufis in this collection, Casiri had frequent occasion to refer to a "Sufi monk" (Suphita monachus) as the author or the subject of a text, as in the following description of two books bound together:

> A work on the solitary life, entitled *The Monastic Science*, whose author is Muhammad ibn `Ali ibn Muhammad al-`Arabi al-Ta'i the Spaniard, leader of the Sufi monks (monachorum Suphitarum) . . . who wrote many books on Mystical Theology…
>
> A book of the Rules and Constitutions of the Sufi Monks [*Qawa'id al-tasawwuf wa usuluhu*], entitled *Fundamentals of the Solitary Life*, by Abu al-`Abbas Ahmad al-Burnus.[41]

It is noteworthy that in the first example, describing one of the works of the great Andalusian Sufi, Ibn `Arabi (d. 1240), Casiri does not hesitate to describe his Sufi writings under the category of mystical theology. Not yet having access to the abstract term Sufism, in translating the second title, Casiri uses the plural noun ("the Sufi monks") to convey the notion of *tasawwuf* as a community practice.

In another passage, Casiri offers a specific definition of the Sufi that emphasizes monastic practice:

> The Sufi is a man who embraces a more exacting and purer discipline, who, renouncing all things, in the manner of prophets and ascetics, withdraws to remote places to give himself freely to the contemplative life. But usually such ascetic Mahometans are distinguished from the rest by white woolen [*suf*] garments: hence the name [i.e., Sufi]. Many lead a coenobitic [monastic community] life outside of the city, where under the Prefect, that is, the Superior General, they are bound by specific laws and regulations, and determinations.
>
> The establishment of this religious life occurred not long before the year 200 hijri [ninth century CE], according to Almakrizi [al-Maqrizi, the

---

[40] Braulio Justel Calaboze, "Casiri a l'Escurial: Catalogue des Manuscrits Arabes," in *al-Dhikri al-mi'awiyah al-thaniyah lil-`Alim al-Maruni Mikhail al-Ghaziri (1792–1992): ra'id al-isti`rab fi Isbaniya: majmu`at muhadirin*, ed. Karam Rizk (al-Kaslik: Ma`had al-Tarikh fi Jami`at al-Ruh al-Qudus, 1999), pp. 25–32.

[41] Casiri 1:222, no. 737.

of something positive that he could compare
Catholic practice of his own day. In fact, the Aca
in its 1694 *Dictionnaire* defined spirituality as '
practice of spiritual things, which concern interi

Herbelot presented a more extended discussic
"Derviche", attending to the origins of monast
which Eastern Christians attributed to Elias or to
patriarchs. He nevertheless noted the relatively
of such practices among Muslims during the Sar
in the ninth century, generally with the understan
gious knowledge is a prerequisite to pursuing the
Herbelot illustrated the subject of dervishes with qu
anecdotes from Persian authors such as Sa`di and H
concluded with the repeated observation that "the
number of books treating the religious life, and the
which it is practiced among the Muslims."[38]

The encounter with books on Sufism, which wa
Herbelot, required the development of descriptive
for classification and cataloging the books and ma
brought from the Middle East and India to the gre
ies of Europe. Another typical example is the great c
the library of Arabic manuscripts in the royal monast
Escorial, near Madrid. This catalog was compiled in La
Lebanese Christian scholar, Miguel Casiri (Mikha'il al-
1710–91), in two large volumes published in 1760 and 1
catalog described over 1,800 Arabic manuscripts, many o
(including volumes originally from the library of Granad
acquired from the Sultan of Morocco.[39] Casiri had taught e
languages in Italy before coming to Spain. Like Herbelot,
received royal patronage (he was official Oriental transla
the king of Spain), and he was chief librarian at El Escori
over two decades. His catalog of the Escorial manuscripts (w
was translated into Arabic in Morocco in 1811) was w

---

[37] "Dictionnaires D'autrefois," s.v. "spiritualité."

[38] Herbelot, s.v. "Derviche."

[39] Miguel Casiri, *Bibliotheca arabico-hispaña escurialensis; sive, librorum omnium mss. arabicè ab auctoribus magnam partem arabo-hispanis compositos bibliotheca coenobii es alensis complectitur* (Madrid: Antonius Perez de Soto, 1760–70).

> Mamluk historian, d. 1442], becoming known at that time when sects and heresies grew among Mahometans; then under the auspices of the Caliphsit spread far and wide; even today throughout the Mahometans' empire it flourishes. Of the rules of the sect, its manners, studies, and the doctrine of the illustrious men, and their piety, quite a few authors have written in praise in their proper place in this library of ours.[42]

While Casiri accepts the etymology of Sufi from the word for wool, he clearly imagines the Sufi as a member of a legally regulated group, indistinguishable from a Catholic religious order, complete with ecclesiastical officials and legal codes as dictated by the Church.

Conclusion

The examples just described of early Orientalist views of Sufis were typical, and the same kinds of categories were repeated by other authors of the time, even though the terminology used to name the Sufis was unstable and variable. Thus, Simon Ockley, in his 1708 English translation of the Arabic philosophical fable *Hayy ibn Yaqzan*, added a footnote describing the doctrine of the Suphians:

> The Suphians are an Enthusiastick Sect among the Mahometans something like Quietists and Quakers; These Set up a Stricter Sort of Discipline, and Pretended to Great Abstinence and Contempt of the World, and Also to a Greater Familiarity and Stricter Union with God than other Sects; they use a great many strange and extravagant actions and utter Blasphemous Expressions.[43]

Here Ockley added here Ockley the Quakers alongside the Quietists, as a marginal and questionable religious group to whom Sufis might be compared. He also entertained the Greek etymology of the word Sufi. Likewise, the British East India Company servant James Fraser (1712–54) made a brief reference to Sufism in the 1742 catalog of the Oriental manuscripts that

[42] Casiri, 1:220.

[43] Muhammad ibn'Abd al-Malik Ibn Tufayl, *The Improvement of Human Reason: Exhibited in the Life of Hai Ebn Yokdhan*, trans. Simon Ockley (London: E. Powell, 1708), p. 18.

he acquired in Western India. In his description of an important Persian Sufi work, *Lawa'ih-i Tawhid*, "Flashes of Unity", by Maulana `Abd al-Rahman Jami, he invokes the category of Quietism once again as he described it as "a Treatise of the *Tusvuff* [*tasawwuf*] Religion, or the Eastern Quietism. With Rules how to acquire a Habit thereof."[44] In a similar fashion, the Orientalist George Sale, famous for his translation of the Qur'an, made the following comments in a popular universal history to which he contributed, published in 1759:

> *Sofi* signifies properly, in *Arabic, a man cloathed in woolen*, from *Sof*, or *Suf*, which signifies *wool*. But there is more reason to believe that the word comes from the *Greek Sofos*: for the Musulmans denote by that a sage, or philosopher, who lives separate and retired from the world, by a kind of religious profession. *Sofi*, therefore, signifies a religious *Mohammedan*, who is called also *Dervish*, or *Darwish*, both in *Turkish* and *Persian*; and in *Arabic, Fakir*.[45]

Sale in this account leaned more in the direction of philosophy and retreat from the world as the adequate account of the Sufi life. Numerous other parallels could be cited from eighteenth-century writings.

The overall impression provided by these early European accounts of Sufis is one of ambivalence, in which etymologies and origins were given great importance. The problem was how to categorize this religious phenomenon, and the classifications that came most easily to hand were adapted from the history of Christianity and from pagan antiquity. Suspicion about the behavior and beliefs of Sufis and dervishes, whether originating with European observers or following the prejudices of Iranian mullahs, encouraged the deployment of terms drawn from the catalog of heretical and marginal Christian groups. More positive assessments had to be phrased in terms of Christian monasticism

---

[44] James Fraser, *A Catalogue of Manuscripts in the Persic, Arabic, and Sanskrit Languages, Collected in the East by James Fraser* (London: W. Strahan, 1742), p. 34.

[45] George Sale et al., *The Modern Part of an Universal History, from the Earliest Account of Time. Compiled from Original Writers. By the Authors of the Antient Part* (London: Printed for S. Richardson, T. Osborne, C. Hitch, A. Millar, John Rivington, S. Crowder, P. Davey and B. Law, T. Longman, and C. Ware, 1759), 5:420–421, note A, with italics of the original.

and spirituality. Sufis were often assumed to be in the same category as Hindu yogis, and they were in addition frequently identified as the epigones of Greek philosophy. Inconsistencies between these rival explanations were not a cause for concern. To be sure, these European writers were drawing upon cues already present in India, where discussions of the relations between religious traditions were definitely taking place at the time. While not as systematic as the efforts of Sir William Jones and his Orientalist colleagues in Calcutta, the early European attempts to describe Sufis employed techniques very similar to the approaches of the Asiatic Society of Bengal, even before the creation of the term Sufism. Describing the unfamiliar other in terms drawn from one's own backyard is of course an age-old procedure for inquiry. As an initial approximation, this is a step towards greater knowledge. But self-assured reflexiveness and implicit critique of others all too often result in a blinkered view of culture that elides contact with the unknown. Whether glimpsed through travel narratives or introduced by scholarly catalogs, the Sufis remained something of a cipher, reflecting back the European concepts that early Orientalism could not avoid.

Index

About the Author

Carl W. Ernst is a specialist in Islamic studies, with a focus on West and South Asia. His published research, based on the study of Arabic, Persian, and Urdu, has been mainly devoted to the study of three areas: general and critical issues of Islamic studies, premodern and contemporary Sufism, and Indo-Muslim culture. He has received research fellowships from the Fulbright program, the National Endowment for the Humanities, and the John Simon Guggenheim Foundation, and he has been elected a Fellow of the American Academy of Arts and Sciences. His publications, which have received several international awards, include *Rethinking Islamic Studies: From Orientalism to Cosmopolitanism* (co-edited with Richard Martin, 2010); *Following Muhammad: Rethinking Islam in the Contemporary World* (2003); and *Teachings of Sufism* (1999).

He is the William R. Kenan, Jr., Distinguished Professor (2005-) and Co-Director of the Carolina Center for the Study of the Middle East and Muslim Civilizations. He and Bruce Lawrence are co-editors of the Islamic Civilization and Muslim Networks Series at the University of North Carolina Press.